Business Finance

C J Higson, BA, MSc, FCA
Principal Lecturer in Finance, Kingston Polytechnic

London
Butterworths
1986

United Kingdom	Butterworth & Co (Publishers) Ltd, 88 Kingsway, LONDON WC2B 6AB and 61A North Castle Street, EDINBURGH EH2 3LJ
Australia	Butterworths Pty, Ltd, SYDNEY, MELBOURNE, BRISBANE ADELAIDE, PERTH, CANBERRA and HOBART
Canada	Butterworths, a division of Reed Inc, TORONTO and VANCOUVER
New Zealand	Butterworths of New Zealand Ltd, WELLINGTON and AUCKLAND
Singapore	Butterworth & Co (Asia) Pte Ltd, SINGAPORE
USA	Butterworth Legal Publishers, ST PAUL, Minnesota, SEATTLE, Washington, BOSTON, Massachusetts, AUSTIN, Texas and D & S Publishers, CLEARWATER, Florida

© Butterworth & Co (Publishers) Ltd 1986

Reprinted 1990

British Library Cataloguing in Publication Data

Higson, C. J.
   Business finance.
   1. Business enterprises—Finance
   I. Title
   658.1'5   HG4026
   ISBN Softcover 0 406 50141 6

Typeset by Phoenix Photosetting, Chatham
Printed in Great Britain by Dotesios Printers Ltd, Trowbridge, Wiltshire

Preface

In *Business Finance* we study the investment and financing decisions of firms. These decisions are often large in scale and uncertain in outcome, and this makes them amongst the most difficult but important that managers have to make, with far-reaching consequences for the welfare of the firm and for society as a whole. However, modern theory provides a powerful analytical framework to help managers think about these problems, and in this book I try to show the uses and limitations of this theory in guiding financial decisions in practice.

The structure of the book reflects the building blocks of business finance: the nature of the firm and its tax environment; the valuation of the individual project; the valuation of the whole firm; the financing decision and the cost of capital; the capital market environment; some important applications, working capital management, merger, failure; and finally, the international dimension.

However elegant the theory, students are right to reject it unless it is clearly grounded in the world they recognise. So this book is in the setting of UK law, companies and institutions. Wherever possible I show how the concepts of business finance can be applied under the constraints of the real world, how they link up with surrounding disciplines: accounting, economics, decision analysis, corporate policy and marketing; and how they relate to some of the wider issues that surround the firm.

The book is intended for students in business, accounting and finance, and economics; but also it will be of interest to students of other disciplines, for example in science and engineering, who increasingly need a knowledge of finance. The book is set at undergraduate, or non-specialist postgraduate level. Equally the book should be of value to professional students, and to practising managers who want a fresh perspective on what they are doing.

Many colleagues have lent time and advice to the development of this book, and I give them my sincere thanks. I owe a special debt of gratitude to my good friend, Dr Paul Auerbach. Not only do the ideas in the book reflect his influence in many places, but I doubt that without his tireless help and encouragement the book would ever have reached completion. I am also indebted to my wife, Kate, and my children, Toby and Louise, for their tolerance and support in a project that took far too much of their share of my time.

C J Higson
March 1986

Contents

xii Contents

Acknowledgments

Grateful acknowledgment is made to the following for their kind permission to reproduce various materials:

Accountancy, Accountancy Age, American Economic Review, Bank of England Quarterly Bulletin, John Carvel, Datastream, Harvard Business Review, Lord Hesketh, International Economic Review, London Business School Risk Measurement Service, Richard Pike, Plessey plc, The Accountant's Magazine, The Financial Times, Unilever plc.

Part I
The background to finance

CHAPTER 1

Introduction

In this book we study the investment and financing decisions of firms – how firms should invest and how they should raise the money to pay for it. These are some of the most important, but also the most difficult of economic decisions.

Firms *invest* when they buy machines, build factories, pay the wages of the research and development department, mount advertising campaigns, build stocks of raw materials, or do anything which involves committing resources in the present to increase income in the future. Firms can *finance* this investment in various ways: by selling shares, by using cash generated from existing projects, by borrowing. Because resources in this world are scarce, investment involves choice and sacrifice. The firm must choose between rival projects, by choosing some it foregoes others. And the people who finance the firm must choose too. By financing firms they sacrifice present consumption, and by financing one firm they forego another. But in each case the choice criterion is the same and is surprisingly simple – the alternative which offers the best stream of returns in the future will be the most valuable. Since firms are owned by their shareholders, we expect firms to make decisions that give the best stream of returns to them, as signalled by their valuation of the firm.

Firms should make the investment and financing decisions *that maximise the value of the firm*. The central aim of this book is to study the effect of these decisions on the value of the firm so as to develop the analysis needed for making the best financial decisions. The characteristic of all decisions is that while their effects lie entirely in the future, the only thing about which we have information is the past. The future is by its very nature *uncertain*. This is what makes investment and financing decisions difficult in practice, since they often have effects stretching for many years ahead. In our study of financial decision-making we have to come to terms with the fact that the decision-maker has only limited information to form his expectations about the future, and there are *costs* to getting more information. So while it is easy to generate neat and well-qualified examples of decision-making in textbooks, in practice quantification is often partial and decisions may be made subjectively and judgementally. This gap between theory and practice tends to make decision-makers impatient with theory and students overly critical of decision-makers. Both reactions are inappropriate so long as we bear in mind that the decision-rules we develop must be useful in a world where obtaining information is costly.

This book is about the financial decisions of firms in 'market' or 'capitalist' economic systems. In reality most economies in the world fall somewhere between the pure 'market' model and the 'centrally-planned' alternative. Most West European countries, for example, have a significant public sector in which financial decisions are made by state and local government and by nationalised enterprises. Since the core of our analysis concerns the efficient allocation of resources, it would be relevant to any system, but the special problems of centrally-planned economies and of the public sector are outside our scope. However we do examine public policy issues where they impinge on the firm. As well, we relate the analysis of financial decisions to other areas of study that are relevant – economics, accounting, decision analysis, corporate policy, marketing. It is not possible to

3

get a useful understanding of business finance in isolation from the world of which it forms a part.

Section I outlines the structure of the book and Section II examines the role of 'theory' in the study of finance, and the concepts of the 'model' and the 'market' in building a theory of finance.

I AN OUTLINE OF THE BOOK

Figure 1 is a simple picture of the investment and financing process. At the centre is the firm. The firm commits resources to projects, which are the basic building-blocks of investment, using funds raised from investors or generated by existing projects.[1]

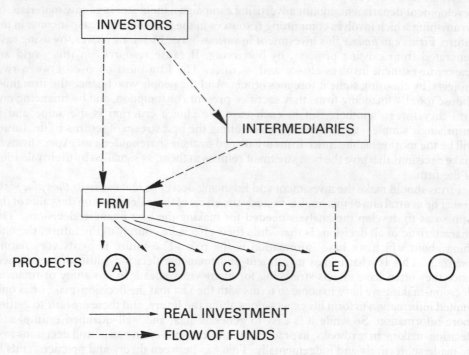

Figure I The investment and financing process

The firm is clearly the major force in modern market economies, active in seeking out investment opportunities and the resources to exploit them, bringing about technological change, and wielding immense economic power. But it is useful to look beyond this monolithic image and see the firm, or rather its managers, as agents investing resources on behalf of the owners.

1 The terminology may confuse. The word 'investment' is commonly used to describe the actual commitment of resources to projects by firms, more accurately described as 'real investment', *and* for the original decision by individuals to forego consumption. The words 'funds' and 'finance' and sometimes 'capital' are all used synonymously to describe the claims on resources that individuals transfer to firms to enable them to undertake the real investment. To describe the whole area of study we are examining we use the words 'Business Finance' or 'Finance and Investment'.

Chapter 2 examines the firm more closely. It considers the legal nature of the firm, and particularly the limited liability joint-stock company. It also raises some important questions: on the one hand – why do firms exist at all, and why is it necessary to have firms intermediating between investors and projects? On the other hand, do managers in fact try to maximise the value of the firm in a world in which managers and owners are separate people? Thinking about these questions sheds some useful light on the investment and financing process. Chapter 3 discusses one aspect of the firm's environment that has a major impact on financial decisions: taxation.

The investment decision of the firm

The building blocks of investment are *projects*. Table I gives an example of a simple project in which, over a period of time, funds are spent on researching and developing a new product, on laying in the necessary productive machinery and stocks of raw materials, on advertising and promotion and subsequently on production costs, which are then to be recovered in revenues.

Table I Project 'X' expected cash flows		
Year		Cash flows £000
1986	Research and Development	(200)
1987	Plant & Equipment	(300)
	Stockbuilding	(50)
	Advertising & Launching	(200)
1988 → 1992	Annual Revenues	600
	Annual Costs	(200)
	Annual Overheads	(50)

To decide whether a project is worthwhile the firm should evaluate all the costs and benefits now and in the future and combine them into a single measure, the *value* of the project. Each project with a positive value that the firm undertakes should increase the value of the firm itself. 'Value' is the measure of success in finance.

However, to find the value of a project the decision-maker has to confront several problems. He must identify the costs and benefits that are relevant to the decision, and he must decide how to compare costs and benefits incurred at different times. But crucially he needs methods of analysis that take into account the uncertain nature of future events. Part II of the book develops the theory of investment decision-making, first assuming that the future is known with certainty and then more realistically that it is not. At this stage we leave aside the financing decision, and assume that the firm is financed entirely by equity.

Financial information and valuation

In Part III we move on to study the valuation of *shares* in firms, and also the valuation of a close relation, *options* to buy or sell shares at a fixed price in the future. The information we want for valuation is information about the future. In forming expectations about the future heavy use tends to be made of accounting data about the past performance of firms and individual projects. The process of forming expectations is a complex and judgemental one in reality so in Part III we examine some aspects of the process. We consider the significance of 'profit' and to what extent future profits can be forecast. We also consider how far it is possible to measure and compare economic performance and efficiency using accounting data.

The financing decision

In Part IV we analyse the second major financial decision of the firm – the financing decision. Part V examines the nature and operation of the capital market and the main financing alternatives available to the firm but first we consider how the firm can choose the best *mix* of financing – the financing policy that maximises the value of the firm. We analyse two key financing decisions – the capital structure decision, – 'what is the right balance of equity and debt?', and the dividend-decision, 'how much of the firm's earnings should it pay out as dividend, and how much should it invest?'

Earlier in the book we studied the investment decision under the convenient assumption the firm was financed entirely by equity – the cost of capital we used was the cost of equity. In the final chapter of Part IV we complete the circle by calculating the cost of capital for project valuation when the firm is pursuing its optimal financing policy.

Financing alternatives

All investment must be financed. Firms raise their finance in various ways, through issuing 'equity', by retaining earnings, by borrowing. These all represent different types of *contract* the firm can make with its suppliers of funds. In Part V of the book we examine the main types of financing contract.

The firm raises its finance in the capital market and in Part V we also address ourselves to the rather important question of the structure of this market and its efficiency of operation. As in other markets demand and supply in the capital market are regulated by a market price, termed from the supplier's point of view his *return*, and from the firm's point of view, the *cost of capital*. This market price has a central role in ensuring the efficient allocation of funds in the economy. Firms which have the most valuable projects can afford to bid higher for the necessary finance, so that if the market is working efficiently it should be the most valuable projects which are undertaken.

The investment decision in practice

Part VI examines some particular applications of investment decision-making. Chapter 23 considers how to determine the optimum balances of working capital for the firm. Chapters 24 and 25 consider the process of investment and disinvestment at the level of the whole firm. So far we have talked about firms investing in single projects, but an alternative and very popular method of growing for firms is to buy up existing projects by acquiring all or part of another firm. We call this growth through 'merger'. Apart from particular issues of decision-analysis, merger raises the whole question of the growth of the firm and the rationale for combining many projects within single firms.

Inevitably projects, and even whole firms, fail on occasion and it is appropriate to disinvest. In the case of the firm, it may be possible to reorganise so that part of the firm survives – otherwise the whole firm must be liquidated. We review the liquidation process and consider when firms ought to be liquidated, and why they are liquidated in practice.

International finance

In the final chapter we widen the view to see what happens to the analysis of the investment and financing decisions when firms can operate internationally. The analysis of the previous chapters applies equally well to the international case, though there are some particular problems to look out for.

II   THE STUDY OF FINANCE

THE ROLE OF THEORY

There exists a well-developed theoretical structure that provides a very powerful way of thinking about real world finance problems. The theory of finance is essentially concerned with building models of how financial assets are *valued* in markets. 'Value' is the key statistic in finance and we identify the objective of managers as the maximisation of the value of the firm. So by modelling the asset-valuation process theorists can help us analyse the various financial decisions managers might make in terms of their impact on the value of the firm. In Chapter 6 we use the seminal model developed by Fisher in 1930 to show that in a world of certainty the firm will maximise its shareholders' wealth by accepting all projects which have a positive value when evaluated at the capital market interest rate. In Chapters 7 and 8 we describe what is currently the cornerstone of contemporary finance theory, the 'capital asset pricing model' (CAPM) developed in the early 1960s to explain how assets will be valued in a world of uncertainty. We can use the CAPM to help the firm calculate its required return when appraising investment projects, and in the context of financing, to show what required return the capital market will require when valuing the securities the firm issues. In Chapter 11 we encounter another model which has found many applications in finance, the model developed by Black and Scholes in the early 1970s to value options. In the late 1950s and early 1960s Modligiani and Miller developed models to analyse the impact on the value of a firm of two key financial decisions, the capital structure decision (which we examine in Chapter 14) and the dividend decision (Chapter 15) in a perfect market.

MODELS

The main analytical tool in finance theory is the *model*. In this context[2] a model is a set of *assumptions* about the world and a set of *conclusions* they *logically* imply:

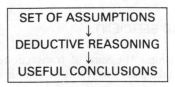

```
SET OF ASSUMPTIONS
        ↓
DEDUCTIVE REASONING
        ↓
USEFUL CONCLUSIONS
```

Models are most valuable when they start from assumptions that can be directly assessed as to their realism, and demonstrate conclusions of which we may have been unaware and which are operationally useful in guiding decisions. Models are exercises in logic, but their assumptions and conclusions are statements about the world. Consider one model we just mentioned – the capital asset pricing model. The CAPM will not mean much to the reader at present, and it is discussed at more length in Chapters 7 and 8. The CAPM shows that:

2   Another type of model is the national economic model. In a general sense these are similar in that they transform a set of assumptions about the world into a set of conclusions, in this case a set of forecasts of significant economic variables. But the emphasis is less on the logical deduction, which is usually mathematically trivial, and more on the generation of the basic equations with their empirical assumptions, and the accuracy of the forecasts or conclusions.

IF	certain assumptions hold, including
	— INVESTORS ARE AVERSE TO RISK
	— THE CAPITAL MARKET HAS NO TRANSACTIONS COSTS
	— THERE IS FULL AND COSTLESS INFORMATION AVAILABLE ABOUT THE RISK AND RETURN OF ASSETS
BY	using deductive reasoning, a mathematical proof
THEN	THE REQUIRED RETURN ON A RISKY ASSET IS THE RISKLESS INTEREST RATE PLUS A SIMPLE MULTIPLE OF THE MARKET RISK PREMIUM

The point to note is that the assumptions are statements about the world which are verifiable, and its conclusions may contain useful rules for guiding investment decisions and judging the efficiency of the capital market.

A feature of models in finance is that they are both *descriptive* and *prescriptive*. On the one hand they describe how the world works so, for example, a good deal of research has gone into seeing if returns on risky assets do actually follow the CAPM rule. But at the same time they make a statement about how the world ought to work. So the CAPM rule is presented as a major aid to investment decisions in the sense that behaving this way will help a decision-maker attain his objectives. The link is that financial models usually assume *rationality* in the behaviour they describe, in other words they *assume* people do what they ought to in their own best interests.

The constant attempt to explain the world better by building better theories is important work. But theory can be very beguiling with its clean lines and logical structure, and there is a temptation to forget that the test of a good theory is its usefulness in the real world. The link between a theory and the world outside is the 'assumptions' the theory makes about the world; so as well as understanding the theory it is important to understand the environment of finance inside and outside the firm – the nature of the individuals and institutions involved, the motives of managers and investors, the structure of the capital market, the impact of government through law and taxation. This permits us to appraise the assumptions of the models we use.

MARKETS: PERFECT AND EFFICIENT

The word 'market' means simply the sum of transactions in a particular commodity wherever and however they take place. In terms of what is transacted or transferred we usually identify three broad groups of markets: the labour market, in which people sell their labour or 'work' to others; the product markets, in which goods and services are transferred; and the capital market in which funds are transferred. Business finance is centrally interested in the capital market. Since, however, the end-purpose of these transfers is investment in real resources business finance must also take an interest in the markets for resources themselves, the labour and product markets and particularly the product market for 'capital assets' – machines and other durable things used in production.

In a market, exchanges between buyers and sellers are determined by a *market price*. Financial decisions made in what is predominantly a market economy use data which is a collection of prices set in markets, and the meaning of this information depends in part on the nature of the market in which it was set. So we have to take an interest in the characteristics of markets, and use the terms 'efficient' and 'perfect' to describe them. Since these terms are used repeatedly throughout the book we will define them here, and give them a closer scrutiny in Chapter 18.

An *efficient* market is defined as one in which *prices always fully reflect all available information*. People looking for efficiency in capital markets usually concentrate on three testable implications of this definition:

1 There is no way of using existing price information to develop consistently profitable trading rules, ie to forecast prices better than the market.
2 When new information becomes publicly available it is correctly and promptly incorporated into market prices.
3 No market participants are able to make above average returns by the use of privileged information.

The efficient market is defined in terms of the characteristics its *prices* have. The *perfect* market is a concept used by theorists and is defined in terms of the characteristics of the *market* itself. The general conditions needed for a market to be perfect are as follows:

1 There is full and costless information available to all participants.
2 There are no transaction costs and the tax system is neutral with respect to the market.
3 There are many buyers and sellers: participants are 'price-takers'.
4 Participants are 'rational': they behave in accordance with certain axioms of rationality such as preferring more to less of a good thing, and less to more of a bad.

Most financial theory assumes perfect capital markets. Perfection is a far more demanding requirement than efficiency, and by assuming perfection theorists can build models with powerful conclusions about the meaning of the prices they yield, and which provide a convenient base from which to analyse the impact of the market imperfections that may occur in practice.

III SUMMARY

Business finance concerns the process of investment by firms. It considers two central and related questions: how firms should choose the investments they make, and how they should raise the necessary finance. In this chapter we outlined the structure of the subject. We also emphasised the relationship betweeen the theory of finance and the world it attempts to describe, and in particular the role that the concepts of the 'model' and of the 'market' play in the theory of finance.

CHAPTER 2
The firm

Business finance is concerned with the investment and financing decisions of firms, so in this chapter we consider 'the firm'. Section I examines the legal nature of the firm and particularly the 'limited liability joint-stock company'. In the second section we study the firm's objective, value maximisation, as well as some 'managerial' alternatives to value maximisation. Section III considers whether value-maximisation is an appropriate objective for some other forms of enterprise, such as publicly-owned corporations, and worker and consumer co-operatives. The final sections of the chapter consider two applications of the 'contractual' approach to finance theory. One is Oliver Williamson's analysis of the question 'why do firms exist?' and the second is the application of 'principal and agent' theory to the capital structure of the firm.

I TYPES OF FIRM – THE LEGAL BACKGROUND

The first step in understanding the firm is to distinguish between incorporated and unincorporated firms. The word 'incorporate' comes from the Latin – *corpus* (a body) and if a firm is incorporated in law this means that legally the firm becomes 'a person', separate from its owners and with certain legal rights and duties a person would have, such as the right to incur debts and be sued on its own account. An incorporated firm is called a 'company' in the UK, and a 'corporation' in the US, though sometimes the US word is used in the UK for a particularly large company.[1] An unincorporated firm is viewed by the law merely as a collection of owners, rather than as a separate legal person, and such a firm is known as a 'partnership' if there is more than one owner, and a 'sole-trader' if there is only one.

UNINCORPORATED FIRMS

To set up in business as a sole-trader or partnership requires no action at all in law. There are few special legal constraints on the internal and external behaviour of partnerships and the relevant statute remains the Partnership Act 1890 which laid down guidelines for resolving internal conflicts between partners. Two important points arise about partnerships.
– The Companies Act 1948 limited the number of partners in a partnership to twenty. But since this was proving a real constraint on the growth of certain professional firms, like accountants, solicitors and stock exchange members, whose governing bodies require them to be partnerships, the Companies Act 1967 relaxed the constraint for these firms, and they were also lifted for other professions.

---

1 Very broadly the word 'firm' describes any unit undertaking economic activity for gain. The word 'business' is a similarly loose term covering the same ground. In this book the words 'firm' and 'company' will be used interchangeably.

– All partners are personally liable to the extent of their personal wealth for the debts of the whole firm, and thus for debts arising from the negligence, incompetence and fraud of other partners. This argues in favour of choosing your partners carefully! It also raises the question of what constitutes a partner. This depends on the circumstances, but receiving a share of the profits tends to be evidence of partnership since it is the hallmark of an ownership or 'equity' interest.[2]

Most of the duties imposed on partnerships are duties individuals have in equity and common law. The law imposes few additional constraints, but it offers no concessions either. This is not the case with companies.

COMPANIES

There are various legal forms a company can take.[3] We are interested in the most common, the company limited by shares and registered under the Companies Act. This has two important characteristics:

Limited liability

Incorporation gives the firm the legal status of a person, able to incur debts and be sued, separate from its owners. But also incorporated firms tend to have 'limited liability': the liability of the owners for a company's debts is limited to their investment in the firm.[4]

Joint-stock

In a company the ownership rights are divided into transferable shares or 'stock'. The company is managed on behalf of its owners by a board of *directors* whose duties towards the shareholders are defined by law and by the company's 'articles of association'.

Public and private companies

Table 1 shows the numbers of public and private companies. Private companies emerge as the predominant type numerically, even allowing for the fact that perhaps only half of the number registered are actually trading, according to Inland Revenue figures. The largest companies are in the main 'quoted'. These are public companies which have decided to seek a wider market for their shares by having them quoted on The Stock Exchange.

Table 1 Types of company in the UK

private	710,662 (1)
public	16,015 (1)
public-quoted	2,431 (2)

(1) Source: Department of Trade 'Companies in 1979' HMSO
(2) Source: Stock Exchange Fact-Book, Numbers are for full and USM markets, on 30 June 1985.

2 However the 1890 Act also deems anyone a partner who 'holds-out' as a partner, that is, gives the impression of being a partner to the outside world.
3 Companies can be incorporated by Act of Parliament rather than registered and can be limited by guarantee, or unlimited. Conversely, it is worth noting that not all partnerships have unlimited liability: it is possible to register a limited partnership, though these are very rare.
4 There is one minor exception to this – if the company has any partly-paid shares the owners can be asked to contribute the balance of the nominal value of these shares to meet the company's debts.

In the UK public companies are identifiable by having Plc (public limited company) after their name, while private companies have 'Limited'. The advantages of 'private' status have diminished over the years. The 1967 Companies Act removed the exemption from filing an annual report and accounts. Also the introduction of corporation tax removed many of the tax advantages which small closely-owned companies, known as 'close-companies', had provided. Since the Companies Act 1980 public companies, like private, may have only two shareholders, and it is no longer the case that private companies are limited to no more than fifty shareholders and are required to restrict share transfers. In practice however most private companies still do have this restriction in their articles of association, which are the rules that control the internal regulation of the company. Private companies do not have to issue a prospectus when raising new capital. Public companies have a statutory minimum share capital of £50,000 of which 25% must be paid-up before it can start trading, whereas there is no minimum for private companies and in theory a private company could have just 2 shares of 1p each.

THE ADVANTAGES OF INCORPORATION

Limited liability looks like 'manna from heaven' for entrepreneurs. They receive the fruits of success yet are protected from suffering the losses beyond a certain level. But in an efficient market, there should be no 'free lunches'. The risk of loss is merely transferred to the creditors of the firm: trade creditors, employees, and other unsecured lenders. Why do they accept this risk? The answer is that in many cases they either do not accept it, or they seek compensation for it. New and unknown companies will find that suppliers insist on cash payament, and that banks require loans to be secured by personal guarantees from the directors. Personal guarantees effectively circumvent limited liability. Further, in an efficient market we would expect those who lend to the company or trade with it and have not covered their risk another way to do so by charging a higher interest rate on their loans or a higher price for their goods and services.

Every year a certain number of firms do go bankrupt leaving creditors partly unpaid. Whether these creditors had 'insured' themselves against this risk in the ways we suggested would be very hard to establish. Few people would suggest that the market is fully efficient in this respect, and cases involving unscrupulous use of limited liability to swindle creditors are regularly reported. But the reader should recognise the existence of processes which reduce the value of limited liability. In one respect creditors may benefit from limited liability. One constraint imposed by the law in exchange for limited liability is the requirement to publish financial information, limited though this may be.

The vital characteristic of companies which provides a strong motive for incorporation is the *joint-stock* principle. Joint-stock permits the *separation of ownership and control*, and hence the separation of two quite distinct inputs to the firm – the provision of finance and the provision of management skills. There is no reason why these two should be possessed by the same people, and to require the same individuals to provide them can impose a real constraint. Anyhow, where managers do possess personal wealth they may prefer to spread their personal risk by investing in other firms.

A second advantage of the separation of ownership and control relates to the continuity of the enterprise. Continuity in management is a thing of value to the firm, continuity in ownership is not. In a joint-stock company free transfer of shares can take place without the running of the business being disturbed. Contrast this with a partnership, where the death or retirement of a partner may mean the repayment of his capital and can impose severe strain on the finances of the firm, or on the other hand where the partner finds a good deal of his personal wealth is tied-up in the firm and can only be released if he resigns. But company status does not solve all continuity problems. The plight of the family company, forced to sell part of the shareholding to outsiders to pay capital taxes is well known. This problem arises because continuity of management dictates a break in ownership, and the family is not prepared to accept a separation of ownership and control, or fears that the loss of ownership will sooner or later lead to a loss of control. Though incorporation permits the separation of ownership and control, in many firms, particularly smaller ones, they are not separate.

Another advantage of joint-stock is that larger investments can be financed this way. A wider ownership can be sought by pooling contributions from many individuals. Instead of their fortunes being entirely bound up in the success of one or two firms these individuals can spread their risk by buying shares in many firms. The real function of limited liability may be as a necessary condition for joint-stock. If shareholders had unlimited liability the purchase of even a small number of shares would render the owners liable to the full extent of their wealth. Of course, this is the case in a partnership. The difference is that in a partnership he or she can monitor and influence the conduct of the business, and control the admission of other partners. But in a joint-stock company they are less able to assess or control their risk.

The separation of ownership and control offers some advantages but it also raises a potential problem. If ownership and control are separate, how can owners *control* managers, and ensure they are pursuing the shareholders' objective? This is the issue we examine in the next section.

II VALUE MAXIMISATION

In finance we assume that when managers make decisions they do so with the objective of *maximising the value of the firm*. Given the number of shares in issue, the objective can be restated as *maximise share price*. We assume this objective because we expect the firm to provide its owners with the best stream of returns through time and the shareholder's evaluation of a share will simply be the value he or she puts on this stream of returns. If you asked the man in the street what the objective of the firm should be, he would most likely say 'profit'.

How does profit relate to the value goal? They are closely related. The returns a shareholder gets from a firm come in the form of a stream of dividends through time. The investors' *evaluation* of the dividend stream will depend on their opinion of its 'quality' – its riskiness and the comparison with returns available on other investments. The dividend stream depends on the profit of the firm, period by period. However, as an objective, profit maximisation is inadequate in coping with the dimensions of time and risk. Profit is essentially a one-period measure of performance whereas the whole thrust of finance is to see the firm as a continuing entity and to see managers as making financing and investment decisions which have effects now and in the future.

Value-maximisation is the cornerstone of finance theory but in reality it is not without problems. For one thing, once we recognise that different shareholders may have different tax positions, then there may be no single or unique financial policy which will be preferred by all of them. What is more, it may be very hard in practice for the financial manager to *know* what the value-effect of a particular financial policy will be – how the shareholders will evaluate it. But the issue that has been a major preoccupation of theorists concerns the motives of managers. Once ownership and control of the firm are separate how can we be sure managers will pursue the owners' objective? There are two questions – first, how will managers' objectives conflict with shareholders'; second, what sort of control do share-holders have over managerial behaviour?

WHAT ARE MANAGERS' OBJECTIVES?

Several arguments have been produced why, unconstrained, managers will pursue different objectives from shareholders. The main ones concern *size* and *security* and *satisficing*.

Size

Managers will be interested in the size of firm if their *rewards* – pay, power, status and so forth – are associated with the size of the firm rather than its value. In practice this appears to be the case. Research suggests that the remuneration of managers is related to the size of the firm,[5] and it seems likely that the same goes for power and status. Size in this context is usually measured by *sales revenue*. It may not be immediately obvious why size and value are conflicting objectives since we usually expect bigger firms to be more valuable. However a conflict will occur when in the pursuit of sales revenue managers undertake projects which have negative value, are 'unprofitable', so that the value of the whole firm is reduced. We demonstrate this possibility in Figure 1, along similar lines to Baumol (1958). Like him, we compare sales with profit rather than value. The profit-maximising

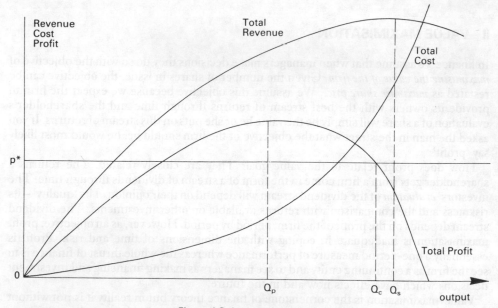

Figure I Sales-maximisation

5   For example, Cosh (1975) found size to be the major explanatory variable in the remuneration of chief executives. When he segmented the sample into larger and smaller firms much the same results applied to the 'larger' firms, but amongst the 'smaller' group profitability performed more strongly as a predictor of remuneration. Meeks and Whittington (1975a) found that 'size is confirmed as being of overwhelming importance in the explanation of the level of directors' pay'. But they argued strongly in favour of examining changes in size rather than absolute levels.

output is Qp but the sales maximising output is higher, at Qs. Profit maximisation occurs where marginal revenue equals marginal cost. Units sold between Qp and Qs still have positive marginal revenue and so increase total sales revenue, though they decrease total profit since their marginal costs exceed their marginal revenue. Beyond Qs the search for revenue can go no further since any further increase in sales volume will be more than offset by the price cutting needed to achieve it.

The virtue of this model is that it reminds us that there *may* be a point beyond which increased sales can only be bought at the expense of profit, or value. Baumol suggested that in practice managers will have *some* interest in profit, to the extent of meeting a minimum profit requirement or constraint set by shareholders. For example the constraint p* in Figure I would restrict sales to Qc.

A problem 'sales maximisation' shares with 'profit maximisation' is its neglect of the time dimension. In practice managers making sales strategy over multiple time periods will be conscious of providing the organisational structure and productive capacity needed to accompany increase in size, and of the response of the shareholders if there were uneven growth: large gains in sales one year, and smaller gains another. Both of these argue in favour of *orderly growth*. For this reason firms often express their size objective in terms of a target *annual growth rate*.

Security and risk

By 'risk' in finance, we usually refer to the variability of a stream of returns. If managers and shareholders are both risk-averse they will both have an interest in reducing this variability and in particular in avoiding the liquidation of the firm which is a negative outcome with particularly heavy costs. But even where managers and owners are risk-averse a conflict of interest may arise if they value risk differently. Managers can reduce the risk of the firm in two ways: they can avoid single projects which are risky, and they can reduce the risk of single projects by *diversification* – pooling projects with different profiles of risk to form a 'portfolio'. In Chapter 7 we show that the risk associated with an investment decision is the effect of the decision on the risk of the overall portfolio. This provides one reason why owners and managers may disagree about a particular decision – they may be evaluating it in terms of different portfolios. Managers may treat the firm itself as the portfolio, while for owners, shares in the firm are probably just one asset in their portfolio. Consider the costs of the extreme outcome – liquidation – to the two parties. To managers, association with a firm which is liquidated will involve costs of two kinds. There will be a short-term loss of income and a good deal of disruption during the period of search for a new job, and there may be long-term lowering of income resulting from the damage to the manager's reputation. For the shareholder there may be a loss of wealth following the sale of the firm's assets at distress prices with associated selling costs.

For shareholders there are costs as well as benefits to diversifying the firm. In a diversified firm the owners of loss-making projects bear the whole loss by setting it off against other projects. However, had each project been independent, part of the loss might have been shifted to creditors, through limited liability. Suppose, to take a simple example, that we have two projects A, B, and two future 'states of the world' which may occur, I, II. A 'state of the world' is a set of external factors – level of demand, weather, etc – which affect the returns on a project. At present we attach equal probability, .5, to each state of the world. Table II shows the 'value' each project would have if either state I or II occurred.

If each project constituted the sole activity of a firm then the expected value of firm A would be .5 × £4m + .5 × £3m = £3.5m. But the expected value of B would be .5 × £3m + .5 × £0m = £1.5m. This is because the shareholders in B are protected from negative

Table II

States of the world and probability		Project values A	Project values B	Firm C's value = A + B
I	.5	£4m	£3m	£7m
II	.5	£3m	(£1m)	£2m

outcomes by limited liability, so the £1m loss would be borne by creditors. Hence, as independent firms, A and B have a total value of £3.5m + £1.5m = £5m. But if a firm C were formed to hold projects A and B then its expected value would only be .5 × £7m + .5 × £2m = £4.5m. The difference is that in the latter case the loss of £1m, with a probability of .5, and thus an expected value of £.5m, has been borne inside the firm rather than by outsiders. However, in practice, the value of limited liability, and thus the loss incurred by losing it, may be reduced by the ability of creditors to extract compensation for the increased risks that limited liability imposes on them. In general, though, liquidation can affect owners and managers in different ways, and they might well disagree on how much risk-avoidance the firm should do.

Satisficing

One important strand in the managerial literature is provided by writers such as Simon (1959) and Cyert and March (1963). These 'behaviourists' considered the possibility that so little precise information relevant to firm profitability was available to the firm that it might well now maximise anything. Simon introduced the notion of 'satisficing' to describe managers who aspire only to a 'satisfactory' rather than an optimal level of attainment of their goals, and for whom the motive to act is a response to a state of affairs that has become unsatisfactory. The characteristic of these writers is that they were looking within the firm to find explanations for its behaviour and not at the external constraints which the environment imposes upon the firm.

Decisions of the firm are in fact decisions of the management group which controls the firm. In practice this group comprises individuals with personal goals which may conflict. Cyert and March suggest that the compromises necessarily reached to resolve these conflicts impose upon the firm a set of unrationalised and conflicting objectives which reflect themselves in a form of inefficiency called 'organisational slack'. This approach has an affinity with the 'contractual' theories of the firm discussed below.

CONTROL OF MANAGERIAL BEHAVIOUR

The divergent personal objectives of managers would not matter too much if shareholders could effectively control managerial behaviour. In principle managers are constrained by legal controls and by market forces.

Legal controls

The assumption of the Companies Acts is that directors are the owners' representatives. Once a year they produce a financial report on the performance of the firm which is independently audited and presented to shareholders at the *annual general meeting*. At the same time some directors offer themselves for re-election, by rotation. So in theory the directors' tenure is contingent on their performance. But there are several major obstacles to this process. One is a lack of information. To judge someone's performance and objectives it is necessary to compare what they did with what they might have done. On the former, the information in the financial report is both limited and is an aggregate of all the firm's activities. On the latter, even managers themselves may not have full information; rejected choices and possibilities are often not quantified and sometimes not even recognised by managers. Owners are forced to make judgements by comparisons with other firms and other time periods, with all the associated problems of comparability.

Another problem is that the attendance of shareholders at AGMs is notoriously poor. Shareholders receive the financial report by post before the meeting, and with it a proxy form in case they will not be attending. Under the proxy system a shareholder is free to nominate anyone to vote for him, but the proxy form usually proposes a director as proxy, thus reinforcing managerial control. As a result the number of shares needed for actual control can be surprisingly small.

Weak shareholder control is sometimes attributed to the inadequacies of individual shareholders. Individuals with small holdings may be too dispersed and isolated to form an effective coalition against the directors. And small shareholders are sometimes painted as financially illiterate, unable to understand the information they are given, and without the resources to analyse it.[6] In contrast, the trend in the UK towards ownership of shares by the 'institutions', pension funds, insurance companies, etc may be significant. By dint of close and continuous scrutiny, experts such as security analysts may be able to form a better view than other outsiders about the performance of managers. Often the investment decisions of individual shareholders are guided by analysts too, but the presumption is that institutions have much closer continuing access to the advice of experts.

But institutions usually claim to avoid interference in management if possible. They see their role as investors, so their more likely reaction if they are dissatisfied with the performance of managers is to sell the shares. However one fund manager we spoke to summed up his experience in dealing with companies in Exhibit I.

Exhibit I The View from the Institutions

'Forget about the idea of the shareholder-wealth-maximising manager. On balance managers prefer to ignore their shareholders and they usually can get away with this and perpetrate their own existence indefinitely. What really excites managers is the game they are playing with the managements of rival companies. What really motivates them is the love of the game, and the charisma and self-esteem that can come with success.

But as institutional shareholders we do intervene when things go too far: probably more often than the public realises. Essentially it is a matter of power, we weigh up whether we have the muscle and the will to shift them, and they make the same calculation. If we have, they usually prefer it to be done quietly. If it's a matter of some directors resigning they will prefer to avoid publicity and leave their reputations intact. Very often once you have decided a manager is going you can find some technical infringement to lever him out – some breach of the articles of association, he may be over age, and so forth. Often, though, I think we intervene too late.

I think the institutions *are* getting more active in intervention. Perhaps this is why managements tend to be so lyrical nowadays about the need for small shareholders; all they get from small shareholders is adulation!'

---

6   Lee and Tweedie (1977) research the private shareholders' comprehension of accounting data and found it to be very weak.

When an institution does intervene it will often gather the support of other institutions through one of the organisations of institutional investors. There was an example of this when the Post Office Superannuation Fund intervened to stop Associated Broadcasting Corporation from giving a large compensation package to the outgoing Mr Jack Gill. The package included £½ million in cash, and the right to buy his company house, currently valued at £275,000, for £165,822. The Financial times [8/11 January 1982] noted that the Post Office was supported by the National Association of Pension Funds [14 members of which had invested in ABC] in its attempt to get a legal injunction against the compensation payment. But it also noted that ABC's equity was split into voting and non-voting shares, and that Lord Lew Grade, Chairman of ABC and supporter of the compensation, owned 27.6% of the voting stock. The FT concluded this would be 'More than enough to combat the dissident shareholders who hold 16% of the shares'.

Market-forces

How far are managers constrained to be value-maximisers by market-forces? Consider the capital-market first. Suppose managers make a decision in which present and future profits are sacrificed for the sake of sales or security. The market value of the firm should fall to reflect this. What has happened is that managers have chosen to use the resources under their command in a way which yields a lower value than alternative strategies. In principle it is now possible for the firm to be bought at this value by investors deploying another management team, in order to reap a capital gain by implementing the higher-value alternative strategy. So *fear of takeover* may constrain managers to maximise value.

The notion of the threat of takeover as a constraint on managerial behaviour is usually attributed to Marris (1964), but it has subsequently appeared as a constraining mechanism in much managerial theory. However there are some obstacles to the effectiveness of the threat. First, the potential acquiror faces the same information problems as existing shareholders in knowing which firms could be doing better. Second is the possibility that it may be 'too late' to usefully transfer the resources to new uses. Once committed, many of the costs associated with a project become sunk and the value of the assets in other cases may be significantly less. Finally, there are the transactions costs of the capital-market itself, including the need to pay a premium over share-price to induce sufficient existing shareholders to sell. In practice these factors can allow some latitude for managerial objectives to be pursued.[7]

The nature of the product markets in which the firm trades will also determine the degree of freedom managers have to pursue their objectives. It only makes sense to discuss a trade-off between sales and value to the extent that managers are able to choose the markets, and the prices and quantities, at which they sell. The degree of control managers have over the firms destiny will depend in part on the degree of market power the firm has in its product markets, and thus on the competitiveness structure of the market.[8]

THE EVIDENCE

The issue of the divergence of owners' and managers' objectives has produced a large literature. Researchers have examined two questions; the extent to which firms are in

---

7 For evidence on the characteristics of firms that get taken over see Chapter 24, and the work of Singh (1975) and Kuehn (1975). Neither of these studies suggests that the threat of takeover is a particularly sharp instrument.

8 For a further discussion of the market as a constraint on the firm see Alchian's famous 'survival of the fittest' argument in Alchian (1950).

practice controlled by their owners, and the extent to which the type of control affects the firm's behaviour. Neither question has found an easy or consistent answer, as might be suspected from the size of the literature.

The actual exercise of control generates few observable signs, so researchers have been forced to define some observable conditions which might confer on owners the *ability* to control the firm. Unfortunately these conditions are of necessity arbitrary, and even if sufficient may not be necessary conditions of owner control. For example, Florence (1961) in his study of the control of UK companies in 1951 used several criteria for owner control: whether the largest shareholder had more than 20% of votes, the largest twenty shareholders more than 30%, or the directors more than 5%. Florence found that the voting strength of UK companies showed a good deal of dispersion, and that in a special study of very large firms where a comparison was drawn with the position in 1936, that the dispersion had increased between 1936 and 1951. But the significance of results such as these have been challenged, most recently by Nyman and Silbertson (1978). Nyman and Silbertson point out the rich and subtle variety of ways in which *influence* and *control* can be exercised in the real world, a variety which cross-sectional research designs find it hard to capture. They observe that 'any individual firm may be related to other corporations, banks, financial institutions, and family owners via complex patterns of shareholdings, interlocking directorates, and kinship networks'. Also, UK law has only recently made it necessary to disclose the beneficial owners of nominee shareholdings, which hitherto could conceal concentrations of voting power. Based on a detailed case-study analysis of the top 250 UK companies in 1975: Nyman and Silbertson conclude: 'the first component of the beliefs held by managerial theorists – that control of large corporations is by and large not in the hands of proprietary interests – is not true for the UK.' But they found significant industry differences; the food, electrical engineering, construction, retailing, merchanting, and miscellaneous and services industries were predominantly owner-controlled. The chemicals, metal goods and building materials industries were predominantly non-owner controlled.

In the UK Stanworth and Giddens (1975) have found a significant increase this century in the prevalence of directorships which interlock between the top fifty industrial companies and the largest financial institutions and public utilities. In the case of banks, it is common to find in the UK some influence being exercised by banks through directorships in the firms which they advise and finance. But though banks are outsiders they are not usually shareholders, and beyond protecting their own capital and interest we cannot predict their objectives in the control of the firm.

Many researchers have tried to test the managerialist view that owner-controlled firms are more likely to pursue owner objectives. Nyman and Silbertson survey ten of the most recent contributions to this literature. The only consistent result they found was an agreement by all seven studies which examined the issue that owner-controlled firms have a higher profit rate than management-controlled firms, but in only two of these studies was the finding statistically significant. Palmer (1973) provides an interesting contribution to the rate of profit issue. He attempted to introduce the nature of product markets as a variable, and found that amongst a sample of large US industrial corporations only in the presence of high barriers to entry did owner-controlled firms have significantly higher rates of profit than management-controlled.

FINAL COMMENTS ON MANAGERIALISM

The idea that a conflict in objectives will follow the separation of ownership and control is not new. Discussing joint-stock companies in 1776 Adam Smith observed:

The directors of such companies, however, being the managers rather of other people's money than of their own, it cannot well be expected, that they should watch over it with the same anxious vigilance with which the partners in a private co-partnery frequently watch over their own ... Negligence and profusion, therefore, must always prevail, more or less, in the management of the affairs of such a company.

The first thing to note is that the debate on the separation of ownership and control essentially concerns larger firms. Small and medium-sized firms are for the most part 'closely-controlled', owned and managed by a small group, often including the founding family. In the larger firms the shareholding is often widely spread, but even in these firms there is not necessarily a divergence of objectives, since many company directors are also shareholders. Indeed the encouragement of share-ownership amongst managers and workers is an obvious ploy by owners concerned about divergent objectives. Prais (1976) found that the holdings by voting shares by directors of the hundred largest quoted manufacturing companies in the UK declined between 1968 and 1972 from a mean of 7.3 to 5.4%. But even this level of share-ownership might encourage a value-maximising orientation amongst managers.

How effective are the available controls and constraints on managers? In practice both the controls provided by company law and the threat of takeover can leave some leeway for managers, but researchers have failed to find compelling evidence that managers are consistently pursuing other objectives, and it may well be that informal controls of the sort proposed by Nyman and Silbertson are effective.

One reason why firms may not *appear* to pursue value-maximisation is that it is not easy to operationalise, to convert into rules for guiding actual decisions. So to the extent that firms overtly set objectives at all they often set 'intermediate' goals 'derived' from the main objective. These more manageable goals may be a certain level of profit, return on investment, sales growth, market share, or some mixture of these. So long as these goals generate the strategy that maximises value, the assumption of finance theory is not violated.

III WORKERS, CONSUMERS, SOCIETY AT LARGE

The claims of certain other groups are sometimes advanced as relevant to the objectives of the firm, notably the claims of consumers, society as a whole and, of course, workers. At present the welfare of these groups tends to enter the decision-making of firms as constraints to be satisfied in attaining the main objective.

The constraint may be a legal one or a behavioural one. Examples of the first are the costs to the firm of complying with consumer legislation such as the date stamping requirement on food retailers, or the costs of fitting anti-pollution equipment on cars destined for the American market. Examples of the second are the cost of meeting workers' demands under threat of strike, or of building a sports club which it is perceived should improve worker morale. In either case these constraints are merely additional costs of operation.

The interesting case arises when the welfare of one of these groups becomes the objective of the firm, the 'thing to be maximised', or to be jointly maximised along with the attainment of other goals. The consumer co-operative movement provides examples of firms designed to set objectives in terms of consumers' interests, and the nationalised industries could be seen as attempts to do the same for society as a whole. In practice nationalised industries in the UK have tended to pursue financial objectives akin to those of the private sector, perhaps because of the difficulty in making an operational objective out of social welfare, the same problem may afflict consumer co-operatives. But in either case the problem is not severe since society or the consumers own the firm. Value-maximisation carries through as the objective – it can serve any master who owns the firm. The same applies when considering the group whose interests have been pressed most vigorously in recent history-workers.

The analysis of the labour-managed firm is still in its infancy. Vanek (1975) provides a useful sample of existing literature in the area, which tends to take a static profit-maximising approach to defining the firm's objectives. A long-run analysis of labour-managed firms is Furubotn (1976). A problem for theorists in this area is that there are currently relatively few examples of labour-managed firms outside of Yugoslavia, and there is no settled legal form, hence they tend to make assumptions about the rights and duties of the participants.

A key assumption in Furubotn's analysis is that workers cannot sell their share of the future profits of the firm when they leave the co-operative, so investment decisions are biased towards projects yielding high returns in the short term. A common prediction of theory is that labour-managed firms may display a preference for *minimising* the size of the workforce, since new workers would acquire an equal share in the 'surplus value' of profitable projects belonging to existing workers. For our purposes it is sufficient to note that the analysis of the labour-managed firm is very similar to that of the conventional firm, with wages taking the place of dividends in combining the roles of payment for a factor of production and in the distribution of the surplus of the firm. The dilution of ownership of this 'surplus value' is equally a problem in conventional firms. It is got round by means of 'rights issues' to existing owners which permit them to capture the benefits from a new issue and which give them a vested interest in the maximisation of firm value. But models of the labour-managed firm have not adapted to the possibility of this sort of institutional device and in general those predictions which deviate from value maximisation can be atttributed to the assumptions about the allocation of ownership and control rights possessed by labour groups, rather than to the firm being labour-managed per se.

IV WHY DO FIRMS EXIST?

The firm is the centre piece in finance, taking funds from investors and investing them in projects. But why do firms exist? The question may seem odd, but there are closely related questions – What is the optimum size for the firm? Are big firms better than small firms? What is the best organisational structure for the firm? – which often arise. The seminal discussion of this topic was by Ronald Coase (1937). Coase said that the *firm* and the *market* were alternative modes of economic organisation and that *transaction costs* would determine whether a given set of transactions were '*internalised*' in a firm or left to the market. We can put this another way. Bearing in mind that market prices are bearers of economic information, the firm will be chosen as a method of economic organisation when it provides a less expensive way of exchanging information than the market. Williamson (1975) provides a recent and highly influential development of this approach.

Williamson

Oliver Williamson depicts economic activity as a set of transactions in which productive inputs or resources are transferred and combined into outputs. These transactions either take place in markets, where individuals contract with each other to supply goods and services, or within *hierarchies*, eg firms, where goods and services are called forth and supplied through relationships of authority and direction between individuals in the firm.

So firms have replaced or 'internalised' markets in certain areas, and the question is; Why this has happened?

As a simple example in which the market and the firm are alternative ways of doing something consider the choice that faces you when you build an extension to your house. You get an architect to draw up the plans, then you can either get a building firm to build it, or organise the building yourself by subcontracting various craftsmen, joiners, bricklayers, electricians, etc, to do the work, and arranging with builders' merchants to supply the materials. In the latter case the job is completed through a series of contracts with individuals, in the former case you contract with a firm and the firm directs the craftsmen it employs to do the job. Even in this simple case, where the nature of the tasks are relatively clear-cut and the time duration relatively short there are problems in the market mode of contracting. For example the exact task facing the bricklayer will not be clear until the foundations are dug, and this and the weather will determine when the joiner, the electrician and so forth will be needed. A contract with these craftsmen which allowed for all these possibilities would be '*complex*', and '*contingent*' on future events. The building firm, on the other hand, avoids these complexities by writing employment contracts. These are known as '*incomplete contracts*' since the nature of the tasks the employee will be expected to undertake is not fully specified at the outset.

It is clear that many of the contracts that would need to be written in the absence of firms would be exceedingly complex and time consuming to write; in other words they would be 'costly'. Hierarchical organisations such as firms replace markets in Williamson's view when it is less costly to use the internal than the external mode

> The shift of transactions from autonomous market contracting to hierarchy is principally explained by transactional economies that attend such assignments.
> (*Williamson*, op cit, p 248)

It is not that relationships within the firm are not contractual, but rather that they involve different types of contract, contracts that are often incomplete or informal. Some writers are more explicit about this

> most organisations are legal fictions which serve as a nexus for a set of contracting relationships among individuals.
> (*Jensen and Meckling* (1957) p 310)

Williamson identifies two sets of factors which will determine the cost of contracting through markets, and thus the likelihood of markets *failing* and being replaced by hierarchies. The first is the uncertainty of future states of the world combined with the 'bounded rationality' of humans. To define bounded rationality he quotes Herbert Simon:

> The capacity of the human mind for formulating and solving complex problems is very small compared with the size of the problems whose solution is required for objectively rational behaviour in the real world.

Uncertainty means that long-term contracts that covered every contingency in the future might need to be very complex. The limitations of the human mind mean that the costs of writing such contracts would be high. The virtue of a firm in this situation is that in a firm there may be less need to anticipate the future, the future can be allowed to unfold, and be dealt with in a sequential fashion.

The second set of factors concern the combination of 'opportunism' where 'opportunism refers to a lack of candour or honesty in transactions, to include self-interest seeking with guile', with 'small-numbers' of participants in a transaction. One reason why hierarchies might be preferred in a world where people behave self-interestedly is that in general 'the internal incentive and control machinery is much more extensive [in a firm] . . .' The relevance of 'small numbers' to this needs explaining. Basic economic theory shows that when the supply of some good or service is monopolised or controlled by a small number of individuals its price is likely to be higher than in a perfectly competitive market. Williamson points out that although contracting often starts as competitive the parties build up specialist knowledge about 'the business which, when subsequent contracts are written, gives them monopolistic powers which permit them to behave opportunistically.'

There are information *costs* associated with firms too. Larger hierarchies tend to have more levels of authority and an increased risk of loss of control as information is delayed and distorted on its way up and down the hierarchy and as top management are plied with more information than they can handle. And if the functional departments of the firm are handling a large range of heterogeneous projects it becomes difficult for top management to get accurate signals of the performance of these separate activities. The solution to this excess of hierarchy suggested by Williamson and practised by many firms since Dupont and General Motors in the early 1920s is to adopt a multidivisional, or '*M-form*' structure. In the M-form firm operations are broken up along product or geographical lines, into semi-autonomous divisions, quasi-firms. According to Williamson the main function of the parent company in the M-form enterprise is as a 'miniature capital market', monitoring divisional performance and allocating funds for investment.

The divisions of an M-form enterprise are only one step removed from separate firms interrelating through the market. Unless the hierarchical 'miniature capital market' is clearly superior to the capital market itself, there is no clear reason not to break the enterprise up into separate firms. At the time of writing this view appears to be gaining ground. In the US there has been a wave of 'demerger', including major corporations such as General Tyre. In the UK the General Electric Company, whose chairman, Sir Arnold Weinstock has been a major advocate of the M-form structure was reported to be contemplating demerger.

The Times of 16.2.1980 said that GEC saw several advantages in a demerger; it would increase the ability of workers to identify with the firm, and divisional managers would get more public recognition for their success. It might also reduce the risk of nationalisation. Against this was the loss of economic 'clout' in a world containing some very large and powerful competitors, and the fact that certain trading inter-relationships and dependencies might have to be severed. But the decisive obstacle at present was the large tax bill many shareholders would face, since under present tax law the demerger would amount to a sale of shares in GEC by shareholders.

V THE COSTS OF AGENCY AND THE SEPARATION OF OWNERSHIP AND CONTROL

Business finance is particularly interested in one subset of the firm's contractual relationships – contracts for the supply of finance. Financial contracts have a time dimension: they give the supplier claims against the future assets of the firm. But this time dimension introduces uncertainty and means that the future assets of the firm, and thus the claims, are '*contingent*' on future '*states of the world*' that cannot yet be known with certainty. Moreover, financial contracts tend to be '*complex*' in that they cover many time-periods and potential states of the world. We saw in the previous section that the costs of writing contracts like this that were complete in that they fully specified claims in all possible states of the world, would be prohibitive. It would mean working out in advance every future action of the firm in every contingency! The contract between the supplier of finance and the firm is usually left 'incomplete', and managers are entrusted with running the firm and making decisions on behalf of the shareholders or creditors sequentially as a future unfolds. So the separation of ownership and control, can be seen as a response to the costs of writing complete complex contingent claims contracts.

We can describe the relationship between the suppliers of finance and the managers as one of *agency*, where an agency relationship is

> ... a contract under which one or more persons (the principal(s)) engage another person (the agent) to perform some service on their behalf which involves delegating some decision-making authority to the agent.
> (*Jensen and Meckling* (1976) p 308)

The application of the theory of agency to problems in finance is relatively recent and still developing, but the paper by Jensen and Meckling gives a taste of the contribution this particular form of 'contractual' approach can make.

Jensen and Meckling

Jensen and Meckling address two questions, whether the value of the firm will be maximised when there is a separation of ownership and control, and why firms choose the capital structures they do. As they freely acknowledge, their analysis is very restrictive. It assumes a simple word in which a manager who initially owns 100% of the equity sells 5% to outsiders, and where there are no taxes, outside equity has no vote, and no financing contracts more complex than debt and equity are possible.

Jensen and Meckling assume that managers make decisions which maximise their own utility, and that this involves not just the cash income, or 'value', of the firm but a whole range of non-cash perquisites,

> ... the physical appointments of the office, the attractiveness of the secretarial staff, the level of employee discipline, the kind and amount of charitable contributions, personal relations ('love', 'respect', etc) with employees, a larger than optimal computer to play with, purchase of production inputs from friends, etc.
> (*Jensen and Meckling*, op cit, p 312)

And leisure, which conflicts with the single-minded quest for profitable projects, will have utility for managers as well. Once it is accepted that managers get utility from non-cash perquisites, it necessarily follows that a separation of ownership and control will reduce the value of the firm. Consider a firm in which the manager initially owns 100% of the equity, then subsequently sells 5% to outsiders. In the former case the manager will expand his consumption of perquisites until at the margin he is sacrificing £1 of cash to get £1 of utility from perquisites. But if 5% of the equity is held by outsiders, 5% of the sacrifice of cash is borne by them too, and the manager only bears 95p of the cost of the £1 worth of perquisites. It will be in the manager's interest to expand his consumption of perquisites further, and reduce the free cash flow, and thus the value of the firm.

The difference between the value of the firm when it is owner-controlled and when there is a separation of ownership and control is a cost of the agency relationship. The principal may incur costs to '*monitor*' the agent's behaviour and the agent may himself find it worthwhile to incur *bonding* costs to demonstrate that his behaviour is not harmful to the principal. The total cost associated with an agency relationship has thus three components: these monitoring and bonding costs, and the '*residual loss*' of value that remains after the optimal amount of monitoring and bonding of taken place.[9] Examples of monitoring and bonding costs include 'auditing, formal control systems, budget restrictions, and the establishment of incentive compensation systems' (p 323).

Jensen and Meckling apply their analysis to the question of the ownership structure of the firm: why it is that firms employ a mix of debt and equity and that the mix varies from firm to firm? The risk to debt holders in a firm in which the manager holds a significant amount of equity is that after the terms of the debt have been agreed the manager will change his policy in favour of undertaking riskier projects, which offer potentially greater gains to equity but a greater risk of loss to debt. Hence there will be a value-loss to debt-holders arising from the agency relationship between debt-holders and management, and as before it will be in the interests of managers that this should be mitigated through monitoring and bonding. So it is common to find clauses in debt agreements that limit the scope of managers to do things like paying dividends, issuing more debt or running down working capital.

The agency costs of inside equity, outside equity, and debt will differ between industries. So in industries such as the bar and restaurant trade where theft, shirking, and favouring of special customers are easy for managers little outside equity will be found, and inside finance will tend to be debt. But in, say, conglomerates where the riskiness of the earnings of the firm can be changed to the detriment of debt-holders by changing the mix of the firm's activities, then debt-financing will be less popular. Again, in highly regulated industries where the scope of managers to undertake risky projects is constrained, debt will be more prevalent.

Agency theory is still in its early stages of development. The theory has not yet entered the main canon of finance theory and its predictions have yet to be subjected to empirical testing. But it can provide interesting insights.

VI SUMMARY

There are many legal forms a firm may take, but the significant one for the study of business finance is the 'limited liability joint-stock company'. With this structure there can be a separation of ownership and control, so that the management of the firm is entrusted to a continuing team of people with management skills, while ownership may be in the hands of a potentially large and changing group of individuals or institutions with savings available to finance the firm. However, the separation of ownership and control raises the potential problem of a conflict of interest between owners and managers.

We reviewed the arguments for a divergence of interest, and the constraints on managerial behaviour which might limit the divergence. Though the arguments have some appeal, and the constraints appear to leave scope, there is no strong empirical evidence that managers are consistently pursuing objectives other than value maximisation.

The final sections of the chapter reviewed the work by Williamson on the rationale for the existence of the firm, and by Jensen and Meckling applying agency theory to analyse problems arising from the separation of ownership and control. This work provides examples of the 'contractual' approach which underlies many current day theoretical developments in finance. Under this approach the framework for economic analysis is a world of rational individuals freely contracting with each other in the face of future events which are complex and uncertain.

9   The 'optimal' amount of these activities will occur where the marginal cost equals the marginal benefit. If the marginal costs are positive it will not be worthwhile to eliminate all of the value loss.

REFERENCES AND BIBLIOGRAPHY

Alchian, A A	'Uncertainty, Evolution and Economic Theory', Journal of Political Economy, 1950, pp 211–221.
Baumol, W J	'On the Theory of Oligopoly', Economica, August 1958, pp 187–198.
Berle, A A and Means, G C	The Modern Corporation and Private Property (1932) Macmillan, New York.
Briston, R J and Dobbins, R	The Growth and Impact of Institutional Investors (1978) Institute of Chartered Accountants in England and Wales, London.
Coase, R H	'The Nature of the Firm', Economica, 1937.
Cosh, A	'The remuneration of chief executives in the United Kingdom', Economic Journal, March 1975, pp 75–94.
Cyert, R M and March, J G	A Behavioural Theory of the Firm (1963) Prentice-Hall, Englewood-Cliffs, New Jersey.
Furubotn, E G	'The Long-Run Analysis of the Labour-Managed Firm: An alternative Interpretation', American Economic Review, 1976, pp 104–123.
Herman, E S	Corporate Control, Corporate Power (1981) Cambridge University Press.
Jensen, M C and Meckling, W H	'Theory of the Firm: Managerial Behaviour, Agency Costs and Ownership Structure', Journal of Financial Economics, Oct 1976, pp 305–60.
Kuehn, D	Takeovers and the Theory of the Firm: An Empirical Analysis of the United Kingdom, 1957–1969 (1975) London, Macmillan.
Lee, T A and Tweedie, D P	The Private Shareholder and the Corporate Report (1977) Institute of Chartered Accountants in England and Wales, London.
Liebenstein, H	'Allocative Efficiency vs "X-Efficiency"', American Economic Review, June 1966, pp 392–415.
Marris, R	'A Model of the "Managerial Enterprise"', Quarterly Journal of Economics, 77, 1964, pp 185–209.
Marris, R and Mueller, D C	'The Corporation, Competition, and the Invisible Hand', Journal of Economic Literature, 1980, pp 32–63.
Meeks, G and Whittington, G	'Directors' Pay, Growth and Profitability', Journal of Industrial Economics, vol 24, Sept 1975a, pp 1–14.
Meeks, G and Whittington, G	'Giant Companies in the United Kingdom, 1948–69' Economic Journal, 1975b.
Nyman, S and Silberston, A	'The Ownership and Control of Industry', Oxford Economic Papers, 1978. Reprinted in Wagner, L. (ed) Readings in Applied Microeconomics (1981) Oxford.
Prais, S J	The Evolution of Giant Firms in Britain (1976) Cambridge University Press, Cambridge.
Sargent Florence, P	Ownership, Control and Success of Large Companies (1961) Sweet and Maxwell, London.
Simon, H A	'Theories of Decision Making in Economics and Behavioural Science', American Economic Review, June 1959, pp 253–283.

Singh, A	'Takeovers, Economic Natural Selection, and the Theory of the Firm: Evidence from the Post-war United Kingdom Experience' Economic Journal, 85, 1975, pp 497–515.
Smith, A	*An Inquiry into the Nature and Causes of the Wealth of Nations* (1776). E. Cannon (ed) (1961) Methuen University Paperbacks, London.
Stanworth, P and Giddens, A	'The Modern Corporate Economy: Interlocking Directorships in Britain, 1906–1970', Sociological Review, 1975.
Vanek, J	*Self-Management* (1975) Penguin, Harmondsworth, England.
Williamson, O E	*Markets and Hierarchies* (1975) Macmillan, New York.

QUESTIONS

1 We tend to associate unincorporated firms with small scale, and limited liability with large scale enterprise. What is the reason for this?

2 In finance we assume managers seek to maximise the value of the firm. Why is this a desirable objective?

3 What constraints exist on managers pursuing their own interests?

4 What objectives should the managers of a public utility be asked to pursue?

5 Markets are usually considered an efficient way of organising economic activity. If this is so, how can we explain the existence of large hierarchical structures called 'firms'?

6 What are the problems of running large firms and how does 'M-form' help overcome them?

7 Explain how the problem of the separation of ownership and control can be described in terms of the principal-agent relationship.

CHAPTER 3

Taxation

This chapter outlines the UK tax system and examines some taxes that have an impact on financial decision-making. The first section gives an overview of the tax system as a whole. In Section II we examine corporation tax, and in Section III some taxes borne by investors, personal income tax, capital gains tax and capital transfer tax. In the final section we examine value added tax to show how even taxes which appear to be borne by others can have an impact on the firm.

I THE UK TAX SYSTEM

Table I shows an outline of the UK tax system in terms of the main sources of tax revenue. The figures in brackets after each source are the percentage it contributed to total government tax revenues in tax year 1984–85. Essentially government extracts three kinds of tax. *Income taxes* are taxes on incomes as they are earned. Companies pay corporation tax on their profits, and individuals including sole traders and partnerships pay two forms of income tax, personal income tax and national insurance contributions.[1] *Commodity taxes* are taxes on expenditure. The most widely felt are value added tax (VAT) and excise duties

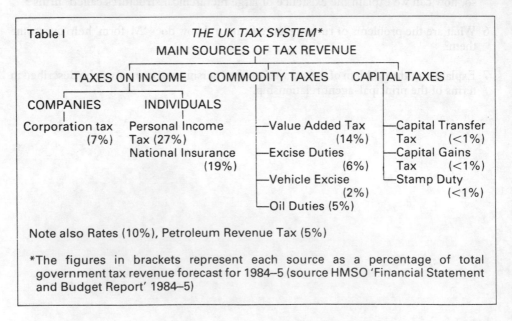

Table I	THE UK TAX SYSTEM*

MAIN SOURCES OF TAX REVENUE

TAXES ON INCOME   COMMODITY TAXES   CAPITAL TAXES

COMPANIES   INDIVIDUALS

Corporation tax (7%)	Personal Income Tax (27%) National Insurance (19%)	—Value Added Tax (14%) —Excise Duties (6%) —Vehicle Excise (2%) —Oil Duties (5%)	—Capital Transfer Tax (<1%) —Capital Gains Tax (<1%) —Stamp Duty (<1%)

Note also Rates (10%), Petroleum Revenue Tax (5%)

*The figures in brackets represent each source as a percentage of total government tax revenue forecast for 1984–5 (source HMSO 'Financial Statement and Budget Report' 1984–5)

---

1 Though easy to overlook, national insurance was second only to personal income tax as a source of revenue in 1984–5, yielding 19% of total revenues.

which are taxes on specific items, notably alcoholic drink, tobacco, gambling, and petroleum. *Capital taxes* are taxes on the disposal of assets. Capital transfer tax (CTT) is charged on a sliding scale on the value of presents or bequests on death. Capital gains tax (CGT) is charged on the surplus made from selling certain types of asset, and stamp duty is charged on the proceeds of sale of certain types of asset, notably land, buildings and securities. In general, if it moves it is taxed! However, since there is no intellectual reason to restrict taxation to things that move, the proposal for a wealth tax is receiving consideration in certain quarters. A tax of this sort already exists in the form of *rates* which are taxes on immovable property, houses, factories etc. Rates are levied by local government and represent a significant tax on firms with approximately 3/5 of total rate revenue generated from industrial and commercial buildings. Of course since most assets yield income even if it is only utility or 'psychic income' the difference between an income tax and a tax on capital stock or wealth is smaller than at first appears, it is a difference of the 'tax base' government uses.

Taxation is and has always been an emotive issue. For one thing people do not like paying tax and tend to complain about it. More significantly the fiscal system provides government with major instruments of economic and social policy, and whichever the government, there are sure to be a lot of people who either disagree with its objectives, or with its means of achieving them.

A major problem is that tax policy often poses a conflict between *equity* and *efficiency*, between who gets the cake and how big the cake is. This problem was evident in the UK personal income tax system. Until recently it was possible for certain individuals to pay a marginal rate of tax of 98% on some of their income. Many people felt that the redistributive (= equity) effects of this tax were outweighed by its disincentive and distortive (= efficiency) effects on economic behaviour. In fact the effect of personal income tax as a disincentive to the supply of effort and to risk-taking has been much researched, but with no strong conclusion emerging. The problem is that, in economic terms, there is a substitution effect, but also an income effect. Though high income tax makes work less attractive at the margin, it also means that more work is needed to achieve a given income. Which of these factors predominates is likely to depend on the income, the social group and the nature of the work of the individual. But one argument which tends to be influential in the low-growth UK is the international comparison. No other advanced country sported such a high marginal rate of personal income tax, and the top rate of personal income tax was reduced to 60% by the Thatcher administration. Since the removal of this 'anomaly' the UK sits fairly well in the middle of advanced economies both in terms of the overall tax burden and in the balance of taxes which it collects.[2] Looking particularly at business taxes, though, and compared to the other main industrialised countries, Kay and Sen (1983) found UK business taxes to be low relative to output and as a percentage of total tax revenues, but high as a fraction of profits. This apparent paradox arises because UK profitability has been relatively low.

Taxes and financial decisions – a look ahead

As a starting point in building the theory of financial decisions we will often assume a perfect capital market with no taxation. But in the real world the earnings of firms are liable to corporation tax, and the returns to investors are liable to personal income tax or capital

2   Some of the efficiency aspects of the tax system are referred to below where they relate to financial decisions, but for a comprehensive introduction and critique of the UK tax system which is easy to read, the reader is referred to Kay and King (1983). In the context of the firm, King (1977) provides a powerful attempt to model the impact of the tax system on the financial decisions of UK companies.

gains tax. So in a taxed world the job of the financial manager is to choose the projects and to find the financing mix that give the best after-tax returns to investors. However the picture can get complicated because effective tax rates may differ between companies, and between investors. Companies can find themselves permanently or temporarily non-taxpaying with the result that they pay no corporation tax or pay at an effective rate which is below the full rate. More problematic is the fact that the investors' tax rates may differ too – some pay tax at higher rates, whereas others may be exempt from tax. The problem is that not only may managers not be sure about their investors' tax-positions, it may be actually impossible to find a financing policy that suits them all. Take dividends as an example: tax-exempt investors may want high dividends, while high taxpayers may prefer to take capital gains.

Taxation complicates financial decisions and raises some questions that theory cannot completely answer. We will be returning to the issues raised by taxation throughout the book. Before we proceed, however, another caution on tax rates.

Traditionally changes to the structure of the tax system and to the rates of tax are made by the annual Finance Act and announced by the Chancellor of the Exchequer each March in his budget, though Chancellors sometimes present interim budgets at other times in the year. So the details of the tax system in this chapter were correct in 1985 but may soon change, though the general principles which they illustrate are less likely to change. And it ought to be remembered that these *are* only general principles; tax law in reality is a mass of special cases and exceptions which generate handsome incomes for lawyers and accountants. There are several regularly updated sources available for the reader who wishes to check the detail of tax law, for example the regularly updated *Simon's Taxes*.

II CORPORATION TAX

Companies pay corporation tax (CT) on their 'taxable profit' at the prevailing rate for the financial year in which the profit is earned: FA 1984 outlined the following CT rates:

Financial year ended 31 March:	1983	52%
	1984	50%
	1985	45%
	1986	40%
Thereafter:		35%

There is a special 'small companies' rate of 30%, which should more accurately be called a small profit rate since it applies when 'profits'[3] are below a given level. At present companies pay this rate when profits are below £100,000 and an intermediate rate on profits between £100,000 and £500,000 after which the full rate applies. For convenience we will assume a CT rate of 40% in examples.

THE IMPUTATION SYSTEM

There are various possible ways of taxing companies, but in the UK since 1973 CT has been collected under the 'IMPUTATION' system. Under this system CT is normally paid in two parts,[4] advanced corporation tax (ACT) and mainstream corporation tax (MCT).

---

3   For this purpose only 'profits' is defined in a slightly different way to the usual 'taxable profit'.
4   Or three, since if the company pays an interim as well as a final dividend it will need to pay two instalments of ACT.

When the firm pays a dividend it must remit to the Revenue fourteen days after the end of the quarter some ACT, an amount of tax equivalent to the basic rate of personal income tax which would have been deducted, as if the dividend were one paid net of income tax.

Consider an example:
Atherton Ltd pays a dividend of £500,000, and the basic rate of personal income tax is 30%. The firm must pay ACT of £214,286. Why? Because £214,286 is the tax that would have had to be paid if £500,000 were a payment net of basic rate income tax, since the gross mount would be:

$$£500,000 + £214,286 = £714,286$$

$$\text{giving: tax } £714,286 \times 30\% = 214,286$$
$$\text{net of tax } £714,286 \times 70\% = 500,000$$

What we have done is to 'gross-up' the £500,000 at 30%. The tax was found by multiplying the net amount by $\dfrac{\text{'tax-rate'}}{1 - \text{'tax-rate'}}$. So in this case, tax $= £500,000 \times \dfrac{.3}{1 - .3} =$ $£500,000 \times \dfrac{30}{70} = £214,286$.

This procedure may seem rather complex at first sight. But it is aimed to prevent a bias in the tax system against paying dividends. The dividend the shareholder receives is deemed to have borne basic rate income tax already, personal income tax is 'imputed' to it, so he does not have to pay this again. The company on the other hand can set the tax off against its overall tax liability, hence it is 'advance' corporation tax. The balance of CT is referred to as MAINSTREAM corporation tax and one redeeming feature for companies is that there is often a significant lag before mainstream tax need be paid. In general companies that were trading before 1965 may not have to pay their mainstream for up to 21 months after the end of their accounting year.

So if Atherton Ltd is a company of this sort and its accounting year ends on 30 April 1986 it will pay MCT on these profits on 1 January 1988, 20 months later. Companies which started trading after 1.4.65 pay the tax nine months after the accounting year-end. In either case the lag amounts to costless finance for the firm, provided by the Inland Revenue.

Developing the previous example, Atherton's dividend was paid on 31 March 1986,[5] out of taxable profits for the year ended 30.4.86 of £2 million, hence the ACT will be payable on 14 April 1986. Its overall tax position is as follows, with the position if it had paid no dividend shown as a comparison

	Position if divi-dend is paid (000's)	Position if no dividend is paid (000's)
Taxable profits	£2,000	£2,000
CT (40%)	800	800
	1,200	1,200
Dividend (net)	500	
Retained profit =	£ 700	£1,200

5 Note, for simplicity we have assumed that the dividend is paid in the accounting year to which it relates. In practice the final dividend is usually paid after the accounting year, and this causes allocation complications since ACT is set off against the CT of the period *in which*, not *for which*, the dividend is paid.

	Position if divi-dend is paid	Position if no dividend is paid
Position of Shareholders		
Dividend received	500	–
Imputed tax	214.3	–
Gross dividend =	£714.3	
Liability of Atherton to Inland Revenue		
ACT payable 14.4.1986	214.3	–
Mainstream payable 1.1.1988	585.7	800
	£800.00	800

The main aim in introducing the imputation system was to remove the incentive to retain rather than pay dividends which the previous system provided. Whether the imputation system *is* neutral in this sense is explored in Chapter 15. In fact the disincentive which remains in the system is one of cash flow. In the example above, by paying a dividend Atherton has also committed itself to paying £214,286 a year earlier than otherwise.

TAXABLE PROFIT

The profit on which the Revenue charges tax is based on the profit reported in the accounts, but with some important changes. Certain expenses are not allowed for tax and have to be added back to profit. Some examples are expenses incurred in entertaining people, other than foreign customers and their agents, charitable subscriptions, fines, general provisions for events that have not yet occurred, and costs of tax appeals! The general principle is that expenses must be *wholly and exclusively* incurred for the purposes of the business.

A principle of taxation with great significance for finance is that though interest – the cost of servicing debt finance – is an allowable deduction in arriving at taxable profit, dividends – the cost of servicing equity finance – are not. With a rate of CT of 40% this almost halves the cost of debt finance and alters the optimal mix of finance in favour of debt. The rationale is that dividends are a distribution of the profits of the firm rather than an expense in earning them. But for most firms dividends are both a distribution and a necessary expense in obtaining equity finance. It could be argued that dividends have two components, the minimum return required by equity to induce them to invest in the firm given its risk and growth prospects, and a premium representing the distribution of surplus profits. We might want to allow the first component as an expense and tax the second. However, the size of these two elements is not directly ascertainable and it seems unlikely that a practical alternative to 'not allowing' dividends could be devised. Part of the popularity of 'convertible loan stock' as a method of financing is that it is debt to the tax man, but offers the appeal of equity to the investor.

On the other hand some revenues are not taxable either. An example is dividends received from other UK companies which are not taxable since they are paid out of profits that are already taxed. Also any profits made on the sale of assets are 'capital gains' under tax law, and as such are taxed at 30%. This is achieved in practice by including in taxable profit a figure of 30/40 of the capital gain. One major difference between accounting and taxable profit concerns depreciation.

Capital allowances

In an effort to stimulate investment, post-war governments have allowed UK firms to accelerate the depreciation they can charge in finding taxable profit, so conferring cash-flow benefits on them by postponing tax. The Revenue ignores the firm's depreciation charge and deducts instead *capital allowances*, in the form of *writing-down allowances*. Additionally, for some assets companies were able to claim a higher *first-year allowance* instead of the writing-down allowance in the year of purchase. For plant and machinery first-year allowances have been 100%, allowing the firm to write-off the whole cost against tax immediately. This reflected the view that a slowness to invest in new machinery embodying more efficient technology had contributed to the low rate of growth of the UK. However the 1984 budget phased-out first-year allowances. For plant and machinery and phase-out was as follows:

Financial period ended 13 March 1984	100%
31 March 1985	75%
31 March 1986	50%
Thereafter	NIL

Henceforth only writing-down allowances are available. Table II shows the current rates.

Table II Writing-down allowances

Plant, Machinery, Ships Aircraft, Vehicles, etc.	25% per annum of the reducing balance
Qualifying Industrial Buildings, Agricultural Buildings and Hotels	4% p.a. straight-line
Other Buildings	NIL

When a company disposes of an asset it may well sell it at a price which is above, or below, its tax written-down value. The tax treatment then depends on whether the asset is 'pooled' or not. If not the Revenue either reclaims the excess allowances by making a *balancing charge*, or allows the write-off of the remaining cost through a *balancing allowance*. However for plant and machinery and motor vehicles, with certain exceptions, the treatment is different. They are added to a *pool* of similar assets, and writing-down allowances are given on the value of the whole pool. When the asset is sold the sale proceeds are removed from the pool. The company still receives in effect balancing allowances and charges. However these are spread into the future as the surplus or deficit left in the pool is written down in future periods, and since writing-down allowances on plant, machinery and vehicles are 25% on a reducing-balance basis, assets are never fully expunged.

Cash grants

As a further incentive, investment in certain underdeveloped regions attracts cash grants from government, and these grants do not reduce the cost of the machine for the purpose of calculating capital allowances. The current rates are in Table III. So a machine costing £1 million, bought in a special development area reduces tax by £1 million × 40% = £400,000, and qualifies for a cash grant of £1 million × 22% = £220,000. The effective cost of the machine to the firm is therefore £380,000.

In addition to regional grants there is a whole range of schemes under which

Table III Cash grants for investment as a % of cost at Jan 1985			
	Regional Development Grants		Capital and Industrial Development Grants
	Special Development Areas	Development Areas	Northern Ireland
New Buildings, Works, Plant and Machinery	22%	15%	30–50%
Sources; Dept of Industry, N Ireland Industrial Dev Office			

government provides cash grants usually up to 33⅓% of eligible costs for projects which boost productivity or stimulate innovation, particularly in the area of new technology.

Whether all these incentives have had a significant effect is hard to say. UK investment has remained low, but might have been lower without them. Governments, in their efforts, have changed the law so often that it is sometimes said that uncertainty about the tax system has itself provided a disincentive to invest.

The effects of inflation

The base for CT is accounting profit with certain adjustments. But as we will see in a later chapter when there is inflation, accounting profit, being based on historic cost, is likely to overstate profit and in particular understates the cost of stocks and fixed assets. This means that under inflation companies are liable to be over-taxed. The reason is that by the time the historic costs are taken into account for tax they understate the cost of replacing the fixed assets and stocks. When UK inflation was particularly high the Revenue was forced to recognise this problem. The system of 100% first-year allowances on plant and machinery did this by allowing tax relief immediately the cost was incurred. In addition between 1974 and 1984 companies could claim STOCK RELIEF by deducting from taxable profits the purely inflationary part of their stock profits. However, in 1984 both these concessions were withdrawn, despite the fact that UK inflation, though lower, was still positive.

Inflation also has an effect through the lag in tax payments. There is a lag of up to 21 months before companies need pay their MCT, and if there is inflation this reduces the real cost of the tax to the firm. On the other hand it reduces the value of the tax-saving associated with any expenses the firm incurs. This effect becomes more significant when the tax payment is postponed still further because the firm is carrying forward tax losses.

TAX LOSSES

For various reasons, because the firm has excess capital allowances, or maybe because it was making an accounting loss anyway, it can make a TAX LOSS. Sadly, the Revenue does not start paying the firm 40% of its losses at this juncture, but losses *can* be used to reduce tax liability. The precise rules depend on how the loss arose, but in general losses can be carried forward to be 'set off' against or to reduce taxable income of the 'same trade' in future periods, or they can be set off against the profits of the whole firm, or of other firms in the same group or consortium, in the present or previous year. So in the latter case it may be possible to reclaim money from the Revenue.

The problem with carrying forward tax losses is that the cash flow benefit is postponed until they are offset. But strategies such as LEASING or MERGER can assist. Firms with excess capital allowances can make mutually beneficial arrangements with other firms which have excess taxable profits. The 'profitable' firm may buy the plant and machinery for the other firm and lease it to them. This way it can qualify for the capital allowances and postpone some of its own CT, and the benefits can be split with the other firm by charging advantageous rates for the lease. Occasionally the tax benefits are so powerful as to justify a permanent merger between a firm expecting chronic taxable profits and a firm expecting chronic tax losses, caused perhaps by heavy investment.

Accumulated past losses do not provide a motive for merger though, and there is no longer a market in firms with accumulated losses. The Revenue allows 'GROUP RELIEF' of *current* tax losses and of unrelieved ACT, but carry-forwards of losses are carefully monitored and are only allowed where there is a clear continuity of ownership and trade. 'Diagonal' set-offs, against future profits of other group members, are not allowed, though there can be some scope for transferring profits to group members with losses by judicious choice of transfer prices.

The combined effect of generous capital allowances and, when it was available, stock relief is that many UK firms have paid relatively little CT. Table IV shows CT as a percentage of profits by 20 of the largest UK companies in 1983. The 1984 budget reduced capital allowances, but average rates are still below nominal tax rates.

DEFERRED TAXATION

It is clear that because of the exclusions and allowances the Revenue makes in measuring taxable profit, few companies will have an accounting profit and a taxable profit which are

Table IV Corporation Tax 1983			
(£m)			
Company	Pretax Profits	Corp Tax	%
Allied-Lyons	145	44	31
Bass Charrington	161	61	38
BAT	979	139	14
Barclays	557	188	34
BP	2,593	579	22
Britoil	306	115	37
Courtaulds	633	85	13
Distillers	209	67	13
GEC	670	224	33
Grand Metropolitan	295	50	17
GKN	95	9	9
ICI	612	198	32
Imperial Group	189	68	36
Marks and Spencer	237	79	33
National Westminster Bank	503	116	23
P & O	53	2	4
Reed International	74	25	34
Rio Tinto-Zinc	575	58	10
Shell	3,020	2	0
Unilever	813	114	14

the same. The differences between the Revenue's and the accountant's methods of measuring income are of two sorts, permanent differences and timing differences. PERMANENT differences relate to revenues and expenses recognised by the accountant, but not taxable or allowable under tax law, or vice versa. Examples are certain types of entertainment expenditure, dividend income, or capital gains which though taxable are not taxable at the full CT rate. TIMING differences relate to items which are recognised by both but in different time periods, so that while in the long run the accounting and tax treatments are the same, in any given year they will differ. Examples are capital allowances and revaluation surpluses.

Consider an example:
A firm buys a machine for £1,000 which it expects to use for 10 years to earn a profit each year before depreciation of £200. Assuming it depreciates the machine on a straight-line basis its accounting profit each year will be:

Profit before depreciation	200
Depreciation	(100)
Accounting Profit	100

On the other hand the firm can claim writing-down allowances of 25% of the reducing balance. This will determine its taxable profit and thus the tax it pays each year. Assuming a CT rate of 40% the taxable profit and tax payable are shown below. Note that in the first year the firm's capital allowance exceeds its profit so the excess has to be carried forward in the first two years.

Year	1	2	3	4	5	6	7	8	9	10	TOTAL
Profit before Depreciation	200	200	200	200	200	200	200	200	200	200	2000
Cap. Allow's limited to	250 / 200	188 / 200	141 / 179	105	79	59	45	33	25	75	1000
Taxable Profit	–	–	21	95	121	141	155	167	175	125	1000
Tax (40%)	–	–	8	38	48	57	62	67	70	50	400

Over the ten years the accounting profit and the taxable profit both add to £1,000. But they are distributed differently, and thus the relationship between the accounting profit and the tax charge is uneven. So in the year 1 the firm earns £100 profit and pays no tax. In year 9 the firm earns £100 and pays £70 tax.

This unevenness has led most firms to adopt an accounting procedure called 'DEFERRED TAX accounting' albeit after some controversy. Under deferred tax accounting firms show in their published income statement a CT charge which is NOT what is actually payable in the year, but is calculated as though tax were charged on the basis of the accounting treatment of items with a timing difference.[6] So in the example, where there are no absolute differences between accounting and taxable profit the tax charge calculated this way would be £100 × 40% = £40 each year. The difference between tax calculated this way, and the

6 Under the present guidelines from the accountancy bodies, SSAP 15, companies need not provide deferred tax if the deferral is permanent or 'semi-permanent'.

actual tax charge is transferred to or from a reserve in the balance sheet. This reserve represents a liability to the Revenue for tax whose payment has temporarily been deferred. The rationale for deferred tax accounting is that of matching revenues with the expenses incurred in earning them, contingent or actual: cash flow is replaced by a measure of the change in the liability position of the firm. On the other hand deferred tax accounting may conceal a fact of real economic significance to firms – the deferment of tax liability. More tellingly much of deferred tax provisions may never be paid because of the continuous replacement policies of most firms and the continuing scaling-up of costs through inflation. Either way deferred tax is a concept that must be understood by anyone who seeks to understand the published accounts of firms.

CLOSE COMPANIES

Corporate status might provide opportunities for tax avoidance. Believing that abuse is most likely in firms that are owned and managed by a small, close group of people, the law has defined a CLOSE COMPANY. Roughly speaking this is a company which no more than five 'participators' control.

'Participator' is defined widely and individuals who tend to act as a unit, for example husband and wife, are defined as one participator. The close company law has been softened a great deal since its inception, but it remains the case that:
1 The Revenue has the right to treat certain profits as dividends above a certain level and if they are surplus to the requirements of the business; they may 'apportion' them and charge shareholders income tax on their share. The purpose of this is to discourage the conversion of income into capital gains which attract a lower rate of tax.
2 If the firm makes loans to shareholders they will have to remit ACT to the Revenue as though the loan had been a dividend. This restricts the advantage of hidden dividends being paid by making loans to shareholders, which are subsequently written off in the books or linger there forever.

Defined in this way, the vast majority of small and medium-sized firms are 'close', and some large firms where control has stayed in the hands of a small number of families. However, an additional clause in the legislation allows that a company may not be 'close' if the 'public' own at least 35% of the voting power, so long as the company's five largest vote-holders do not between them hold more than 85% of the voting power. This perhaps explained the decision by some firms to 'go public'.

III PERSONAL INCOME TAX AND CAPITAL GAINS TAX

It is impossible to understand the behaviour of individuals in the capital market without considering the taxation of the individual's income and capital gains.

Income tax

In the UK an individual is liable to pay tax on his or her taxable income which is basically all income from any source, at home or abroad, less certain 'allowances'. So for example all single persons and the wage-earners in married couples receive a 'personal allowance'. If the Chancellor has set the personal allowance at £2,000 for the year, then the first £2,000 of income would be tax free for all individuals. Another allowance that is significant for many individuals is the facility to deduct from taxable income the amount of interest paid on loans of up to £30,000 for the purchase or improvement of their private residence.

As well as generally available allowances the law allows certain expenses associated with earning the income to be set-off in calculating taxable income. This depends on the type of income, and there are several different sets of rules, or 'schedules', defining in each case how taxable income is calculated, what expenses are deductable, and when the tax is payable. Individuals who are employees usually have income tax deducted by the employer under the 'Pay-as-you-earn' (PAYE) system. Income from employment is dealt with under 'Schedule E', which offers very little scope for setting-off expenditure, or for postponing payment of tax. But self employed people, sole traders and partnerships, pay tax under 'Schedule D' which offers considerably more potential for individuals to arrange their affairs so as to reduce tax and postpone paying it. One key difference is that to be deductable under 'Schedule E', expenses have in general to be 'wholly, exclusively and *necessarily*' incurred in earning the income, whereas under 'Schedule D', they only have to be 'wholly and exclusively' incurred.

Personal income tax is 'progressive'. In the first portion of income, to the extent of any allowances, the individual pays no tax. Then the first portion of taxable income is taxed at the BASIC RATE of 30%, then subsequent bands of income are taxed at progressively higher rates up to a maximum of 60%. However, institutions such as pension funds and insurance companies, and also charities, are not liable to income tax. The upshot is that the marginal tax of a firm's investors can range from zero if they are institutions, to 60% if they are high income individuals.

Capital gains tax (CGT)

Gains made by selling assets may be taxed as CAPITAL GAINS. The rules for determining just what gains qualify in this respect are complex, but they need not concern us beyond noting that if buying and selling the particular type of asset effectively constitutes a trade then the gains will be taxed as income. Hence, for example, the law attempts to distinguish people who buy and sell shares short term for speculative gain from those who buy shares to hold as income producing assets. In the former case gains would be taxed as income, in the latter case as capital gains.

The taxpayer can deduct from the gain, inflation as measured by the RPI during ownership of the asset. The rate of CGT is 30% and companies also pay tax at 30% on their capital gains. Pension funds, charities etc do not pay CGT on any gains they make from 'dealing' in assets rather than holding them. Unlike personal income tax the rate is not progressive and herein lies its significance. The distinction between capital and income is in many cases arbitrary, and it is possible in certain situations to choose how a gain will be taken.

Consider an example:
On 1 November Cynthia owned shares with a value of £1,100 which she had bought for £900. The increase in value partly reflected the fact that the shares were about to pay a dividend of £100, going 'ex div' on 2 November, and on 3 November their value was expected to fall to £1,000. Cynthia's marginal rate of tax was 60%. If she sold the shares on 1 November her position would be:

	£
Capital gain	1,100 − 900 = 200
Tax (CGT)	200 × 30% = 60
Net gain	140

If she sold the shares on 3 November her position would be:

$£$

Capital gain	$1,000 - 900 = 100$
Tax (CGT)	$100 \times 30\% = \underline{30}$
	70
Dividend	100
Income tax[7]	$\underline{43}$
	$\underline{57}$
Net gain	127

So Cynthia avoids £13 tax by selling cum div.

In practice the gap between CGT and personal income tax can be even wider because postponement can make the *effective* rate of CGT much lower. CGT is not paid as gains accrue, but only when they are realised. The longer the asset is held the longer the tax payment is postponed. King (1977) found that in the UK in 1971 the average effective tax rate on capital gains was 14.9% whereas the mean income tax rate on all shareholders was 44.1%.

Capital transfer tax (CTT)

The final tax we need to mention is CTT. CTT is a tax on gifts of assets and transfers at death. The tax is assessed by adding all the liable transfers made by an individual during his lifetime and at death, and charging tax on the total, at progressive rates of up to 30% on lifetime transfers, and 60% on transfers on or within three years of death. The lifetime rate depends on the cumulative total in any ten year period.

The significance of CTT in the context of business finance is the problem it raises for the transfer of owner-controlled 'family' firms. There is partial tax-relief on the transfer of 'relevant business property'. But where the ownership of a firm forms a significant part of the wealth of an individual they or their estate may have to sell part of it to meet the CTT liability. This may be damaging on personal grounds – they would probably have preferred to leave the firm intact to their family, and possibly on efficiency grounds – the tax burden is forcing a change in ownership which may not be compatible with economic efficiency.

IV   VAT AND THE SHIFTING AND INCIDENCE OF TAX

To give a full picture of the government's overall fiscal impact on the firm would be a large task. It would mean looking at the taxation and subsidies borne directly and indirectly by the firm, its investors, customers and suppliers; at the effect of government consumption and expenditure on the pattern of economic activity in the economy, and of the pricing and investment decisions of government controlled firms. These are all issues that the firm

---

7 The income tax liability is a little complicated. Under the Imputation System a dividend is deemed to have already borne tax at the basic rate. If the basic rate is 30%, and the individual's marginal tax rate is 30%, then the additional tax liability is 30% (=60%−30%) of the 'gross equivalent' of the dividend, $£100 \times \dfrac{100}{70} = £142.86$ (hint, £142.86 is the amount which after deducting 30% gives £100). So, tax = $£142.86 \times 30\% \simeq £42.86$.

should be alive to, but they would be expensive to quantify on a regular basis though this might be justified in the context of a particular project.

So far we have examined some taxes that bear most directly on the firm. But to undermine the easy notion that the rest of the tax system is irrelevant to the firm we will briefly examine the INCIDENCE of taxation as against its SCOPE. The incidence of a tax describes who actually bears the tax, the scope who nominally bears it. In practice most tax is 'shifted' at least partially onto firms or individuals other than those for whom it was planned. Take VAT as an example.

Value added tax (VAT)

VAT is a tax on consumption. It is currently charged at a rate of 15% on the sale price of most goods and services. In principle the tax is merely collected by firms on behalf of the taxman (in this case the customs and excise authorities). The tax is charged even on sales from one firm to another, but most firms can set off the VAT they pay against the VAT they collect or get a refund if they have paid more than they have collected. This way VAT is intended to be passed on through the economy to final consumers who must bear the tax. Firms act as unpaid collectors of VAT. They have to remit quarterly to the Customs & Excise the excess of collections over payments and they have to be able to account in detail for all VAT-bearing transactions. This accounting imposes a cost on firms, and for some firms it meant the introduction of an accounting system where none previously existed, and thus perhaps a larger liability to tax than previously existed! However we are interested in another cost, relating to the fact that firms not only collect the tax, but may indirectly suffer the burden of it.

Figure I depicts some conventional upward and downward sloping supply-SS and demand-DD schedules for a product, say shoes. The present equilibrium price is £10 giving a sales volume of 50,000 units. Suppose 15% VAT is introduced. This is equivalent to a vertical shift in SS of 15% to S'S', which at the former equilibrium would involve VAT of £1.50 per pair. According to the legislation VAT is a tax on consumption,

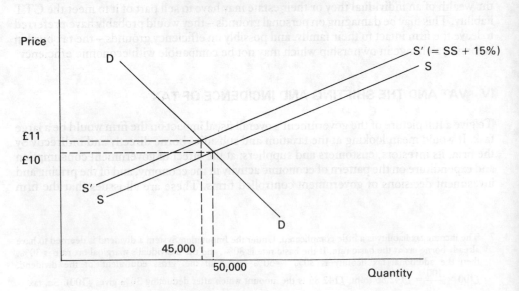

Figure I

collected by the producer who must pay the government £1.50 for each pair of shoes sold. But there will be a new equilibrium at the intersection of DD and S'S'.

Not only has the producer been left with lower sales of 45,000 but the new equilibrium price is only £11. This is the 'gross' price, of which the producer must remit 3/23 to the Customs & Excise. So the VAT is £1.43 leaving the producer £9.57. The firm has borne part of the consumption tax. So incidence of the tax clearly depends not so much on the intentions of the government as the elasticity of demand and supply in the market. Had the demand been infinitely inelastic (vertical) inspection of the diagram shows that the whole tax would have been borne by the consumer. Infinitely elastic (horizontal) demand would shift the whole tax to the producer.

The same arguments could be applied in the markets for labour and capital, and the recognition that the incidence of taxes can differ from their scope bedevils discussions of tax policy. One current controversy of this sort is whether the firm's social security contribution is a tax on the firm, or the employee concerned.

V SUMMARY

This chapter has examined those taxes that are encountered most frequently in business finance; corporation tax, personal income tax, capital gains tax and capital transfer tax. All of these taxes can have an impact on financial decision-making. The aim has been to depict the general structure of the relevant taxes but in practice detail and minutiae are of the essence of the tax system, and the law and rates of tax are constantly changing, so the reader must be on the look out for this. We examined those taxes whose impact on the financial decisions of the firm is relatively direct, but many other taxes such as VAT affect the firm indirectly and their impact will be implicit in the analysis of project cash flows.

REFERENCES AND BIBLIOGRAPHY

Kay, J A and King, M A	*The British Tax System* (3rd edn, 1983) Oxford.
King, M A	*Public Policy and the Corporation* Chapman and Hall (1977) London.
James, S and Nobes, C	*The Economics of Taxation* (1977) Philip Allen, Oxford.
Simon's Taxes	Yearly.
Kay, J A and Sen, J	'The Comparative Burden of Business Taxation' Fiscal Studies, 1983.

QUESTIONS

1 Fred Ltd pays an interim dividend to its shareholders on the 2 July 1986. How much ACT will Fred have to pay, and when? How will this affect Fred's overall corporation tax liability?

2 Plato plc buys an oil tanker for £3 million during tax year 1986/7, then sells it for £1 million during 1990/1. Assuming the corporation tax rate is 40% throughout, how will the tanker affect Plato's tax bill from 1986/7 to 1990/1?

3 Suppose that without the oil tanker Plato expected to be earning profit before tax of £3 million and paying corporation tax of £1 million, each year. Show how Plato's profit after tax will be affected each year if he opens a deferred tax account for the oil tanker.

Part II
The investment decision

CHAPTER 4

Relevant information for decisions

In practice the effects of investment decisions spread through time, and this affects the analysis in two ways. First, the money tied up in a project has a time-value, and second, the effects of the decision, the project costs and benefits, will be more risky and uncertain the further into the future they occur. These two issues are taken up in subsequent chapters. But it is convenient at this stage to abstract from the impact of time in order to develop some basic principles. The sort of decisions we are interested in in this chapter are ones in which these two effects are insignificant.

Section I considers what costs and benefits of a project are relevant in making a decision about undertaking it, and derives a decision-rule in terms of the 'contribution' of the project. This section is essentially concerned with how the effects of a project should be quantified. It is easy to generate neat and well-quantified examples of decisions in textbooks, but in practice quantification is often partial and decisions may be subjective and judgemental. A project can have a multitude of effects, direct and indirect, and the question also arises of how far the decision-maker should go in tracking down and quantifying the costs and benefits of a project. Section II discusses this question in terms of information costs. In Section III a commonly used approach in business decision-making, 'break-even analysis', is examined in the light of the concepts developed earlier, and Section IV applies the 'relevant cost' approach to the pricing decision of the firm.

I RELEVANCE AND CONTRIBUTION

Relevance

For decision-making purposes, the costs and benefits of a project[1] are the *effects* of the project, beneficial or costly, wherever and whenever they occur. In other words, the only aspects of an alternative that are *relevant* in deciding whether or not to choose it, are those aspects that depend on the decision. Only the *increment* in costs and benefits as a result of the decision are relevant; benefits we would receive irrespective, and costs which we would have had to incur are irrelevant. On the other hand, we should consider *all* the effects of the decision, however remote. The more relevant data we consider, the better the decision.

The only thing that can be changed by decision-making is the future – the past is immutable. It follows from this that past, historic data can *never* be 'relevant' for decisions. The phrase *sunk cost* has acquired a pejorative as well as a descriptive sense for just this reason. It describes costs which have been committed to a project in the past, and are therefore irretrievable. Of course there is a sense in which the past *is* relevant. By virtue of its immutability it is the only thing about which we can be certain, and upon which we can

---

1 The word 'project' is normally used in this book in the context of investment decisions, where the effects spread through time. But for convenience we are using it in this chapter to describe activities such as pricing and output decisions as well.

base our expectations of the future. It is the data from which we predict future costs and benefits, but should never be included as a cost or benefit itself.

Consider an example:
Some years ago Marvell Ltd acquired ten litres of technologically advanced metallic paint at a price of £100, the price reflecting the special nature of the paint. Unfortunately the product for which it was bought was never produced and it remains in the stock room, unused and now technologically superceded. The maintenance man has approached the manager. He has to paint the men's washroom and suggests using up the old metallic paint for the job. He will have to mix £5 worth of thinner with it, but will thereby avoid paying £20 for a new tin of industrial emulsion.
Should the manger accept the idea?
The answer must be yes. The *relevant* effects of using the paint are:

BENEFIT – saved on new paint   £20
COST – thinner   (£ 5)
                                                      +£15

The fact that we once paid £100 for the paint is sad, but irrelevant.

But the determined reader might still persist: 'There may be a better use for this special paint which we will think of tomorrow, saving *more* than £20'. We reply that we know there will not. Can we be certain? No. But in this chapter we *assume certainty*. The vital topic of uncertainty will be introduced later.

Opportunity cost[2]

Unfortunately, when used for decision-making the everyday concept of 'cost', which tends to be the accountant's historic cost – 'what was paid for it' – turns out to be inadequate.

Suppose project G requires an input of 5 tons of material X. If undertaking project G means buying an extra 5 tons of X at £20 per ton, then the cost is truly what is paid for it, the *replacement cost*. This is consistent with the relevance principle which says it is the effect, or increment in cost as a result of undertaking project G that should be considered as the cost to the project.

The other possibility is that we have *already in stock* some or all of the material. This opens up new possibilities for costing, all of which are instructive. Assume the material cost £15 per ton when bought. The storekeeper has it in his records at £15 per ton. For his purpose – control – this is appropriate. But for our purpose – decision-making – the cost will not be £15 other than by chance. 'Cost' depends on context and purpose. To find the cost of material X in the current context, the effects of using it on project G have to be examined. This means looking at alternatives.

Suppose material X can be used on project K as well. In the normal course of events the firm will use the material now and replace 5 tons when it is needed for project K. So, again, the cost of X to project G will be £100, the replacement cost. But X may be well nigh irreplaceable at a reasonable price. The effect of using X on G is that K will be impossible: K will have to be sacrificed with the loss of its contribution to profits. So the cost of X in this case would be the loss of profit from K.

The alternative 'project' may be outside the firm. It may be possible to sell the material

---

2   For a classic exposition of the concepts of relevance and opportunity cost see Coase (1938). A sound textbook treatment of the issues from an accounting perspective is Arnold and Hope (1983).

to outsiders, if only for scrap. In this case the *net realisable value*, the proceeds of selling the material after deducting any costs associated with selling, is the cost of using it on project G.

The final case to consider is the extreme, but important real-world case where a resource has no other uses either inside or outside the firm. (This was the case with the metallic paint in the example earlier.) The cost of such resources for decision-making purposes is *zero*, because using them has no effects at all.

This variety may appear confusing, but the underlying principle is simple. In decision-making only *effects* are relevant. To find the cost of a resource we simply examine the effects of using it; which means examining alternative uses inside and outside the firm. This type of cost is called *opportunity cost*, which is the *benefit foregone from the best alternative use*.

Opportunity benefits?

If opportunity costs are so important, why is more not heard of opportunity benefits? The criterion of relevance is equally important on the benefit side. Suppose another firm is considering a product P which will yield revenues of £1 million per annum, but partly at the expense of lost sales on the existing product R which will fall by £.2 million per annum. In deciding whether to launch P the real benefit to the firm is £1 million – £.2 million = £.8 million. We might call £.8 million the opportunity benefit, the benefit after allowing for foregone alternatives. In practice this would be accounted for in two parts, revenue would be held at £1 million, and the £.2 million entered as a cost to the project. There would otherwise be a serious risk of double-counting, given the similarity between opportunity costs and benefits.

A DECISION RULE IN TERMS OF RELEVANT COSTS

In analysing decisions it is customary to split the measurement of the overall worth of a project into two stages.

The opportunity cost of the resources used in the project is deducted from the incremental revenue of the project to find the *contribution*.

incremental revenue   xxx
opportunity cost of resources used (xxx)
     CONTRIBUTION xx

From this is deducted the opportunity cost entailed by having to sacrifice other projects to undertake the project in question, in other words the contributions of those projects, to find the *net benefit*.

CONTRIBUTION   xx
opportunity cost of other projects xx
     NET BENEFIT   x

Assuming the objective of maximising the wealth of the owners we can define a *decision-rule* in terms of contribution, this is: choose all projects with a positive contribution. These are all projects which are 'covering their own costs' and making a contribution to the central burden of committed resources ('overheads') and to the profit of the organisation.[3]

It will be observed that it is only when the decision-maker is forced to *choose between* projects by limited resources or because of the nature of the service that he wishes to have provided, that the second stage will be relevant. And that only one project out of a group from which we may only choose one, which is known as a *mutually exclusive* group, will have a positive net benefit. This is because the opportunity cost of each project is the contribution of the best alternative.

Some projects are 'naturally' mutually exclusive. For example, the choice of a new photocopier for the office. Only one photocopier is wanted, it is a matter of choosing the best. But in practice decisions very often involve mutually exclusive projects for another reason, because of *constraints*.

CONSTRAINTS

The two-part decision rule in the previous section provided a motive for choosing between mutually exclusive projects. When the choice is being forced by a 'constraint', we have a different way of expressing the same rule. We choose that project or projects which *maximise the contribution per unit of the constraint*.

Consider the following example:

Tanner Ltd makes two products x and y with the following costs and revenues:

per unit	x £	y £
Selling price	18	15
Labour	(12)	(6)
Materials	(5)	(6)
CONTRIBUTION	3	3

Which product should Tanner make?

Both products have incremental benefits greater than incremental costs, that is, a positive contribution. So it would be worth Tanner's while to make both x and y up to the limits of demand by the market at the ruling prices.

But suppose demand for the existing price exceeds the capacity of the firm to produce. In other words suppose the firm's resources are insufficient to meet the demand. Which product should be produced? The answer is the product yielding the best contribution per unit of the constraint. So the production plan depends on which factor is limiting or constraining output. Suppose labour is the constraining factor, then:

$$\text{contribution}/\text{£ labour} \qquad \overset{x}{£3/12 = 25\text{p}} \qquad \overset{y}{£3/6 = 50\text{p}}$$

The best plan would be to produce as many y as possible, and produce x only when demand for y is satisfied. But if materials are scarce then the following figures suggest the reverse strategy:

---

3   The reader who has studied some economics and wonders what all this has to do with it, should note that 'choose all projects with a positive contribution' is the same as 'set output where marginal cost equals marginal revenue', the short-run profit maximising rule in economics. The difference is merely one of terminology. Where economists think in terms of increasing output until the marginal revenue from the last unit just exceeds its marginal cost, we are talking of accepting projects up to those whose incremental revenue just exceeds their incremental cost.

contribution/£ materials
$$\overset{x}{£3/5} = 60p \quad \overset{y}{£3/6} = 50p$$

Another possibility is that the constraint may be one not costed in the contribution calculation – for example factory capacity. The decision-maker will have to get estimates of how much 'capactiy' each product uses, perhaps in machine-hours, or plant square-footage, to quantify the demand on limited resources.

This example, though instructive, is excessively simple for most practical cases. It assumed only one constraint. But in practice there may be hundreds, and finding the best production plan needs a mathematical programming technique capable of processing this complexity.

Managerial effort as a constraint[4]

Managers regularly appear to choose a smaller set of projects than they might on the basis of our analysis so far. That is, they sometimes reject or, what is the same thing, fail to seek out projects with a positive contribution even where tangible resources, plant, materials, labour, could be obtained to service them. This behaviour appears more rational if we recall that managerial effort is a limited resource, though one which may be hard to quantify. Indeed we would expect rational managers to choose the set of projects which maximise contribution per unit of managerial time.

Constraints are factors which are limited in the short-term (this is what 'short-term' means in economics). But in the longer-term decision makers should seek ways to remove the constraints, and thus increase contribution. The managerial effort constraint can be one of the hardest to remove. Skilled management may need to be trained over a long period of time, though good manpower planning should anticipate these needs. Also, where the manager is the owner of the firm he may well resist the introduction of new managers to permit expansion. I Ie may fear a dilution of control and may get considerable psychic benefits from the intimate nature of the status quo.

II WHAT COSTS AND BENEFITS TO INCLUDE

Consider the following example:
Bundy Ltd an engineering company, is short of work to the extent that it is planning to make some of its skilled machinists redundant. An old customer rings up to ask if Bundy can complete special fabrication work at a price of £2,000. When the job is costed, the figures look like this:

		£
Revenue		2,000
Costs:	Materials (bought out)	(1,800)
	Labour (machinists)	(1,200)
	Fixed overhead (pro rata on labour)	(600)

The job would permit Bundy to postpone sacking the machinists for 3 months. Should the job be accepted? (Ignore redundancy pay).

In analysing this problem, the message of the previous pages is seek *relevant* costs and benefits. In this case, the 'fixed overhead' is clearly irrelevant, it has to be paid whether or not we take the job. So the relevant figures are:

4   For an early exposition of this problem see Robinson (1934).

	£
Revenue	2,000
Incremental Costs 1800 + 1200	(3,000)
CONTRIBUTION	(1,000)

Bundy would be using other resources on the job, namely the factory, but as the factory would otherwise be idle, its opportunity cost is zero.[5] With a negative contribution of £1000 should the job be accepted? In practice, few people would categorically say no, for the simple reason that so many considerations have been left out of the analysis, for example:

(a) The revenue is poor, but the customer may withdraw his goodwill if Bundy does not accept, thereby losing future business.
(b) If Bundy sacks the machinists it may be costly or impossible to replace them if trade improves.
(c) Bundy may feel a moral duty to keep the machinists employed.
(d) On the other hand the prospects for Bundy's survival in the long-term may be poor anyhow.

In fact, it is very uncommon for decisions to be so 'cut and dried' as at first appears. Decisions have a whole host of effects, DIRECT and INDIRECT. Moreover the effects are very often not quantified, they are *qualitative*, and so even if discovered may be hard to incorporate into the calculation.

An INDIRECT effect is one whose impact is on another project or department of the firm. Effect (a) above is of this sort, rejecting the current project will have an effect on revenues from future projects.

We encountered another effect of this sort when we talked about 'opportunity benefit' earlier. There, the launch of a new product involved taking sales away from an existing product of the firm, an effect which could not be ignored. These effects are at least in principle in quantitative form, though in practice their measurement causes considerable problems. But consider effect (c): Bundy may feel a moral duty to keep the machinists employed. This sort of consideration could be decisive in a decision to take on new work. How can it be incorporated in the decision? The first thing to note is that in principle this effect *could* be quantified just by asking the management of Bundy to put a price or value on it. The key question would be 'how much are you willing to pay to avoid sacking your workers?' This measures the cost of sacking them, the benefit of not doing. In practice this sort of measurement is rarely attempted.

THE COSTS AND BENEFITS OF BETTER INFORMATION

We claimed above that the more information about the effects of a decision that can be incorporated into the decision the better. Information may be deficient in two ways:

1 The decision-maker may lack relevant information: *new information is needed*.
2 The decision-maker may have all the relevant information, but in judgemental not quantified form: *existing information is judgemental*.

In one respect these two are the same. Most information can be acquired in quantified form at some cost. But the guiding principle is that the decision-maker should acquire better information when the *benefits of better information exceed the costs of acquiring it*.

5   In the short-run the opportunity-cost is zero. In the long-run the factory could be sold.

In practice information that is routinely collected in a firm's accounting system can be used at a low or zero cost. The cost and revenue information in the Bundy example is of this sort. Information for which collection techniques are well-established, but which is not routinely collected will have a greater cost. Items (a), (b) and (d) concerning the external environment of Bundy are of this sort, and could presumably be illuminated by consultants: market researchers, economists, financial analysts. Information that is rarely collected, such as (c), the ethical implications of laying off workers, might be very expensive to quantify.

The cost and benefits of better information can typically be represented as in Figure I.

Figure I assumes that the cost of information is a linear function of the quantity, but that the benefit from having it is a reducing function; in other words the benefits from extra information eventually become fairly small. But the shape of the lines is not critical. What matters is the notion that there is some point, K, where the net benefit of extra information (the gap between the lines) is at a maximum.

The reader may accept that we can calculate the cost of getting more information; we know the cost of running the computer, the fees usually charged by market researchers and so forth. But how can we know what the benefits of better information will be before we know what the information will be? At this stage we ask the reader to accept that decision-makers may make judgements about the value of information.

QUANTIFICATION VERSUS JUDGEMENT

A key issue in the study of financial decision-making is the role of *quantified* information. In 'B Ltd' we encountered an example where the decision-maker was presented with certain quantitative information, but where some non-quantified information might be decisive. It should be possible, at some cost, to quantify these views and combine them in

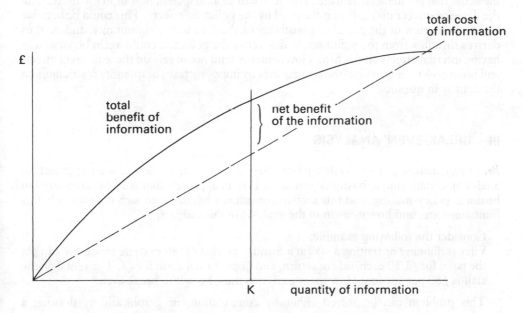

Figure I Information costs and benefits

the quantitative presentation. Our previous rule suggests doing this if the benefits exceed the costs. When there are benefits in quantifying data which decision-makers already possess judgementally or in 'externalising' information which managers already possess 'internally', 'inside their heads'?

The benefits of quantifying information are:

1 The information may be improved by quantification. Forcing decision-makers to externalise their views may force an ordering or reappraisal of the information, and perhaps reveal data with internal inconsistencies.
2 Quantification, and thus recording, of all the inputs into a decision may be necessary for *control* when decisions are decentralised to subordinates. This will occur in any organisation where some decisions are not taken by those ultimately responsible; in other words most organisations of any size.

Often the benefits of quantification will be exceeded by the costs. In these contexts managers *may* be behaving rationally in apparently irrational decisions; such as choosing projects with a negative contribution, rejecting projects with a positive contribution, etc.

EXTERNAL EFFECTS

One set of effects of a project can generally be ignored by the firm in making decisions about it: the *external* effects, the effects on outsiders. Sometimes firms do appear to take some account of 'externalities' in their decisions. For example, a firm may voluntarily decide to install expensive pollution control equipment to reduce pollution to the surrounding countryside. This can come about for two reasons: the firm may fear a future reaction to the pollution, from government or consumers, and may be seeking to forestall this. In this case the pollution has indirect *internal* effects which the decision-maker should allow for. On the other hand the effects of the pollution may be purely external in the sense that no financial damage to the firm can be anticipated, now or in the future. But the decision-maker may still be influenced by the pollution effects. This could be because he has some view of the moral responsibility of the firm to the community, and he thus derives disutility from the pollution. In this sense the pollution could again be viewed as having internal effects on the firm. Governments tend not to rely on these indirect effects and often seek to 'internalise' the externalities by imposing taxes or quantity restrictions on the activity in question.

III 'BREAK-EVEN' ANALYSIS

Break-even analysis, or cost-value-profit analysis as it is also known, is an approach to analysing certain simple business problems. It is an approach that is still encountered in business policy-making, and this section considers what the approach involves, what its limitations are, and how it fits in to the analysis of this chapter.

Consider the following example:
Vijay is thinking or renting a stall at a Sunday market to sell cassette tapes. He can get the tapes for £1.50 each, sale or return, and hopes to sell them for £4. The rental on the stall is £80 per session. How many cassettes must he sell to break even?

This problem can be solved either by computation, or graphically by drawing a break-even chart.

Computation

To find the break even sales we start by noting that
    Sales – Variable Cost – Fixed Cost ≡ Profit
    So if X = number sold
X. Unit selling price – X. Unit variable cost – Fixed cost ≡ Profit
If we define CONTRIBUTION MARGIN = Unit selling price – Unit variable cost, then
Profit ≡ X. Contribution Margin – Fixed Cost, and noting that at 'break-even' profit is

zero, we can solve for X to find BREAK-EVEN SALES (=X) = $\dfrac{\text{Fixed Cost}}{\text{Contribution margin}}$

In Vijay's case:

CONTRIBUTION MARGIN   = £4 – £1.50 = £2.50

BREAK-EVEN SALES   = $\dfrac{£80}{£2.50}$ = 32 tapes

Suppose more realistically that Vijay will only consider the stall if the operation will leave him £20 in his pocket. The break-even analysis can cover this since the desired profit is equivalent to an additional fixed cost. Now we have

BREAK-EVEN SALES   = $\dfrac{£80 + £20}{£2.50}$ = 40 tapes

Break-even chart

The same approach can be illustrated by constructing a chart. Figure II charts the initial break-even decision above.

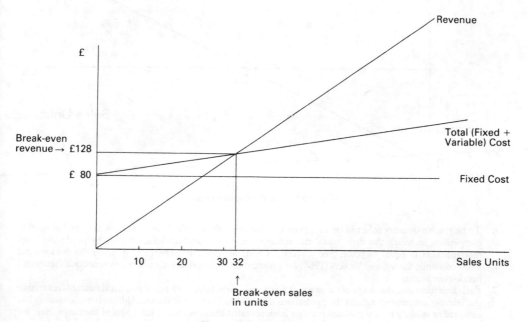

Figure II Break-even chart

The break-even chart displays the standard cost and revenue assumptions of break-even analysis. The break-even point is at sales of 32 units, with revenue of £128. The profit or loss at sales above or below this point is the vertical distance between the Revenue and Total Cost lines, in Figure II. This information is sometimes plotted on to a 'profit-volume chart' which simply shows the profit or loss at each level of sales, as in Figure III.

AN ANALYSIS OF BREAK-EVEN ANALYSIS

The Vijay problem was possibly as simple a business problem as could be imagined, but break-even analysis is applied to larger business decisions too, and the user needs to be aware of the limitations inherent in the approach.

(1) Shape of the curves   The most obvious weakness of break-even analysis as it is usually presented is the assumption of linearity in the revenue and cost curves since linearity appears to conflict with our beliefs as to how costs and reserves behave. On the revenue side it implies that any amount can be sold at the given price, whereas economics holds quantity sold to be a function of price.[6] On the cost side it implies a clear distinction between some costs which are fixed over the whole range of output, and a variable cost which is constant per unit. This seems to preclude step-like fixed-cost functions, or marginal variable costs which increase or decrease because learning effects, imperfections in input markets, stockbuilding, and so forth.[7]

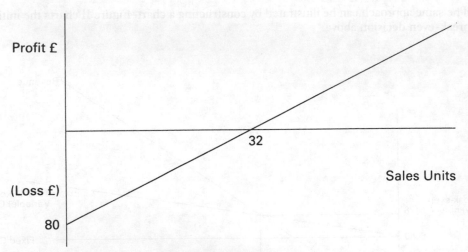

Figure III Profit-volume chart

6   To be precise quantity sold will be a function of price other than in the limiting case of perfect, 'atomistic', competition in which the firm 'takes' the ruling market price and optimises output by producing until marginal cost is equal to price. See a standard text, for example Scherer (1980), on the background microeconomic theory, and Vickers (1960) for a discussion of the relationship between economic theory and break-even analysis.

7   Each firm must find the shape of its own cost function. There have been many empirical cost studies testing the linearity assumption against the predictions of traditional economic theory. Although no consensus has emerged or is likely to, a significant number have revealed linearity over at least part of the range. See, for example, Silbertson (1972).

In practice these problems may not be severe. First, if the analysis is restricted to a small range of outputs linearity may be a reasonable approximation over that range. Second there is no reason why the cost and revenue functions need be linear on a break-even chart. The analyst can use more realistic functions if he wishes. But the computational approach to break-even anaylsis will cease to be simple once the simple assumption of constant contribution margin disappears.

(2) Concept of cost   A more insidious weakness of break-even analysis is that it appears to embody the wrong concept of cost. We know that for decision-making purposes the appropriate measure of cost is opportunity-cost. Consider 'fixed-costs'. In the 'Vijay' example 'fixed-cost' was a misnomer since Vijay could have avoided them by not taking the stall, but 'fixed-cost' usually refers to the cost of 'overhead', of using productive capacity already owned. The cost of using capacity depends on what else is happening. If the enterprise is working at less than full capacity the opportunity cost of using capacity is zero. If the enterprise is at capacity, the cost is the contribution lost from the displaced alternative. The sensitivity of costs to other opportunities is rather hard to embody in a break-even chart.

(3) Indirect effects   An associated weakness of the break-even analysis is its failure to represent the indirect effects of decisions. For example in a multi-product firm there often exist relationships of substitution or complementarity between products, in other words, sales of one product may diminish or enhance sales of another. This would clearly be a relevant effect for decision-making, but is rather hard to incorporate in a break-even chart.

(4) Future effects   Another dimension of complexity which tends to be overlooked in break-even analysis is time. In reality few decisions have effects which all occur within one time period, but unless this is the case the timing as well as the level of costs and revenues becomes important.

Why do people use break-even charts? Apart from indicating the break-even level of sales the strength of break-even charts is their ability to depict the rate at which sales generate profits and to show how the fixed charges of the business, the financial and operating leverage, increase the volatility of that profit. But the problem with traditional break-even charts is that they can suppress a lot of relevant information in the process. This is inevitable, since any attempt to depict a complex process in a two-dimensional graph involves a great deal of selectivity as to what is depicted. They may severely mislead the decision-maker in any but the most simple situations.

IV   RELEVANT COSTS IN THE PRICING DECISION

Pricing decisions exemplify the importance of using the right cost concept, and also the limitations of costs in decisions. Earlier, a problem involving the decision whether to accept an order was examined. The problem decision is the same problem viewed from the other end: the decision to charge £10 for a product y is the decision that orders for y will not be accepted at less than £10.

We will examine the pricing problem in two contexts: first, when the firm has spare capacity; second, when the firm is working at or near full capacity.

Spare capacity

It is well known that a firm which is short of work, has spare capacity, would be wise to accept any job or project which offers a positive contribution. The reason is that the incremental revenue from such a job will cover the incremental costs and contribute something at least, to the overheads of the organisation (by 'overheads' is meant anything that does not change on this occasion, for example if it is not practicable to hire and fire labour at will, labour is an overhead). In pricing terms, this means that the firm would be wise to accept any price for a job, so long as it covers incremental costs.

The value of this perception is that is will prevent managers being misled by the standard output of cost accounting systems, which often includes overhead with labour, or with some other cost, on a pro rata basis. Overhead, by definition a cost which does not change if the job is accepted, is irrelevant for decisions. The opportunity cost of the resources it represents is zero, since there is spare capacity.

But this rule needs some qualification!

First, as we saw in the Bundy example, consideration of all the relevant effects might even condone a price yielding a negative contribution.

Second, 'contribution-pricing' suggests a minimum price. It would be pointless to charge this price if the market would accept a higher price for the same volume. Indeed it could be damaging to the firm to signal its problems by charging 'distress' prices.

Third, a firm which is not 'covering its overhead', and sees little prospect of doing so, would be advised to withdraw from the market as quickly as possible, albeit earning any contribution it can on the way.

Full capacity

We turn now to the 'normal' situation where firms are at or near full capacity.

Research suggests[8] that many pricing decisions by firms are based on *cost plus*. That is, prices are calculated thus:

incremental cost	xx
+ overhead (pro rata)	xx
+ required profit (% on cost)	x
'COST-PLUS' PRICE	xxx

Consider the following example:

Smythe measures its annual activity level in terms of its labour cost. This year its budgeted activity level for labour is £500,000 and fixed overheads are expected to be £200,000.

Smythe expects to earn a pre tax return on capital employed of 25%.

This year it is employing capital of £600,000.

Job No 73 is estimated to have the following direct costs:

labour	£6,000
materials	£2,000

A cost-plus price for this job could be calculated as follows:

First Smythe must re-set its profit objective in absolute terms:

25% of £600,000 = £150,000.

Assuming that labour is the appropriate measure of capacity usage of Smythe, the overhead recovery and profit requirement can be set in terms of labour:

---

8   The pioneer study in this area was Hall and Hitch (1939). Several subsequent studies in the UK have confirmed their general findings. See Hague (1971) and Skinner (1970).

Overhead = 200,000/500,000 = 40% of labour
Profit = 150,000/500,000 = 30% of labour

So the job can be fully-costed or priced thus:

			£
Job No 73	Labour		6,000
	Materials		2,000
			8,000
	Overhead recovered	6000 × 40%	2,000
	Profit	6000 × 30%	1,800
	COST-PLUS PRICE		12,200

In practice this would be presented more simply as

Labour at 170%*	10,200
Materials	2,000
	12,200

*100% Labour plus the two mark-ups.

Rationale for cost-plus

Cost-plus pricing is often criticised. Critics suggest that by ignoring demand it can lead the firm to a suboptimal position, assuming a firm is facing a downward sloping demand-curve DD for its product, and has a corresponding average cost curve CC (see Figure IV).

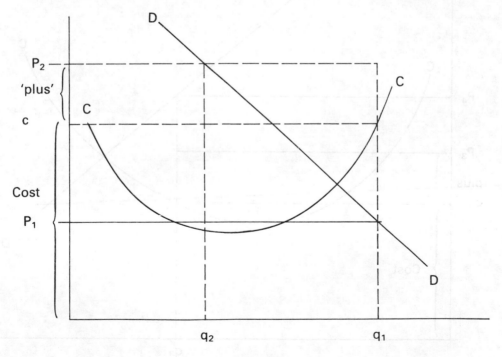

Figure IV

The firm is a cost-plus pricer. It chooses its desired output or activity level q_1, it discovers the average cost c at this level, and applies a profit mark-up, the 'plus'.

Suppose the firm chooses $q = q_1$ in Figure IV. This leads to a planned price and quantity combination, $p_2\ q_1$. But the market will not accept this, it is to the right of the demand curve. The firm will be forced to revise its plans. The actual outcome will depend very much on the speed with which the firm receives information back from the market, and the extent to which resources have been irrevocably committed to producing q_1. Two things are sure.

1 The actual outcome *must* be a price/quantity combination on or to the left of the demand curve.
2 The actual outcome will be sub-optimal, whether it sells planned q_1 at price p_2, or q_2 at planned price p_1, the firm will not make its planned profit.

Similar arguments apply if the firm aims too low and chooses p and q below the demand curve, say $q = q_3$, $p = p_3$ in Figure V. In this case the market would bear a higher price, and the firm could, for example, increase the price to p_4 to the pure benefit of profit.

Cost-plus as a response to information costs

We described in a previous section how decision-making involves two sets of information, the quantitative and the judgemental. Some data are quantified, then combined with the remaining non-quantified data judgementally by the decision-maker. The problem with the above critique of cost-plus pricing is that it ignores the judgemental part of decision-making.

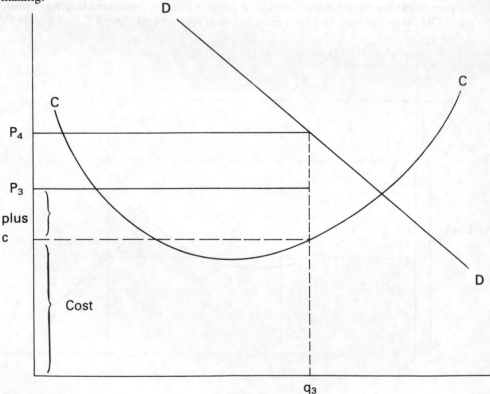

Figure V

The reality of cost-plus pricing for most firms is that it provides a base figure which can be adjusted by decision-makers using their experience of demand, and competition, in the light of their marketing strategy. The profession of marketing attempts to provide techniques for ordering, analysing and quantifying this sort of information. But the acquisition of quantified market information is costly. The benefits are more likely to exceed the cost, the more the product is homogeneous and of high volume, and the more homogeneous the market. This will be the case when soap powder or baked beans are the product. But for many products, and in many firms, these conditions do not pertain.

At the beginning of this chapter the importance of using relevant costs was emphasised. Are the costs in a full-cost price – overhead allocated on a pro rata basis, and a proportionate profit mark-up – relevant measures of the cost of using 'capacity'? When the firm has idle capacity it is appropriate to treat the cost of using overhead as zero. But when the firm is at or near full capacity projects or jobs compete for resources. The best position is found by choosing those projects that have the highest contribution per unit of limiting factor. Faced with the problem of applying this criterion in a multi-product firm of any size, where jobs may be heterogeneous, possibly made to order, and where pricing and order-acceptance are decentralised to sales clerks, cost-plus pricing provides an excellent decision aid. If overhead and profit are allocated *pro rata to the constraining factor*, be it labour, machine-hours or whatever, the cost-plus price will indicate the contribution necessary for a job to be chosen. The firm should be happy that customers accept or reject individual jobs on the basis of such prices. If there is a preponderance of rejections then this is a signal that a downward revision of the profit mark-up is called for, and if excess demand an upward revision.

V   SUMMARY

This chapter has explored decision-making in the relatively simple cases where one can ignore the effects of time. We saw that in this case the firm should accept projects, fix output, set prices, or whatever, so as to maximise 'contribution'. If some factors are in limited supply this can be done by choosing the projects that maximise contribution per unit of limiting factor. 'Contribution' is the appropriate decision-statistic and is measured as the surplus of the incremental revenue over the incremental cost resulting from the project, where these are measured at 'opportunity cost'. Only the effects of a project, the changes in cost and benefit associated with the decision to undertake it are relevant in analysing the decision. But often these effects can be indirect and it will only be rational to quantify them when the benefit of doing so exceeds the cost of getting the further information. The chapter concluded by applying these concepts to break-even analysis and to the pricing decision.

REFERENCES AND BIBLIOGRAPHY

Arnold, J, and Hope, T   *Accounting for Management Decisions* (1983) Prentice-Hall International, Englewood-Cliffs.

Coase, R N   'The Nature of Costs', The Accountant, London, 1.10.1938–17.12.1938, reprinted in Solomons, D. (ed) *Studies in Cost Analysis* (2nd edn, 1968) Sweet & Maxwell, London.

Hague, D C   *Pricing in Business* (1971) Centre for Business Research, University of Manchester, George Allen and Unwin, London.

Hall, R L, and Hitch, C J   'Price Theory and Business Behaviour', Oxford Economic Papers, May 1939.

Lindley, D   *Making Decisions* (1971) Wiley, London

Robinson, E A G   'The Problem of Management and the Size of the Firm', Economic Journal, 1934.

Scherer, F M   *Industrial Market Structure and Economic Performance* (2nd edn 1980) Rand McNally, Chicago.

Silbertson, A   'Economies of Scale in Theory and Practice', Economic Journal, March 1972.

Skinner, R C   'The Determination of Selling Prices', Journal of Industrial Economics, July 1970, pp 201–277.

Vickers, D   'On the Economics of Break-Even', The Accounting Review, July 1960.

Walker, R G   'The Judgement Factor in Investment Decisions', Harvard Business Review, 1961.

QUESTIONS

1 Trubshaw makes two sorts of smoke-detector, W and WPW. The company allocates overheads on the basis of direct labour hours. The budgeted costs, selling price and estimated annual sales and production are:

Per Unit	W	WPW
	£	£
Direct labour (£2 per hour)	6	14
Direct material	13	10
Fixed overhead	9	21
	28	45
Selling price	32	44
Annual sales/production in units	20,000	4,000

As WPW is making a loss should this product be discontinued? (What will be the overall effect on profitability?) If the company could purchase WPW from another company at £30 each would it be worthwhile doing so? What assumptions have you made in arriving at your answers?

2 Grimshaw makes two sorts of door-bell, type A and type B, with the following costs and selling price:

	A	B
	£	£
Selling price	10	11
Direct material (50p per lb)	2	1
Direct labour (£2.00 per hour)	4	6
Profit per unit	4	4

What production/sales programme should be chosen if:

(1) materials are limited to 1,000 lbs but labour is unlimited?

(2) only 4,000 direct labours are available but materials are unlimited?

3 Patel Engineering produces and sells for £250 control device for which there is a heavy demand but which the company is prevented from satisfying because of a shortage of skilled labour. The direct material and labour costs of the machine are £118 and £45 respectively. The labour force is paid 150p per hour. All other costs may be regarded as fixed. The company has been invited by one of its customers to supply, for £20,000, a batch of machines of modified design which the customer wishes to incorporate into his own product.

   Patel's estimator has calculated that to execute the order, 2,000 direct labour hours would be required and the cost of material would be £8,000 excluding the cost of special switches which could be bought in for £1,000 or, alternatively, made by the company for a material price of £550 and labour time of 100 hours.

   Advise the Patel management of whether to accept the order. What factors other than those mentioned are likely to be relevant in practice?

4 (a) From the following profit and loss statement, construct a break-even chart and determine:
   (i) the break-even point
   (ii) the P/V ratio
   (iii) the sales necessary to obtain profit of £10,000

Profit and Loss Statement

		£	£
Sales			84,000
Costs	Materials	20,000	
	Labour	20,000	
	Sales Commission	2,100	
	Direct Overhead	13,900	
	Fixed Overhead	14,000	
	General Administration		
	(apportioned)	10,000	80,000
	Profit		4,000

(b) What assumptions underly the traditional break-even chart? Evaluate break-even charts as a tool for managers.

CHAPTER 5

Valuing projects under certainty

The effects of an investment decision spread through time, and the capital tied-up in a project has a time-related cost. In this chapter we see how to take the time-value of money into account in valuing projects.

In the previous chapter the worth of a project was measured by its 'contribution'. We now encounter the concept of *net present value*, which is the time-adjusted equivalent of contribution. We recommend firms to undertake all projects that have a positive net present value. In the next chapter we will show why this should lead to attaining the objective of maximising the firm's value.

Section I introduces the arithmetic of present value and shows how discounting allows the cost of capital to be embodied in the valuation of a project. In Section II we consider how to value a typical investment project. In Section III we examine the effect of inflation on project appraisal. At the moment we are continuing to leave to one side the question of risk and we are abstracting from the financing decision by assuming firms are all-equity financed.

I THE ARITHMETIC OF PRESENT VALUE

Financial decisions have effects which spread through time. The effects we are interested in are a stream of cash flows positive and negative, and to evaluate the decisions we have to find the *net present value* of the stream. We assume money has a positive 'time-value' so that the decision-maker values a pound received in the future less than a pound received today. Money has a time-value because like other inputs to projects it has an opportunity cost. This is the return, r, the investor can get from alternative investments. We value the stream of cash flows using the *discounted cash flow* (DCF) technique.

The first step in developing the DCF analysis is to recall some elementary mathematics.

Compounding

If £100 is invested today (at time, t_0) at 10% per annum interest, then one year later (t_1) the investor will have £100 × (1 + .10) = £110.

If he leaves the capital and interest to earn interest for another year he will have by the end of the second year (at t_2)

$$£110 \times (1 + .10)$$
$$= £100 \times (1 + .10) \times (1 + .10)$$
$$= £100 \times (1 + .10)^2$$
$$= £121$$

This process of reinvesting capital and interest to earn interest for another period is called *compounding*. We call the outcome of this process the *future value* of the initial amount, compounded at a certain rate of interest for a given number of time periods.

Symbolically if
> FV = Future value
> PV = Initial outlay
> r   = Periodic rate of interest (expressed as a decimal)
> n   = Number of periods for which the sum is invested

then FV = PV $(1 + r)^n$ (1)

For simplicity we will assume that interest is paid annually, in other words we assume *annual compounding*. In practice examples are commonly found in semi-annual compounding (banks, building societies, may pay interest twice a year) right down to daily compounding. Formula (1) applies to all these cases provided r is the semi-annual, daily, or whatever rate of interest, and n is the number of half-years, days, etc. We consider the important case of continuous compounding later on.

Consider an example:
An acquaintance approaches you and says:

> My father is giving me £5,000 in two years time. The trouble is I want to sail round the world now. If you'll just lend me the £5,000, I'll return it when I get back in two years.

Does this seem a good deal to you? Probably not. For one thing he might easily perish in the Megallon Straits. Secondly, inflation during the two years may seriously erode the value of the £5,000. But ignoring these risks, by lending the money to him you are prevented from investing it at a real rate of interest elsewhere. The *opportunity cost* of the loan is the interest you could earn elsewhere.

You decide to calculate the amount you would need in two years to compensate for the loss of £5,000 now, the future value of the £5,000. You discover you could invest at 7%.

$$FV = £5,000 (1 + .07)^2$$
$$= £5,725$$

Clearly £5,725 in two years is equivalent in value to £5,000 now. If the rate of interest is 7%, no one would accept less than £5,000 now for £5,725 in two years, and no one would offer more.

Discounting

Having established the equivalence between a present sum and a future sum, the logic of compounding can be reversed to find the *present value* (PV) of a known future amount.

For the situation where we know FV, and wish to find its present value, PV we can

rearrange (1) $PV = \dfrac{FV}{(1 + r)^n}$ (2)

Consider an example:
I want to have £1,000 in 3 years time. I can invest at 9%. How much do I need to invest now?

To solve this problem we merely have to find the PV of £1,000 received in 3 years time,

where $PV = \dfrac{1,000}{(1 + .09)^3}$

$$= \frac{1,000}{1.295} = £772,20$$

The reader can confirm that £772.20 compounded at 9% for 3 years yields £1,000. The procedure we just adopted was unwieldy in one respect. £1,000 was multiplied by $\dfrac{1}{(1 + .09)^3}$, which is called the *discount factor*, and which had to be calculated. Tables of these factors have been calculated, and are reproduced at the end of the book. They are called *discount tables*, or *present value tables*, and they give the PV of £1 received after n years at interest rate r. To find the value of $\dfrac{1}{(1 + .09)^3}$ inspect the 9% column and 3 year row of the table: the factor is .772.

Consider an example:
I will inherit £20,000 in six years time. I want to sell the right to my inheritance. What is it worth now, if the interest rate is 14%? The 14%, 6 year discount factor is .456, so the present value of the inheritance is

PV = £20,000 × .456 = £9,120

Another piece of terminology: the % rate used for discounting, 14% in the previous example, is commonly called the *discount rate*.

Annuities

Annuity tables provide a useful supplement to discount tables. Suppose one wants to find the present value of an equal sum of £200 received each year for the next 5 years, discounting at 10%. This can be calculated as follows:

t	=	1	2	3	4	5	Total
cash (£)		200	200	200	200	200	
		×	×	×	×	×	
10% discount factors		.909	.826	.751	.683	.621	
present value		182	165	150	137	124	£ 758

This is correct, but it would have been quicker to sum the discount factors then multiply the total by £200, saving computations. Even better, tables exist which do this: they are reprinted at the end of the book. Using *annuity tables* to perform the above calculation we inspect the 10% column, 5-year row: the annuity discount factor is 3.791. (You can check this, .909 + .826 + .751 + .683 + .621 = 3.790.)
So the present value of the annuity is £200 × 3.791 = £758.

If a discount factor is wanted for a run of equal cash flows, but starting some time in the future, this can be found by combining annuity factors. Suppose we wish to find the present value of an annual amount of £300 to be received in the 12th to the 16th years from now, with a 10% discount rate

16 year, 10% annuity factor	7.824
subtract the 11 year, 10% annuity factor	(6.495)
12 to 16 year factor	1,329
So the present value is £300 × 1.329	£ 393

Why cash flow?

We use the words *cash flow* instead of the rather looser word 'effect' to describe the future events to be discounted. Once *time* becomes a critical factor in decision-making it is important to identify exactly *when* costs and benefits arise. For decision-making purposes costs are incurred when cash is committed and benefits are realised when cash is released. This is because cash-flow marks the time when the firm will start, and cease, incurring a cost on the capital involved.

Continuous compounding

When FV is the future value of a sum, and PV the present value, r is the annual rate of interest and n the number of years for which the sum is invested, then

$$FV = PV (1 + r)^n \tag{3}$$

However, if interest is paid twice a year:

$$FV = PV (1 + \frac{r}{2})^{2n}$$

If four times:

$$FV = PV (1 + \frac{r}{4})^{4n}$$

In general if interest is compounded m times per year:

$$FV = PV (1 + \frac{r}{m})^{mn} \tag{4}$$

One important case is the one where m tends to infinity, and thus interest is compounded continuously. To help to interpret this case we recall from mathematics that the value 'e' is defined as the limiting value of $(1 + \frac{1}{m})^m$ as m tends to infinity.

$$e = \lim_{m \to \infty} (1 + \frac{1}{m})^m = 2.718 \tag{5}$$

substituting e in (4) gives

$$FV = PV\, e^{rn} \tag{6}$$

and conversely

$$FV = FV\, e^{-rn} \tag{7}$$

It should be clear from comparing (6) and (3) that e^{rn} is the continuous compounding equivalent of $(1 + r)^n$. Continuous compounding is interesting in several ways. One great virtue is that value becomes a continuous function of time, so that value functions are differentiable with respect to time.

For this purpose it is worth noting that

$$\frac{d}{dn} (e^{-rn}) = -r e^{-rn}$$

Since e forms the basis of *natural logarithms*, future values are easy to evaluate using natural logs. The future value of £1 continuously compounded for n years at r% is

$$FV = e^{rn}$$

taking logs of each side

$$\ln FV = rn. \ln e$$
$$= rn \text{ since } \ln e = 1$$

If £100 is to be continuously compounded at 8% per annum for 3 years

$$\ln FV = kn = .08 \times 3$$
$$= .24$$

If we look up natural log tables we find that the number with a natural log of .24 lies between 1.27, which has a natural log of .23902, and 1.28 which has a natural log of .24686. Interpolating we get $\dfrac{98}{98 + 686} = 0.125$, so the number we seek is 1.27125. Hence in 3 years at 8% £100 will compound to £127.13. Conversely the present value of £100 received in 3 years at 8% is $\dfrac{£100}{1.27125} = £78.66$.

In many situations it *is* more realistic to assume that cash is received continuously throughout the period, but even if this is not the case the shorter the periods, and the lower the interest rate, the less significant is the difference between continuous and periodic compounding. For example the following are the present values generated by various compounding periods of £100 invested at 8% per annum for 3 years:

compounding period	present value (£)
annual	79.38
six months	79.03
three months	78.85
continuous	78.66

In summary, the present value, PV, of a future sum, FV, received at time n, is given by $PV = \dfrac{FV}{(1 + r)^n}$, under discrete compounding and $PV = FV^{-rn}$, under continuous compounding.

A DECISION RULE FOR PROJECTS

In project appraisal we want to find the present value of the whole bundle of cash flows, positive and negative, which result from undertaking the project. The term *net present value* (NPV) is used for this. If C_t is the cash flow (+ or −) in period t, and r is the required periodic return, then the logic of discounted cash flow suggests that:

$$NPV = \sum_{t=o}^{n} \frac{C_t}{(1 + r)^t} \tag{8}$$

Discounting cash flows enables us to take account in project decisions of the fact that the cash tied-up in projects has a time-related cost. It implies a decision rule: *accept all projects with a positive NPV*. NPV is the time-adjusted equivalent of 'contribution' – it is the contributions yielded by a project in different time-periods, discounted at the cost of capital and summed. By discounting we now also ensure that the capital tied-up in the project is fully costed. Moreover the concept of cost remains 'opportunity cost': r is the investors' opportunity cost of capital, the return they could get on the best alternative investment. The NPV of a project measures the amount of cash the owners could immediately withdraw as a result of the project: the immediate increase in the owners' wealth associated with owning the project. In the next chapter we show the theoretical foundation of the NPV decision rule – why choosing projects with a positive NPV is the policy that maximises shareholders' wealth.

II   VALUING A TYPICAL INVESTMENT PROJECT

This section considers how to identify the cash flows associated with an investment project, and how to calculate its NPV.

Consider the following example:
Anglo-Precision is considering buying a machine to make bearings. The machine costs £1.2 million and will last 5 years. Scrap value of these machines is currently £200,000. An investment of £150,000 in working capital will be needed initially. The accountant has prepared the following estimated annual trading account for the project:

	£
Bearing sales	1,400,000
Materials, labour	(800,000)
Depreciation	(200,000)
Fixed overhead allocated	(250,000)
ANNUAL PROFIT	150,000

A-P's discount rate is 10% per annum, and the company pays a marginal rate of tax of 40%. What is the NPV of this project?

Incremental costs and benefits

A general point; the principles established in the previous chapter apply equally to this. The relevant effects for appraising a project are the incremental costs and benefits; and the cost of employing resources is their opportunity cost. Purely for convenience we assume all cash flows take place on the last day of the year. Specifically we also assume that the machine acquired at t_0, was actually bought on the last day of the previous year. In reality cash flows can arise on any day of the year, and computer packages to calculate NPV take account of this and discount for the appropriate number of days.

Asset cost

For NPV calculation the cost of the machine is the cash outlay, when it occurs. In the A-P example the anticipated scrap value means there will be a cash receipt in period 5.

t	=		0	1	2	3	4	5
Cash flow machine	(£)	(1,200,000)	–	–	–	–	200,000

Depreciation

Depreciation should be ignored in DCF, as it is a non-cash expense. Depreciation is an accounting contrivance designed to inject a measure of capital consumption into the measurement of annual performance. Since DCF considers all time-periods at once, including the periods when the cash flows occur, depreciation is unnecessary.

Interest

Interest payments should not be included as cash flows. The cost of capital is measured directly by the discount rate.

Overheads

Overheads, if they would be incurred anyway and are merely allocated to the project, should be ignored. This follows from the ruling principle that only increments in cost as a result of the project are *relevant*. So the trading proceeds of the project can be calculated:

	each year
Bearings Sales	1,400,000
Materials, labour	(800,000)
Cash flow = Trading proceeds	£ 600,000

Working capital

Projects usually require an investment in additional working capital. But unlike fixed capital, working capital is not consumed by the project in which it is used. Rather it represents an advance payment, or 'stockpiling', of inputs that are already costed in the project. So the appropriate treatment is to charge the outlay as a cost when it is incurred, and add back the same amount at the end of the project. The rationale is that in the final year of the project cost savings can be achieved on materials by running down stocks. Thus the effective cost of the investment in working capital is the 'interest cost' during the period in which it is held. In the case of A-P this means:

t =	0	1	2	3	4	5
capital (£)	(£150,000)	–	–	–	–	150,000

Taxation

The tax system was discussed in Chapter 3. For project appraisal the following aspects of the tax system are important:

(I) Costs and revenues are with some exceptions[1] tax-deductible and taxable, respectively, at the prevailing corporation tax rate. Assuming a tax rate of 40% then the Inland Revenue will take .4 of the revenues and, effectively, pay .4 of the costs (– the latter because tax deductibility means allowing the firm to avoid paying tax it would otherwise have had to pay).

(II) Lags in assessment and collection of company tax mean that tax is not paid until between 9 and 21 months after the year in which the income arises.[2] For convenience we assume that tax effects are lagged by 1 year.

(III) Tax relief on the cost of the machine is given through capital allowances. In this case the machine qualifies for a writing-down allowance of 25% on the reducing balance. Hence annual capital-allowances are:

---

1   Some expenses, for example entertaining UK businessmen, the Revenue will not in general allow for tax deduction at all. Other expenses, such as industrial buildings and 'company cars', are allowed only piecemeal.

2   In practice the simple timing structure we are presenting here may be considerably complicated. When the tax effects of a particular project are felt depends on the overall tax-paying position of the firm. For example, if the firm is making a loss overall, of a 'tax-loss' created by heavy capital allowances, then the tax is in a tax-paying position, which could be some years hence. In general the decision-maker should seek professional guidance from the company's tax adviser as to the tax implications of the project in question.

t =	0	1	2	3	4	5	6	TOTAL
25% WDA (£)	300,000	225,000	168,750	126,563	94,922	84,765		1,000,000
Tax saved (40%)		120,000	90,000	67,500	50,625	37,969	33,906	400,000

Because we assume that the machine was bought on the last day of the previous year, the first WDA (of $1,200 \times 25\% = 300$) is credited to that year, enabling tax relief of 120 (= $300 \times .4$) to be claimed at t_1. Subsequent WDA's are 25% of the reducing balance, which means that when the machine is finally scrapped for 200,000 the balancing allowance in the final period is 84,765.

Assembling these cash flows, and using 10% as the discount rate, we can now calculate the NPV of A-P's bearings project, as an Exhibit I. The project has an NPV of £625,942. We have seen how to set up the cash flows for calculating NPV, but we have neglected some key issues. Where does the discount rate come from? How do we know how long the project will last, and for that matter, how do we know what the cash flows will be? How does inflation affect the analysis?

THE DISCOUNT RATE

The discount rate should measure the cost of the capital used in the project – the investors' opportunity cost, the best return they could get elsewhere. In a perfect capital market where the future is known with certainty there will be just one cost of capital or discount rate, a uniform rate of interest prevailing throughout the market. This is what we assume in this chapter. Once the assumption of certainty is removed then we expect the cost of the capital invested in a project to reflect the riskiness of the project. Subsequent chapters dicuss how the risky discount rate for a project can be found.

In this chapter we are also assuming that the firm is financed entirely by equity. However, in the world of certainty the distinction between equity and debt is meaningless. Later on we relax this assumption and consider the financing alternatives available to the firm. Again, we can show that in a perfect capital market the way in which the firm raised its finance would not affect its cost of capital and the investment and financing decisions of firm would be independent of one another. In reality though, financing decisions may affect the cost of capital.

In this chapter we just take the discount rate as 'given' but this does not mean its importance should be neglected. The study of business finance is all about the transfer of capital from investors to projects through firms. The cost of capital is the key statistic in that process since it is the market price of what is being transferred.

ECONOMIC LIFE

Deciding on the life, or time horizon of the project is difficult yet crucial. The NPV of the project may be significantly affected by the decision to add another year's cash flow to the appraisal, but the year in question is the remotest from now, the one about which we know least. The project life decision confronts us with the inadequacy of the 'certainty' assumption we are making in this chapter. The existence of uncertainty probably explains the popularity of the decision rule that concentrates on *payback-period*. It also raises the possibility that the firm will have to make decisions about *abandoning* or *disinvesting* in projects when the future does not unfold as well as was expected. We discuss these issues in subsequent chapters.

Exhibit I DCF appraisal of bearings project

	t = 0	1	2	3	4	5	6
Machine – cost	(1,200,000)					200,000	
– tax		120,000	90,000	67,500	50,625	37,969	33,906
Trading proceeds		600,000	600,000	600,000	600,000	600,000	
– tax			(240,000)	(240,000)	(240,000)	(240,000)	(240,000)
Working capital*	(150,000)					150,000	
ANNUAL CASH FLOWS	(1,350,000)	720,000	450,000	427,500	410,625	747,969	(206,094)
10% Discount factors	1	.909	.826	.751	.683	.621	.564
PRESENT VALUES	(1,350,000)	654,480	371,700	321,053	280,457	464,489	(116,237)

TOTAL = NPV = £625,942

*Note the working capital cash flow has been assumed to have no tax effects

But the assumption of certainty we are making at present is a convenient one for highlighting another feature of project life. In discussions of project appraisal, and in computer packages for calculating DCF, the 'life' of the project tends to be treated as a parameter, as part of the data of the project. It is important to see that on the contrary the life of a project should be calculated *simultaneously* with its NPV.

The *physical life* of, say, the machinery used on a project may be a datum. But this rarely constrains a project in practice since it is usually possible to buy or lease extra years of machine services, *where it is economic to do so*. Similarly, further investments of marketing or design expenditure can often bolster the sales of a flagging product.[3] Whether it is worth prolonging the life of a project another year depends on the effect of the costs and benefits of doing so on the NPV of the project. Hence we can define the *economic life* of a project as the life which *maximises NPV*. In practice we may need to explore different assumptions about termination and reinvestment to find the economic life.

III THE EFFECT OF INFLATION ON PROJECT VALUE

The impact of inflation[4] on the value of projects could be significant. We know that NPV = $\Sigma \frac{C_t}{(1 + r)^t}$. Inflation is likely to affect both our estimates of the cash flows C_t, and the required return, r. There are two aspects of inflation that need to be separated. First, that it exists, and second, that it is uncertain. So if we are working out the cash flows associated with operating a machine for making widgets it will be important to know that while widgets sell for £2 each this year they will be selling for £5 in two years time. That would be a case of 'certain' inflation. But in reality the rate of inflation is not known, so that in two years time the best that could be predicted may be that widgets will be selling between £3.50 and £5.50. The latter problem we will leave until later as part of the general problem of the *uncertainty* of future cash flows, and consider here what to do about inflation in a certain world.

At first sight the best thing to do about inflation might be to ignore it. Suppose there was a *uniform* expected rate of inflation across the economy, i. Then actual or 'nominal' future cash flows, C_t, would be related to their 'real' or 'current price' equivalents, C_t', as follows:

$$C_t = c_t' (1 + i)^t \qquad (9)$$

and, as Fisher (1930) suggested, nominal interest rates, r, would be related to real rates, r', as follows:

$$1 + r = (1 + r')(1 + i) \qquad (10)$$

This is the so-called 'Fisher effect'. So long as the market is efficient, we can expect nominal interest rates to fully embody inflationary expectations.

It follows from (9), (10), that $NPV = \Sigma \frac{C_t}{(1 + r)^t} = \Sigma \frac{C_t (1 + i)^t}{(1 + r')^t (1 + i)^t}$

and the i terms cancel, so $\Sigma \frac{C_t}{(1 + r)^t} = \Sigma \frac{C_t'}{(1 + r')^t}$

In the case of uniform inflation we get the same answer working in current prices with

---

3 Marketing often talks about the *life-cycle* of a product but recognises there are various ways the life-cycle can be stretched. See, for example, Kotler (1985) ch 12.
4 For fuller discussions of this topic see Carsberg and Hope (1976), Friend, Landskroner and Losq (1976), and Nelson (1976).

the real discount rate as with inflated prices and the nominal discount rate. In practice, though, ignoring inflation is both unsafe and more difficult than it might look. We can see this by looking at the cash flows and the discount rate again.

CASH FLOWS

Inflation strikes unevenly. The decision-maker just cannot assume that the prices of the particular inputs and outputs that make up his cash flow will inflate uniformly and at the average or general expected rate the market builds into the nominal interest rate.

Taxation provides a good example of non-uniform inflation. Tax receipts and payments are fixed in terms of the expense or income to which they relate, but follow it with a lag of, we assume, 12 months. If my tax rate is 30% and I earn £100 today, I will have to pay £30 tax in a year's time, whether the rate of inflation in the intervening period is 20% or 200%. In this sense taxation is subject to zero inflation.

DISCOUNT RATE

If we decide to use 'real' rather than 'nominal' cash flows we need the real cost of capital to discount them. Unfortunately we cannot directly observe the real rate. The costs of capital, r, that we observe in the market are nominal ones. They reflect the return required by providers of funds to give a real return, r', AND to compensate for the loss in the purchasing power of the capital due to inflation, i.

As we saw in (10)

$$1 + r = (1 + r') (1 + i)$$
$$\text{so} \quad r = r' + i + r'i$$

assuming the likely magnitudes of r' and i make the r'i term insignificant,

$$r = r' + i \tag{11}$$

To find the real return r', we need to deduct i from the market rate, r, where i is the market's expectation of future inflation. But we do not know what i is. After the event we know what inflation *was*, but not what people thought it was going to be; we know the 'ex post' but not the 'ex ante'. In fact the market rate is one of our main sources of information about the market's inflation expectations, so the process of estimating r is likely to be circular and conjectural. But if our knowledge of the composition of r is circular and conjectural, how can we know that r fully reflects future inflation? In general we may prefer to assume the market is correct on the pragmatic grounds that, before the event, we lack the evidence to assume otherwise.

In summary, our prescription for handling inflation in project appraisal is to forecast cash flows at nominal values, and discount them using the nominal cost of capital.

IV SUMMARY

This chapter showed how discounting incorporates the opportunity cost of capital into project valuation. We saw how to find the net present value of a typical investment project, and discussed the problem of inflation, and the concepts of the cost of capital and of the 'economic life' of the project. In the next chapter we examine the theoretical base of the NPV decision-rule and consider how robust it is in real world conditions.

REFERENCES AND BIBLIOGRAPHY

Carsberg, B and Hope, A	*Business Investment Decisions under Inflation: Theory and Practice* (1976) Institute of Chartered Accountants in England and Wales, London.
Fisher, I	*The Theory of Interest* (1930) Macmillan.
Friend, I Landskroner, Y and Losq, E	'The Demand for Risky Assets under Uncertain Inflation', Journal of Finance, Dec 1976, pp 1287–1297.
Kotler, P	*Marketing Management, Analysis, Planning and Control* (5th edn, 1985). Prentice-Hall, London.
Nelson, C R	'Inflation and Capital Budgeting', Journal of Finance, June 1976, pp 923–931.
Van Horne, J C	'A note on Biases in Capital Budgeting Introduced by Inflation' Journal of Financial and Quantitative Analysis, Jan 1971, pp 653–58.
Westwick, C A and Shohet, P S D	'Investment Appraisal and Inflation' Institute of Chartered Accountants in England and Wales, Research Committee, Occasional Paper No 7, 1976.
Wilkes, F M	'Inflation and Capital Budgeting Decisions'. Journal of Business Finance, Autumn 1972, pp 46–53.

QUESTIONS

1 I desire to have £5,000 in four years time. The interest rate is 11%. How much money do I need to invest now? If interest rates are 13% how much do I need?

2 If interest rates are 12% how much would I expect to pay for an annuity of £2,500 per year for the next five years?

How would the answer be different if I want the annuity to start in five years for the subsequent five years?

3 A project has the following expected cash flows over its four year life:

t =	0	1	2	3	4
Cash flows	(17,800)	8,000	4,000	6,000	6,000

Work out the project's NPV at the following discount rates:

0%,   6%,   9%,   12%,   15%,   18%,

and plot your results on a graph.

4 Sharpcrease plc is considering the possibility of opening a new factory to produce inlaid rosewood trouser-presses. The company expects to be able to sell each one for £2,000. The factory will cost £700,000 to build and equip, and will have annual fixed costs of £40,000. The company purchased the site for the factory for £200,000 two years ago, and have already spent £20,000 on excavation of it. If they decide not to open the new factory, they will sell the site as it stands for £350,000.

The production costs per trouser-press will be as follows:

Materials	£400
Direct labour	£300
General Administrative Overhead	£200

Although the company can sell unlimited quantities for £2,000 each, the materials used in its production are so specialised and scarce that only enough can be purchased to produce 250 per year.

The market for the presses is expected to last for 10 years, at which point ABC will sell the site complete for £400,000. The company's discount rate for appraising such projects is 15%; and the company does not expect to pay tax for the foreseable future.

How much better off will Sharpcrease be if it accepts the project?

What annual production level will be just sufficient to allow Sharpcrease to break-even on this project?

What other information would you find useful in appraising this project?

5 How would your answer to (4) be affected if
   (a) all the project costs and revenues were expected to rise in line with the RPI over the life of the project, and the RPI itself is expected to rise at 5% per year,
   (b) materials and labour costs will rise by 2% per annum more than the RPI?

6 Evaluate the following project. Your company's cut-off rate for investment projects is 12%

Cost of machine	£40,000
Scrap value, aftrer 5 year life	£2,000
Annual net revenues from machine	£14,000

Tax is payable one year in arrears. The tax rate is 40%, and the company will receive 25% per annum writing down allowance on the reducing balance.

CHAPTER 6

NPV and IRR

The last chapter showed how to find the *net present value* of a project, and said that the firm should invest in projects which have a positive NPV. We now look at the theory behind NPV, and at another DCF-based measure of project worth, the internal rate of return.

In Section I we present the model developed by Jack Hirshleifer from Irving Fisher's pioneering work. The Fisher-Hirshleifer model provides a rigorous proof of why in a world of certainty accepting all projects with a positive NPV maximises the wealth of shareholders. In doing this the model illustrates the central relationships in finance, the relationship between projects, firms, investors and the capital market.

Section II considers a particular application of NPV analysis, the problem of finding the optimum replacement period for an asset. Section III considers how the NPV rule needs to be modified in the face of a common market imperfection – capital rationing. In this case the firm has to choose between worthwhile projects. The complexities of choosing the best bundle out of a large set of possibly interrelated projects point to the use of mathematical techniques such as linear programming, so we explain how linear programming can be used in project choice, and how the results should be interpreted.

A seemingly equivalent measure of project worth to NPV emerges from the Fisher-Hirshleifer model in the form of 'internal rate of return' or 'IRR'. But though NPV stands up well when we relax some of the assumptions of the Fisher-Hirshleifer model, the IRR runs into real problems. We discuss the IRR and its limitations in Section IV.

I THE FISHER-HIRSHLEIFER MODEL[1]

We asserted that the firm could maximise the wealth of its shareholders by accepting all projects with a positive NPV. This section demonstrates why.

Consider a simple world with only two time periods, this one and the next, which we can call t_0 and t_1. There is an investor with an amount of cash X, and with some production opportunities available to him, projects which require an investment of cash now, at t_0, but will yield a return of cash in one year's time at t_1. So the investor can split the X he holds between consumption at t_0, and investment, which will yield consumption at t_1. His objective is to get the best balance of consumption in the two periods, to get the mix which he values most highly or, as we usually term it, which *maximises his wealth*. There are going to be two sides to consider. On the one hand his decision will depend on how much t_1 consumption can be gained by sacrificing t_0 consumption – on the returns to investing in projects, in other words. On the other hand there is the investor's preferences for a pound next year as against a pound this – his 'rate of time preference'.

---

1 The graphical analysis of Fisher (1930) was explored and extended with respect to capital market imperfections in Hirshleifer (1958). A more rigorous and full account of the theory of investment is found in several texts, notably Fama and Miller (1972).

The return to projects

Figure I plots the consumption the investor can obtain in each period if he invests in projects. We can call it the 'production opportunities curve'. Points X and Y are the two extremes.

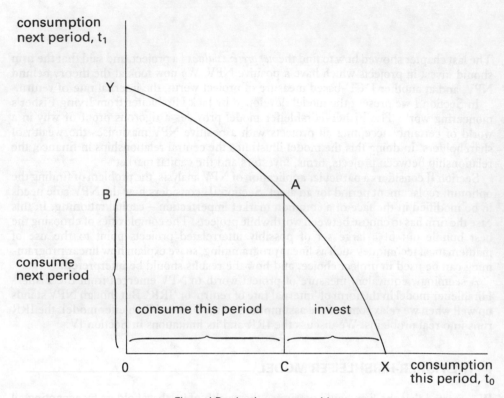

Figure I Production opportunities

If he invests nothing now he can consume all his X this period, but nothing next period, while by consuming nothing this period and investing the whole X he can obtain a maximum consumption of Y next period. Most likely he will move to an intermediate position such as A requiring investment of X – C in projects, and yielding consumption of C this period and B next. But why is the curve the shape it is? The shape is determined purely by assumptions we are making. We assume projects are infinitely divisible and that projects are independent of one another so that accepting one does not affect the returns on another. This gives a smooth curve. We assume that not all projects yield the same return, so for example £1 invested in one project might yield £1.10 of consumption next period while in another it might yield £1.30. Since the rational investor will choose the best projects first, this gives a curve which is concave to the origin. The slope of the production opportunities curve at any point indicates the marginal return to investment at that point, the consumption at t_1 that can be got from sacrificing £1 of consumption at t_0. Towards Y the curve flattens out, indicating that as nearly all the £X is invested the marginal returns are low.

The investor's preferences

We can depict the investor's preferences about various mixes of consumption this period and next in terms of a set of indifference curves. Indifference curves are familiar from microeconomics. They join points of equal utility for the individual, and if the individual's preferences follow the basic axiom of rationality in that he prefers more to less then he will seek to be on the highest possible indifference curve.

As before we assume smooth curves, this time convex to the origin. This convexity reflects the assumption of diminishing marginal utility to consumption in either period, that is, the investor will require increasing amounts of consumption in one period to compensate for successive units of consumption sacrificed in the other period. The slope of the curve at any point measures the rate at which the investor is prepared to trade present for future consumption, his *marginal rate of time preference*.

Superimposing the relevant part of our investor's preference map onto the production opportunities curve, in Figure II, we can see why he chose position A. Since A is the point of tangency between the production opportunities and an indifference curve, it puts him onto the highest possible indifference curve; it is his utility-maximising position.

The capital market opportunities

We will now make a major innovation into the analysis by introducing a capital market. A *capital market* is a place where funds, claims on resources, are exchanged, and it provides a

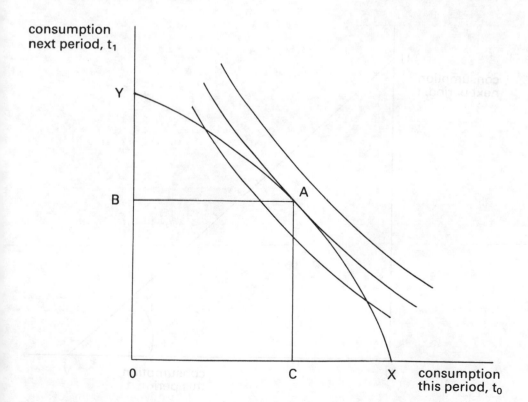

Figure II The investor's preferences

different sort of 'opportunity' for mixing consumption in different time-periods. If there is a capital market and our investor wishes to postpone some consumption he can lend at the prevailing interest rate until the next period, alternatively he can bring forward some consumption by borrowing against future funds he will receive. The capital market opportunities are depicted in Figure III as line UV. Why is the capital market opportunities line straight? This is because if we assume a perfect capital market the rate at which consumption this period can be traded for consumption next period is the same all over the market and for every pound invested.

There is a common rate of interest or rate of return, r, so that V invested at t_0 returns U at t_1 where $U = V (1 + r)$. Hence $(1 + r)$ is the slope of the capital market line. The contrast is with the production opportunities curve, where there were good and not so good projects and the behaviour of the investor in choosing the good ones first gave a curve concave to the origin.

Figure IV combines capital market and production opportunities. Recall that the pre-capital market equilibrium was A. The introduction of a capital market permits a new equilibrium at E, which is a point of tangency to a higher indifference curve and so represents an increase in the investor's utility. The investor achieves this in two stages. He invests in projects, that part of the initial funds X which are needed to give the mix of present and future consumption represented by D. He chooses D because, as the tangency point, it permits him to get on to the highest capital market opportunities line. He then exchanges D for E on the capital market. He is free to do this since D and E are both

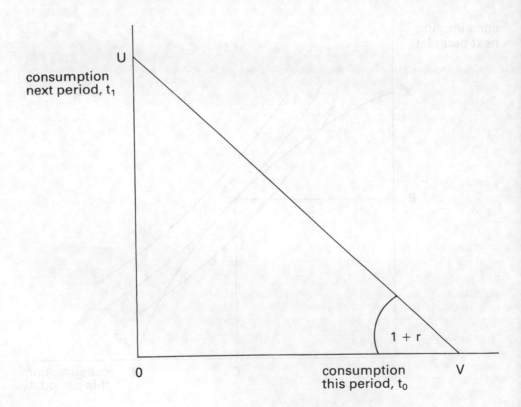

Figure III The capital market opportunities line

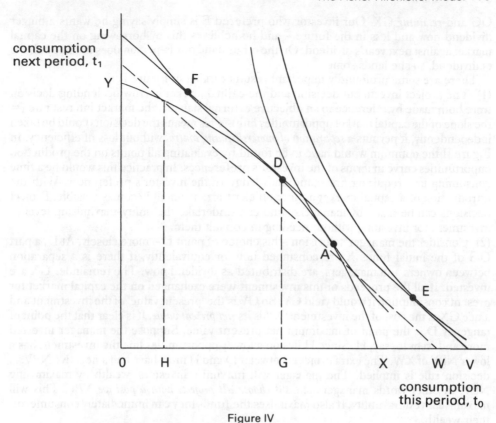

consumption
next period, t_1

U

Y

F

D

A

E

0   H   G   X   W   V

consumption
this period, t_0

Figure IV

on the same capital market opportunities line. In this case getting from D to E is a matter of selling some future consumption to receive more present consumption – 'borrowing'. To summarise, our investor finds that by undertaking some productive projects that yield relatively high consumption at t_1, then borrowing against those future returns to make up his t_0 consumption, he is better off overall.

The firm

We have talked about the investment decision of the individual investor, but the argument extends easily to firms. The only difference is that in a firm there will probably be more than one investor, with managers running the firm on their behalf. If there were more than one investor each with different tastes, *and no capital market*, managers could face a problem in finding an investment policy to suit everyone's tastes, since each investor might want the firm to choose a different point on the production opportunities curve. But once we introduce the capital market, each investor can choose their own mix of consumption and saving in response to the going rate of interest, *independent* of the behaviour of the others. Another investor with a relative preference for future consumption might find her point of tangency at F in Figure IV, compared to our initial investor's choice of E.

The firm has done its best by all its investors by investing up to point D.

At D the firm is investing GX and freeing OG for consumption, it is paying a *dividend* of

OG and *retaining* GX. Our investor who prefered E is simply saying he wants a bigger dividend now and less in the future – and he achieves this by borrowing on the capital market against next year's dividend. On the other hand our F-person does not need all the t_0 dividend, so she lends some.

There are some profoundly important results lurking in Figure IV:

(1) The project investment decision and the capital market borrowing/lending decision were both made by reference to an objective external statistic, the market interest rate (= the slope of the capital market opportunities line). This means the decisions could be taken independently, it permits a *separation of ownership and control* without loss of efficiency. In Figure II the optimum would have to be found by evaluating all points on the production opportunities curve in terms of the investor's preferences. In practice this would be a time consuming task requiring first-hand knowledge of the investor's preferences. With the introduction of a capital market a more efficient arrangement becomes feasible. Project decisions can be made by managers, who can undertake the utility-maximising level of investment for investors, without needing to consult them.

(2) Consider the manager's decision – his choice of point D – more closely. At D, a part OG of the initial funds X are consumed now or equivalently, if there is a separation between owners and managers, are distributed as dividend now. The remainder GX are invested. If all the proceeds of this investment were exchanged on the capital market for present consumption it would yield GV. So GV is the 'present value' of the investment and since GX is the cost of the investment, XV is its *net present value*. It is clear that the point of tangency D is the point of maximum net present value. Suppose the manager invested more and went to, say, H. Since H lies on a lower opportunities line the investment has a lower NPV of XW. The extra projects between D and H must have had a negative NPV. A decision rule is implied. The manager will maximise investors' wealth by maximising NPV, in other words managers should *choose all projects with a positive NPV*. This will maximise investors' utility. It also maximises the funds they can immediately consume, or, their wealth.

(3) The rule could be expressed another way. Since D is the point of tangency between the production possibility curve and the capital market line, the slopes, the marginal return to investment, more commonly called *internal rate of return*, and the rate of return in the market, are equal at D. So the manager would arrive at D if he were to: *invest until the market rate of return equals the IRR of the marginal project*. So in this case we can recommend managers to accept all projects whose IRR is greater than the cost of capital.

THE ASSUMPTIONS OF THE MODEL

What about the assumptions of the Fisher-Hirshleifer model? Throughout the argument we made the following assumptions:

1 Rational shareholders
2 Certainty
3 Two time-periods
4 Perfect capital markets
5 Project divisibility and independence

How does a model derived under such artificially simple assumptions stand up in the real world?

Rational shareholders and certainty (Assumptions 1 and 2)

The assumption that future cash flows are known with certainty is of course utterly unrealistic. This assumption is relaxed in the next chapter. The assumption that share-holders are rational might sound questionable to some people too. But all we are assuming here is that shareholders prefer more dividends to less in all time periods.

Two time-periods (Assumption 3)

It was convenient to assume investment decisions were being made over just two time periods, so as to present the argument graphically. But this is not a critical assumption. The existence of a capital market permits firms to raise finance and investors to spread their consumption over many periods. The NPV rule is completely robust over multiple time periods, but as we will see in the next section the IRR becomes difficult to interpret.

Perfect capital markets (Assumption 4)

We will be looking at the capital market in some detail in later chapters. In fact, though the market appears to be fairly efficient in its operation, it is not perfect. This is likely to have two effects on the analysis: borrowing and lending rates may diverge; and in some circumstances the firm may not be able to borrow at all.

Suppose the borrowing rate is higher than the lending rate. Then we get the outcome in Figure V.

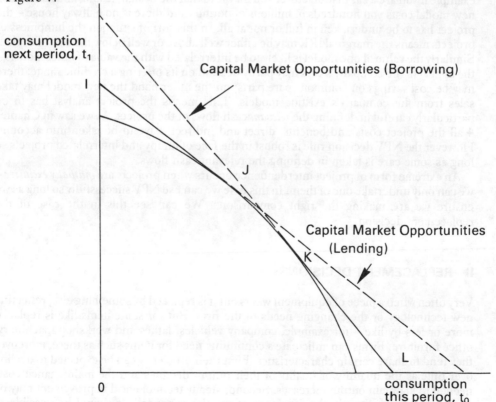

consumption next period, t_1

Capital Market Opportunities (Borrowing)

I

J

Capital Market Opportunities (Lending)

K

L

0

consumption this period, t_0

Figure V When borrowing and lending rates differ

Since the market rate of return determines the slope of the capital market opportunities line, different borrowing and lending rates effectively mean different lines, as the opportunities facing a lender are different from those facing a borrower. So investors whose preferences place them between I and J will seek to *lend* from this period's income to increase next period's consumption and will prefer the manager to invest up to J. Similarly others will be *borrowers*, and prefer K, and others still will prefer an outcome 'in the middle', on the curve between J and K. Different borrowing and lending rates bring indeterminacy into the analysis: different groups of shareholders may have conflicting views on the firm's investment policy, and the best the firm can do may be to choose a policy and stick to it, knowing that the dissatisfied investor can always invest elsewhere.

If there are actually quantity limits on the finance the firm can raise, we say the firm is suffering *capital rationing*. In this case capital is a constraining factor and it is necessary to modify the NPV decision rule so as to maximise NPV per unit of capital – we explore the practicalities of this in a later section.

Project divisibility and independence (Assumption 5)

We assumed that projects were infinitely divisible, giving a smooth and continuous production opportunities curve. Also we assumed that projects were independent in that the cash flows of one project were not affected by the acceptance or rejection of another. In practice neither of these may hold – projects can be 'lumpy' and highly interrelated. For example if you are a car manufacturer you may find that the design, testing and launch of a new model costs you hundreds of millions of pounds and there is no halfway house – the project has to be undertaken in full or not at all. In this sort of situation the lumpiness of projects means the marginal IRR may be either well above or well below the cost of capital. Similarly the value of one model is likely to be interrelated with the value of other models – the appeal of the company's cars may partly depend on its offering a credible range; there may be cost savings on common spare parts; on the other hand the new model may take sales from the company's existing models. This means the project analyst has to be particularly careful in defining the *relevant* cash flows of the project. As we saw in Chapter 4 all the project costs and benefits, direct and indirect, have to be taken into account. However the NPV decision rule is robust in the face of lumpy and interrelated projects so long as some care is taken in defining the relevant cash flows.

An extreme form of project interdendence occurs when projects are *mutually exclusive* – we can only undertake one of them. In this case we can use NPV successfully so long as we ensure we are making the right comparisons. We can see this in the case of the replacement decision.

II REPLACEMENT DECISIONS

Very often when a piece of equipment wears out it is replaced by something else, reflecting new technology or the changing needs of the firm. But for some items like is replaced more or less by like – for example, company vehicles, lathes and workshop machinery, office furniture. Firms can anticipate a continuing need for items such as these, moreover they tend to share certain characteristics. First their efficiency can be expected to decline over time as the quantity or quality of their output declines and the maintenance costs needed to maintain output increases. Second, steady technological improvement may be expected through time in the efficiency of the 'latest model'. It should be possible to estimate both of these factors. Third, these are well established second-hand markets in all these items, so the realisable value of equipment of any age can be ascertained from dealer's lists. These features make it feasible to calculate an *optimal replacement period* for the asset.

Consider an example:
Antioch Manufacturing is trying to establish a replacement policy for a lathe with the following characteristics:

Year	0	1	2	3	4
Machine Values					
Purchase cost	5,000				
Second hand value		4,000	3,600	3,000	2,000
Net cash flow during period		2,000	1,800	1,600	1,400

Incorporated into the cash flows is a 10% per annum expected decline in efficiency of the asset in use. We are ignoring taxation, inflation and technical improvements in the new machine, and assume a discount rate of 10%.

The firm is considering the alternatives of replacing the machines every 1, 2, 3 and 4 years. Denoting the NPV of a machine kept for one year as NPV_1, for two years as NPV_2 etc, then:

$$NPV_1 = (5,000) + \frac{2,000}{1.1} + \frac{4,000}{1.1} = 455$$

$$NPV_2 = (5,000) + \frac{2,000}{1.1} + \frac{1,800}{(1.1)^2} + \frac{3,600}{(1.1)^2} = 1,281$$

$$NPV_3 = (5,000) + \frac{2,000}{1.1} + \frac{1,800}{(1.1)^2} + \frac{1,600}{(1.1)^3} + \frac{3,000}{(1.1)^3} = 1,762$$

$$NPV_4 = (5,000) + \frac{2,000}{1.1} + \frac{1,800}{(1.1)^2} + \frac{1,600}{(1.1)^3} + \frac{1,400}{(1.1)^4} + \frac{2,000}{(1.1)^4} = 1,830$$

Effectively each replacement policy represents a rival project. As a set they are mutually exclusive. However we cannot just compare these NPVs as they stand: since each project covers a different time period we would not be comparing like with like. The different policies must be compared over equal time horizons. The one-year policy involves a yearly cycle of purchase and replacement. To compare this with the two-year policy we must look at a two year time horizon, involving two runs of the one year cycle. So the appropriate NPVs for comparison would be:

$$\text{NPV of 1 yr policy} = (5,000) + \frac{2,000}{1.1} + \frac{4,000}{1.1} + \frac{(5,000)}{1.1} + \frac{2,000}{(1.1)^2} + \frac{4,000}{(1.1)^2} = 868$$

$$\text{NPV of 2 yr policy} = \text{as originally} = 1,281$$

Now the NPVs are being calculated in comparable fashion. The calculation of the NPV of the one year policy could have been simplified by noting that it is

$$NPV = NPV_1 + \frac{NPV_1}{1.1} = 455 + 413 = 868$$

To compare all four policies we must find a time horizon which permits completed cycles of all the policies. This is the lowest common denominator of 1, 2, 3 and 4 years, which is 12 years. So we would compare 12 cycles of the yearly policy, 6 of the two-yearly and so forth. The calculations for this are clearly rather onerous. If we allow the possibility of a five-year policy, the appropriate time horizon is 60 years!

Surprisingly, a solution is to take each policy to an *infinite* time horizon since this permits us to use the formula for the sum of a geometric progression. The NPV of the one-year policy repeated each year to infinity is

$$\mathrm{NPV}^{\infty}_1 = \mathrm{NPV}_1 + \frac{\mathrm{NPV}_1}{1.1} + \frac{\mathrm{NPV}_1}{(1.1)^2} \cdots \infty = \mathrm{NPV}_1 \sum_{t=0}^{\infty} \frac{1}{(1.1)^t}$$

Similarly the NPV of the two-year policy repeated to infinity is

$$\mathrm{NPV}^{\infty}_2 = \mathrm{NPV}_2 + \frac{\mathrm{NPV}_2}{(1.1)^2} + \frac{\mathrm{NPV}_2}{(1.1)^4} \cdots \infty = \mathrm{NPV}_2 \sum_{t=0}^{\infty} \frac{1}{(1.1)^{2t}}$$

and so forth. Now, in general if $k > 0$, where m is the replacement period.

$$\sum_{t=0}^{\infty} \frac{1}{(1 + k)^{tm}} = \frac{1}{1 - \dfrac{1}{(1 + k)^m}}$$

So the NPV of the one-year policy to infinity simplifies to

$$\mathrm{NPV}^{\infty}_1 = \frac{\mathrm{NPV}_1}{1 - \dfrac{1}{(1 + k)^m}} = \frac{455}{1 - \dfrac{1}{1.1}} = 5{,}005$$

similarly
$$\mathrm{NPV}^{\infty}_2 = \frac{1{,}281}{1 - \dfrac{1}{(1.1)^2}} = 7{,}381$$

$$\mathrm{NPV}^{\infty}_3 = \frac{1{,}762}{1 - \dfrac{1}{(1.1)^3}} = 10{,}051$$

$$\mathrm{NPV}^{\infty}_4 = \frac{1{,}830}{1 - \dfrac{1}{(1.1)^4}} = 5{,}773$$

Inspection of the NPVs to infinity shows that the optimal replacement period is 3 years, Antioch should replace every 3 years.

III   CONSTRAINED INVESTMENT DECISIONS

In an ideal world decision-makers would accept all projects with a positive NPV. But in practice investment decisions may be constrained by scarcity of resources so that the firm has to *choose between* projects which have positive NPVs. In this section we will consider the case where just one resource is fixed: FINANCE This restriction is imposed for two reasons, one virtuous, one not-so-virtuous. The not-so-virtuous reason is, as the reader will soon discover, that making investment decisions with just one constraining factor is quite complicated enough. And anyway the analysis of one resource limited in several time periods is effectively an analysis of several constraints. The other reason is that the assumption of investment funds as the only constraint is probably realistic in a great many cases. We start by explaining why this is so.

The notion of resource constraints is essentially a short-run one. In the longer-run economists prefer to think that managers can arrange the supply of all the inputs they require, albeit at a price. So in appraising capital investments, which are essentially longer-term projects, we do not expect to find serious shortages of labour, raw materials and plant. These can be hired or trained, bought, and built as appropriate. Why does the same not apply to investment funds? Extra funds should be available from the market at some rate of interest.

Capital-rationing can come from inside or outside the firm. Earlier in the book we observed that firms may undertake less projects than would be worthwhile 'rationally' because of a hidden resource constraint, that of 'managerial effort'. We can expand this concept of the scarce resource of managerial effort to include not just limitations of managerial time, but also situations where the aims and objectives of managers about the growth rate of the firm imply a limit on the scale of investment to be undertaken. Managers may choose to restrict the growth rate of the firm because of uncertainty about the future, or because the absolute size of the firm, or its rate of growth may pose a threat to their ability to exercise control. Managers may prefer orderly, sustainable growth. One way managers can control the growth of the firm is through limiting the investment funds available during any period.

The previous comments related to the top, policy-making level of the firm where the power to raise new investment funds resides. Capital rationing can also be encountered lower down the firm, for if investment decisions are decentralised to divisions and an annual budgeting system is in operation which requires funds to be allocated to divisions prior to the decisions on how to use them, decision-makers find themselves confronted by a fixed ration of investment funds. The sort of capital rationing we have been describing, which the firm imposes upon itself, is usually called *soft* capital rationing.

But we cannot ignore the possibility that a firm may face externally imposed or *hard* capital rationing, when the supplier of funds, say a bank, will not provide finance at any price. This could arise if the bank itself were constrained, perhaps because the government had imposed lending limits on banks as part of its money supply policy. This would be a situation in which the suppliers of finance agreed that the firm had potential projects with a positive value but were unable to help. Alternatively though, the constraint may arise because of a disagreement between the firm and the supplier of funds as to the value of the project, and particularly as to its risk. There is a real problem here since much of the relevant information about, for example, the skill of management and the realism of their expectations, is hard to quantify. It is often said that the capital market is too cautious in lending, particularly to small firms where the information problem is greatest. This question is discussed in some more detail in Chapter 19.

Hard capital rationing implies imperfections in the capital market, beyond the control of the firm, while soft capital rationing is within the firms's control. But all capital rationing involves lost opportunities. The extent to which the firm imposes capital rationing on itself depends on the extent to which it is prepared to trade one objective, value, off against others such as orderly growth.

We start by analysing the situation where funds are limited in only one time period, then introduce two-period and multiperiod constraints.

ONE PERIOD CAPITAL RATIONING

If capital rationing only holds for one period we have a simple constrained maximisation problem of the sort we investigated in Chapter 4. The decision-rule is *choose the projects which yield the highest NPV per unit of the constraint.*

Consider an example:
Harlequin plc has the following possible projects available:

Project	Initial Capital Outlay	NPV	NPV per £1 capital
	(1)	(2)	(2) ÷ (1)
1	£75,000	7,663	.1022
2	£30,000	7,906	.2635
3	£25,000	150	.0060
4	£160,000	25,814	.1613
5	£50,000	7,195	.1439
6	£10,000	1,011	.1011
7	£30,000	2,892	.0964
	£380,000		

Harlequin has a capital budget of £250,000 for the year. Which projects should it undertake?

The solution is to rank the projects in terms of NPV per unit of constraining factor which in this case is capital. The final column provides the necessary data.

The ranking is:

Project	Cumulative Capital requirement
2	30,000
4	190,000
5	240,000

£250,000
cut-off point

1	315,000
6	325,000
7	355,000
3	380,000

So the firm should accept projects 2, 4, 5 as they yield the best NPV per unit of capital. This uses £240,000 capital. The remaining £10,000 would best be used by undertaking a proportion $\dfrac{10,000}{75,000}$ of project 1. This will give a total NPV of $7,906 + 25,814 + 7195 +$

$\dfrac{10}{75} \times 7,663 = £41,937.$

Project indivisibility

But is it realistic to assume we could undertake a fractional project, such as $\dfrac{10}{75}$ of project 1?

If we can do that, the reader may counter, why not go to the other extreme, and undertake project 2, $\dfrac{25}{3} = 8\frac{1}{3}$ times. If the firm could do it this would give the best solution of all, with an NPV of 7,906 × 8⅓ = £65,883. Commonly, though, projects will be *indivisible* and in this case our decision rule will not always give the best solution.

In the present case, if project 1 is indivisible, inspection suggests that the best alternative wil be project 6, which will just use up the £10,000 of capital budget left unused. Project 1 is better than 6 in terms of $\dfrac{\text{NPV}}{\text{capital}}$ but does not 'fit' so well. The lumpiness, or indivisibility, or projects has meant that some shuffling of projects is necessary to make the best use of the budget. Improvements like this are not always so easy to spot by eye and the task of shuffling to find the best set is better left to a computer. Implicitly we have had to relax our decision-rule. Now, when projects are indivisible, the rule is *choose those projects that maximise NPV subject to the constraint*.

If a firm expects capital rationing each period it would clearly be unwise to treat the problem as a one-period one. The danger is that when the second period arrives insufficient funds will be available to complete the committed investment projects. However, if management experience is that this danger is not real, and that residual financing requirements from previous years' projects never exceed subsequent years' capital rations treating capital rationing in this simple one-period way may be feasible. Each period's capital ration will simply be the uncommitted residue of new financing. But the treatment will never be optimal, it ignores too much information, it considers one period's cash flows and constraints, and ignores future periods.

TWO-PERIODS

The choice between capital investment projects under multiple constraints is best handled by using the linear programming (LP) technique. In this section we consider a simple two-project, two-period, investment problem, and in the next section how more complex problems could be handled.

Consider the following example:
Gerald & Co, builders, have two designs of factory to offer. They have just acquired a large green field on which they plan to build these factories. Unfortunately, the factories take two years to build, and Gerald have strictly limited investment funds in the next two years. The capital requirement during building, and estimated NPV of the two sorts of factory is:

Factory	A	B
Capital Year 1	3	8
Year 2	4	4
NPV	6	14

(figures are in £ millions)
The firm has £24 million to invest each year. How many of each factory should the firm build?

The constrained decision-rule is *choose those projects that maximise NPV subject to the constraints*. The question is how to choose.

The first step is to set the problem up in linear programming form:

Maximise:	$NPV = 6\,x_A + 14\,x_B$
Subject to constraints:	$3\,x_A + 8\,x_B \leqslant 24$
	$4\,x_A + 4\,x_B \leqslant 24$
	$x_A , x_B \geqslant 0$

where x_A = number of A factories built
    x_B = number of B factories built

Again we face the indivisibility problem since this formulation permits the building of fractions of factories. The reader must bear with this problem, which is a limitation of the simple technique being used. Economic sense could be given to the idea of part-factories if it is possible to undertake a joint venture with someone else to complete the factory. The requirement of part-factories can be avoided by using more sophisticated techniques such as integer programming.

Because a simple two variable problem was chosen it can be solved graphically:

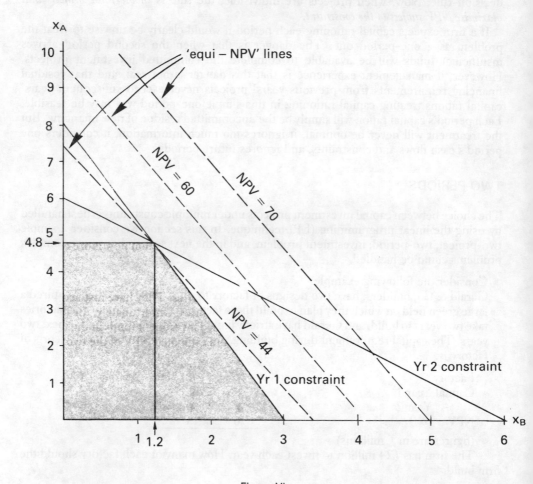

Figure VI

Figure VI graphs the two constraints. For example, in the first year the firm could have $\frac{24}{3}$ = 8 of A, or $\frac{24}{8}$ = 3 of B, or some linear combination of these. There is a similar constraint in the second year.

A feasible solution must comply with all the constraints, including the requirement that only positive quantities of factories can be built. The shaded area in figure VI is the feasible set.

To find the best combination of factories from this feasible set, we superimpose on the diagram a set of equi-NPV lines. These lines link the various combinations of projects that yield a particular NPV in total, they are the dashed lines on figure VI. The best combination is the member of the feasible set which lies on the highest NPV line. By inspecting the graph we can see the optimal solution consists in building

$$4.8 \text{ of A}$$
and $$1.2 \text{ of B}$$

The NPV of this solution will be: $6 \times 4.8 + 14 \times 1.2$
$$= \text{£}45.6 \text{ mn.}$$

MULTIPLE-PERIOD CAPITAL RATIONING[2]

The main virtue of the two-period, two-project case is that it permits the solution of the programming problem to be presented graphically. But real-world problems can be very complicated, and are best solved using a computer package. We now consider how a more complicated problem would be solved using a package. Suppose a firm is contemplating four projects extending over three years as follows:

Projects		1	2	3	4	Capital Available
Capital Required:	Time 1	11	20	40	25	120
	2	40	40	80	50	80
	3	60	20	0	55	60
NPV		39	20	79	60	

(Figures are in £ millions)

We can set the problem up in linear programming form as before:

Maximise   NPV $= 39x_1 + 20x_2 + 79x_3 + 60x_4$
Subject to constraints:

$$11x_1 + 20x_2 + 40x_3 + 25x_4 \leqslant 120 \quad (1)$$
$$40x_1 + 40x_2 + 80x_3 + 50x_4 \leqslant 80 \quad (2)$$
$$60x_1 + 20x_2 \qquad\qquad + 55x_4 \leqslant 60 \quad (3)$$
$$x_1 \leqslant 1 \quad (4)$$
$$x_2 \leqslant 1 \quad (5)$$
$$x_3 \leqslant 1 \quad (6)$$
$$x_4 \leqslant 1 \quad (7)$$
$$x_i \leqslant 0 \ i = 1 \text{ to } 4 \quad (8)$$

Constraint (8) says, as in the previous example, that the firm cannot undertake negative amounts of projects. But now we are also stipulating in (4) – (7) that the firm cannot undertake any project more than once. The constraints are all inequalities at present, but we can convert them to equalities by introducing 'slack' variables. Letting S_1, S_2, S_3 represent the capital unused at time points 1, 2, 3 respectively and S_4 to S_7 represent the unpurchased proportion of projects 1 to 4, the problem becomes:

2   For further reading on this topic the reader is referred to Lorie and Savage (1955), Weingartner (1963), Weingartner (1977), Bernhard (1969), Bhaskar (1976), Hughes and Lewellen (1974).

Maximise $\qquad$ $39x_1 + 20x_2 + 79x_3 + 60x_4$

Subject to constraints $\qquad$
$$11x_1 + 20x_2 + 40x_3 + 25x_4 + S_1 = 120$$
$$40x_1 + 40x_2 + 80x_3 + 50x_4 + S_2 = 80$$
$$60x_1 + 20x_2 \qquad\quad + 55x_4 + S_3 = 60$$
$$x_1 + S_4 = 1$$
$$x_2 + S_5 = 1$$
$$x_3 + S_6 = 1$$
$$x_4 + S_7 = 1$$
$$x_i \geqslant 0 \qquad i = 1 \text{ to } 4$$

This problem was processed using the LINDO package. A final solution was reached after 2 iterations as the printout below:

```
LP Optimum found at step 2
Objective function value : 89.625
VARIABLE      VALUE
X1            0.0
X2            0.0
X3            0.375
X4            1.0
ROW        SLACK      DUAL PRICES
(S1)       80.0          0.0
(S2)        0.0          0.9875
(S3)        5.0          0.0
(S4)        1.0          0.0
(S5)        1.0          0.0
(S6)        0.625        0.0
(S7)        0.0         10.625
```

The printout indicates that the optimum return in terms of NPV is £89.625 mn. This is obtained by purchasing all of project 4 ($x_4 = 1$) and three-eights of project 3 ($x_3 = 0.375$). This investment leaves spare capital at time 1 of £80 mn ($S_1 = 80$) and £5 mn at time 3 ($S_3 = 5$). The project slack variables confirm what we know from the x values. In the optimum solution projects 1 and 2 are unused ($S_4 = 1$, $S_5 = 1$) and project 3 is only .375 used ($S_6 = .675$).

The computer package uses the so-called *simplex* method of solution and the *dual* or *shadow price* is a valuable piece of information generated by simplex solutions. It tells you how much the value of the objective funtion would have increased if a particular constraint had been relaxed by one unit. In other words it tells you the opportunity cost of the constraint. By definition, the dual is only positive when the corresponding slack is zero and vice versa: a constraint only has an opportunity cost when it is binding. Capital was a binding constraint in period 2 ($S_2 = 0$). The dual tells us that had another £1 million of capital been available at time 2, the value of the objective function would have increased by £987,500. Similarly we can see that had we been able to undertake project 4 twice instead of once this would have added £10,625,000 to total NPV.

AN ASSESSMENT OF LP

The LP approach is powerful but it has its limitations, some only apparent, some real:

Linearity

As the name implies, the objective function and the constraints must be linear. In practice this is not a severe restriction since it is usually possible to approximate a non-linear relationship with a series of linear relationships.

Divisibility

The assumption that projects are divisible is again not as severe as at first seems. If the assumption that projects can be scaled up or down and their NPVs scaled up or down proportionately, does too much violence to the facts, in other words if the projects use resources with significant indivisibilities, then integer programming models can be used.

Opportunity cost of capital

A more perplexing problem in capital rationing is what discount-rate to use. In the example above the NPVs of the alternative projects were worked out using the opportunity cost of capital, which was taken to be known and constant for the duration of the projects. The trouble is that, on the face of it, capital rationing is exactly the situation when this cannot be assumed! The opportunity cost of capital in any period is the return on the marginal project in that period. But we do not know what the marginal project is until we have gone through the optimising process, and we cannot do that without the discount rate! However, the distinction between 'soft' and 'hard' capital rationing is important here. It is the investors' opportunity cost of capital that is significant, but this will vary with the composition of the firm's optimal bundle of projects only if the capital market has imperfections and there is 'hard' capital rationing. If the capital market rationing is 'soft', self-imposed by the firm, then it will not affect the investors' opportunity cost of capital and we are safe to go on using the firm's cost of capital as a discount rate.

Uncertainty

Perhaps the most telling limitation of LP is its requirement of certainty about cash flows from future projects, and about capital constraints. At present no very satisfactory way has been devised of incorporating uncertainty into the model. In reality, though, in an uncertain and changing world, opportunities and constraints are constantly changing and unfolding. But this limitation is common to all optimising techniques including DCF analysis itself. The answer is to recognise that optimising must be a continuous, rather than a 'once-for-all' process, with plans being constantly revised in the light of new information. But decisions still have to be made, and LP can be a valuable aid in project choice.

IV THE INTERNAL RATE OF RETURN

We saw that our investment decision-rule could be specified in terms of a project's internal rate of return: accept all projects with an IRR greater than the cost of capital. In practice IRR is in widespread use in decision-making. Unfortunately, though NPV is robust to relaxing most of the Fisher-Hirshleifer assumptions, IRR is less so. On closer inspection IRR betrays major weaknesses as the basis for a decision rule.

CALCULATING PROJECT IRRs

The IRR measures the yield of a set of cash flows in percentage terms and is the discount rate which makes the NPV of the cash flows equal zero. Mathematically it is R in the following formula:

$$\text{NPV} = \sum_{t=0}^{n} \frac{C_t}{(1 + R)^t} = 0 \tag{1}$$

Consider the project that comprises an initial outlay of £12,500 followed by 4 annual receipts of £4,000. We can find the IRR by repeated solving with different discount rates in order to find the discount rate that gives NPV = 0. Try 8% first.

t =	0	1	2	3	4	Total
cash flows (£)	(12,500)	4,000	4,000	4,000	4,000	
8% discount factor	1		3.312			
present value	(12,500)		13,248		NPV = £748	

Discounting at 8% yields a positive NPV of £728, so a higher rate is needed to reduce the impact of the future inflows. Try 10% and 12%:

We derive the following results:

Discount Rate	NPV
8%	748
10%	179
12%	(352)

Hence the IRR is between 10% and 12%. We can estimate it with greater accuracy by *interpolating*[3] between 10% and 12% thus:

$$\text{estimate rate} = 10\% \quad + \quad 2\% \quad \times \quad \frac{179}{179 + 352}$$

	↑	↑
	interval between 10% and 12%	distance along the interval which gives NPV = 0

$$= 10.7\%$$

This type of solution method is called an *iterative* process. It involves converging on a solution by informed trial and error. In fact, there is no other way of finding the IRR. Manual solution of IRR can be very time consuming, but the task is the sort that computers thrive on and DCF packages that calculate IRR are widely available.

The relationship between the IRR and the NPV of a project is as follows:

NPV is the project's value using the cost of capital as the discount rate

IRR is the discount rate which makes a projects's NPV zero

For 'conventional' projects in which an initial outflow of cash is followed by a succession of inflows, the relationship between IRR and NPV is shown in Figure VII. This would be the relationship under the Fisher-Hirshleifer assumptions. We can see that IRR and NPV

---

3   This is still slightly inexact because we have used 'linear' interpolation on what is, as Figure VII shows, a curvilinear relationship.

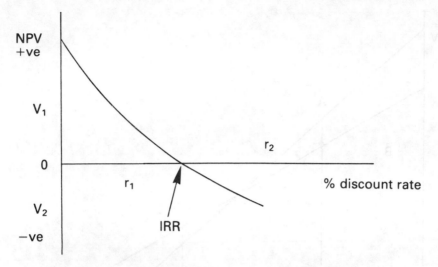

Figure VII The relationship of the NPV and IRR of a project

give completely consistent signals – when IRR > r, NPV is positive, when IRR < r_2, NPV is negative. However if some of the Fisher-Hirshleifer assumptions are relaxed this may not be so.

Project interdependence

If projects are not independent (assumption 5) IRR may fail. Suppose projects are *mutually exclusive* – the firm might be choosing a new computer and though there are many acceptable makes available it only wants one. In this case the decision maker needs additional information to *rank* the computers in order of merit.

IRR cannot be relied upon to rank projects correctly. Consider the mutually exclusive projects J and K:

	Cash Flows			
	Yr 0	Yr 1	IRR	NPV at 10%
Project J	(£100)	£150	50%	£36
Project K	(£300)	£400	33%	£64

On this basis of IRR we would choose J, on the basis of NPV, K. We can rely on the NPV signal – it tells us how much projects J and K would increase our wealth. The IRR is merely beguiling – project J does offer a higher percentage return per pound invested, but this is not the appropriate criterion for project choice. In the case of mutually exclusive projects the relative efficiency of the smaller project is *irrelevant*, it is the absolute level of NPV that counts. In this example the problem was caused by the fact that the competing projects were of different *scale*. But more generally the ranking problem can arise whenever two projects' NPV functions intersect in the positive quadrant. Figure VIII shows the nub of the problem. The NPV for two projects A and B is graphed at different discount rates. The IRR of B is higher than that of A, as its line cuts the X axis at a higher discount rate. But, because the A and B lines intersect, which project has the better NPV *depends on the choice of discount rate*. If the discount rate is x, A has the higher NPV. If it is y, then B is preferred. The discount rate is crucial. It provides the correct rate for reinvest-

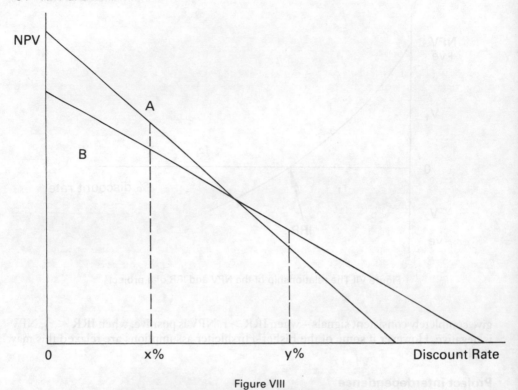

NPV

A

B

0   x%   y%   Discount Rate

Figure VIII

ment, and it reassures us that the capital which is used in the project is fully costed, and that a uniform measure of the cost of capital is being used for *every* project being pursued. On these grounds we have confidence in NPV as always giving an accurate ranking.

The problem of IRR with mutually exclusive projects can be solved however. The solution is to combine projects into one project for appraisal by taking one from the other and appraising the difference.

Consider the following cash flows of projects A, B and the difference A−B

Cash flows	t_0	t_1	t_2
A	(500)	100	600
B	(500)	500	150
'A − B'	0	(400)	450

Calculating NPV and IRR for A and B at a 10% discount rate we get

	NPV	IRR
A	87	20%
B	79	25%

with IRR perversely favouring B. But if we are determined to use IRR we can find the IRR of 'A − B', which is 13%. Since the IRR of 'A − B' is greater than the cost of capital, A is preferred, and this is consistent with the NPV analysis.

Multiple time periods

Once projects stretch beyond two time-periods in length (assumption 3) it becomes possible they will not have a 'conventional' profile of cash flows, ie an initial outlay followed by positive inflows in all future periods. If the cash profile is any different it may have multiple solutions to its IRR, or even no IRR at all. Consider the following project:

Year	0	1	2	3
cash flow	(25)	150	(275)	150
sign of cash flow	−ve	+ve	−ve	+ve

This project has three IRRs: 0%, 100%, 200%! The decision-makcr would be hard put to interpret this information.

The problem is that the IRR formula

$$\text{NPV} = \sum_{t=1}^{n} \frac{C_t}{(1 + R)^t} \text{ is a}$$

polynomial with n roots of which the number of *real* roots, which are the IRR values, can be up to but not greater than the number of sign changes in the cash flows, C_t.[4] In the case of the previous project there were three sign changes and three solutions.

In reality there are very many projects with unconventional cash flows. For example, processes which require re-equipping halfway through; projects with heavy contractual costs at the end for refurbishment; orders for which the customer makes a significant advance payment; and so forth. In terms of the NPV function all these projects share the characteristic of cutting the x-axis more than once, hence their multiple IRRs. Figure IX depicts this for the project mentioned above.

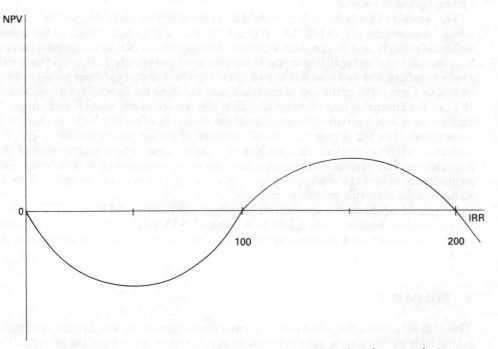

Figure IX The relationship of NPV and IRR for the multiple-sign-change project

4 This follows from Descartes' 'rule of signs'. Lorie and Savage (1955) and Fawthrop (1971) discuss this problem in more detail.

Varying costs of capital

Another problem where there are multiple time periods is that IRR gives an average return over the life of the project. This may not matter too much if the cost of capital is constant through time, but forecasting a constant cost of capital is usually a simplifying assumption forced by lack of better information. Suppose we have the following data about a 5-year project.

Project IRR   12%

	Yr.	1	2	3	4	5
Forecast cost of capital:		8%	8%	10%	14%	14%

We could not ascertain the project's acceptability without further analysis – it would be simpler to calculate NPV at the outset.

THE ECONOMIC SIGNIFICANCE OF IRR

The fundamental problem with IRR is rather simple. IRR tells us what the cost of capital *would need to be* to give NPV = 0. This is interesting, but only indirectly related to our real concern which is what NPV *is* at the ruling cost of capital. The problem is that to make the calculation we assume the cost of capital to be different from what it actually is: we assume that the firm can borrow needed cash and invest spare cash during the project at the project's IRR rate. This is the so-called *reinvestment* assumption. This is a safe assumption, one that does not yield confusing or downright misleading results, only in the Fisher-Hirshleifer world.

The appeal of IRR is that it is expressed as a rate of return, and these are the terms in which businessmen like to talk. Our objection is that it attracts attention to the wrong feature of projects, and this can be dangerous. The oddness of IRR as a decision-criterion becomes clearer if we recall that capital is just one input to a project. Labour and materials might be others, and we could just as well calculate what the cost of labour would need to be to give a zero NPV, or the cost of materials, and call these the internal return on labour, IRL, or the internal return on materials, IRM. As we see in the next chapter, firms do explore these issues as part of the analysis of the sensitivity of project NPVs to changes in assumptions. But the appropriate *overall* measure of project worth remains NPV. We encounter a similar problem when we look at some decision criteria such as *payback* in a later chapter. The payback criterion says *choose the project which recovers its initial outlay first*. Again, speed of payback is one component of a project's success, but by raising it to the status of a decision-rule problems arise.

In general we have two reasons for prefering NPV. First, NPV provides a robust decision-rule in situations where IRR fails. Second, NPV relates directly to the objective of value maximisation, it measures the amount by which a project adds to the value of the firm.

V   SUMMARY

This chapter showed that when projects have effects spreading through time, the appropriate decision rule for choosing between them is based on the *value* of the projects. The Fisher-Hirshleifer model shows how by adopting the decision-rule – *choose all projects with a positive NPV* – the wealth of shareholders will be maximised. The assumptions of the Fisher-Hirshleifer model appear rather restrictive, but the NPV decision rule is quite robust even when they are relaxed. The associated rule in terms of *internal rate of return* does not fare so well and runs into significant difficulties of interpretation under fairly realistic assumptions about projects.

The NPV has to be modified when capital is rationed, either by outside suppliers of finance or internally as a policy decision. The solution is an application of the constrained-resource analysis of Chapter 4: we recommend the firm to choose the bundle of projects with the highest NPV. We pointed out that the more likely form of capital rationing encountered was internal, and that here the loss of value was often more apparent than real since the imposition of capital rationing might well be a method of accounting for risk and for indirect costs that are hard to quantify. The practical problem of choosing between positive valued projects can be handled by using linear programming, though the usefulness of a technique such as this is in practice limited by its inability to cope with the uncertainty of the real world.

REFERENCES AND BIBLIOGRAPHY

Bernhard, R H	'Mathematical Programming Models for Capital Budgeting – a Survey, Generalisation and Critique', Journal of Financial and Quantitative Analysis, June 1969, pp 111–158.
Bhaskar, K N	'Linear Programming and Capital Budgeting: The Financing Problem', Journal of Business Finance and Accounting, Summer 1976, pp 159–194.
Dudley, C L	'A Note on Reinvestment Assumption in Choosing Between Net Present Value and Internal Rate of Return', Journal of Finance, Sept 1972, pp 907–915.
Fama, E F, and Miller, M H	*The Theory of Finance* (1972) Dryden Press, Hinsdale, Illinois.
Fawthrop, R A	'Underlying Problems of Discounted Cash Flow Appraisal', Accounting and Business Research, Summer 1971, pp 187–198.
Fisher, I	*The Theory of Interest* (1930) Macmillan, New York.
Hirshleifer, J	'On the Theory of Optimal Investment Decisions', Journal of Political Economy, 1958, pp 329–372, reprinted in Archer and D'Ambrosio *Theory of Business Finance*.
Hughes, J S, and Lewellen, W G	'Programming Solutions to Capital Rationing Problems', Journal of Business Finance and Accounting, Spring 1974, pp 55–74.
Keane, S M	'The internal rate of return and the reinvestment fallacy', Abacus, June 1979.
Levy, H, and Sarnat, M	*Capital Investment and Financial Decisions* (1978) Prentice-Hall International, London.
Lorie, J H, and Savage, L J	'Three Problems in Rationing Capital'. Journal of Business, Oct 1955, pp 227–239.
Pointon, J	'Taxation and Mathematical Programming', Journal of Business Finance and Accounting, Spring 1982, pp 43–50.
Scholefield, H H	'Replacement of Equipment' Accounting and Business Research, 1972, pp 316–324.
Walker, R G	'The judgement factor in investment decisions', Harvard Business Review, 1961.

Weingartner, H M   *Mathematical Programming and the Analysis of Capital Budgeting Problems* (1974) Kershaw, London.

Weingartner, H M   'Capital Rationing: "n" Authors in Search of a Plot', Journal of Finance, Dec 1977, pp 1403–32.

Wilkes, F M   'On Multiple Rates of Return' Journal of Business Finance and Accounting, 1980, pp 569–583.

QUESTIONS

1 Explain why in a perfect capital market under certainty firms maximise shareholders' wealth by choosing projects with positive NPV, or with IRR greater than the cost of capital.

   Show how the equivalance of IRR and NPV may break down under more realistic assumptions.

2 Jack Ltd is considering two projects A and B with the following cash flows

	t = 0	1	2
Project A	£(8,000)	£6,000	£4,000
Project B	£(2,000)	£1,000	£2,000

   Calculate the NPV's of projects A and B using a discount rate of 10% and 25%, and their IRRs

   Which project(s) should Jack choose if A and B are (i) mutually exclusive (ii) not mutually exclusive?

3 The Smith Company has a lathe of a sort for which an active new and secondhand market exists. The net revenues from using the lathe are £21,000 per year. The lathe could be retained for six years or replaced at any point at a replacement cost of £60,000.
   The secondhand prices for such lathes are

Years old	Market value
1	£50,000
2	£42,500
3	£37,500
4	£30,000
5	£16,000
6	£3,000

   What is the optimal replacement policy assuming a 10% cost of capital? What will your answer be if the net revenues are £30,000 p a not £21,000?

   Explain the apparent paradox that an optimum exists at all, assuming a perfect market for a secondhand asset, with rational buyers.

4 A choice has to be made of some combination of six available projects in such a way as to maximise the net present value of the returns. The projects require investments during the next three years, and these together with the net present value of the returns are given below (in £000s).

		PROJECT					
		I	II	III	IV	V	VI
	Year 1	25	5	18	22	4	13
Investment	2	10	20	18	–	10	5
required	3	–	5	18	–	18	5
NPV of returns		48	40	65	40	36	32

Capital is rationed to 65 per year.

(i) Formulate (without solving) this as a linear programming problem assuming that it would be possible to purchase any proportion of each project.
(ii) Explain how you would interpret the solutions to the LP, including the shadow prices on the constraints.

CHAPTER 7

Risk aversion and portfolio building

We have seen how the firm would choose its projects if the future were known with certainty. But the future is far from certain and we need to be able to make investment decisions under conditions of risk.

This chapter examines the theory behind risk-analysis. In Section I we consider what risk means in finance. Section II introduces the fundamental assumption that investors are risk-averse, and Section III shows how investors can reduce their risk by building portfolios of assets. Section IV brings together these two elements, the preferences of investors and the asset portfolios they can build, to analyse risky investment decisions. The 'capital asset pricing model' which we describe in Section V gives an expression for the return we should expect to get on any risky asset, and in the next chapter we use this as the basis for a decision-rule for choosing risky projects.

I MEASURING RISK

Suppose we are not certain what return we are going to get from an investment decision. The variety of possible outcomes the decision can have can be described in terms of the value, r_i, of each outcome i, and the probability p_i, of it happening. The probability of a certain outcome is 1, and of an impossible outcome 0. The probabilities of all possible outcomes must sum to 1, that is $\sum_{i=1}^{n} p_i = 1$ where n is the number of possible outcomes.

Example
Hardcastle Manufacturing Company is wondering what return it will get from its umbrella division if it keeps the division going next year. It decides the results of the last ten years were representative; these were:

Umbrella Division									
year 19*0	1	2	3	4	5	6	7	8	9
% return 9	14	14	8	15	17	17	10	14	22

To describe a probability distribution like this we can use two statistics, the *expected value* and the *variance*. The expected value is the mean of the outcomes, r̄, where

$$\bar{r} = \sum_{i=1}^{n} r_i p_i \tag{1}$$

100

The variance is a measure of the spread of the various possible outcomes around this mean. We measure the variance, σ^2, of a distribution as

$$\sigma^2 = \sum_{i=1}^{n} (r_i - \bar{r})^2 p_i \tag{2}$$

So the $\bar{r}$ and σ^2 for the Umbrella Division are

r_i	p_i	$r_i p_i$		$r_i - \bar{r}$	$(r_i-\bar{r})^2 p_i$
8	.1	.8		-6	3.6
9	.1	.9		-5	2.5
10	.1	1.0		-4	1.6
14	.3	4.2		0	0
15	.1	1.5		1	.1
17	.2	3.4		3	1.8
22	.1	2.2		8	6.4

expected value $= \bar{r} = \underline{14.0}$ variance $= \sigma^2 = \underline{16.0}$

An alternative way of describing the spread which is sometimes more convenient is the *standard deviation*. The standard deviation, σ, is simply the square-root of the variance, so the umbrella division's σ is $\sqrt{16} = 4\%$. In one sense, σ may be easier to interpret than σ^2 since it provides a measure of spread which is of the same scale as the original data.

In finance theory we use variance and standard deviation to measure risk. The greater the variance of outcomes from a project, the more risky we will say the project is; the greater the variance in returns from a division, or from the firm as a whole, the more risky the division or firm. Measuring risk this way, we can proceed to build a theory of how individuals choose risky assets. But before we do that there are one or two important cautions to bear in mind.

The first is a technical point. Probability distributions can come in all shapes and sizes, and not all of them can be completely described in terms of mean and variance. Variables that follow the so-called 'normal distribution' *do* have this property – if you know the mean and the variance you can work out the whole distribution and the probability of each outcome. For example we know from mathematical tables that 95% of the area of a normal distribution lies within 1.96 standard deviations either side of the mean, and 99% is within 2.58 standard deviations. Applying this to the umbrella division, we know that the mean return, $\bar{r}$, is 14%, and the standard deviation, σ, is 4%. So if the division's returns are normally distributed, there is a 95% probability that the returns in any year will be between 6% and 22% ($= 14 \pm 1.96 \times 4$), and a 99% chance they will be between 4% and 24%.

Figure I.i shows the symmetric, bell-shaped pattern of the normal distribution. A remarkable number of variables in nature follow this distribution, but do the returns to projects and firms? In the long run returns to firms are likely to be 'skewed' as in Figure I.ii. This is because while there is no upper limit to the returns a firm can earn, firms earning inadequate returns will sooner or later go out of business. Despite this it is convenient to assume 'normality' so long as it does not do too much violence to the facts.

The second thing we might question about variance is whether variance is really what people worry about when they consider risk. In calculating variance, positive and negative deviations from the mean get equal weight, but are people really indifferent between positive and negative? Surely the preoccupation of most decision makers is with the

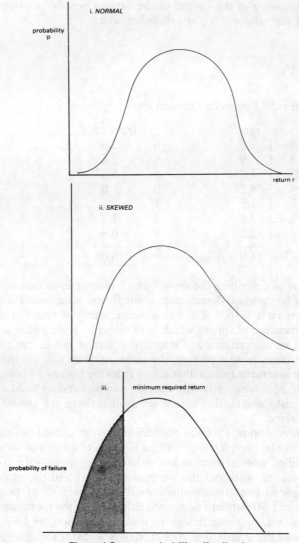

Figure I Some probability distributions

so-called *downside risk*, and in particular the risk of failure, the shaded area in Figure I.iii? As we develop the story in this chapter it will become clearer why finance theory does not pay more attention to this. Finance theory envisages people holding bundles of assets, projects, or shares in firms, so that the risk of failure on one individual asset *is* balanced by the possibility of success on another, and it is overall risk and return that matters. In any case if returns are normally distributed standard deviation will be a perfect *proxy* for downside risk. We will assume that people choose assets on the basis of their mean and variance. But how far decision-makers actually think this way is another question and it may be that finance theory should pay more attention to downside risk.

One final reservation before we proceed. We can talk about risk when we have sufficient information to estimate the mean and variance of the distribution of outcomes. But this still requires a relatively high level of information. At the other extreme we may find decision-makers operating under such *uncertainty* that they are unable to produce any clear views about future outcomes. This situation does not provide such attractive material for finance theorists but may describe the predicament of many decision-makers. The prevalence of uncertainty puts a limit on the usefulness of risk-analysis and we return to this topic at the end of the next chapter.

II RISK AVERSION

In everyday usage of the word, 'risk' is clearly 'a bad thing', something to be avoided.
  Consider the following example:

You are offered the choice of two deals:
either (a) the certainty of £100
or   (b) a .5 chance of £150 and a .5 chance of £50 to be decided by the toss of a coin.
Which would you prefer? Don't forget that the 'expected value' of (b) is .5 × £50 + .5 × £150 = £100

Your answer will indicate if you are 'risk-averse' or not. The riskier alternative is clearly (b) – the expected values of (a) and (b) are the same, but the spread of actual outcomes around that value is higher in the case of (b). If you
    prefer (a) you are RISK-AVERSE
    prefer (b) you are RISK-PREFERRING
    are indifferent you are RISK-NEUTRAL
  Probably most people would prefer (a). But why do we believe people are risk-averse? We can show that risk aversion is logically implied by the 'diminishing marginal utility of wealth', expressed diagrammatically in Figure II.i. Here an individual's total utility or satisfaction is plotted against his wealth. The curve is drawn so that successive increases in wealth yield successively smaller increases in utility, until eventually the curve almost flattens out, at which point the individual attaches hardly any value to extra wealth. This is known as the 'diminishing marginal utility of wealth' (DMUW). An individual whose attitude to wealth was one of this sort would be risk-averse.
  Consider Figure II.ii. which is Figure II.i with the earlier example superimposed. The

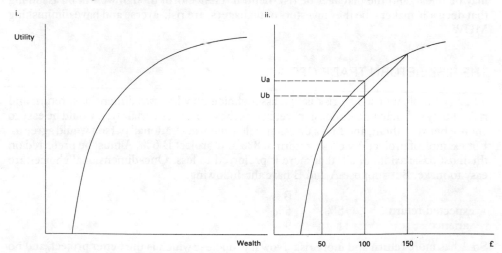

Figure II Diminishing marginal utility of wealth

expected return from an equal gamble of £50 and £150 is £100. The expected *utility* of the gamble is the mean of the utilities of £50 and £150, which is point U_b halfway along the straight line connecting the £50 and £150 utilities. However, the shape of the curve means that U_a the utility of the *certain* prospect of £100, is higher than U_b, the expected utility of the two uncertain prospects, £50 and £150.

Demonstrating risk-aversion as a logical implication of DMUW is only helpful if DMUW can be validated some other way. The idea that the more wealth you have the less you value money is intuitively appealing – we have an image of the tycoon lighting his cigar with a $1,000 bill with the pauper agonising over the loss of a coin. But the idea needs some qualification. For example does MUW diminish over its whole range, or is it constant (linear) over part of the range? Constant marginal utility of income would imply risk-neutrality. Moreover, the concept of DMUW was developed to describe the individual consumer. Does it apply equally to the decision-maker in a firm? We can think of two reasons why managers may exhibit DMUW.

Target setting

Managers' performance is often appraised by comparing actual performance to a pre-ordained target or budget, and the manager may prefer to be on target, rather than below *or* above it. He or she may prefer a certainty of achieving budgeted sales of say £100 to an equal change of achieving £50 sales and £150 sales. Under-performance may have damaging career implications, over-performance may involve the need to set targets next period which are hard to live up to. The lower the risk, the better the manager's control over his or her future.

Bankruptcy

For most managers bankruptcy is to be avoided at all costs, and outcomes which make bankruptcy possible have a particularly heavy 'disutility'.

But if neither of these factors is present: if there is no institutional risk-aversion created by the appraisal system, and if there is no real risk of bankruptcy then the manager's MUW may be linear, and the manager be risk-neutral. Henceforth though we will be assuming that decision-makers, be they investors or managers, are risk-averse and have diminishing MUW.

THE RISK RETURN TRADE-OFF

The key problem posed by risk is that asset choice now has two dimensions, return and risk. If they only had one dimension, return, as they do under certainty, it would be easy to choose between them, and find a decision-rule which any 'rational' person would agree to. For example if project A yields a return of 8% and project B 6%, A must be preferred on the most basic axiom of all, that more is preferred to less. One-dimensional choices are easy to make. But suppose A and B have the following:

	A	B
expected return	8%	6%
variance	11	9

So A has more return and more risk. Now it is unclear which is the better project, and no amount of studying the projects will make it clearer. To find which is the better project it is necessary to study the decision-maker, and the relative valuation he puts on risk and return, his *risk-return trade-off*. Any decision-rule needs to take account of subjective data, the preferences of the decision maker.

In finance theory we depict these preferences between risk and return as a set of concave indifference curves as in Figure III.

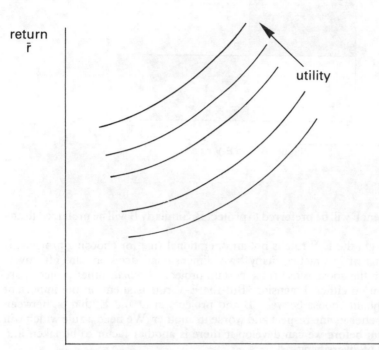

Figure III The individual's preferences

The E-V rule

Underlying Figure III is a fundamental assumption: that people choose assets according to the EXPECTED RETURN-VARIANCE Rule.[1] It says Project A will be preferred to project B if

1 Expected return of A exceeds (or is equal to) the expected return of B and the variance of A is less than the variance of B, or

2 Expected return of A exceeds that of B and the variance of A is less than (or equal to) that of B.

The rule is easily understood in a graph.

---

1 The E–V rule was first presented by Harry Markowitz (1952). The theory of choice under uncertainty shows that given certain fundamental axioms about their preferences, people will seek to maximise their expected utility of wealth. They can do this by choosing according to the E–V rule, but only if asset returns are normally distributed, or if the individuals have quadratic preferences. The theory behind Figure IV is described in more detail in Fama and Miller (1972).

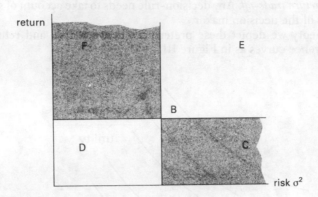

Figure IV The E-V rule

Any project in segment F will be preferred to project B. Similarly B will be preferred to any project in C.

As it stands, though, the E-V rule is not an operational rule for choosing projects. It correctly points out that in practice many 'two-dimensional' decisions are effectively 'one-dimensional' in the above sense since certain projects *dominate* other projects; are not worse than them on either dimension. But the E-V rule is silent on the important question how we should choose between B and projects in D and E, that is, between projects which are better in one respect and worse in another. We need a rule which will cover these cases but before we can develop it there is another factor to be taken into account, the effects of diversifying risk.

III PORTFOLIO-BUILDING

Few firms have just one project, and few investors own shares in just one firm. People like to spread their risks, hold *portfolios* of assets. In everyday life the advice is 'don't put all your eggs in one basket'. We can get the idea behind this if we compare Hardcastle's umbrella division with another of its divisions, deckchairs. Figure V plots the returns of the two divisions through time, and also the return of the two divisions together. If the two divisions are combined the expected return is summed, but not the variability. The return of the joint project fluctuates less than the individual projects because their fluctuations have cancelled each other out to some extent.

Before we can be more precise about portfolio risk and return, however, we need to understand the concept of covariance.

COVARIANCE AND CORRELATION

Closely linked to variance is another key concept, *covariance*. If we know the distribution of returns to an asset we can work out the expected value, and the variance will tell us how widely the actual outcomes are likely to be spread around this expected value.

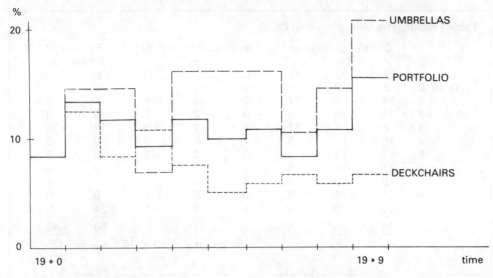

Figure V Hardcastle returns

But suppose we have *two* assets. It will be useful to know the extent to which the returns on these two assets vary together. Do high returns on one asset tend to occur when the other asset has high returns, or when it has low returns, or is there no relationship? Covariance measures this. The covariance between two assets j and k, σ_{jk}, is calculated as follows:

$$\sigma_{jk} = \sum_{i=1}^{n} \quad (r_{ij} - \bar{r}_j) \quad (r_{ik} - \bar{r}_k) \, p_i \tag{3}$$

Formula (3) is similar to the variance formula we met before except that now, instead of being squared, each deviation from the mean is matched with the corresponding deviation for the other asset. In fact variance is a special case of covariance. The variance of a series of numbers is simply its covariance with itself.

Hardcastle Manufacturing has a Raincoat and a Deckchair division, as well as the Umbrella division we met earlier. In Table I we chart the divisional results and work out the covariance between Raincoats and these two other divisions.

The covariance between umbrellas and raincoats is 5.9. In absolute terms this does not mean much, but we can interpret it by relating it to the standard deviations of the two divisions to measure the *correlation* between them.

The *coefficient of correlation* between two variables j and k, R_{jk}, is measured by

$$R_{jk} = \frac{\sigma_{jk}}{\sigma_j \sigma_k} \tag{4}$$

The value of R_{jk} can range from $+1$ in the case of perfect correlation, where the two variables always move together, to -1 in the case of perfect negative correlation, when the two variables always move in opposite directions. If R_{jk} is around 0 then there is obviously no association between the variables, and we say they are *independent*.

Table I Hardcastle Manufacturing Co

	Divisional Returns (%)			Deviations from mean $(r_i - \bar{r})$			Product of Deviations	
	U	R	D	U	R	D	UxR	UxD
Yr 19*0	9	9	9	−5	−1	1	5	−5
1	14	6	12	0	−4	4	0	0
2	14	8	9	0	−2	1	0	0
3	8	8	11	−6	−2	3	12	−18
4	15	10	8	1	0	0	0	0
5	17	13	5	3	3	−3	9	−9
6	17	13	6	3	3	−2	9	−6
7	10	10	7	−4	0	−1	0	4
8	14	10	6	0	0	−2	0	0
9	22	13	7	8	3	−1	24	−8
	14%	10%	8%				59	−42

$$\text{So, } \sigma_{UR} = 59 \div 10 \quad \sigma_{UD} = -42 \div 10$$
$$= 5.9 \quad\quad\quad = -4.2$$

In Hardcastle's case we know $\sigma_{UR} = 5.9\%$, and $\sigma_U = 4.1\%$. The reader can check that $\sigma_R = 2.3\%$, so $R_{UR} = \dfrac{5.9}{4.1 \times 2.3} = .63$

The returns are highly correlated, and this partly reflects the close relation between demand for umbrellas and raincoats. With deckchairs though it is a different story. There we have $\sigma_{UD} = -4.2\%$, $\sigma_U = 4.1\%$, and again the reader can confirm $\sigma_0 = 2.1\%$, so $R_{UD} = \dfrac{-4.2}{4.1 \times 2.1} = -.49$. There is a fairly strong inverse correlation between the returns on umbrellas and deckchairs.

THE RISK AND RETURN OF A TWO-ASSET PORTFOLIO

The expected return and variance of a two-asset portfolio are given by

$$\text{expected return} = \bar{r} = p_j\bar{r}_j + p_k\bar{r}_k \tag{5}$$
$$\text{variance} \quad = \sigma^2 = p_j^2\sigma_j^2 + p_k^2\sigma_k^2 + 2p_jp_k\sigma_{jk} \tag{6}$$

where p_j, p_k, are the proportions of the two assets in the value of the portfolio.

The expected return is just the weighted average of the returns of the two assets. To understand the variance, though, it will be useful to substitute

$$\sigma_{jk} = R_{jk}\sigma_j\sigma_k, \text{ to get}$$
$$\sigma^2 = p_j^2\sigma_j^2 + p_k^2\sigma_k^2 + 2p_jp_k R_{jk}\sigma_j\sigma_k \tag{7}$$

Now suppose the two assets are perfectly correlated, so that $R_{jk} = 1$, then (7) reduces to

$$\sigma^2 = (p_j\sigma_j + p_k\sigma_k)^2$$
and $\sigma = p_j\sigma_j + p_k\sigma_k$

At worst the standard deviation of a portfolio is the weighted average of the individual standard deviations, and there are no gains to diversification. This will happen when the asset returns are perfectly correlated. Anything less than perfect correlation means a reduction in standard deviation. So by building portfolios we can potentially reduce risk for no loss of return.

Recall what we know about Hardcastle and its divisions:

	$\bar{r}$	σ^2	σ	
umbrellas	14%	16%	4%	$R_{UR} = .63$
raincoats	10%	5.2%	2.3%	$R_{UD} = -.49$
deckchairs	8%	4.6%	2.1%	

Suppose Hardcastle only owned the umbrella and raincoat operations, and had the same investment in each, so that $p_U = p_R = .5$. We can find Hardcastle's overall return and risk thus:

expected return $= \bar{r} = (.5 \times 14) + (.5 \times 10) = 12\%$
variance $\qquad = \sigma^2$
$= (.5^2 \times 16) + (.5^2 \times 5.2) + (2 \times .5 \times .5 \times .63 \times 4 \times 21.)$
$= 7.9\%$

Now, suppose Hardcastle only invested in umbrellas and deckchairs but this time in the proportions 2:1. We choose this proportion so the return would be, as before,

$\bar{r} = (\frac{2}{3} \times 14) + (\frac{1}{3} \times 8) = 12\%$

but the risk would be

$\sigma^2 = (\frac{2}{3}^2 \times 16) + (\frac{1}{3}^2 \times 4.6) - (2 \times \frac{1}{3} \times \frac{2}{3} \times .49 \times 4 \times 2.1)$
$= 5.8\%$

Even though deckchairs look less attractive on their own than raincoats – they have a lower return and only marginally less risk – their negative covariance with umbrellas makes them ideal for *diversification*. In Figure VI we plot the standard deviation and return of the three divisions and different permutations. The dotted line shows what would have happened if deckchairs had *perfectly* negatively correlated with umbrellas. When r = −1 there is some investment proportion that will eliminate risk altogether. In this case it turns out to be $p_u = .344$, $p_D = .656^2$.

With these proportions the portfolio has

$\bar{r} = .344 \times 14 + .656 \times 8 = 10\%$
$\sigma^2 = .344^2 \times 16 + .656^2 \times 4.6 - 2 \times .344 \times .656 \times 4 \times 2.1 = 0$

PORTFOLIO RISK WITH MANY ASSETS

What happens to portfolio risk as we add more assets? The general formulae for the risk and return of an n-asset portfolio are

2 When R = − 1, and $\sigma^2 = 0$, the variance formula becomes
$0 = p_j^2\sigma_j^2 + p_k^2\sigma_k^2 + 2p_jp_k\sigma_j\sigma_k$
$= (p_j\sigma_j - p_k\sigma_k)^2$
$= p_j\sigma_j - p_k\sigma_k$
so $\dfrac{p_j}{p_k} = \dfrac{\sigma_k}{\sigma_j}$

so in this case $\qquad \dfrac{p_u}{p_D} = \dfrac{\sigma_D}{\sigma_U} = \dfrac{2.1}{4}$

so $p_U = .344$, $p_D = .656$

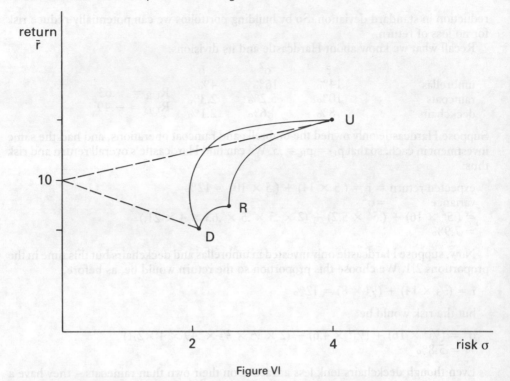

Figure VI

$$\bar{r} = \sum_{j=1}^{n} \bar{r}_j p_j \tag{8}$$

$$\sigma^2 = \sum_{j=1}^{n} \sum_{k=1}^{n} p_j p_k \sigma_{jk} \tag{9}$$

Equation (9) says that the variance of a portfolio is the sum of an $n \times n$ matrix of covariances, $p_j p_k \sigma_{jk}$, depicted in Figure VII.

When n was 2 in equation (6), we find two variance terms $p_j^2 \sigma_j^2$ and $p_k^2 \sigma_k^2$, and two covariance terms $2\,p_j p_k \sigma_{jk}$. In general with n assets we get n variance terms, and all the rest, n^2-n, are covariances between assets. So in a 20 asset portfolio, the variance would be an average of the 20 individual variances, and 380 ($=20^2-20$) covariances. As the portfolio grows the covariances between assets become the dominant factor in determining risk.

The diagonal terms in Figure VII give each asset's covariance with itself, i e its variance. We can see what this means in practice in Figure VIII. If we build an equally weighted portfolio of assets, chosen at random[3], then plot the variance of the portfolio against the number of assets, we find the portfolio variance drops sharply up to about 10 assets, then levels out rapidly. We can achieve the benefits of full-diversification with 10–20 assets.

However as Figure IX shows, risk can be minimised, but not eliminated entirely. To build a zero-variance portfolio we would need assets whose returns had perfectly negative

3   Various writers have done this. See for example Fama (1976).

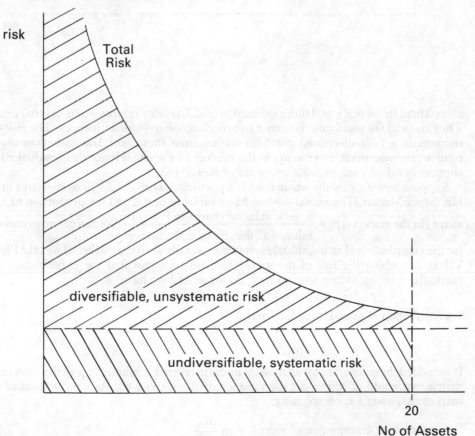

asset	1	2	3	4	→ n
1	$p_1^2\sigma_1^2$	$p_1p_2\sigma_{12}$	$p_1p_3\sigma_{13}$	$p_1p_4\sigma_{14}$	
2	$p_2p_1\sigma_{21}$	$p_2^2\sigma_2^2$	$p_2p_3\sigma_{23}$		
3	$p_3p_1\sigma_{31}$	$p_3p_2\sigma_{32}$	$p_3^2\sigma_3^2$		
4	$p_4p_1\sigma_{41}$				
↓ n					

Figure VII The variance of an n-asset portfolio

risk

Total Risk

diversifiable, unsystematic risk

undiversifiable, systematic risk

20

No of Assets

Figure VIII The effect of diversification on risk

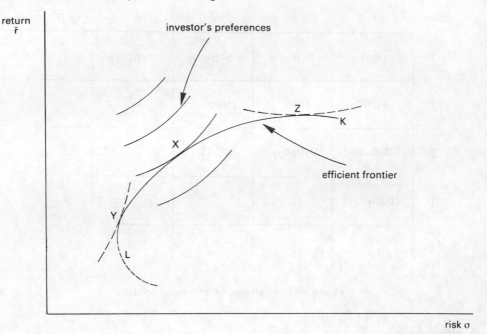

Figure IX

correlation. In the real world these are hard to find. In reality returns *covary* to some extent. They rise and fall together in response to overall economy-wide influences. The risk that remains in a fully-diversified portfolio comes from these correlations between asset returns, the systematic movements in the market as a whole. Hence this residual risk is commonly called *undiversifiable, systematic* or *market* risk.

Suppose now we view the whole market a portfolio, say all the 2,500 or so shares in the UK Stock Market. The *market-porfolio* has a variance of σ_m, and the proportion of each share j in the market is $p_j = \dfrac{\text{value of shares in j}}{\text{value of all the shares in the market}}$. We can get an expression for the contribution of an individual asset to the overall risk of the market. If we take Figure VII as describing the risk of the market/portfolio we can find the contribution of a particular asset by adding across a row. So for asset 1 we have:

$$\text{contribution of asset } 1 = p_1 \sum_{j=1}^{n} p_j \sigma_{ij}$$

$$= p_1 \sigma_{1m}$$

If we added these together for all n assets in the market, that is added up all the rows in the matrix, we would of course get the variance of the market, σ_m^2. As a proportion of this market risk, asset 1 is contributing:

$$\text{proportionate contribution of asset } 1 = p_1 \frac{\sigma_{1m}}{\sigma_m^2} \tag{10}$$

So the relative riskiness of an asset depends on $\dfrac{\sigma_{jm}}{\sigma_m^2}$, which we call the asset's *beta*. Beta tells us how risky an asset is compared to the market as a whole, and is a key statistic later on.

IV THE OPTIMAL INVESTMENT DECISION UNDER RISK

Supppose Mr Xavier has £1,000 to invest. How will he make his investment decision? To start with, we will limit him to risky assets. There is any number of different portfolios he can hold out of all the risky assets on the market and these investment possibilities are the shaded area in Figure IX bounded by the line LXK.

The efficient frontier

The first thing to note is that no rational investor, that is no investor choosing according to the E–V rule, would ever choose a portfolio on the interior of LXK. For every point within LXK there is a point on the frontier giving the same risk but a higher return. By the same token rational investors will only choose points on the solid part of the frontier. Points on the broken line below L, where the frontier bends back, are dominated by points on LXK. So we call LXK the *efficient frontier*.

To find out which portfolio on the efficient frontier Mr Xavier will choose we introduce his preferences in the form of a set of indifference curves. He will choose the portfolio that gets him on to the highest indifference curve, which is X, the point of tangency with the efficient frontier. But different investors may have different points of tangency, for example Ms Young is a more risk-averse individual and finds her optimum at Y, while Zoltan, a less-risk-averse person, might prefer Z. Investors with different preferences over risk and return will choose different portfolios from the efficient frontier.

Borrowing and lending

However as we found in the Fisher-Hirshleifer model the analysis is transformed if we assume investors can borrow and lend at a rate of interest, r_i, and at no risk. In other words we are allowing investors to include a new asset in their portfolios, a 'riskless asset' with a return of r_i, and $\sigma = 0$.

Now our investors can put part of their £1,000 into risky assets and lend the rest, or if they prefer they can buy more than £1,000 worth of risky assets and borrow the extra. Figure X shows that these new possibilities yield a new efficient frontier, which is a *straight-line* from the riskless asset at R tangent to our old efficient frontier at M. RM is the so-called *capital market line* and it shows the risk and return characteristics of all efficient portfolios in the market.

To see why the new frontier is a straight line we just need to recognise that the investor's new portfolio now contains two components, the riskless asset, R, and a composite of the risky assets, M. We know that the mean and variance of this two-asset portfolio are:

mean $= \bar{r} = p_i r_i + p_M \bar{r}_M$

variance $= \sigma^2 = p_i^2 \sigma_i^2 + p_M^2 \sigma_M^2 + 2 p_i p_M \sigma_{iM}$

But the variance of the riskless asset, σ_i^2, is by definition zero so the variance of this two-asset portfolio reduces to $\sigma^2 = p_M^2 \sigma_M^2$, and its standard deviation is $\sigma = p_M \sigma_M$. If we use standard deviation as the measure of risk, RM is a straight line.

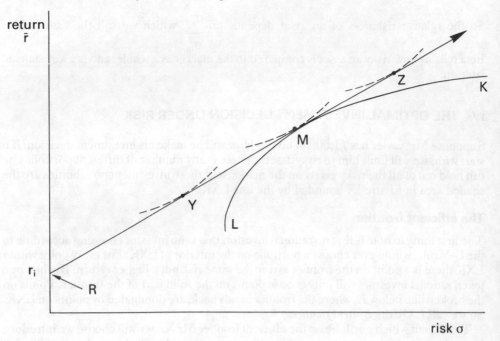

Figure X The capital market line

There is any number of straight lines we could draw between R and the set of risky portfolios LMK, but the tangent RM gives the efficient frontier because, as before, it offers a higher return for the same variance than any interior point.

The reason borrowing and lending transforms the analysis is even clearer when we add back the investor's preferences from Figure XI. As before our investors have different preferences between risk and return and so have different points of tangency on RM. An investor with tangency at M invests 100% of the £1,000 in risky assets. In terms of proportions, $p_m = 1$, $p_i = 0$. If the tangency is at Y, investors hold some M and some R. But investors can borrow as well as lend, so there is nothing to stop them choosing Z if they prefer. Here he or she buys more than £1,000 worth of risky assets, and borrows the money to do it. Now, the portfolio proportions are $p_m > 1$, $p_i < 0$, with, as always, the proviso $p_m + p_i = 1$. This possibility explains why we can extend the efficient frontier out past M.

The thing that does not change is the tangency between RM and the set of risky portfolios. Investors all combine risky assets in the same relative proportions M, their only difference is in how much of M and R to hold. The composition of the optimal portfolio of risky assets is independent of the preferences of investors. This is the *separation theorem* and it is exactly equivalent to the separation result we got in the Fisher-Hirshleifer model. In both cases introducing borrowing and lending opportunities means that each investor can make his own investment choice independent of other investors, and independent of the determination of the optimal portfolio, of investment projects in the case of Fisher-Hirshleifer, and of risky assets in the present case.

V THE CAPITAL ASSET PRICING MODEL

Let us concentrate now on point M in Figure X, the optimum portfolio of risky assets chosen, in some proportion, by all investors. M must be the market portfolio. This, follows because everyone, we assume, has the same view so if one person decides an assets return is too low no-one else will want it either, and its price will fall, and return rise, until it is included in the risky portfolio again. Of course this does not mean that all individuals have to have in their portfolios some of every asset in the market. What matters is that every asset earns a return relative to its risk, equivalent to that earned by all other assets in the market portfolio. If so, all assets will be perfect substitutes for one another. What is this relation between risk and return? During the 1960s the *capital asset pricing model* (CAPM)

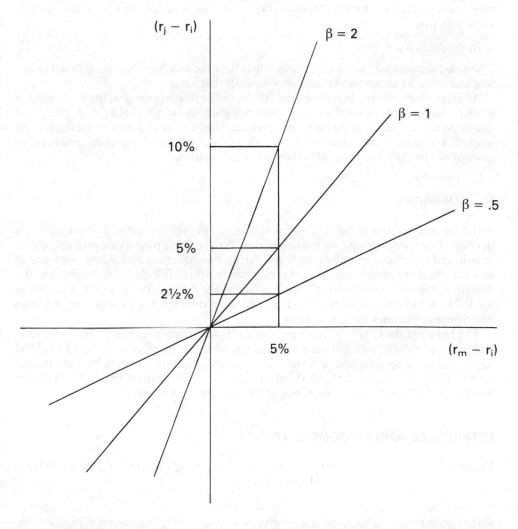

Figure XI

was developed to provide the answer to this question.[4] The CAPM shows that in equilibrium the return, r_j, on a risky asset j can be calculated as

$$r_j = r_i + \beta_j (r_m - r_i) \tag{11}$$

where as we saw earlier in this chapter $\beta_j = \dfrac{\sigma_{jm}}{\sigma_m^2}$, a measure of the volatility of assets j's return relative to the market. This equation is sometimes known as the *security market line*. The capital market line told us the relationship between the risk and return of efficient portfolios. The security market line tells us the relationship between risk and return of the individual assets in an efficient portfolio. It says that the return on any risky asset is the riskless interest rate plus a risk premium which is a multiple β_j of the premium on the market as a whole. What the CAPM is saying is this: We know the return to risky assets on average, which is the return on the market portfolio, so the return to any asset will be in proportion to its risk compared to the average. This becomes clearer if we rearrange (11) slightly so that

$$(r_j - r_i) = \beta_j (r_m - r_i) \tag{12}$$

The risk-premium on j should be a proportion β_j of the risk premium on the market as a whole. Figure XI shows this relationship for different betas.

An asset whose return always rises and falls by the same percentage as the market so has a risk premium of 5% when the market has a risk premium of 5%, has a $\beta = 1$. The $\beta = 2$ line depicts a so-called 'aggressive' asset, whose return rises and falls by more than the market. A 'defensive' asset has $\beta < 1$. So with a β of .5 we would expect the return on an asset to rise by only 5% for a 10% increase in the market.

VI   SUMMARY

An investment decision is risky if it has more than one possible outcome. In this chapter we developed the theory behind the analysis of risk. We saw that investors are probably averse to risk, and that they can reduce their risk for no loss of return by holding portfolios of assets. Indeed in a perfect capital market everyone will hold full-diversified portfolios and the only risk investors will be unable to eliminate will be the 'specific' risk of each asset they hold. The CAPM shows us that this risk is measured by the asset's beta, and in such a world beta determines the price of risk.

The beauty of the CAPM is that it gives us a rule for quantifying risk in terms of return, and in the next chapter we will use it to find a discount rate for risky projects. The CAPM has found many applications in finance and is appealing for its simplicity and intuitive appeal. The problem with the CAPM is the rather restrictive assumptions under which the model holds. We will take a closer look at these in the next chapter.

REFERENCES AND BIBLIOGRAPHY

Blume, M E   'On the Assessment of Risk', Journal of Finance, March
                              1971, pp 1–10.

---

[4] The key articles in the development of the CAPM are Markowitz (1952), Sharpe (1964), Lintner (1965), Mossin (1966).

Fama, E F and Miller M H	*The Theory of Finance* (2nd edn, 1972) Holt, Rhinehart and Winston.
Friedman, M and Savage, L J	'The Utility Analysis of Choices Involving Risk', Journal of Political Economy, Aug 1948, pp. 279–304.
Lintner, J	'The Valuation of Risk Assets and the Selection of Risky Investments in Stock Portfolios and Capital Budgets', Review of Economics and Statistics, Feb 1965, pp 13–37.
Markowitz, H	*Portfolio Selection*, (1959) Yale University Press, New Haven.
Mossin, J	'Equilibrium in a Capital Asset Market', Econometrica, Oct 1966, pp 768–783.
Pratt, J W	'Risk Aversion in the Small and in the Large', Econometrica, Jan–April 1964, pp 122–136.
Sharpe, W F	'Capital Asset Prices: A Theory of Market Equilibrium under Conditions of Risk', Journal of Finance, Sept 1964, pp 425–442.

QUESTIONS

1 The Bouncy Beachball Company has experienced the following series of returns over the last five years:

19×1	19×2	19×3	19×4	19×5
4%	−6%	13%	24%	18%

Find the mean and variance of this series.

2 Sam's Sailboard Company had the following returns:

19×1	19×2	19×3	19×4	19×5
8%	2%	18%	25%	30%

Calculate the covariance and coefficient of correlation between Sam and Bouncy. Would Sam and Bouncy join well in a portfolio?

3 You are given the following choices:

a) a gift of £1,000, or
b) a 10% chance of getting £5,000, and a 90% chance of getting some other amount.

How much would the other amount have to be for you to be indifferent between the two alternatives if you were risk-neutral?

4 Why might the finance theorist be troubled if he found some people were taking out fire insurance on their houses and also filling-in football pools?

5 Cedric is considering three projects with the following mean and variance of returns:

	mean	*variance*
project A	20	20
B	15	15
C	18	13

All we know about Cedric's preferences is that he is risk-averse. What can we say about his ranking of these projects?

6 The ordinary shares of Black Ltd and White Ltd have the following expected returns and standard deviations:

	Black	White
Expected Return	8%	18%
Standard Deviation	16%	20%

Calculate the expected return and variance for the following portfolios;

(i)   100% Black
(ii)   75% Black + 25% White
(iii)   50% Black + 50% White
(iv)   25% Black + 75% White
(v)   100% white

Assuming that the returns have a coefficient of correlation $R = +0.5$ graph the resulting transformation curve.

7 Explain the difference between an efficient and an optimal portfolio, and show how the possibility of borrowing and lending at 5% affects the investors' opportunities in question (6). What are the relative proportions of Black and White in the optimal portfolio?

CHAPTER 8
Project investment under risk

In the last chapter we developed a theory of how investors will choose risky assets. The fruit of this was the capital asset pricing model, which yielded a very simple formula relating the return on any asset to its risk, measured by beta. Now we consider the firm's project investment decision under risk. Section I establishes the need for a simple and reliable method of adjusting the project discount-rate for risk, and in Section II we explain how beta could be used this way. The beta-technique is simple and intuitive but the underlying capital asset pricing model seems to rest on some fairly unrealistic assumptions. In Section III we examine its assumptions and empirical support, and consider the usefulness of beta in practice.

We then assess some alternatives. In section IV we consider how risk can be handled when managers cannot use beta, and in section V we recognise that very often in practical situations managers will be working under extreme uncertainty and have nothing like the information needed to calculate beta or variance. So we present alternative techniques, of necessity cruder, which permit decision makers to make efficient use of what information they have.

I A DECISION-RULE FOR RISKY PROJECTS

A good decision-rule will have the following properties. It should be *economical*, not requiring too much costly information. And what is much the same thing, it should be easy to *delegate* to subordinates. In large organisations it is essential to be able to delegate decisions, but it will only be feasible if checking and controlling subordinates is not too costly in terms of information. Making investment decisions under certainty we said 'choose all projects with a positive NPV' where

$$NPV = \sum_{t=0}^{n} \frac{C_t}{(1 + r)^t}$$

How can we modify this rule for a world where the cash-flows, C_t, are not known with certainty? Suppose there are two projects, one whose cash-flows are known with certainty, the other whose cash-flows have the same *expected* value, but whose actual outcomes are risky. Assuming the decision-maker is risk-averse, so that risk is a 'bad thing', it follows that the risky project should have a lower value than the certain one. Inspection of the NPV formula shows that we can give it a lower value in two ways, by reducing the cash-flows (the numerator), or by increasing the discount rate (the denominator).

Certainty-equivalence

The first approach handles risk by replacing the expected value of risky cash flows by the 'utility' to the decision-maker of those cash flows, that is, the *certain* sum of money the decision-maker values equally to the risky cash-flows. We can find these amounts by using the decision-maker's utility of wealth schedule. Figure I recalls the information from Figure II of the last chapter where we were comparing the utility a decision-maker attached to a certainty of £100 as against a 50/50 chance of £50 and £150. If the cash-flow of £100 we are using in our NPV formula is in fact the expected value, or mean, of a 50/50 chance of £50 and £150, then its *certainty-equivalent*, the certain sum of money giving the same utility, can be found by inspecting the utility schedule at U_c. The certainty equivalent is £80 in this case.

The certainty-equivalent approach is conceptually sound: if we calculated NPVs using certainty-equivalents instead of cash-flows then 'choose all projects with a positive NPV' this will still lead to value-maximising choices, even in a world of risk. But it is rarely attempted in practice since it does not meet our requirement for a good decision-rule. Its heavy demand for information about the decision-maker's utility of each cash-flow would make it uneconomical and difficult to decentralise.

The risk-premium

A more common approach is to adjust the discount rate for risk. Since, the higher the

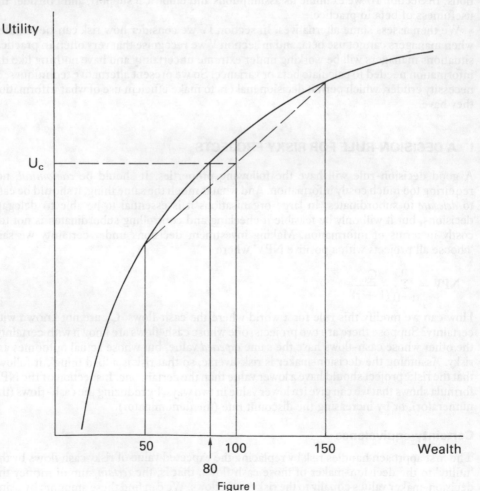

Figure I

discount rate the less value we are attaching to future cash-flows, this means adding a *risk premium* to the discount-rate we would use for risk-free cash flows.

We need $r_j = r_i + r_p$ where r_j = required return on risky asset j

$$r_i = \text{risk-free rate}$$
$$r_p = \text{risk premium}$$

The practice of using a higher discount rate to value risk is widespread, but in the past readers of textbooks must often have been puzzled when they looked for instructions on how to calculate the risk-premium. The problem was that theorists had not worked out how to calculate a risk-premium that was theoretically sound, i e would lead firms to make value maximising investment decisions, but was economical to use and easy to delegate. There appeared to be two problems:

Portfolio effects   We saw that what matters is the impact of a project on the risk of *the portfolio* in which it is included. So, on the face of it, before a project's risk can be appraised a study is needed of its inter-relationship with all the other projects in the firm. This requires a lot of information; if the firm has 100 projects there are 100 variance, and 9,900 covariance terms in the calculation of its overall portfolio risk.

Subjectivity   To use a risk premium to evaluate risk is to put a price on risk in terms of return. But how risk averse are the investors? This is a subjective evaluation which requires knowledge of the decision-maker's preferences between risk and return. This sort of information is costly to obtain.

These information requirements seemed to undermine the idea of the risk-premium as a quick and efficient tool. But in the 1960s a model for the valuation of risky assets was developed which revolutionised finance theory: the *capital asset pricing model* (CAPM). We described the CAPM result at the end of the last chapter. As we saw, if we make certain assumptions about investors, assets and the capital market the required return from an asset j, r_j, can be calculated as

$$r_j = r_i + \beta_j (r_m - r_i) \tag{1}$$

where r_i is the return on riskless borrowing and lending and r_m is the return on the market as a whole. Hence we have a *decision-rule* for risky projects *which makes no mention of other projects or the preferences of the decision maker*. The rule is *accept projects with a return greater or equal to* $r_j = r_i + \beta_j (r_m - r_i)$.

In the next section we see how to find project betas in practice. There are some real practical problems here, and as we will see later there are some conceptual problems too, so it would be foolish to think beta gives any easy answers. But used carefully the CAPM can give useful insights into the problem of analysing risk in the real world.

II   USING BETA TO MEASURE PROJECT RISK

The problem facing the project appraiser is what risk-premium to build into the discount rate for a risky project. The capital asset pricing model gives us a simple and intuitive formula for calculating risk-premiums on assets. It says: 'You know the *average* risk-premium on the market as a whole. The risk-premium on your project will be proportionate to this, and the proportion is easily found in terms of the covariance of the project with the market.' How is beta measured in practice? As a first step we will see how to find the beta of a share. There are two ways of getting the beta for a share; we can estimate it ourselves or we can use one of the published estimates that are available.

ESTIMATING SHARE BETAS

We want to estimate the beta of shares in South Pacific Tropical Packers plc. The beta of an asset j is defined as, $\beta_j = \dfrac{\sigma_{jm}}{\sigma^2_m}$ where m relates to the market as a whole. So we need two things, the returns on South Pacific over a period of time and the returns on the market over the corresponding period. What exactly do we mean by 'return' in this context? The return on a share has two components, the dividend-yield and the capital gain,

so return in period $t \to t + 1 = \dfrac{DIV_{t+1} + (S_{t+1}-S_t)}{S_t}$

where DIV_{t+1} = dividends received in period ended $t + 1$
S_{t+1} = share price at $t + 1$

In the case of 'the market' we can get the equivalent information by looking at the return on a market index such as the FT Actuaries, and the dividend yield on the index. These are published weekly in the Financial Times.

Table I shows the returns data for South Pacific and the market over the last ten years.

Table I Returns on South Pacific and the Market						
	South Pacific				Market	
Date	Share Price	Dividend	Return %	Index	Div. Yield %	Return %
1 Jan 19*0	46			530		
31 Dec 19*0	50	4	17	564	5	11
1	49	4	6	602	4	11
2	60	5	33	586	4	1
3	48	5	(12)	443	5	(19)
4	52	5	19	567	7	35
5	58	5	21	651	6	21
6	54	5	2	683	5	10
7	59	5	17	789	4	20
8	63	6	17	832	4	9
9	63	6	10	882	5	11

We found the 19*0 return of South Pacific as $\dfrac{4 + (50 - 46)}{46} = 17\%$.

Since the dividend figures for the market are already in yield form, we got the market return by simply adding the percentage capital gain in the market index to the dividend yield, for 19*0 this gave $\dfrac{564 - 530}{530} + 5 = 11\%$. These points are plotted in Figure II.

To find the straight line that best describes the relationship between South Pacific returns and market returns the statistician would run simple linear regression of South Pacific on the market. The best line would be the 'least squares' line. This is found by measuring the distance of each of the ten actual observations from the line, squaring them and adding them up. The 'least-squares' line is the one which minimises this sum. We can express this line as

$r_{jt} = \hat{a}_t + \hat{b}_t r_{mt} + \hat{e}_t$

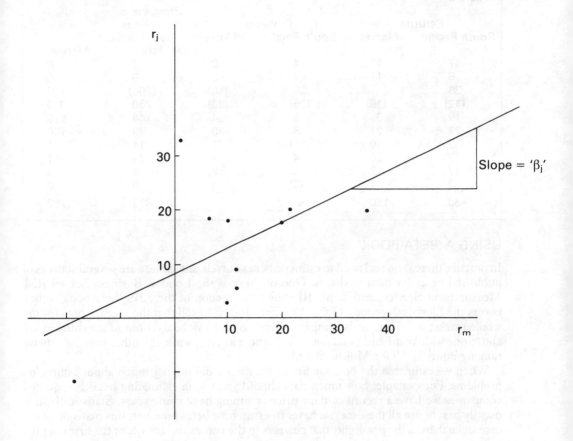

Figure II Returns on South Pacific and the market

where a and b are the intercept and the slope, and e is the error. Readers who know some statistics will recall that the slope coefficient is found by $b = \dfrac{\sigma_{jm}}{\sigma_m^2}$ This is beta! In other words we do not need the theoretical framework of the CAPM to give us beta, it is something anyone interested in the responsiveness of the return on a particular share to movements in the market as a whole will calculate. From Table II we can calculate South Pacific's beta as follows:

$$\sigma_{jm} = \frac{813}{10}, \qquad \sigma_m^2 = \frac{1762}{10}$$

so, $$\beta_j = \frac{813}{1762} = \underline{\underline{.46}}$$

Table II					
Returns		Deviations		Products of Deviations	
South Pacific	Market	South Pacific	Market	South Pacific X Market	Market²
17	11	4	0	0	0
6	11	(7)	0	0	0
33	1	20	(10)	(200)	100
(12)	(19)	(25)	(30)	750	900
19	35	6	24	144	576
21	21	8	10	80	100
2	10	(11)	(1)	11	1
17	20	4	9	36	81
17	9	4	(2)	(8)	4
10	11	(3)	0	0	0
130	110	0	0	813	1,762

USING A 'BETA-BOOK'

In practice there is no real need to estimate beta yourself, since there are several sources of published betas for quoted shares. One of these is the London Business School Risk Measurement Service, and Table III shows the section of the LBS 'beta-book' which covers the Electricals section of the All–Share Index. Recall that the average beta for the whole market is 1. Electricals companies tend to have low betas. Four of the thirteen are above one with Ward and Goldstone the highest at 1.12, while the other nine have betas ranging down to .69 for Muirhead Ltd.

When we estimated the beta for South Pacific we did not say much about estimation problems. For example, how much data should you use in estimating beta? For quoted companies we have a record of daily prices running back many years. Statistically, it is usually best to use all the data you have. In estimating betas however, this may not be the case since there is the possibility that changes in the nature and activity of the firm over the years may make earlier observations unrepresentative. LBS estimate their betas on monthly prices over the previous five years. Another important issue with linear regression is the *strength* of the relationship between the two variables. The figures following the LBS beta estimates are very informative on this. Take MK Electric. Its beta of 1.12 has a standard error of .16 and an R^2 of 27%. The R^2 tells us what proportion of the variance in the independent variable a model is explaining. In this case, 27% of MK's variance is market risk. LBS give us the information to observe this in another way. MK's total 'variability' (= standard deviation) was 36%. The part *not* explained by beta was 31%, which is of course the 'specific risk' of MK.[1]

It may seem that beta does not explain very much. In Table IV we get a view on this, when we list the industries with the lowest and highest average R^2. It is no surprise to find that beta explains most for Investment Trusts, and that they also have a beta not too far from 1. Since investment trusts are simply portfolios of other shares on the market, we would have worried if things had been otherwise. At the other end we find beta explains least for Gold, which also has the lowest beta of any industry group. For other basic commodities

---

1   The two *do* reconcile. MK's variance was $36^2 = 1296$, of which $31^2 = 961$ was unexplained, so 335 was explained. $\frac{335}{1296} = 26\%$, 27% after rounding.

Table III Electrical Industry Betas

SEDOL Number	Company Name	S.E. Industry Classification	Market Capit'n	Market ability	Beta	Varia-bility	Specific Risk	Std Error	R-Sq'rd	Qly Ab Return	Ann Ab Return	Ann Act Return	Gross Yield	P/E Ratio	Price
	ELECTRICALS														
96162	B.I.C.C.	ELECTRCL	502	0TO	1.08	29	23	.13	40	-9	-11	22	5.7	12.1	263
196207	Chloride Group Ltd	ELECTRCL	46	0 A	.95	52	49	.18	10	36	57	89	.0	.0	36
251240	Dale Electric Intl	ELECTRCL	12	.2 A	.70	34	32	.16	13	1	0	25	6.7	9.4	92
278807	Dowding & Mills	ELECTRCL	18	2TA	.87	33	30	.16	19	-8	-11	18	5.7	11.7	54
550301	M.K. Electric Grp plc	ELECTRCL	125	0TA	1.12	36	31	.16	27	4	-24	10	3.5	15.1	341
609203	Muirhead Ltd	ELECTRCL	13	0TA	.69	45	43	.18	7	-8	-11	14	4.7	11.3	153
646880	Northern Engineering Ind	ELECTRCL	184	0TA	.98	32	27	.15	29	-24	-25	6	8.3	7.2	84
665045	Oxford Instruments plc	ELECTRCL	143	0 A						-4			.4	47.9	321
683649	Petbow Hldgs Ltd	ELECTRCL	7	.6 A	.95	46	43	.18	13	-15	0	31	.0	.0	49
779388	Scholes (G. H.) & Co.	ELECTRCL	23	.4TA	.71	33	31	.16	13	-24	-37	-11	6.8	9.2	358
821405	Sound Diffusion	ELECTRCL	203	0TA	1.07	46	42	.18	16	-12	32	66	.3	65.8	146
929042	Victor Prods (Wall)	ELECTRCL	8	2TA	.74	30	28	.15	18	-27	-57	-29	6.6	7.6	100
939007	Ward & Goldstone	ELECTRCL	19	.2TA	1.18	51	47	.18	15	7	19	56	2.7	34.4	123
964430	Wholesale Fittings	ELECTRCL	47	.4TA	.89	31	27	.15	22	15	-15	14	2.3	22.0	335

Source: LBS Risk Measurement Service, April 1984

Table IV Industries with high and low R^2 on beta

Stock Exchange Industry Classification	Beta	Variability	Specific Risk	R^2
Investment Trusts	1.03	23	15	58
Cement and Concrete	1.09	27	20	48
Hotel and Catering	1.09	29	22	43
Insurance (Life)	1.00	26	20	43
Toys and Games(*)	.87	45	42	11
Tin	.91	46	43	11
Motor Vehicles	.84	67	65	5
Gold	.54	41	40	6

Source LBS Risk Measurement Service April 1984

* Three other industries also had an R^2 of 11

such as tin and rubber, market risk also explains little. Does the low R^2 we often find with betas matter? The CAPM says NO. It tells us not to worry about specific risk, since in a fully diversified portfolio only market risk matters. Table IV suggests that if we do not accept the CAPM beta may not be a reliable risk measure, since it explains only a small part of total risk in many cases.

FINDING PROJECT BETAS

Betas for quoted shares are fairly easy to find, we have a reliable and well-documented history of market-values to work from. This is not the case with projects. Projects are not quoted on the stock-market, and in any case the most difficult projects to value are the ones that are new and untried. Projects usually fall into one of the following categories:

1 expanding existing capacity
2 replacing and improving technology in existing capacity
3 moving into adjacent product areas
4 moving into new areas of activity

In the case of 1 and 2 the project may have a history on which a beta could be calculated. But these investments tend to be fairly uncontroversial anyhow. The projects that worry managers most are types 3 and 4. These are the ones with no history and whose future is most uncertain. There are two strategies for finding a beta in this case. In theory the decision-maker could build a *simulation*, that is, model the returns to the project under different scenarios about the future, then find the implied beta. In practice this would require a lot of information, so that even if they felt capable of it managers would only be interested in doing it for major projects.

An easier alternative is to find a share beta to proxy for the project beta, or at least to serve as a starting point. If we are going to do this, however, we need a good grasp of what determines systematic risk, and what characteristics to look for in a proxy.

(1) The prime factor is LINE OF BUSINESS. We need to find a firm which is 'doing the same thing' as the project. We cannot expect to find a perfect match: details of markets, technology, and management style may differ, but these may not affect beta too much. A real problem, however, is diversificaiton. Most firms have a variety of projects, and their share betas are an average of the betas of these different activities. Unless we are confident the proxy company we are looking at is predominantly engaged in the activity in question, it

may be safer to use the *industry beta* in the hope that these extraneous factors cancel out in aggregate.

(2) Much of the variability in returns from a project or a company comes from its cost structure and in particular the relationship of fixed to variable cost, which we call GEARING. The lower the gearing, that is, the more its costs are variable, the better able the firm is to absorb increases or decreases in revenues by corresponding increases or decreases in costs. A particularly important source of gearing is *financial gearing* the proportion of debt financing the firm uses, and this can differ between firms within the same industry. So far in this book we have assumed projects are all-equity financed and we continue this assumption now. But in a subsequent chapter we will show how betas can be adjusted for financial gearing.

Tuckwell foods is planning to open a chain of freezer centres, where frozen foods are sold in bulk. Jack Berry, the corporate planner of Tuckwell wants to find a beta for this activity. He chooses Bejam plc as a quoted company in this line of business. LBS Risk Measurement Service shows Bejam's beta to be .81. Should Tuckwell use this for its project? Before it does, Berry needs to ask these questions:
— What else does Bejam do?
— What is Bejam's financial structure?
— Have we any other clues that might be relevant?

Bejam's annual report gives some answers to the first two questions. It shows that 75% of Bejam's business is in food sales, and the rest is mainly in hardware, freezers and ovens. This matches fairly well with Tuckwell's expected revenue mix. Berry also found that Bejam has little or no long-term debt, and is effectively all-equity, so he adopts .81 as a good proxy for the project beta.

USING BETA TO FIND THE COST OF CAPITAL

We have seen how to find a project's beta, β_j. To calculate the discount rate for a project we also need estimates of the future values of the market return, r_m, and the riskless rate, r_i. All three of these need to be forecasts: we want values that will be appropriate over the future life of the project.

The riskless rate

How can we know what the risk free interest rate will be during the future life of the project? Unless we feel we have special knowledge the best we can do is take the market's view embodied in the spot rate for the appropriate period. For a ten-year project this means the prevailing rate on ten-year loans at the start of the project, since this tells us the market's required return on a risk-free investment lasting ten years, including compensation for the inflation the market expects during that period. As a proxy for this we can use the yield on government bonds of the appropriate duration.

Market return

From one year to the next the return on the market can vary dramatically. But this is the *actual* return the market earns and it reflects unanticipated events that push up, and down, the present and expected future profits of companies. But what returns do investors *require* from the market? One way to estimate this is to take the average of achieved returns on the market over a long period. Franks and Broyles (1979) did this and found that the historic *after tax* risk premium on the UK market has been 7½%. There are times, in wars, depressions and so forth, when the risk to business activity in general rises, and other times when it falls. If decision-makers feel that the duration of the project will be such a period they can adjust the premium up or down accordingly. Otherwise we recommend using $r_m - r_i = 7\frac{1}{2}\%$.

Jack Berry can now find a discount-rate for Tuckwell Foods' freezer centre project. The project has a ten-year time horizon. He finds the after-tax yield on ten-year government bonds to be 11%, and estimates the market risk-premium at $7\frac{1}{2}\%$. A suitable beta for freezer-centre projects was .81 so Berry calculates a required return of $r_i = 11\% + .81 \times 7\frac{1}{2}\% = 17\%$

Beta

There is a forecasting problem with beta too, though when we described how to estimate a project beta, we did not say much about it. Can we be sure that betas drawn from historic data will still be relevant over the life of a project lasting, say, ten-years? In other words, are betas stable through time? The evidence suggests that share betas may not be too stable through time, though industry betas are more stable. This argues, again, for not using single share betas without keeping an eye on the rest of the industry.

It is clear that the step from a past share beta to a future-oriented project beta requires a good deal of judgement and the project-appraiser still needs to use all his or her instincts about the project in hand when he is measuring its beta. But like all the theory we encounter, the real role of beta is to aid the thinking of managers rather than substitute for it.

III   HOW USEFUL IS BETA?

Apart from any practical problems in using beta, there are some theoretical problems too. The capital asset pricing model that underlies it rests on some apparently unrealistic assumptions. So how useful is beta?

The key to understanding beta is 'diversification': *beta is the risk measure for full diversified investors* in a world where all investors are fully diversified. We said there seemed to be two problems in finding a decision-rule for risky assets: the computational problem of working out the *portfolio* effect of each individual asset, and the apparent *subjectivity* of the risk-return trade off. The assumptions of a CAPM world are designed to make these problems go away.

Portfolio effects

The effect on the investor's risk of acquiring another asset depends on the asset's covariance with the portfolio the investor is adding it to. But in a fully-diversified portfolio only market risk remains, and investors can ignore the interrelationship of an asset's risk with the other assets they hold. To find an appropriate risk premium they look outside to the market, where they will find the asset's risk premium as the market premium multiplied by the asset's beta. The assumptions of the CAPM describe a world in which investors *will* be fully-diversified. They will want full-diversification because they are risk-averse, and they will be able to fully diversify because in a perfect market there are no barriers to doing it.

Subjectivity

The second problem was that we needed to know the decision-maker's preference about risk and return. Under the CAPM assumptions, though, all investors have the same trade-off between risk and return at the margin. The line of argument is a familiar one in micro-economics. Consider a world where bananas sell for 10p each, and oranges for 20p, in other words, where two bananas trade for one orange. Suppose an individual visits the market and observes this rate of exchange. He also reflects that as far as he is concerned oranges are worth more than that; he would trade three bananas for one orange given his tastes for bananas and oranges. His response is to buy less bananas and more oranges. However, as he does this his interest in oranges will diminish as his appetite for them is satisfied, yet the appeal of bananas will grow. The individual's consumption pattern will only be in equilibrium when his preferences between marginal increments in consumption are in line with market prices. For bananas and oranges read return and risk. The risk-premium on an asset is the market price of its risk in terms of return. An investor whose preferences do not accord with this market evaluation will adjust his consumption of risk and return until they do. He can adjust the proportions of risk and return he consumes by lending or borrowing at the risk-free rate.

THE ASSUMPTIONS OF THE CAPM WORLD

The CAPM is derived on the following assumptions; the first four of which are our usual perfect market assumptions. About the market:
1 There are no taxes, and no 'transactions costs' – costs to buying and selling.
2 Information is fully and freely available.
3 There are many buyers and sellers, so none can influence prices.
About investors:
4 Investors are rational, that is, risk-averse and wealth-maximising.
5 They have homogeneous expectations about the future.
About assets:
6 Assets are all marketable and infinitely divisible, and have normally distributed returns.
7 There is a riskless asset.

Some of these assumptions are innocuous, but others are not so. Let us consider some of the apparently unrealistic ones.

In reality asset returns are subject to *taxation* at rates which can differ between investors and between firms and so yield differing after-tax returns on the same asset. The effect of this is rather like investors having different *expectations* about the future and Lintner (1969) suggested that the existence of differing views about the future among investors did not seriously undermine the conclusions of the CAPM. But the effect on the CAPM of the complex tax possibilities of the real world has yet to be fully investigated, though Brennan (1970) examined tax effects in the context of dividend policy and found that it was necessary to add an extra term to the beta-equation to explain asset returns in a world where dividend-policy has tax effects.

There are other frictions in the market besides tax. Buying and selling shares incurs costs: the jobber's turn, broker's fees, stamp duty and VAT, and these may inhibit investors from fully adjusting their portfolios. Transactions costs will also have the effect of driving a wedge between borrowing and lending rates. Put another way, the buying and selling prices of the riskless asset will differ.

Is there a *riskless asset* anyhow? In reality no asset has a future return which can be known with certainty. Three-month Treasury Bills are the closest thing we have to a riskless asset. The risk of default is, we hope zero. But only the *nominal* return is certain, the future rate of inflation and so the *real* return on treasury bills, is unknown. However, Black (1972) showed that the conclusion of the CAPM can be derived without a riskless asset, but using instead a portfolio of zero-beta assets – assets whose records are uncorrelated with the market portfolio.

In developing the CAPM we assumed that the distributions of asset returns are *normal*. In reality returns tend to have infinite variance and to be skewed, since firms can make any amount of positive returns, while negative returns are restricted by limited liability.

It is fairly easy therefore to challenge the CAPM assumptions, and show that some of them are unrealistic. But does it matter? Is the theory completely invalidated or is the damage slight and the CAPM still a reasonable approximation to the way the market prices risk? This is the important question, and it can only be answered empirically, by seeing if the beta-equation accurately describes how assets are priced in practice.

A large number of research studies have examined this[2], with perhaps the best-known by Fama and Macbeth (1973). The easiest way to understand their findings is to recall the beta-equation and consider some of its properties. Expressed in terms of 'excess returns' the CAPM says

$$r_j - r_i = \beta_j (r_m - r_i) \tag{2}$$

If the excess return on security j is plotted against its beta we get the solid line in Figure III. This is the *theoretical* market line and it has the following properties:
— It is straight, that is, the return on an asset is a linear function of its beta
— It slopes upward, that is, return is an increasing function of risk as measured by beta
— It goes through the origin, that is, no other factor influences return
— The slope on beta is $r_m - r_i$

Typically, researchers have grouped shares into portfolios of shares with similar betas to avoid the measurement problems associated with individual securities, and regressed the excess returns and betas of these portfolios. The *empirical* market line they have found this way has usually looked like the dotted line in Figure III.

We can see some similarities and some differences between theory and practice. Excess returns are a linear and increasing function of beta. But the slope is less, and the intercept is above the origin. Hence it seems that in practice low beta securities earn a higher return than the CAPM would predict, and high beta a lower return. Moreover researchers have found that beta is not the only factor that explains return, for example size appears to be a factor, with small firms earning higher returns than large.

However, Roll has raised serious doubts about the possibility of ever testing the CAPM. He points out that the CAPM is a theory of the pricing of assets, shares, but also land, human capital, oil paintings, and so forth. Any test of the CAPM is also a test of the efficiency of the whole market portfolio. But for reasons of data availability, empirical testing tends to be restricted to the securities markets, and this makes it difficult to interpret empirical results as decisively accepting or rejecting the CAPM.

The limits to diversification

The cornerstone of the CAPM is the notion of the fully-diversified investor. The CAPM world is one in which investors will want to be fully-diversified, and the capital market will contain no obstacles to their achieving it. But how does diversification by the *firm* fit into

2   The main studies into the performance of the CAPM are listed in the bibliography to this chapter. But a good place to start is Roll (1977, 1978), and in Sharpe (1978).

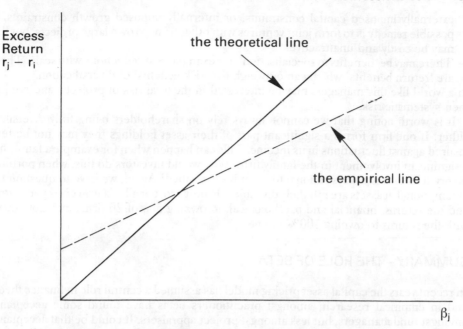

Figure III The empirical market line

this? Since we assume investors are risk-averse 'fully-diversified' is something the rational *investor* will seek to be, but is diversification a strategy *firms* should pursue? In a perfect capital market the answer is NO, diversification by the firm would not be a thing of value. As the reader works through the book the argument for this will become familiar. In a perfect capital market there are no transactions costs, firms and individuals have the same information, face the same taxes and can borrow and lend at the same rate, and so forth. The up-shot is that many financial strategies can be pursued just as well by individuals as by the firms they own. So, for example, in a perfect capital market it becomes *irrelevant* what capital structure the firm has and what dividend policy the firm adopts, because share-holders can recreate the policy themselves at no extra cost.

The same applies to portfolio-building. In this ideal world there is no need for firms to diversify, since the owners of the firm can do it for themselves by buying shares in the potential subsidiaries. Investors will be fully-diversified and will use beta; so managers, who are simply the agents of shareholders, should use beta when choosing projects for them. In practice, though, managers do not seem to behave like this. Rather than taking a shareholder view of risk, they often seem to take a company view. We explored the reasons for this in Chapter 2. First, if there are significant bankruptcy costs it might actually be in shareholders' interests for managers to protect the firm by diversification. In a perfect market no one would worry about bankruptcy – the assets of the firm would just slide smoothly and costlessly to their next best use at a price that fully reflected their economic value. In reality there *are* costs to bankruptcy and people do care about avoiding it. Second, managers may be self-interested, and diversify the firm to protect their jobs. In other words they may trade value-maximisation off against managerial objectives.

However, diversifying a firm is not so easy as diversifing a portfolio of shares for the following reasons:
— Real projects are often large and indivisible while the size of the firm may be limited by

externally imposed capital constraints, or internally imposed growth constraints. A possible remedy is to form joint ventures with other firms to own large projects, but this may be costly and unattractive.

— There may be 'benefits to specialisation', for example cost reductions with scale. These are 'return benefits' which can outweigh the 'risk benefits' of diversification.

In a world like this managers may be interested in the total risk of projects, and not just their systematic risk.

It is worth noting that we cannot always rely on shareholders being fully diversified either. If one firm forms a significant part of their asset holdings they may not be fully insured against fluctuations in its income. This can happen when for example a family has a significant involvement in the family firm. Why would investors do this, when portfolio theory tells us it is always rational to be fully-diversified? Again, we have to question the assumption that assets are infinitely divisible. Owning most or all of a firm gives you *control*, and the returns, financial and psychological, to owning 5% of 20 firms may not equate with the returns to owning 100% of one.

SUMMARY – THE ROLE OF BETA

In recent years the capital asset pricing model has assumed a central role in finance theory and in empirical research; amongst practitioners betas have found some acceptance amongst fund managers, but less amongst project appraisers. It could be that acceptance of beta will grow slowly, as it has done with DCF. But before recommending beta wholeheartedly, we need a balanced view of the pros and cons of using it in practice.

The beta formula is based on an elegant theory of how people choose risky assets. But the theory uses some seemingly unrealistic assumptions, and the evidence suggests that in determining the return on risky assets beta is an important part of the story, but not the whole story. Researchers are now looking at multi-factor asset pricing models to get a better explanation of the return to risky assets. Unfortunately a more complex model will probably not meet our requirement for a decision-rule which is simple and economical to use.

When we apply the CAPM to project appraisal we meet two problems. The first is a practical one; investment projects are often unique events for which estimating a beta may be far from straightforward. The second is more fundamental. Beta is the measure of risk for fully-diversified investors. Unless this is the context in which managers are working, they may want to look at the total risk of projects they are appraising.[3] But the fundamental appeal of beta is that it provides a method for getting risk-premiums which is simple and intuitive but theoretically based. In the next two sections we look at risk analysis in a world where we cannot assume the CAPM. This may be the world most managers inhabit. The problem is that, now, risk analysis involves a trade-off between simplicity and soundness.

IV   RISK IN A NON-CAPM WORLD

What do we do when the assumptions of the CAPM are so significantly breached by the facts of the case that beta cannot be used? Unfortunately there are no easy answers. In the rest of this section we will see what can be done when the decision-maker at least has enough information to estimate the distribution of future outcomes. In the final section we consider the all too common case of extreme uncertainty.

3   Strictly, of course, the CAPM does not hold in a world where some investors are optimising and others are not. Unless it is appropriate for everyone, it will not be appropriate for anyone.

A TOTAL-RISK APPROACH

If the investor is less than fully-diversified he will need to take account of total risk, that is, systematic *and* unsystematic risk. The following discussion is conceptual rather than practical since no simple technique is available.

Suppose Specialised plc is trying to choose some combination of three projects, I, II, III, to add to its existing investments. The problem facing the decision-maker who is using a 'total risk' approach is how to select the best portfolio out of the eight depicted in Figure III. Each point in Figure IV represents the risk and expected value of the firm's return under the eight possible combinations of projects (I + II + III, I + II, I + III, . . . 0) added to the existing firm.

Some combinations can be eliminated immediately using the expected return/variance rule. These portfolios are 'dominated' by one of the others: there exists a portfolio which is better in one respect and not worse in the other. Points B, C, F and G can be eliminated this way.

We have a portfolio choice problem similar to the one we encountered in the last chapter, except now we are leaving aside borrowing and lending, and we are assuming the projects are indivisible so we have discreet points instead of a continuous efficient frontier. As before, to find Specialised's choice we must introduce its preferences between risk and return in the form of risk-return indifference curves. D turns out to be the preferred combination.

This looks straightforward in a diagram, but how will it work in practice? These

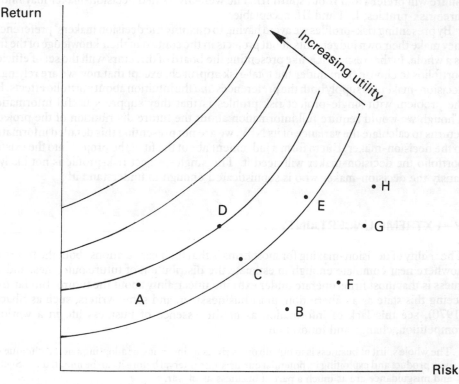

Figure IV Specialised's decision problem

decisions have heavy information requirements. Once we reject the CAPM, we are back with calculating the impact of each project on the portfolio risk and return of the whole firm and with mapping the decision-makers' preferences over risk and return. The example we just took was a simple one. In general if there are n assets, there are 2^n different combinations of those assets (including zero). So a firm with 20 projects to choose from would have $2^{20} = 1,048,576$ portfolios to think about if it wanted to be *sure* of getting the right choice.

If we believe that the corporate view of the board of directors correctly embodies the organisation's preferences then we can perhaps avoid overtly measuring the organisational preference function by presenting them with data on alternative policy implications and expecting them to make the right decisions. But there will be no theoretically sound way of decentralising these decisions.

SINGLE-PROJECT RISK PROFILES

A step down in sophistication from the total-risk approach is to ignore portfolio effects and present the decision-maker with the risk profiles for single projects. So he or she might be presented with a probability distribution of net present values, to accompany the expected value information on each project being appraised. Consider the three profiles in Figure V. Project I is relatively riskless, project II is riskier, and project III has some risk of negative outcomes.

The risk-averse decision-maker who prefers to avoid variance, positive or negative, will prefer I. The decision-maker who may be less generally risk averse but is averse to the risk of failure will prefer I and II but spurn III. The well-diversified decision-maker may find all three risk-profiles, I, II and III, acceptable.

By presenting risk-profiles we avoid having to quantify the decision makers' preferences; they make their own judgements about projects in the context of their knowledge of the firm as a whole. In that respect it is like presenting the board of directors with the set of efficient portfolios to choose from under the total-risk approach, except that now we are relying on decision-makers to supply both the preferences *and* the intuition about portfolio effects. But the problem with single-project risk profiles is that they suppress useful information. Though we would require full information about the future distribution of the project's returns to calculate the variance of its NPV, we are not presenting this detailed information to the decision-maker. But to form a judgement about the fit of the project into the existing portfolio the decision-maker will need it. The single-project risk-profile is not likely to satisfy the decision-maker who is sophisticated enough to understand it!

V EXTREME UNCERTAINTY

The reality of decision-making for most firms is that their expectations about the future are nowhere near complete enough to estimate the distribution of future outcomes, and our guess is that most firms operate under extreme uncertainty about the future. But far from seeing this state as an aberration, most businessmen and some writers, such as Shackle (1970), see this lack of information as of the essence of business life in a world of competition, change and innovation.

> The whole spirit of business is to out-do one's rivals by inventing or adopting a new technique or a new product and exploiting its potential during some interval before it can be imitated . . . Secrecy and misguidance are as much a part of business as of war.
> From Shackle GLS (1970) p 94.

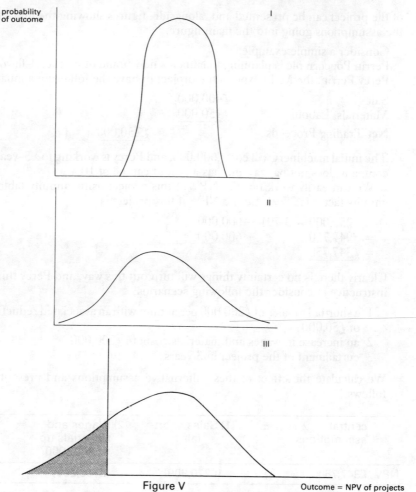

Figure V

Outcome = NPV of projects

But even in such a world the decision-maker must attempt rational. We are going to describe two approaches to decision making in a world of extreme uncertainty, 'sensitivity analysis' and 'payback'.

SENSITIVITY ANALYSIS

In sensitivity analysis key aspects of the project are identified and their values changed to see what effect this has on the expected value of the project as a whole. In other words we see how sensitive the project is to changes in assumptions. We recommend this very strongly as an approach to uncertainty. Sensitivity analysis is the equivalent of feeling one's way on a foggy road – by repeated touch an outline is developed of what is there. Its relationship to the drawing of risk profile is that it represents an exploration of possibilities rather than a calculation of probabilities. Sensitivity analysis enables the firm to use as much of the subjective data it has as possible. It disaggregates the problem and lets the firm identify those aspects that seem most at risk and that cause most concern. Also it provides information in a form that decision-makers can easily digest and use. The expected value of the project can be presented and, alongside, figures showing the impact of changes in the assumptions going into the main figure.

Consider a simple example:
Perrin Popcorn plc is planning to launch a new brand of mackerel-flavoured popcorn. Percy Perrin, the M-D expects the project to have the following annual cash-flows:

Sales	£400,000
Materials, Labour	£150,000
Net Trading Proceeds	£250,000

The initial machinery will cost £600,000, and Percy is working to a 5-year horizon. The company does not pay tax and has a cost of capital of 10%.

We can easily work out the NPV of this project using annuity tables. The 5-year annuity factor is 3.791. So the NPV of this project is:

$$250,000 \times 3.791 - 600,000$$
$$= 947,750 \quad\quad - 600,000$$
$$= £347,750$$

Clearly there is no certainty things will turn out this way, and Percy thinks it might be instructive to consider the following scenarios;

1 a shortfall in sales of £200,000 per annum with an associated reduction in expenses of £50,000
2 an increase in wages and materials costs to £200,000
3 curtailment of the project in 3 years

We calculate the effect of these alternative assumptions and present the results as follows:

	central assumptions	(1) Sales short-fall	(2) Wages and materials up to £200,000	(3) 3 year life
NPV	£347,750	(£220,900)	(£158,200)	£21,750

Alternatively, decision-makers often like to know how far key parameters could fall before the project makes a loss, in other words to know their break-even values. In the present example it is easy to find these:

If X is the break-even level of trading proceeds, assuming a 5-year life then

$$3.791X - 600,000 = 0$$
so,
$$X = £158,270$$

So the project will have a positive NPV if it can clear more than £158,270 per year. Alternatively we can examine the time horizon. If X is the 10% annuity-factor which just breaks-even assuming £250,000 annual trading proceeds, then

$$250,00 X - 600,000 = 0$$
$$X = 2.4$$

Exploring the annuity tables we find that this implies about 2 years of life.

With a more complicated series of cash-flows we would have to do this sensitivity analysis by trial and error, or by using one of the available computer packages that permit sensitivity analysis.

PAYBACK AS A DECISION-RULE

Is it possible to develop decentralisable decision rules under extreme uncertainty? Payback – 'accept the project or projects with the shortest payback period' – is such a rule. It works by taking just one element, the length of time to the recovery of the initial investment, from the sensitivity analysis of a project, making it paramount and ignoring all the others. By ranking all projects on his one dimension it is decentralisable since no information about preferences is needed to make one dimensional choice. Decision-makers who adopt this criterion are implicitly asserting that very low utility is attached to uncertain outcomes and that uncertainty increases with time, as it does with distance on a foggy road.

VI SUMMARY

In reality decisions give rise to a range of possible outcomes in the future, and this causes problems in the search for an economical and decentralisable decision-rule. Under the assumptions of the CAPM, we can derive a rule which is simple and economical to use. Otherwise sound decisions will need a good deal of information, both about the preferences of the decision-makers, and about the inter-relationships between projects. Very often the situation of the decision-maker is one of extreme uncertainty about the future. In this case we recommend techniques such as sensitivity analysis which help him or her to make the best of the information available, and to explore those aspects of projects that are of particular concern.

REFERENCES AND BIBLIOGRAPHY

Black, F Jensen, M C and Scholes, M	'The Capital Asset Pricing Model: Some Empirical Tests' in *Studies in the Theory of Capital Markets* ed M. C. Jensen (1972) Praeger, New York, pp 79–124.
Bierman, H and Schmidt, S	'Application of the Capital Asset Pricing Model to Multiperiod Investments' Journal of Business Finance and Accounting, Autumn 1975, pp 327–340.
Copeland, T E and Weston, J F	*Financial Theory and Corporate Policy* (2nd edn, 1983) Addison-Wesley, Reading, Mass.
Fama, E F	'Risk, Return and Equilibrium', Journal of Political Economy, Jan/Feb, 1971, pp 30–55.
Fama, E F and Macbeth, J D	'Risk, Return and Equilibrium: Empirical Tests', Journal of Political Economy, May/June 1973, pp 607–636.
Foster, G	Finance Statement Analysis (1978) Prentice-Hall, Englewood-Cliffs, New Jersey.
Franks, J R and Broyles, J E	*Modern Managerial Finance* (1979) Wiley.
Jensen, M C	'Capital Markets: Theory and Evidence' Bell Journal of Economics and Management Science, Autumn, 1972, pp 327–398.
Levhari, D and Levy, H	'The Capital Asset pricing Model and the Investment Horizon', Review of Economics and Statistics, 1977, pp 92–105.

Myers, S C and Turnbull, S	'Capital Budgeting and the Capital Asset Pricing Model: Good News and Bad News' Journal of Finance, 1977, pp 321–332.
Roll, R	'A Critique of the Asset Pricing Theory's Tests' Journal of Financial Economics, March 1977, pp 129–176.
Ross, S A	'The Arbitrage Theory of Capital Asset Pacing' Journal of Economic Theory, Dec 1976, pp 343–362.
Ross, S A	'The Current Status of the Capital Asset Pricing Model (CAPM)' Journal of Finance, June 1978, pp 585–601.
Rubinstein, H E	'A Mean-Variance Synthesis of Corporate Financial Theory' Journal of Finance, March 1973, pp 167–182.
Shackle, G L S	Expectation, Enterprise and Profit (1970) George Allen and Unwin, London.

QUESTIONS

1 Exotic Specialities is thinking of starting-up a tinned pilchard operation to supplement its product-range. It wants to know what return one would require from such a project, and brings you in as a consultant. You find that Portugese Pilchards, a single-product firm, had the following dividend and share price data, relative to the markets:

Portugese Pilchard

	Share Price	Dividend	Market Return
1986	300	20	20%
1985	240	20	30%
1984	195	20	(10%)
1983	240	10	10%
1982	200	10	(10%)
1981	240		

Find an appropriate beta for Exotic's pilchard operation and show how you would use it to derive a required return on equity for the project.

2 Orange-Blossom Cosmetics seek to determine a CAPM-based cost of capital, and identify Musk Ox, a quoted firm, as being similar in its mix of activities.

Orange-Blossom ascertains the following data about Musk Ox and the market over the last ten years:

Standard deviation of Musk Ox equity returns	8%
Standard deviation of FT Actuaries index	12%
Correlation Musk Ox/FT Actuaries	+ .6
Average return on FT Actuaries	18%
Average return on 3-month Treasury Bills	11%

Estimate a cost of capital for Orange-Blossom to use in evaluating future investment projects, noting any assumptions you are making.

3 What are the assumptions of the CAPM? Say whether they appear realistic, and how robust the conclusions of the CAPM would be to their not holding.

4 What considerations would guide a firm wondering whether to use the CAPM to measure risk in project appraisal? How would you recommend firms that cannot use CAPM to choose amongst risky assets?

CHAPTER 9

Project choice in practice

The value-maximising firm should choose all projects with a positive net present value, but in practice firms often seem to make their investment decisions in rather different ways. We start this chapter by considering evidence on how one large corporation, Unilever, made its investment decisions. In Section II we examine the findings of a recent survey by R H Pike of investment practices in the UK. He found, as others have, that although the use of DCF analysis seems to be on the increase, other apparently conflicting decision-rules are also widely used. Amongst small and medium-sized firms, and even in large corporations it is common for projects to be chosen on the basis of rather simple criteria such as their *payback period* or their *average accounting rate of return*. It is easy to devise situations in which these criteria will lead to choices which do not maximise value. But it is not just these so-called *rules-of-thumb* that pose this threat. Many major corporations structure their investment decision-making using strategic planning models which seem to emphasise variables such as market share, and growth rate in sales, rather than value.

These alternatives to DCF are too widespread to be lightly dismissed and in Sections III and IV we examine their relationship to DCF analysis in more detail and consider the reasons for their popularity.

I INVESTMENT DECISIONS AT UNILEVER

Unilever is one of the UK's largest and most successful industrial firms. When it submitted evidence[1] to the Wilson Committee in 1977 it gave some interesting insights into the way a firm of this size and sophistication was making its investment decisions and how its practice matched up with the theory we have been describing.

In terms of basic technique Unilever used a mixture of DCF and the so-called 'rules-of-thumb', payback period and accounting rate of return. The prime measure of project performance was internal rate of return or 'DCF yield' which it calculated in constant prices. But 'in appropriate cases' Unilever looked at the prospective trend in the project's accounting rate of return, and for particularly risky projects at payback period. When it comes to risk, Unilever said the following:

> To assist the assessment of risk, we test the sensitivity of the DCF yield to variations in the main assumptions. We also calculate the payback period and give particular attention to this measure in situations of high risk. A considerable part of the assessment of risk, however, is a judgement of the credibility of the yield calculation. We have found from bitter experience that project profitability obtained in the event is on average significantly below project profitability estimated in advance . . . It must be stressed that in modern conditions, the allowance for risk in even an average risk proposal has to be substantial. Moreover, although formal methods of evaluation of risk can help in a number of cases the overall assessment of risk has to be mainly a matter of judgement rather than scientific calculation.

1 Unilever's submission to the Wilson Committee (1977).

There is no mention here of variance and portfolio effects! If projects were perceived as risky, Unilever relied on the techniques of sensitivity analysis and payback we mentioned in the previous section. But a new dimension to risk emerged from Unilever's statement, the problem of 'reliability of source'. Unilever recognised that managers tend to be optimistic, and some are more optimistic than others.

Our main thrust in the last chapter was to find a robust way of adjusting the cost of capital for risk, but Unilever was not using a risk-adjusted discount-rate. Indeed one reason Unilever used IRR may be that, unlike NPV, it did not require a specific measure of the cost of capital. Perhaps because it was written in a period of high and uncertain inflation Unilever was sceptical about the cost of capital:

> The cost of capital also cannot be scientifically established. Working in constant prices, the marginal cost of capital in the form of extra borrowing is often negative, ie interest rate less tax is less than the inflation rate . . . Calculations of average cost of capital taking account both of shareholders funds and of borrowings are highly theoretical and controversial and can produce a wide range of answers depending on definitions. Partly for this reason we have never set any rigid minimum DCF return.

Another issue which comes out strongly in the Unilever submission is the question of strategy. In practice, project appraisal in the sense we have been discussing it is the second stage in the overall investment decision. Firms do not choose projects in a vacuum, they choose them in the context of a *strategy*. Unilever were clear about this:

> In making decisions on investment proposals, the main criteria are:
>
> 1 Does the proposal fit into the agreed strategy for the company involved?
> 2 Is the prospective yield adequate in relation to the risks involved and the cost of capital?

In deciding strategy at Unilever, 'current and prospective profitability . . . are over-whelmingly the most important considerations'. They pointed out, though, that in practice a lot of investment was in projects that yield no direct profitability but contribute to the necessary infrastructure of the firm, and in the replacement and maintenance of existing operations. The question of how firms determine an investment strategy is one we will return to later on.

The third issue that Unilever raised is the question of timing in capital investment. This is another area which can be important in practice, but about which theory does not have much to say.

> . . . although we do our utmost to maintain stability in our capital expenditure programmes, they are influenced particularly in their timing by liquidity considerations. The strength of our balance sheet makes this factor less important for us than for the majority of companies. Nevertheless, major funds outflows . . . undoubtedly cause some low priority capital expenditure to be deferred.

In theory if the capital market is efficient firms can always borrow more money, albeit at a higher price. In practice, as we see later in the book, firms tend to put a high priority on using internally-generated funds and if these are not available investment may get postponed.

II PIKE'S EVIDENCE ON INVESTMENT DECISION-MAKING

R H Pike (1983) surveyed the capital budgeting techniques of 208 UK manufacturing and retailing companies, the largest in terms of market capitalisation. He got a response rate to his questionnaire of 83.7%, very high for this sort of survey. He asked firms to describe their investment appraisal practices in 1980, and to compare this with what they did in

1975, and he regressed these responses on size and industry measures. We present some of his results in Table 1. They throw some interesting light on how large firms make their investment decisions in practice.

In terms of administration, Pike found relatively few companies had a full-time capital budgeting staff, though by 1985 85% had a formal review body for projects. 65% of his sample were budgeting more than two years ahead in 1980.

Finance theory gives some clear instructions on how to appraise projects, but is silent on how to generate worthwhile projects in the first place. About half Pike's respondents said they had difficulty in finding enough projects to meet their investment plans. Having generated proposals, nearly all firms subject them to some form of financial appraisal. However even by 1980 only 37% of firms were formally assessing risk and these tended to be the largest firms; in the majority, risk assessment was subjective. As we saw in the case of Unilever one 'risk' factor that concerns firms is the reliability of managerial forecasts and the tendency to optimism among some project proposers. The only way to check for biases of this sort is the conduct past-completion audits. While 80% of firms monitored project performance, Pike found that only 48% conducted past-completion audits.

Table I   Investment practices of large firms

| | % of companies | | Significance level* | |
	1975	1980	size	industry
ADMINISTRATION				
Full time capital budgeting staff	25	27	0.0001	0.03
Formal review body	78	85	0.10	0.05
Budget more than two years ahead	56	65	0.01	0.10
EVALUATION AND CONTROL				
Formal financial evaluation	91	96	0.7	0.2
Formal analysis of risk	25	37	0.02	0.05
Monitor performance	68	80	0.8	0.7
Post-completion audit on major projects	32	48	0.5	0.3
EVALUATION TECHNIQUES				
Inflation ignored	30	11	0.20	0.20
Risk: Shortened payback	23	30	0.85	0.45
Increased required return	33	36	0.04	0.55
Sensitivity analysis	24	38	0.0001	0.02
Probability analysis	10	12	0.03	0.55

Source: Pike (1983)
*Note: the lower the significance statistic the more significant the relationship.

The technical aspects Pike investigated were the treatment of risk, of inflation, the use of subjective judgement, and most fundamentally, the investment criteria themselves. There was a significant fall between 1975 and 1980 in the number of firms ignoring inflation altogether in their calculations. Only 11% were doing this in 1980. Amongst the remainder however there was a fairly even spread of techniques, with the larger firms tending to favour the specification of different rates of inflation for different costs and revenues and other firms either forecasting at constant prices with a 'real' required return or making a general inflation adjustment. A number preferred to analyse inflation at the risk analysis/sensitivity analysis stage.

Firms seemed averse to formal risk-analysis, and some claimed to have tried it and rejected it. The preferred method of adjusting for risk amongst the smaller firms was to shorten the payback period, with larger firms evenly spread between raising the required return, and sensitivity analysis. Pike found a particular growth in the popularity of sensitivity analysis between 1975 and 1980.

In earlier chapters we have emphasised the importance of judgemental factors in investment decisions. Pike's research bears this out. He asked firms to weigh on a semantic scale the importance they attached to judgemental aspects in decision making. Only 5% of respondents discounted it as of little importance, and overall he found amongst firms of all sizes equal weight being attached to qualitative and quantitative aspects of appraisal. In the next section we concentrate on one aspect of quantitative appraisal, the choice of investment criteria.

III   RULES OF THUMB

While DCF analysis has gained in popularity over the years there is plenty of evidence that many firms, including large corporations, are still using 'rules of thumb' for investment decisions. These are simple statistics such as *payback period* or average *accounting rate of return*. Table II shows Pike's findings. Pike found, as previous studies had done, a gradual growth in the adoption of DCF. But payback still emerges as the most popular technique, used in 79% of firms. 26% of firms were using single criteria, with payback and ARR the most popular. Most firms, in fact, used a combination of DCF and rules of thumb techniques. Also, it is worth noting that of the DCF techniques, firms seem to prefer IRR to NPV despite the fact that, as Chapter 6 showed, NPV is theoretically stronger. A survey by Schall, Sunden and Geijsbeck (1978) has found a continuing trend towards the use of DCF techniques in the US also. They found 86% of firms in their sample now using NPV or IRR, but that the DCF techniques have not displaced rules of thumb but are used alongside. Only 16% of their sample used a DCF technique without also using a rule of thumb. In small and medium-sized firms the proportion is probably much higher.

There have been many studies of investment criteria over the years and some are listed at the end of this chapter. What emerges so strikingly from them is the major role rules-of-thumb still play in the appraisal tool kit. This is particularly so when we note that it is nearly always the largest firms that are being surveyed, and we would expect these firms to be most likely to use 'sophisticated' techniques. The Wilson committee surveyed the investment practices of 'medium sized' companies. They concluded:

> DCF techniques were used by only a fifth of companies, usually for the larger incremental projects. These were nearly all the larger companies. But even in cases where DCF was used there was often some scepticism about its value in practice . . . So investment appraisal in the majority of companies combined a relatively unsophisticated – or rule of thumb – assessment of payback and 'flat' (accounting) return on capital which were largely seen to go together. Other smaller companies, as we have said, did not even go this far in their financial quantification. (Wilson 1978)

We know that NPV is a robust and reliable investment criterion and that if the firm undertakes projects on the basis of NPV it will maximise value. The trouble with simple rules of thumb like payback and accounting rate of return is that they may not give results that are consistent with NPV.

Table II   Combinations of Investment Criteria

	Percentages 1980	1975
No method	–	4
PB	11	12
ARR	8	14
IRR	4	6
NPV	3	1
Single method	26	33
PB, ARR	11	10
PB, IRR	12	10
PB, NPV	6	5
ARR, IRR	3	1
ARR, NPV	1	3
IRR, NPV	4	3
Two methods	37	32
PB, ARR, IRR	10	7
PB, ARR, NPV	6	6
PB, IRR, NPV	10	8
ARR, IRR, NPV	1	1
Three methods	27	22
PB, ARR, IRR, NPV	10	9
Key:	100	100

PB = Payback
ARR = Accounting rate of return
IRR = Internal rate of return
NPV = Net present value

Source: Pike (1983)

PAYBACK

The 'payback' period of a project is the number of years it takes to recover the initial cash outlay. It is found by summing the annual cash flow until the initial outlay is recovered. It has an associated decision-rule – *accept the project or projects with the shortest payback period*. Consider Exhibit I, where the cash flow of two projects x and y are displayed.

Exhibit I

	Project X		Y
Net Cash Flow t = 0	(500,000)		(500,000)
1	300,000		200,000
2	300,000	← payback	200,000
3	–	payback →	100,000
4	–		100,000
5	–		100,000
6			100,000

The payback period of the two projects is x = 1.7 years
                                         y = 3 years

So under the payback criterion project x is preferred. However, the NPV's of the two projects (at 10%) are x = £20,650
                                  y = £109,080

On this criterion project y is vastly superior.

The key defect of payback is that in setting-up the speed of recovery of the outlay as the choice criterion, it ignores the rest of the project's life. In the example the subsequent cash flows of project y were decisive.

Another defect of payback compared to DCF is its failure to discount the future cash flows. Some firms calculate *discounted payback* to cure this defect: the *discounted* cash flows from the project are summed and compared with the initial outlay.

Of course payback does not always give contrary results. Sarnat and Levy (1969) showed that in certain circumstances payback is consistent with IRR: for investment proposals with an IRR greater than 30% and with project lives exceeding ten years the 'payback reciprocal' provided a good estimate of the discounted rate of return. The problem with payback is rather like the problem with IRR itself, which we noted in Chapter 6. It concentrates on just one aspect of a project's performance and ignores others. NPV, on the other hand, is all embracing.

ACCOUNTING RATE OF RETURN

The *accounting rate of return* (ARR) is the accounting profit of the project divided by the book value of the assets employed in it. Though it is usually called the ARR in the rules of thumb literature, it is nothing other than the return on investment we encounter in Chapter 13. The ARR can be calculated annually or as an average over the life of the project, and in the context of investment appraisal it is common to calculate it on the average investment in the project. ARR tends to have associated decision-rules such as *accept the project or projects with the highest ARR* or *accept projects with an ARR above the predetermined cut-off rate.*

Suppose project X has an annual accounting profit of £5,000 net of depreciation, and there are no taxes. The initial investment is £24,000 which is written-down, straight-line, to zero over the four-years of the project life. The average investment in the project is £12,000 $\left(= \dfrac{24,000 + 0}{2} \right)$ and the average ARR will be 5,000/12,000 $\simeq$ 42%. This project will be accepted or rejected on the ARR criterion by comparing this 42% with the ARR from other projects or with the firm's cost of capital.

Is this sort of procedure likely to lead to the right projects being chosen? Again, the best approach is to investigate the relationship of ARR and IRR; IRR is not always a reliable signal of value but at least we know its shortcomings and its relation to NPV. We investigate this question in Chapter 13 and will see that we *can* relate the IRR of a project and its series of ARRs, but the IRR turns out to be a fairly complicated weighted average of the annual ARRs plus an error-term which depends on the discrepancy between book and market values at the beginning and end.

In a project which fully consumes its capital we can ignore the error term, but the IRR only becomes the simple mean of the ARRs when, additionally, the ARR is constant throughout the period. We cannot rely on the simple averages of forecast ARRs that firms commonly use for investment appraisal to be a good proxy for IRR. Still less can we rely on a single-year's ARR.

WHAT IS THE APPEAL OF RULES OF THUMB?

If rules of thumb can lead firms to choose the wrong projects, why do firms use them? The first thing to note is that it is *inevitable* that rules-of-thumb give the wrong answers sometimes. If we could find a simple rule that *always* gave the same answer as a more sophisticated rule, then the more complicated rule would disappear – no one would ever talk about it. The question is, does the cost of using rules-of-thumb, which is the cost of choosing inferior projects sometimes, outweigh their appeal? Various explanations for the appeal of rules of thumb have been proposed, some more apparent than real.

Firstly, of course, they are more *simple* to operate. Payback and ARR are fairly intuitive concepts while to know about DCF the manager will probably need some management education. The growth in such education since the war probably explains the spread of DCF. But why do many large firms, with procedural manuals and training departments, still use rules-of-thumb, often alongside DCF?

Second, payback emphasises the *liquidity* rather than the profitability aspect of investment decision-making. It tells the decision-maker how soon he will get his cash back. This fact should be of no significance to the 'rational' decision-maker, since the DCF approach incorporates accurately the cost of capital, the cost of 'laying out cash'. However some managers persist in attaching importance to speed of payback. And if they perceive capital as tightly rationed, this will not be so irrational since the opportunity cost of funds will be high and will favour early payback.

Another factor which induces managers to think about speed of payback, in particular, is *uncertainty*. If they find it very hard to forecast beyond a short time horizon then early cash flows will be particularly valuable. Again, we can make allowance for uncertainty when calculating NPV – by increasing the discount rate or adjusting downward the expected value of later cash flows. But the more uncertain we are about later cash flows the more we will prefer early-payback projects. So payback may be a rough and ready way of screening-out uncertainty, and this may be why some firms use it alongside DCF.

In terms of the value-maximising model of the firm, one of the attractions of DCF analysis is that it forces managers to fully quantify projects. You cannot calculate NPVs without being very specific about your expectations of future cash flows. But this may be precisely why managers are unhappy with DCF. A lot of organisational literature has discussed the politics and psychology of decision making. It is suggested that decision makers are uncomfortable with sophisticated and specific decision rules. Investment projects are often initiated by relatively junior managers and the initiation of successful projects will enhance a manager's prospects. The less specific he is about the project at the outset the less chance there is of it conflicting with the personal objectives of superiors whose sponsorship it will need, and the less damaging will be the subsequent revisions of assumptions to the reputation of those involved. Firms tend to require full quantification of de-centralised decisions for control purposes. But for the same reason individual decision-makers tend to resist quantification in order to increase their freedom.[2]

Maybe one unfortunate side effect of the dramatic improvement in analytic techniques and computational power available to the decision maker is that successful decision-

---

2 For a readable discussion of reasons why firms do not always use the most sophisticated techniques, see Cooper (1975).

making can appear to be measured by the sophistication of the decision-rule. We firmly believe that the decision maker should use the best rule available, nor do we think the DCF rule is too sophisticated for any manager to employ. But one thing is worth remembering. Given a set of bad projects the most sophisticated choice rule will choose a bad project, but stick a pin into a set of good projects and you get a good project. If a firm has resources to invest in either improving its decision techniques or improving its performance in generating ideas for new projects it might be better to choose the latter.

IV   STRATEGIC PLANNING MODELS

Once we consider the practicalities of project choice we run up against the question of strategy. Given a set of potential investment projects the value of the firm will be maximised by choosing the ones with a positive NPV. But how does the firm *find* these projects? How does it develop its choice of activities, of products and markets, so as to ensure the best supply through time of valuable projects? This is the question students of *business strategy* attempt to answer, and it is closely-linked to the investment appraisal issue.

Many large firms use 'strategic portfolio matrices' to assist in strategy formulation. Wensley (1981a) describes the underlying principal of strategy models as follows: 'They are decision rules or heuristics for detecting areas of sustainable competitive advantage'. Perhaps the best known of these is the so-called 'Boston-Box' model developed by the Boston Consulting Group (BCG).

STRATEGIC PORTFOLIO MATRICES

In strategic portfolio matrices two key strategic variables are emphasised: *market-share*, and *market growth rate*. To understand why this is so, we need to sketch in some background.

Strategy Models get part of their intellectual support from the 'PIMS' ('Profit impact of market strategies') research project carried out at Harvard in the early 1970s. The key issue in business strategy is what sort of strategies yield maintainable profits. PIMS addressed itself to just this question; its aim was to identify and measure 'the major determinants of return on investment (ROI) in individual businesses'. PIMS collected data from 57 large US corporations on 620 individual businesses they owned. The data covered financial and market information for the separate businesses, and firms were asked to provide estimates of other variables including market share. The major conclusion of PIMS was that return on investment is strongly related to market share. These results are shown in Figure I.

On average a 10% difference in market share entailed a 5% difference in pretax ROI. PIMS found several factors contributing to this phenomenon.[3] As market share rose asset turnover tended to stay steady but profit margin tended to rise sharply. The main cost difference between high and low share businesses was in the purchases-to-sales ratio, but marketing costs also appeared to decrease relatively as market share rose. Finally PIMS found that higher share business tended to have developed 'unique competitive strategies' and to be able to charge higher prices and sell higher quality products. In terms of *where* the market share/ROI relationship was most likely to hold, PIMS found market share to be more important for infrequently purchased products, and in businesses where buyers are fragmented.

3   The best description of the PIMS results is Buzzell, Gale and Sultan (1975).

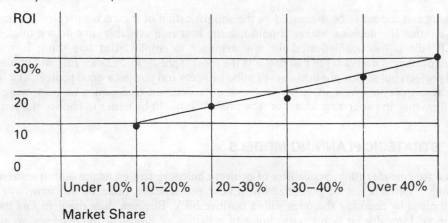

Source: Buzzell, Gale and Sultan (1975).

Figure I The relationship between market share and pretax ROI

To gauge the significance of market growth rate as a strategic variable we look at the notion of the *product life cycle* (PLC). PLC is a widely used concept in marketing.[4] It attempts to identify four stages in a product's sales history, each stage having distinctive characteristics.

Figure II depicts these stages as they are usually conceived for a 'typical' product.

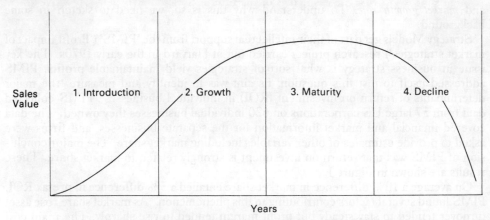

Figure II A typical product-life cycle

The four stages in a product's life are Introduction, Growth, Maturity, and Decline. In the introductory stage, sales growth is very slow as the market becomes familiar with the product. Once the market accepts the product a period of rapid growth will ensue. In both the introductory and growth stages, the product can be expected to make heavy demands on cash – there will be high investment in research, marketing, plant, and stock-building.

4   All standard marketing texts carry a section on the PLC. See, for example, Kotler (1980) ch 12.

Only later in the growth stage will buoyant revenues start to recoup this cash outflow. The introductory stage is conventionally depicted as having low, even negative, profitability as the periodic write-off of the initial investment is set against low revenues, but in the growth stage profitability increases. In the maturity stage sales flatten out as the potential for new customers is exhausted. The product now generates a lot of cash as investment is confined to replacement investment, and 'profits peak in this period and start to decline because of increased marketing outlays to sustain the products position against competition' (Kotler (1980) p 290). In the decline stage sales, profits and cash-flow fade away to zero.

Strategic portfolio matrices offer users a technique for analysing and structuring their product portfolio. The two key dimensions of strategy, market share and market growth rate, are depicted on a two-dimensional matrix as depicted in Figure III. We have seen that these two variables can be considered in some ways as proxies for profitability and cash flow. The firm inserts activities into the matrix as circles, with the diameter of each circle proportional to the sales volume of the activity. The matrix is commonly divided into four boxes assigned names that have now entered business strategy jargon:

'problem children'   = low share, high growth
'stars'   = high share, high growth
'cash cows'   = high share, low growth
'dogs'   = low share, low growth

The firm's strategic objective can now be defined. The firm's long-term objective is to develop and maintain a *balanced portfolio*. Cash cows should generate cash, while problem children will probably use cash. Stars and dogs are expected to break even on the whole. In a balanced portfolio, there will be enough cash cows to support the problem children, and enough stars to provide the cash cows of the future. So the matrix generates investment and disinvestment strategies, known as 'holding' and 'building', and 'divesting' strategies in BCG parlance. The firm will want to build or expand chosen problem children, divest the remainder of its problem children and dogs, and hold its investment in stars and cash cows.

The imaginary firm whose projects we have marked on Figure III has two cash cows, A and B.

A, in particular, is a major source of revenue and cash, though its market share is only marginally greater than its nearest competitor. (Note that it is conventional in this context to measure the market share axis in terms of market share proportional to the market leader). However project C combines high growth and a commanding market position and this could become a major cash generator in the future. The firm needs to decide whether to invest in one or both of E and D in order to enhance their market share. These decisions could not be made without more information on the competitive structure of the markets, and thus the likely costs of buying more market share. The same applies to F, but the presumption must be that in a low growth market the costs of buying more market share is unlikely to be justified.

A FINANCIAL ANALYSIS OF STRATEGY MODELS

Like all strategic analysis strategic portfolio matrices confront the most fundamental question of all – how to succeed in business. But despite their popularity they have received some fundamental criticisms. A major thrust of criticism has been that the world is far more complex than the simple prescription suggests, and that the underlying PIMS

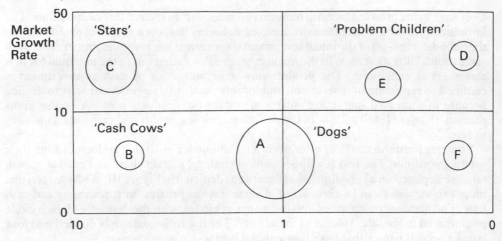

Figure III An example of a Strategic portfolio matrix

relationship between market share and market growth is not sufficiently strong to merit the role it is given in the analysis.[5] We have described a particular strategy model, but there are several portfolio models that firms can currently choose from, and each has its own emphasis and method of scaling the key variables. Wind, Mahajon and Swire (1983) applied various models to 15 sample businesses, and found that only one business was classified the same, as a 'star', by all models. Indeed it seemed that a given business could emerge as any of dog, star, cash cow or problem child depending on the model. They concluded the 'any strategic generalisations concerning them [are] suspect and at best unstable', and suggested that each user would tend to choose the model which met its organisational objectives.

The search for the ingredients and recipe for above-normal returns is the modern alchemy. However the merits of the rival strategy models are outside our scope. But we *are* concerned with how these strategy models relate to the logic of business finance. It is convenient to think of the investment process in two stages: first the firm generates a set of potential projects, then it chooses the ones it is going to undertake. In finance books, and certainly in this one, we talk as though this distinction is nice and clear-cut, and financial analysis only enters the picture when the finance-manager is presented with a set of well-quantified projects to evaluate. But once we start to consider strategy models the distinction ceases to be so clear-cut. By telling the firm where it should be going, the strategy model effectively opens up some options and closes-off others. So, even if most or all of the corporations employing strategy models are using DCF analysis as well, the bundle of potential projects that reach the DCF investment appraisal stage will be a pre-selected one. We found just the same problem with 'rules-of-thumb'. Some firms use 'rules-of-thumb' alongside DCF, but using DCF *as well* does not render the rules-of-thumb harmless. If rules-of-thumb are used at any stage in the process there is a chance that positive valued projects will be rejected. Finance theory indicates that firms should choose projects on the basis of their NPV, evaluated making suitable allowance for risk.

5   For some of these criticisms see Wensley (1981a) and Wensley (1981b).

The question is, does a strategic portfolio matrix select on a consistent basis with NPV? If not, the firm may be overlooking valuable activities.

The model described advocates a portfolio which is 'balanced' in terms of market growth rate and market share. There is a link between these and financial variables if market share is a proxy for return on investment, and market growth rate is a proxy for financing requirements. *If* market share is a good proxy for ROI, and ROI a good proxy for value then it will make sense to hunt down valuable projects by looking for high market share. We note the limiting conditions under which ROI is a proxy for value in Chapter 13 and a main thrust of criticism of the strategic portfolio matrix has been that the world is not so simple – market share is not a perfect proxy for value.

However, there are two other respects in which strategy models run counter to the logic of finance. First, they usually make no allowance for the *riskiness* of alternative activities, whereas putting a proper price on risk is one of the central preoccupations of finance. Second, the notion of a 'balanced portfolio' in terms of cash requirements has no financial rationale. Implicitly, in the model, all new investment must be financed from retained earnings and the portfolio is balanced to yield sufficient cash-generating projects to support projects with high investment needs. In reality, as we see in Part IV of the book, firms do raise most of their cash internally. But there is no reason why this should be the limiting factor on investment. If the capital market is efficient new funds will be available to finance valuable projects and a positive NPV on a project is evidence that it should yield a surplus after covering its cost of capital. The logic of finance is to cost capital directly rather than leave the supply of capital as a constraint on the investment decision.

In terms of financial logic, therefore, strategy models seem to have some key deficiencies. But how can we explain the fact that firms, in this case some of the most sophisticated corporations, use them and seem happy with them? What benefits do strategy models offer to make up for their limitations? Perhaps the overwhelming attraction of strategy models is that they help the firm *think*. The task of deploying the firm's resources today so as to ensure the best supply of valuable projects in the future is, particularly in a large diverse corporation, complex and beset by uncertainty. Strategy models attempt to structure this problem and to deploy research results that might be useful. They focus the firm's attention on apparently important variables. The limitations of such models is perhaps inevitable given the difficulty of the problem, but strategy models can help in the formulation of strategy even if the firm does not adhere slavishly to their prescriptions. As usual, where we find actual management practice diverging from finance theory, we have to hope the leeway is made up by sound judgement.

V SUMMARY

In this chapter we considered the practice rather than the theory of project decision-making. In the first section we examined the findings of Pike about the practice of large UK firms. Though companies do seem to be growing more sophisticated, judgement and rule-or-thumb still play a major part.

In the second and third sections we reviewed two approaches to investment decision making that appear at odds with DCF analysis. Even in sizeable firms 'rules-of-thumb' such as payback and accounting-rate-of-return maintain considerable support, despite their apparent short-comings; and many of the largest companies develop their investment strategy using 'strategy models' which seem out of line in some respects with the logic of finance. We accounted for this behaviour in various ways, but the common theme was that they are both responses to the extreme uncertainty and complexity facing decision-makers in practice.

REFERENCES AND BIBLIOGRAPHY

Buzzell, R, Gale, B T, and Sultan, R G M — 'Market Share – a key to profitability' Harvard Business Review, 1975.

Carsberg, B V, and Hope, A — *Business Investment Decisions Under Inflation: Theory and Practice* (1976) Institute of Chartered Accountants in England and Wales, London.

Gitman, L J, and Mercurio, V A — 'Cost of Capital Techniques Used by Major US Firms: Survey and Analysis of Fortune's 1000', Financial Management, Winter 1982.

Hellings, J — 'The Case for Payback Re-examined', Journal of Business Finance, 45, Spring 1972, pp 99–102.

Klammer, T — 'Empirical Evidence of the Adoption of Sophisticated Capital Budgeting Techniques', Journal of Business, July 1972, pp 387–397.

Kotler, P — *Marketing Management. Analysis, Planning and Control* (1980) Prentice-Hall International, Englewood-Cliffs, New Jersey.

Moore, J S, and Reichert, A K — 'An analysis of the Financial Management Techniques Currently Employed by Large US Corporations', Journal of Business Finance and Accounting, Winter 1983, pp 623–646.

Petty, J, Scott Jr, D F, and Bird, M M — 'The Capital Expenditure Decision-Making Process of Large Corporations', Engineering Economist, Spring 1975.

Pike, R H — *Capital Budgeting in the 1980s* (1982) Institute of Cost and Management Accountants, London.

Pike, R H — 'A Review of Recent Trends in Capital Budgeting Processes', Journal of Accounting and Business Research, Summer 1983, pp 201–208.

Sarnat, M, and Levy, H — 'The Relationship of Rules of Thumb to the Internal Rate of Return: A Restatement and Generalisation', Journal of Finance, June 1979.

Schall, L D, Sundem, G L, and Geijsbeck Jr, W R — 'Survey and Analysis of Capital Budgeting Methods', Journal of Finance, March 1978, pp 281–292.

Wensley, R — 'Strategic Marketing: Betas, Boxes or Basics', Journal of Marketing, Summer 1981(a).

Wensley, R — 'The Market Share Myth', London Business School Journal, Winter 1981(b).

'Wilson Committee' — 'Committee to Review the Functioning of Financial Institutions – Survey of Investment Attitudes and Financing of Medium-Sized Companies', Research Report No: 1, HMSO, 1978.

Wind, Y, Mahajan, V, and Swire, D J — 'An Empirical Comparison of Standardised Portfolio Models', Journal of Marketing, 1983, pp 89–99.

QUESTIONS

1 For each of the following projects calculate its payback period, and its accounting rate of return using straight-line depreciation:

Project

Year	0	1	2	3	4	5
1	(5,000)	1,400	1,400	1,400	1,400	1,400
2	(10,000)	3,300	3,700	3,000	1,000	
3	(15,000)	2,000	2,000	4,000	4,000	12,000
4	(20,000)	15,000	5,000			

Find the NPV of the four projects using a 10% discount rate.

2 Researchers have found that although there has been a trend towards the use of 'rigorous' techniques of investment analysis such as DCF in recent years many large firms still retain judgemental and rule-of-thumb methods for project choice. Explain why firms might use payback period in preference to DCF in investment analysis.

3 Finance theory suggests choosing those projects that yield the maximum net present value, subject to any capital constraint the firm might be under. However, many major companies use strategic portfolio matrices to choose their product portfolios, and often use this, alongside traditional DCF techniques. Contrast the key features of these two approaches and explain whether they are in fact consistent.

Part III
Financial information
and valuation

CHAPTER 10

Valuing shares

An understanding of the arithmetic of share-valuation is a vital tool in finance. Finance theory is built on the assumption of value-maximisation, so the share price of the firm is the key statistic in assessing the theoretical effect of financial decisions. In a practical context finance managers need to value shares when they are fixing the terms of a new issue, appraising another firm for merger or when they are assessing the effect of their own financial decisions on the firm's share price. Once we have mastered share valuation the valuation of other forms of security, such as debt contracts, is quite straightforward. Moreover, as we will see, the value of a security and the cost of the associated capital are inseparable notions. Section I shows the general relationship between the value of a security and the cost of capital. Section II explores the arithmetic of share valuation to derive some usable rules for finding the value of shares, and Section III considers some practical issues in implementing them.

This chapter is essentially about practicalities. It tells you *how* to value shares in practice. The important question of *why* a given firm's market value is what it is, and of the effects of financial policy upon it, are the topics of subsequent chapters.

I THE GENERAL RELATIONSHIP BETWEEN THE COST OF CAPITAL AND VALUE

With most commodities that are bought and sold the market price is easy to determine, the total payment is agreed by the parties when the transaction is made. But with finance the price – which is the return to the supplier, and the cost to the user – usually needs some calculating. This is because a financing contract involves the right to *use* an amount of finance for a limited or unlimited period, so the return or cost is a *rate per unit of time*. The payment will consist of cash flows in different time periods, and these may not be fully specified at the time the contract is made. In the case of equity the payment is an uncertain stream of dividends, with a final payment in the form of the proceeds from selling the shares or a liquidation dividend.

In general the relationship between the present outlay of finance, V_o, the subsequent inflows of cash, C_t, and the cost or return, r, when the financing contract lasts for n periods, is given by the present-value formula:

$$V_o = \sum_{t=0}^{n} \frac{C_t}{(1 + r)^t} \qquad (1)$$

If we know the present value, V_o, and the future cash flows, C_t, we can find the actual return, r. Conversely if we know the C_t associated with a contract and if we know the *required* return, which is the cost of capital, r, we can value it. This chapter is concerned with the mechanics of doing this in practice. As always in finance the central problem is knowing the future, in this case, the future cash flows – C_t. Most of the formulas and rules of thumb we encounter simply reflect different attempts to tackle this problem by making assumptions about the future values of C_t.

II   TECHNIQUES OF SHARE VALUATION

The profits of a firm belong to the shareholders, but their ability to get hold of them is limited since this depends on their power to influence the dividend policy of the directors. If the company is wound up the residue belongs to the shareholders, but in practice most firms are only wound up when they are in severe difficulties, and the residue can be negligible. The law gives shareholders the right to monitor the performance of the firm by receiving financial reports, and to elect the directors. But the quality of the information shareholders get and the effeceiveness of their control over the firm can be limited.

THE DIVIDEND-VALUATION MODEL

The *return* to a shareholder from owning shares has two components: *dividends* and *capital gains*. Suppose I buy a share today for 100p with the expectations of getting a dividend of 10p in a year's time, and then selling it for 105p. I can find my return, r_e, from holding the share as follows:

$$100 = \frac{10 + 105}{(1 + r_e)}$$

$$1 + r_e = \frac{115}{100}$$

$$r_e = 15\%$$

In general, if S_o and S_1 are the values of the share at t_o and t_1 and DIV_1 is the dividend received at t_1

$$S_o = \frac{DIV_1 + S_1}{(1 + r_e)} \tag{2}$$

rearranging, to find the return in terms of the dividend-yield and capital gain, we get:

$$r_e = \frac{DIV_1 + S_1}{S_o} - 1 \tag{3}$$

$$= \frac{DIV_1}{S_o} + \frac{S_1 - S_o}{S_o} \tag{4}$$

What determines the current share price, S_o? The share in the previous example gave a dividend yield of 10% and a capital gain of 5%, so r_e was $10\% + 5\% = 15\%$. But just suppose investors would have been happy with a 10% return – the return they could get on investments of similar risk elsewhere. In this case the share is under-valued and demand would bid up its price until it gave a return of 10% too. People who had the same expectations about its future value and dividends, and had the same required return of 10% would be prepared to pay 104.5p for a share like this, since $104.5p = \dfrac{10p + 105p}{1 + .10}$, so in an efficient market 100p would not be an equilibrium price.

This does not mean that all shares always yield the market's required return, *ex post*. An efficient market sets share-prices to do this *ex ante*, but these prices reflect investors' *best guesses* about the future. As the future unfolds it often turns out in ways investors did not anticipate. In a later chapter we will be taking a close look at the stock market and its efficiency in setting share prices.

We have seen that the present value of a share held for a year depends on the investors' required return r_e, which is their opportunity cost of the capital invested in the share, i e

$$S_o = \frac{DIV_1 + S_1}{(1 + r_e)}$$

What determines S_1? Clearly the next person to buy the share is buying the right to future dividends and a subsequent capital gain too. Suppose he or she in turn receives a dividend after one year of DIV_2, then sells for S_2. The share's value to this investor at t_1 will be, similarly,

$$S_1 = \frac{DIV_2 + S_2}{(1 + r_e)} \tag{5}$$

Substituting (5) into (2) we get

$$S_o = \frac{DIV_1}{(1 + r_e)} + \frac{DIV_2}{(1 + r_e)^2} + \frac{S_2}{(1 + r_e)^2} \tag{6}$$

Pursuing this argument indefinitely we can see that the value of a share is the present value of its future dividend stream summed to infinity,

$$S_o = \sum_{t=o}^{\infty} \frac{DIV_t}{(1 + r_e)^t} \tag{7}$$

Expression (7) is the *dividend valuation model* which is our fundamental share valuation model. If the firm is liquidated at some point, rather than surviving indefinitely, we can still use the model – in this case there is a final liquidation dividend and subsequent dividends are zero.

It is useful to see that the valuation of the firm is simply an extension of the valuation of individual projects. The firm is effectively a bundle of projects, and whereas in project appraisal we were finding the present value of the cash flows generated by a single project, the dividend valuation model is simply finding the present value of the firm as a whole. The big difference, however, is in the quality of the information being used. In project appraisal the valuation is being done by insiders with best access to information for estimating likely cash flows. Share valuation is usually done with highly aggregated information, and often by outsiders.

Another problem with the dividend valuation model is the immense quantity of information apparently needed to service it. Rather than being limited to the life span of one project, it sums to infinity. To find S given r_e, or to find r_e given S, both require forecasts of the dividends on the share in *all* future time periods. But these will depend not only on the future internal performance of the firm, but on external factors such as future levels of demand, the behaviour of other firms, and the macro-economic environment, all forecast into the distant future! We seem to need the future history of the world to value one share. In practice we do not know the future of the world but we do need to value shares, so we have to make the best use of the information we have got.

One way we might make life easier is by working to a *time horizon*. The idea of a dividend stream to infinity is fairly daunting, but discounting means that more distant dividends become relatively insignificant. Table I shows what proportion of the value of a perpetuity, which is a constant amount received each year for ever, is accounted for by the earlier years under different discount rates. These proportions are easy to find using annuity tables. We can see that if we cut the calculation off at 7 years we would get 29% of the value when the discount rate is 5%, but 62% if it is 15%. Bearing in mind that we are allowing no growth in the cash flow so the discount rate is effectively a 'real' rate, then 5% may be the more realistic. Either way the earlier cash flows predominate in valuation.

Table I Percentage of the value of a perpetuity contributed by different years

Discount rate		5%	10%	15%
first	1 year(s)	5%	9%	13%
	2	9%	17%	24%
	3	14%	25%	34%
	4	18%	32%	43%
	5	22%	38%	50%
	7	29%	49%	62%
	10	39%	61%	75%

In practice financial analysts tend to respond to the information problem by valuing shares using *dividend-yields* and *price-earnings ratios* (P/E). These express share price as a multiple of current dividends and earnings, and analysts develop a view on the right multiple from studying other firms and industry averages. As we show next, dividend-yield and P/E are closely-related to the dividend valuation model and can be derived from it by making simplifying assumptions about what dividends are going to be.

DIVIDEND-YIELDS

If we *assume* that dividends will grow at a constant rate indefinitely then the dividend valuation model can be re-expressed

$$S_o = \sum_{t=0}^{\infty} \frac{DIV_t}{(1 + r_e)^t} = \sum_{t=0}^{\infty} \frac{DIV_o (1 + g)^t}{(1 + r_e)^t} \qquad (8)$$

Now *so long as* $r_e > g$ the sum of this infinite series is[1]

$$S_o = \frac{DIV_1}{r_e - g} \qquad (9)$$

Assuming a constant g, less than r_e, the value of the share is the first year dividend capitalised using the 'dividend yield', which is $r_e - g$, the required return less the growth rate in dividends. Rearranging (9) we get

---

1   The proofs of this and the subsequent theorem are in the Appendix to this chapter.

$$r_e = \frac{DIV_1}{S_o} + g \qquad (10)$$

So the cost of equity is the dividend yield plus the expected growth rate in dividends. This model is often known as the 'Gordon growth model' following an early statement of it in Gordon and Shapiro (1956).

Globule Ltd, is expected to pay a dividend of 20p per share this year. The market's required return from a firm of Globule's risk is 12%. We forecast that Globule will maintain an annual growth in dividend of 4%.

So $DIV_1 = 20p$, $r_e = .12$, $g = .04$, and the value of a Globular share, S_o, is

$$S_o = \frac{20p}{.12 - .04} = 250p$$

Cum div and ex div values

We say a share is 'cum div' when its owner also gets the right to the latest declared dividend, and it goes 'ex div' when that right lapses. When we set up the dividend valuation model we assumed the first dividend would be received one year hence, and since it is derived from the dividend valuation model, the Gordon growth model makes the same assumption too. Hence, we are implicitly finding an 'ex div' share price. Suppose we want to value a share 'cum div'. Then we simply add the latest dividend, DIV_o, to the 'ex div' value:

$$\text{'cum div' value} = \frac{DIV_1}{r_e - g} + DIV_o$$

If we find that the latest declared dividend on a Globule share was 18p then the 'cum div' value of Globule is 250p + 18p = 268p.

PRICE-EARNINGS RATIOS

The other commonly-used relationship in share valuation is the price-earnings (P/E) ratio where

$$P/E = \frac{\text{share price}}{\text{earnings per share}} = \frac{S}{E}$$

The relationship of the P/E ratio to the dividend valuation model is not quite so direct as it was with dividend yield. To examine it we will make two new assumptions. Instead of assuming a constant growth rate, g, in dividends *assume*

(a) the firm maintains a constant ratio of dividends to earnings, or 'payout ratio' which for convenience we will describe as $(1 - b)$, where b is the ratio of retentions to earnings; and it is entirely financed by these retentions;

(b) the firm can invest retained earnings in projects within the firm which have an internal rate of return, R.

One useful result follows immediately – if we assume a constant payout ratio the growth rate in earnings is the same as the growth rate in dividends. This must be so, since DIV is a constant proportion, $1 - b$, of E at all times. The new assumptions are rather powerful since they define the earnings of the firm in all future time periods! Suppose the firm has earnings of E_1 in year 1. Earnings in the second year, E_2, will be E_1 (since the firm continues to earn the same yield on existing capital) PLUS the return R on that part of E_1 that was reinvested, bE_1.

so
$$E_1 = E_1$$
$$E_2 = E_1 + bE_1R = E_1 (1 + bR)$$

similarly $E_3 = E_2 + bE_2R$
$$= E_2 (1 + bR) = E_1 (1 + bR)^2$$
$$E_4 = \dots\dots\dots = E_1 (1 + bR)^3, \text{ etc}$$

Evidently the growth rate in E is a constant, bR. Since we saw that dividends and earnings growth rates are identical if there is a constant payout ratio, then

$$bR = g \tag{11}$$

In other words an assumption about a constant payout ratio, and a given internal rate of return are sufficient to define a constant growth rate in dividends. We defined

$$DIV = (1 - b) E \tag{12}$$

Substituting (11), (12) into the dividend yield formula, $S_0 = \dfrac{DIV_1}{r_e - g}$

we get $S_o = \dfrac{(1 - b) E}{r_e - bR}$ \hfill (13)

This defines the value of the firm in terms of current earnings, the payout ratio, the internal rate of return of the firm, and the required return from the firm. Next consider the special case where the firm's internal rate of return equals the required return from the firm. If $R = r_e$, (3) reduces to

$$S_o = \frac{(1 - b) E}{(1 - b) r_e} = \frac{E}{r_e} \tag{14}$$

Hence $r_e = \dfrac{E}{S_o}$ \hfill (15)

The ratio of earnings to price, the reciprocal of the price earnings ratio, measures the cost of equity.

To summarise, if we assume a constant payout ratio and a constant internal rate of return, it follows that the earnings and dividend growth rates are identical and constant. In the special case where $R = r_e$, we can value the share by capitalising earnings at the cost of equity rate and $\dfrac{E}{S_o}$ is a good measure of r_e.

Fisher-Hirshleifer revisited

This is a convenient place to take another look at a fundamental result in finance, the Fisher-Hirshleifer theorem that the all-equity firm should use the investor's required return as its discount-rate for projects. Recall that there are only two things a firm can do with its earnings, pay a dividend or reinvest them.[2] If the firm is maximising shareholder wealth it will choose the policy which has the highest value to shareholders.

Suppose a firm is trying to decide whether to pay a dividend of £DIV or reinvest the

2   Funds held 'idle' in the firm are simply being reinvested at zero return.

money, and assume we are in a simple Fisher-Hirshleifer world with no taxes. The value to the shareholder of the dividend, DIV, paid at time t_o is simply DIV since this is the value of the alternative investment that he can make with the money. The value of DIV reinvested in the firm is the present value of the infinite stream of future dividends generated by the extra investment. By the end of the first year the DIV investment will yield earnings of RDIV of which the proportion $(1 - b)$ will be distributed, and b reinvested. By the end of the second year the earnings from the initial DIV investment will have grown to RDIV $(1 + bR)$ of which the proportion $(1 - b)$ will be distributed, and so forth. Hence, the reinvestment will generate a stream of dividends which will be valued thus:

$$\text{Value of reinvestment} = \frac{(1 - b)RDIV}{1 + r_e} + \frac{(1 - b)RDIV(1 + bR)}{(1 + r_e)^2} + \frac{(1 - b)RDIV(1 + bR)^2}{(1 + r_e)^3} \cdots \infty$$

As we show in the Appendix this infinite series sums to

$$\frac{(1 - b)RDIV}{r_e - bR} \tag{17}$$

The shareholders will prefer reinvestment when the value of reinvestment exceeds the value of the dividend i e

$$\frac{(1 - b)RDIV}{r_e - bR} > DIV$$

Dividing each side by DIV, and multiplying out the top line of the LHS the criterion becomes

$$\frac{R - bR}{r_e - bR} > 1$$

Clearly, when $R = r_e$ the shareholder is indifferent between the two policies – he values them equally. He prefers reinvestment when $R > r_e$ and he prefers a dividend when $r_e > R$. Hence the firm will maximise the shareholders' wealth by using r_e as the cut-off rate for projects.

A CLOSER LOOK AT GROWTH

In deriving the dividend-yield and P/E ratio we saw that the question of valuing shares hinges on 'g' – the growth rate in dividends. This is no surprise since the growth rate is simply a compact way of describing the future time-profile of dividends, which is the great unknown in valuation. Let us take a closer look at growth.

There is good growth and bad growth

'Growth' has a virile sound to it, but recall that $bR = g$. Any firm with $b > o$, and $R > o$ will have positive growth, even though it may be retaining hardly anything and the internal rate of return R may be very low. If this sounds surprising it is because we are forgetting that accounting earnings are net of depreciation. Hopefully any necessary amounts for replacement, to maintain the productive capacity of the firm, have been deducted in measuring earnings so that *any* reinvestment augments the firm's productive capacity.

In Table II we show the growth rate and value of a firm with current earnings, E, of 1,000 and a required return, r_e, of 10%, under various assumptions about internal rate of return and retention policy. The value of the firm in each case is calculated using expression (17) above.

Table II   Growth Rate and Value when £ = 1,000, r_e = 10%

	1 Internal Rate of return R		2 Retention Policy b	3 Growth Rate g = bR	4 Value of the firm $= \dfrac{(1-b)E}{r_e - bR}$
	5%	.25	1.25%	8571
		.5	2.5%	6667
		.75	3.75%	4000
E = 1000	10%	.25	2.5%	10000
		.5	5.0%	10000
r^e = 10%		.75	7.5%	10000
	15%	.25	3.75%	12000
		.5	7.5%	20000
		.75	11.25%	∞

Several things are worth noting in Table II.

— If $R = r_e$ shareholders are indifferent between reinvestment and dividends, and the value of the firm is £10,000 in each case. This follows since when $R = r_e$ the value of the firm reduces to $\dfrac{E}{r_e}$ which is independent of b. In this case $\dfrac{E}{r_e} = \dfrac{1000}{10\%} = 10,000$.

— If $R < r_e$ then the more the firm reinvests, the worse-off the shareholder is. But if $R > r_e$, then the reverse holds and it is in the shareholders' interests that the firm reinvest as much as possible. In the first three rows of Table II the firm is achieving growth through reinvestment but it is 'bad' growth, since it is bought at the expense of shareholders.

— With .75 retention and 15% internal return, the value of the firm approaches infinity! This embarrassing result arises because the value is the sum of an infinite series which is growing faster (at 11.75%) than the rate at which we discount it (10%). In other words we have broken the condition of the 'dividend yield model' – that $r_e > g$. Further on, we consider whether it is feasible that a firm could have $g > r_e$ indefinitely.

Can growth be forecast?

We have talked widely about using g in valuation. But in Chapter 12 we will spend some time showing that for most firms earnings are unforecastable. The 'random-walk' literature has demonstrated convincingly that annual earnings cannot be forecast! The time-series behaviour of earnings has been shown to follow a random-walk-with-drift process where the 'drift' is a common growth factor across all firms.

We can reconcile this apparent paradox in two ways. First even in a random-walk context it still makes sense to try and forecast the general 'drift' factor for all firms and a specific growth rate when we can. Second, empirical research in this area can only work with a narrow range of published data – viz the past earnings series of firms. In practice the analyst has a great deal more information available – detailed information about the firm gleaned from close scrutiny and close contact with the firm's management. Having said this, the random walk results provide a valuable caution, a reminder that the future is inherently unknowable and the rather neat and shiny models described in textbooks do nothing to change that. At best they provide a framework for marshalling our thoughts.

Can super-normal returns be maintained?

We cannot use the dividend yield model when $g > r_e$, since it yields infinite share values. In practice though, we regularly come across firms which achieve, over periods of years, very high annual growth at rates which must be above their cost of capital. This is often interpreted as a weakness in the Gordon model, though of course the dividend valuation model also yields an infinite solution where $r_e < g$. The problem is with the assumption of $g \geqslant r_e$ *indefinitely*.

We know that $g = bR$, and we expect that $o \leqslant b \leqslant 1$. So we will get infinite solutions – the valuation models will 'diverge' rather than converge – when the firm can maintain internal returns, R, which are sufficiently above r that even the proportion bR is greater than r. Hence $R > r_e$ is not sufficient on its own for $g > r_e$. In Table I we saw that only when an R of 15% was combined with a retention of .75 did the value of the firm become infinite. With a b of .25 the firm would need to maintain a return of over 40% to yield $g > r_e$. But there are compelling reasons (apart from a desire to preserve the reputation of the valuation model!) why this cannot last.

First, as the firm gets relentlessly larger, it will need to find more and more projects yielding the high R to service its growth, yet because of what we might call diminishing marginal efficiency of investment, this cannot happen. Faced with a variety of potential projects the rational firm chooses first the ones that yield the highest return, and once the potential of these products and markets has been exhausted, it turns to others. For a firm to find a return of R wherever it turns there must be *constant* returns throughout the economy. But if there is a constant return throughout the economy it must be r_e!

We can make this argument from the other end, in terms of r_e. 'r_e' is the shareholders' required return from the firm, based on the returns available elsewhere in the market. But as our cuckoo-like firm relentlessly expanded, it would start to dominate the market and eventually swamp it. Under the influence of our firm's returns the market r_e will rise and tend towards R, preventing S from ever reaching ∞. In any case we expect that firms and projects yielding excess returns to attract competition, which drives returns to a 'normal' level.

In practice, what research exists on the topic suggests that some firms do maintain above-normal returns for long periods[3], yet they remain finite in size and do not swamp the economy. We must presume that they do this by containing their reinvestment rate in the long term so that $r_e > bR$.

If there are firms with $bR > r_e$ for a limited period we need to know how to value them. Consider a firm with 'super-growth' of g_s for 3 years which then reverts to a normal growth rate g. We know that from year 3 onward the firm will have constant growth, so we can find its value at $t = 3$ as $S_3 = \dfrac{DIV_4.}{re - g}$ To find its value today we value this and the first three years' dividends.

$$S_o = \frac{DIV_1}{(1 + r_e)} + \frac{DIV_1 (1 + g_s)}{(1 + r_e)^2} + \frac{DIV_1 (1 + g_s)^2 + S_3}{(1 + r_e)^3}$$

For example, suppose Sparkler plc is expected to pay a dividend of 40p per share at the

---

3 Mueller (1977) studied the persistence of profit rates above the firm for a sample of 472 firms on the US Compustat tape over 24 years. His findings supported the hypothesis that 'the positions of above-normal monopoly profits can and will be sustained over time'.

end of this year, and to increase this by 50% per annum for the next two years, after which it will settle back to 5% growth. The required return is 15%.

The dividends for the next four years will be

Yr	1	2	3	4
DIV	40p	60p	90p	94.5p

The share value at the end of year 3 will be

$$S_3 = \frac{94.5}{.15 - .5} = £9.45$$

Today's share value is

$$S_o = \frac{40p}{1.15} + \frac{60p}{(1.15)^2} + \frac{90p + £9.45}{(1.15)^3} = \underline{£7.60}$$

A STRATEGY FOR VALUING SHARES

We can assemble what we know about the arithmetic of share valuation into a strategy:

1 If you can estimate it, use the dividend valuation model:

$$S_o = \sum_{t=0}^{\infty} \frac{DIV_t}{(1 + r_e)^t}$$

Note that we do not actually need to estimate dividends to infinity. Later dividends will be discounted to insignificance, so we will not go too far wrong by working to a finite horizon.

2 If our best guess is that dividends will grow at a constant rate g, use the dividend yield formula:

$$S_o = \frac{DIV_1}{r_e - g}$$

This will give the right answer so long as g is constant and maintainable. But we know that $g > r_e$ is *not* maintainable.

3 If the firm has a g_s which is only maintainable for n periods we can use the formula for a limited period of super-growth

$$S_o = \frac{DIV_1}{(1 + r_e)} + \frac{DIV_2}{(1 + r_e)^2} \cdots \cdots \frac{DIV_n}{(1 + r_e)^n} + \frac{DIV_{n+1}}{(r - g)(1 + r_e)^n}$$

4 A study of earnings is useful. If b and R are constant and maintainable we can use them to estimate g, since

$$g = bR$$

Also, compare the earnings price ratio $\frac{E}{S}$, to the dividend yield estimate r_e. It will give a good estimate if $r_e = R$. If $\frac{E}{S}$ is significantly less than r_e we can expect $R > r_e$. This in turn may signal a g that is not maintainable.

III VALUING SHARES IN PRACTICE

If we make some assumptions, we can express the value of a share in terms of r_e and g. This does not solve the information problem, it just expresses what we need to know more compactly – the future divided stream in terms of a constant growth rate, g, and the required return in terms of the cost of capital, r_e. In fact, though we have not said much about it, the assumption of a *constant* and *knowable* r_e is just as heroic as assuming g. The required return, r_e, measures the opportunity cost of investing in this firm – so it reflects the future return from the best alternative asset we could invest in. However in a world of limited information these probably reflect the best we can do, and at the very least they help concentrate the mind on the relevant issues. If the analyst feels he has better information he can always attempt to estimate the full dividend valuation model.

How can we find r and g?. There are two approaches to the problem. One is to *forecast* them directly, the other is to find a *comparable firm* which has a market price, and use the 'r_e – g' implied by this.

If the firm maintains a constant payout policy then its growth rate in earnings will measure its growth rate in dividends. How can we forecast earnings growth? In Chapter 12 we will see that the earnings of most firms follow a random path through time. So using only earnings data the best we can do may be to find the general drift factor. To improve on this we must do what analysts do which is to construct, formally or informally, an economic model of the firm. This means getting more information about the cost and demand functions of the firm's various activities, and figuring out the likely future environment and how the firm might perform in it. In the latter case the analyst will probably use the sort of analysis we discuss in Chapter 12 to get an indication of the firm's strength and position relative to other firms, and an indication of factors, like the skill of the management team, that might affect future performance. If we use data gleaned from a 'comparable' firm the same set of considerations arise in assessing the similarities and differences between the two firms.

USING A COMPARABLE FIRM

Consider an example:
We are trying to value the shares of Powell and Lawson Ltd, an industrial cleaning company. Pritchard Systems is a comparable company with a market quotation of 61p and currently paying a dividend of 3.8p per share. So Pritchard's dividend yield is $\frac{3.8p}{61p} \times 100 = 6\%$.

Powell and Lawson currently pay a dividend of 2p so assuming that 6% is the appropriate dividend yield for them too, we can value a share in Powell and Lawson thus:

$$\frac{2p}{6\%} = 33p$$

But how do we 'know' the two firms are comparable? No two firms are identical. In some firms the chairman drives a Rolls and the receptionist is called Doris, in other firms it is a Jaguar and Boris. But in comparing two firms in a valuation exercise we need only ask two questions:
— Have I any reason to expect their growth rates, g, to differ?
— Have I any reason to expect them to differ in the riskiness of their dividend stream, and thus in required return, r_e?

Differences between firms are only relevant as they affect g and r_c.

By using Pritchard's dividend yield we implied it had the same r_c and g as Lawson and Powell. But even if the two firms are not identical in this respect it is an easy matter to adjust the dividend-yield so long as we can quantify the difference.

Suppose we find Pritchard's expected earnings growth to be 12%, while from Powell and Lawson we only expect 6%. Pritchard's dividend yield was 6%, so an appropriate yield for Lawson and Powell is 12%. To see why, recall that dividend yield = r_c − g. For Pritchard, dividend yield = 6%, g = 12%, therefore r_c = 18%. For Lawson and Powell we assume the same r_c applies, so r_c = 18%, g = 6%, therefore, dividend yield = 12%.

Similarly, if we can quantify the difference in required return on account of risk we can adjust the dividend yield too. Suppose the growth rate of the two firms were the same, but because of risk we require a 1% higher return from Lawson and Powell. This implies a dividend yield of 6% + 1% = 7%.

This all hinges on finding a comparable firm with quoted shares, but why should we trust market values? Existing market prices are, after all, based on the analysis of other analysts, all of whom are mortal and all of whom are setting prices largely by reference to the market. The price setting process looks worryingly circular. There is a good deal of evidence that the market is 'efficient' in setting prices. Market prices reflect the activity of large numbers of buyers and sellers, each striving to anticipate the future better than the rest, and the prices that result appear to embody the relevant information quickly and fully. However, the residual possibility that the market is universally and consistently getting it wrong cannot be ruled out. Until we have hard evidence on this issue though, it must remain in the realm of philosophical doubt. Market prices set in an efficient market remain the best indicators of value we have.

What makes for comparability?

The factors to look for in assessing the comparability of two firms are anything that will affect r_c or g. One factor must be line of business. Both the potential for growth and the variability of returns are closely associated with the firm's line of business and so we would expect to find a comparable firm to be in a similar line of business.

A second factor is the financial structure of the firm. The impact of the economic risk of the firm's activities will be 'geared-up' by any prior claims the firm has issued to debt. A third factor which might be relevant is the size of the firms. The general expectation, which is supported by research evidence, is that the returns of small firms are more volatile than large and, therefore, require a higher r_c. Another candidate is the marketability of the share. It is usually claimed that quoted shares have a higher value, other things being equal, than unquoted shares.

Data on quoted firms

Information on the prices of shares quoted on the London Stock Exchange is available daily from a variety of sources. Table III shows an extract of information from the Financial Times of 5.11.1985.

Table III

(1) 1985 High	Low	(2) Stock	(3) Price	(4) + or −	(5) Div. Net	(6) C'vr	(7) Y'ld	(8) P/E
99	61	Pritchard Sys. 5p	61	−	3.8	1.8	8.9	(7.5)

Source: Financial Times 5.11.1985.

This information relates to Pritchard Limited, a company in the INDUSTRIALS group. The shares in question are the 5p ordinary shares of the company. Column (3) indicates that at close of business on the previous day the shares were traded at 61p each, and this can be compared in (1) with the highest and lowest prices reached so far in 1985, and in (4) with the change on the previous day. In this case the shares showed no change on previous day.

Earnings

The P/E of Pritchard is 7.5, which means that valued at 61p, the share price is 7.5 times the *earnings per share* (EPS) reported in the latest, annual or half-yearly, report. The EPS of a firm is usually measured as historic cost profit after taxation,[4] minority interests and preference dividends, but before extraordinary items: divided by the number of issued equity shares ranking for dividend during the period.[5] There are 'non-economic' factors affecting the earnings of firms arising from choice of conventions available under historic cost accounting – these can distort comparisons of EPS and may require adjustment. Some care is needed in interpreting variations in EPS if the firm has issued new shares. If the shares were issued for new money there is not a problem, and the movement of EPS up or down tells us something about the relative profitability of the latest finance. But if there were a 'stock split' the EPS will fall proportionately without there being any change in profitability or asset base. In this case the analyst needs to adjust the figures to make sure they are on a consistent base throughout the period under review.

Dividends

The Dividend Yield of Pritchard is 8.9%, and its dividend was 3.8p per share covered 1.8 times by profit after tax, calculated on the 'net' basis. Although the 3.8p is the net dividend which the shareholder actually receives, the *yield* and *cover* use the gross equivalent – the dividend grossed-up by the ACT tax credit given to the shareholder. Hence, assuming a basic rate of income tax of 30%.

$$\text{gross dividend yield} = \frac{\text{net dividend}}{\text{share price}} \times \text{grossing factor} \times 100$$

$$\text{Pritchard's Dividend yield} = \frac{3.8}{6.1} \times \frac{100}{70} \times 100 = 8.9\%$$

However, if we are applying dividend yield to net dividends we have to use net dividend yield, which for Pritchard is $8.9\% \times \frac{70}{100} = 6.2\%$, which we used in the previous example.

CURRENT VERSUS HISTORIC-COST EARNINGS

We know that current-cost profit can diverge dramatically from historic-cost profit, and

---

4 Taxation can be an ambiguous figure since, under the imputation system, the amount of corporation tax a firm pays can be affected by the amount of its dividend – but the level of dividends is determined after profits are struck. The problem is that the amount of dividends affects the extent to which certain tax liabilities can be set-off against mainstream corporation tax. EPS calculated net of the company's own unique tax charge including these variable components is known as EPS on the 'net distribution' basis. The 'nil distribution' basis leaves out the variable components. Companies usually report EPS on the 'net' basis, but if it differs significantly from the 'nil' they report that also. The Financial Times shows the P/E in brackets where the net is more than 10% different from the nil basis, as it is in this case.

5 The detailed recommendation of the accounting bodies on calculating EPS can be found in SSAP 3.

the degree of divergence may differ between firms, and analysts are now using current-cost figures increasingly in their appraisal of firms. In theory the mechanics of costing and valuing equity using 'real' ie inflation-adjusted figures are the same as for nominal. We know that if the payout ratio is constant, and if the internal rate of return is constant and equal to the cost of equity then earnings form a reliable basis for costing and valuing equity, so

$$S = \frac{E}{r_e}$$

The important thing is to be consistent top and bottom – to capitalise *real* earnings using a *real* required return or cost of equity, r_e. Though this may sound obvious, recent research has suggested analysts may not always do it.[6] However, the problem is that although current-cost earnings are interesting, in the context of valuation we do not understand them. As yet there is no theory which tells us of the relation between the value of a firm and its current cost profit. It might be said that the same applies to historic cost, but in this case analysts have had long experience in using HC figures.

THE ROLE OF ASSET VALUES

So far we have talked about finding the *economic value* of the firm – the value of its future income stream. But analysts commonly look at the *realisable value* of the underlying assets too. How does this fit into the valuation process? The realisable value of the firm's assets measures their economic value in their next best use – it is the best price the firm could get for the assets if they were sold. On the face of it, therefore, if resources are allocated to their best uses, realisable values are irrelevant since they will always be lower than economic value. But calculating realisable values is useful for several reasons. For one thing the process of efficient resource allocation requires a constant comparison with values in other uses. It can emerge that the ecomomic value of a firm *is* less than its asset value, with the implication that the assets should be transferred to other uses. A second motive is the inherent uncertainty of economic values. Realisable value gives the valuer some indication of the extent of the loss if expectations about the earnings of the firm are disappointed. The relative importance of realisable values depends on the *control* the shareholder has over the firm. Shareholders will only be in a position to enforce the sale of the firm's assets or their redeployment if they are planning to own a controlling interest in the firm.

Calculating realisable values is not as easy as first appears. Traditional accounting provides the 'historic-cost' valuation of the firm's assets, current cost accounts usually measure at replacement cost. Probably the best the outsider can do is use replacement cost figures as a surrogate for realisable value. Another problem is that replacement cost valuations tend to be values of individual assets. They do not say what economic value groups of those assets might yield together.

IV SUMMARY

In this chapter we showed how the dividend valuation model for valuing shares was derived. In reality the great problem is knowing the future stream of dividends attaching to a share, so we make simplifying assumptions and derive rules of thumb in terms of dividend-yields and earnings-price ratios, and we look round for comparable firms with a market price, to help in the valuation process.

6 Modigliani and Cohn (1978) suggested that, partly because analysts were capitalising 'real' earnings using 'nominal' capitalisation rates they were undervaluing US stocks by 50%. We discuss the support for the M & C view in some more detail in Chapter 18.

APPENDIX – SOME DERIVATIONS

1 The 'Gordon growth model'

Assuming a constant rate of growth in dividends, g, the dividend valuation model becomes

(i) $\quad S_o = \sum\limits_{t=0}^{\infty} \dfrac{DIV_o\,(1 + g)^t}{(1 + r_e)^t}\,,$

expanding, we get:

(ii) $\quad S_o = \dfrac{DIV_o\,(1 + g)}{(1 + r_e)} + \dfrac{DIV_o\,(1 + g)^2}{(1 + r_e)^2}\,\ldots\ldots\,\dfrac{DIV_o\,(1 + g)^\infty}{(1 + r_e)}$

Multiplying (ii) by $\dfrac{1 + r_e}{1 + g}$ gives

(iii) $\quad S_o\dfrac{(1 + r_e)}{(1 + g)} = DIV_o + \dfrac{DIV_o\,(1 + g)}{(r + r_e)}\,\ldots\ldots\,\dfrac{DIV_o\,(1 + g)^\infty}{(1 + r_e)^\infty}$

Subtracting (ii) from (iii) gives:

(iv) $\quad S_o\dfrac{(1 + r_e)}{(1 + g)} - S_o = DIV_o - DIV_o\dfrac{(1 + g)^\infty}{(1 + r_e)^\infty}$

If we *assume* $r_e > g$, then $DIV_o\dfrac{(1 + g)^\infty}{(1 + r_e)^\infty} = 0$, so

(v) $\quad S_o\dfrac{(1 + r_e)}{(1 + g)} - S_o = DIV_o$

(vi) $\quad S_o\dfrac{(1 + r_e) - (1 + g)}{1 + g} = DIV_o$

(vii) $\quad S_o\,(r_e - g) = DIV_o\,(1 + g)$

and since $DIV_1 = DIV_o\,(1 + g)$

(viii) $\quad S_o = \dfrac{DIV_1}{r_e - g}$

2 Expression for the value of reinvestment

$\begin{aligned}\text{Value of}\\ \text{reinvestment}\end{aligned} = \dfrac{(1 - b)RDIV}{1 + r_e} + \dfrac{(1 - b)RDIV(1 + bR)}{(1 + r_e)^2} + \dfrac{(1 - b)RDIV(1 + bR)^2}{(1 + r_e)^3}$

$\qquad\qquad + \ldots\ldots\ldots\ldots\ldots\ldots\ldots\,\infty$

$= \dfrac{(1 - b)RDIV}{(1 + r_e)}\left[1 + \dfrac{1 + bR}{1 + r_e} + \left(\dfrac{1 + bR}{1 + r_e}\right)^2 + \left(\dfrac{1 + bR}{1 + r_e}\right)^3 + \ldots\ldots\,\infty\right]$

$= \dfrac{(1 - b)RDIV}{1 + r_e}\left[\sum\limits_{i=0}^{\infty} x^i\right]$ where $x = \dfrac{1 + bR}{1 + r_e}$

Now for any $|x| < 1$, $\sum\limits_{o}^{\infty} x^i = \dfrac{1}{1 - x}$, so assuming $bR < r_e$

$$= \frac{(1-b)RDIV}{1+r_e} \cdot \frac{1}{1-x}$$

$$= \frac{(1-b)RDIV}{1-r_e} \cdot \frac{1+r_e}{r_e - bR}$$

$$= \frac{(1-b)RDIV}{r_e - bR}$$

REFERENCES AND BIBLIOGRAPHY

Gordon, M J and Shapiro, E	'Capital Equipment Analysis: The Required Rate of Profit', Management Science Oct 1956, pp 102–110.
Mueller, D C	'The persistence of profits above the norm', Economica, Nov 1977, pp 369–380.
Sharpe, W F	*Investments* (1978) Prentice-Hall, Englewood-Cliffs, New Jersey.

QUESTIONS

1 Wheel is expected to pay a dividend per share of 10p next year. The market requires a return of 18% from companies of Wheel's riskiness, and Wheel's dividends are expected to grow at a constant 10% indefinitely. Value a Wheel share.

2 Heel is in the same business as Wheel, but its dividends are only expected to grow at 5%. Value a Heel share.

3 At the same time as valuing Wheel, we need to value Snail. Snail anticipates 8% growth indefinitely, and has a beta of 1.5 as against Wheel's 1.0. The expected return on short-term government securities is 11%. Value a share in Snail.

4 Slug is expected to have earnings per share of 20p at the end of the current year. Slug retains 50% of its earnings, and has an internal rate of return of 14%. From a share of Slug's risk, the market requires a return of 20%. Value a Slug share.

5 What is the expected share price of Lizard, today and in three years time, if Lizard's dividend in a year's time is expected to be 30 pence per share and to grow at 40% for another two years, then 6% thereafter. The required return of Lizard's shareholders is 17%.

6 What is the required return of Snake's shareholders if Snake has a share price of £1.64, and has just paid a dividend of 10p, which is expected to grow indefinitely at 8%?

CHAPTER 11

Valuing options

In the last chapter we saw how one would value a share. In this chapter we see how to value a closely-related security – the option to buy, or sell, a share, at a given price, at some time in the future. In share valuation we were trying to value the whole distribution of future dividends. In option valuation we are trying to value just a part of the distribution, because the value of the option depends on the future returns from the share being above a certain level.

There are two reasons for being interested in options. For one thing there is a market in options, and people need to know how to value them. But once we understand options we will see that many other contractual arrangements in finance turn out to embody options. For example, warrants and convertible loan stock create options to buy shares; underwriting agreements create options to sell shares to the underwriter; call provisions in debt contracts give the firm an option to buy back the debt. Most fundamentally, the relationship between the different classes of debt and equity in a firm turn out to hinge on implicit option contracts between them.

Section I explores the nature of share options in more detail. Section II derives some general principles of option valuation and Section III presents a specific option-valuation model, the Black-Scholes model, and shows how to use it. In Section IV we discuss some applications of option pricing theory in finance. The Appendix contains some mathematical tables that are useful for option valuation.

I THE NATURE OF OPTIONS

The option to *buy* something is known as a *call* option, and to sell, a *put*. The price at which the purchase or sale is to be made is the *exercise price*. As to the date of exercise there are two possibilities. We call an option that must be exercised on a specific date a *European* option, and one that may be exercised anytime up to and including the exercise date, an *American* option. You can write options to buy or sell any asset, and there are highly developed markets in closely related areas such as commodities futures. But our interest is in options on shares. We can get a good idea of how share-options work by looking at the London traded-options market.

Buying calls on the London Market

The variety of financial contracts that are available is a good measure of the sophistication of a capital market, just as we can judge a product market by the range of goods it offers. In Chicago there is a well-established and very active traded-options market. In London The Stock Exchange's traded-options market is fairly recent in origin and still fairly small.

Suppose Phil Smith wants to buy call options on GEC on the London Market. Table I shows the prices at which options on GEC were being traded on 15.11.1983.

On the London Market 'American' options are traded with a life of nine months, and

Table I   Options on GEC shares : 15.11.1983

GEC share price on 15.11.1983 : 210p

Exercise Price	Call			Put		
	Jan	April	July	Jan	April	July
180	36	42	48	2	5	7
200	21	28	32	7	10	14
220	9	16	22	18	20	24
240	3	7	–	32	34	–
260	1	–	–	–	–	–

Source: Financial Times

there are expiry dates every three months, so investors always have options with three different dates to choose from. In November 1983 Smith could buy GEC options expiring in January, April or July 1984, and he could choose five different exercise prices, between 180p and 260p, compared to the current price of a GEC share which was 210p. The exercise price can be above or below the current share price. Options with exercise prices below the current share price are commonly known as *in the money* and if the reverse applies they are *out of the money*. Option prices or *premiums* are quoted per share and options are traded in units or *contracts* of 1,000 shares.

Smith believes that by April 1984 GEC shares will be sufficiently above 220 to justify paying 16p now for the option to buy them. He instructs his broker to buy one contract for 1,000 April call options, at a total cost of 16p × 1000 = £160. When April arrives there are two possibilities. If GEC shares are, say, only 200 Smith will have to tear up his option and forget about it – no-one wants an option to buy for 220 something that is only worth 200. But suppose Smith's hunch was correct and GEC shares are now 250. Smith can exercise his options and buy the shares for 220, or he can just sell the options to someone else. Most often, in fact, people buy calls with no ultimate intention of taking the shares. Either way he can calculate his profit as follows:

Share price	250
Exercise price	(220)
	30
Cost of option	16
profit	14p × 1,000 = £140

In reality Phil Smith's profit will be less than this because of transactions costs. His broker will charge a fixed commission per contract, and since time elapsed between buying the options and exercising them, he has foregone some interest on the premium money as well. Also he will have to pay capital gains tax on the profit. But leaving these points aside Figure I shows Smith's payoff. The solid line shows how the option's payoff is related to the share price on the day the option expires. If the share is worth less than the exercise price, 220, then the option is worth nothing. After that, the payoff increases pence for pence with share price, as the 45° line. Since Smith paid 16p to buy the option in the first place his return is given by the lower broken line. If share price fell to zero, he would lose 16p, and he breaks even when share price is 236. Any increase in share price after that goes straight onto his return.

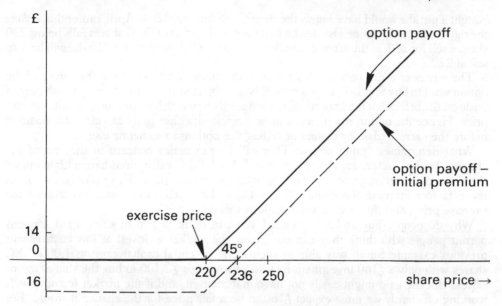

Figure I Smith's pay off to buying a GEC call

One difference between options and the underlying shares is where they come from. All GEC shares were, at some time or other, issued by GEC. But options on GEC shares have nothing at all to do with GEC. They are created by another investor being prepared to sell GEC shares at a fixed price sometime in the future. Suppose in the present case that person was Sharon Brown. All Brown had to do to sell or *write* options at 220 for April was to instruct her broker to do so for her. The day after the options are sold Brown will receive £160 for the options from her broker. Figure II shows Brown's return. It is the mirror image of Smith's.

When the GEC share price goes above 220 and Brown is forced to deliver them at 220 she is going to be sorely tempted to run away and renege on the deal. Because of this risk there are market rules which force the writer to lodge some *collateral* with his broker. This could be the share certificates, or if as is likely, Brown does not actually own any GEC shares, she can put up her collateral or *margin* in the form of government securities or cash. It is important, by the way, not to confuse selling a call with buying a put. If Brown had

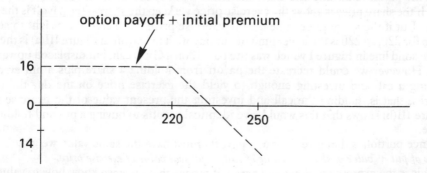

Figure II Brown's return to selling GEC calls

bought a put she would have *bought* the right to *sell* for, say, 220 in April, rather than *selling* the right to *buy* to someone else. In the first case, if the price of GEC shares falls below 220 she *can* sell for 220, in the second case, if the price of GEC goes above 220 she will have to sell at 220.

The writer of a call option need not own the underlying shares nor the buyer of the option want to buy them. The option itself is the object of the transaction and both parties trade on the belief that the option will subsequently be worth less, or more, than its current price. Hence the option never needs to be exercised; either party can close his position before the exercise date by buying or selling the options to someone else.

What determines option prices? This will be our major concern in the rest of the chapter, but two factors are already clear in Table I. GEC call options have a higher price the lower the exercise price and the longer the period to expiry. This makes sense. Both these factors increase the chance that GEC's share price will eventually exceed the exercise price, and this is what gives options value.

Why do people buy and sell options? We can think of two motives. First, options permit people who think they can out-guess the market to invest at low cost. In our previous example Smith was able to secure the potential capital gain on 1,000 GEC shares with only a £160 investment instead of investing £2,100 to buy the shares themselves. But the gain might easily not have materialised, and if the market for options is working efficiently we must expect £160 to be a fair price for the chance it would. For every buyer there is always a seller. Smith was obviously just as convinced the shares would move the other way.

Another motive for buying and selling options is risk-reduction. Suppose Smith had already owned 1,000 shares in GEC, which he bought at 170 as against the current 210. If he wanted to protect his capital and part of that profit, yet still back his belief that GEC was going to carry on rising he could sell his GEC shares, and buy options, yielding 210p − 16p = 194p per share in cash.

It is possible to *hedge* all the risk in holding shares by using options. This exploits the fact that option prices increase with the price of the underlying share. So by holding shares and selling a suitable number of options the investor can balance increases in his share position by falls in his option position, and vice versa. We look at hedging portfolios in more detail later on.

Put options

The value of a put option is closely linked to the value of the equivalent call. Figure III(a) plots the payoff to owning one GEC share and a put option on it with an exercise price of 220. If the share price is above the exercise price we keep the share – the payoff is the share price. But if the share price is below the exercise price we exercise our right to sell the share for 220, so 220 is the lower limit of our payoff. The payoff in Figure III(a) is the same as the solid line in Figure I which was the payoff on a GEC call, but displaced upwards by 220. However we could recreate the payoff from holding a share plus a put *exactly* by holding a call and investing enough to yield the exercise price on the day the option expires, that is, holding the call and investing the present value of the exercise price. Figure III(b) shows that this would give identical payoffs to buying a put and holding the share.

Since portfolios that give the same payoffs must have the same value we get:

value of put + value of share = value of call + present value of exercise price.

This is the expression of *put-call parity*, it means that once we know how to value calls this will permit us to value puts as well.

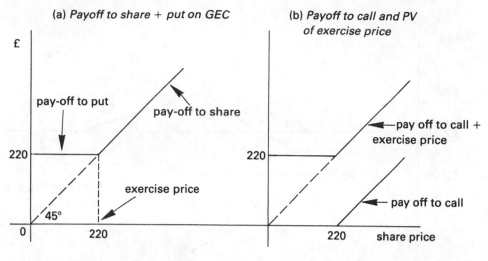

Figure III

A simple 'states of the world' model of option value

We saw in the previous chapter that the value of a share, S_o, is the present value of the future dividend stream, DIV_t, discounted at the shareholders' required return, r_e:

$$S_o = \sum_{t=o}^{\infty} \frac{DIV_t}{(1 + r_e)^t}$$

This is the 'dividend valuation model'. The big problem facing investors in valuing shares is that the dividend stream, and the underlying earnings, are uncertain. It is helpful to restate this problem in terms of 'states of the world'. A *state of the world* is an exhaustive description of the firm's environment at a given time – we are thinking of the state of competition, technology, tastes, government policy, the macro-economic environment, the internal environment of the firm, its financial policies, and so forth. We will say that each state of the world uniquely determines the firm's earnings, in other words, *given* the state of the world the firm's earnings are *certain*. All the uncertainty about future earnings and dividends, therefore, is uncertainty about states of the world. Take a simple case in which we are valuing a share and there are three possible states of the world. Figure IV depicts the problem.

The present value of a share (at t_o) is S_o. This value reflects the market's evaluation of the firm's earnings subject to future states of the world. If between $t_o \rightarrow t_1$ state of the world W_1 occurs, then at t_1 the value of the share will be S_1^1; if it is W_2 then the value will be S_1^2, and so on. And in subsequent periods there will be further branching. We can put some numbers into the picture. Suppose the value of the share at t_o is £2. How much would we be prepared to pay for the option to buy the share at t_1 for an exercise price, E_1, of £2.50? Clearly the option will only be worth exercising if S is greater than £2.50 at t_1. This is a question of whether W_1 occurs in the next time period. Suppose, in fact, we know there is a .3 probability of W_1, and if W_1 does occur, S_1^1 will be £3. If we exercised the option at t_1 we would be (£3 – £2.50 =) 50p better off. Since the probability of W_1 is .3, the expected value of this outcome will be 50p × .3 = 15p. So we should be prepared to pay the present value of 15p to secure the option.

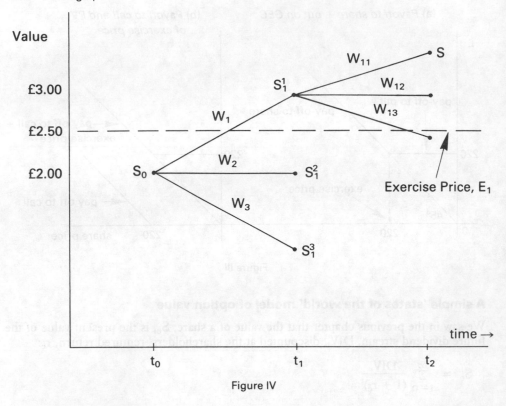

Figure IV

On the face of it, option valuation looks just as hard as valuing shares. It requires the same sort of information about the future. But all the information relevant to valuing the option should already be embodied in the value of the share, *which is known*. The trick in option valuation is to disentangle that proportion of the overall share value that relates to the option. In the simple example we just looked at this was easy, there were only three possible states of the world, and we knew their probabilities. In practice the possibilities for future states of the world, and for future share values, are infinite and we have to make some assumptions about the process of share prices through time to generate the future distribution. This is what Black and Scholes do in the specific option valuation model we look at later.

II THE PROPERTIES OF AN OPTION PRICING MODEL

We are going to work towards an option valuation model in two stages. In this section we derive some of the general properties that all option prices must have, before presenting a specific option valuation model that meets these requirements in the next section.

As we have seen before, a 'model' in finance is a logical construction in which we make certain *assumptions* about the world, then derive certain *conclusions* from them using a logical argument or *proof*. In this section the conclusions are a set of 'theorems' about the factors which affect option prices, and the nature of their effect. Option prices turn out to depend on the value of the underlying share (S), the variability of the share's return (σ), the exercise price (E), the time to exercise (t), and the risk free interest rate (r_it). Option prices turn out to be *unaffected* by the level of the share's return, and by by preferences of investors.

The assumptions needed to get these results are as follows:

1 Capital markets are perfect
2 The risk-free interest rate is constant
3 The underlying share pays no dividends

To get the specific Black-Scholes model in the next section we will have to add one or two more assumptions. Of the three assumptions above, 3 is the most troublesome. In practice nearly all shares do pay dividends, and though theorists have been able to analyse the dividend-paying case it does not have a simple solution.

We consider European call options at the moment, but we will see later how the results transfer to the more general case of the American call. The symbol c will denote the value of a European call, and C an American call, and we denote the value of a call dependent on given values of S, t and E as c = c (S, t, E).[1]

SOME THEOREMS ON THE PRICING OF EUROPEAN CALL OPTIONS

I   Option prices cannot be negative

ie   c (S, t, E) $\geq$ o.

This follows from the fact options are optional! If the exercise price turn out to be below the share price on the day the option expires, you can just tear it up.

II   On expiry, an option is worth the greater of zero or the difference between the share value and the exercise price

ie   c (S, 0, E) = MAX [0, S − E]

On the day the option expires, either S > E so that the option is worth exercising and has a value of S − E, or S ≤ E in which case the option will not be exercised and its value will be zero.

III   An option price must not be less than the greater of zero or the difference between the underlying share price and the present value of the exercise price

ie   c (S, t, E) $\geq$ MAX $[0, S - \dfrac{E}{e^{r_i t}}]$

The proof of theorem III uses a 'dominance' argument. 'Dominance' is a common method of analysing relative value in finance. If we can show that one investment will give a higher return than another in some future states of the world and not less in the rest, then it cannot have a lower value now.

Consider two alternative investment strategies, A and B −

---

1   In this, as in most of this section we are following Merton (1973). Merton's account is invaluable reading for anyone requiring to deepen their knowledge of option pricing.

A: Purchase an option at price c(S, t, E) and invest an amount of $\dfrac{E}{e^{r_i t}}$ at the continuously compounded riskless interest rate, r_i (this will just yield the exercise price, E, after t periods).[2]

B: Buy one share for S.

Let S* be the value of the share on expiry of the option. At that time the value of investment B is clearly S*.

On expiry, the value of the option will be the greater of 0 or S* − E (by theorem II), and the investment $\dfrac{E}{e^{r_i t}}$ yields E, so adding these two the overall value of A is the greater of E (= 0 + E) or S* (= (S* − E) + E). Hence A 'dominates' B, it offers a higher return in some states of the world and no less in others; at worse A is worth S*, but if the exercise price is higher it is worth E. So the present value of A must be no less than B.

$$c\,(S, t, E)\ +\ \frac{E}{e^{r_i t}}\ \geqslant S$$

and
$$c\,(S, t, E)\qquad\qquad \geqslant S\ -\ \frac{E}{e^{r_i t}}$$

and since option prices cannot be negative

$$c\,(S, t, E)\ \geqslant\ MAX\ [0,\ S\ -\ \frac{E}{e^{r_i t}}]$$

IV   An option cannot be worth more than the underlying share

ie   c (S, t, E) $\leqslant$ S

If c (S, t, E) > S, no-one would buy the option. It would be cheaper to buy the share now and hold on to it.

Theorems I – IV already provide us with some boundaries within which an option price must lie, relative to share price. We depict these in Figure Va.

The 45° line through the origin, the share price plotted on itself, provides the upper bound. This follows theorem IV – an option cannot be worth more than the underlying share. The lower bound is provided by theorem III. The option price cannot be less than $S - \dfrac{E}{e^{r_i t}}$ (which we depict as the 45° line shifted $\dfrac{E}{e^{r_i t}}$ to the right) or less than zero.

But how does the option price behave within these boundaries? To investigate this we need some more theorems:

V   If the share price is zero, the price of an option written on it is zero

ie   c (o, t, E) = 0
       Proof:

The proof follows from theorems I and IV.

---

2   What is $\dfrac{E}{e^{r_i t}}$, the reader may ask? It is the continuous time equivalent of $\dfrac{E}{(1+r_i)^t}$. See Chapter 5.

(a) *Boundaries of option prices*

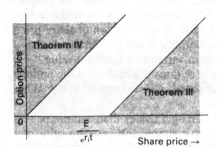

(b) *The shape of the option function*

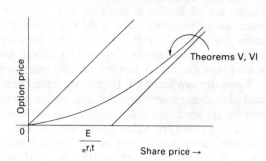

Figure V

VI   The option price is a 'convex' function of share price

We say a function is convex when, if we draw a straight line between any two points of the function no intermediate value of the function lies above that line. This is expressed formally as:

for all λ, $0 < \lambda < 1$
if $S_3 = \lambda S_1 + (1 - \lambda) S_2$
then $c (S_3, t, E) \leqslant \lambda c (S_1, t, E) + (1 - \lambda) c (S_2, t, E)$

The proof of this theorem uses the dominance approach again.

Figure Vb shows what theorems V and VI do for us. They tell us what shape the relationship between the option price and the share price will have. It will be a line passing through the origin, convex to the horizontal axis.

So far we have only considered the relationship between option price and share price. We have been holding constant other factors that might affect option value. But we can develop some theorems on these too.

VII, VIII, IX   The lower the exercise price, or the longer the period to expiry, or the higher the risk-free interest rate, then the more valuable the option

We group these three theorems together because they are essentially all about the same thing. Each is a factor which will affect the present value of the exercise price. We can see by examining theorem III:

$$c (S, t, E) \geqslant MAX [0, S - \frac{E}{e^{r_i t}}]$$

that anything which lowers the present value of the exercise price will raise the option value, all other things equal.

X The more risky the share the more valuable the option

We saw how option value was affected by factors such as S, E, t, r_i. We have assumed these things are all known at the time the option is valued. The great unknown in option valuation is the expiry value of the underlying share, S^*. To know that, we would need to know the process which links S^* to S. However if the future distribution of share price outcomes can be described by its variance and the past variance of returns on the share is a good proxy for this we can capture the relation between variance and option value.

Consider two firms i, j. Both firms have shares with options outstanding. The options and underlying shares are identical except for the variance, and we know $\sigma_i^2 > \sigma_j^2$. What can we say about the values of the respective options?

Merton (1973) provides a proof that an option written on a riskier share cannot be less valuable, other things being equal. The intuition of this is simple. The present value of a share, S, represents an expectation of good and bad outcomes in different states of the world. In the case of a riskier share with the same value more extreme future values are balancing to give the same expected value. However the option valuer does not need to take a balanced view. He is only interested in outcomes above the exercise price, and attaches zero value to others. For him the higher the variance of future outcomes the better, since this means outcomes above his exercise price will have higher value.

THE PRICING OF AMERICAN CALLS

An American call can be exercised on or before the exercise date, whereas a European option can only be exercised on the exercise date. What difference does this make to the valuation of an American option? The key thing to note is that if an American option is not exercised until expiry it is effectively a European option.

XI If the underlying share does not pay dividends an American call will not be exercised until expiry and thus has the same value as a European call.

When an option is exercised its value is MAX $[0, S - E]$. But if it still has time to run, i e t $> o$, its value is MAX $[0, S - \dfrac{E}{e^{r_i t}}]$ which is not less than MAX $[0, S - E]$ for positive r_i and t. So it is always worthwhile to keep an option live rather than exercise it.

If the underlying share does not pay dividends our previous theorems on European options will apply to American options too.

THE EFFECT OF DIVIDENDS

So far we have *assumed* that dividends are not paid on the underlying share. This is clearly unrealistic, so what effect will dividends have on option valuation? When we explored the relation between dividends and share valuation in Chapter 10 we found that share price falls after a dividend, 'ex-div'. This is simply because part of the assets whose value was embodied in the cum-div share price have now been distributed to the shareholders. Since we know that option value is an increasing function of the value of the underlying share, we would expect this drop in share value to engender a corresponding drop in option value. We know that the value of an option kept 'live' is always more than its value exercised, but if the loss in value due to the dividend is greater than this premium it might be rational for the holder to exercise it early, if he can. Hence the existence of dividends may lead to the premature exercise of American options. Furthermore, since the European call holder would have preferred to exercise early too, but could not, we can expect American calls to sell for a higher price in a world of dividends.

In practice it is feasible to build clauses into option agreements protecting them from dividend payouts.[3] The value of a fully-protected option is unaffected by dividend payouts, however, in practice few options are fully-protected. But dividend policy is just one of the management decisions that can affect the value of the option by affecting the value of the underlying share. In this respect options are vulnerable like all other claims on the firm, to management decisions.

III THE BLACK-SCHOLES MODEL OF OPTION VALUATION

We know the general relationship between option value and share price, and we know that option value is an increasing function of r_i, t and σ^2, and a decreasing function of E. But we do not yet know *precisely* what function option value is of all these variables. The problem, as always in finance, is one of knowing the future. In the case of options the key unknown is the share price on exercise, and the only way to get round this problem is to make assumptions about the future 'process' linking the present and future share price. In a seminal paper Black and Scholes (1973) did this, and by doing so were able to derive a specific option valuation model. We will give some insights into their model, though we will not derive it (the mathematics is far too advanced for this text), and we will show how it is used.

THE MODEL

In the Black-Scholes model:

$$c\,(S, t, E) \;=\; S \cdot N\,(d_1) \;-\; \frac{E}{e^{r_i t}} \cdot N\,(d_2)$$

$$\text{where } d_1 \;=\; \frac{\ln\,(S/E) + r_i t + \sigma^2\,t/2}{\sigma\,\sqrt{t}}$$

$$d_2 \;=\; \frac{\ln\,(S/E) + r_i t - \sigma^2\,t/2}{\sigma\,\sqrt{t}}$$

$N(d)$ = 'cumulative normal density function', i e the area to the left of D under a normal distribution of unit variance and zero mean; ln is the natural log.

In words, BS are saying that the value of a European call option is the difference between share price and present value of the exercise price, but with weights N (d) attached. The model is deterministic, it gives a unique value for the option, and it has all the properties we derived in the last section.[4]

The ASSUMPTIONS Black and Scholes make in addition to the ones we have made already are as follows:

---

3 Merton (1973) shows the derivation of a protection clause.
4 If we took partial derivatives we would find:
$$\frac{\delta c}{\delta S} > 0, \quad \frac{\delta c}{\delta \sigma^2} > 0, \quad \frac{\delta c}{\delta t} > 0, \quad \frac{\delta c}{\delta r_i} > 0, \quad \frac{\delta c}{\delta E} > 0.$$

4 The share price follows a special sort of random process known as 'geometric Brownian motion'.

5 There is continuous trading, and there are no restrictions on 'short-sales'. 'Short-selling' is having a negative holding.

Assumption 4 permits BS to estimate the future distribution of share values using knowable parameters, the present share price and variance of return. But perhaps the key insight Black and Scholes had was that using shares and options investors could build 'perfectly-hedged', riskless, portfolios. For this they required assumption 5.

Hedging

Black and Scholes saw that the existence of call options permits an investor to construct a perfectly *hedged* portfolio, ie a portfolio with zero risk. The overall return on such a portfolio must be the risk-free rate, r_i. The formula for creating such a portfolio is simple, and will be discussed below.

Figure VI plots the relationship between option price and share value from Figure Vb, this time with numbers attached.

The slope of c(S) shows how much the price of the option increases as the price of the share rises by one unit. Consider a discrete increase in share price from 50p to 54p. We see that the option on the share responds by increasing in price from 20p to 22p. An investor holding one of these shares has a risky asset – an asset whose price fluctuates over time.

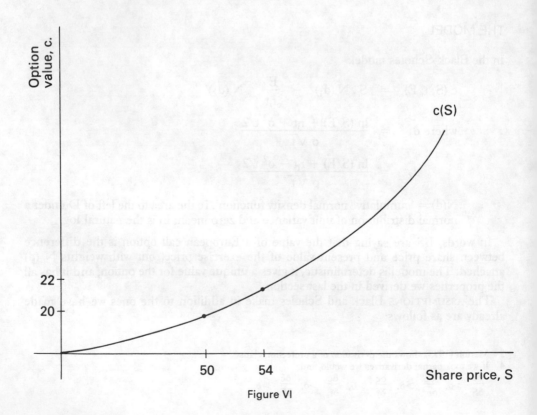

Figure VI

Suppose he would rather hold a riskless position. The existence of a separate security, an option, whose price moves in concert with the share permits him to achieve this. All the investor needs to do is sell-short two options. Now when the value of the share increases by 4p this gain is exactly compensated by the loss on the short position in options – it will cost our investor an extra 4p to replace the two options. Similarly, if the share price falls the investor is also protected. He loses 4p on his share, but will need to pay two pence less to replace each of the two options he has sold. This is the hedging process, and it depends on the investors ability to sell-short; hence the necessity for the assumption that there are no restrictions on short sales.

We looked at small changes in share price, and assumed the effects on option price were symmetrical. However the HEDGE RATIO – the number of options you need to sell for each share – is the slope of the option valuation curve $c(S)$, and since $c(S)$ is convex its slope changes over the range of share price. The implication is that the investor will need to keep constantly rebalancing his portfolio as the hedge ratio changes with share price. Hence the need for the assumption that there is continuous trading in the market.

VALUING A CALL

Shares in Primal plc are presently selling for 300p and the standard deviation of Primal returns is 40%. The riskless interest rate is 10%. What is the value of a 90 day call-option on Primal with a 250p exercise price?

We can feed the following values into the BS model:

$$
\begin{aligned}
S &= 300 \\
E &= 250 \\
r_i &= .10 \\
t &= .25 \\
\sigma &= .4
\end{aligned}
$$

It will also be useful to work out:

$$
PV(E) = \frac{E}{e^{r_i t}}
$$

$$
= 243.82
$$

The natural log of S/E, where $S/E = \dfrac{300}{250} = 1.2$, we can find from natural log tables.

In $(1.2) = .1823$

$$
\text{So } d_1 = \frac{.1823 + .10 \cdot .25 + (.4)^2 \cdot .25/2}{.4 \cdot \sqrt{.25}} = 1.1365
$$

$$
d_2 = \frac{.1823 + .10 \cdot .25 - (.4)^2 \cdot .25/2}{.4 \cdot \sqrt{.25}} = .9365
$$

$N(d_1)$ and $N(d_2)$ are the areas under the unit normal distribution 'to the left' of d_1 and d_2. From the Table in the Appendix we get:

$N(d_1) = .8713$ $N(d_2) = .8246$

So the value of the call option in Primal is

$$c = 300 \times .8713 - 243.82 \times .8246$$
$$= 261.39 - 201.05$$
$$= \underline{60.34p}$$

The BS formula is straightforward to operate, but an alternative is to use 'option-tables'. The user 'plugs-in' the key parameters, and the tables show the premium, as a percentage of S, that should be added to $S - E/e^{r_i t}$ to get the option value.

The hedge ratio

The Black–Scholes formula also gives us the *hedge ratio* – the number of options the investor must sell short to create the perfectly hedged portfolio. In the example we had earlier the option price rose from 20 to 22 when the share moved from 50 to 54. The slope of the curve in this vicinity was $2/4 = \frac{1}{2}$, and the hedge ratio was 2, which was 1/slope. Actually, $\frac{1}{2}$ was only an approximation of the slope over a discrete interval, in reality, the slope changes continuously round the curve. The BS formula tells us what the slope is at any point. We know that

$$c\,(S, t, E) = \; S.N\,(d_1) \; - \; \frac{E}{e^{r_i t}} \;.\; N\,(d_2).$$

The slope of this curve is $\dfrac{dc}{ds} \; = \; N\,(d_1)$.

To see whether this tells us how to build a hedged portfolio we can use the Primal example.

$N\,(d_1)$ for Primal was .8713. This implies a hedge ratio of $\dfrac{1}{.8713} = 1.1477$.

So if we owned 1,000 shares of Primal we could hedge by *selling* $1{,}000 \times 1.1477 = 1147$ calls.

The value of our portfolio will now be:

$$1{,}000\,.\,S - 1148\,.\,c$$
$$= 1{,}000 \times 300 - 1147 \times 60.34 = \underline{£2{,}307.90}$$

If the share price rises to 301, the option price will rise to £61.24 (you can check this using the BS formula).

The value of the portfolio will be:
$$1{,}000 \times 301 - 1147 \times 61.24 = \underline{£2{,}307.56}$$

The decrease in the value of the short position in options has almost perfectly offset the increase in share value. And the reader can check for himself that if share price falls to 299p the portfolio value will be $\underline{£2{,}307.35}$.

The discrepancy of a few pence in each case is explained by the fact we explored a change of 1p around the share price. This may seem a small enough interval, but for perfect hedging one would need to readjust the hedge ratio continuously, as assumed by BS.

Valuing a put

Now we can value a call we can value a put, using the *put-call parity* result:

Put + share = Call + PV (exercise price)

In the case of Primal:

Put + 300 = 60.34 + 243.82
Put = 4.16p

The value of a put in Primal, if the share price is 300, is 4.16p.

Empirical evidence

The evidence shows that, allowing for transactions costs, the market efficiently prices options. Black and Scholes (1972) studied the prices of options on the over-the-counter market from 1966 to 1969. They found that abnormal returns could not be earned using the option pricing model to identify under- and over-valued options. Interestingly, they found that the option pricing model performed much better when ex post (ie actual) variances were used in its estimation than when ex ante (ie calculated on past history) variances were used. Galai (1977) studying option prices during seven months in 1973 on the Chicago Board Options Exchange found abnormal returns could be made using the option pricing model, but that transactions costs wiped these out.

IV   SOME APPLICATIONS OF OPTION THEORY

The beauty of option theory is the insights it can give into other financial contracts. In this section we point out some of the applications.

Warrants and convertibles

Some firms issue 'share-options' as part of the remuneration package of employees. The employee gets the right to buy company shares at an agreed price. The main difference between share-participation schemes like this and traded-options is that the option is exercised for new shares issued by the firm, instead of existing shares held by another investor. More generally, companies can issue *warrants* which give the holder the right to buy shares from the company at a fixed price sometime in the future. This sometimes happens at the time of a merger, or detachable warrants may be issued with loan-stock. Warrants are tradeable securities, unlike employee share-options which are usually not, and which also often require the employee to hold on to the shares for a period after he has bought them.

A common alternative to issuing loan-stock with warrants is to issue *convertible* loan-stock which gives the investor the option to exchange the debt for equity at a certain price at some time in the future. A convertible is like debt plus a warrant, except that the warrant cannot be detached, and the debt has to be redeemed when the option is exercised.

In all these cases the company is selling call options on its shares. Another sort of option is sometimes embodied in debt contracts. When debt is *callable* the firm has effectively bought a call option from the debtholder. We consider these issues in Chapter 21.

Underwriting

In Chapter 20 we will see that to protect themselves from the risk of undersubscription firms often have new issues of shares *underwritten*. The underwriter agrees to buy any unsold shares at the issue price, in exchange for a commission. It should be clear by now that the firm is simply buying a put option from the underwriters. The commission is the option price, and the exercise price of the option is the issue price of the shares.

The relationship of debt and equity

Debt and equity effectively split the ownership of the firm between them, but in a particular way. If the total value of the firm exceeds the value of the debt claim, then the surplus belongs to equity. But if the value of the firm is less than the debt claim, equity are protected by limited liability from making good the debt. The position of equity is analytically the same as it would be if debtholders owned the firm and had sold a call option on it to equity holders at an exercise price set at the value of the debt claim. If the value of the firm exceeds the value of debt, equity exercise the option, pay off debt, and keep the surplus. If it does not, equity just walk away. We analyse the relationship between debt and equity in Chapter 14.

We can get a better idea now why options are important. Finance contracts specify the claims that providers of finance will have in the future. But these are claims on returns that are uncertain and depend on unknown future states of the world. We call a finance contract more *complex* the more states of the world it covers, and complex contracts are aggregates of *simple* contracts that cover a subset of states of the world. Equity and debt are complex contracts, but option contracts are simple. We can get a better idea of how to value complex contracts by studying the simple contracts that make them up.

V SUMMARY

Options are 'simpler' contracts than shares, they are a claim on just a part of the future distribution of returns to the share. It is straightforward to develop general boundaries for the value of options in terms of the underlying share price and exercise price, and to see in which direction factors such as time to exercise, the riskless interest rate, and the variance on the share's return will push option values. To get a specific model of option valuation, however, it is necessary to make some assumptions about the process linking present and future share values. Black and Scholes did this, and derived a model that permits us to get deterministic value for options.

Option theory is relatively new in finance, and its importance stretches beyond the valuation of traded options. Option theory is a powerful tool for explaining various other contractual arrangements in finance.

APPENDIX – AREA UNDER THE NORMAL CURVE

x	N(x)	x	N(x)	x	N(x)	x	N(x)	x	N(x)	x	N(x)
0.00	0.5000	0.50	0.6915	1.00	0.8413	1.50	0.9332	2.00	0.9773	2.50	0.9938
.01	.5040	.51	.6950	.01	.8438	.51	.9345	.01	.9778	.51	.9940
.02	.5080	.52	.6985	.02	.8461	.52	.9357	.02	.9783	.52	.9941
.03	.5120	.53	.7019	.03	.8485	.53	.9370	.03	.9788	.53	.9943
.04	.5160	.54	.7054	.04	.8508	.54	.9382	.04	.9793	.54	.9945
.05	.5199	.55	.7088	.05	.8531	.55	.9394	.05	.9798	.55	.9945
.06	.5239	.56	.7123	.06	.8554	.56	.9406	.06	.9803	.56	.9948
.07	.5279	.57	.7157	.07	.8577	.57	.9418	.07	.9808	.57	.9949
.08	.5319	.58	.7190	.08	.8599	.58	.9429	.08	.9812	.58	.9951
.09	.5359	.59	.7224	.09	.8621	.59	.9441	.09	.9817	.59	.9952
0.10	0.5398	0.60	0.7257	1.10	0.8643	1.60	0.9452	2.10	0.9821	2.60	0.9953
.11	.5438	.61	.7291	.11	.8665	.61	.9463	.11	.9826	.61	.9955
.12	.5478	.62	.7324	.12	.8686	.62	.9474	.12	.9830	.62	.9956
.13	.5517	.63	.7357	.13	.8708	.63	.9484	.13	.9834	.63	.9957
.14	.5557	.64	.7389	.14	.8729	.64	.9495	.14	.9838	.64	.9959
.15	.5596	.65	.7422	.15	.8749	.65	.9505	.15	.9842	.65	.9960
.16	.5636	.66	.7454	.16	.8770	.66	.9515	.16	.9846	.66	.9961
.17	.5675	.67	.7486	.17	.8790	.67	.9525	.17	.9850	.67	.9962
.18	.5714	.68	.7517	.18	.8810	.68	.9535	.18	.9854	.68	.9963
.19	.5753	.69	.7549	.19	.8830	.69	.9545	.19	.9857	.69	.9964
0.20	0.5793	0.70	0.7580	1.20	0.8849	1.70	0.9554	2.20	0.9861	2.70	0.9965
.21	.5832	.71	.7611	.21	.8869	.71	.9564	.21	.9865	.71	.9966
.22	.5871	.72	.7642	.22	.8888	.72	.9573	.22	.9868	.72	.9967
.23	.5910	.73	.7673	.23	.8907	.73	.9582	.23	.9871	.73	.9968
.24	.5948	.74	.7704	.24	.8925	.74	.9591	.24	.9875	.74	.9969
.25	.5987	.75	.7734	.25	.8944	.75	.9599	.25	.9878	.75	.9970
.26	.6026	.76	.7764	.26	.8962	.76	.9608	.26	.9881	.76	.9971
.27	.6064	.77	.7794	.27	.8980	.77	.9616	.27	.9884	.77	.9972
.28	.6103	.78	.7823	.28	.8997	.78	.9625	.28	.9887	.78	.9973
.29	.6141	.79	.7852	.29	.9015	.79	.9633	.29	.9890	.79	.9974
0.30	0.6179	0.80	0.7881	1.30	0.9032	1.80	0.9641	2.30	0.9893	2.80	0.9974
.31	.6217	.81	.7910	.31	.9049	.81	.9649	.31	.9896	.81	.9975
.32	.6255	.82	.7939	.32	.9066	.82	.9656	.32	.9898	.82	.9976
.33	.6293	.83	.7967	.33	.9082	.83	.9664	.33	.9901	.83	.9977
.34	.6331	.84	.7995	.34	.9099	.84	.9671	.34	.9904	.84	.9977
.35	.6368	.85	.8023	.35	.9115	.85	.9678	.35	.9906	.85	.9978
.36	.6406	.86	.8051	.36	.9131	.86	.9686	.36	.9909	.86	.9979
.37	.6443	.87	.8078	.37	.9147	.87	.9693	.37	.9911	.87	.9980
.38	.6480	.88	.8106	.38	.9162	.88	.9699	.38	.9913	.88	.9980
.39	.6517	.89	.8133	.39	.9177	.89	.9706	.39	.9916	.89	.9981
0.40	0.6554	0.90	0.8159	1.40	0.9192	1.90	0.9713	2.40	0.9918	2.90	0.9981
.41	.6591	.91	.8186	.41	.9207	.91	.9719	.41	.9920	.91	.9982
.42	.6628	.92	.8212	.42	.9222	.92	.9726	.42	.9922	.92	.9983
.43	.6664	.93	.8238	.43	.9236	.93	.9732	.43	.9925	.93	.9983
.44	.6700	.94	.8264	.44	.9251	.94	.9738	.44	.9927	.94	.9984
.45	.6736	.95	.8289	.45	.9265	.95	.9744	.45	.9929	.95	.9984
.46	.6772	.96	.8315	.46	.9279	.96	.9750	.46	.9931	.96	.9985
.47	.6808	.97	.8340	.47	.9292	.97	.9756	.47	.9932	.97	.9985
.48	.6844	.98	.8365	.48	.9306	.98	.9761	.48	.9934	.98	.9986
.49	.6879	.99	.8389	.49	.9319	.99	.9767	.49	.9936	.99	.9986

REFERENCES AND BIBLIOGRAPHY

Black, F, and Scholes, M	'The Valuation of Option Contracts and a Test of Market Efficiency' Journal of Finance, May 1972, pp 399–418.
Black, F, and Scholes, M	'The Pricing of Options and Corporate Liabilities', Journal of Political Economy, May/June 1973, pp 637–659.
Black, F	'Fact and Fantasy in the Use of Options' Financial Analysts Journal, 1975.
Cox, J C, Ross, J C, and Rubinstein, M	'Option Pricing: A Simplified Approach' Journal of Financial Economics, Sept 1979, pp 229–263.
Galai, D	'Tests of Market Efficiency of the Chicago Board Options Exchange', Journal of Business, April 1977, pp 167–197.
Galai, D, and Masulis, R	'The Option Pricing Model and the Risk Factor of Stock', Journal of Financial Economics, Jan/March 1976, pp 53–82.
Merton, R C	'Theory of Rational Option Pricing', Bell Journal of Economics and Management Science, Spring 1973, pp 141–183.
Rubinstein, M, and Cox, J C	*Option Markets* (1980) Prentice-Hall, Englewood-Cliffs, New Jersey.

QUESTIONS

1 Musicstand has a share price of 60p, and monthly returns on Musicstand have displayed a variance of 40% over the last five years. The riskless interest rate over the next six months is expected to be 12%. Using the Black-Scholes model, value a six-month call option on Musicstand with a 70p exercise price.

2 Using diagrams, derive the put-call parity result, 6-month call options on Ankle with an exercise price of 150p are currently selling for 30p. Ankle's share price is 100p and the riskless interest rate is 10%.

Using put-call parity, value a six-month put on Ankle.

3 Derive a theorem that shows whether the value of a call option will in general be an increasing or decreasing function of the exercise price, the riskless interest rate, and the time to expiry. What assumptions are you making?

4 Derive the limits of the Black-Scholes model as time to expiry tends to zero, and to infinity. Explain the intuition behind the result you get.

5 Choose two forms of contractual arrangement found in finance and show how option-pricing theory can help in analysing them.

CHAPTER 12

Income and value

The economic value of a firm or a project depends on the expected level and the risk of its future cash flows. Investors have to develop their expectations about the future from knowledge of the past, and information about past performance is often in the form of accounting data. In this chapter we examine the relationship between accounting measures of income and value, and financial valuation. We want to know how good accounting value is as a measure of economic value, and how good past earnings are as a predictor of future cash flows.

Section I discusses 'historic cost' valuation, and Section II considers 'current-cost' and its relationship to economic value. Section III considers past 'cash-flow' as the focus for reporting performance. In Section IV we consider the question, how 'good' a basis is past accounting data for forecasting the level and risk of future cash-flows, and encounter the puzzling research finding that the path through time of most firms' profits is a 'random-walk'. In the final section we suggest that to form expectations about the future we would need to look behind the highly aggregated accounting data and develop an economic model of the process that generates it.

I HISTORIC COST ACCOUNTING

The key to understanding accounting data is the relationship between asset valuation and income measurement. The *income*[1] of a firm during a period is the increase in its asset value over the period, less the net distribution to shareholders, that is the difference between dividends paid and new equity funds received.

So, $\qquad P_t = C_t + (A_t - A_{t-1})$ $\qquad\qquad\qquad\qquad\qquad$ (1)

$\qquad$ where P_t $\quad$ = income in period $t-1 \rightarrow t$
$\qquad\qquad A_t$ $\quad$ = asset value at time t
$\qquad\qquad C_t$ $\quad$ = net distribution to shareholders

We are defining income broadly in (1) and the firm may not put all of this through its profit and loss account. However the important implication of (1) is that a change in the value of assets will imply a change in income

$\qquad \triangle$ assets $\equiv \triangle$ income

We need to be a little more precise about what we mean by 'the assets' of the firm. Exhibit I shows the balance-sheet and profit and loss account for Plessey for the year ended 1 April 1983. The balance-sheet is effectively two lists: a list of the net assets of the firm, and a list of the sources of finance for those assets. We can see that Plessey's net assets of £418

---

1 We will be using the words 'income', 'profit' and 'earnings' interchangeably. Readers who are unfamiliar with accounting terminology and the content of accounting reports should consult a standard accounting text such as Glautier and Underdown (1982).

million were made up of fixed assets of £190.4 million, deferred tax receivables of £46.5 million, and current assets, including stocks, debtors, short-term investments, and bank balances, of £753.6 million. Netted-off against the total or 'gross' assets to give the net assets figure are the firm's liabilities: short-term creditors, loans and overdrafts of £385 million, and longer-term liabilities and provisions of £187.5 million.

However, since we are interested in valuation from a shareholder point of view 'net assets' is not quite the asset measure we need since we can see from Plessey's accounts that 'minority interests' owned £10.2 million of the net assets. This arose because Plessey has consolidated the accounts of subsidiaries that were partly owned by outsiders. The value of the equity asset in Plessey is the 'shareholders funds' of £407.8 million in 1983 and £359.6 million in 1982, an increase of £48.2 million. Plessey declared a dividend of £24.5 million in 1983 but raised £4.1 million of net equity, a net distribution of £20.4 million, so income according to equation (1) is £68 million.

According to the P+L, however, Plessey retained profits of £57 million in 1983, which does not tie up with our £68 million. The difference is explained in the notes to the accounts, and is caused by revaluations and write-offs which are not passed through the P+L.

The underlying reality behind a set of accounts is stocks and flows of assets and liabilities associated with the individual activities of the firm. These assets and liabilities are valued and aggregated into the published accounting numbers. The problems in using accounting numbers come from the level of aggregation, and the method of valuation.

There is not much we can do about the aggregation problem except note it. Ideally we would want the details of assets and liabilities, and the associated costs and revenues, project by project, or at least for each division. In practice we cannot rely on finding even sales, profit and asset figures at the divisional level. Plessey's accounts are fairly forthcoming, and analyse sales and profit into five main product categories. Sales are also analysed by main markets at home and abroad.

HISTORIC-COST

The basic valuation method firms use for financial reporting is *historic-cost* (HC). We know from Chapter 5 that to find the value of a *project* we need the cash flows it will generate in the future and discount them to the present. The firm can be viewed as a bundle of projects, and Table I represents this, as though we could identify all the projects that make up firm Z and lay out the cash flows associated with them in a table.[2] So project h, for example, is a project with a five-year life, starting in 1986. The NPV of project h at its commencement at the beginning of 1986 is £1,601 (discounted at 10%).

In project appraisal we take a single project and evaluate it by looking at all its cash flows through time. The accountant who is asked to measure historic-cost profit has to do the opposite. His job is to produce a useful picture of the performance of the firm based on the cash flows of the whole firm in just one year. So the accountant measuring, say, the 1988 profit of firm Z has as his starting point a series of cash-flows reflecting inflows and outflows at different points on the life-cycles of the various projects that are alive in 1988. The problem with taking this sideways view of the firm is that just as one year's cash flow might not in isolation tell you much about the worth of a project, one year's cash flow for the firm as a whole may not be representative of the performance of the firm through time.

2   In practice of course it will usually be impossible to identify separately the component projects in a firm, because of the inter-relationships and dependencies, the joint costs and benefits, between projects.

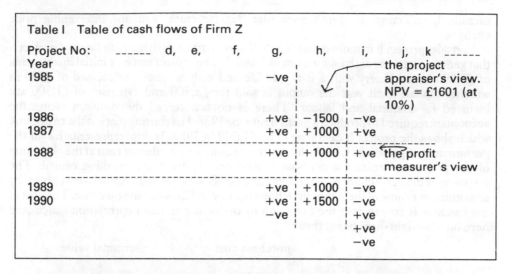

Table I   Table of cash flows of Firm Z

Project No:	d,	e,	f,	g,	h,	i,	j, k
Year							the project
1985				−ve			appraiser's view. NPV = £1601 (at 10%)
1986				+ve	−1500	−ve	
1987				+ve	+1000	+ve	
1988				+ve	+1000	+ve	the profit measurer's view
1989				+ve	+1000	−ve	
1990				+ve	+1500	−ve	
				−ve		+ve	
						+ve	
						−ve	

So accountants try to make a more representative income figure by re-allocating costs where necessary to the period in which the matching revenue was earned. This is the 'accruals' convention of accounting. However since the 'accruals' convention seems to allow plenty of scope for transferring cash flows between periods, accountants are expected to be guided by the 'prudence' convention. Under the prudence convention revenues and profits are not anticipated, but are recognised '. . . only when realised in the form either of cash or of other assets the ultimate cash realisation of which can be assessed with reasonable certainty' (SSAP2).[3] The resulting figure is known as *historic-cost profit*. The costs that have not been expensed in the period, and are expected to generate revenue and so be expensed in future periods, are assets at the end of the period valued at historic cost. So in historic-cost accounting asset values are accumulated unused costs.

Two aspects of historic-cost valuation tend to concern people: the effect of price-changes, and the discretionary nature of the valuation process.

The effect of price changes

There are lags in the productive process between buying the inputs and selling the outputs, and it is because of these lags that financing is needed. But these lags have implications for profit measurement as well. Historic-cost accounting measures profit by reallocating costs between time periods so that revenues are matched with the actual, 'historic' cost of the relevant inputs. If price levels are in general rising through time, the longer the lag between purchase of inputs and sale of outputs the higher the apparent profit of the firm. Historic-cost profit may provide a misleading signal for financial decisions in this situation. It will become harder to make meaningful comparisons between firms because the measured return of a firm will reflect both its operating performance in converting inputs into outputs, *and* the set of prices in which those inputs and outputs are

---

3 'The law' on what companies have to report is consolidated in the Companies Act 1985. The recommendations of the accounting bodies are contained in a series of Statements of Standard Accounting Practice (SSAP) produced by the Accounting Standards Committee (ASC). Companies quoted on The Stock Exchange are required to produce a report twice a year, and have some additional accounting requirements.

measured, reflecting the firm's particular 'lag structure' and any intervening price changes.

Consider project h in more detail. Table II shows the underlying cash flows of project h that generated the net cash flow we saw in Table I. The project involves initial investments of £2,000 in machinery with a five-year life and with no resale value, and of £500 in working capital. Each year the output is sold for £2,500 and expenses of £1,500 are incurred for material and labour. There is no tax. Recall the problem facing the accountant required to produce a profit figure for 1988. His starting place is the cash-book which shows the project h cash flow to be £1,000 in 1988. Is this 'representative' of the performance of project h? Clearly not, since it required an outflow of cash at the beginning of the project to create the necessary investment in fixed and working capital. The response of the accountant is to convert the cash-flow series into 'historic-cost profit' by smoothing out some of the lumpy cash flows over time. Consider the machine. The cost of the machine is spread over the five years by deducting annual depreciation (calculated here on a 'straight-line' basis) thus:

$$\text{depreciation} = \frac{\overset{\text{purchase cost}}{\underset{\downarrow}{2000}} - \overset{\text{terminal value}}{\underset{\downarrow}{0}}}{\underset{\underset{\text{useful life}}{\uparrow}}{5}} = \text{£400 per annum}$$

This gives an annual profit figure of:

revenue	2500
labour and materials	(1500)
depreciation	(400)
Historic-Cost Profit	£ 600

But suppose that the purchase price of the machine the firm uses is inflating at 20% per annum so that by 1988 a new machine to replace the old one would cost $£2,000 \times (1 + .2)^2 = £2,880$. Recall that our firm consumes one fifth of such a machine each year, so if it valued the machine at replacement cost it would have had annual depreciation of $£2,880 \times \frac{1}{5} = £576$ and an annual accounting profit of $£1,000 - £576 = £424$ in 1986. Assuming none of the other cash flows were affected by inflation, £424 is the *current-cost* profit of the project in 1986.

Table II   Table of cash flows for project h (£)

date incurred	1.1.1986	end 1986	−1987	−1988	−1989	−1990	total
machinery	(2000)						
working capital	(500)					500	
revenue		2500	2500	2500	2500	2500	
labour and materials		(1500)	(1500)	(1500)	(1500)	(1500)	
	(2500)	1000	1000	1000	1000	1500	3000
1986 Cash Flows	(1500)						

NPV of project h at 10% = £1,601

Since Z Ltd actually did pay £2,000 for the machine it might seem rather perverse to charge depreciation at replacement cost. Surely it is the good fortune of the firm to have bought the machine when it did? Under current-cost accounting, assets are revalued annually at current prices. This reflects any benefit to the firm of owning assets whose value has increased, but it also implies a higher cost in the income statement of using these assets. We will look at current-cost accounting later.

ARE HISTORIC-COST VALUES DISCRETIONARY?

Valuing assets at what they cost sounds objective, but in practice firms have some discretion as to how they do it. The primary problem is that historic-cost valuation involves allocating costs between present and future periods, so it depends on the firm's necessarily subjective expectations about future revenues. In the particular case of stocks it is not always easy to ascertain what historic-cost was anyhow. Another complication is that the 'historic-cost' accounting that firms practice is usually a mixture of historic- and current-cost. For example, firms are expected to write-down or write-off altogether assets like stock and debtors when their current value falls below cost, and they sometimes write-up or revalue property, though there is no consistent practice amongst firms on this.

Write-off policies for long-lived assets

To determine the depreciation policy for an asset requires estimates of its useful life and its terminal value. But these will be determined by future demand for outputs and by the future supply of more efficient technology neither of which is known with certainty. The problem is the one we encountered in Chapter 5 when we were discussing 'project life' and it is particularly acute with intangibles such as goodwill, advertising or R & D expenditure. Consider advertising. The expenditure on the advertising launch of a new product may generate sales over several years – in that sense an asset has been created which provides service in several periods and which could be depreciated accordingly. But the uncertainty surrounding the duration of the benefits is such that most firms write-off their advertising, and often R & D and goodwill, immediately.

Write-off policies for current assets

If current assets are not likely to be realised for what they cost, the *conservatism* principle of accounting indicates writing them down to what they will realise. Most firms write-down stock rigorously, but the firm which is in difficulties may be reluctant to do so. It has a dilemma – it can least afford to write stocks off, but it is most likely to have redundant stocks since its failure and its low stock values may well spring from the common source of insufficient demand. A similar problem arises with debtors. Some debtors never pay, for good or bad reasons. They may genuinely dispute the quality or delivery of the goods, or they may not have sufficient funds to pay. The firm should constantly be looking out for debts that will turn 'bad' in this way and should eliminate them. But, again, to write-off a £100 debt means sacrificing £100 of profit ($\triangle$ assets $\equiv$ $\triangle$ income). Most firms write off their bad debts, but the occasional firm will be reluctant or slow to do this, particularly if the firm is failing.

Finding the cost of stocks

Stocks are the raw materials, partly completed work ('work-in-progress') and finished goods that the firm is holding. Firms can have thousands, even millions of items in stock

Exhibit I

Consolidated Profit and Loss Account
for the 52 weeks ended 1 April 1983

	Notes	1983 £000	1982 £000
Turnover	1	1,074,750	963,074
Cost of sales		772,757	712,910
Gross profit		301,993	250,164
Other operating expenses (net)	2	182,989	150,024
Operating profit		119,004	100,140
Share of profits less losses of related companies	3	6,651	4,420
Investment income	4	33,431	22,271
Profit before interest payable		159,086	126,831
Interest payable	5	12,724	15,393
Profit on ordinary activities before taxation	1 and 6	146,362	111,438
Taxation on profit on ordinary activities	9	60,528	38,540
Profit on ordinary activities after taxation		85,834	72,898
Minority interests		3,036	2,032
Profit before extraordinary items		82,798	70,866
Extraordinary items less taxation	10	1,349	2,892
Profit attributable to members of the holding company		81,449	73,758
Dividends	11	24,455	20,960
Retained profit for year		56,994	52,798

Earnings per share

Before extraordinary items	33.99p	29.31p
After extraordinary items	33.43p	30.51p

Based on weighted average number of
shares outstanding – 243,627,500 shares
(1982 – 241,759,091 shares).

The profit and loss account includes the results of the Company and of its subsidiaries. Under the provisions of the Companies Act 1948, the Company is not required to publish its own profit and loss account. The profit attributable to members of the holding company, dealt with in the accounts of the Company, is £69,071,000 (1982—£70,787,000).

These extracts from the 1983 Plessey Report and Accounts and those on pp 208–209 are reproduced with kind permission of the Plessey Company plc. Responsibility for the accurate presentation of any extract rests with the author.

Consolidated Balance Sheet
as at 1 April 1983

	Notes	1983 £000	1983 £000	1983 £000	1982 £000
Fixed assets					
Tangible assets	12		171,788		143,549
Investments	13		18,566		10,732
				190,354	154,281
Deferred taxation asset	14			46,506	26,139
Current assets					
Stocks	15	254,135			223,445
Debtors	16	227,965			177,332
Investments	17	227,747			192,530
Cash at bank and in hand		43,805			45,217
			753,652		638,524
Current liabilities					
Creditors: amounts falling due within one year					
Loans and overdrafts	18	25,880			30,252
Other	20	359,155			307,455
			385,035		337,707
Net current assets				368,617	300,817
Total assets less current liabilities				605,477	481,237
Creditors: amounts falling due after more than one year					
Loans and overdrafts	19		31,414		25,515
Other	20		58,915		22,594
				90,329	48,109
Provisions for liabilities and charges	23			97,129	65,428
Net assets				418,019	367,700
Capital and reserves					
Called-up share capital	27			122,096	121,252
Share premium account	28			57,048	53,798
Revaluation reserve	28			2,902	2,727
Other reserves	28			864	834
Profit and loss account reserve	28			213,016	173,433
Attributable share of related companies' reserves	28			11,849	7,528
Shareholders' funds				407,775	359,572
Minority interests				10,244	8,128
				418,019	367,700

and keeping individual records of the cost of all these items would be prohibitively costly, so in order to value them it is usual to make some arbitrary assumptions. The firm may assume that the stocks on hand are the ones most recently acquired, thus they can be valued at current prices. This is the 'FIFO' (first in, first out) assumption. An alternative is to assume that the final stocks are representative of the whole year's purchases, then they can be valued at average prices for the period. Another alternative is to assume 'LIFO', that final stocks are the earliest purchases. Though LIFO is not commonly used in practice in the UK it is worth noting that valuing stocks at LIFO is effectively replacement cost accounting.

For example, suppose a firm regularly buys 1,000 items of a particular component each month. At the annual stock check on 31 December the storeman finds they have 2,000 in stock. The price of this component has gone up three times during the year as follows:

	period	price (£)
	→ 31 March	2.56
1 April	→ 31 May	2.90
1 June	→ 30 November	3.00
1 Dec.	→	3.10

How should the components be valued? If we make the FIFO assumption, that the ones on hand are the most recent, then the stock represents November and December purchases and would be valued thus:

			£
FIFO	bought in November:	1,000 @ 3.00	3,000
basis	bought in December:	1,000 @ 3.10	3,100
		2,000	£6,100

But if the firm feels its stock comprises items bought throughout the year it might value at an average price:

Average basis $\left\{ \begin{array}{l} \text{average price of 3 months @ 2.56, 2 @ 2.90, 6 @ 3.00.} \\ \text{1 @ 3.10 =} \\ \quad\quad \text{2000 items @ 2.88 = } \underline{£5,763} \end{array} \right.$

Revaluations

The picture is complicated by the fact that historic-cost accountants are prone to 'revalue' land and buildings, that is, to substitute current-values for book-values, though there is no requirement on firms to do this regularly or indeed at all. Also we saw that stock and debtors should be written down to realisable value. However stocks may be valued at realisable value even when it is above cost. This can occur in valuing work-in-progress on long-term contracts. Accounting practice permits firms to 'take profit' early by increasing work-in-progress value in the direction of final realisable value.

Monitoring by auditors and analysts

Historic cost accounting appears to offer plenty of scope for variation in the way firms value their assets, and thus measure their income. This raises problems of comparability and the possibility of manipulation. The smaller the profit of the firm relative to its assets, the greater the impact of asset-valuation changes which may appear relatively innocuous.

Consider a simple example:

Pigott Resins has	(£ million)
Profit	1.0
Assets	
– fixed	3.0
– debtors	4.0
– stocks	5.0
– creditors	(2.0)
Return on capital employed = 10%	

Pigott decides to revalue upwards its stocks by 5% = £250,000. This increases profit by £250,000 = 25%. Return on capital is now just under 12½%.

$$(= £\frac{1.25}{3.0 + 4.0 + 5.25}\text{mn.})$$

However outsiders can reduce their vulnerability to misleading accounting by spending money to monitor the firm. First, the law requires companies to be audited by independent firms of professional auditors. The auditors' job is, amongst other things, to confirm that assets are being valued on consistent principles and that any change in principles is disclosed in the annual report. Second, firms come under close scrutiny from the *analysts* employed by financial institutions. The job of analysts is to become as familiar as they can with the firms in a particular sector and to narrow the information gap between outsiders and insiders as far as possible. They undertake economic analysis, use a wide range of information sources, and are usually in regular contact with managers in the firms in question. As a result analysts are unlikely to be hindered by the apparent limitations of accounting numbers. As we will see in Chapter 18 there is a good deal of research evidence that, probably because of this monitoring, the market incorporates the new information associated with the annual report well in advance of its publication, and also that the market is not misled by differences in accounting treatment.

II CURRENT COST

An alternative to historic cost is to value assets at current prices. We need to distinguish buying and selling prices. We call the buying price of an asset its replacement cost (RC), and the price it can be sold for its realisable value (RV).

If asset markets were perfect the buying and selling price would be the same, but in practice replacement costs exceed realisable values by some margin. Transactions in any asset will incur transactions costs which must be borne by buyers and sellers. These will include the costs of market intermediaries who provide the necessary expertise and organisation. For regularly traded items like vehicles, workshop machinery and office buildings these will be the main costs. But other assets may be much more 'thinly-traded' and in this case the gap between RC and RV can widen dramatically. The realisable value of an asset depends on its value in its next best use, which may be well below its replacement cost. Consider the case of a chemical plant which costs £100 million to construct but whose design is totally specific to the manufacture of one chemical. If demand for that product collapses there are likely to be no other uses for the plant, except perhaps as a museum of industrial archaeology. If the site value is low, but the authorities insist the plant is demolished on environmental grounds the realisable value could even be negative! The owner has to pay someone to take it away.

In Chapter 4 we said the right way to measure cost was *opportunity cost*. How do the concepts, realisable value, replacement cost, economic value, relate to that? Bonbright (1965) was the first to show that you can get an accounting measure of opportunity cost by combining them. This composite measure is usually known as 'deprival value' or 'value to the business'.

In 1980 UK firms were asked to produce a supplementary 'current-cost' balance-sheet and income-statement under accounting standard SSAP16 using value-to-the-business as the measure of cost. SSAP16 defined value-to-the-business as '(a) net current replacement cost; or if a permanent diminution to below net current replacement cost has been recognised, the recoverable amount . . . [which is] the greater of the net realisable value of an asset and, where applicable, the amount recoverable from its further use'.

Figure I depicts this. All it says is that to find the opportunity cost of an asset to the firm you should ask what the maximum loss would be if the firm were deprived of it.

Consider an example:
The Gomez Garment Manufacturing Co uses a computer controlled cutting table. Gomez reckons it could get £30,000 for the one it has, though it would cost £40,000 to replace. Suppose the economic value (EV) of the machine to Gomez, the present value of the contribution the machine will earn, were either £20,000, £35,000, or £60,000. How would Gomez find the value-to-the-business of the machine in each case?

If the EV is only £20,000 Gomez would be better off selling the machine for £30,000. So if Gomez were deprived of the machine, it would lose the opportunity to sell it, and its opportunity cost is £30,000. Value-to-the-business is £30,000 in this case. If the EV is £35,000, however, it would not be worth Gomez's while replacing the machine, but since it has one, Gomez is better off using it. In this case the value-to-the-business is £35,000.

Hopefully the 'normal' situation is the third one, where EV is £60,000. In this case EV > RC, and in terms of our normal finance terminology the machine has a 'positive net present value' of £60,000 − £40,000 = £20,000. If Gomez were deprived of the machine it would want to replace it and so the value-to-the-business is £40,000. In

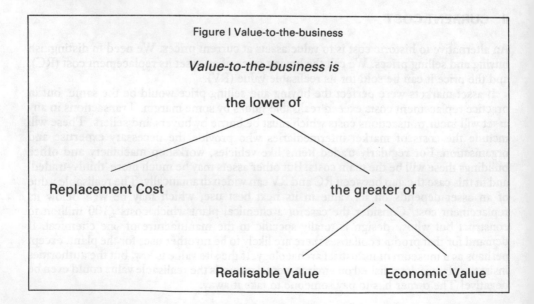

Figure I Value-to-the-business

Value-to-the-business is

the lower of

Replacement Cost   the greater of

Realisable Value   Economic Value

practice, assuming most assets in use have a positive NPV, we would expect replacement cost to be the dominant valuation method.

NPV AND TOBIN'S q

Deprival value reminds us that the relationship between economic value and current-cost is at the heart of investment decision-making.

In the case of an *investment* decision, investment is worthwhile if the present value of cash flows generated is greater than the initial cost of acquiring the necessary assets that is, if

$$EV > RC$$

Since $NPV = EV - RC$, this is simply another way of stating our project decision rule, *accept all projects with a positive NPV*.

In the case of *disinvestment* decisions, which we examine in Chapter 25, the rule is parallel except now the question is whether the present value of cash flows from assets in their present use is greater than in alternative uses, as measured by what we could dispose of the assets for.

So disinvest if $EV < RV$

We have already noted the general relationship between HC, RC and RV. If there is inflation in asset prices then we will find $RC > HC$, and in general $RC > RV$ by a margin that depends on the nature of the particular asset markets. But the big question is how EV relates to RC. Why do positive net present values occur? Put another way, what enables firms to undertake projects that yield 'rents', that is, yield a return above the cost of capital? The search for profitable opportunities is the central quest of economic life, and if we had a reliable treasure map we would have solved our own and everybody else's economic problems a long time ago. But it *is* possible to describe the relationship of EV and RC at a theoretical level. In a world with perfect markets EV, RC and RV will all coincide. In perfect markets there are no positive NPVs, no abnormal profits. As soon as any appear they are eliminated by competition, and in a perfect market there are no barriers to the competitive process.[4] Positive NPVs arise when markets are not perfect, and the search for positive-valued projects can be described as the search for exploitable market imperfections. An implication of this is that in a world of perfect markets valuing the firm would be easy – we could read the economic value of the firm off the current cost balance sheet. In practice though, we have no clear idea of the relationship between accounting values and economic value so we have to estimate the level and risk of the future cash flows of the firm.

It is sometimes interesting to make a measure at the level of the whole firm, similar to the NPV of a project. The relationship between the economic value and the replacement cost of the whole firm can be expressed as the statistic known as 'Tobin's q'[5] where

$$\text{'q'} = \frac{\text{MARKET VALUE OF THE FIRM}}{\text{REPLACEMENT COST OF THE FIRM}} = \frac{EV}{RC}$$

A 'q' of unity is the equivalent at the level of the firm to an NPV of zero in the case of a

---

4   Introductory economics texts describe the competitive equilibrium in a world of perfect markets. On the relationship between EV, RC and RV, see Bromwich (1975).
5   The 'q' notion is usually attributed to James Tobin. See, for example, Tobin (1971).

project. The firm with a 'positive NPV' will have q > 1, and is earning a return above the required return of shareholders. Conversely, the firm with q < 1 is not covering its cost of capital.

When we look at Tobin's q for the UK industrial sector an interesting picture emerges. Figure II plots the aggregate q for the UK through the 60s and 70s. In the early 1970s the market valuation of UK industrial and commercial companies fell below the replacement cost of their assets and q has remained < 1 ever since. The implication is that the average return of UK companies has been below the cost of capital since the early 1970s, providing what the Bank of England Quarterly Bulletin described as a 'very weak inducement to invest'. Put another way, the aggregate NPV of UK firms appears to be negative! One source of comfort is that just the same phenomenon occurred in the other developed countries. Modigliani and Cohn (1979) argued that the falling q reflected inflation-induced errors in share valuation. They asserted that Western stock markets are under-valuing shares so that a truer 'q' would be above unity. However, this assertion has not received widespread support. Researchers are currently working on 'q' and until we understand it better it would be dangerous to draw sweeping conclusions using 'q'. The question is whether the equilibrium value of 'q' really is unity. For one thing the replacement cost of the individual assets of a firm drawn from a current-cost balance sheet may not adequately measure the cost of reproducing the whole firm. For another, the gap between replacement costs and realisable values means we would not necessarily want to dismantle a firm just because EV/RC < 1.

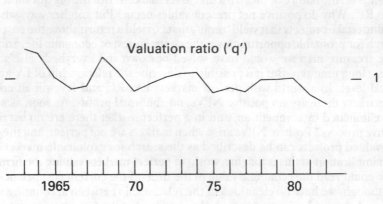

Valuation ratio ('q')

1965   70   75   80

Source: Bank of England Quarterly Bulletin, June 1982

Figure II 'Tobin's q' for UK industrial and commercial companies, 1963–81

CURRENT-COST ACCOUNTING

We now turn to the practicalities of producing current-cost accounts. In current-cost accounting, since assets are regularly revalued, the distinction between 'operating' and 'holding' gains is particularly important. Holding gains are profits made from owning assets whose value increases; operating profits are the profits made by the company's business operations and which are passes through the P & L account. The same distinction is employed in historic-cost accounting when surpluses on revaluing property are taken directly to a reserve in the balance-sheet.

In principle, to find current-cost operating profit you should cost each input at the price ruling on the day the corresponding output was sold. In practice the information costs of doing that would be large, so SSAP 16 recommended firms to make four adjustments to historic-cost profit to correspond to four main categories in the balance sheet: fixed assets, stocks, monetary working capital and net borrowing:

— An additional *depreciation* charge to bring depreciation up to what it would be if it were calculated on the replacement cost of fixed assets.
— A *cost of sales* adjustment to provide for the cost of replacing at current prices the stocks consumed during the year.
— A similar adjustment for *monetary working capital*, which is essentially debtors and creditors, to reflect the fact that changing output and input prices will require the firm to maintain proportionately changed levels of debtors and creditors.
— A *gearing* adjustment. Since the amount of loans made to and by the firm is fixed in money terms the real value of the firm's net borrowing will fall during a period of inflation. In an efficient market we expect this loss of value to be reflected in higher interest rates. The market interest rate r has two components, $r = r' + i$, where r' is the real rate of interest, and i is the expected rate of inflation during the period of the loan. In historic-cost accounting the full interest payment r is deducted as an expense, but to find current cost profit the firm must add back an amount to reflect that part of r which is in effect an early repayment of capital.

Normally, if price levels are increasing, the depreciation, cost of sales, and monetary working capital adjustments will be negative ie deductions from profit, reflecting the increased cost of replacing the respective inputs. Since net borrowing is effectively a negative asset, the reverse applies to the gearing adjustment. If the firm is a net borrower the nominal interest charge overstates the real cost of borrowing and this is reflected in a positive gearing adjustment. If the firm is a net lender this adjustment should be negative, though under the particular rules of SSAP16 companies did not need to make an adjustment in this case.

We saw the historic-cost accounts of The Plessey Company. But Plessey's 1983 current cost accounts show the following adjustments to profit:

	£m
'working capital adjustment' (= stock adjustment plus monetary working capital adjustment)	(4.3)
additional depreciation	(11.0)
gearing adjustment	–
net reduction in profit	(15.3)

Because Plessey was a net lender in 1983 it did not show a gearing adjustment. These adjustments reduce Plessey's net profit from £81 million to £66 million. Plessey paid a dividend of £24 million in 1981, so 'dividend cover', which is the ratio of earnings to dividend, calculated on the two bases was

Historic-cost dividend cover : 3.4
Current-cost dividend cover : 2.8

Plessey's current-cost balance sheet shows that if net assets are revalued at current-cost, shareholders' funds rise from £408 million to £439 million. Calculating return on investment as earnings after extraordinary items over shareholders' funds:

Plessey 1983 Return on Investment:

Historic-cost $\quad \dfrac{81}{408} \times 100 = 19.8\%$

Current-cost $\quad \dfrac{66}{439} \times 100 = 15.0\%$

How does current-cost accounting affect companies in general? Berry and Gray (1982) made a study of the effect of CC accounting in the reports of companies in the FT Actuaries published in 1980 and 1981. They were not able to sample all the companies in the FT Actuaries, and their coverage varied from industry to industry as we see in Table III.

In certain industries CC adjustments were sufficient to eliminate all profits. In 1980/81, for example, mechanical engineering, metals and metal-forming, motors. In others, electricals, health and household products, textiles, chemicals, profits fell dramatic-

Table III The effect of CC accounting on firms in the FT Actuaries Index					
Industry	Sample as % of FT Actuaries coverage	(1) HC Net Profit Total (£m)	(2) CC Net Profit Total (£m)	(2) ÷ (1) (where meaning- ful)	Average HC Dividend Cover	Average CC Dividend Cover
Building materials	59	308.4	144.1	47%	3.29	1.44
Contracting and Construction	54	196.0	137.0	70%	4.17	2.70
Electricals	30	137.8	45.0	33%	3.80	1.44
Engineering Contractors	55	70.6	45.1	64%	3.38	2.43
Mechanical Engineering	30	158.6	(18.9)	–	3.07	1.02
Metals and Metal Forming	69	14.8	(143.4)	–	2.17	0.90
Motors	76	31.4	(107.3)	–	2.11	0.78
Other Industrial Materials	80	174.3	14.8	8%	2.38	0.75
Brewers and Distillers	35	516.9	263.7	51%	3.19	1.64
Food Manufacturing	48	536.1	298.0	56%	4.25	1.56
Food Retailing	64	94.9	76.1	56%	3.76	2.68
Health and House- hold Products	43	32.1	6.6	21%	2.75	0.69
Packaging & Paper	40	12.4	(70.8)	–	1.73	0.22
Stores	36	335.6	190.1	57%	3.16	1.67
Textiles	43	(103.9)	(220.7)	–	1.55	0.56
Tobaccos	100	359.2	156.2	43%	3.92	2.45
Chemicals	60	(11.0)	(295.0)	–	2.15	0.82
Shipping & Transport	50	110.1	59.9	54%	3.30	1.75
Miscellaneous	29	129.1	37.0	29%	3.05	1.27
Oils	42	1,510.7	606.3	40%	3.59	1.25
Totals		4,614.1	1,223.8		3.04	1.40

Source: Berry and Gray (1982)

ally under CC accounting. Profits were most robust in contracting and construction, electrical contracting, and food retailing. Berry and Gray found that, in aggregate, profits attributable to shareholders under CC accounting were only 27% of HC.

What use are current cost accounts?

Current-cost data is just as highly aggregated as historic-cost, and areas of discretion still remain in current-cost accounting – managers still have to make judgements about depreciation policies for fixed and intangible assets, about the realisable value of debtors and stocks and so forth. But current-cost accounting provides a balance-sheet in which the firm's assets are displayed at current prices and an income statement in which revenues and costs are measured in consistent prices. This reduces problems in comparing income and asset figures through time and between firms.

But although replacement cost has a long and respectable tradition in national income accounting, in business accounting it remains controversial. Some accountants argue that other concepts of 'cost' should be used, some argue that another method altogether would be better, and some argue that no attempt at all should be made to improve on historic cost.[6] At the time of writing SSAP16 has been withdrawn.

III CASH FLOW

Historic and current-cost accounting are both attempts to improve on cash flow as a measure of the firm's economic performance. An alternative is to use the firm's series of cash flows over several years as the basis for judging its performance.[7] This way profit-measurement problems are avoided, but the problem of the unrepresentative nature of single-period cash flows is reduced as well.

An example of this approach was the analysis of the cash flow of the beleaguered British Leyland by Tom Lee (Financial Times 23.11.81), reproduced as Table IV. Lee presented the annual cash deficit of BL from 1974 to 1980 in terms of the firm's annual operating cash flow less payments for capital expenditure, interest, tax and dividends. BL generated a cash deficit of £1,762 million over the seven years, which was financed by share issues and bank borrowing. A cash flow analysis like Table IV can give a clear picture of the failure or success of a firm. In the case of BL we see a firm whose operating cash flows were negative nearly every year, but which was committed to a heavy and increasing capital expenditure programme. The necessary borrowing itself introduced an increasingly significant interest burden over the period. One thing which emerges clearly is that it is cash flow rather than profit which measures the financing requirement of a firm. The total cash deficit, and thus the financing requirement of BL over the period was £1,762 million, whereas the historic cost loss after tax and dividends amounted to a little over half of that, at £963 million.

Of course the difference between the cash flow and profit of BL is largely explained by the heavy capital expenditure towards the end of the period, undertaken in the hope of moving BL into profitability in the 1980s. So it could be claimed that the cash flows in Table IV are unrepresentative in precisely the way that profit-measurement attempts to

6   Baxter (1975) and Sandilands (1975) provide good discussions of some of the alternatives. For a thorough empirical review of the issues, see Carsberg and Page (1984).
7   See Egginton (1984), Lee (1985), Lawson (1985) and Egginton (1985) for a stimulating debate on the rival merits of profit and cash-flow.

Table IV BL Ltd Cash Flow Results	1974 £m	1975 £m	1976 £m	1977 £m	1978 £m	1979 £m	1980 £m	Total £m
Sales receipts	1,603	1,805	2,835	2,557	3,031	2,940	2,991	17,762
Less: operating payments	1,560	1,890	2,848	2,594	3,029	2,960	3,034	17,915
	43	(85)	(13)	(37)	2	(20)	(43)	(153)
Less: capital [expenditure] payments	99	84	118	144	226	238	250	1,159
	(56)	(169)	(131)	(181)	(224)	(258)	(293)	(1,312)
Less: interest payments	17	38	47	54	56	66	94	372
	(73)	(207)	(178)	(235)	(280)	(324)	(387)	(1,684)
Less: tax payments	7	7	13	13	11	10	5	66
	(80)	(214)	(191)	(248)	(291)	(334)	(392)	(1,750)
Less: dividend payments	9	3	–	–	–	–	–	12
TOTAL CASH DEFICIT	(89)	(217)	(191)	(248)	(291)	(334)	(392)	(1,762)
Financed by: Share issues	–	–	198	–	444	148	295	1,085
Bank borrowings	89	217	(7)	248	(153)	186	97	677
Financing	(89)	(217)	(191)	(248)	(291)	(334)	(392)	(1,762)
Historic cost loss after tax and dividends	(24)	(124)	(44)	(52)	(38)	(145)	(536)	(963)
Source: Financial Times 23.11.81								

correct. Moreover, though Table IV presents a good picture of what has happened in the past, it is not clear how much it tells us about what we really want to know, which is how BL will do in the future. In practice, both the cash flow and the income of the firm give valuable information about performance, and the analyst can use them both in the expectations-forming process.

How to calculate cash flow

Though cash-flow is the 'basic series', the firm does not publish its cash-flow as such, and the analyst has to construct it. To see the link between profit and cash recall that the profit of a period 'explains' the change between one balance-sheet and the next. So profit can be re-expressed as a series of changes during the period in the levels of the various assets and liabilities of the firm. Companies do this by producing a 'statement of sources and applications of funds', commonly known as a *funds flow*. This analyses the funds flow of the firm into its main sources: operating at a profit; new finance; reducing assets, and increasing liabilities; and into its main uses: operating at a loss; disbursing dividends, interest and tax; increasing assets and reducing liabilities. The funds flow of Plessey Ltd for 1983 is Exhibit II. We have used it to construct an analysis of Plessey's 1983 cash flow in Table V.

Table V   Plessey 1983 Cash Flow Analysis

	(£000)
Cash flow from operations	134,396
Interest received	20,707
Tax paid	(34,072)
Net capital expenditure	(72,437)
'Free cash flow'	48,594
Dividend payments	(21,118)
Net financing	6,329
Increase in cash balances	33,805

The reader can check if he gets the same answer.

The relationship between profit and cash flow

Since historic-cost accounting reallocates cash flows through firms, cash flow and profit can sometimes give contrary signals. On the one hand, products reaching the end of their life-cycle and requiring little further investment can be large cash generators – the so-called 'cash-cows' in business strategy parlance. On the other hand fast-growing and heavily investing firms may be profitable but be heavy users of cash. Indeed the failure of companies is sometimes attributed to *over-trading* – growing faster than their resources will allow. But as we have seen the right signal for the supply of finance to the firm is 'value' not profit. If the firm has a positive value this shows that its early negative cash flows can be financed and still leave a surplus. Firms with positive value can borrow against future cash in an efficient capital market. If the capital market were withholding finance from such firms it would indicate market inefficiency. On the whole the evidence is that the market is not inefficient, and if firms are failing through overtrading we need to look for other explanations. Managers may be misled by positive profits and simply overlook the need for financing until it is too late. Or the mistake may be an investment one in that high initial profits may induce over-optimism about longer-term prospects. Additionally, fast growth may impose a capital-structure which is 'over-geared', that is, too much of the firm's capital is borrowed rather than equity-financed so that the firm is particularly vulnerable to fluctuations in future profits.

IV   FORECASTING FUTURE EARNINGS

Our real interest in the accounting numbers produced by firms is for the assistance they can give in forming expectations about the future. The dividend valuation model requires us to forecast the level and risk of the future dividend stream of the firm, but given the dependency of dividends on earnings we normally use earnings as a proxy.

In this section we discuss the forecasting of earnings. We immediately meet an apparent contradiction. On the one hand there is a widespread belief that it is possible to find positive-value projects, and that some firms are consistently successful at finding them. These firms are usually described as 'growth-stocks' and accorded a market value that

Exhibit II

Source and Application of Funds
for the 52 weeks ended 1 April 1983

	Currency retranslation (note 1) £000	Acquisitions and disposals (note 2) £000	Funds flow (note 3) £000	1983 Total £000	1982 Total £000
Funds from operations					
Operating profit	—	—	119,004	119,004	100,140
Dividends from related companies	—	—	107	107	903
Investment income less interest payable	—	—	20,707	20,707	6,878
Depreciation of tangible fixed assets	—	—	25,994	25,994	23,130
Net amount written off fixed asset investments	—	—	286	286	7
	—	—	166,098	166,098	131,058
Funds from other sources					
Sales of tangible fixed assets	—	75	2,218	2,293	10,460
Grants on purchases of tangible fixed assets			1,615	1,615	1,249
Sales of fixed asset investments	—	78	2	80	—
Issues of shares	—	—	4,094	4,094	3,548
Currency retranslation	708	—	—	708	4,179
	708	153	7,929	8,790	19,436
Total inflow of funds	708	153	174,027	174,888	150,494
Application of funds					
Increase in tangible fixed assets	5,407	6,730	45,511	57,648	35,085
Investment in new subsidiary business	—	14,361	29,516	15,155	—
Increase in fixed asset investments	13	—	2,248	2,261	317
Minority interests	829	—	2,264	1,435	1,506
Corporate taxation	853	7,763	27,162	34,072	18,858
Dividends	7	—	21,125	21,118	18,429
Extraordinary items	—	189	1,172	1,361	5,230
	3,731	321	128,998	133,050	68,331
Net inflow of funds	3,023	168	45,029	41,838	82,163
Utilised as follows:					
Movement in working capital					
Stocks–*increase*/decrease	11,229	20,104	643	30,690	23,313
Debtors–*increase*/decrease	8,809	9,731	32,093	50,633	4,545
Creditors–increase	6,378	15,748	17,543	39,669	30,953
Provisions–increase	2,192	14,564	15,338	32,094	32,766
	11,468	477	1,431	9,560	91,577
Movement in net liquid funds:					
Borrowings–increase/*decrease*	14,955	282	13,146	1,527	1,703
Current asset investments–*increase*	150	—	35,067	35,217	153,913
Cash at bank and in hand–*increase*/decrease	314	27	1,753	1,412	21,530
	3,023	168	45,029	41,838	82,163

Notes
1 The currency retranslation column indicates the extent to which the increases and decreases in assets and liabilities have been directly affected by the movement in currency exchange rates during the year.
2 The acquisitions and disposals column shows the net effect on the level of assets and liabilities arising from the acquisition and disposal of businesses during the year.
3 The funds flow column, therefore, reflects the source and application of funds attributable to the underlying, ongoing business of the Group.

Consolidated profit and loss accounts

	1982/83	1981/82	1980/81	1979/80	1978/79
	£M	£M	£M	£M	£M
Turnover	**1,074.8**	**963.1**	**844.5**	**751.0**	**648.3**
Operating profit	**119.0**	**100.1**	**86.0**	**66.3**	**44.6**
Related companies	6.7	4.4	3.1	3.5	10.5
Investment income	33.4	22.3	7.9	2.6	2.2
Interest payable	12.7	15.4	12.5	12.3	11.0
Profit on ordinary activities before taxation	**146.4**	**111.4**	**84.5**	**60.1**	**46.3**
Taxation on profit on ordinary activities	60.5	38.5	29.0	19.0	14.2
Profit on ordinary activities after taxation	**85.9**	**72.9**	**55.5**	**41.1**	**32.1**
Minority interests	3.1	2.0	1.6	1.5	1.2
Profit before extraordinary items	**82.8**	**70.9**	**53.9**	**39.6**	**30.9**
Extraordinary items less taxation	1.4	2.9	1.5	4.7	2.9
Profit attributable to members of the holding company	**81.4**	**73.8**	**52.4**	**34.9**	**28.0**
Dividends	24.4	21.0	18.5	16.5	15.0
Retained profit for year	**57.0**	**52.8**	**33.9**	**18.4**	**13.0**
Earnings per share					
Before extraordinary items	**34.0p**	**29.3p**	**22.5p**	**16.7p**	**13.1p**
After extraordinary items	**33.4p**	**30.5p**	**21.9p**	**14.7p**	**11.8p**
Dividend per share	**9.9p***	**8.6p**	**7.6p**	**6.9p**	**6.3p**

*For comparative purposes, the 1982/83 proposed dividend is shown on the basis of the equivalent dividend prior to the new capitalisation proposals.

Consolidated balance sheets

	1983	1982	1981	1980	1979
	£M	£M	£M	£M	£M
Fixed tangible assets	171.8	143.6	141.0	133.0	133.5
Fixed asset investments	18.6	10.7	11.8	12.5	11.5
Deferred taxation asset	46.5	26.1	3.7	1.6	—
Cash and short term investments	271.5	237.7	62.3	21.0	19.1
Other current assets	482.1	400.8	428.6	397.3	362.5
Loans and overdrafts	57.3	55.8	54.1	62.3	71.7
Other creditors	418.1	330.0	255.3	225.8	199.5
Provisions for liabilities	97.1	65.4	33.1	22.5	13.8
	418.0	367.7	304.9	254.8	241.6
Called-up share capital	122.1	121.3	120.3	119.1	118.5
Reserves	285.7	238.3	177.5	128.7	116.6
Shareholders' funds	407.8	359.6	297.8	247.8	235.1
Minority interests	10.2	8.1	7.1	7.0	6.5
	418.0	367.7	304.9	254.8	241.6

reflects their growth potential. On the other hand research suggests that many of the statistical models popularly used to extrapolate past profit flows into the future do not work, and that the best model is the one which simply asserts that earnings are a 'random-walk' through time.

Time series analysis of earnings

There are several popular approaches to modelling past earnings, each reflecting those aspects of the past which the forecaster feels are most relevant to predicting the future.[8]

If we expect that the earnings, X, of the firm at time t, $E(X_t)$, will be some average of recent earnings we might use a *moving-average* model in which $E(X_t)$ is an average of earnings in the previous n periods, each with weight W_t:

$$E(X_t) = \sum_{i=1}^{n} W_{t-i}X_{t-i}$$

Where
$$\sum_{i=1}^{n} W_{t-i} = 1 \tag{2}$$

The simplest moving average assumes equal weights. For example, if we expected X_t to be an equally weighted average of the last three years, then:

$$E(X_t) = \tfrac{1}{3}(X_{t-1} + X_{t-2} + X_{t-3})$$

But if we attached greater importance to recent observations we might attach weights of, say, ·6, ·3, ·1 thus:

$$E(X_t) = ·6. X_{t-1} + ·3. X_{t-2} + ·1. X_{t-3}$$

Often forecasters look at the nature of *changes* in past data, and extrapolate from this into the future. Forecasting models of this sort are known as *autoregressive* models, in which $E(X_t)$ is a function of X_{t-1} and some past rate of change in X. A common example is the process of *finding the trend* – the rate of growth (or decline) in past observations which is assumed to be a guide to the future.

Plessey's 'five-year summary' Exhibit II, shows the following earnings per share data for the five years to 1981 for earnings before, and after, extraordinary items. We have calculated the year-on-year growth rates so that, for example

$$16.0\% = \frac{34.0p - 29.3p}{29.3p} \times 100$$

	1982/83	1981/82	1980/81	1979/80	1978/79
EPS. before extraordinary items	34.0p	29.3p	22.5p	16.7p	13.1p
% change year-on-year		16.0%	30.2%	34.7%	27.5%
EPS. after extraordinary items	33.4p	30.5p	21.9p	14.7p	11.8p
% change year-on-year		9.5%	39.3%	50.0%	24.6%

Suppose the analyst wants to find the future growth rate in earnings of Plessey, which of these growth rates should he use? The first question is whether to use earnings before or

8   This section is a brief survey of some commonly used approaches to forecasting. For a fuller survey of forecasting in the context of accounting numbers see Foster (1978) or Firth (1977).

after extraordinary items. Though it is earnings after extraordinary items that constitute the net earnings available to equity, the trend should be better measured before extraordinary items since the whole purpose in identifying extraordinary items is to identify significant items of a non-recurring nature. The next step is to check that there have been no capital changes which might distort the comparison of earnings per share over the five years under review.

The analyst must now form his judgement about future growth in earnings from past growth rates, and it is common to do this by taking an average of previous years' growth rates. But a moment's inspection of the year-on-year changes in Plessey's earnings before extraordinary items shows the difficulty of this approach. Plessey's growth rate has risen and fallen over the five years. So the average 1978/79 – 1980/81 rate is (27.5% + 34.7%) $\div$ 2 = 31.1% per annum, and 1980/81 $\to$ 1982/83 = 23.1%, while the average 1978/79 $\to$ 1982/83 is 27.1%. Which of these is the 'correct' trend in Plessey earnings? The analyst might appeal for more data, say ten years, and would doubtless get a different figure again. But the extra information will relate to more remote years whose relevance to future growth rates is obscure. Alternatively he might try to extrapolate the observed rate of change in growth rates.

But which way Plessey's growth rate is going is far from clear in the data, and the analyst can only choose between these rival contenders for the 'trend' by referring to other information. In particular he must decide which elements of the past are most representative of the future. So the widespread practice of estimating future growth rates by 'finding the trend' in past data is highly judgemental. But calling it 'judgemental' is in no way a criticism. As we saw in Chapter 4 the costs of quantifying information very often make judgemental decisions most efficient. The important thing is to recognise that the quantified information, the past series of earnings in this case, is only a part of the information that is being used in the forecast. It may indeed be a minor part whose main function is to provide the analyst with a framework for marshalling his thoughts on the issue of what it is about the firm's past that is relevant in forecasting its future.

If the role of the forecasting model is seen in this light it may prove counter-productive for the forecaster to look beyond the simple moving-average and auto-regressive models to something more sophisticated. But the forecaster who does and has access to computing facilities can make use of techniques of *statistical analysis* which are now widely available in 'package' form. Statistical packages of this sort are able to test the observed time-series against a wide range of model-specifications and para meterisations of these models, in order to find the model that fits the data best.

The empirical evidence: earnings are random

Anyone choosing a forecasting model for earnings should note that research has shown that the actual time-series behaviour of earnings is best described by *random-walk* models. In the *martingale*, or simple random-walk process,

$$E(X_t) = X_{t-1}$$

so that the best estimate of earnings this period is earnings last period. A related model is the *sub-martingale*, or random-walk with drift process, in which

$$E(X_t) \geqslant X_{t-1} \text{ estimated as } E(X_t) = X_{t-1} + \delta$$

where δ is a *drift factor* with a non-negative expected value. The martingale model implies that the only information of value in prediction is last period's earnings. The sub-martingale allows a role for the past growth in earnings in predicting a general drift factor for firms in the sample which is added to the previous year's earnings of the specific firm to generate its expected earnings at time t. The drift factor might reflect general factors such as inflation and economic growth. In the first case earnings are random around X_{t-1}, in the second around $X_{t-1} + \delta$.[9]

The pioneering empirical work was by Little (1962) and Little and Raynor (1966). Little and Raynor found that the earnings behaviour of the 529 UK quoted firms they studied during the period was best described by the random-walk model. US studies, for example Ball and Watts (1972), also found earnings to be best modelled by a martingale or sub-martingale. Of course, these results are average across large samples. Brealey found that though earnings changes were mainly random, there was a small tendency for the earnings of some firms to be 'mean-reverting', ie to exhibit a negative relationship in successive earnings changes and Lintner and Glauber (1972) found a small number of firms that displayed positive correlation beween earnings changes.

The randomness of earnings seems at variance with a belief in the existence of firms which are consistently successful at finding positive value projects, and with the notion of 'finding the trend'. In Chapter 18 we will see that share prices follow a random-walk too. But the cases are quite different. The randomness of share prices reflects a well-functioning stock market, since in such a market all the information existing at time $t-1$ that is relevant to share prices at time t will be fully incorporated in the price at $t-1$. Therefore any price change between $t-1$ and t must be unanticipated, random. We cannot explain the randomness of earnings this way.

It may be that the higher inflation levels of the 1970s have created an expectation of positive growth in nominal earnings which makes randomness seem surprising. Second, the results are averages but within the samples tested firms have been found which do display maintained growth. Finally, the random walk results assert not that earnings are random, but that a random walk model performs better than any other model *tested* in predicting future earnings. The basic problem could be that a statistical model of earnings, however well chosen, may not be the right way to forecast earnings. We will consider this possibility further in the next section.

9   There are various ways of testing for randomness, but the most common is to measure the serial correlation, r_s, between the change in earnings at time t and the change s periods prior to t. The coefficient of serial correlation is then calculated thus:

Given a series of n earnings observations, X_t, for a firm, the price change in any period can be defined as

$$C_t = X_t - X_{t-1}$$

The average price change is thus

$$\bar{C} = \frac{1}{n-1} \sum_{t=1}^{n-1} C_t$$

The coefficient of serial correlation of order s, is then

$$r_s = \frac{\Sigma(C_{t-s} - \bar{C})\,(C_t - \bar{C})}{\Sigma(C_t - \bar{C})^2}$$

The coefficient of serial correlation can be interpreted as follows:

If r_s = zero then successive changes are independent, and the variable is random.

If r_s < zero then any change tends to be followed by a change of opposite sign and the process is described as 'mean-reverting'. If r_s > zero then there is positive dependency between changes.

Can risk be forecast?

For share valuation we need to be able to forecast the riskiness of future earnings too. We already encountered this topic in Chapter 8 when we saw that the betas of firms do not appear to be stable through time. This slightly undermines the notion of the firm whose future risk is determined by fundamental economic characteristics and is *knowable*. Some researchers have investigated whether risk, as measured by beta, can be forecast from accounting data. Beaver, Kettler and Scholes (1970) found that accounting data did have some predictive value in forecasting beta. The prediction of risk from accounting data is discussed in some detail in Foster (1978) Chapter 9.

V THE NEED FOR AN ECONOMIC MODEL

The earnings figure which the firm presents to outsiders is a complex and highly aggregated number. To see this consider Figure III which is a stylised representation of some of the components of an *economic model* of the earnings of the firm. This is the sort of model a firm must build when it is preparing its budget or corporate plan for the coming year.

The basic relationships of such a model are the revenue and cost functions of the firm, which reflect the quantities and prices of the firm's outputs and of its inputs. From these

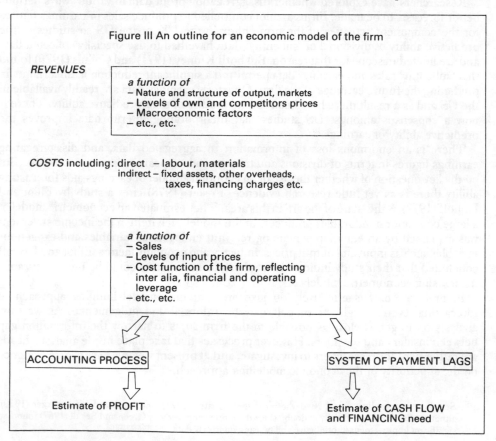

Figure III An outline for an economic model of the firm

REVENUES

a function of
- Nature and structure of output, markets
- Levels of own and competitors prices
- Macroeconomic factors
- etc., etc.

COSTS including: direct – labour, materials
indirect – fixed assets, other overheads,
taxes, financing charges etc.

a function of
- Sales
- Levels of input prices
- Cost function of the firm, reflecting inter alia, financial and operating leverage
- etc., etc.

ACCOUNTING PROCESS

Estimate of PROFIT

SYSTEM OF PAYMENT LAGS

Estimate of CASH FLOW and FINANCING need

the firm can derive its earnings forecast, reflecting the set of accounting rules it employs, and can derive its cash forecast and thus its financing plan, which will be related to the revenues and costs through a set of payment lags.

The ability of the firm to maintain growth in earnings during the coming year or years is determined by a complex of external factors such as the nature of competition, the structure of markets, levels of input and output prices, and the level of demand in the economy. It is also determined by internal factors: the shape of its cost function which reflects the response of various costs, including overheads, taxes, and financing charges to a change in output; and by the particular set of accounting conventions adopted by the firm. When developing its corporate plan the firm will attempt to estimate each of these components separately, just as macro-economic forecasters find it necessary to decompose the complex process that determines national income by building a 'model' of the economy.

Furthermore profit figures are *aggregated* across the various activities of the firm and through time. The more diversified the firm, the less similar will be the cost and revenue functions of its component activities. Additionally there is no particular reason to expect the conventional accounting period of a year to correspond to the natural economic cycle of events that faces the firm.

Given the complex and aggregate nature of the profit figure it is not so surprising that attempts to find a statistical model of its time-series behaviour have not been more successful.

Researchers have explored whether disaggregating profit data in various ways permits better forecasts to be made. Firms are not compelled to produce sales or earnings figures for the component activities of the firm either in the UK or the US so studies of the predictive ability of divisional or 'subentity' data have had to use specially collected data and are limited in scope for that reason. But both Kinney (1971) and Collins (1976) found that 'subentity' sales and earnings data permitted a significant reduction in uncertainty in predicting the future earnings of the firm. Quarterly earnings data are readily available in the US and as a result there have been several studies of their predictive ability. There is now a consensus amongst US studies that incorporating interim data improves the predictive ability of earnings.[10]

There is an enormous loss of information in aggregated data, and disaggregating earnings figures in terms of divisions and time periods appears to improve forecasts. But on the key question of whether the use of an economic model of earnings aids forecasting ability there is as yet little research evidence. Foster (1978) cites a study by Elliot and Uphoff (1972) as the 'state of the art' in this area. They estimated an econometric model of a large consumer nondurables producer. In the model each item in the income statement was explained by an equation containing relevant endogenous variables and exogenous variables such as input and output prices, industry and economy factors. Elliot and Uphoff concluded that their study indicated that short-term forecasts could be more accurately made using econometric models.

In practice analysts effectively do take an economic model-building approach to forecasting, even though the models may be informal and judgemental. As we saw, analysts try to get as close as possible to the firm so as to narrow the information gap between insiders and outsiders. However processes that take place inside analysts' heads are rather hard for researchers to investigate, and at present we only have sparse evidence on the superiority of the economic modelling approach.

10 See, for example, Brown and Niederhoffer (1968), Coates (1972), and Jones and Litzenberger (1970), although this result was initially in doubt, since the pioneering study by Green and Segall (1967) found no significant improvement in predictive ability using quarterly data.

VI SUMMARY

Share valuation depends on expectations about future dividends. But in an uncertain world the process of forming those expectations are complex and judgemental, and a major input to it is the accounting data of firms. This chapter examined the asset valuations produced by accountants, and their associated income measures. 'Historic cost' is the principal accounting method used by firms, however it has certain inherent weaknesses. It allows the firm some discretion in valuation, and, when price-levels are changing, historic-cost values may become misleading. Current-cost valuation offers a partial remedy to these problems.

However accounting-values will only measure economic-value under the most unlikely circumstances, and to estimate economic values, analysts are more likely to study past earnings and cash flow series.

But there is no simple relationship between any of these figures and the future cash-flow of the firm. Despite the popularity among analysts of activities such as 'finding the trend' in past data, there is a body of empirical research to show that earnings series effectively follow a random walk. This may simply testify to the complexity of the earnings-generating process. Firms attempt to solve the complexity by building an economic and financial model and forecasting the component variables. The well-informed analyst may be able to combine much the same information in a 'judgemental' forecast of the future cash flow of the firm.

REFERENCES AND BIBLIOGRAPHY

Accounting Standards steering Committee	'SSAP 16, Current Cost Accounting', London, 1980.
Ball, R, and Watts, R	'Some Time Series Properties of Accounting Income', Journal of Finance, June 1972, pp 663–681.
Baxter, W T	Accounting Values and Inflation (1975) McGraw-Hill.
Baxter, W T, and Davidson, S, (eds)	Studies in Accounting (1977) London.
Beaver, W, Kettler, T P, and Scholes, M	'The Association Between Market Determined and Accounting Determined Risk Measures', Accounting Review, Oct 1970.
Berry, R N, and Gray, S J	'The Impact of Current Cost Accounting: Some Industry Comparisons', The Accountants Magazine, Jan 1982.
Bonbright, J C	Valuation of Property (1937) McGraw-Hill, New York.
Bromwich, M	'Asset Valuation with Imperfect Markets', Journal of Accounting and Business Research, 1975.
Brown, P, and Niederhoffer, V	'The Predictive Content of Quarterly Earnings', Journal of Business, Oct 1968, pp 488–497.
Carsberg, B, and Page, M, (eds)	Current Cost Accounting: The Benefits and Costs (1980) Institute of Chartered Accounting in England and Wales.
Coates, R	'The Predictive Content of Interim Reports – A Time Series Analysis', Empirical Research in Accounting: Selected Studies, Journal of Accounting Research, 1972.
Collins, D W	'Predicting Earnings with Sub-Entity Data: Some Further Evidence', Journal of Accounting Research, Spring 1976, pp 163–177.

Edey, H	'The Nature of Profit', Journal of Accounting and Business Research, 1970, pp 50–55.
Egginton, D A	'In defence of profit measurement: some limitations of cash-flow and value-added as performance measures for external reporting' Accounting and Business Research, 1984.
Egginton, D A	'Cash Flow and Performance Measures for External Reports: a Rejoinder' Accounting and Business Research, 1985.
Elliott, J W, and Uphoff, H L	'Predicting the Near Term Profit and Loss Statement with an Econometric Model: A Feasibility Study', Journal of Accounting Research, 1972.
Firth, M	*The Valuation of Shares and the Efficient-Markets Theory* (1977) Macmillan, London.
Foster, G	*Financial Statement Analysis* (1978) Prentice-Hall, Englewood-Cliffs, New Jersey.
Glautter, M W E, and Underdown, B	*Accounting Theory and Practice* (2nd edn, 1982) Pitman.
Green, D, and Segall, J	'The Predictive Power of First-Quarter Earnings Reports', Journal of Business, Jan 1967.
Hicks, J R	*Value and Capital* (1939) Oxford University Press.
Jones, C P, and Litzenberger, R H	'Quarterly Earnings Reports and Intermediate Stock Price Trends', Journal of Finance, March 1970, pp 143–152.
Kinney, W R	'Predicting Earnings: Entity versus Subentity Data'. Journal of Accouning Research, Spring 1971.
Lawson, G H	'The Measurement of Corporate Performance on a Cash Flow Basis: A Reply to Mr Egginton', Accounting and Business Research, 1985.
Lee, T A	'Cash Flow Accounting, Profit and Performance Measurement: a Response to a Challenge'. Accounting and Business Research, 1985.
Lintner, J, and Glauber, R R	'Higgledy Piggledy Growth in America', in *Modern Developments in Investment Managment* (1972) Praeger, New York.
Little, I M D	'Higgledy Piggledy Growth', Bulletin of the Oxford Institute of Statistics, Nov 1962.
Little, I M D, and Raynor, A C	*Higgledy Piggledy Growth Again* (1966) Blackwell, Oxford.
Modigliani, F, and Cohn, R A	'Inflation, Rational Valuation and the Market', Financial Analysts Journal, March/April 1975, pp 24–43.
Sandilands Report	Inflation Accounting (Cmnd 6225)
Tobin, J, and Brainard, W C	'Asset Markets and the Cost of Capital', ch II of Balassa, B., Nelson, R. (eds) *Economic Progress, Private Values and Public Policy* (1977) North-Holland, Amsterdam.

QUESTIONS

1 Forecast growth in earnings is a key component of share valuation. Is this consistent with the research finding that earnings are random?

2 What accounting issues should the analyst be aware of in using the past series of accounting profits as a basis for estimating future growth?

3 What accounting issues should the analyst be aware of in using the balance-sheet value of the shareholders' interest as a basis for valuing shares?

4 Explain the terms – 'economic value'; 'historic cost'; 'replacement cost'; 'realisable value'. What do the relative values of these numbers tell us about a firm?

5 We have the following information about Brassdock Ltd, as at 31.12.1986:

			£
Balance-Sheet			
Fixed Assets			100,000
Goodwill			10,000
Current Assets	Debtors	60,000	
	Stock	20,000	
	Cash	20,000	
		100,000	
Current Liabilities		(60,000)	40,000
			150,000
Share Capital (£1 ord shares)			50,000
Reserves			80,000
Shareholder's Interest			130,000
Long-Term Debt			20,000
			150,000
Net profit after tax for year ended 31.12.1986			£20,000
Proposed dividend for year			10p

£40,000 of fixed assets represents the cost of a town-centre property recently revalued at £140,000.

Debtors include £10,000 due from X Ltd, now in receivership. Brassdock owns a patent, not shown in the balance sheet, for which an American electronics firm offered £14,000 during 1980.

The average dividend-yield in the industry is 3% and the average P/E is 12 : 1.

Value a Brassdock share on the basis of its assets, its earnings and its dividends. How do you account for the differences? Which basis should an analyst use? What other information would you have liked?

6 From the following data derive a 'current cost' profit for Zoo Ltd for year ended 21/12/86:

Balance Sheets	*31/12/86*	*31/12/85*
Machine (cost 1,500 on 1/1/85; 10 year life)	1,200	1,350
Stock (valued on FIFO basis)	400	250
Debtors	400	200
Creditors	(150)	(100)
Cash	770	250
	2,620	1,950

	Balance Sheets	*31/12/86*	*31/12/85*
Equity		1,820	1,150
10% Debentures 1996		800	800
		£2,620	£1,950

'Historic Cost' Profit for 1986 was £670.

Assume the Retail Price Index rose by 6% in 1986.

The relevant stock price index at 31/12/85 was 167.3

and at 31/12/86 was 198.2

A replacement machine could have been purchased for £1,950 on 31/12/85 and for £2,535 on 31.12.86.

CHAPTER 13
Measuring performance

The process by which the market forms its expectations about the future cash flows of firms is complex and judgemental. An important part of the process is the comparative analysis of the performance and efficiency of the firm. The hope is that by assessing the firm's current strengths and weaknesses, and particularly the skill of its management team, the analyst can throw some light on its competitive position in the future.

In general, to assess the performance of anyone we have to compare what they did with what they might have done. Unfortunately, in the case of management teams we have no direct evidence of what they might have done. Though managers do have objectives and do make plans they are not required to publish them. Even less do we have evidence on the opportunities missed and the ideas the firm never had. So the judgement on managerial performance tends to be made by comparison with the performance of other firms, and with the firm's own performance in previous periods.

Section I discusses what 'efficiency' means in the context of a firm. Section II describes some commonly-used accounting measures of efficiency and considers the problems of comparing these measures cross-sectionally, and through time. Perhaps the most commonly used accounting measure of performance is *return on investment* (ROI). ROI is used within organisations to appraise the performance of projects and divisions, and by shareholders and other outsiders such as government, to appraise the firm as a whole. In Section III we discuss the use of ROI in these contexts.

I MEASURING EFFICIENCY

We can say that an economy, a firm, or any other form of economic system is *efficient* when there is no way of using or organising available resources which will increase the 'welfare' of the system. But economic activity can have different effects on different groups of people. It can make some people better off and some people worse off. To say whether we have an improvement in welfare in this case implies we can measure the effects on the welfare of the individuals and then make a judgement about the relative importance of these individuals' changes in welfare. Economics tends to side-step this problem by adopting the rather restrictive Paretian criterion for an efficiency gain. An economic activity is said to be 'Pareto-efficient' if it makes some individuals better off but no-one worse off. This has proved a useful basis for building economic theory, but it clearly cannot handle many of the situations that confront decision-makers in practice.[1]

The efficiency of the firm

In the theory of finance the 'system' we are interested in is the firm, and we assume that the

---

1 The basic notions in welfare economics are covered in general texts such as Scherer (1980), which is a good introduction to industrial economics and related issues. A comprehensive treatment of welfare economics is to be found in de Graaf (1967).

welfare of the system is the welfare of the firm's shareholders and can be measured by the value of the firm. The objective of managers is thus to maximise the value of the firm.[2]

In practice we want to be able to judge performance and efficiency using accounting data. Managers need to make a detailed analysis of existing activities either at the level of the individual project or of the department or division. This permits *control* and *decision-making*.

Shareholders' control on the firm is rather indirect. By assessing the firm's current strengths and weaknesses they hope to judge its competitive position in the future and so develop their expectations in order to value the firm. Analysing existing performance is a prior activity to valuation for managers and shareholders.

Most *accounting* measures of efficiency are $\dfrac{\text{output}}{\text{input}}$ ratios. Other things being equal, an operation becomes more efficient if its output increases relative to its inputs, that is, if the ratio $\dfrac{\text{output}}{\text{input}}$ increases. Consider a simple productive operation, the production of shirts using cloth and labour.

Last week 2 men made 15 shirts out of 1 piece of cloth. This week by cutting better they make 20 shirts out of the same cloth. That they became more efficient can be seen by comparing the $\dfrac{\text{output}}{\text{input}}$ ratios last week (time t_0) and this week (time t_1).

$$\frac{(20 \text{ shirts})}{(2 \text{ men} + 1 \text{ piece of cloth}) \ (t_1)} \quad \text{is greater than} \quad \frac{(15 \text{ shirts})}{(2 \text{ men} + 1 \text{ piece of cloth}) \ (t_0)}$$

But suppose, more realistically, that the extra production was bought at the cost of employing another man. Is the new position more efficient?

$$\text{Is} \quad \frac{(20 \text{ shirts})}{(3 \text{ men} + 1 \text{ piece of cloth}) \ (t_1)} \quad \text{greater than} \quad \frac{(15 \text{ shirts})}{(2 \text{ men} + 1 \text{ piece of cloth}) \ (t_0)}$$

This inequality cannot be evaluated until we add *prices* to reduce the various components to a common measure.

Suppose the inputs and outputs in our example have the following prices:

shirts = £5
men = £20 per week
cloth = £25 per piece

Now the two ratios can be evaluated:

$$\frac{100}{(60 + 25)} \quad (t_1) = 1.18$$

$$\frac{75}{(40 + 25)} \quad (t_0) = 1.15$$

2 In the light of the previous paragraph we can see that this is a rather restrictive measure of welfare. As we saw in Chapter 2 it takes no direct account of the impact of the firm on certain people who might be thought to be 'part of the system', notably managers, workers, and society in general. Also an increase in the value of the firm need not be Pareto-efficient. For example we can envisage a firm with shareholders in significantly different tax positions instigating a change in dividend policy which made most shareholders better off but some worse off. Various writers have discussed the problem of divergent shareholder preferences, see, for example, King (1977).

So this week, productive efficiency has increased, in terms of the ratio $\dfrac{\text{Value of output}}{\text{Value of input}}$

The importance of prices

It is only possible to appraise diverse economic activities if their effects are reduced to a common measure using *prices*. But the problem is ensuring that the prices are 'right'. We can only be confident that an improvement in a ratio of the values of some of the firm's outputs and inputs will imply an overall increase in the value of the firm if we know that the change left all other things equal. Similarly, in comparing two firms we can only conclude that one is more efficient on the basis of some ratio if all other things are equal. This would not have been the case in the shirt example if the man who was imported into the shirt operation at a salary of £20 per week had been, say, taken off productive work elsewhere in the factory on which he had been earning a *contribution* of £30 per week. This is the problem encountered in Chapters 4 and 5 when finding the relevant measures of cost and benefit for the appraisal of projects. We saw that the problem is solved by ensuring that the prices used measure *opportunity costs*. But in project appraisal the decision-maker is an insider, with access to all relevant information, while the analyst measuring the performance and efficiency of the firm may be an outsider, with only restricted access.

In practice the difficulty in knowing whether 'other things are equal' when you use a ratio, or in being able to rely on the prices embodied in the ratio correctly measuring the opportunity cost of the inputs involved puts severe limitations on the usefulness of ratios. 'Ratio analysis' is a very popular tool of financial analysis but great care is needed in drawing conclusions about firms from ratio analysis.

II RATIO ANALYSIS

In this section we describe some of the commonly used ratios. First we describe some *specific* ratios that attempt to examine the efficiency with which the firm uses particular inputs. In these ratios the usual measure of output is sales revenue, so the ratio describes how the firm economises on the use of a particular input per unit of sales. We then describe some measures of the overall performance of the firm.

SOME SPECIFIC MEASURES OF EFFICIENCY

Labour efficiency

One input, *labour*, has acquired great importance in efficiency analysis. This is partly because labour is a major expense in most firms, but mainly because capital-intensity tends to be seen as the key to efficiency in modern business. Since labour and capital may be substitutes, analysts tend to take economy in the use of labour as an indicator of the extent to which firms are investing in labour-saving technology. A common measure is

$$\text{Sales per employee} = \frac{\text{SALES}}{\substack{\text{AV NUMBER} \\ \text{OF EMPLOYEES}}}$$

where the numerator is sales for the period, and the denominator is employees at the beginning and end of the period, averaged. Problems of comparison arise in interpreting the 'number of employees' when working weeks are of different lengths or different amounts of overtime worked, or when firms use a significant number of part-time workers, since some firms report the number of 'full-time equivalent' workers, and others the numbers of workers.

Fixed asset efficiency

We can get another view of capital-intensity by comparing the fixed asset and labour expense of the firm, then examining how the balance between these has moved through time, and compares to similar firms.

These are measured as follows:

$$\text{Fixed asset expense ratio} = \frac{\text{DEPRECIATION}}{\text{SALES}} \qquad \text{Labour expense ratio} = \frac{\text{WAGES}}{\text{SALES}}$$

You should avoid analysing labour and fixed assets efficiency with a blind belief in the superiority of capital. The relative appeal of these two factors is determined by their prices and it is not necessary to be a Luddite to remain open to the possibility that in some cases relative prices may favour the substitution of capital by labour.

Working capital efficiency

As we see in Chapter 23 the firm should hold as small an investment in debtors and stocks as possible subject to the constraint of sufficiency for planned levels of operation. The indicator of debtor efficiency is

$$\text{'Debtor collection period'} = \frac{\text{AV DEBTORS}}{\text{SALES}} \times 365$$

This tells us how many days' credit the firm's debtors are taking on average. As a numerator, the average of opening and closing debtors, ideally with VAT excluded from UK debtors, is used so as to provide a figure which is comparable with sales, and which relates to the whole period. It is tempting to use just closing debtors in order to form a view of the firm's latest debtor policy, but if there is any trend up or down in sales during the period this will be a distorted measure. To assess the latest debtor policy closing debtors would have to be related to annualised sales for the last month or two, but these figures are not normally available.

Strictly *sales* above should be *credit sales*, but this figure is, once again, not normally available. If a firm with significant cash sales is being appraised but the overall sales figure is used in the debtor ratio, there will be no distortion for *comparative* purposes so long as the proportion of cash sales can be assumed to be constant.

A similar ratio can be calculated for stocks, and similar comments apply.

$$\text{'Stock turnover'} = \frac{\text{AV STOCKS}}{\text{SALES}} \times 365$$

The stock ratio is sometimes calculated using 'cost-of-sales' ie direct materials and labour, in the denominator, but this ignores two facts. A large part of stocks consists of work-in-progress and finished goods, as well as raw materials, and anyhow the cost-of sales figure is not always available to outsiders. Using sales will be distorting *only if* raw materials are a significant proportion of stock *and* the relationship between purchases and sales is changing, that is if the gross profit margin is not constant.

Using mainly the data from Chapter 12, we can calculate these ratios for the Plessey Company. As soon as we start calculating ratios in practice the need for caution becomes apparent. Sales per employee and labour expense are straightforward in Plessey's case. They provide a good deal of disaggregate information on average employee numbers and costs, though we use the totals. To calculate the numerator of the fixed asset expense ratio we have to aggregate Plessey's depreciation charge with its expenditure on hire and leasing of equipment. In 1983 the relative magnitudes of these were: depreciation £26.5 million, hire, leasing, etc £22.8 million. To find *average* debtor and stock figures for 1982 we have to go to the previous year's accounts for an opening balance. Since a good deal of Plessey's work is on contract, the stock figures are net of progress payments.

	1983		*1982*	
		(Figures are in £000)		
Sales per employee	$\dfrac{1,074,750}{40,872} =$	£26,295	$\dfrac{963,074}{42,929} = $ £22,434	
Fixed asset expense	$\dfrac{49,278}{1,074,750} =$	.046	$\dfrac{39,573}{963,074} = $ .041	
Labour expense	$\dfrac{376,876}{1,074,750} =$	.351	$\dfrac{331,199}{963,074} = $ .344	
Debtor collection period	$\dfrac{202,649}{1,074,750} \times 365 = 69$ days		$\dfrac{179,605}{963,074} \times 365 = 68$ days	
Stock turnover	$\dfrac{238,790}{1,074,750} \times 365 = 81$ days		$\dfrac{235,102}{963,074} \times 365 = 89$ days	

Sales per employee have improved by 17% over the year, helped by an increase in sales and a reduction in employees. There has been a slight increase in the costs of labour and fixed assets per pound of sales. A significant change is the improvement in stock turnover between 1982 and 1983.

Expense efficiency

We are also interested in the relationship between the size of the various expense outlays, and the firm's level of activity.

In general firms analyse their revenue and expense in the following way:

SALES	xxxx
less 'COST OF SALES' – direct materials and labour	(xxx)
GROSS PROFIT	xxx
MANUFACTURING EXPENSE,	
Factory overheads, depreciation	(xx)
ADMINISTRATION EXPENSE,	
Office overheads, salaries	(xx)
SELLING EXPENSE	
Cost of the sales force, advertising	(xx)
OPERATING PROFIT	xx
FINANCIAL EXPENSE	
Interest charges	(xx)
NET PROFIT	xx

In each case the analyst would be interested in examining how the firm controls its expenditure relative to its level of activity, by calculating $\dfrac{\text{EXPENSE}}{\text{SALES}}$.

Unfortunately the outsider may have access to *none* of these expense details about the firms, since normal accounting conventions do not require firms to publish them. One expense ratio of particular interest in determining the basic trading position of the firm is

$$\dfrac{\text{DIRECT MATERIALS AND LABOUR}}{\text{SALES}}$$

or equivalently (since gross profit + direct materials + labour = sales)

$$\text{GROSS PROFIT MARGIN} = \dfrac{\text{GROSS PROFIT}}{\text{SALES}}$$

The non-availability of gross profit data is a major obstacle for outsiders analysing a firm's performance.

In fact Plessey discloses this information to outsiders, and we can calculate their expense and gross profit ratios as follows:

		1983 (figures in £000) % of sales		1982 % of sales
Gross Profit	301,993	28%	250,164	26%
Marketing, Selling	99,525	9.3%	87,738	9.1%
Administration	42,720	4.0%	33,389	3.5%
R & D	45,065	4.2%	31,672	3.3%

Plessey enjoyed an improvement in its gross profit margin, which was, however, effectively consumed by increased operating costs.

Ultimately the firm must be judged on its overall performance. The study of specific efficiencies may be useful in explaining differences in overall performance of firms, but it is hard to make judgements about overall performance by looking solely at specific assets and expenses. Many different and conflicting combinations of specific policy can go to form an overall efficient strategy. For example in retailing we find successful stores which adopt 'price-competitive' strategies, with small gross margins and intensive use of shop floor space, and we find successful stores which adopt 'quality and service – competitive' strategies, with high gross margins and more generous applications of labour and floor-space.

OVERALL EFFICIENCY

Net profit margin, price-cost ratio

The measures of efficiency we have looked at so far have had the general form $\dfrac{\text{output}}{\text{input}}$ and used sales as the measure of output. An overall performance measure of this sort would relate sales to total costs. Since Net Profit = Sales − Total Cost, this can be captured by calculating the *net profit margin*

$$\text{net profit margin} = \dfrac{\text{NET PROFIT}}{\text{SALES}}$$

The *marginal* equivalent of this ratio, which relates the revenue and cost associated with an extra unit of sales is the *contribution margin*.

$$\text{contribution margin} = \frac{\text{CONTRIBUTION PER UNIT}}{\text{UNIT PRICE}}$$

or equivalently the *price-cost ratio*

$$\text{price cost ratio} = \frac{\text{UNIT PRICE}}{\text{UNIT MARGINAL COST}}$$

A key deficiency of the net profit margin as a measure of overall performance is that it omits the cost of equity capital. So a higher net profit margin is not automatic evidence of greater efficiency. It may simply indicate higher investments in assets, or more risk taking. Either of these will lead shareholders to *require* a higher return from the firm. Put in terms of value, if there had been an increase in the riskiness of returns, or in the capital employed in the firm, an increase in net profit margin does not necessarily signal an increase in the value of the firm.

There is no easy solution to this problem, since the cost of equity is not explicitly stated anywhere. In fact it is implicit in the value of the firm, but this is the end product of the financial analysis. The *return on investment* tackles this problem by relating profit to the capital employed in the firm.

Return on investment

The return on investment (ROI)[3] can be defined in a number of ways depending on what measure of investment we use. We will adopt the following formulation:

$$\text{ROI} = \frac{\text{NET PROFIT BEFORE TAX AND INTEREST (NPTI)}}{\text{NET ASSETS}}$$

In any ROI measure it is important to measure the numerator and denominator consistently. In this case, since net assets are funded by both equity and debt, interest, the reward to debt, is added back to the numerator.

It is usual to add back corporation tax in calculating ROI. One argument for this is that tax is externally imposed and therefore will distort the view of the operating efficiency of the firm. On the other hand it could be argued that since taxes are real costs borne by firms, the efficient firm will attempt to minimise them. Another problem is that many firms estimate the tax charge in the profit and loss account on the deferred tax[4] basis, rather than showing tax actually paid in the period.

Other variants of the denominator are found. Gross assets (= fixed assets + current assets) are sometimes used, and it is common to deduct intangible assets from the capital measure, reflecting a lack of faith in the worth of assets such as goodwill, R + D expenditure, and so forth. In practice it may be useful to calculate ROI on several bases, in order to see if the change of basis makes any significant difference to the comparison.

Having identified a change in ROI the analyst usually sets about explaining the change. It is often informative to disaggregate ROI as follows:

3   Also known as 'return on capital employed' or 'accounting rate of return'.
4   See Chapter 3.

$$ROI = \frac{NPTI}{SALES} \times \frac{SALES}{NET\ ASSETS}$$

$$\underset{\text{'MARGIN'}}{\uparrow} \qquad \underset{\text{'TURNOVER'}}{\uparrow}$$

In other words, ROI = Margin × Turnover.

The overall return of a firm can be decomposed into the margin of profit achieved on each sale, and the volume of sales achieved on the given asset base.

In the next section we examine the economic significance of ROI a little more closely.

In calculating ROI it is most important to be consistent 'top and bottom'. If we use as a numerator Plessey's 'profit before interest payable', which is also before tax, minority interests, and extraordinary items, the denominator must measure the claims of equity *and* debt. Plessey's 'net assets' are also 'net' of debt claims, they effectively measure the equity interest in the firm so we add back Plessey's short and long-term loans and overdrafts. For example in 1983 this gives an asset figure of (£000) 418,019 + 25,880 + 31,414 = £475,313.

	1983		1982	
ROI $=$	$\dfrac{159,086}{475,313} = 33.5\%$		$\dfrac{126,831}{423,467} = 30.0\%$	

Alternatively we could calculate 'return-to-shareholders' as 'profit attributable to members of the holding company'/'shareholders funds' i e:

	1983		1982	
'Return to shareholders' $=$	$\dfrac{81,449}{407,775} = 20.0\%$		$\dfrac{73,758}{359,572} = 20.5\%$	

The return to shareholders does not show the same advance in 1983 as did the wider measure, and this appears to be explained by the jump in tax charge in 1983. We can analyse the ROI change into 'margin' and 'turnover'

	1983		1982	
'margin'	$\dfrac{159,086}{1,074,750} = 14.8\%$		$\dfrac{126,831}{963,074} = 13.2\%$	
'turnover'	$\dfrac{1,074,750}{475,313} = 2.26$		$\dfrac{963,074}{423,467} = 2.27$	

The level of assets needed to support £1 of sales stayed very constant in 1983, and the change in ROI appears to be explained by an advance in the profit margin on sales.

PROBLEMS IN COMPARING RATIOS

Ratios do not say much in isolation, only when compared with something else. There are two ways in which accounting ratios are compared:
1 with the numbers of the same firm in previous time periods – TIME-SERIES ANALYSIS,
2 with other firms in the same time period – CROSS-SECTIONAL ANALYSIS.
In general comparisons may be invalidated if the figures use different prices and/or different accounting conventions. This problem is most severe in comparing firms in

different industries, but even the time-series analysis of the single firm can be distorted if, for example, there has been a changing rate of inflation, or if the firm has changed its accounting conventions.

The problem of price comparability can be largely solved by using current cost figures, which at least ensure that each firm's ratio is measured in internally consistent figures. We return to this in the next section.

Firms can display some differences in accounting conventions even under current cost, for example, with regard to depreciation rates on fixed assets, and write-off policies on intangibles. If enough information is available to identify specifically the difference in treatment, analysts often recalculate the profit and capital employed figures to put them on a comparable basis.

TIME-SERIES COMPARISONS

The prime motive for studying a historic series of accounting numbers is the search for regularities that might continue into the future: the forecasting motive.

Dealing with price-level changes

One problem in time-series is dealing with changing price levels. There are two things to attend to here:

(1) Current-cost There is as yet no evidence or theory to show that current-cost accounting numbers provide a better predictive base than historic-cost. But one great virtue of current-cost figures for comparative purposes is that they attempt to be *internally-consistent*, and this removes some of the uncertainty the analyst faces in interpreting accounting numbers. So where possible current-cost numbers should be used.

(2) Inflation There is still a need to take account of inflation even when current-cost figures are being used. If a financial report has been drawn up using current-cost accounting we can rely on the report being internally consistent in terms of prices. But the current-cost prices will be specific to the date of the report, and if we want to compare with other year's results or with a firm using a different reporting date, then we must 'index' the figures we are using to eliminate any inflationary distortions.

Plessey's sales over a five year period were:

	1979	1980	1981	1982	1983
(£m)	648.3	751.0	844.5	963.1	1074.8

Before we can interpret these figures it would help to index them. Table I shows the retail price index (RPI) over the five calendar years 1978–1982.[5] From this, coefficients can be derived to calculate all the sales figures in 1978 prices.

	1979	1980	1981	1982	1983
Reported Sales	648.3	751.0	844.5	963.1	1074.8
Price deflator[5]	× 1	× .88	× .75	× .68	× .63

5 We have used the RPI average for the calendar years most closely corresponding to Plessey's financial years; which end at the end of March in the subsequent year. To be ruthlessly accurate we could have calculated an average to match Plessey's financial year.

SALES AT
1978 prices   648.3   660.9   633.4   654.9   677.1

% growth in
'real' sales   + 2%   − 4.2%   + 3.4%   + 3.4%

Once we index Plessey's sales, by recalculating them at 1978 prices in this case, we get
a clearer view of the trend of 'real' sales.

Table I Retail Price Index (Source CSO Annual Abstract of Statistics)				
Year	1978	1979	1980	1981	1982
Index	197.1	223.5	263.7	291.2	314.3
Deflator to convert to 1978	1	$\frac{197.1}{223.5}$	$\frac{197.1}{263.7}$	$\frac{197.1}{291.2}$	$\frac{197.1}{314.3}$
=	1	.88	.75	.68	.63

Indexation is only needed when comparing *values* at different times, such as 'sales-revenue' in different years or between firms with different reporting dates. Obviously it is not necessary to index *real* figures, such as 'number of employees'. But remember that the ratio of two values is a real figure, while the ratio of a value and a real figure is a value. So if we are comparing Debtor Turnover $= \dfrac{\text{Sales}}{\text{Debtors}}$, we do not need to index, but if we are calculating, say Sales per employee $= \dfrac{\text{Sales}}{\text{No of employees}}$ we must index.

Earlier on, we calculated the 'sales per employee' for Plessey as

$$1983 = £26,295 \qquad 1982 = £22,434$$

But if we re-express the 1983 figure in 1982 pounds by multiplying it by $\dfrac{291.2}{314.3} = .926$,

so that 'real' sales per employee in 1983 is £24,362, we can compare 'real' growth in sales per employee. Of course, we have assumed RPI is an appropriate price index for Plessey's sales. We discuss this assumption next.

Which index?

In the previous example RPI was used to index 'sales'. We could have used the specific price index relating to the particular types of goods and services Plessey produces. But a general index such as RPI has certain advantages:
— specific indices may not be readily available[6]
— in a multi-product firm an appropriate composite index would have to be calculated. This requires information about the composition of published figures that the outsider does not have

6   The RPI is published monthly in the 'Employment Gazette', by the Department of Employment. It gives a monthly RPI for the past two years, and an annual index for more than ten years. Specific indices are produced by a variety of agencies. *Price Indices for Current Cost Accounting*, published by HMSO in the Business Monitor series give current cost indices for a variety of specific goods and services. Failing this, many trade associations produce their own price indices.

— the application of a specific index to a composite figure like 'profit' would require very close interpretation. Part of the skill of management lies in responding to the differences between inflation rates on inputs and outputs, and we would not want to mask this.

In general we recommend using a general index unless there is reason to believe it will lead to a significantly misleading interpretation.

Can ratios be forecast?

As with earnings, the analyst who implicitly or explicitly attempts to forecast ratios needs to be aware of the existing evidence in this area. There is, in fact, little work available on the time-series properties of ratios. Several writers have found that the random-walk model performs less well for 'deflated' earnings series such as ROI, than it does for the earnings itself (see for example, Ball and Watts (1972)). So it may be possible to find trends in ROI. But as for other financial ratios, Foster (1978) examined auto correlations for 12 assorted liquidity, gearing, profitability and turnover ratios calculated on available firms on the US Compustat tape between 1957 and 1975. He concluded that 'a random-walk model could, on average, have considerable descriptive validity'. We saw the implications of this in the previous chapter. If ratios are random they have no predictive content and so future values cannot be directly forecast from the past series of the same ratio.

However researchers have had a good deal of success in using ratios to predict economic events such as the failure of the firm. We consider failure prediction models in Chapter 25.

CROSS-SECTIONAL ANALYSIS

Since we cannot know in isolation whether a firm is efficient we might try to form a judgement by comparing it with other firms. But what is a comparable firm? There are few single-product, single-market firms. Most firms produce multiple products and sell them in several markets, and each product can be expected to require a different configuration of assets and costs for its production, and each market for inputs and outputs to set prices under potentially different conditions of demand and competition. A useful comparison of efficiency or performance between two firms must hold these factors constant. The usual way of doing this is to use as a 'control' a firm producing similar products in similar markets. But there may be few if any firms with a similar range of activities. The problem is compounded by the fact that firms are not obliged to report to outsiders on their separate activities. The outsider may hope for some breakdown of sales revenue into activities, but he will not often find disaggregated data on assets and costs.

Data sources

There are several levels at which the analyst can look for comparable data.

(1) The individual firm Data on individual firms is available as follows:

—ANNUAL REPORTS The annual report of all registered companies can be inspected at Companies House in London or Cardiff.[7] To reduce the inconvenience, 'search agencies' advertise in the financial press who will make the visit and post the results, in exchange for a fee.

—DATA BASES The financial data of larger firms are collected and published by various

7 . . . if the company has filed them. Some companies fail to.

agencies. EXTEL publishes 'cards' containing financial, and some historical and institutional data on 8000 firms. It also produces EXSTAT, a computerised source of financial data to subscribers. The DATASTREAM teletext service is another source of data on individual firms.

(2)   *Aggregate data*   There are various sources of financial data aggregated over industries. DATASTREAM and EXTEL provide this. The government provides industry averages in *company finance*, a publication in the Business Monitor series. Many industry and trade associations compile average financial data on members.

(3)   *Inter-firm comparisons*   One problem, with aggregate or firm-level published data is that it contains only the information that firms are required to publish – it is 'outsider' information. A firm can get access to more detailed information about competitors by joining an inter-firm comparison agency such as PIMS, or the Centre for Inter-firm Comparisons. In return for providing confidential information that it would not normally publish, the firm receives an analysis of similar data provided by other firms.

Interpreting the comparison

Anyone who wants to compare financial numbers of firms has to be exceedingly careful. Leaving aside issues of comparability, there remains the question of what conclusion to draw once the comparison has been made. There is always a danger of making a 'standard' for comparison out of the thing which is compared. If one firm is compared with other individual firms we have to ask what the status of those firms is, and what reason there is to believe them satisfactory. The problem is not removed by looking at the 'average' firm in the industry, at the whole industry, or even at the performance of all the firms in the economy. There is sometimes a blind faith in the 'average' as a standard for comparison. But there is no reason why the average should be of any significance in appraising the individual firm.

III   ROI IN ECONOMIC APPRAISAL

ROI is perhaps the most commonly used accounting ratio. Within the firm managers make judgements about the performance of single projects and divisions using ROI, and outsiders evaluate the performance of whole firms this way. Accounting numbers are only useful in *comparison*, and we have already encountered some of the problems in using ROI this way. Comparisons rely on consistency in terms of price data and accounting treatment, and the outsider may have some difficulty ensuring this.

So far we have simply asserted that 'if other things are equal' ROI will be a consistent signal of the value of the firm, but now we will examine the relationship between ROI and value more closely. We will do this by seeing whether, and in what situations, ROI is a good proxy for the internal rate of return, IRR. If we can establish the status of ROI this way then it will make some sense to compare the ROI of projects, divisions and firms with the cost of capital. We know from Chapter 6 that IRR itself can be troublesome and provide an inconsistent signal on occasions, but we leave these problems to one side in this discussion.

ROI AS A PROXY FOR IRR

The relationship between ROI and IRR was explained by John Kay in Kay (1976). We will describe the version of the relationship produced by Peasnell (1982). The building blocks for Peasnell's theorem are two accounting identities we are familiar with already plus the definition of net present value. The first is the profit identity we met as equation (1) in the last chapter.

$$P_t \equiv C_t + (A_t - A_{t-1}) \tag{1}$$

where P_t is profit in period t, C_t is the dividends or cash distributed by the project or firm in the period, and A_t is the accounting or book value of the firm's assets at time t. The second is his definition of return on investment, a_t, where

$$a_t \equiv \frac{P_t}{A_{t-1}} \tag{2}$$

We can define net present value as the present value of the net cash flows plus the present value of the terminal realisable value of the assets, less the initial cost.

$$NPV = \sum_{t=1}^{N} \frac{C_t}{(1+r)^t} + \frac{R_N}{(1+r)^N} - C_o \tag{3}$$

Where C_o is the initial outlay on assets, and R_N is the terminal value of the assets. We will not reproduce Peasnell's proof, but it is quite simple and proceeds by noting that both the accounting identities and the NPV formula contain the cash-flows, C_t, so one can be substituted into the other by eliminating C_t. Also we know that the internal rate of return, which we will call r^*, is the discount rate that gives NPV = 0. By some manipulation Peasnell derives the basic theorem, which shows the internal rate of return from a firm or a project over a number of periods to be a weighted average of the periodic accounting rates of return, plus an error term relating to the discrepancy between book value and market value of assets at the beginning and the end.

$$r^* = \sum_{t=1}^{N} W_t a_t + E \tag{4}$$

where the period weights and the error term are defined as

$$W_t = \frac{A_{t-1}/(1+r^*)^{t-1}}{\sum_{j=0}^{N-1} A_j/(1+r^*)^j} \quad \text{where} \quad \sum_{t=1}^{N} W_t = 1 \tag{5}$$

$$E = \frac{E_N - E_o}{\sum_{j=1}^{N} A_{j-1}/(1+r^*)^j} \tag{6}$$

where $E_N = (R_N - A_N)/(1+r)^N$
$E_o = C_o - R_o$

Taken together the theorem embodied in (4), (5), and (6) looks fairly intimidating, but it contains within it some interesting results.

Some implications of Peasnell's theorem

1 If $E = 0$, then $r^* = \sum\limits_{t=1}^{N} w_t a_t$

ie if there are no opening and closing valuation errors, or they cancel out, the internal rate of return is a weighted average of the return-on-investment series. There will be no opening and closing valuation errors if the market values of the assets equal their book values at the beginning and end.

2 If $E = 0$, and $a_1 = a_2 = a_3 \ldots = a$, then

   $r = a$

if the ROI is constant and there are no opening and closing valuation errors then the ROI is a good proxy for IRR.

Kay and Peasnell derive various other special cases, but an interesting one is

3 If $E_N = E_0$ and if the book value of the firm's assets grows at a constant rate which is less than the IRR, the IRR will be more closely related to earlier IRRs. If the rate of growth is greater than the IRR, the IRR is more closely related to later ROIs.

The key implication of Peasnell's theorem is that a series of ROI or the ROI of a single period provide a good proxy for IRR only under apparently limiting assumptions: only if the differences between the book value and market value of the firm's assets at the beginning and end of the period are either zero, or cancel each other out. Otherwise an adjustment has to be made to allow for the opening and closing valuation discrepancy. The logic of this is clear – if there is effectively no change in the value of assets during a period, then the ROI of the period will tell us all we need to know about economic performance. This has implications for the various uses people put ROI to.

PROJECT APPRAISAL

In Chapter 9 we saw that managers commonly use 'rules of thumb' to make project investment decisions. One of these involves deriving either the average ROI from a project, or the ROI for a single year, and comparing this with the cost of capital. We can see now that we can only be sure the average ROI will be a good proxy for IRR if the average uses the weights in equation (5) and if the assets are fully consumed on the project and have no resale value at the end so that there is no valuation discrepancy.

To show how the formula for calculating IRR would work in project appraisal, Peasnell produces a simple example. Consider a machine which costs £10,000 and which has a useful life of six years with no terminal value. The machine produces cash flows of £2,296 each year. DCF analysis of the project would show that it has an IRR of 10%, and an NPV of £614 using an 8% discount rate. However, using Peasnell's formula we can get the same result by analysing its stream of accounting rates of return. Table II shows how this works out.

Net profit each year is £629, the annual cash flow less the annual depreciation. To find ARR this is divided by the *opening* asset value (as Peasnell's formula requires). So in year 1, ARR is $629/10000 = 6.29\%$. The weights are calculated using expression (5) and the IRR is simply the sum of these, since, because the machine is completely consumed on the job, there is no valuation error term.

Peasnell's formula shows that a series of ARRs can be meaningful economically, but he is not necessarily recommending we should calculate IRR this way. In the example, it would have been more straightforward to calculate it conventionally.

Table II   Peasnell's formula applied to a project

Year	0	1	2	3	4	5	6	
Cash flow	(10,000)	2,296	2,296	2,296	2,296	2,296	2,296	
Profit before depreciation		2,296	2,296	2,296	2,296	2,296	2,296	
Less: depreciation		1,667	1,667	1,667	1,667	1,667	1,667	
(1) Net profit		629	629	629	629	629	629	
(2) Written down value of machine	10,000	8,333	6,667	5,000	3,333	1,667	0	
ARR (1) ÷ (2)		6.29%	7.55%	9.44%	12.58%	18.88%	37.78%	
Weights		.332	.251	.183	.125	.075	.034	
total		2.09	1.90	1.73	1.57	1.4	1.28	= 10%

THE ROI OF THE FIRM

Does it make sense to compare the ROI of a firm with the firm's cost of capital? Exactly the same comments apply. If there are no valuation discrepancies, then ROI will be a good proxy for IRR and we can compare it with the cost of capital, embodying the market's perception of the firm's riskiness. But if the value of the firm is changing as well we cannot rely on ROI as a measure of IRR. For example if the firm is 'building for growth', investing heavily now in the anticipation of future profits, its current ROI may be low but its market value will be increasing and this will generate a positive error-term so that the IRR will be above ROI.

DIVISIONAL CONTROL: ROI AS AN OBJECTIVE

Perhaps the most common method of organising a large firm is as a group of more or less autonomous 'divisions'. The question of just how much decision-making should be decentralised to divisions and how much control retained at head office is an important one. Head office has to balance the benefits of tight control and efficient co-ordination of the overall enterprise against the dangers of over-centralisation – high information costs, slowness of response, loss of morale at the divisional level, and so forth.

The question arises of how to ensure that the behaviour of the autonomous divisions will conform to the objective of the firm as a whole – value-maximisation. One practice is to appraise the achieved ROI of each division and since the rational and ambitious divisional manager will respond to this appraisal system by maximising ROI, this is tantamount to setting the maximisation of ROI as the divisional objective.

Some of the problems in making ROI an objective should be clear by now. It is important that the prices of inputs and outputs should reflect the opportunity costs to the firm of the resources involved. This may not happen unless divisions sell goods and services to each other at the right *transfer prices*. Unless transfer prices are carefully set the performance of different divisions may be over or understated and they may well over- or under-produce in response.[8] This applies particularly to finance. If capital is not priced at its opportunity cost it may be inefficiently allocated within the firm and the situation can

8   The classic analysis of this problem is Hirshleifer (1956).

arise where one division is starved of funds for projects which have a higher return than some that actually get undertaken in other divisions. The allocation problem can be helped by requiring divisions to bid competitively for the available supplies of capital within the firm.[9]

But the real problem with appraising managers in terms of ROI can be seen from studying equation (4). It imparts a bias in favour of projects with positive returns in early years and against projects which may have a positive value but earn their returns in subsequent periods. In fact given high rates of job turnover amongst managers, the cynical manager can enhance his own reputation and tarnish the reputation of his successor by choosing just these projects! In terms of equation (4) managers will have an incentive to choose projects with high a and low or negative E.

ROI is the wrong objective

Even if ROI is a good proxy for IRR, this does not imply we should *maximise* it. Consider Table III which shows three projects A, B, C, yielding differing profits in perpetuity. Suppose the firm can choose to undertake any or all of the projects A, B and C, which should they choose?

The reader will recall that the rational firm would invest until the IRR of the marginal project equals the cost of capital. Such a firm will choose all three projects, since they all yield a return which covers the cost of capital. But the ROI maximiser will choose only A. B and C are both worthwhile but will be rejected because of their tendency to dilute the achieved ROI.

Table III				
Project	Annual Profit (£)	Capital Employed (£)	ROI	Cumulative ROI
A	300,000	1,000,000	30%	30% (A)
B	200,000	1,000,000	20%	25% (A & B)
C	100,000	1,000,000	10%	20% (A & B & C)
	Cost of Capital: 8%			

There is no easy solution to the divisional control problem, for two reasons. First, we are trying to find a measure of present performance, when what we really want is a measure of value-performance which depends on effects which lie partly in the future and are as yet unknown. Second, we want a control on divisional performance which preserves as far as possible the benefits of autonomy. By virtue of its inside position head office is in a position to monitor the detailed plans and budgets of the division, and to exercise more direct control than the shareholder. But the closer this control, the less autonomy remains.

9 In many organisations investment decision-making is retained at head-office, but when divisional managers can control their own investment base it has been suggested they should be appraised on the basis of the *residual income* they generate, where residual income is accounting profit less a charge for the cost of the capital used by the division. This way it is hoped to provide the appropriate price-signals for optimal behaviour. For the main lines of this debate see Flower (1971), Bromwich (1973), Tomkins (1975), Emmanuel and Otley (1975).

ROI AS A MEASURE OF 'EFFICIENCY'

Are firms with higher ROI 'better' in a broader sense?[10]

Consider an example:
Arthur Shaw Ltd is a general manufacturer whose income statement last year was as follows:

	£ million
Sales	1.0
Materials	(.2)
Labour	(.3)
Overheads	(.1)
Profit	.4

Capital Employed was £1m, and ROI 40%

Arthur Shaw, the chairman and owner of the firm was pleased with the results, but was well aware of the importance in achieving this result of the loyalty of the customers and the diligence of the workers. So he decided to reward them this year with a 15% price cut and a 30% bonus respectively. Nothing else changed this year, either in quantities of inputs or outputs, or in their prices, so the results were

	£ million
Sales	.85
Materials	(.20)
Wages	(.39)
Overheads	(.10)
Profit	.16

Capital Employed £1m, and ROI 16%

Was Arthur Shaw less efficient this year? The answer depends on what 'efficiency' we are talking about. Since the fall in profit will presumably lead to a fall in the value of the firm, it seems that the change in ROI does signal a reduction in efficiency. The reason this conclusion may feel uncomfortable is that there was no change in the 'efficiency' with which the firm converted physical inputs into outputs, and the profits change simply reflects a voluntary redistribution of the surplus, which may well have led to an increase in social welfare overall.

We might be happier with the conclusion that efficiency had fallen if the changes in sales price and wages had not been voluntary, but forced by changes in the respective output and input markets, that is, if Arthur Shaw Ltd had been forced to trim its prices by increased competition, and to pay higher wages by increased outside demand for this type of labour. In general, changes in the return of firms will signal a parallel change in welfare of society as a whole, as well as in the welfare of shareholders, only if the prices of inputs and outputs measure their relative utility and scarcity. If prices are of this sort it will be feasible to make comparisons between firms to judge relative efficiency. But do prices do this job? The only world that economists have identified in which one could be confident that prices are accurately measuring the relative utility and scarcity of resources is the

10   Amey (1969) provides a detailed investigation of this issue. For a short and stimulating contribution see Skinner (1965). The numerical example follows Skinner's.

world of perfect competition in input and output markets. If this does not obtain, it may be the case that comparisons between firms will mislead.

The arbitrary price changes that Arthur Shaw imposed could not have happened in a world of perfect markets because his return on capital would then be the competitive return, just sufficient to stay in business, and his act of generosity would have driven his return below this necessary level. In the example we looked at Arthur Shaw who was effectively fixing the prices of his inputs and outputs, whereas in a perfect market all participants must 'take' prices and accept the market prices.

In practice markets are not perfect, and it follows that it is dangerous to conclude that a firm with higher ROI is necessarily more efficient or desirable in a social sense. The difference in results may simply reflect the fact that one firm is a monopolist in its input or output markets while the other operates in highly competitive markets. In the UK an obvious example of this is the public utilities. It becomes difficult to compare the performance of state monopolies such as gas, electricity and post, which are able to fix their own output prices, with firms in more competitive markets.

THE PERFORMANCE OF UK FIRMS

The performance of UK firms in aggregate over the last twenty years is shown in Table IV. From 1963 the pre-tax historic-cost rate of 'return on trading assets' of industrial and

Table IV   Rates of return on trading assets of industrial and commercial companies

	Pre-tax historic cost	Pre-tax real	Post-tax real (1)
1963	15.9	11.4	7.4
1964	16.6	11.9	7.8
1965	15.8	11.2	7.3
1966	14.2	9.9	5.9
1967	13.6	10.0	5.8
1968	14.8	10.1	5.7
1969	14.9	9.9	6.0
1970	14.4	8.6	5.2
1971	15.2	8.9	6.1
1972	16.8	9.3	6.5
1973	19.7	9.1	8.1
1974	20.0	6.0	6.6
1975	18.4	5.2	3.9
1976	20.4	5.5	5.5
1977	21.1	6.9	7.2
1978	21.1	7.2	7.1
1979	20.4	5.2	6.3
1980	15.6	3.6	4.2
1981	13.2	2.7	3.8

Industrial and commercial companies, excluding their North Sea activity.
(1) using the 'backward-looking' measure of tax liability.
    Source: Bank of England Quarterly Bulletin, June 1982.

commercial companies was remarkably constant, 15.9% in 1963 and 13.2% in 1981. But in the same period the UK moved from low to relatively high levels of inflation. The second column shows the effects of making depreciation and stock adjustments to the historic-cost series. 'Real' return on trading assets fell dramatically from 11.4% in 1963 to 2.7% in 1981. Tax mitigated these effects slightly, so that the post-tax real return of UK firms in 1981 was 3.8%.

The most dramatic downturn of real profitability occurred in 1975, and it was sufficiently severe to move the Chancellor of the Exchequer to introduce changes in tax legislation to aid company liquidity. After 1975 real profits rose slightly to 1978 and then declined further.

As yet there is no generally accepted explanation for the fall in real returns over the period, or for that matter of the strange constancy in nominal, historic-cost returns.[11] But there has been general agreement that declining profitability has made it difficult for industrial and commercial firms to generate internal funds for investment.

IV SUMMARY

The process of measuring the performance of the firm in practice is indirect. We have no direct information on what managements might have done or even what they wanted to do. In practice the analyst is forced to judge performance by comparing present performance with the performance of other firms, and the same firm in other periods. In this chapter we presented some of the ratios commonly used in comparison and discussed their use. The overriding lesson that emerges is the need for care in making judgements about firms using ratios. The relationship between accounting ratios and economic value is at best indirect, and the analyst depends heavily on the price data that goes into ratios being consistent and comparable.

REFERENCES AND BIBLIOGRAPHY

Amey, C R	*The Efficiency of Business Enterprises* (1969) Allen and Unwin, London.
Ball, R and Watts, R	'Some Time Series Properties of Accounting Income', Journal of Finance, June 1972, pp 663–681.
Bromwich, M	'Measurement of Divisional Performance – A Comment and Extension', Accounting and Business Research, Spring 1973.
Burgess, G J and Webb, A J	'Rates of Return and Profit Shares in the United Kingdom', Lloyds Bank Review, April 1974.
de V Graaf, J	*Theoretical Welfare Economics* (1967) Cambridge.
Emmanuel, C R and Otley, D T	'The Usefulness of Residual Income', Journal of Business Finance and Accounting, 1976, pp 43–52.
Flower, J F	'Measurement of Divisional Performance', Accounting and Business Research, Summer 1971.

11   The fall was first catalogued by Glyn and Sutcliffe (1972) who provided a socialist interpretation and saw it as signalling a crisis of capitalism. Subsequent work in this area included Burgess and Webb (1974) and King (1975). Statistics on aggregate profitability are published annually, with an interpretation, in the June edition of the Bank of England Quarterly Bulletin.

Foster, G	*Financial Statement Analysis* (1978) Prentice-Hall, Inc Englewood-Cliffs, New Jersey.
Glyn, A and Sutcliffe, R B	*British Capitalism, Workers and the Profits Squeeze* (1972) Penguin, London.
Hirs Hleifer, J	'On the Economics of Transfer Pricing', Journal of Business, 1958, pp 172–184.
Kay, J A	'Accountants, Too, Could Be Happy in a Golden Age', Oxford Economic Papers, 1976.
King, M A	'The United Kingdom Profits Crisis: Myth or Reality?', Economic Journal, March 1975, pp 33–54.
King, M A	*Public Policy and the Corporation* (1977) Chapman and Hall, London.
Layard, R (ed)	*Cost-Benefit Analysis* (1972) Penguin, Harmondsworth.
Pearce, D W and Nash, C A	*The Social Appraisal of Projects* (1981) Macmillan, London.
Peasnell, K V	'Some Formal Corrections Between Economic Values and Yields and Accounting Numbers', Journal of Business Finance and Accounting, 1982.
Prest, A R and Turvey, R	'Cost-Benefit Analysis: a Survey', Economic Journal, 1965, pp 685–705, reprinted in part in Layard (1972).
Scherer, F M	*Industrial Market Structure and Economic Performance* (2nd edn, 1980) Rand McNally, Chicago.
Skinner, R C	'Return on Capital Employed as a Measure of Efficiency', Accountancy, June 1965.
Tobin, J	'A General Equilibrium Approach to Monetary Theory', in Essays in Economics: Macroeconomics, Vol 1, Chicago, 1971.
Tomkins, C	'Another Look at Residual Income', Journal of Business Finance and Accounting, Spring 1975, pp 39–54.

QUESTIONS

1 What difficulties arise in using ROI to compare the performance of two firms?

2 What difficulties arise in setting ROI as a target for managers?

3 You are personal assistant to the manager of a large branch of a leading commercial bank. Thrusting the file into your hand, your manager explains that tomorrow the chairman of Northampton Engineers Ltd, is coming to discuss their loan facility. Northampton are seeking to increase their overdraft by £200,000 to finance the acquisition of badly-needed modern equipment. Your manager is very concerned about the existing level of the overdraft. As background he tells you that Northampton have been associated with your bank for 40 years, and that they are an important employer in the town.

The file contains the recent accounts of Northampton. You also obtain from the bank's economics section some performance indicators for Northampton's sector of the engineering industry as a whole.

Industry sector figures: 1986

Return on total assets	10%
Debt ratio	45%
Profit margin on sales	4%
Acid test ratio	1.2
Current ratio	2.5
Stock turnover	8 times
Debtors' turnover	14 times

NORTHAMPTON – Balance sheets (31 December)

ASSETS EMPLOYED	1985	1986
Land and buildings	293,700	275,400
Machinery	284,580	243,180
Stocks	1,147,500	1,859,040
Debtors	624,240	872,100
Cash	64,260	45,900
Creditors and accruals	477,360	862,920
Overdraft	229,500	642,600
	1,707,420	1,787,100
FINANCED BY		
Ordinary shares (£1 at par)	826,000	826,000
Retained earnings	789,480	881,280
Debentures	91,940	79,820
	1,707,420	1,787,100

– Income statements (year ended 31 December)

	1985	1986
Sales	6,196,500	6,426,000
Cost of sales	4,957,200	5,140,800
Gross profit	1,239,300	1,285,200
General expenses	698,040	826,200
Depreciation	229,500	275,400
Net income	£311,760	£183,600

Prepare a brief for your manager suggesting how he should respond to Northampton. Consider what further information would be useful.

Part IV
The financing decision

CHAPTER 14
The capital structure decision

There are two types of finance: equity – new issues and retained earnings; and debt – long, medium and short-term, and disguised debt finance such as leasing. The question is, which should the firm use? We call the mixture of financing a firm uses its 'capital structure', so the purpose of this chapter is to show how the firm's optimal capital structure is found, that is, the capital structure that maximises the value of the firm.

As so often, the best way to approach the capital structure problem is first to envisage what would happen in a perfect capital market, then to consider the effect of introducing realistic market imperfections into the analysis. In a classic study, Modigliani and Miller (1958), 'MM', showed that in a perfect capital market it does not matter what capital structure the firm chooses, its value will be unchanged – in other words capital structure is *irrelevant* to the value of the firm. The argument is that different mixes of financing contract are merely different ways of cutting and distributing a given cake, the cake being the level and risk of the firm's earnings stream. Just as the nature of a cake is unaffected by who eats the cherries and who eats the sponge, so the total value of the firm is unaffected by the detail of the distribution of risk and return to providers of finance. This is the case in a perfect capital market, but when we introduce the market imperfections of tax, bankruptcy costs, and information costs we find the value of the firm *is* affected by capital structure.

In Section I we discuss the nature of financial and business risk. The analysis of the capital structure decision in a perfect market is presented in Section II. In Section III we examine the effect of introducing market imperfections into the model. Section IV considers the duration of the financing mix. In the final section we examine the evidence on the capital structures that firms actually have, and try to generate some recommendations for choice of capital structure. At this point we concede that at the present state of knowledge we cannot fully explain the capital structures we observe in the real world.

I RISK; BUSINESS AND FINANCIAL

In previous chapters we saw that the future returns to projects cannot be known with certainty – what we face when looking at the future is a distribution of possible outcomes and we use the 'variance' of this distribution, a measure of dispersion, to measure the riskiness of future returns. The returns to the firm as a whole are also risky, being the aggregate of the returns from its individual projects. But this aggregate risk depends on how the component projects fit together as a portfolio and managers might try to diversify the component projects of the firm in order to achieve a relatively low-risk return from the firm as a whole.

The risk we have been talking about so far – the economic risk innate in the firm's operations – we now label *business risk*. Various factors cause some projects and thus some firms to have relatively more business risk than others: the structure of the market and the industry, the rate of change of tastes and technology, the exposure to macroeconomic variables, the 'operating leverage' of the firm. The discussion of risk in the first part of the book was independent of financing. But when we consider financing alternatives we encounter a new aspect of risk: *financial risk*. Financial risk is a function of the proportion of debt in the total financing of the firm. We will use the word *gearing* for this proportion, though the US term *leverage* is also used in practice. We define 'gearing' as:

$$\text{GEARING} = \frac{\text{DEBT}}{\text{DEBT} + \text{EQUITY}}$$

$$= \frac{D}{D + S} = \frac{D}{V} \tag{1}$$

where D = market value of debt
S = market value of equity
V = D + S = market value of the firm

Debt includes all borrowing that is intended should form part of the long term financing of the firm. An alternative specification which is commonly used is

$$\text{GEARING} = \frac{\text{DEBT}}{\text{EQUITY}} \tag{2}$$

(1) Is perhaps more convenient, since it has a possible range to 100% rather than to infinity. When analysing the impact of the firm's capital structure it can be useful to explore the 'income' aspect of gearing as well. We can define

$$\text{INCOME GEARING} = \frac{\text{Interest payments}}{\text{Earnings before interest}} \tag{3}$$

As we shall see the impact of gearing is related to the commitment to fixed interest payments relative to a varying underlying income stream – income gearing measures this directly.

Gearing and the creation of financial risk

Consider Arc plc, which is choosing between two alternative and rather extreme capital structures, a low-geared structure with £100,000 of debt and £1m of equity (gearing = .09), and a high-geared structure with £1m of debt and £100,000 of equity (gearing = .91). Arc can issue debt at a cost of 5%, which is below its cost of equity. Arc expects future profits to be either £100,000, £75,000 or £50,000, each equally probable, and Table 1 presents the return to equity and to debt under each of these outcomes and under each gearing situation, assuming all surplus profits are distributed to equity as dividends so that earnings per share (EPS) and dividend per share are the same.

At both gearing levels and at all levels of profit the return to debt is the same – a constant 5p in the £1, or 5% – this was our assumption. But in the second and fourth rows we see the impact on the returns to equity of gearing-up with lower cost debt. With high-gearing the average earnings per share, π, is 25p as against only 7p with low-gearing – by importing more cheap finance the residual profits increase dramatically relative to the reduced number of equity shares.

But the gearing also increases the riskiness of the equity return. At low-gearing, the standard deviation of EPS assuming all three profit outcomes are equally likely, is 2p. At high-gearing it is 20p. The variability, which is risk per unit of return $\frac{\sigma}{\pi}$, is

Table I Arc: Interest and Dividends

LOW-GEARED	Profit £100,000 Total	Interest per £1/EPS	£75,000		£50,000		
Interest on £100,000 debt	£5,000	5p	£5,000	5p	£5,000	5p	
Dividends on £1m equity	£95,000	9p	£70,000	7p	£45,000	4p	$\pi = 7p$ $\sigma = 2p$

HIGH-GEARED							
Interest on £1m debt	£50,000	5p	£50,000	5p	£50,000	5p	
Dividends on £100,000 equity	£50,000	50p	£25,000	25p	£0	£0	$\pi = 25p$ $\sigma = 20p$

low-gearing, $\dfrac{2}{7} = .28$

high-gearing, $\dfrac{20}{25} = .8$

Gearing has given equity a higher return but at the cost of bearing a higher risk. It is this extra risk which we call 'financial' risk. We can measure the extent of the financial risk component by finding the variation in equity returns in the no-gearing case. With no debt the whole financing will be provided by 1,100,000 £1 shares. Average equity earnings in total will be (100,000 + 75,000 + 50,000) ÷ 3 = £75,000. So average EPS is £75,000 ÷ 1.1 million = 6.8p. The standard deviation of this return is .01p, and this is a measure of the underlying business risk of the firm. Now we can identify the components of the risk borne by Arc equity in the high-geared case as follows

σ of EPS with NO GEARING   = .01 ← BUSINESS RISK
σ of EPS with HIGH GEARING = .80
Difference = .79 ← FINANCIAL RISK

Gearing increases the return to equity but also the risk, but these risk and return effects come from quite separate sources. Gearing pushed up the return to equity because we *also* *assumed* that debt was cheaper than equity. There are good reasons for this assumption in practice – the tax-deductibility of interest payments, and the lower risk associated with debt. But if debt happened to have a higher cost than equity, the effect of gearing would be to reduce the return to equity. The risk effect of gearing on the other hand, occurs because the return to debt is fixed, irrespective of whether debt is cheaper or not. By agreeing to give debt a larger risk-free slice of earnings the firm is reserving all the variation in earnings for equity, but on a lower absolute return. Figure 1 depicts this under Arc's two gearing alternatives. For convenience we express the assumption that earnings of £100,000, £75,000 and £50,000 are equi-probable by showing earnings fluctuating between these values through time.

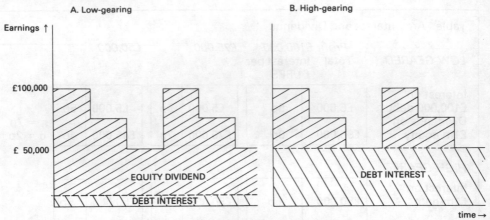

Figure I The division of Arc earnings between equity and debt

EQUITY AS AN OPTION ON THE FIRM

Another way to analyse this relationship between debt and equity is using option theory. Though the idea can seem rather strange at first, some thought will show that the returns to debt and equity are the returns they would receive if debt owned the firm and had sold a call option on it to equity at an exercise price equal to the redemption value of the debt, the amount debt-holders receive when the debt expires. Suppose D is the redemption value of the debt, and V the value of the whole firm when debt is redeemed, with S the value of the equity. When the debt is redeemed debt get D if V > D, but if the firm's assets are insufficient, i e D > V, debt get V. So the return to debt will be MIN (D, V). If V > D, equity get what is left, i e V − D, but if D > V then equity get nothing. So the return to equity will be MAX (0, V − D) which we can recognise as the pay-off to a call option.

If we assume V is given and is invariant to the split between debt and equity (this is the assumption we will be exploring in the remainder of this chapter), once we know equity is an option we could use the Black and Scholes option pricing model to give us insights into the determinants of both S and D (= V − S). Recall from Chapter 11 that, other things equal, the value of an option is an increasing function of the risk of the underlying asset. This was because the option value depends entirely on positive variances above the exercise price – the more risky the asset, the more of these there will be. As we discuss elsewhere, once the debt-contract is signed and sealed it is in the interests of equity to increase the riskiness of the firm. Now we can see exactly why this is so. Option theory provides a method for evaluating the effect of changes in risk on the value of debt and equity, and of other financing changes the firm might have in mind, such as increasing the amount of debt (= the exercise price of the option) or the duration of debt (= the time to exercise).

II THE ANALYSIS OF THE CAPITAL STRUCTURE DECISION

If equity investors are risk-averse they will only be interested in gearing if they are compensated by higher returns. The key question we now turn to is whether and under what circumstances gearing will lead to a net gain to shareholders, as signalled by an increase in the value of the firm.

SOME NAIVE MODELS OF VALUATION

We will start by considering two extreme views, and one somewhere in the middle, of how the firm is valued relative to its capital structure. The two extreme positions are best described in terms of the 'net income' (NI), and the 'net operating income' (NOI), of the firm[1]. NOI is the firm's basic earnings stream before dividends and interest, NI is NOI less interest payments, I.

To start with we are going to describe a simple world in which there is no growth in earnings, all earnings are paid out as dividends, and the cost of equity is r_e; and in which debt is a perpetuity and receives a constant annual interest payment I. We will assume there is no taxation so that the cost of debt is simply r_d. We saw in Chapter 10 that if there is a constant growth rate in dividends, g, then the value of a share is $\dfrac{DIV_1}{r_e - g}$. If we assume further that all earnings are paid out as dividends, so $DIV_1 = NI$, and there is no growth in earnings, so g = o, then the value of equity is $S = \dfrac{NI}{r_e}$. Similarly, $D = \dfrac{I}{r_d}$ The overall value of the firm is

$$V = D + S$$

so
$$V = \frac{I}{r_d} + \frac{NI}{r_e} \tag{1}$$

Suppose a firm has an NOI of £3,600, pays interest of £600 and distributes the remaining £3,000 as dividend. Its costs of debt and equity are 5% and 12% respectively. In this case the overall value of the firm

is $V = \dfrac{600}{.05} + \dfrac{3,000}{.12}$

$= 12,000 + 25,000 = £37,000$

We can also say something about the average price it pays for its finance, which will be the cost of the individual types weighted by the proportions it uses of each. We define the *weighted average cost of capital*, WACC, or r_a, as

$$r_a = \frac{D}{D + S}r_d + \frac{S}{D + S}r_e \tag{2}$$

In the present case

$r_a = \dfrac{12,000}{37,000} \times .05 + \dfrac{25,000}{37,000} \times .12$

$= 0.016 \qquad + 0.081 \ = \underline{9.7\%}$

Our interest is in what happens to the value of the firm, V, and its overall cost of capital, r_a, when gearing changes. The NI model and the NOI model represent two different views about how equations (1) and (2) will respond. The NI model says that r_d and r_e are constant. If $r_d < r_e$ then switching to cheaper debt must reduce r_a, the average cost of capital. And switching from dividends to interest must increase V as well, because in (1) we

1   This follows the analysis by Durand (1952).

are capitalising interest at a higher value than dividends. The NOI approach is quite different. It says that the overall amounts, V and r_a, are constant, and r_d is constant too. Something must give if (1) and (2) are to hold at different gearing levels, and it is r_e which changes. We can see this in action with numerical examples.

The NI model

Table II shows the NI approach in our firm with NOI of £3,000 and a cost of debt of 5% and cost of equity of 12%. In the first column we assume it has £12,000 of debt as before. In the second column it has £24,000 of debt and therefore pays £1,200 interest.

Table II The NI approach to valuation		
	Gearing I	Gearing II
NOI	3,600	£ 3,600
Interest, I	600	1,200
NI	3,000	2,400
equity capitalisation rate, r_e	.12	.12
Value of equity, S	25,000	20,000
Value of debt, D	12,000	24,000
Value of firm V	£37,000	£44,000

Because of the lower capitalisation rate on debt the total value of the firm is increased by issuing debt instead of equity. There is no limit on the benefits to this policy and the relationship between value and gearing are depicted in Figure IIa. The value maximising position appears to be 100% gearing, and this would also give the lowest overall cost of capital, which would just be r_d.

In practice most firms stop a long way short of 100% gearing. One reason for this could be a fear that extreme gearing will lead to bankruptcy. So when gearing is perceived as getting too high both debt and equity may increase their required return to compensate themselves for the increased risk, thereby causing a downturn in the valuation of the firm at high gearing levels. We depict this modified NI model in Figure IIb. This picture, with benefits to cheaper debt 'up to a point', is known as the *traditional view*. It will make a useful comparison later on.

The NOI model

Under the NI Model debt and equity were valued independently, using appropriate capitalisation rates. The value of the firm was the sum of the two. Under the NOI approach the value of the firm is determined directly by capitalising the NOI of the firm using an overall capitalisation rate, r_a, which is constant and given for the firm.

$$\text{Hence } V = \frac{\text{NOI}}{r_a}$$

It follows immediately that, since NOI and r_a are constant and given, V is invariant to gearing. But it remains the case that $V = D + S$.

Now if we still assume that r_d is constant then debt can be valued independently as

$$D = \frac{I}{r_d}$$

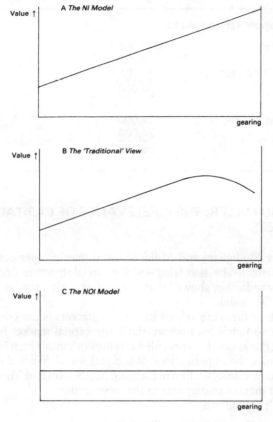

Figure II

Hence the value of equity, S, is the residual $S = V - D$

and r_e, the return on equity, is determined within the system since

$$r_e = \frac{NI}{S}$$

We will use the NOI Model on the previous example. We assume $r_d = 5\%$ as before, but this time assume an overall capitalisation rate for the firm, $r_a = 10\%$. The equity rate, r_e, is to be found. This time the valuation process is described in Table III.

Under gearing 1 the implicit cost of equity is

$$r_e = \frac{NI}{S} = \frac{3,000}{24,000} = 12.5\%$$

Under gearing 11, $r_e = \frac{2,400}{12,000} = 20\%$

The value of the firm is thus invariant to gearing and is found directly by capitalising NOI. This is depicted in Figure IIC.

As they stand the NI and NOI models are just exercises in arithmetic, no more. Next we analyse which of them is likely to describe the workings of the real world.

Table III The NI approach to valuation

	Gearing I	Gearing II
NOI	3,600	3,600
Overall capitalisation rate, r_a	.10	.10
Value of the firm, V	36,000	36,000
comprising		
Debt, at values as before, D	12,000	24,000
Equity , S	24,000	12,000
	36,000	36,000

MODIGLIANI AND MILLER; THE IRRELEVANCE OF CAPITAL STRUCTURE IN PERFECT MARKETS

In their 1958 paper Modigliani and Miller showed that in a perfect capital market the value of a firm is unaffected by its gearing – so the capital structure decision is irrelevant to valuation. In other words, they showed that in a perfect capital market firms will be valued according to the NOI model.

The analysis of how firms are valued in perfect markets is the cornerstone of finance theory. This is not so much because we think the capital market is perfect but rather because the perfect market analysis provides a framework into which we can systematically introduce and evaluate the imperfections of the real world. We will adopt this approach with the capital structure analysis, first presenting Modigliani and Miller's argument, then relaxing the perfect market assumption in the next section.

MM derive two 'propositions'

Proposition I   The market value of any firm is independent of its capital structure and is given by capitalising its expected return at the rate r_a appropriate to its [risk-]class.

Hence $V = \dfrac{NOI}{r_a}$

Putting this the other way round:
The average cost of capital to any firm is completely independent of its capital structure and is equal to the capitalisation rate of a pure equity stream of its class.

Hence $r_a = \dfrac{NOI}{V}$

Proposition II   The expected yield of a share of stock is equal to the appropriate capitalisation rate r_a for a pure equity stream in the class, plus a premium related to financial risk equal to the debt-to-equity ratio times the spread between r_a and r_d.

Hence $r_e = r_a + (r_a - r_d)\dfrac{D}{S}$

In their original 1958 paper MM made a variety of assumptions in order to derive their propositions. Since then theorists have worked to reduce the assumptions that are necessary to support the theory. This process is central to the scientific method of economics. The fewer assumptions necessary for a theory, the stronger the theory.

One feature of original MM work which looks rather strange now is their requirement that firms belong to homogeneous 'risk-classes'. These are the classes MM refer to in the statements of their propositions we quoted above, and their overall capitalisation rate, r_a, is a rate appropriate to firms *in the risk-class*. MM were writing before the CAPM gave us a method of directly evaluating differences in risk between firms, so they had to eliminate risk from their discussion by working with firms within a constant-risk class. (This is more evidence, for the reader who might be doubting it, why the CAPM represented such a major advance in finance thinking.)

The necessary assumptions

The assumptions necessary for the MM propositions are those that define a 'perfect market'. In particular, we need the following attributes of a perfect market.
1   The tax system is neutral with respect to capital structure.
2   Individuals and firms can borrow and lend at the same rate.
3   There are no costs associated with the liquidation of the firm.
4   Information is freely available to all participants in the capital market.
   When we have established the MM propositions we will investigate these assumptions in turn.

Deriving the MM propositions

The proof of MM's proposition I is important because it employs two concepts that we use constantly in thinking about finance: the concepts of *arbitrage* and the *home-made alternative*.

   The test of any financing or investment decision is whether it enhances value. Since the value of firms is set in the market place this means studying the market reaction to the decision. In a perfect market two identical commodities must sell for the same price. Indeed we can define a 'perfect market' this way. If the prices of two identical commodities are out of line in such a market owners will switch from the dearer to the cheaper to make a profit. But this process of selling and buying drives prices down and up respectively until in equilibrium the prices are equal and there is no more incentive to switch. We call the process by which prices are driven into line in this way the *arbitrage* process. In the case of the capital market the 'commodities' are the shares or debt of firms, both of which offer claims over an uncertain stream of future returns. For us to be sure that two different 'commodities' in this market were 'identical' we would have to be sure they gave the same return in every possible future state of the world. MM's proof of irrelevance does precisely this. It shows in the case of capital structure that the sum of the shares and debt of a firm remains an 'identical commodity' whatever the split between the two, hence the operation of arbitrage in the market will ensure that two firms different only in capital structure must have the same value.

   Another concept MM employ in reaching their conclusion is the notion of the 'home-made alternative'. Often we see firms, or intermediaries in the capital market, doing things which appear to benefit investors. But in general these will only add value to the firm if they are things the investor could not have done for himself. In the MM world investors can borrow just as easily as firms, and at the same cost. In this world no one would pay more for a firm just because it borrows. Home-made gearing is a perfect substitute. Home-made alternatives cease to be equally valuable once market imperfections enter the picture. In a world of taxes, transactions costs and information costs, capital-structure and dividend policy may be relevant to the value of the firm.

   Consider two firms, 1 and 2, with the same expected profit (NOI), X, and in the same risk-class. Firm 1 has all-equity financing, firm 2 has some debt. Suppose also, in line with the 'traditional' view of capital structure, that the geared firm, 2, is accordingly more valuable. Figure III may help to envisage what is going on. The capital structure of the two firms is represented by two boxes and the height of each box indicates the total value of each firm, V_1 and V_2. In the case of firm 2 this value is made up of D_2 of debt and S_2 of equity.

Let Y_1, Y_2 be the incomes an investor gets from owning the proportion α of the equity of each firm. We represent the proportion he owns horizontally in Figure III.

Hence $Y_1 = \alpha X$.

But because firm 2 has to pay interest at the rate r_d on its debt D_2 the equity profit is correspondingly reduced so

$$Y_2 = \alpha \ (X - r_d D_2)$$

Now, by assumption, firm 2 is more valuable than firm 1,

$$V_2 \ (=S_2 + B_2) > V_1 \ (= S_1)$$

This opens up a profitable strategy to the investor in firm 2. He can take the following steps:

1 Sell his equity stake in firm 2, αS_2.
2 Raise a loan, exactly equal in size to α of firm 2's debt, αD_2.
3 Spend the proceeds, $\alpha(S_2 + D_2)$ on shares in firm 1.

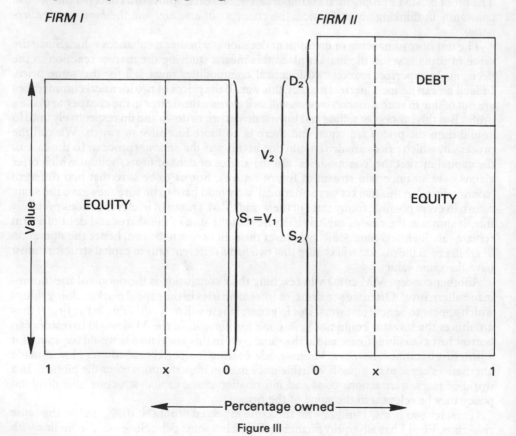

Figure III

Step 2 should be no problem since he can offer as security his shares in firm 1, which represent claims on the same underlying assets that firm 2 could offer its debt-holders.

Using this strategy the investor increases his income at no cost. The investor's old income was $\alpha(X - r_dD_2)$. If he had bought α of firm 1, his new net income would be the same: αX, less the cost of servicing his loan, $\alpha r_d.D_2$. However his income from firm 1 will be higher than αX, since his proceeds from the sale and the loan enable him to buy more than α of firm 1. We know this because, by assumption, $S_2 + D_2 > S_1$, so that $\alpha(S_2 + D_2) > \alpha S_1$. Though his income increases, his risk is unchanged. He now has personal borrowing in the same proportion $\dfrac{D_2}{D_2 + S_2}$ as firm 2 had. Arbitrage will take place until $V_2 (=S_2 + D_2) = V_1 (=S_1)$. By an equivalent argument we could also show that the value of the geared firm cannot be lower than the ungeared.

Consider an example:
Suppose there are two firms in the market, Argon plc and Neon plc, which are effectively identical in that they have the same expected NOI of £200,000, and this profit has the same risk. The market rate of interest is 12%. Argon is an all-equity firm valued at £1 million. Neon has £800,000 of equity and £400,000 of debt, so Neon's total market valuation is £1.2 million. Both firms pay out 100% of net income as dividends.

Griselda Grasby owns £80,000, or 10%, of Neon's equity and notices the valuation discrepancy, so she does the following:
— sells her Neon shares, realising £80,000
— takes out a loan equivalent in size to 10% of Neon's debt, £400,000 × 10% = £40,000
— invests £120,000 in Argon's equity
As a result of these transactions Grasby's income is increased. She used to receive a dividend of 10% of Neon's earnings, £15,200. She now gets *12%* of Argon's NOI of £200,000, which is £24,000 and has to pay £40,000 × 12% = £4,800 of loan interest, leaving a net £19,200. She has an equity of £80,000 on underlying assets of £120,000 just the same proportion as Neon had.

One question we cannot answer is what the equilibrium value of Neon and Argon would be in the previous example. Which value adjusts would depend on which firm was out of line with the market as a whole.

Proposition II can easily be derived now. Dropping subscripts and bearing in mind we are talking about a geared firm, we know that if r_e is the rate of return on equity then

$$S \, r_e = X - r_d D$$

we also know $X = r_a(S + D)$

eliminating X and rearranging we get proposition II:

$$r_e = r_a + (r_a - r_d)\frac{D}{S} \tag{3}$$

We can see that Proposition II is none other than the weighted average cost of capital formula we net earlier. Rearranging (3) we get

$$r_e = (1 + \frac{D}{S})r_a - \frac{D}{S}r_d$$

$$= (r_a - \frac{D}{D + S} r_d) \frac{D + S}{S}$$

$$\text{so, } r_a = \frac{D}{D + S} r_d + \frac{S}{D + S} r_e$$

III THE EFFECT OF MARKET IMPERFECTIONS

Under the MM assumptions the capital structure of the firm is irrelevant to its valuation. We now investigate the realism of those assumptions to see what modifications we may have to make to the irrelevance proposition.

TAXATION

If there is a corporation tax, against which debt interest is a deductible expense but equity dividends are not, the tax system will not be neutral with respect to capital structure. The effect of CT is to make the value of the firm an increasing function of gearing, and thus the cost-of-capital a decreasing function. To see why, we have to modify the NOI valuation model to allow for corporation tax. Now it is *after-tax* returns that investors will capitalise, using a capitalisation rate, r_a, which we will now assume to be an appropriate *after-tax* rate.

Consider two identical firms with NOI before tax of £2,000. The CT rate is 40% and the after-tax capitalisation rate, r_a, is 20%. One firm is presently financed entirely by equity, the other has £3,000 of 12% debt. What will be the relative value of these two firms? We will proceed in two stages: first assuming CT exists but interest is not tax deductible, second calculating the value-effect of the tax deductibility of interest payments, the value of the 'tax-shield' provided by interest.

When there is CT but interest is not tax-deductible, the picture is our usual NOI one – the total valuation of the firm is unaffected by gearing. What happens once interest is tax deductible? The value of the debt is unchanged, but now the Revenue rebates to the firm an amount which is the rate of corporation tax times the interest payment. If the interest payment is $r_d.D$ and the tax rate is T, then the tax rebate is $T.r_d.D$. What discount rate should we use to value this rebate? It is effectively an increase in the after-tax NOI of equity, so maybe the overall capitalisation rate, r_a, might be appropriate? But tax rebates are, unlike NOI, a low risk stream. *Given* the continuation of the tax system, and assuming the company has sufficient taxable earnings, the tax rebate is as certain as the interest payments to which it relates. And except for the risk of bankruptcy we can consider interest payments a certain stream. Hence it is appropriate to capitalise tax savings using the debt capitalisation rate, r_d.

Assuming the payment of debt interest is a perpetuity – the firm always intends to have gearing of this extent – then we can value the tax saving thus

$$\text{Value of tax-saving} = \frac{T r_d D}{r_d}$$

$$= TD$$

The value of tax savings is the value of debt times the corporation tax rate. In Table IV we see that this amounts to £3,000 × 40% = £1,200.

Table IV The NOI approach with Corporation Tax

(1) Assuming CT but interest is not tax deductible

	Ungeared firm	Geared firm
NOI	2,000	2,000
CT @ 40%	800	800
After tax NOI	1,200	1,200
capitalisation rate, r_a	.20	.20
Value of firm	£6,000	£6,000
Comprising equity	6,000	3,000
debt	—	3,000
	£6,000	£6,000

(2) Effect of tax deductibility

Interest paid £3,000 @ 12%	= £ 360
Tax-saving £360 @ 40%	= £ 144
capitalisation rate, r_d,	= .12
VALUE OF TAX SAVING	£1,200

Hence value of geared firm = value of ungeared firm + value
of tax saving = £6,000 + £1,200 = £7,200

MM's after-tax propositions I and II

Using subscripts G, U for the geared and the ungeared firm respectively, MM derived the following:[2]

After-tax proposition I $V_G = V_U + TD$
The value of a geared firm is the value of the ungeared firm plus the value of the tax-savings.

After-tax proposition II $r_e = r_a + (1 - T)(r_a - r_d)\dfrac{D}{S}$

The after tax return on the equity of the geared firm is that for the ungeared firm plus a premium relating to the CT rate, the return on debt and the degree of gearing.

If T = 0, these reduce to the pretax propositions I and II.

As it stands, MM's after-tax proposition I implies the firm should have 100% gearing since value is an increasing function of gearing with a positive CT rate – we have the 'extreme corner solution' depicted in Figure IV. Clearly this does not happen in practice. To understand why we must bring in some other market imperfections.

The effect of personal tax

One problem with MM's tax analysis is that it only considers corporation tax. But other taxes affect the after-tax receipts of debt and equity investors too – personal income tax on

2   MM's first attempt at incorporating corporation tax, in their 1958 article, was mis-specified. MM (1963) represents their corrected attempt.

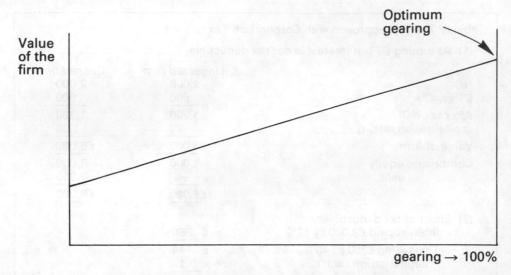

Figure IV The value of the firm under MM's after tax analysis

dividends and interest, and capital gains tax. Miller (1977) developed a more general model. He proposed the following modifications of MM's after-tax proposition I:

$$\text{let } A = \text{tax advantage of gearing} = \left[1 - \frac{(1 - T)(1 - Tpe)}{(1 - Tpd)} \right] D$$

where, now, T = corporation tax rate and
       Tpe = personal tax rate on dividends
       Tpd = personal tax rate on interest

We can see that MM were effectively assuming the special case where the rate of tax on dividends and interest are the same. If $Tpe = Tpd$, Miller's model for the tax advantage to gearing reduces to our earlier TD. So if the corporation tax rate were 40% the tax advantage to debt would be .4D.

Now consider a tax system in which, additionally, interest suffers personal tax, but dividends do not. This is effectively the situation under an 'imputation' tax system such as the UK one. In the UK dividends are taxable, but the basic rate of tax is deemed to be already covered by the company's CT payment. So if investors are paying tax at the basic rate of 30% we might have:

$T \quad = 40\%$
$Tpe = \quad 0\%$
$Tpd = 30\%$

in which case, $A = [1 - \dfrac{(1 - .4)\,(1 - 0)}{(1 - .3)}]D = .14D$

In this case the benefit to debt is reduced. The reason is clear – when we look at the whole tax system we see that the corporation tax saving on interest is partially balanced by personal tax on interest.

In general, to get an adequate picture of the tax-effects of the firm's capital structure decision we need to look at the particular tax-position of the firm and of its investors, and the effective rate of personal tax faced by a firm's clientele of investors can vary enormously depending on their personal circumstances. While charities are exempt tax, some individuals pay tax at up to 60% of income. It is hard to generalise about the effect of a tax system on the basis of its statutory characteristics since tax systems allow so much variety of individual treatment. In this situation the best we can do is recommend each firm to evaluate the tax positions of its own investors in appraising its optimal capital structure. Exactly the same doubts arise about the tax position of the firm itself. Though the nominal corporation tax rate might be 40%, the effective rate for many firms is considerably reduced because they are 'tax exhausted', they have zero taxable earnings in some periods. If the firm is not in a taxpaying position it cannot relieve its ACT, and the tax withheld from dividends becomes a real tax again. Consider the extreme case when the effective tax rates facing a firm and its investors are:

$$T = 0, Tpe = 30\%, Tpd = 30\%$$

then $A = (1 - \frac{1}{1})D = 0$. In this case the advantage to debt is zero, and capital structure is, again, irrelevant.

Miller uses his model to draw some general equilibrium conclusions. He suggests that in practice Tpe will be so low as to be effectively zero, and he points out that for equilibrium, at the margin the tax advantage to debt must be zero. Looking at his equation we can see this will occur when $Tpd = T$, when the tax rate of the marginal debt holder just equals the corporate tax rate. This will determine the overall amount of corporate debt, but since all companies will face the price of debt set by this marginal tax rate, there will be no optimum gearing for any individual firm, and gearing will again be irrelevant.

Bankruptcy costs

To escape from the extreme corner solution implied by MM's after-tax analysis theorists have also turned to bankruptcy costs. In an MM world there were no costs to bankruptcy. But if there are, and if gearing increases the risk of bankruptcy, then this will imply an interior solution, an optimal gearing just where the value loss from possible bankruptcy starts to outweigh the value-gains from tax-savings. The argument is appealing since bankruptcy[3] is a bogey-word. In bankruptcy, investors lose their money, workers lose their jobs and managers lose their reputations. There is never any problem arguing the case that bankruptcy is a bad thing and that investors will shy away from it.

In Chapter 25 we identify several costs to bankruptcy: when a firm is liquidated its assets may be sold at a discount on their economic value; the proceeds of liquidation will be subject to transactions costs such as liquidator's fees; and the process of receivership and liquidation may impose managerial costs. All of these may cause the owners to lose a proportion of the value of the firm if it is liquidated. If this proportion is L and the value of the firm is V, then they will lose LV. However liquidation is an uncertain event, and we can express the expected value of these bankruptcy costs in terms of the probability of bankruptcy, p, which we assume to be some function of gearing.

so expected bankruptcy costs = pLV

Hence we can extend our valuation formula for the geared firm thus

$$V_G = V_u + TD - pLV.$$

---

3 We follow the American practice on this and use the word 'bankruptcy' interchangeably with 'liquidation' which is the correct word in the UK for company failure.

Now, assuming p only becomes significant at higher levels of gearing the relationship between value and gearing will be as depicted in Figure V.

The crucial intellectual step is to see that in a perfect capital market *bankruptcy is of no importance*. Firms will use assets just so long as their economic value within the firm exceeds their value outside. If the profitability of the assets declines to such an extent that this ceases to be the case, then they should be sold. If such a large proportion of the firm's assets fall into this category that the firm cannot continue to exist without them, then the firm will be liquidated. Since the realisable value is now the economic value of the firm, no loss will be associated with liquidation so far as owners are concerned if the firm is liquidated in a perfect market.

How important are bankruptcy costs in practice? The evidence is very thin. The transactions costs in liquidation are real enough, though as a percentage of value they may not be large. A study by Warner (1977) of US railroad bankruptcies showed that they averaged only 3.5% of the value of the firm in question, though the percentage may be much higher for smaller firms. Do the assets of liquidated firms sell at below their economic value? The implication is that asset markets are inefficient and perhaps that receivers do not seek out best prices when selling assets. There is no hard evidence on this topic. To some extent the problem may be one of perceptions. Investors may have lost touch with the real value of the firm and the event of bankruptcy may cause a sudden awakening to losses that have been accruing for some time. The managerial costs of failure – the extra time spent in dealing with receivers, liquidators, bankers; the lost opportunities embodied in the constraints on behaviour imposed by these people – are similarly hard to quantify. But costs that are hard to quantify may still be real.

The second question is the relationship between gearing and the probability of bankruptcy. One view is: 'Gearing increases the firm's fixed commitments to interest payments. These commitments are legally enforceable. Hence gearing increases the likelihood that outsiders can enforce liquidation on the firm'. The trouble with this view is that it ignores the *economics* of failure and looks only to the *legal* event. The task of a receiver is to explore alternative uses for a firm's assets and ascertain the best use. Though it is easy to see that higher gearing may trigger the appointment of a receiver sooner rather

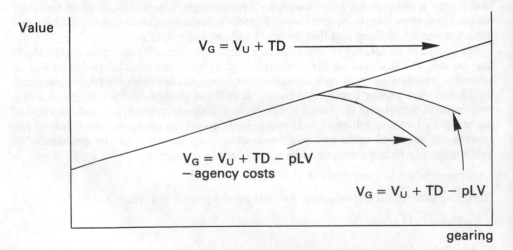

Figure V The effect of gearing on value with market imperfections

than later, it is not so clear why this will make bankruptcy more likely. The decision to liquidate should reflect the economic value of alternative possibilities, and this appears to be independent of the appointment of a receiver. Again the problem may be one of confusing cause and effect. A succession of losses will drive-up gearing simply by eroding the equity base. The underlying cause remains the economic performance of the firm.

CAN INDIVIDUALS AND FIRMS BORROW AND LEND AT THE SAME RATE?

The central plank of the MM propositions is the notion that homemade and corporate leverage are perfect substitutes. A necessary condition for this is that individuals and firms can borrow and lend at the same rate. In practice there may be market forces at work which lead investors to prefer firms to do the borrowing and which accordingly raise the value of geared firms. First, there are economies of scale in borrowing which make it cheaper for the firm to borrow rather than the individual. Second there may be restrictions on the ability of institutions to borrow. Some institutions such as pension funds and charities have restrictions in their trust deeds limiting the proportion of funds they can invest in different types of asset, and thus limiting their ability to indulge in home-made leverage. These market imperfections may create a demand from investors for geared companies.

THE COSTS OF INFORMATION; THE AGENCY PROBLEM

The relationship between debt-holders and management is one of agency. Managers are the debt-holders' agents, stewarding assets over which the debt has claims. As we saw in Chapter 2, agency relationships have costs, springing from the fundamental divergence in interest between principal and agent and the fact that it would be prohibitively expensive to write a complete contract at the outset – a contract that specified what management should do in every possible future state of the world. Up to a point it will be worthwhile the principal incurring costs on monitoring the agent, and the agent incurring costs in 'bonding' himself to the principal in order to reduce overall agency costs.

The problem facing debt is that, once the debt contract has been written, subsequent actions of managers may reduce the value of debt-holders' claims – the firm may issue other senior debt, pay large dividends to equity, increase the risk of the firm, and so forth. In response debt will try to protect itself by writing protective covenants into the debt-contract, limiting the actions of management. But debt only partly protects itself this way: greater protection would require more complete contracts and prohibitive costs in monitoring the subsequent actions of managers. Since the risks to debt get greater with gearing and the agency costs of controlling those risks will be prohibitive, agency costs argue for limiting the gearing of the firm.

Figure V shows the effects of CT, bankruptcy costs, and agency costs, on value. The final picture is very similar to the 'traditional view' we presented earlier in the chapter.

THE ROLE OF 'SECURABLE ASSETS'

Firms differ in the assets they can offer as 'security' for debt. In practice we find companies such as property companies may have substantially more debt than firms with less securable assets. But the possession of securable assets is just one manifestation of the underlying business risk of the firm. What characterises the 'securability' of an asset is the degree of certainty that we can have about its future resale value. So while 'business risk' describes the variability of the returns from the firm's assets in their 'first-best' use, the resale value of the firm's assets reflects the forgone returns from second-best uses. The greater the security that can be given to debt financiers, the less the monitoring costs they will need to incur in protecting their debt.

IV   OPTIMAL CAPITAL STRUCTURE WITH RESPECT TO DURATION

The analysis so far has considered the optimal balance between debt and equity for the firm. In other words we have been looking at the best mixture of contracts for the firm to write in terms of risk and return. But we are also interested in the duration of the finance the firm raises – the balance between long-term finance, equity and long-term debt, and short-term finance such as bank-borrowing. There is a traditional rule of thumb which says the firm should match the term-structure of its financing to the term-structure of its assets. The rule says that the long-term finance of the firm should be at least as great as its fixed or long-term assets. In terms of the simple balance-sheet below, the difference x should always be positive and the firm should never finance any part of its long-term assets with short-term finance.

A simple balance-sheet

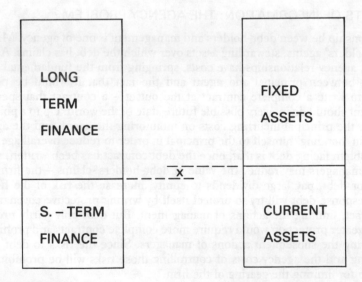

In its 'Money for Business', the Bank of England states a similar principle.

For a business with a sound balance-sheet, long-term funds are in general appropriate to help finance investment in productive assets with a long-life, such as industrial buildings or heavy plant machinery. .... Medium-term finance ... is appropriate for the purchase of most plant and machinery, and to finance a proportion of working-capital. Short-term funds are appropriate to meet fluctuations in working capital and for the finance of trade.
(p 11–12)

This principle is the equivalent of the old banking adage 'never borrow short and lend long'. At first glance it sounds eminently sensible, but subjected to the hard logic of finance, it loses some of its force. The aim may be to avoid the danger that the firm will be unable to repay if short-term finance is withdrawn, without selling-off fixed assets and thus dismantling the fixed capital of the firm. In an efficient capital market it is hard to see the logic in this. For one thing, if finance were withdrawn there should be no more reason to consider a loss of fixed capital more significant than a loss of current assets. In a firm which is not carrying redundant assets both are vital. But anyhow in an efficient capital market we find it hard to conceive that short-term finance would be withdrawn yet the firm be unable to replace it, unless there had been a deterioration in the economic value of the firm. If the effect of gearing up with long term finance is to limit the option the investor has to withdraw his funds, should there be a fall in the value of the firm, then we can expect him to want compensating for this reduction in his options.

V THE CAPITAL-STRUCTURE DECISION IN PRACTICE

By starting from an MM world with no taxes then considering different market imperfections it is possible to build up a picture of the factors that are likely to determine optimal capital structure. These factors will differ from firm to firm, depending on the tax position of the firm and its particular clientele of investors, the scale of potential bankruptcy costs and the risk of bankruptcy, and the difficulty in writing financing contracts that protect debt. But the fact is, theory cannot at present fully explain why firms choose the capital-structures they do.

The empirical evidence

Though it is interesting to see how different industries shape-up in terms of capital structure, data like this cannot be more than suggestive. The key question is how capital structure affects value, but this question is hard to research. No two firms are identical and firms differ in other ways that might affect value the most notable being economic risk, and growth rates. Researchers have adopted various approaches to this problem. Modigliani and Miller (1958) choose two industries in the US which had fairly large populations of apparently homogeous firms – electric utilities and oil companies. They regressed cost of capital on capital structure and found no apparent influence of capital structure. MM were unable to reject the null hypothesis of the irrelevance of capital structure. However MM's 1958 work can be criticised in that their sample groups are not truly homogeneous in either economic risk, or growth rates. Weston (1963) and MM (1966) made some allowance for this and got results which suggests there is a positive tax advantage to gearing. Masulis (1978) devised a different methodology. He studied 163 occasions between 1962 and 1976 on which firms had exchanged equity and debt. By studying financial exchanges within given firms he hoped to hold the effect of economic risk and of growth constant. He found evidence of statistically significant tax advantage to gearing. However, there is a good deal more research needed before we have a full explanation of the effects of capital structure on value.

International comparisons; gearing in Japan

People often point to the financing practices of overseas firms when looking for reasons why the UK economy has performed relatively badly.[4] In particular they point to Japan

4 See for example Carrington and Edwards (1979).

where companies seem to have gearing levels over 80%. The argument then runs: 'debt is cheaper than equity, high geared firms have a lower average cost of capital, therefore they invest more'.

Modigliani and Miller have taught us to be highly suspicious about arguments like this, and we would need to see a rather special configuration of market imperfections to support it. There are certain special features of the Japanese capital market but whether they reduce the cost of capital is unclear. One is the extraordinarily high level of savings in Japan.[5] Japanese households customarily save 20% – 25% of disposable income – much more than in other developed countries. Another is the role of banks, which have traditionally been far and away the main sources of finance for Japanese firms. A significant place in the Japanese economy is held by 'zaibatsu' – loose groups of industrial and commercial firms with significant cross-holdings of shares, and often including a bank and other financial institutions within the group. Also the Japanese tax system seems to offer tax savings to corporate debt.

Elstron (1981) tried to assess the gearing of Japanese companies. He found that the 'equity ratio' of Japanese industry (equity as a percentage of total assets) had not always been so low. It had fallen from a level of 60% in the 1930s to a low-point of 17% for manufacturing firms in 1975/1976, compared with 35% – 40% in W Germany, 50% in the UK and 50 – 60% in the US. But Elstron then suggested that there might be a problem of measurement. He pointed to three factors tending to understate equity: i) a serious under-valuation of assets like land due to a lack of inflation accounting, ii) the classification of certain equity reserves as debt, and iii) an overstatement of total assets by failing to net off certain balances due to and from smaller associated firms. Adjusting for these, Elstron suggested the 1975 ratio could have been 40% – 50%, comparable to other developed economies. The example indicated the danger of measuring gearing in book values – the problem would not have arisen without market values.

VI   SUMMARY

Finance theory cannot yet fully explain the capital structures that firms adopt in practice, but – with the help of Modigliani and Miller's analysis, and a careful inspection of real world market imperfections we can get a good idea of the factors that will affect the capital structure decision. In a perfect capital market the capital-structure of the firm would be 'irrelevant' to its value. But in reality the underlying tax subsidy on debt provides a strong incentive to 'gear-up', but it is impossible to generalise about the tax-effects on gearing. The size of the tax advantage to debt depends very much on the particular tax-positions of the firm and its shareholders. However, whatever the tax advantage to debt, there will be limits on the gearing of firms. Both bankruptcy costs, and agency costs, make debtholders reluctant to provide high levels of gearing to firms.

REFERENCES AND BIBLIOGRAPHY

Baron, David P   'Default Risk and the Modigliani-Miller Theorem: A
                                Synthesis'. American Economic Review, March 1976.

---

5   This section draws heavily on C D Elstron, 'The financing of Japanese industry' Bank of England, Quarterly
    Bulletin: Dec 1981

Carrington, J C and Edwards, G T	*Financing Industrial Investment* (1979) Macmillan, London.
De Angelo, H and Masulis, R W	'Optimal Capital Structure under Corporate and Personal Taxation' March Journal of Financial Economics, 1980, pp 3–30.
Durand, D	'Cost of Debt and Equity Funds for Business; Trends and Problems of Measurement' in 'Conferences on Research in Business Finance', National Bureau of Economic Research, New York, 1952.
Fama, E F	'The Effects of a Firm's Investment and Financing Decisions' American Economic Review, June 1978, pp 272–284.
Hamada, R	'The Effect of the Firm's Capital Structure on the Systematic Risk of Common Stocks Journal of Finance, March 1972, pp 435–452.
Haugen, Robert A and Senbert, Lemma, W	'The irrelevance of Bankruptcy Costs to the Theory of Optimal Capital Structure' Journal of Finance, March 1978, pp 383–393.
Jensen, M C and Meckling, W H	'Theory of the Firm's Managerial Behaviour, Agency Costs and Ownership Structure' Journal of Financial Economics Oct 1976, pp 305–360.
Marsh, P	'The Choice between Equity and Debt: An Empirical Study', Journal of Finance, March 1982, pp 121–144.
Masulis, R	'The Effects of Capital Structure Change on Security Prices: A Study of Exchange Offers', Working Paper 2–79, Study Center in Managerial Economies and Finance, University of California, Los Angeles, Dec 1978.
Miller, M H	'Debt and Taxes' Journal of Finance, May 1977, pp 261–275.
Modigliani, F and Miller, M H	'The Cost of Capital, Corporation Finance and the Theory of Investment', American Economic Review, June 1958, pp 261–297.
Modigliani, F and Miller, M H	'Corporate Income Taxes and the Cost of Capital: A Correction', American Economic Review, June 1963, pp 433–443.
Modigliani, F and Miller, M H	'Some Estimates of the Cost of Capital to the Electric Utility Industry', American Economic Review, June 1966, pp 333–391.
Modigliani, F and Miller, M H	'Reply to Heins and Spreckle' American Economic Review Sept 1969.
Myers, S C	'Determinants of Corporate Borrowing' Journal of Financial Economics, Nov 1977, pp 147–176.
Rendleman, Richard, J	'The Effects of Default Risk on the Firm's Investment and Financing Decisions'. Financial Management. Spring 1978, pp 45–53.
Rubinstein, M	'Mean Variance Synthesis of Corporate Financial Theory' Journal of Finance, March 1973, pp 167–181.
Scott, J H Jn	'A Theory of Optimal Capital Structure' Bell Journal of Economics, Spring 1976, pp 33–54.

Stiglitz, J E   'On the Irrelevance of Corporate Financial Policy', American Economic Review, Dec. 1974, pp 851–866.

Warner, J   'Bankruptcy Costs: Some Evidence' Journal of Finance, May 1977, pp 337–348.

QUESTIONS

1 Ios and Knossos are identical firms with the same expected stream of net operating income, NOI. However, Knossos has some debt in its capital structure while Ios does not, and the market value of Knossos is higher as follows:

	Ios	Knossos
NOI	10,000	10,000
Loan interest	—	2,000
Net income	£10,000	£8,000
Value of debt (market rate) of interest − 10%)	—	20,000
Value of equity (equity capitalisation rate − 20%)	50,000	40,000
Value of the firm	£50,000	£60,000

If the world is as described in MM's before tax capital structure analysis are these equilibrium values? If not, describe a profitable arbitrage strategy which will exploit the situation, and suggest when equilibrium might be reached. Work out the existing, and equilibrium, costs of equity, debt, and the overall weighted average cost of capital in each case.

2 What difference would it make to your answer to 1, if there is a 40% corporate tax, but no personal tax?

3 What was Miller's expression for the tax advantage to debt in a world of personal and corporate tax? What tax rate would the marginal debtholder have to have in a UK context for capital structure again to be irrelevant?

4 Theorists now generally consider the following assumptions to be necessary to support the basic MM analysis; no taxes, no bankruptcy costs, freely available information, a single borrowing and lending rate. How does relaxing each of these assumptions affect our predictions for the existence of an optimal capital structure? Which of MM's assumptions seem *least* likely to hold in reality?

CHAPTER 15
The dividend decision

Retained earnings are the main source of finance for most firms, and since retaining earnings and distributing them are alternatives the dividend decision is a key financing decision. We spend this chapter analysing the dividend decision. Section I introduces some of the background concepts in dividend policy and examines the evidence on the actual dividend policies of firms. In Section II we examine two approaches to the analysis of the dividend decision. The first is the 'naive' though rather appealing idea that the firm should just hold on to the earnings it needs to finance its positive valued projects each period, and distribute the rest. The second is the classic demonstration by Miller and Modigliani that under the assumptions of a perfect capital market it does not matter what dividend policy the firm adopts – in such a market dividend policy is irrelevant to the value of the firm. As with the capital structure decision, the MM analysis provides a good basis for a systematic review of the effect of market imperfections on dividend policy. We provide this in Section III and draw some conclusions on the determinants of dividend policy in practice. In the final section we review the research findings into the relationship between dividends, earnings and the valuation of the firm.

I DIVIDEND POLICY – CONCEPTS AND TERMINOLOGY

Public companies commonly pay a dividend twice a year: an *interim dividend* halfway through the year and a *final dividend* after the year-end when the firm has full information about the year's earnings. For example in the financial year ended 1.4.1983 Plessey paid the following dividends:

Plessey Ltd, dividends for the year ended 1.4.1983	
Interim	4.073p
Final	5.835p
Total dividend per share	9.908p

The final dividend was payable on 2.1.84, but to qualify, the shareholder had to be registered as the owner of the share at the close of business on 10.11.1983. Hence we say the share was 'cum div' up to that date, and 'ex div' thereafter. This is rather important since the person buying the share wants to know if he is getting it cum div or ex div.

In analysing firms' dividend policies the key statistic is the *payout ratio* which is the proportion of distributable profit actually distributed:

$$\text{Payout ratio} = \frac{\text{Dividend per share}}{\text{Earnings per share}}$$

Alternatively we talk about *dividend cover* which is the reciprocal of the payout ratio – the number of times the dividend could have been paid from the earnings. In year ending 1983 Plessey's EPS was 33.43p, so its payout ratio was 30% ($= \dfrac{9.9}{33.4} \times 100$) and its cover was $1/.3 = 3\frac{1}{3}$.

The UK shareholder who receives a dividend from Plessey is also entitled to a tax credit of 3/7ths of the dividend, assuming the basic rate of income tax is 30%. Hence the 9.908 dividend is worth $9.908 \times \dfrac{10}{7} = 14.154$p to him, and cover and payout ratios are sometimes calculated using this gross figure. When using payout figures it is useful to be clear which figure you are dealing with.

It is still conventional to use historic-cost earnings per share to calculate payout ratio. The Plessey figures were HC, and the research studies on dividend policy which we refer to later also use historic-cost. But it is also useful to assess dividend policy on current cost profits too, since current cost provides a measure of earnings after maintaining the capital of the business at current prices. Of course there is some controversy about how to measure CC earnings just as there is with HC, but the fact remains that a firm which has a replacement cost payout ratio of >100% is paying dividends out of capital, as far as we can estimate it. Paying dividends from capital is a cardinal sin in company law but luckily for some UK firms company law has not caught up with current-cost accounting yet.

If the analyst is interested in the availability-of-cash aspect of dividend policy, rather than the capital maintenance aspect, he might compare dividend per share to cash-flow per share. The cash-flow is the historic cost profit with non-cash expenses, notably depreciation, added back. Plessey's payout ratios calculated are as follows:

PLESSEY Y/E 31.3.1983	Historic-cost £000	Current-cost £000
Total profit/cash flow	81,449[1]	65,800[1]
Total dividend	24,445	24,445
Payout ratio	30%	37%
(1) after extraordinary items		

Table I shows the payout ratios for the main UK industry groups at the end of 1983. The figures are the unweighted averages of firms on the Datastream list. Most UK

Table I   UK Payout Ratios: 1983 Industry Averages

Industry	Payout	Industry	Payout
Metals and Metal Forming	69%	Food Retailing	42%
Mechanical Engineering	53%	Contracting	41%
Newspapers and Publishing	53%	Shipping and Transport	37%
Engineering Contractors	52%	Office Equipment	37%
Food Manufacturing	48%	Packaging and Paper	35%
Textiles	47%	Electricals	33%
Chemicals	45%	Leisure	33%
Stores	43%	Tobacco	28%
Brewers and Distillers	42%	Oil	28%
Motors and Distributors	42%		

Source: Datastream

industries were paying out between 35% and 55% of profit as dividend. At the low-payout end we can find some recognisable growth industries such as Leisure, Electricals, Office Equipment, and at the high-payout the beleaguered Engineering and Metal-working industries. These are industry averages, and within some industries there is a wide dispersion of individual firms. In Stores, at one end of the distribution 23% of firms had an average payout of 69%, while at the other end, 5% of firms were paying out only 8%.

LINTNER'S STUDY ON DIVIDEND POLICY

The classic study of the actual dividend behaviour of firms was Lintner's (1956) study. Lintner proceeded in two stages. First he conducted a series of interviews with businessmen to form a view of how they went about their dividend decisions. He then formed a model on the basis of these interviews which could be tested on a larger data set. It emerged from the interviews that investment needs were not a major consideration in the determination of dividend policy, rather that the decision to change the dividend was usually a response to a significant change in earnings which had disturbed the existing relationship between earnings and dividends.

Lintner modelled this dividend behaviour as follows:

$$\Delta D_{it} = a_i + c_i (D_{it}^* - D_{i,t-1}) + U_{it}$$

where ΔD_{it} = change in dividends per share of company i in year t
c_i = speed of adjustment factor
D_{it}^* = target dividend payout
$D_{i,t-1}$ = last period's dividend per share
a_i = constant
U_{it} = normally distributed random error term

Lintner fitted this model to dividends and earnings data from 1918 to 1941. He found that firms appeared to have a target payout ratio of .5 and to adjust towards this at a rate of 30% per year. His model explained 80% of changes in dividends in the firms he studied.

In a later study Fama and Babiak (1968) tested a variety of models of dividend behaviour against dividend data for 201 firms from 1947 to 1964. They found that Lintner's model performed well and was only improved by suppressing the constant term and introducing a lagged earnings term. Lintner's findings suggest a pattern of dividends through time rather like the one depicted in Figure I.

In Figure I dividends move in a lagged response to earnings, maintaining a constant payout ratio in the long term. Managers like a smooth and increasing dividend per share through time and are wary of increasing dividends if they might have to be reduced later on. This is not to say firms never cut dividends, they sometimes have to. If there is a general slump in earnings across the economy so that many firms are cutting dividends, then the embarrassment is reduced though it is still an agonising decision for the first few firms to take the plunge. GKN was in just this position in 1980. Lack of earnings meant it could not offset against corporation tax the ACT as its dividends, so increasing their cost, and GKN would have had to borrow cash at high interest rates just to maintain the previous year's dividend. Moreover GKN was in the process of making 10,000 workers redundant, so it was not clear why shareholders should not share some of the misery. In the end GKN cut its interim.

In the following sections we analyse the dividend decision and try to explain these dividend-paying practices of actual firms.

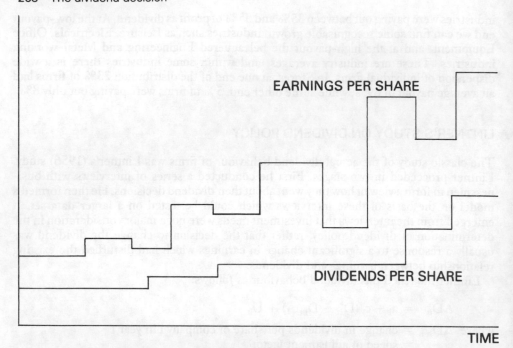

Figure I

II THE ANALYSIS OF THE DIVIDEND DECISION

First we will consider the 'naive', but very appealing, theory that firms should use the earnings they need for profitable investment and pay the rest out as dividends.

A 'NAIVE' MODEL: DIVIDENDS AS A RESIDUAL

Gordon Grub Limited is a manufacturer with a net profit this year of £1 million and the following set of investment projects available.

Gordon Grub Limited
Available investment projects

Project	Capital required £	NPV £
A	250,000	50,000
B	150,000	40,000
C	100,000	35,000
D	100,000	30,000
E	100,000	(20,000)

We know that to maximise the value of the firm, Grub should select projects A, B, C, D. If the projects have been properly appraised using a discount rate which measures the return that shareholders could earn elsewhere, their NPV measures the surplus generated by using the funds inside the firm rather than distributing them for investment outside.

This investment decision appears to imply a dividend decision. Surely the firm should hold on to the capital it needs, namely the capital required for projects A, B, C, D which is £600,000 (£250,000 + £150,000 + £100,000 + £100,000) and distribute the rest as dividend? To do anything else would be to reduce the value of the firm, either it would imply holding on to funds which could be better invested outside, or distributing funds that could be better invested inside. If follows that the payout ratio would be determined year by year, by the investment projects available to the firm that year. Dividends would be a residual. Figure II depicts this theory.

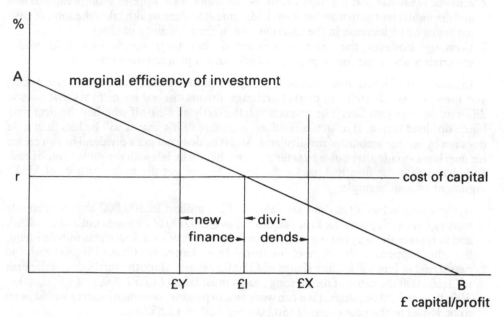

Figure II A naive model of the dividend decision

Line AB in Figure II depicts the investment projects the firm has available in the year, ranked in order of return – this is the familiar marginal efficiency of investment schedule. Efficient investment dictates investing up to the point where the return on the marginal investment just equals the cost of capital, r, implying an investment outlay of I. If profits in the year are X a surplus of X−I can be distributed as dividend. If profits are only Y, new financing of I−Y will be implied.

In practice retentions *are* the major source of finance, and Wilson (1980) reported 'In the evidence we have received from companies there are frequent allusions to external finance being regarded essentially as a means of making good any shortage of internal funds . . .' (p 148). But Lintner showed that firms do not appear to behave in line with the 'naive' model. Their preoccupation seems to be with maintaining a long-run target pay-out ratio. In practice firms not only pay dividends and raise new external finance at the same time – a bizarre activity under the 'naive' theory – they are often inclined to *increase* dividends around a new share issue. To understand this behaviour we need to analyse the determinants of dividend policy carefully.

THE MILLER-MODIGLIANI MODEL: DIVIDEND POLICY IN A PERFECT MARKET

In their 1961 paper Miller and Modigliani (MM) analysed the effect of dividend policy on the value of the firm in a perfect capital market. Just as they had with capital structure, they showed that dividend policy is irrelevant; given their assumptions 'the current value of the firm must be independent of the dividend of the firm'. MM made the following assumptions:

1 *Perfect capital markets*   that is: markets in which buyer and seller are price takers, free and fully available information, no transactions costs, neutral taxation.
2 *Rational behaviour*   which MM define as 'investors always prefer more wealth to less and are indifferent as to whether a given increment to their wealth takes the form of cash payments or an increase in the market value of their holdings of shares'.
3 *Certainty*   however they also demonstrated that their conclusions hold under uncertainty about the future profits and investment programme of the firm.

In such a world home-made financial policy is a perfect substitute for corporate policy, and there are no obstacles to market arbitrage driving the values of firms that pursue different policies into line. The investor is left exactly as well-off whether the firm pays him a dividend or not. If he gets a dividend the value of his shares will be less than if he does not by just the amount of the dividend. And if he does not get a dividend he can create his own home-made alternative by selling shares: he will be left with the same value of cash and shares as if the firm had paid a dividend. We can get the main features of MM's argument with an example:

Irrelevance plc has a total market value of £1.2 million in 300,000 shares presently worth £4 each. Suppose the firm decides to pay £150,000 of its assets out as a dividend, and to replace them by issuing new shares. The owner of each share gets 50p dividend, but what happens to the value of his share? In exchange for their £150,000 cash the new shareholders will require shares of £150,000 value. Since the total value of the firm is £1,200,000 the value of the existing shares must fall to £1,050,000, or £1,050,000 ÷ 300,000 = £3.50 per share. (We can work out, in passing, how many shares would need to be issued to the new equity, £150,000 ÷ £3.50 = 42,857.)

Hence the owner of one share in Irrelevance plc is in the same position whether or not the firm pays a dividend:

	Dividend paying	*No dividend*
Value of dividend	.50	–
Value of share	3.50	4.00
Shareholder's wealth	£4.00	£4.00

What would have happened to the value of a share if Irrelevance had decided to pay the dividend but *not* to replace the cash from outside? We cannot say because that would require knowing the NPV of the £150,000 used in the firm. By assuming that the cash is *replaced* we are leaving the firm, its assets and earnings capacity, unchanged, and thus can expect the value of the firm to be unchanged. Reducing the size of the firm would be an investment decision, and that would obscure the analysis of the dividend decision.

Two points to note in the argument are (1) that the firm's investment plans were unaffected by the dividend policy, so that the distributed cash had to be replaced – this is probably the main psychological barrier to accepting the irrelevance proposition – since we tend to associate retention with reinvestment. (2) That replacing the cash meant transferring an identical amount of share value to new investors. However both these depend on the proposition that the total value of the firm is unaffected by the dividend.

To demonstrate that the irrelevance proposition holds under uncertainty as well as certainty MM extend their 'rationality' assumption. They assume 'symmetric market rationality', that is, every trader in the market is rational and imputes rationality to every other trade in forming his expectations. In this case MM suggest that two otherwise identical firms with different dividend policies could not sustain different values in the market. It is important to note that uncertainty introduces the possibility of the firm replacing cash through issuing debt, as an alternative to equity. Does the use of debt affect the value of the firm? This of course is the subject of MM's 'other', 1958, article in which they show that under similar perfect market assumptions the level of gearing does not affect the value of the firm. We can now assess systematically the impact of certain *market imperfections* that may occur in practice.

III   THE EFFECT OF MARKET IMPERFECTIONS

TAXATION

The present UK system of company taxation, the imputation system, is often held to be neutral with respect to dividends. Consider a firm wondering whether to distribute £100. The appropriate comparison is between the alternatives of (a) distributing £100 and issuing £100 of shares, and (b) retaining £100.

If the firm distributes £100, it must remit $£100 \times \dfrac{30}{70} = £42$ to the Revenue in the next

quarter as a payment of ACT (assuming a basic rate of income tax of 30%). The Revenue deems the ACT to cover the shareholders' basic rate of tax. So the £100 is 'net' to the shareholders, and the £42 paid by the firm is an advance payment of a corporation tax liability the firm would have had to pay anyhow. Under the imputation system, therefore, the dividend costs the firm £100 and the shareholder receives £100. If he reinvested this money by buying £100 of shares, he and the firm would be just as well off as if the firm had retained the £100 in the first place. In practice, though, the effects of taxation may not be neutral. For one thing there is a cashflow cost. The time-lag between paying ACT and paying mainstream corporation tax can be considerable. In the present example, if the lag were only one year and the firm's cost of capital was 10%, then the cost of the early payment is $£42 \times 10\% = £4.20$. Additionally there will be some fairly small tax costs associated with issuing the £100 of new shares – stamp duty, VAT on brokerage. On the other hand, if the £100 is retained the shareholders incur a potential liability to capital gains tax, which at a CGT rate of 30% is £30, though if the shareholders do not plan to sell in the near future the present value of the CGT liability may be substantially less.

The argument so far might seem to favour distribution, on the grounds that the CGT effect might outweigh the others. But, as we did with capital structure, we have to take account of the diversity of tax positions of the firm and its investors, and this makes it hard to generalise about the impact of the tax system on dividend policy.

If the firm is not in a tax-paying position then the ACT cannot be offset, at least until the firm returns to a tax-paying position. At the limit this could be never, and the £42 will become a pure cost of distribution, sufficient to tip the balance toward retention. Firms in this position might in any case be high-growth, with a lack of mainstream corporation tax due to high capital allowances. As to the shareholders, we assumed they were paying 30% CGT and basic rate income tax, but this combination of events may be unlikely. CGT is not payable on the first slice of annual gains by an individual. The shareholder who is only paying basic rate income tax would often not be paying CGT, so his receipt will be the same under dividend or retention. But there are two other significant groups of share-holders. Some shareholders, notably institutions like pension funds and charities, do not pay tax and can reclaim the ACT paid on their dividends. Other individual shareholders may be paying up to 60% tax on their income, but just the flat 30% on capital gains. The former may favour distribution, the latter retention, so each firm will have to assess the composition of its shareholding and weigh their tax-paying positions and its own, in determining its dividend policy. The outcome may be on either side of neutrality.

The clientele effect

Since investors' tax positions may give them positive preferences for dividends or growth, we can expect a company to develop a clientele of shareholders who like its dividend policy. There are other market imperfections which generate this sort of preference, besides taxation. For example some institutional investors are constrained by their trust deeds from making current expenditures from capital. And though the hard logic of finance implies indifference between dividends and capital gains, it is easy to conceive of elderly investors who impose a similar constraint on themselves. They prefer high income shares and shudder at the thought of 'living off capital'. They conflict with MM's assumption of rationality.

MM themselves suggested that the formation of clienteles would permit the market to absorb certain tax imperfections, and that even if there was not a perfect match between the distribution of shareholder preferences and the distribution of company payout ratios, investors could build their own payout ratios by buying appropriate proportions of what was available. Only if the distribution of preferences was heavily skewed to one end would the perfect market results be impaired.

Do firms develop clienteles? Recent research in the US by Llewellen, Stanley, Lease and Schlarbaum (1978) has shed some light on the significance of the clientele effect in practice. Llewellen *et al* surveyed 2,500 clients of a large broker by questionnaire, and received 914 responses from investors holding interests in 1869 different shares in all. They ranked the dividend yields of these shares into ten groups then used multiple discriminant analysis to determine any significant differences between the characteristics of investors in the groups. They conclude

> it seems to us, that a substantially sharper profile of differences would be necessary to raise much of a concern about investor specialisation along tax lines, or to suggest to corporations a 'tax-tailored' dividend policy . . . [and] we . . . are unable to find in the data much evidence to support the notion that an important dividend-tax-clientele effect is in fact present.

But other studies in the US have concluded the opposite. Pettit [1977] who also studied the portfolios of brokerage clients concluded that there was a portfolio effect since he was able to explain a significant part of the variation between the dividend-yields of individual investor's portfolios in terms of factors such as the investor's age, family income, and marginal tax rates. In an earlier study Elton and Gruber [1970] also found support for a clientele effect using a rather different methodology.

TRANSACTIONS COSTS

One market imperfection which creates a strong bias towards retention is the existence of issue costs on new shares. As we see in Chapter 20 these are of two sorts, *administrative* costs which for a relatively small 'issue for sale' can be of the order of 6% and *issue discount* which can be 15% or more if shares are issued to new equity. In a rights issue the costs are less – issue discount is not a cost, and the administrative costs may be lower. These costs make retained earnings a cheaper source of finance than new-issue finance.

Also, if firms do build up clienteles of investors, the transactions costs associated with the purchase and sale of shares will provide an incentive for firms to maintain a stable dividend policy – *homemade dividend policy* will have a cost attached to it.

LEGAL CONSTRAINTS ON DIVIDENDS

On the whole companies can pay the dividends they want to, but they sometimes meet legal constraints of two sorts: there is an amount of law about dividends, and governments sometimes take powers to limit dividend payments as part of an 'incomes policy'.

Case law

Most of the dividend case law has arisen in the context of firms in financial difficulties, so it does not attempt to dictate policy to healthy firms. And since it is couched in terms of historic cost profit its strictures lose their edge with inflation. The main provisions of the case law are:

— Dividends cannot be paid if it would lead to a loss of solvency.
— Dividends can be paid if there is a current operating profit, even if there are current losses on fixed assets, or operating losses from previous years that have not been made up.
— Undistributed past profits can be distributed in future years.
— Even unrealised capital gains can be distributed if the articles permit and all the assets have been revalued.

Incomes policy

The most recent period during which dividends were controlled in the UK was from 1973 to 1979 as part of a counter-inflation package of price and wage controls. During this period companies were only permitted to increase dividends by a percentage of the previous year's dividend, and the permitted percentage went from 5% to 12½% and back to 10% during the period. The controls were not renewed by the new Conservative administration in 1979, and many companies responded by not only increasing their current dividend significantly, but also paying out a 'backlog' of dividend. The Financial Times of 30.7.79 reported that BP had promised to pay a special interim dividend of £47 million and to increase its 1979 dividend from £97.3 million to £212 million net. Shell Transport and Trading had built up unpaid dividends worth £296.9 million net since 1972 and was about to decide what to do with them, while Unilever was due to pay out its backlog of £52.9 million on the following Wednesday.

Representatives of the workers were probably dismayed by all this paying of backlogs, but the logic of finance suggests that the backlog and the dividend controls were largely *irrelevant*. Instead of dividends the shareholders had been given retained earnings for six years, and the cost to them, if any, was merely the loss of value caused by the divergence between actual and desired dividend policy – the extent of this loss is determined by the significance of the market imperfections we have been discussing in this chapter.

UNCERTAINTY AND THE SUPPLY OF INFORMATION

There seem to be two conflicting views on the effect of uncertainty on dividend policy. The future cash flows from firms are uncertain, and it is sometimes argued that dividends are 'relevant' because they resolve some of this uncertainty. On the other hand MM claimed that their irrelevance proposition still held under uncertainty.

The conflict between these views is reduced when we distinguish two things – first, that the future is uncertain, second, that the information which can help form expectations about this uncertain future may not be freely and equally available to everyone. The first is an immutable fact about the world, the second is a potential market imperfection.

The evidence from testing of the efficient markets theory suggests that information is not 'equally' available in practice. In particular we distinguish two levels of access – the *insider* level and the *outsider* level. The insiders are management and their advisers who should have the best access to the relevant information for forecasting the firms' future cash flows, and who in part determine it by their decisions. The outsiders are shareholders who receive a limited diet of highly aggregated information about the past performance of the firm. Shareholders employ analysts to try and bridge this gap by close scrutiny of the firm, but analysts are unable to completely bridge the gap and as tests of the strong-form EMT indicate, possession of inside information remains a thing of value. In this context the dividend decision is a significant signal of future prospects. Its significance as a signal springs from a general belief that managers do not like reducing dividends below the previous year's level. So when management sets a dividend it is implicitly making a statement that the dividend can be maintained in future periods, and thus a statement about expected future profit levels. On this view the dividend-decision becomes a quasi profit forecast.

MM recognised the informational role of dividends. They noted

> ... in the real world a change in the dividend rate is often followed by a change in the market price (sometime spectacularly so). Such a phenomonon would not be incompatible with Irrelevance to the extent that it was merely a reflection of ... 'the information content' of dividends ...

> ... where a firm has adopted a policy of dividend stabilisation with a long-established and generally appreciated 'target payout ratio', investors are likely to (and have good reason to) interpret a change in the dividend rate as a change in management's views of future profit prospects for the firm. The dividend change, in other words, provides the occasion for the price change though not its cause ...
> *Miller and Modigliani* (1961)

MM are saying that the test of relevance is the effect of dividend policy on the value of the firm, but dividend policy does not alter the value of the firm, only the timing of the recognition of its value. Of course if dividends have an information role which management and shareholders recognise as important this will lead to a dividend policy that is different some or all of the time from what it would otherwise have been. In this case the firm will be retaining more, or on the other hand raising more from other sources, than it would have done. Surely this entails a cost? Not per se, only if some of the other market imperfections we have discussed, such as tax costs and transactions costs, are real.

THE FACTORS THAT SHAPE DIVIDEND POLICY

Putting together the observations of Lintner and others, the arguments of MM, and our knowledge of real world market imperfections we can get a picture of the factors that will shape the dividend policy of the firm:

1 High-growth firms will probably have lower payout ratios. Issue costs make retained earnings a cheaper source of finance than new issues, other things equal. Hence the firm's target payout ratio will reflect investment needs in the long-run, in line with the 'naive' model.

2 In the short-run, the firm will be conscious of the information signalling properties of dividends. The firm will be keen to show a regular advance in dividend per share, but be aware of the risk of having to reduce dividends in the future.

3 Around these general conclusions, the relative preferences of the firm and its shareholders as to dividend policy will depend very much on their individual tax positions. High retention policies will appeal to shareholders with high personal tax rates, and to firms which cannot offset their ACT.

IV EVIDENCE ON THE DETERMINANTS OF THE VALUE OF THE FIRM

Researchers have investigated whether the level of a firm's dividends affects its value, and whether changes in dividend policy affect value; the former to test the dividend irrelevance hypothesis, the latter to explore the informational content of dividends.

Effect of dividend yield on value

There has been a long tradition of research studies investigating the relative importance of dividends and retentions in determining share prices, but it was not possible to undertake this sort of research properly until researchers had a satisfactory measure of relative risk.[1] Risk is a key determinant of relative share prices yet is likely to be strongly associated with levels of dividends and retained earnings.

Black and Scholes (1974) added a dividend payout coefficient to the CAPM and tested the explanatory powers of this augmented model on firm data for 1936–1966. They found that for all periods and sub-periods the coefficient on dividends was not significantly different from zero, and concluded that it could not be shown that the returns on high and low yield ordinary shares differed, before or after tax.

In the light of the Black and Scholes findings we can say more about the existence of clientele effects. As we saw earlier the evidence for clienteles is mixed. But even if there is a tendency, as seems intuitively likely, for investors to cluster round the shares offering the mixture of dividends and growth they prefer, Black and Scholes are telling us that there is no imbalance between the preferences of investors and the supply of suitable firms that would lead to a premium on certain firms.

Effect of dividend changes on value

Various writers have investigated if dividend change announcements affect share value. Watts (1973) concluded that no significant value gains could be made with prior access to dividends announcements but Pettit (1972) concluded that dividend information was used by the market in determining the value of shares. These studies seem to imply that dividend announcements do have an information content, and the stock market appears to be efficient in using this information. Of course dividend information is not the only data used by the market in determining share prices.

Foster (1978) Chapter II provides a good description of research studies into the impact of various earnings-relevant announcements on share value.

---

1 Friend and Puckett [1964] provide a pre-CAPM study of the relationship between dividends and share price yet are aware of the limitations of the existing methodology.

V SUMMARY

Dividend policy is a key financing decision, since dividends determine retentions and these are the main source of finance for most firms. The most obvious dividend policy would be the one which just distributed those earnings the company could not profitably reinvest. MM showed that under perfect market assumptions it would not matter what dividend policy the firm chose, the value of the firm would be unaffected by whether it used retentions or new issue finance for its investment. In practice firms have target payout ratios in the long term, and these tend to reflect their financing needs. In the short-term though firms do not payout a set proportion as earnings rise and fall. They like a smoothly-rising dividend per share and strongly dislike cutting dividends. This gives dividends a signalling role: it indicates that management think current dividends can be maintained. The neutrality of the tax system with respect to dividends is hard to generalise on, and depends very much on the particular tax situation of the firm and the shareholders. There is no doubt, however, that the cost of new issue finance provides a strong incentive to retain earnings.

REFERENCES AND BIBLIOGRAPHY

Bhattacharya, S — 'Imperfect Information, Dividend Policy, and the "Bird in the Hand" Fallacy'. Bell Journal of Economics, Spring 1979, pp 259–270.

Black, F, and Scholes, M S — 'The Effects of Dividend Yield and Dividend Policy on Common Stock Prices and Returns', Journal of Financial Economics, May 1974, pp 1–22.

Brennan, M J — 'A Note on Dividend Irrelevance and the Gordon Valuation Model', Journal of Finance, 1971, pp 1115–1122.

Briston, R J, and Tomkins, C R — 'The Impact of the Introduction of Corporation Tax Upon the Dividend Policies of the UK Companies', Economic Journal, Sept 1970, pp 617–637.

Elton, E J, and Gruber, M J — 'Marginal Stockholders' Tax Rates and the Clientele Effect', Review of Economics and Statistics, Feb 1970, pp 68–74.

Fama, E, and Babiak, H — 'Dividend Policy: An Empirical Analysis', Journal of the American Statistical Association, Dec 1968, pp 1132–61.

Foster, G — Financial Statement Analysis (1978) Prentice-Hall, Englewood-Cliffs, New Jersey.

Friend, I, and Puckett, M — 'Dividends and Stock Prices', American Economic Review, Sept 1964, pp 656–682.

Lintner, J — 'Distribution of Incomes of Corporations Among Dividends, Retained Earnings and Taxes', American Economic Review, May 1956, pp 97–113.

Lintner, J — 'Dividends, Earnings, Leverage, Stock Prices and the Supply of Capital to Corporations', Review of Economics and Statistics, 1962.

Litzenberger, R H, and Ramaswany, K — 'The Effects of Personal Taxes and Dividends on Capital Asset Prices: Theory and Empirical Evidence', Journal of Financial Economics, June 1979, pp 163–196.

Llewellen, W G, Stanley, K L, Lease, R C, and Schlarbaum, G G	'Some Direct Evidence on the Dividend Clientele Phenomenon', Journal of Finance, Dec 1978, pp 1385–1399.
Miller, M H, and Modigliani, F	'Dividend Policy, Growth and the Valuation of Shares', Journal of Business, Oct 1961, pp 163–96.
Miller, M H, and Scholes, M S	'Dividends and Taxes', Journal of Financial Economics, Dec 1978, pp 333–364.
Pettit, R R	'Dividend Announcements, Security Performance and Capital Market Efficiency', Journal of Finance, Dec 1972, pp 993–1007.
Pettit, R R	'Taxes, Transactions Costs and Clientele Effect of Dividends', Journal of Financial Economics, Dec 1977, pp 419–436.
Theobald, M	'Intertemporal Dividend Models – An Empirical Analysis Using Recent UK Data', Journal of Business Finance and Accounting, Spring 1978, pp 123–35.
Watts, R	'The Information Content of Dividends', Journal of Business, 1973, pp 191–211.

QUESTIONS

1 According to the MM model, the shareholder is just as well-off if the firm retains £1 as if they pay him a dividend of £1 and replace it with a new share issue. What assumptions are necessary for this conclusion? Does irrelevance hold under realistic assumptions?

2 MM say dividend policy is 'irrelevant' and so should not affect share prices. But in Chapter 10 we showed that the value of a share is the present value of the future dividend stream. Is there a conflict here?

3 The following in condensed form is a letter published in *Accountancy Age* on 3.2.1983 on the topic of current cost income, dividends and the capital market:

> I have yet to see a company report which says that because of CCA figures the dividend has been proportionally reduced and in fact, in many instances, dividends have been maintained out of historically calculated profits when the CC accounts have shown an apparent loss. Neither does it appear that the stock market in general pays much attention to CCA figures otherwise prices would be dramatically reduced. If companies were to base their dividends on CCA there would inevitably be a collapse of stock market prices.
>
> Therefore management will continue, so long as historically produced profits permit, to maintain dividends in order to protect themselves. In the meantime industry will, as it always has, keep its shareholders happy and the wolf from the door by over distribution and will rely on raising new capital from its happy shareholders to finance the replacement of assets and working capital.

Comment on this letter.

CHAPTER 16

The cost of capital

The cost of capital is the link between the firm's investment and financing decisions. Our aim in this chapter is to show how the firm should cost the finance input when making investment decisions.

In Section I we pull together some lessons about the determinants of the cost of capital from other parts of the book, and we look at the costs of different types of finance in the UK.

As soon as we start to describe actual procedures for finding the cost of capital we run into a familiar problem. The simplest approach is to calculate a weighted average cost of capital (WACC) for the whole firm. This has the great virtue in a world where information is costly of being easy to calculate, and decentralisable to subordinates. The problem is, it ignores the fact that individual projects may have different costs of capital. In Section II we describe the WACC and its calculation, and in Section III show how to derive a WACC that is project-specific just in risk. In Section IV we describe how *all* the specific financing costs of a project could be taken into account by calculating its 'adjusted present value' (APV). In valuing a particularly large and unrepresentative project it can be worthwhile calculating APV. For more routine evaluations we suspect firms will prefer WACC, hopefully supplemented by judgement based on an understanding of the pitfalls.

I THE DETERMINANTS OF THE COST OF CAPITAL

WHAT WE ALREADY KNOW

Elsewhere in the book we find most of the raw materials for our discussion of the cost of capital:

The risk-premium

In Part II we abstracted from the financing problem and discussed investment appraisal under the assumption that the firm was entirely financed by equity. Our main interest, there, was to see whether we could find a cost of capital for use in project appraisal that correctly reflected the risk of the project and led to value-maximising investment decisions. We found that if the assumptions of the capital asset pricing model held the required return from a risky asset j was the riskless interest rate plus a proportion, beta, of the risk premium on the whole market, so

$$r_j = r_i + \beta_j (r_m - r_i)$$

We usually reckon risk to be the key determinant of relative returns, and we saw how to price risk in Part II. But the price of finance may also reflect its duration and the quantity raised. As to the former, lenders may require a higher price for longer-term loans. The amount of finance raised has an effect on the cost of capital because of market costs which have a fixed component that, in the case of new issues of securities, can be significant. We will need to take issue costs into account when we calculate the costs of specific types of finance.

The dividend valuation model and the cost of equity

In Part III we explored the arithmetic of share valuation, which is also often used for estimating the cost of capital. The value of a firm, or of the equity, S, where the firm also has debt finance, is the present value of the future dividend stream, discounted at the shareholders' required return, so

$$S_o = \sum_{t=0}^{\infty} \frac{DIV_t}{(1 + r_e)^t}$$

However, if we know S_o we can equally well use the dividend valuation model to find r_e, the required return or cost of capital which is implied by the valuation S_o. The Gordon Growth Model gives a convenient simplification of the dividend valuation model if there is a constant growth in dividends, g, which is less than r. In this case

$$r_e = \frac{DIV_1}{S_o} + g, \text{ the cost of equity is the dividend yield plus the}$$

expected growth rate. These simple growth models assume a known and constant growth rate, g, less than r_e. If the reality is more complex we have to use a derivative of the dividend valuation model that allows for this. We also saw how inflation will affect the required return. Following Fisher, we can break down the 'nominal' return r into the 'real' return r' and the expected inflation rate, i, so

$$r = r' + i$$

Equity finance can be raised in two ways, by issuing new shares and by retaining earnings. The specific cost of equity raised in each of these ways will differ because of *issue costs*. For new issues there are significant capital market costs which we can express as a percentage N of the nominal amount raised S. So we have

$$\text{as before, cost of retentions} = \frac{DIV_1}{S_o} + g$$

$$\text{but now, cost of new issues} = \frac{DIV_1}{S_o(1 - N)} + g$$

The issue cost, N, has two components which can both be significant in practice: *transaction costs* – professional fees, stamp duty and so forth, and *issue discount* – the discount on market value often offered to subscribers for new shares. Making new issues through a *rights issue* to existing shareholders avoids the issue discount. So the cost of rights lies somewhere between the cost of retentions and of new issues to the public.

The cost of debt

We can find the cost of debt in a similar way. Lags in tax payments require a more complicated model, but if we ignore tax lags and assume perpetual debt with a constant coupon, C, and a present value, B_o. Then

$$r_d = \frac{C}{B_o}$$

Financing and investment are not independent

In the last two chapters we explored the relationship between the financing decision and the value of the firm to see if we could identify a 'best' financing policy. We found that under the assumptions of MM the value of the firm was independent of the financing policy. Put the other way round, under MM the firm's cost of capital is unaffected by how it is financed, so under MM the firm's investment and financing decisions are independent of each other. The firm need only know its overall cost of capital, r_a, and can ignore the specific costs of equity and debt, r_e and r_d, and the gearing ratio, G. So in an MM world our approach in Part II, which was to assume the firm was all-equity financed, would be a reliable and convenient one to adopt in practice, even though the firm had debt. In reality, though, we cannot assume the world is MM, and we need to take account of the fact that financing policy can affect the cost of capital.

THE PRICE OF FINANCE IN PRACTICE

We have a good idea now of what factors determine the price of finance. Take as a base-point the real, riskless, short-term interest rate, which is the return investors would want on a completely riskless short-term loan if no inflation was expected. Onto this, investors will add a premium for anticipated inflation, a risk-premium for the relative riskiness of the return, and for longer-term loans, a duration-premium reflecting the term-structure of interest rates. For some types of finance the cost to the user will be raised further by the market costs of raising finance. We can get an idea of the term-structure and the shape of the *yield curve* by looking at the yield on riskless loans of different durations. Table I shows yields on a selection of inter-bank loans and government bonds in September 1982. At that time the yield on riskless loans was around 11%, with the exact yield varying with the duration of the loan.

Table I Yields in the money-market and on government bonds at September 1982			
Money-market	%	*Government Bonds*	%
Inter-bank overnight	10⅞–11	15% Treasury Stock 1985	10.83
7 days	10⅞–11	13% Exchequer Stock 1987	10.90
1 month	10¹⁵⁄₁₆–11¹⁄₁₆	13% Treasury Stock 1990	11.91
2 months	10⅞–11	13% Treasury Stock 2000	11.52
3 months	10¹³⁄₁₆–10¹⁵⁄₁₆		
Treasury Bills	10.33%		

Source: CSO Financial Statistics, HMSO

These yields are 'nominal'. How much of this is expected inflation? We can gauge this by looking at the yield on *index-linked* bonds. In index bonds inflation is taken care of, because the repayment of principal is indexed. So the observed yield on the bonds is a real return. In September 1982 2% Treasury Index-linked Bonds, 1996, were yielding 3.15%. Historically, this figure is rather high. Over the years the real rate of return has been closer to 0%.

The default risk on UK government bonds is effectively zero, but this does not mean these loans are risk-free. The main component of nominal returns is expected inflation and since actual inflation is uncertain, to this extent government bonds are a risky investment. However it is conventional to use the yield on 3 month Treasury Bills as the risk free rate since we can be relatively sure about inflation over a 3 month time-horizon.

The risk premium the market will demand on risky assets depends on the risk of each investment. But for those risky assets traded on the stock-market we can observe the *average* risk-premium. The return on the market in any period has two components, the dividend yield and the capital gain, which is the percentage increase in the market index over the period. We show this in Table II for the years 1978–1982, and also the yields on more senior (less risky) company securities – debentures and loan-stock.

Table II Yields on FT Actuaries				
	Ordinary Shares			*Debenture and Loan Stock*
	Capital Gain	Div Yield	Total Return	Redemption Yield
1978	12.9%	5.5%	18.4%	12.75%
1979	13.3%	5.8%	19.1%	13.23%
1980	10.5%	6.3%	16.8%	14.16%
1981	13.5%	5.9%	19.4%	15.44%
1982*	15.6%	5.6%	21.2%	12.60%

*year to Sept 1982

Source: CSO Financial Statistics, HMSO

Not surprisingly ordinary shares have offered a higher return than company bonds, but we cannot directly infer the risk premium on equity from the difference between these series of returns. There is clearly a good deal of variability in the equity returns, which ranged during the 5 years between 16.8% and 21.2%. This variability comes about because we are looking at series of 'achieved', ex post, returns containing an unanticipated 'surprise' component. To get at the average risk-premium on equity we need to look at the differences between equity returns and the Treasury Bill rate over a long period when we assume expectations will be realised *on average*. Doing this, Franks and Broyles (1979) found the average after-tax risk-premium in the UK market to have been approximately 7½%. For the US, Ibbotson and Sinquefield (1976) derived a figure of 8.8%.

Looking just at the yields in Table II it is clear that the *redemption yields* on debentures are *higher* than the *dividend yields* on equities. The difference between the yields on higher-coupon government bonds and the yields on equities is even greater. This difference is usually known as the *reverse yield gap*, the implication being that yields are somehow the wrong way round, given the relative risks. Of course there is only a paradox in the reverse yield gap because we ignore the capital gain component of the return to equity. The reason bond-holders need higher yields is that they do not get capital growth as equity may.

II THE WEIGHTED AVERAGE COST OF CAPITAL

Perhaps the easiest way to find a cost of capital for use as a discount rate in project appraisal is to see what the firm pays for its finance *on average*. We can do this by calculating the *weighted average cost of capital* (WACC), with

$$r_a = (1 - T)\frac{D}{D + S}r_d + \frac{S}{D + S}r_e \qquad (1)$$

here r_a = weighted average cost of capital

r_d = cost of debt

r_e = cost of equity

T = corporate tax rate

D,S = value of debt, equity

This is the same as the WACC we encountered early in the last chapter, except that now we have included a $(1-T)$ term to allow for the tax-deductibility of interest. Once we know the specific costs of debt and equity the WACC is easy to find. But certain points need care.

Market not book values

Gearing should be measured at market values, not at the book values of the debt and equity.

$$ie \frac{D}{D + S} = \frac{\text{market value of debt}}{\text{market value of debt and equity}}$$

'Book' values taken from balance-sheets are historic figures which do not measure the current capital structure of the firm. In measuring the WACC we want to know what it would cost to deploy another £1 of finance today – maintaining today's capital structure and using today's costs of capital.

In practice we do not always have market values available – often we will find ourselves calculating WACC for an unquoted firm and will need to estimate the market values. And even with a 'quoted' firm there is a strong chance the debt will not be quoted, so that we have to estimate the market value of debt. We can do this by capitalising the firm's interest expense using a capitalisation rate culled from a similar firm which does have its debt quoted.

$$ie \text{ value of debt, } D = \frac{\text{interest}}{x}$$

where x = interest/value of debt, for a similar firm.

Wide or narrow gearing?

How should gearing be measured – 'narrowly' to include only long-term debt, or 'widely' to include 'short-term' finance such as overdrafts? This really depends on what the permanent capital structure of the firm is expected to be. If 'short-term' sources of finance are expected to be a permanent feature of the balance-sheet, as is often the case in practice, then it would be appropriate to use a concept of gearing which includes them.

Target not actual gearing

Similarly, if the firm is not presently at its optimal capital structure it is the firm's *target* rather than its *actual* gearing we should use. This can seem perplexing at first. But a similar situation arises when the firm *is* on target, but does not raise finance in those proportions. Consider a simple example: Zoom Ltd has a capital structure containing 50% debt, and feels its present gearing is optimal. Its specific cost of debt is 5% and of equity 15%. Zoom is planning an expansion programme which involves investing £1 million this year, and £1 million next. Because of the high fixed costs associated with issuing capital Zoom's finance director has decided to finance this year's investment by an issue of debt, and next year's by an issue of equity. He is wondering whether to appraise this year's investment using the actual cost of the funds they will use, 5% or the WACC, 10%.

The finance director must use 10% as his discount rate, reflecting his *target* gearing. Suppose he uses 5% this year, then, for 'consistency', 15% next year. He will be accepting projects with, say, an IRR of 8% this year but rejecting 12% projects next year. The point is that 5% is not Zoom's cost of capital. Zoom does not plan to continue raising finance at this cost, *nor could it*. The capital market only allows Zoom debt at 5% because Zoom is also raising half its finance in the form of equity yielding 15% – the costs of the component types of finance a firm uses are interdependent as we saw in Chapter 14.

THE PROBLEM WITH WACC

WACC is a very convenient way to get a discount rate. The company treasurer can figure out the target gearing for the firm and the costs of its specific sources of finance, and the resulting discount rate can be promulgated round the firm, permitting decentralised investment appraisal. But this convenience is bought at a price. The WACC is an average for the whole firm, whereas the capital used by each individual project may have its own cost, in particular

1 projects may have different risk levels,
2 project financing may bring differing tax advantages and differing issue costs.

In the rest of the chapter we will consider what can be done about this.

III WACC AND PROJECT RISK

We examined the treatment of risk in Chapters 7 and 8. We saw that given the assumptions of the CAPM we can use *beta* to get a project specific risk premium which is decentralisable and economical to use. If the perfect market assumptions do not hold there is no easy and reliable way of analysing risk, but in this chapter we will assume it *is* appropriate to use beta.

The firm is effectively a bundle of projects. If those projects have different risks the WACC will be an average of the risky discount rates for the firm's component projects. Figure I shows the problem of using WACC as a discount rate when project risks differ. It plots project return against project beta.

The WACC implies a constant discount rate whatever the project beta, hence in Figure I it plots as a horizontal line. We contrast this with the CAPM. The problem with using WACC is now clear. For certain projects, such as X and Y, WACC will yield the wrong investment decision. X would be rejected and Y accepted, since their expected returns are below and above the firm's average cost of capital respectively. But projects X and Y are significantly less, and more, risky than the firm as a whole, and using the CAPM to get a project cost of capital we can see X is earning a more than adequate return, and Y a return less than its cost of capital.

However we can combine the notions of WACC and beta by using beta to find r_e. So long as the debt is riskless so that no project risk is coming through in r_d, this will give us a WACC which is project specific in risk. We saw how to find project betas earlier in the book. At that stage we were assuming the firm was all-equity financed. Since then we

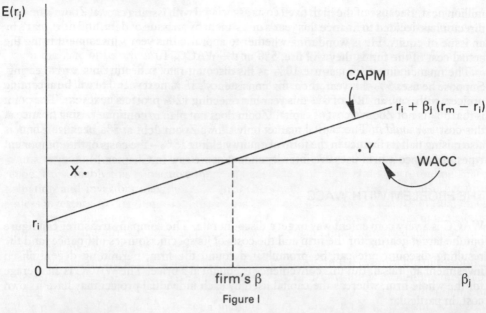

Figure I

have seen not only that the firm is likely to have some borrowing, but that gearing adds a new dimension of risk to equity. Now the risk of equity, measured by beta, will be determined by the variability of the basic income stream – the firm's 'business risk' – *and* by the 'financial risk' introduced by gearing. If we are using a beta derived from regression analysis, or from a surrogate firm we need to be sure it reflects the same gearing as the firm in which it is to be used. If not, we can adjust the beta for differences in capital structure. To do this we will introduce a simple but very useful formula. Because in the CAPM world the relationship between return and risk is linear, it follows that the beta of a portfolio of securities is simply the weighted average of the betas of the component securities. Similarly, the overall beta of a firm, which is often known as its 'asset beta' is the weighted average of the betas of its debt and equity, as follows:

$$\text{asset beta} = \frac{D}{D + S} \, \beta \text{ debt} + \frac{S}{D + S} \, \beta \text{ equity}$$

We will assume the beta of the debt is zero, ie the debt is riskless. This is by no means necessarily the case, especially for highly geared firms in which debt is bearing significant risk, but it will serve as a useful approximation. Hence

$$\text{asset beta} = \frac{S}{D + S} \, \beta \text{ equity}$$

This gives us an expression for ungearing the observed equity beta of one firm, to find a suitable beta for an otherwise similar firm with different gearing.

Suppose we want to estimate a beta for Court Ltd. We notice that Ball plc is a similar company with similar business risk, and its shares have a beta of 1.2. Ball has 30% gearing, while Court has 50% debt in its capital structure. We can find the underlying asset beta by ungearing Ball's beta,

$$\text{asset beta} = \frac{7}{10} \times 1.2 = .84$$

This is the beta an ungeared firm with this business risk would have. Gearing the beta up for Court gives

$$.84 = \frac{5}{10} \times \text{Court's beta, so}$$

Court's beta $= 1.68$

IV MYERS' ADJUSTED PRESENT VALUE

Myers (1974) pointed out that there are other ways, besides risk, in which a project's cost of capital can diverge from the average for the firm. He suggested that rather than attempt to adjust the cost of capital for these effects the firm should value them directly by finding an *adjusted present value* (APV) for its projects.

For one thing, the project's particular cash flow profile will determine the contribution it makes to the firm's overall financing requirement, and thus the amount of external financing it will require. If this external financing has to be by new issues of securities there will be *issue costs* which can add a hefty premium to the cost of capital, relative to retained earnings. As we saw in Chapter 9, strategy models try to address the fact that projects differ as cash generators. The recommendation there was to build a balanced portfolio of 'cash cows' that generate cash, and 'stars' that use it. Myers' recommendation is to put a value on the issue costs incurred or saved when finding the individual project's NPV.

Second, and perhaps most important, there can be tax advantages to gearing, and projects may differ in the extent to which they can be financed by debt. This can happen if individual projects create assets which are more or less able to form security for loans than the average for the firm. For example, suppose a firm with overall gearing of 50% undertakes an investment involving highly securable assets which can be financed 75% by borrowing. The project will bring tax advantages to the firm which would be understated if it were evaluated using a WACC with 50% gearing. The problem will also occur if the ability of the project to support debt changes through the project's life.

Of course issue costs, and the tax advantages to borrowing, are already reflected in the WACC, the tax advantage is $(1 - T)$, and the issue cost was subtracted in finding r_e. Myers is simply saying that we cannot assume that all projects are average in these respects, as we would be doing if we used WACC as the discount rate. Instead, he suggests we proceed in two stages:

1 Find the NPV of the project as though it were all-equity financed, using an equity rate that properly reflects the project's business risk,
2 Find the value of the tax savings associated with borrowing, and any other unique financing costs and benefits the project brings. Add 2 to 1 to find the Adjusted Present Value of the project.

We will calculate APV for the simple project we mentioned earlier. Prenderville Ltd is thinking of investing £500,000 in a project against which it can secure loans of 75% of the written-down value of the assets. The project generates net cash flows of £135,000 per annum for 5 years. The asset value declines on a straight line to a zero resale value after 5 years. The company's marginal tax rate is 40%, it can get 25% per annum writing down allowances on the asset, and pays tax with a one year lag. Prenderville's cost of equity is 12%, and of debt 7%, and it has 50% gearing. First we will appraise the project using conventional WACC, then using Adjusted Present Value.

Weighted average cost of capital

The formula for the weighted average cost of capital is

$$\text{WACC} \quad = (1 - T)\frac{D}{D + S}r_d + \frac{S}{D + S}r_e$$

In Prenderville's case we have $r_e = 12\%$, $r_d = 7\%$, $T = 40\%$, and $\dfrac{D}{D + S} = .5$

So WACC $= (1 - .4). .5 .7\% + .5 .12\% = 8.1\%$

Prenderville will get the following capital allowances, at 25% of the reducing balance:

Year	0	1	2	3	4	Total
	125	94	70	53	158	500

Using 8.1% as a discount rate we can find the project NPV as follows:

PROJECT APPRAISAL USING WACC (£000)

Year	0	1	2	3	4	5	6
Asset cost	(500)	–	–	–	–	–	–
Tax on capital allowances at (40%, lagged 1 year)		50	38	28	21	63	–
Revenues		135	135	135	135	135	–
Tax on revenue			(54)	(54)	(54)	(54)	(54)
Annual cash flows (500)		185	119	109	102	144	(54)
8.1% discount factors	1	.925	.856	.792	.732	.678	.627
PRESENT VALUES	(500)	171	102	86	75	98	(34)

$$\text{NPV} = (\pounds 2)$$

Using WACC the project has a negative NPV of £2,000

Adjusted present value

Given its atypical debt structure it would be safer to calculate the project's APV. We do this in two steps.

(1) What would be the value of the project, all-equity financed? To find this we can use the same annual cash flows we had before. But discounted at what rate? The all-equity discount rate is *not* 12%, but the return equity would require if the firm were all-equity financed.

For convenience we will assume the project has the same risk as the whole firm. We can disentangle the appropriate all-equity rate for the firm from the data we have, using MM's after-tax proposition II:

$$r_e = r_a + (1 - T) (r_a - r_d)\frac{D}{S},$$ where r_a is the all-equity, or 'ungeared' cost of equity.

Substituting-in the values we have,

$$.12 = r_a + .6(r_a - .07)\frac{1}{1}$$

$$r_a = 10.1\%$$

The fact that r_a is less than 12% provides a check we have got the answer right. When the firm is ungeared the equity is relatively less risky, so we expect equity-holders to accept a lower return.

Discounting the annual cash flows at this new rate gives

Year	0	1	2	3	4	5	6
Annual cash flows	(500)	185	119	109	102	144	(54)
10.1% discount factors	1	.908	.825	.749	.681	.618	.561
PRESENT VALUES	(500)	168	98	82	69	89	(30)

$$NPV = (£24)$$

If the project were all-equity financed it would have a negative NPV of £24,000.

(2) What is the value of the tax advantage to debt? We can find this as follows. We know that each year the firm borrows 75% of the asset value of the project, and that the asset value is depreciating at 20% per year. We find the value of the tax saving as the discounted present value of the annual tax savings on interest, using $r_d = 7\%$ as the discount rate since this is a low risk stream.

Tax advantages to debt

Year	1	2	3	4	5	6	Total
1) Written down value of assets (£000)	500	400	300	200	100	–	
2) Debt (.75 of 1))	375	300	225	150	75	–	
3) Interest (.07 of 2))	26.25	21	15.75	10.5	5.25	–	
4) Tax saving (.4 of 3))	–	10.5	8.4	6.3	4.2	2.1	
PV of Tax savings at 7%		9.17	6.86	4.8	3.0	1.4	25.23

The value of the tax savings is £25,230. Added to the all-equity NPV this gives the following APV:

adjusted present value $= -£24,000 + £25,230 = £1,230$

The tax saving has been sufficient to make this project worth undertaking.

Though tax is probably the main one, there can be other costs to particular forms of financing. Suppose in the above example, there were issue costs of 4% of the amount raised on new equity, but the debt was bank borrowing, which was considered to have negligible financing costs. We could also add to the APV the issue costs saved, of £500,000 × 75% × 4% = £15,000.

APV VERSUS WACC

Myer's is simply telling us to use MM's proposition I, rather than II, to appraise projects. MM's after tax proposition I was

$$V_G = V_U + TD$$

The value of the geared firm is the value of the ungeared firm plus the value of tax savings.

Myers says we can apply this to projects too, and avoid the averaging assumptions of WACC.

However, the problem with APV is that, though conceptually sound, it is less simple and more time consuming to implement in practice. WACC is essentially a *rule of thumb*. Like all rules-of-thumb it embodies a trade-off between accuracy and economy. There is a danger that using WACC will lead the firm to make some wrong investment choices. But the great virtue of WACC is that it is easy to calculate and to pass to subordinates to permit decentralised decision-making. The firm has to weigh the costs and benefits. We suspect that APV will only be attractive when the project in question is sizeable and the firm believes its financing costs – tax advantages, issue costs, and so forth – are significantly out of line with the rest of the firm.

DIVISIONAL COST OF CAPITAL AS A COMPROMISE

There is a temptation to dismiss the use of rules-of-thumb as irrational and uneducated. It can be, but rules-of-thumb have great appeal in a world where collecting information and analysing it are costly activities. In this sort of world rules-of-thumb make a lot of sense, especially when they are combined with the judgement of people who understand the theory and know the pitfalls. The WACC is effectively a rule of thumb embodying a trade-off between accuracy and economy of operation. We saw that we could solve one shortcoming of WACC by combining it with project betas. But immediately we do this, we lose the advantage of convenience. An effective compromise is to work out *divisional* betas and costs of capital. There will not be much loss of efficiency in this so long as most of the diversity in the firm's risk lies between its divisions, while within divisions projects are fairly homogeneous as to risk. The extent to which most risk-differences *are* inter-divisional will vary from firm to firm and will reflect the type of economic logic behind the firm's organisational structure. We know the sort of factors that are likely to cause differences in business risk and thus in beta; the operating leverage, the competitive structure of input and output markets, the rate of technological change, the sensitivity of demand to macroeconomic fluctuations, and so forth. So long as projects are fairly homogenous in factors like this within divisions, it will be safe to use a divisional cost of capital for appraising projects.

V SUMMARY

The cost of capital is the link between the firm's financing and investment. The firm will only make value-maximising investment decisions if it is correctly measuring the opportunity cost of its finance. We considered some of the determinants of the cost of capital of the firm, and examined some figures on the cost of capital in practice. When it comes to estimating the cost of capital the firm has a choice. It can use the weighted average cost of capital for the firm as a whole as a discount rate for individual projects. This has the great advantage of being convenient to calculate and economical in information. Head Office can calculate a discount rate which can be used in decentralised decision-making. The problem with WACC is that it assumes all projects have the same opportunity cost of capital as the average of the firm. In reality they differ in risk and in the tax advantages to gearing and the issue costs they generate. We can modify the WACC to include a project specific risk measure and where most of the differences in risk lie between divisions we may be able to use divisional costs of capital as an adequate proxy. To capture all the specific financing effects Myers has suggested an alternative procedure which involves calculating an all-equity value for the project then evaluating its additional financing effects separately. But, in a world where information is costly firms favour simple decision-procedures.

REFERENCES AND BIBLIOGRAPHY

Arditti, F D	'The Weighted-Average Cost of Capital: Some Questions on its Definition, Interpretation and Use', Journal of Finance, Dec 1973, pp 1001–1013.
Brealey, R A Hodges, S D and Capron, D	'The Return on Alternative Sources of Finances', Review of Economics and Statistics, 1976, pp 469–480.
Franks, J R and Broyles, J E	Modern Managerial Finance (1979) Wiley.
Franks, J R and Pringle, J J	'Debt Financing, Corporate Financial Intermediaries and the Value of the Firm' Journal of Finance, June 1982, pp 751–761.
Gordon, M J and Gould, G I	'The Cost of Equity Capital: A Reconsideration', Journal of Finance, 1978, pp 849–862.
Ibbotson, R G and Sinquefield, R A	'Stocks, Bonds, Bills and Inflation: Year-by-Year Historical Returns (1926–1974)', Journal of Business, Jan 1976, pp 11–47.
Miles, J A and Ezzell, J R	'The Weighted Average Cost of Capital and Project Life: A Clarification' Journal of Financial and Quantitative Analysis, 1980, pp 719–730.
Miller, M H and Modigliani, F	'Some Estimates of the Cost of Capital to the Electric Utility Industry; 1954–1957', American Economic Review, June 1966, pp 333–391.
Modigliani, F and Miller, M H	'Corporate Income Taxes and the Cost of Capital; A Connection', American Economic Review, June 1963, pp 433–443.
Myers, S C	'Interactions of Corporate Financing and Investment Decisions – Implications for Capital Budgeting', Journal of Finance, March 1974, pp 1–25.
Stapleton, R C and Burke, C H	'Taxes, the Cost of Capital and the Theory of Investment: A Generalisation to the Imputation System of Dividend Taxation', Economic Journal, 1975, pp 888–890.

QUESTIONS

1 The balance sheet of Rodent plc gives the following information about share capital, reserves and long-term liabilities:

	£m
Share capital, 1,000,000 shares of £1	1.0
Reserves and retained profit	0.5
	1.5
4% irredeemable debentures	1.0

The dividend paid by the company has been 20 pence per share for many years and is expected to remain at this level indefinitely if no investment is made this year. A dividend of 20 pence has just been paid and the current market price of the shares is £2 each. The market price of £100 nominal of debentures is £40. The company's marginal tax rate is 40%.

The company has an investment project available with the following cash flows:

	Now £	End of each year in perpetuity £
Cash flow	−100,000	8,000

Report to Rodent's directors on the company's cost of capital, and whether the project should be accepted.

2 Rodent's managing director replies to your report. He says that, because debt is manifestly cheaper he intends to finance only with debentures from now on. Reply to him.

3 Tobin plc has asked you to calculate its required rate of return for project appraisal. You do some preliminary work and discover that the standard deviation of the returns on Tobin's equity has been 14%, and on the market equity as a whole, 8%, and the coefficient of correlation between the returns on Tobin and on the market is 0.5. Tobin has 40% debt in its capital structure.

Estimate Tobin's beta coefficient.

Indicate how you would estimate the remaining information needed to calculate the required rate of return.

Estimate a beta for an otherwise similar company with 30% gearing.

4 Alberto Industrial Fasteners is planning to invest £80,000 in an automated widget nurdler. Under a technology support scheme the government will lend 75% of the cost at normal market interest rates, the loan to be repaid in equal instalments over the asset's life. The machine is expected to generate a net cash flow of £36,000 per year and to be scrapped after three years with no residual value. The corporation tax rate is 40% and the machine will qualify for a first year allowance of 50% and 25% writing-down allowances subsequently.

Alberto is 30% financed by borrowing, and its debt and equity investors require 12% and 18% returns respectively. The costs of raising debt are considered to be more-or-less zero, whereas issuing new equity involves 5% issue costs.

Value this project using Myer's APV method, and the traditional weighted average cost of capital.

5 What are the relative merits of WACC and APV for investment decision making?

Part V
The financing alternatives

CHAPTER 17

The capital market

This chapter examines the nature of the capital market as it affects firms. First, we identify the main 'types' of finance the firm can raise. These are in effect different types of contract the firm can make with its suppliers of funds. In the second section we look at the flow of funds between the four main sectors of the economy. The factors that determine the supply of these funds and determine the demand of other sectors, determine the financial environment of the firm. The third section introduces the intermediaries – banks, institutions, and specialist agencies – through which most transfers of finance in the capital market pass. We try to explain the existence of intermediaries and to assess their role. In the fourth section we discuss the Stock Market, which is a particularly important part of the capital market.

The capital market exists to help savings to be transferred to net investors, like firms and the government, who invest more than they save, from net savers, such as households, who save more than they invest. As in all markets demand and supply in the capital market are balanced by a market price, which is the 'return' to the supplier and the 'cost of capital' to the firm. In the final section we examine the nature of the return in the capital market and what determines it.

I TYPES OF FINANCING CONTRACT

THE TERMS OF A FINANCING CONTRACT

When a firm raises finance it makes a contract with the suppliers of the funds, and when we talk about the different *types* of finance a firm can get we are really talking about different terms that that financing contract can have.

The TERMS of a financing contract should determine the following:

— QUANTITY: the amount of finance provided.
— DURATION: how long the finance has been provided for. Finance can be provided over any period but people commonly distinguish short-term, medium and long-term, and permanent finance. *Short-term* finance is provided initially for less than a year. *Medium* and *long-term* is finance of fixed or finite duration but longer than a year. *Permanent* finance is issued with the intention it will never be repaid.
— RISK: the risk associated with the returns on the finance. The underlying riskiness of the firm's income stream is determined by economic factors, but the distribution of this risk to the various suppliers of finance is contractual and is determined by their respective claims over the firm's assets and income stream. So the contract might make the supplier an *owner* of the firm or a *creditor* of the firm. Finance which acquires ownership rights is called *equity* and to equity belong any surpluses or deficits the firm makes, and in most cases some influence on the policy of the firm through voting-rights. All other finance is *debt*. Creditors are entitled to recover their interest and capital in priority to equity, but

there is a pecking order within creditors. For example, *secured* loans acquire a lien over a particular asset or class of assets, giving them priority over other creditors.

— RETURN: the terms for payment of interest and repayment of principal. Some finance — for example postponed payment to trade creditors or the Inland Revenue – has no overt cost. Loan finance involves regular *interest* payments, but again the terms of the contract may differ, for example the rate of interest may be fixed at the outset or may be variable at the discretion of the supplier. In the case of equity the periodic payment is called a *dividend* and the level of dividend is set by management.

The main types of finance

In practice there is no limit to the variety of financing contracts that can be made, but for analysis we categorise them. The prime distinction is between equity and debt.

Equity is finance which gives ownership rights on the firm. There are two sources of equity finance: new money raised from outside by *share issues*; and the savings of the firm, including depreciation provisions, held back from shareholders as *retained earnings*. In the main, equity finance is permanent – the law severely limits the firm's ability to repay equity.

Debt is finance which makes the supplier a creditor of the firm. Under 'debt' we include medium and long-term loans at fixed interest. One form of this is the *debenture* or *loan stock* which is a security that can be bought and sold on the market. Debt also includes short-term arrangements such as *bank overdrafts*. But we can also identify a variety of other arrangements that effectively constitute debt-financing – for example, stretching trade creditors, and the use of factoring and leasing. We will refer to these as 'quasi-debt'.

Table I shows the relative importance of some of these types of finance to industrial and commercial companies in recent years. Retained earnings emerge as the major source, with bank borrowing second. Despite the importance given to them in finance books, including this one, new issues of shares are a relatively minor source of finance. But we can still justify paying a good deal of attention to the analysis of shares. The value of ordinary shares reflects the shareholders' whole interest in the firm whether it arose through new issues or the retention of profits.

II THE FLOW OF FUNDS ON THE ECONOMY

Once upon a time economic transactions were restricted to barter – to the exchange of tangible goods or labour services, and the wealth of a man was restricted to the tangible goods physically in his possession. The constraints of this cumbersome way of doing things were eased in due course by the use of very compact and durable goods like gold, but were removed altogether by the use in transactions of 'claims' on resources, rather than resources themselves. A claim on resources is a legally enforceable property right – banknotes and cheques are examples of generalised claims – and this final stage awaited suitable social institutions, notably a legal system which could enforce claims. The purpose of this story is to make it clear that by the 'flow of funds' in the economy we mean the transfer of claims on resources.

Examining the flow of funds in the economy is a good way to get a clearer idea of the factors that might influence the supply of finance to firms. Following national income accounting, we can classify economic units in the economy into four sectors:

The BUSINESS sector, comprising industrial and commercial firms, and financial and banking firms.

Table I   UK industrial and commercial companies

Main sources and uses of funds 1980 and 1984 (£million)

SOURCES OF FUNDS	1984	1984%	1980	1980%
Undistributed income	30,974	74	14,824	63
Credit received, tax balances, capital transfers	401	1	598	3
Ordinary share issues	1,127	3	897	4
Debenture and preference issues	249	1	423	2
Bank borrowing	8,011	19	6,640	28
Loans and mortgages	592	1	667	3
Overseas	357	1	(598)	(3)
	£41,711	100	£23,451	100
USES OF FUNDS				
Fixed capital formation (Gross)	18,858		14,503	
Stock-building	4,736		1,866	
Bank deposits and cash	1,418		3,306	
Credit given	535		666	
Overseas	4,590		2,341	
Other + balancing item	11,574		769	
	£41,711		£23,431	

Source: CSO Financial Statistics

The PERSONAL sector, representing households but also unincorporated business, sole traders and partnerships. In theory, unincorporated businesses should be included in the business sector, but government statisticians have insufficient data to reclassify them.

The PUBLIC sector, consisting of central government, local authorities and public corporation such as nationalised industries.

The OVERSEAS sector, comprising flows of funds to and from abroad.

It is also conventional to divide the funds flow in the economy into two 'accounts'. The CURRENT account concerns the flows of income and expenditure of the sectors. The difference between the income and expenditure of a sector is its saving, and the CAPITAL account concerns the transfer of savings between sectors. Although we are concerned with capital transactions it is useful to start by examining the current account.

These are some examples of current account transactions:

The business sector buys labour or 'work' from the personal sector and there is a flow of wages in return. The personal sector will pay part of this income to government as tax, spend part and save the rest. The spending results in a flow of funds to business in exchange for goods and services, and also in a flow to the public sector since some goods and services are bought from nationalised industries and since expenditure taxes are paid on some of the expenditure. By the same token the public sector pays wages to the personal sector and trades goods and services with the business sector. The surplus of the business sector receipts over its expenditure, its 'profits', are subject to tax, and the remainder constitute its savings. The personal sector similarly pays tax on its income. These flows are depicted in Figure I.

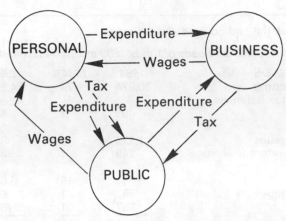

Figure I Some current flows between domestic sectors

THE CAPITAL ACCOUNT

All three domestic sectors, personal, business and public, invest. But there is no reason why a sector's investment should match its saving to the extent that its investment is not covered by its saving a sector must raise *finance*, i e use the savings of another sector. Table II shows how much the three domestic sectors invested and saved in 1984.

Table II UK Domestic Sectors' Savings and Investment, 1984 (£million)			
	BUSINESS		
PUBLIC	FINANCIAL	IND. & COMM.	PERSONAL
Saving(1) 909	7,310	30,804	27,371
Fixed investment + stockbuilding (13,678)	(6,646)	(23,594)	(16,387)
Surplus (deficit) (12,587)	664	7,210	10,984

(1) including capital transfers
Souce: CSO Financial Statistics

The personal and business sector emerge as the large net savers, the public sector as a net investor.

It is the function of the *capital market* to transfer savings between sectors, and also within sectors since individual units within a sector may be net savers or investors. For example, within the business sector one firm may finance another, and within the public sector profitable nationalised industries may subsidise government. In the personal sector a popular destination for personal savings is building societies. Building societies mainly reallocate savings within the personal sector to households which wish to invest in housing. To some extent the personal sector transfers funds direct to business by buying shares and debentures, but in recent years these purchases have been exceeded by sales – households have been reducing their direct investment in firms. The reason is that nowadays most flows of household and other funds for investment pass through *financial intermediaries*, the 'financial firms' part of the business sector – banks, unit trusts, pension funds etc.

An increasingly important factor in recent years has been the role of government as a competitor of business for personal savings. Governments have needed to finance not only their investment but also their dis-saving – the excess of their current expenditure over their current income (which is largely tax revenues). This is the 'public sector borrowing requirement' (PSBR). Again though the personal sector can lend direct to government by buying government bonds, on the whole government, like business, goes through financial intermediaries for its funds. The overseas sector is also significant in the capital account both as a destination for the savings of the UK personal sector, and as a source of finance for government and business. In fact the overseas sector always has been important for the UK, but the spate of 'oil money' on the world capital markets has brought this sector to prominance.

Figure II depicts the capital account flows that we have been talking about.

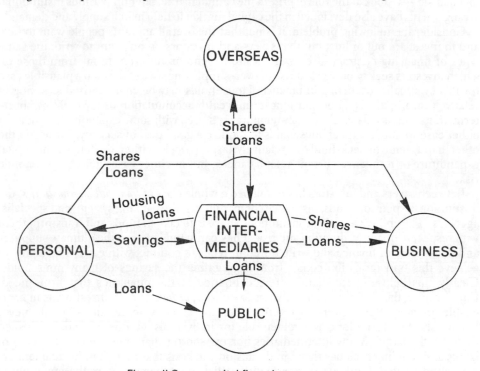

Figure II Some capital flows between sectors

SOME INFLUENCES ON THE SUPPLY OF FINANCE

Thinking about the flow of funds in the economy helps in understanding the environment in which the overall supply of funds to the firm, and the terms on which they are supplied, are set. Amongst other things the financing of firms will be influenced by:

— the level of saving by households, which will be influenced by the level and distribution of incomes, and by government tax policy.

— the competition for these household savings from other sectors, notably the government's borrowing requirement and the personal sector's own house-building plans.

— the role of the overseas sector in taking or providing funds, which will be influenced by the relative returns available in the UK and abroad.

— the firm's need for outside financing in the first place will be determined by the level of its retained earnings relative to the investment opportunities available.

III   CAPITAL MARKET INTERMEDIATION

Matching supply and demand

Demand and supply in the capital market are brought into equilibrium by the price mechanism – we look at the role of *price* in the capital market later on. Various institutional arrangements have also developed in the capital market to help match supply and demand.

Consider the following problem: it is not that the overall amounts people want to save and to invest are out of line, but that savers and investors do not want to write the same types of financing contract – ie savers desire to lend on different terms from those on which investors seek to borrow. At risk of over-simplifying we can develop a plausible case for this eventuality occurring in practice. Households may be characterised as saving in relatively small parcels, either for long-term wealth accumulation or for building short-term 'transactions balances' – money temporarily stored with some expenditure in view. In either case we might expect households to require a good deal of security. Firms, on the other hand, tend to seek funds in relatively large parcels, either for long-term capital expenditure or to finance current asset balances, but in either case subject to economic risk.

Between savers and investors has developed a whole class of *financial intermediaries*: the 'institutions' – pension funds, insurance companies etc; the banking system; and specialist agencies. The ability all of these institutions share is to take in funds and transform them with respect to quantity, duration and risk. They can stand between the ultimate suppliers and demanders of finance and write different types of contract with each. The ability to achieve this transformation comes from aggregating the savings of many households. Clearly this helps intermediaries provide finance in the quantities that firms need. Furthermore, the ability of intermediaries to build a *portfolio* of risky investments in firms enables them to offer a lower-risk return to their investors. As to duration, the rule 'never borrow short and lend long' is a golden rule for individuals but does not hold with such force 'in the large'. Many intermediaries borrow shorter than they lend. In the case of banks and building societies they can do this on the basis that though individual lenders may withdraw their funds at will, new lenders will present themselves, so the sum is not as volatile as its parts. Also they take care not to commit themselves to fixed borrowing and lending rates, and in extremis are able to rely on the support of other banks and building societies.

The homemade alternative

This ability to 'transform' the terms of financing contracts is the customary explanation of the function of financial intermediaries; but it does not actually explain why they exist.[1] In

1   Goodhart (1975) provides a good introduction to the theory of intermediation.

finance, when we are confronted by some institutional arrangement we always have to ask ourselves what it does that the people it serves could not have done equally well for themselves. This is a particularly pertinent question with intermediaries. A little thought suggests that firms themselves could collect together the savings of many households into the quantities they need. If they want longer-term finance than savers wish to provide, they could always refinance with new short-term securities when the previous capital is withdrawn. As for savers, if they are unhappy with the risk associated with investing in a single firm they can build their own portfolios of securities. In other words all the benefits provided by intermediaries could, on the face of it, be 'homemade' by households and firms. In a perfect capital market this would be the case, but in reality households and firms find it advantageous to use intermediaries. We can interpret this in terms of the information costs and transactions costs associated with the capital market in practice. Many savers would find it prohibitively expensive to acquire or buy the necessary expertise to appraise investments and monitor firms, and the fixed costs associated with buying securities tend to make very small holdings uneconomic. Similar considerations will influence the firm.

THE INSTITUTIONS

Perhaps the most discussed feature of the capital market in recent years has been the power of 'the institutions'. The institutions are collectors of long-term savings: pension funds, insurance companies,[2] investment trusts and unit trusts. The institutions had a net inflow of funds of £8.8 billion in 1978 (Wilson (1980) p 46). The Wilson Committee[3] estimated that by the year 2,000 the pension funds alone would be disposing of £8 billion per annum. In recent years households have reduced direct investment in company securities in order to save through institutions. There are several reasons for the appeal of the institutions to household savers. They may provide other services – such as insurance – as well as a method of saving. There are tax incentives to this form of saving, pension contributions are usually tax deductible while the pension and assurance companies are effectively free of tax. In the case of pensions, employees often have little choice but to contribute since contributing to the pension scheme is often a condition of the job, and employers usually provide an incentive by at least matching the employee's contribution. Unit and investment trusts dispose less funds than pension and insurance companies, and they use the funds in a rather different way, as can be seen in Table III. The investment policies of the pension and insurance companies derive from their particular business objective: maintaining a fund which will generate cash flows up to a fairly long time horizon, sufficient to meet foreseeable pension or insurance liabilities and improve them if possible. Hence these institutions feel no special compunction to invest in the business sector, or at least in company securities, and their portfolios contain significant proportions of property and property loans and of government securities.

Unit and investment trusts take a different approach. Households invest in particular trusts on the basis of the specific range of assets in which the trust will invest. The higher proportion of company securities in the portfolios of unit and investment trusts reflects the wishes of their investors. Households may find less difficulty in investing in property and

2 Strictly speaking it is life *assurance* companies who take household savings, but since insurance companies have tended to be net investors these two are usually grouped together.

3 In this chapter we are taking only a brief overview but for the reader who wants a richer discussion the Report and Evidence of the Wilson Committee (1980) provides an invaluable and highly readable account of the workings of the UK capital market in all it aspects.

government securities for themselves, and may feel that their pension and life assurance rights represent fairly riskless assets, so they look to unit and investment trusts to provide investments in more risky company securities.

There was a shift towards investing overseas after the removal of exchange controls in October 1979. There was alarm in some quarters at the flood of institutional funds abroad that followed the new legislation.[4]

Table III Pattern of asset holdings of investing institutions at end 1978

Per cent of total assets[1]

	Insurance long-term	Companies' general	Pension funds	Investment trust companies	Unit trusts
Cash and other short-term assets (net)	4	17	5	5	10
Public sector securities	27	28	22	4	1
Company securities[2]	38	36	53	91	89
Mortgages and loans	8	3	3	–	–
Property[3]	22	11	17	–	–
Other investments	1	5	1	1	–
TOTAL ASSETS[4]	100	100	100	100	100
£ billion	37.8	7.1	31.3	6.7	3.9

1 Assets held in respect of UK business
2 Including unit trust units
3 Including property unit trust units
4 Total assets for insurance companies do not include agents' balances etc and for pension funds are before deducting long-term liabilities

Souce: Wilson (1980)

Since the institutions effectively account for all of the personal sector's new investment in company securities, their investment policies are important. There is some evidence that the criteria the institutions apply in choosing investments implies a bias against smaller firms. Prais (1976) found that institutions prefer to hold securities that are readily marketable, hence they have a preference for quoted securities. Also they prefer minimal transactions costs – which implies large holdings, but holdings which can be sold without too much disruption – which thus implies large companies. Wilson (1980) found that pension funds were concentrating investment in the 200 largest companies, but that insurance companies were not so concentrated. However Moyle (1971) and Briston and Dobbins (1978) both provided evidence that insurance companies avoid small firms too.

THE BANKS

Banks are major suppliers of finance and financial services to the business sector. The name 'bank' can be used by an institution which has obtained permission from the Bank of England to take deposits from the public.

4 The Bank of England Quarterly Bulletin, Sept 1981, noted that the percentage of pension funds' cash flow invested abroad had risen from 7% pre-abolition to 20 or 25%, post-abolition. For insurance companies the figures were 4% and 17%.

Clearing banks

Clearing banks are the 'high-street' banks, Barclays, Nat West, etc. These banks offer a wide range of financial services but it is their role in providing 'current account' banking, the clearance of receipts and payments, which explains their importance in financing. It is a natural development from this to providing an overdraft facility, which permits the customer to spend more than he has. The overdraft is a very flexible and convenient type of finance. Overdraft limits can be raised quickly and cheaply, and interest is only paid on the daily balance. The current account service also means that all firms already have a relationship with a clearing bank whether or not they need finance. For these reasons it is easy to see why bank finance is the most popular type after retained earnings.

Merchant banks

Merchant banks provide a variety of services. They take deposits from the personal and business sectors and lend these funds, though in the main they only deal in 'large amounts'. They provide investment and portfolio management services to clients. They are the prime advisors of firms on 'new issues' of long-term finance, and if they are 'issuing houses' they are able to take-up whole issues of shares for subsequent sale to clients, other institutions or the public.

Finance houses

Finance houses are intermediaries which fall in the banking area, since in many cases they are subsidiaries of banks. Finance houses purchase assets on behalf of clients and lease them to the client, or sell them under hire purchase or deferred sale agreements. Thus they provide a form of indirect or 'off-balance sheet' finance.

SPECIALIST AGENCIES

The capital market also contains a host of specialist agencies which were often created to fill gaps in the supply of finance and in particular to accept higher risks and longer payback periods than the market normally accepts. These agencies are usually owned or financed by the institutions, the banks or the government so they can be classed as intermediaries, since they share their parent's ability to transform the terms on which funds are supplied. We note some of the leading ones.

In 1973 the UK clearing banks, contributing 85% (the Bank of England contributing 15%) set up Finance for Industry (FFI) as the holding company for a variety of subsidiaries providing finance for the business sector, the funds coming from the clearing banks and from public issues. The Industrial and Commercial Finance Corporation (ICFC) is a subsidiary which provides finance in a variety of forms to small and medium sized firms. Finance Corporation for Industry (FCI) is the other main operating subsidiary, providing medium-term loans in larger amounts, of £1 million – £25 million. ICFC itself has two subsidiaries worthy of mention. Estate Duties Investment Trust (EDITH) provides capital to ease the payment of capital transfer tax without interfering with the control of the firm. Technical Development Capital (TDC) finances high risk technological innovation. In 1977 the institutions set up Equity Capital for Industry (ECI) to fill a perceived gap in the supply of equity to small and medium-sized industrial companies. However, demand for ECI finance has been slow. There are also some very significant government-backed specialist agencies. The National Enterprise Board (NEB) was set up in 1975 by the Labour administration both with an objective of financing manufacturing industry and of promoting industrial reorganisation. A change of administration changed the objectives of the NEB, and its mandate moved towards the promotion of technological innovation in the area of microelectronics. The National Research Development Corporation (NRDC) has a more general role in this area. It provides finance through joint ventures, grants, equity or loans to smaller companies for the development and exploitation of inventions.

The NEB and the NRDC have now together formed the British Technology Group (BTG). The BTG provides finance in three main forms:

— Equity and debt on a venture capital basis
— Working capital loans
— Joint venture finance, with BTG contributing 50% of a project's cashflow and recovering the money through a sales levy.

IV THE STOCK MARKET

We have been talking about some institutions and intermediaries in the capital market. The word 'market' is this sense connotes the whole network of exchanges between the suppliers and demanders of funds. It is usual to subdivide this into two, reserving the title 'capital market' for the market in long-term claims and distinguishing the short-term 'money-market'. One part of the capital market, the STOCK MARKET, requires special attention. The stock market is a market in the securities of domestic and foreign companies and of local authorities and the UK government. It is a market in the everyday as well as the economic sense. It has a physical location: there are a number of regional exchanges in the UK but The London Stock Exchange is by far and away the biggest. And it has market traders, called *jobbers*, who are essentially stall-holders specialising in buying and selling particular classes of security. But one difference with an ordinary market is that the buyer or seller may not enter the market area and deal direct with jobbers, he must use an agent called a *stock broker*. Just who can trade as a broker or jobber is strictly controlled by The Stock Exchange Council, and recognition involves, inter alia, passing a qualifying examination. Jobbers and brokers are remunerated in different ways. The jobber's income comes from the 'turn' he can make on buying and selling, that is the difference between the prices at which he buys-in and sells-out. The broker's income comes from a percentage commission on the value of the transactions he handles.

Jobbers and brokers

It might not be quite obvious why it is necessary to have brokers *and* jobbers. Imagine a fruit and vegetable market with a barrier round it patrolled by a policeman, and a special class of person with the sole right to take orders from housewives at the barrier and execute them at the stalls. Of course it would be very relaxing for the shopper to have someone do the shopping and advise them on the best buys. But after a while they will start to ask questions. How do I know he is finding the best bargain? Is his help and advice really worth all the money I am paying him? Is he really necessary? People have asked the same questions about the broker/jobber system. There are perhaps two features of the market for securities that may explain the existence of stock brokers. First there are many securities to choose from, and their customer-appeal depends on characteristics of growth prospects and risk which require some analysis. Hence there may be a need for a specialist adviser. Second, the buyers and sellers of securities are geographically spread, and often have a high opportunity cost for their time. It is useful for them to employ an agent whom they can instruct by letter or telephone. However, many countries seem to get along without separate jobbers and brokers. In fact, as the Wilson Committee reported:

> The jobbing-system of market-making is unique among major capital markets. In most other countries securities firms can, to a greater or lesser extent, combine the roles of principal and agent, though there are usually rules governing the separation of the two and compelling disclosure to clients of the role in which a firm is acting.
> (Wilson (1980))

It may seem that for many transactions there is need for neither a broker nor a jobber, and buyer and seller could make contract via a computer such as exists for second-hand cars. Some years ago such a system was started by institutional investors, known as ARIEL. However, to date this system has yet to capture a significant market share.

Accounts

To simplify accounting and settlement The Stock Exchange calendar is divided into fortnightly 'accounts'. All purchases or sales during an account are paid for on the settlement day, which is usually the second Tuesday after the end of the account. This convention is significant since it gives scope to speculative behaviour. If you think the market price of a share will rise during the fortnight, you can buy at the beginning and sell later on, making a profit without having to lay out any money. Similarly, if you expect the price to fall you can sell 'short', that is without actually owning the shares you sell, and buy the shares you need to deliver later on. Like all speculation, the costs of a faulty judgement can be dramatic.

The primary and secondary market

The stock market is both a *primary* market and a *secondary* market, that is a market where new securities are issued and where existing securities are traded. The volume of secondary business far exceeds the primary. The relatively small amount of new finance that firms raise through stock market issues reflects the fact that there are less costly types of finance available that firms prefer to use. This is sometimes taken as an indictment of the stock market, but this view is misplaced. The secondary market provides services of great importance. First, the market prices of shares traded on the stock market provide a measure of the economic value of firms. This piece of information is the linchpin of the capital market investment process – it signals the return shareholders will receive by providing finance to the firm, and it signals the cost of capital to the firm itself. Second, the existence of a secondary market enables the stock market to perform its vital 'intermediation' function. All the securities traded on the stock market represent permanent or long-term finance. Equity finance is in principle permanent, most loan-stock is long in term. Investors may not want to provide finance for this length of time, or at least will not be certain they will want to, but if the financing contract is in the form of a security with a ready market this does not matter too much. The supplier of funds can enter into the financing contract with confidence that he will be able to sell the security whenever he wants to withdraw. The existence of a securities market means that finance can be simultaneously permanent from the point of view of the firm yet liquid as far as the investor goes.

THE COSTS AND BENEFITS OF LISTING

Only the securities of companies that are 'listed', 'quoted', can be traded on The Stock Exchange. The requirements of stock exchange listing tend to restrict the market to the few large companies. To be listed a firm must meet the following requirements, amongst others:

Size

The firm must have securities with an initial market value of at least £500,000.

Securities on the market

At least 25% of each class of equity or convertible must be owned by the public, though large firms may get exemption to this.

Stock exchange rules

The Stock Exchange information requirements are rather more demanding than company law. Firms have to report to shareholders twice a year instead of once, and a new issue has to be accompanied by a 'PROSPECTUS' which provides potential investors with some information about the present state and future prospects of the firm.

History

Applicants for full listing normally need a five-year trading history with audited accounts to support it.

Cost

At present it costs an initial amount of between £1,000 and £15,000 for the largest plus an annual fee of £500 to £3,500 to be listed. On top of these formal charges are the cost of meeting The Stock Exchange information requirements in terms of additional reporting, prospectuses, etc.

Against these costs the company must weigh the advantages of listing. In terms of new finance, the company will find its securities much more attractive to the all-important institutional investor. Similarly, owners of existing securities will find their assets more marketable. This can be particularly important in family-owned firms where the family is planning a move away from the business or preparing for death taxes. Company law used to allow a degree of privacy to private as against public companies, but this is no longer the case. However, listing does imply greater public access to information about the company and greater public interest. Some companies will welcome this, others may not.

THE UNLISTED SECURITIES MARKET

The problem with stock-exchange listing has traditionally been its all-or-nothing nature, it precluded firms which sought a wider market but either did not meet all the criteria for full listing or did not want it. In many overseas capital markets this need has been met by a thriving intermediate, or 'over-the-counter', market, but in the UK until recently the only comparable facilities were the market offered by M J H Nightingale to a limited number of unlisted companies, or the possibility for informal dealing offered by The Stock Exchange's rules 163(2) and 163(3) which allowed buyers and sellers of unlisted shares to be brought together under certain circumstances.

The apparent demand for these facilities led to the creation of the Unlisted Securities Market (USM) in November 1980. The USM is a properly constituted market but with less stringent requirements than full listing: only 10% of the firm's capital need be put on the market, the advertising requirements on entry are less stringent than for a full listing, and firms are accepted with a three year trading record or in some cases with no history but only 'fully researched projects' to offer. As to cost, USM listing bears a fixed annual fee of £1,500 and no initial fee. But it is not clear that issue costs will be less on the USM than for fully listed firms. In fact, as we see in Chapter 20, the high fixed costs associated with public issues are likely to make small issues particularly expensive.

The existence of an active over-the-counter market has given researchers in the United States an opportunity to examine the 'value' of a full-listing. If marketability is a thing of value to investors we might expect the value of a firm that is promoted to full-listing from over-the-counter listing to experience an increase in share price. Interestingly, studies by Furst (1970) and Van Horne (1970), examining the price of shares before and after listing in the US found no significant value benefits to listing. Indeed in the UK based on a more limited experience of over-the-counter shares, it has been suggested that over-the-counter prices tend to be higher, since the companies to which this market appeals tend to be in sectors of which The Stock Exchange has been traditionally suspicious.

V   THE MARKET PRICE OF FINANCE

As in other markets the supply of finance and the demand for finance are brought into equilibrium by the price mechanism. In this section we see what determines the market price in the capital market.

THE OVERALL LEVEL OF RETURNS

In general the ruling price in the capital market will be the return which brings into equilibrium aggregate saving and investment. We can depict this using conventional demand and supply analysis as in Figure III.

The upward-sloping supply curve in Figure III reflects the willingness of savers to sacrifice more present consumption in response to higher returns. The downward-sloping demand curve reflects the increasing supply of projects that become worthwhile as the cost of capital falls.

To explain the actual level of the equilibrium return it is useful to recall the analysis by Fisher which we encountered in Chapter 5. Fisher said the market return or cost of capital, r, has two components. It comprises the investors required real return, r′, and the expected rate of inflation, i, so that

$$r = r' + i$$

Various researchers have investigated whether the above theory actually explains the process by which the price of capital is formed. In a well-known study Fama (1975) showed that between 1953 and 1971 not only did changes in nominal interest rates in the US perform very well as predictors of inflation, but that the underlying real return, r′, was remarkably constant during the period. Nelson and Schwert (1977) have since suggested, however, that this stability of real returns was perhaps a particular feature of the period Fama studied. It seems clear, though, that expectations about inflation are a major determinant of observed nominal market returns.

The factors that determine the underlying *real* return are those real factors that determine the aggregate supply of savings and demand for investment funds in the economy. We identified some of them earlier in the chapter. Other factors include the level and distribution of incomes, government tax policy, demand for investment funds from government and from overseas, and so forth.

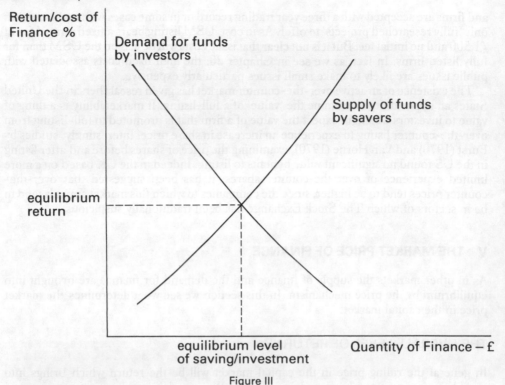

Figure III

RELATIVE RETURNS

Having looked at the overall level of returns we now consider the variations in return on different types of finance. The terms of financial contracts can differ with respect to quantity, duration and risk, and if the market is to be in equilibrium the value of each contract must be balanced by the return it offers. We have seen how various institutions in the capital market, including the stock market itself, *intermediate*, ie absorb differences between the terms required by savers and investors. To the extent that these cannot be absorbed they will affect the relative return on different types of finance.

The quantity premium – the effect of transactions costs

Even allowing for the cost savings achieved by using intermediaries, there can be significant transactions costs associated with lending and borrowing in the capital market. These costs have a fixed component which makes the average cost lower, the larger the amount involved. On the savings side we can see that large investors tend to have access to deposit rates which are a percentage point or two above what the general public are offered. On the cost side there has been a good deal of research into this topic since economies of scale in financing might inhibit the access of small firms.

The duration premium – the term-structure of interest rates

In practice the market return may vary with the duration of a loan, there may be a 'term-structure'[5] in interest rates. Explaining this phenomenon has been a major preoccu-

---

5   Be careful not to be confused by the new use of the word 'term' in this context.

pation of theorists, though as yet no neat consensus has emerged. The debate concerns whether and under what circumstances investors will require a different return on a long-term loan than on a short-term loan.[6]

First we must distinguish a SPOT rate from a FORWARD rate. A 'spot' rate is a rate fixed today on a loan made today for some period, and a 'forward' rate is a rate fixed today for a loan to be made at some point in the future. We will denote a rate that applies to a loan running from time m to time n as $_m r_n$ so $_2 r_4$ would be the rate on a loan starting at $t = 2$ and ending in $t = 4$. Hence spot rates all have a zero prefix, and forward rates a non-zero prefix.

The 'null-hypothesis' on term-structure is the EXPECTATIONS THEORY which expresses the relationship that would hold between interest rates of different terms if investors were indifferent as to term.

The expectations theory says that the relationship between spot rates of different terms must be such that any rate spanning several periods will be the geometric mean of the present and expected successive one-period spot rates covering those periods. This is less complicated than it sounds. Consider today's three year spot rate $_0 r_3$. The expectations theory says it must relate to today's one year spot, $_0 r_1$, and the spot rates that are expected to hold next year $E(_1 r_2)$, and the year after $E(_2 r_3)$, as follows:

$$(1 + _0 r_3)^3 = (1 + _0 r_1)(1 + E(_1 r_2))(1 + E(_2 r_3))$$
$$\text{So } (1 + _0 r_3) = ((1 + _0 r_1)(1 + E(_1 r_2))(1 + E(_2 r_3)))^{1/3}$$

In other words, the return you get from investing long must be the same as would be expected on present information from a succession of short investments. If it were not, investors would move toward the higher return strategy until the rates adjusted to remove any advantage to investing either short or long. Hence if you observe an $_0 r_1$ of 11% and an $_0 r_2$ of 12% the only explanation for this under the expectations theory is that the future spot rate, $_1 r_2$, is expected to be higher. However, various arguments have been produced for the existence of a 'term-premium' independent of expectations. The LIQUIDITY-PREFERENCE theory of Hicks (1939) suggests that, even with the assistance of the intermediation process we described earlier, there may remain an imbalance between the desires of savers and investors. The risk aversion of savers will lead them to prefer to lend short-term, while the risk-averse firm will prefer to borrow long. A term-premium will be needed to balance supply and demand in these circumstances. And theories like the MARKET SEGMENTATION approach of Culbertson (1957) and the PREFERRED HABITAT theory of Modigliani and Sutch (1966) develop further the notion of savers who have strong preferences as to the maturity of loans they make in order to provide explanations for the emergence of a term-premium. The term structure of interest rates has yet to enter the core of finance theory.

The risk-premium

We assume that the suppliers of finance in the capital market are risk-averse. Other things being equal they will require a higher return the more risky that return is. The question is exactly how much extra return will they require? Since the development of the capital asset pricing model (CAPM) this is a question that, given certain assumptions, finance theory is now in a position to answer. The CAPM was described in some detail in Chapters 7, 8 and the reader might wish to review these chapters now.

6 For an introduction to this topic see Goodhart (1975). Cox, Ingersoll, and Ross (1981) provide a recent critique of the main theories.

We assume that risk can be measured in terms of *variance* of returns. Investors may own many return-yielding assets, company securities, government bonds, land, antiques and so on, and the first thing to perceive is that the rational investor will think in terms of the risk and return on his overall *portfolio* of assets rather than on each individual asset. Moreover we find that within a portfolio some of the riskiness of the individual assets cancels each other out. The extent to which this will happen depends on the extent to which individual returns are uncorrelated with each other and on the number of assets. We call this the degree of *diversification* of the portfolio. The only component of risk that cannot be eliminated by diversification is movements in the returns of the market as a whole – the so called *systematic* risk. But the investor can diversify the overall risk on his portfolio down to this level, and in a perfect capital market he can do this costlessly. So if he is a rational investor in a perfect capital market he will do this. In such a world we can calculate the required risk premium on any asset, including company securities.

In the CAPM framework the return on a risky asset j, r_j, is given by:

$$r_j = r_i + \beta_j (r_m - r_i)$$

where r_i is the riskless interest rate, r_m is the return on the market portfolio and β_j is the coefficient measuring the responsiveness of the return of the asset j to the return on the market as a whole. A conclusion of chapter 8 was that although analysis of the assumptions of the CAPM, and empirical work of asset pricing in practice, throws some doubt on the descriptive validity of the model, it remains the best model presently available for explaining the premium on the return of a risky asset.

VI SUMMARY

The capital market exists to allow the transfer of savings from net savers in the economy, such as households, to net investors such as firms. By studying the capital market we can understand the factors that determine the supply of finance to the firm, and which determine the market price of that finance – the cost of capital, which is the key statistic in financial decision-making.

The overall supply of savings in the economy, and the overall cost of capital is determined by the factors that condition the saving and investment behaviour of the main economic sectors. The relative cost of different types of finance depends on the particular terms of the financing contract with respect to quantity, duration and risk. There is a variety of arrangements in the capital market that help to transform the terms on which finance is supplied by 'intermediating' between savers and borrowers. The 'institutions' – pension funds, insurance companies, investment and unit trusts – perform this function, as does the banking sector. And the existence of a stock market within the capital market in which the securities of certain firms can be readily bought and sold enables firms to raise long-term finance in a form which is highly liquid from the saver's point of view.

Any residual differences in quantity, duration or risk must be reflected in differences in return. In finance theory we assume that of these three, risk is the main determinant of relative returns.

REFERENCES AND BIBLIOGRAPHY

Briston, R M, and Dobbins, R   *The Growth and Impact of Institutional Investors* (1978) Institute of Chartered Accountants in England and Wales, London.

Carleton, W T, and Cooper, I A	'Estimation and Use of the Term Structure of Interest Rates', Journal of Finance, Sept 1976, pp 1067–1083.
Cox, J C, Ingersoll, J E, and Ross, S A	'A Re-examination of Traditional Hypotheses about the Term Structure of Interest Rates', Journal of Finance, Sept 1981, pp 769–80.
Culbertson, J	'The Term Structure of Interest Rates', Quarterly Journal of Economics, 1957, pp 489–504.
Fama, E F	'Short-Term Interest Rates as Predictors of Inflation', American Economic Review, 1975, pp 269–282.
Furst, R W	'Does Listing Increase the Market Price of Common Stocks?', Journal of Business, 1970.
Goodhart, C A E	Money, Information and Uncertainty (1975) Macmillan.
Hicks, J	Value and Capital (1939) Oxford University Press, London.
Modigliani, F, and Sutch, R	'Innovations in Interest Rate Policy', American Economic Review, 1966, pp 178–197.
Moyle, J	The Pattern of Ordinary Share ownership 1957–1970 (1971) Cambridge University Press.
Nelson, C R, and Schwert, G	'Short-Term Interest Rates as Predictors of Inflation: on Testing the Hypothesis that the Real Interest Rate is Constant', American Economic Review, 1977.
Prais, S J	The Evolution of Giant Firms in Britain (1976) Cambridge University Press.
Van Horne	'New Listings and their Price Behaviour', Journal of Finance, Sept 1970, pp 783–94.
Wilson, Sir H, (Chairman)	Committee to Review the Functioning of Financial Institutions, 'Report' (Cmnd 7937).

QUESTIONS

1 What are the main differences between equity and debt in a financing contract?

2 What types of equity and debt are most important for financing firms in practice, and why?

3 What role do financial intermediaries play in channelling savings to investment?

4 The stock market has been likened to a casino. Does it have a useful role in reality?

5 In the UK the roles of jobber and broker are separate, whereas in the US they are not. What are the virtues of the alternative systems?

6 What are the relative advantages and disadvantages of a full stock exchange quotation, a USM quote, and being unlisted?

7 We believe the price of finance will reflect the risk, the duration, and the quantity raised. How are each of these factors priced?

CHAPTER 18

Capital market efficiency: the EMT

An important feature of a well-functioning capital market is that the prices of securities traded in the market should always fully reflect all available information. The theory that capital markets actually do this is called the 'efficient markets theory' (EMT) and has been subjected to a great deal of empirical testing in recent years in the US and elsewhere. The results of these studies have suggested fairly convincingly that the market is efficient in pricing securities. In Section I we describe the EMT in more detail and review the research evidence. In Section II we assess the implications of the EMT for business finance.

There are other aspects of market performance that are important. Not all firms have securities traded on the stock market and even quoted firms raise a large portion of their funds by other means. More broadly, even if finance were allocated efficiently between firms, it might be the case that firms as a whole were crowded-out by other sectors in the competition for the savings of the economy. Largely for reasons of data availability the only aspect of capital market efficiency that has been investigated in anything like a thorough way is the EMT. On these other issues the best we can do is to outline the problem and such evidence as exists. We do this in the next chapter.

I THE EFFICIENT MARKETS THEORY

The most thoroughly researched aspect of capital market efficiency is the efficiency of the stock market in its use of *information* in valuing securities and particularly company shares. The *efficient markets theory* is the theory that *security prices always fully reflect all available information*.

Suppose the EMT did not hold and share prices only reflected new information slowly or not at all. By reacting more quickly and anticipating price changes, certain investors might be consistently able to make above-normal returns through trading on the market. It is this potential for abnormal returns that researchers look for in testing the EMT. The fact that some market operators might be able to gain at the expense of someone else is perhaps not particularly important in itself. Its significance is as an indicator that, for a period, a security was not correctly valued.

The present value of a security, V_o, is the future stream of cash flows from the security, C_t, discounted at the appropriate required return, r, where

$$V_o = \sum_{t=o}^{n} \frac{C_t}{(1-r)^t}$$

Information is relevant to valuing a security if it tells us something about the level and risk of the future cash flows. It is convenient to identify three levels of rigour in tests of the EMT reflecting different degrees of *availability* of information:

In the WEAK-FORM of the EMT the set of available and relevant information is the price

310

history of the security itself. The market is weak-form efficient if it is not possible to make abnormal trading gains by analysing past patterns of security prices.

Tests of the SEMI-STRONG form of the EMT investigate whether all publicly available information is embodied fully and instantaneously in share-prices.

The market is STRONG-FORM efficient if it is impossible to make abnormal gains using any information at all, including information that is not publicly available.

In the rest of this section we review the evidence on the EMT. In the main, tests have shown the market to be weak, and semi-strong efficient, but not strong-form efficient.[1] People with inside information appear to be able to make abnormal gains. Also there is puzzling evidence on the volatility of market prices and on the market's response to inflation, on 'weekend effects' and other seeming inefficiencies.

WEAK-FORM EFFICIENCY: SHARE PRICES ARE RANDOM

The striking conclusion from research into weak-form efficiency is that share prices follow a *random-walk* through time. But a moment's thought shows that this is just what we would expect in an efficient market. The market is weak-form efficient if it is not possible to make profitable predictions of share prices using the information implicit in past prices. The reason is simply that in such a market all the available information has already been used, and embodied in share prices. It follows that prices in an efficient market will be random, since random means unpredictable. If prices *are* random this directly contradicts the underlying assumption of much traditional investment analysis. The belief of 'technical analysis' or 'chartism' is that share prices can profitably be forecast by studying past movements in prices. Technical analysis is a widely practiced art and it has a developed vocabulary with analysis looking for conventional patterns and trends in prices.

Researchers have used two sorts of test of weak-form efficiency. They have examined whether share prices actually do behave like a random series of numbers, and they have tested some of the investment rules implied by technical analysis.

Tests of randomness

There are two common ways of looking for randomness. One involves measuring the *serial correlation* between price changes in different time periods. The serial correlation between price change in time t and the change n periods previously, at time $t - n$, is known as the 'nth-order serial correlation'. For a random variable all orders of serial correlation should be zero, in other words there should be no discernible association between price changes at different times. Another approach to randomness is the *runs* test. A 'run' is a series of consecutive price changes of the same sign, and the 'runs test' investigates whether observed runs occur with the same frequency as would be expected in a random series.[2]

Many studies have used these tests to investigate price behaviour in the major stock markets. The earliest way by Louis Bachelier in a study of the French Bourse published in 1900. He found that commodity prices moved randomly. Nowadays this sort of work is made easier by the existence of computerised data-bases. Most researchers have found that in fact there are dependencies between successive price changes, but have usually

---

1 The classic exposition of the EMT and survey of its tests is Fama (1970). Firth (1977) is a useful source of references to research into the EMT and Keane (1983) provides a recent survey.
2 The measurement of serial correlation was described in more detail in Chapter 12, in the context of randomness in profit streams. A fuller description of runs and serial correlation tests can be found in Foster (1978).

concluded that they are too small to generate investment strategies that can cover their own transaction costs.[3]

Mechanical trading rules

Researchers have also tested some of the mechanical trading rules with which practising investment advisers have claimed to successfully predict share prices. One example of a mechanical trading rule is the *filter rule*. A 'filter rule' is a rule which tells an investor when to buy and sell a particular share. It is of this form – 'buy when the price rises by more than X% from its last low point, sell when it falls by X% from a previous high'. The critical percentage, X. is determined by the analyst. Implicitly the filter rule is saying that past price movements are an indication of future movements so a successful filter rule would be evidence that the market was inefficient. Alexander (1964) and Fama and Blume (1966) examined the performance of filter rules. They found, as has often been found in weak-form testing of the EMT, that prices are not perfectly random and in the absence of transactions costs it might be possible to make very small abnormal returns using filter rules. But once transactions costs are taken into account this ceases to be the case. Dryden (1970a) used filter tests to investigate share price movements in the UK, and found that they could not generate profitable investment strategies. Other trading rules have been investigated. In the main they have been shown unable to yield price forecasts that are profitable after allowing for transactions costs.[4]

SEMI-STRONG EFFICIENCY: THE EFFECTS OF NEW INFORMATION

The market is semi-strong efficient if prices always fully reflect all *publicly available* information. There is now an impressive body of evidence that the market is semi-strong efficient.

It is fairly easy to check the speed with which share prices respond to any new information that becomes public. The evidence is usually that the market embodies new information fully by the time it is formally announced. But it is rather harder to know if the market is getting prices 'right' and what the exact effect on prices of news about, say, a merger or a dividend *ought* to be. The researcher would have to say he knew better than the market how the news affected expectations of future cash flows, and how those cash flows should be evaluated. It is easier to find situations where new information has apparently no economic content and check that prices do not change. One study of this sort was the study of 'stock splits' by Fama, Fisher, Jensen and Roll (1969). We will examine this study fairly closely as it is a model of efficient markets research.

Do stock-splits boost value?

The *stock split* is an event whose theoretical impact we can calculate precisely – it should have no impact on the value of the firm. A stock-split takes place when a firm gives its existing shareholders extra shares in proportion to the share they already own.[5] A stock-split is not a 'real' event, merely a distribution of additional share certificates, so the total value of the firm should be unchanged by a stock-split.

3　For examples of work in this area see the early studies by Fama (1965) and Moore (1964) in the US and work on UK data by Kendall (1953), Brealey (1970) and Dryden (1970b).
4　For a list of some of these studies see Firth (1977).
5　'Stock-split' is the US terminology. In the UK stocks-splits are usually known as 'scrip' or 'capitalisation' issues. On this occasion we find the US term more explicit.

Suppose Splitz Ltd has 200,000 shares in issue, selling for £5 each. Splitz decides to issue its shareholders with another share for each one they own. The total market value of the firm is £1 million, and since the stock split should not change this value we would expect the post-split share price to be £1 million/400,000 = £2.50.

However, there is a widespread belief amongst financial advisers and similar personnel that stock-splits do increase the value of the firm, and on the face of it the evidence bears this out. In practice Splitz share price might well settle at, say, £3 after the split giving a total market value of £1.2 million.

The puzzling phenomenon described above, was investigated by Fama, Fisher, Jensen and Roll (1969) in what is a classic study.

Fama *et al* agreed that firms splitting their shares *did* experience abnormal value gains. But they explained this by hypothesising that stock-splits carried valuable information about future dividends. We saw in Chapter 15 that one reason why dividend policy may be relevant to the value of the firm is that managers are known to dislike cutting dividends. Hence the setting of a new level of dividends is interpreted as a statement that this new level of dividends can be maintained in the future, and therefore provides important new information for outsiders. Since managers often try to maintain dividend *per share* when they split stock, a stock-split is often accompanied by a dividend increase.

The 'market model'

Semi-strong tests are concerned with the impact of new information: they compare the share price which resulted with what it would have been without the new information. However the elapse of time causes a problem here. We find that in an efficient market investors are able to anticipate new information and start to embody it in share prices well before it is formally announced. There can be a gap of months between the true pre-information price and the post-information price, during which time many other relevant external factors may have changed.

To handle this problem many studies use the 'market-model' which provides a method of estimating what the price of a share 'would have been'. We know that under the assumptions of the CAPM there is a stable linear relationship through time between the return on an asset j and the market, m, such that:

$$r_j = r_i + B_j (r_m - r_i) \tag{1}$$

where r_j = return on asset j
r_m = return on the market portfolio
r_i = riskless rate
B_j = coefficient specific to project j, reflecting the covariability between asset j and the market portfolio.

This theoretical model suggests the following linear estimating equation, known as the 'market-model', to determine the relationship between the return on the market and return on a particular share j:

$$r_{jt} = a_j + b_j r_{mt} + e_{jt} \tag{2}$$

where a_j, b_j are the parameters of the regression, and e_{jt} is an error term which is independent of r_m and has an expected value of zero.

The return on a share in the period ending at t, r_{jt}, is defined as follows:

$$r_{jt} = \frac{V_{jt} - V_{jt-1} + DIV_{jt}}{V_{jt-1}} \tag{3}$$

where V_{jt} = Value of share j at time t

DIV_{jt} = Cash dividend paid in period t

The return on the market is calculated in a similar way, using a portfolio built for the purpose, or a published market portfolio such as the FT Actuaries.

Fama *et al* used the market-model to test their hypothesis. First they had to establish that extraordinary returns were in fact associated with stock splits, and to abstract from the changes in the returns of a firm that occur anyway because of general market conditions. They had a sample of 622 different shares that were involved in 940 splits from 1927 to 1959. For each security they estimated a version of the 'market model' using data on the returns on the security and on the market for as many periods as were available, but excluding periods immediately prior to the split. (The last point is crucial in using the market model and we will explain it shortly). Having estimated the model, the 'abnormal returns' earned on the share during any period can be calculated as the difference between actual returns and returns predicted by the model in each period, in other words as the 'residuals' or error terms, e_{jt}, in equation (2). (Hence the 'market model' technique is often known as 'residual analysis'.) For each month before and after the split Fama *et al* averaged the residuals across all the stock splits they studied, then found the cumulative total of these residuals month by month from 30 months before the effective date of the stock split to 30 months after. This is shown in Figure I.

The shape of the cumulative average residual curve in Figure I is very much what we have come to expect in research using the market model. The vertical height of the curve at

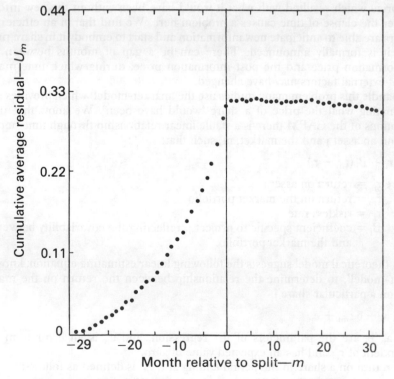

Reprinted with permission of the International Economic Review.

Figure I Cumulative Average Residuals from Fama et al (1969)

t = 0 measures the extent of the extraordinary returns which had accrued by the time of the split. The flatness of the curve there-after can be taken as evidence of market efficiency – the new information had been 'fully' incorporated in share prices by the date of the split. The shape of the curve prior to the split is interesting, since it shows that the market started to anticipate gains up to 30 months in advance. It is common to find a good deal of anticipation in market model studies. Since splits were only announced a month or two in advance Fama *et al* concluded that these anticipated gains could not have been caused by the split, rather that the split *and* the extraordinary returns were jointly caused by '. . . a sharp improvement, relative to the market, in the earnings prospects of the company sometime during the years immediately preceding a split' (Fama *et al* (1969)).

Since extraordinary gains can start to arise well before the event with which they are associated it is important to restrict the estimation of the market model to the 'normal' period prior to the onset of these gains, otherwise there will be estimation bias. But the problem is that until the model is estimated the period of extraordinary gains cannot be identified. To overcome this, Fama *et al* estimated the model twice for each share, the first time to form an idea as to the likely period of extraordinary gains, and the second time excluding this period.

In order to test their hypothesis further Fama *et al* split their sample into shares whose dividend increased subsequent to the split, and those which failed to show the anticipated increase. They found that the latter showed rising cumulative average residuals in the months before the split, but once the anticipated dividend increase failed to materialise the market corrected its error so that the cumulative average residual 'plummeted' in the few months following the split.

The Fama *et al* study provides a good example of the use of the market model in finance research and it shows how careful investigation can unravel the inner logic in a situation in which even the participants themselves may not perceive it. But it remains unclear where the positive advantage lies to the firm in splitting its shares. When asked, managers tend to justify stock splits in terms of a lower share price being more 'convenient' for shareholders to transact, and having the appearance of a bargain. Both of these seem of dubious importance in a market dominated by institutional investors. Managers also justify splits in terms of their beneficial effect on the value of the firm and as a way of signalling success to the market. Fama *et al* showed that in an efficient market the stock split itself is of no intrinsic value, it is only valuable for the dividend increases associated with it. Similar results were found by Firth (1977) in his study of stock splits in the UK.

Creative accounting

Accounting profit reflects various accounting conventions and there seems to be a widespread view amongst managers that it can be worthwhile 'massaging' profits by a suitable choice of conventions. Also many firms give a good deal of thought and spend a good deal of money on the presentation of their accounting information to the outside world. But none of this affects the future cash flow of the firm so in an efficient market it should not affect the firm's value either.

Beaver and Dukes (1973) studied the effect of choice of depreciation method on value. They compared the price-earnings ratios of two groups of firms, one employing straight-line depreciation and the other accelerated depreciation. The average P/E of each group differed, and Beaver and Dukes were able to show that the difference could not be explained in terms of risk or growth differences between the groups. But when depreciation, and thus earnings, were put on a comparable basis the difference in P/E was largely eliminated. Hence it appeared the market was efficiently peering through the 'veil of accounting practice' and valuing the firms consistently. Kaplan and Roll (1972) used residuals analysis to examine the share price behaviour of a group of firms that changed their depreciation method and a group that changed their method of accounting for investment tax credits. In both cases the market appeared to behave efficiently with respect to these changes in accounting method.

Other studies

We have considered the impact on values of some apparently irrelevant events – stock splits and accounting changes. Researchers have also studied the response of prices to the issue of information that *is* relevant to the valuation of shares, but we leave examination of these results to the appropriate chapters in the text. In Chapter 24 we consider how the gains or losses associated with merger are incorporated in share prices, and in Chapter 15 we consider the effect on share prices of earnings and dividend announcements. The evidence suggests the market handles this sort of information efficiently. In Chapter 20 we look at the behaviour of the market in valuing new issues, but here the efficiency conclusion is less clear.

STRONG-FORM EFFICIENCY

Strong-form tests of the efficient markets theory have considered two rather important and interesting questions. The first is whether certain people, 'insiders', have privileged access to information that can be used profitably in market trading. The second is whether any particular group appears to be consistently successful in trading.

Insider trading

Unsurprisingly, research has shown that it is possible to make abnormal gains on the stock-market if you have access to relevant information ahead of the market, so the market does not appear to be strong-form efficient. The benefits from insider trading are hard to research fully because much of it is never publicised. But researchers have been able to examine some occurrences of insider trading. For example, Lorie and Niederhoffer (1968) were able to use SEC records in the US to identify trades in company shares by people with insider information. They found that these insider trades yielded returns above the market average. Jaffe (1974) found similar results when he investigated insider trades on SEC records.

After many years of discussion, the Companies Act 1980, s 68 finally made insider trading illegal in the UK with a maximum penalty of two years imprisonment and an unlimited fine. The prohibition relates to individuals who have been 'connected' with the company either as a director or employee, or through a business or professional relationship. Trading on information got from an insider is prohibited too, as is getting someone else to trade for you. However the act does not create a civil offence, so aggrieved shareholders cannot sue for damages or have the share transaction made void.

The value of reputation

We are talking about the value of knowing before the market that a share price will rise or fall, but sometimes individuals may be in a position to make this happen. For instance it has been said that certain financial journalists have acquired a sufficient reputation to be able to affect the price of a share by recommending it; and that on occasion a City institution, or its chairman, acquires such a golden reputation that its buying and selling behaviour provides a trigger for the rest of the market. An individual who can affect the price of a share can profit by making appropriate purchases or sales on his 'own account' at the same time. Such behaviour by a journalist is deemed highly unethical, and might indicate a semi-strong as well as a strong form breach of efficiency since the market would appear to be responding to irrelevant information. Unfortunately, or perhaps fortunately for the reader with faith in human nature and efficient markets, there is no systematic evidence on this topic. But some rather similar insider trading possibilities have been investigated.

The effect of buying and selling large blocks

Increasingly, buying and selling in the stock market is done by 'institutions' with very large funds at their disposal. Institutions generally profess reluctance to take a holding which is so large that its purchase or sale could affect the share price. But institutional managers are sometimes in a position to do this, and this opens the sort of possibility for personal gain that we mentioned above. Similarly the broker handling a large transaction on the part of a private client might be able to make a personal gain if the share price were affected.

In principle it is unclear why the price of a share should be affected by a 'block trade', since if they are properly priced all shares should be perfect substitutes for one another, and the block could not be significant relative to the volume of all shares on the market. However various studies on the New York Stock Exchange have shown that block trades can lead to significant price changes, in which prices fall temporarily then regain some of their former level. Dann, Mayers and Raab (1977) chose a sample of 298 block sales between July 1968 and December 1969. They included any share which showed a significant fall in price between the opening of trading and the sale of the 'block'. Dann *et al* found that share prices did dip after a block sale but then returned very quickly to their new equilibrium level. Indeed the return was so fast that they concluded the market was weak-form efficient in this respect. An investor in a position to invest $100,000, the maximum they considered, in *every* block trade they examined would have accumulated an annual return of 203% after tax and commission. But such is the speed of return of prices that had he bought at the price ruling exactly *one minute* later his annualised return would have been −4%! However Dann *et al* cautiously suggested that there might be a strong-form inefficiency here because New York Stock Exchange dealers could be in a superior position to capture any abnormal gains associated with block trades. First they would be better placed to participate at the 'bargain' block sale price: second, they have significantly lower transactions costs, and in the Dann *et al* study trading profits were very sensitive to transactions costs.

The value of expertise

Insider trading is about people with privileged access to information, but what about people with special skills in analysing what information there is? Institutions such as investment trusts and unit trusts often claim such skills when advertising their services. Researchers have found that in general institutional investors do not achieve a superior performance to the market. For example Jensen (1968) examined the performance of 115 funds, and found they were not out-performing the market, even before deducting their costs of operation. In the UK, Firth[6] studied the performance of unit trusts between 1965–1975. He found they did not out-perform the market, and that some did significantly worse. The existence of institutions can be explained in other ways – they can transform

6 Referenced in Firth (1977).

the terms of financing contracts and can enable small investors to participate in a diversified portfolio, they provide pension and insurance services, and so forth – but this research casts some doubts on the wilder claims of institutional managers.

One group of experts which does appear to beat the market is the well-known US Value Line Survey, and the Value Line predictions have received a large amount of attention from researchers. Value Line rank shares on the basis of a complex mixture of factors including the price history of the firm, and its earnings performance, through time and relative to other firms. While researchers have disagreed on what methodology to use, even the more unfavourable have found that *some* abnormal gains could be made using Value Line predictions, and this implies semi-strong market inefficiency. A recent example of a value line study is Copeland and Mayers (1982). Research in this area is constrained by availability of data. There may also be other individuals who consistently beat the market, but keep it quiet.

The Briloff factor

It might seem that the EMT paints a dreary picture of a capital market where security prices respond to new information with machine-like efficiency that allows no hope for the talented, and where only inside information can consistently beat the market. In practice few market participants see it that way, and the case of Abraham Briloff is worth considering. Dr Briloff is a leading American accounting professor at City University, New York. He believes that firms *do* mislead the market through accounting manipulation and he has devoted a lot of effort to exposing these practices. Perhaps his best known prey was McDonald's Corporation.[7] In an article in Baron's Magazine of 8 July 1974 entitled 'You deserve a break . . . McDonald's Burgers Are More Palatable Than Its Accounts' he accused McDonald's of various accounting ploys. For one thing Mr Kroc, the chairman of McDonald's had distributed shares to friends and employees without declaring this in the accounts. More significantly, in pursuit of one of his favourite themes, Briloff accused McDonald's of 'dirty pooling' in accounting for acquisitions. In 1973 McDonald's brought new subsidiaries into the accounts at their 'book' value of $6 million even though they cost 'over £50 million' in terms of the value of the shares issued to buy them. This way, Briloff maintained, McDonald's would reduce the depreciation charge on these assets, and enhance profits, in future years.

Briloff's revelations had an apparently dramatic effect on McDonald's share price. Foster (1978) notes that McDonald's price fell from 47⅞ on 7.5.74 to 38⅜ on 7.8.74. In June and July 1974 McDonald's shareholders experienced returns of minus 12% and minus 20%. Returns on the market fell too, but by only 1% and 7%, and McDonald's beta had been 1.7. Of course it cannot be proved that the fall in McDonald's share price was caused by Briloff – it may have been caused by something else. But if it was, it implies semi-strong and strong inefficiency. The market was misinterpreting publicly-available information; and it took an expert to point it out.

SOME COUNTER-EVIDENCE

We now look at some other studies that challenge market efficiency.

---

7 This case is well written-up in Foster (1978) pp 409–420. For more good examples of the Briloff approach see his 'Unaccountable Accounting' (Briloff 1972)).

Does inflation distort share prices?

Modigliani and Cohn (1979) claimed to find a major inefficiency in the valuation of shares in the US stock market. They noted that since the mid-1960s the nominal value of the Standard and Poor's 500 index of US stock prices had remained relatively constant, while in real terms its value had fallen to 60% of its 1965–1966 level. The 'q' ratio, the ratio of value to replacement cost, of US non-financial corporations had fallen from over unity to less than two-thirds in the same period. Modigliani and Cohn argued that this fall did not reflect any underlying real change in the performance of the US economy but that the value of the S + P 500 was wrong, reflecting two inflation-induced errors made by investors in valuing shares. Investors were using the 'P/E' approach to valuing shares, but were multiplying the *wrong* measure of earnings by the *wrong* P/E ratio. We saw in Chapter 12 that to measure current-cost income it is necessary to make four inflation adjustments to historic-cost profit; three which we might normally expect to be negative, reflecting the need to replace fixed assets, stocks, and debtors and creditors at higher prices, and the fourth, normally positive, reflecting the eroding real liability of company borrowing. According to Modigliani and Cohn investors were deducting depreciation and stock adjustments but failing to add back a gearing adjustment, so understating profit.

The P/E ratio is the reciprocal of the required earnings yield. To capitalise a 'real' earnings stream it is appropriate to use a 'real' capitalisation rate, but Modigliani and Cohn believed that, moreover, investors were basing P/Es on the higher 'nominal' interest rates prevailing in the market and thus deriving P/Es that were too low. Correctly-valued, Modigliani and Cohn claimed, the level of the S + P 500 would have been 200 in 1977, rather than 100.

The negative relationship between inflation and share values occurred in all developed countries in the 1970s (see Cohn and Lessard (1981)). But the key question is the link between the two events, and the Modigliani and Cohn argument in terms of market inefficiency is by no means universally accepted. Feldstein (1980) argues that the phenomenon can be explained in terms of the impact of certain features of the tax law, though his argument is specific to the US tax system. Moore (1980) has attempted to explain the UK experience in terms of an inflation-induced failure by companies to maintain the real value of dividends.

The Modigliani and Cohn hypothesis demonstrates the great difficulty in efficient markets research of knowing what share values *ought* to be. They produce published descriptions of the valuation procedures adopted by analysts to support their contention that shares were being wrongly valued. By substituting 'correct' procedures they restore the trend line for the S + P index very much to where they expected it to be. But this does not constitute *proof* of their hypothesis. The share valuation process is based on expectations of the future and is essentially unobservable. It remains possible that some sea-change in the future level and risk of the returns of companies, possibly associated with inflation, perhaps with the 'oil crisis', book place in the 1970s, and was correctly identified by investors. Cohn, in his 1981 paper with Lessard, draws a more tentative conclusion than before.

> The interesting question for further exploration is whether the observed relationship between interest rates, inflation and stock prices is the result of systematic errors in valuation on the part of investors or linkages between structural causes of inflation and factors that reduce long-term earnings potential for firms (pp 287–288).

Are share prices too volatile?

The man-in-the-street often seems perplexed by the responsiveness of the Stock Market indices to information such as macroeconomic indicators, political comings and goings, etc. He finds it hard to see how the effects of these large and hard to assimilate events can be so closely quantified in rises and falls in the index. People with a grasp of finance are usually quick to reasure him that share values are the sums of discounted expectations about the future, so that events that cause a reappraisal of the future can lead to dramatic changes in prices. Recently this comfortable analysis of share price volatility has been challenged by tests, mainly associated with Robert Schiller, which appear to show that, historically, share prices volatility has been far too great to be consistent with valuation in an efficient market (see Schiller (1981a) and Schiller (1981b)).

'Volatility tests' are based on restrictions on the volatility of share prices which can be logically derived from the basic share valuation model. We will show how the simplest of these tests is derived, following Schiller.

The basic dividend valuation model asserts that the value of a share at time t is the discounted value of future dividends to infinity. If S_o^* is the price we could fix at time t_o with perfect knowledge of dividends, DIV_t and using a discount rate, r, then

$$S_o^* = \sum_{t=0}^{\infty} \frac{DIV_t}{(1 + r)^t}$$

But at t_o we do not have perfect knowledge, and so have to work with *expectations* of future dividends, E (DIV_t) in setting the actual price, S_o, so

$$S_o = \sum_{t=0}^{\infty} \frac{E(DIV_t)}{(1 + r)^t} = E(S_o^*)$$

There will be a forecasting error, U, associated with E (S_o^*) which we can define as

$$U = S_o^* - S_o$$

rearranging, $S_o^* = S_o + U$

Since we know that in an 'efficient' forecast, the error, U, must be uncorrelated with the forecast, S_o, we know that the variance of $(S_o + U)$ is the *sum* of the variances of the two terms (the covariance will be zero).

Hence, var (S_o^*) = var (U) + var (S_o)
Variances cannot be negative, hence

var (S_o) ≤ var (S_o^*), or expressed in terms of standard deviations
$\sigma(S_o)$ ≤ $\sigma(S_o^*)$

This inequality, derived from the basic share valuation model and the concept of an efficient forecast shows that the standard deviation of the series based on full knowledge of future dividends cannot be less than that of the actual series, if rationally valued. Schiller estimated the 'expost rational price', the price using hindsight knowledge of what dividends turned out to be for the shares in the Standard and Poor's Composite Stock Price index from 1871–1979, and compared this with the actual price series. We show this in Figure II. It is clear that the actual series, P, is dramatically more volatile than the expost rational series.

Schiller's work is too recent for its implications to be assessed yet. But Lintner (1981)

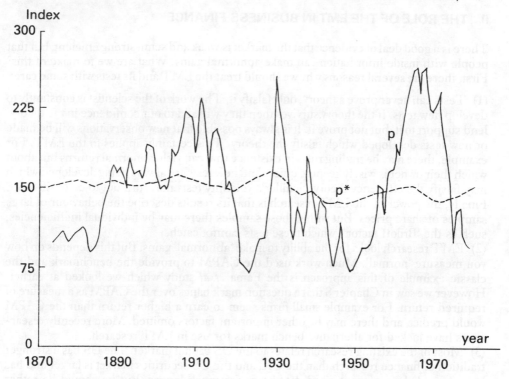

Source: Schiller 1981 (b)

Reprinted with permission of the American Economic Review.

Figure II Actual (p) and Rational (p*) prices of S + P index 1871–1979

makes two comments on the significance of the volatility tests as tests of market efficiency. First, he suggests that the model of the EMT implicit in Schiller's test is a particularly restrictive specification. Second he points out that in common with other efficiency tests, the volatility tests are in fact tests of a joint hypothesis – namely that the market is efficient *and* that the model being used to test for efficiency is appropriate to the task. A failure may reflect falsification of either of these joint hypotheses.

Weekend effects

It seems that shares are more likely to earn negative returns on Mondays! This is the so-called 'weekend effect'. French (1980) looked at the returns on the 500 largest firms on NYSE from 1953 to 1977, and found a very significant negative Monday return overall, and in each five-year sub-period. There also appears to be a year-end effect. Various studies, for example Reinganum (1982), have found a tendency for returns to fall in December, and rise the following January.

There seems to be no obvious explanation for the weekend effect, though the year end effect in the US may well be a result of buying and selling for tax reasons. Also these effects do not appear to be very strong, not strong enough to cover the transactions costs of buying and selling shares. However they would offer abnormal gains to investors who retimed purchases and sales they were going to make anyway.

II   THE ROLE OF THE EMT IN BUSINESS FINANCE

There is a good deal of evidence that the market is weak and semi-strong efficient, but that people with inside information can make abnormal gains. What are we to make of this? First, there are several reasons why we should treat the EMT and its tests with some care:

(1) Tests can never prove a theory, only falsify it. The work of the scientist is constantly to develop new tests. If the theory survives then they will add to our confidence in the theory, lend support to it, but not prove it. It is always possible that new observations will be made or new tests developed which falsify the theory. This certainly applies to the EMT. For example, there may be trading rules in existence that can yield abnormal returns but about which their owner is wisely keeping quiet. And new tests are always being developed which may falsify the efficiency theory. Schiller's volatility tests may turn out to be of this sort. Finally, the power of the EMT research is that its results describe the behaviour of large samples of share prices. But within those samples there may be individual inefficiencies, such as the 'Briloff factor', which these tests cannot catch.

(2) EMT research looks for the ability to make 'abnormal' gains. But this depends on how you measure 'normal'. Much work used the CAPM to provide the benchmark and the classic example of this approach is the Fama *et al* study which we looked at earlier. However we saw in Chapter 8 that a question mark hangs over the CAPM as a measure of required return. For example small firms seem to earn a higher return than the CAPM would predict, and there may be other important factors omitted. More recently researchers have looked for alternative bench marks for use in EMT research.

(3) Most of the existing research relates to the US capital market. The US has a stronger tradition of finance research than the UK, and the US securities market is larger and has been recorded on computerised data bases for much longer. But he should be rather cautious in drawing conclusions about the efficiency of other markets from the US research. All we can do is note that the results of UK studies do appear to conform to those in the US.

(4) Tests of the EMT examine the pricing of the securities of quoted firms. There are about 2,500 quoted firms in the UK, yet over 700,000 companies registered at Companies House. Of course quoted firms are the largest and account for the major part of economic activity in the UK, but the concentration of research effort on these firms cannot be entirely explained this way. It also reflects availability of data. Only quoted firms have continuously recorded market prices, which are the necessary data base for rigorous testing of the EMT. But there are a lot of other important questions we might want to ask about the performance of the capital market. Does the market discriminate against small firms? Are bank loans properly priced? Is the whole company sector correctly allocated its supply of funds? We will look at some of these issues in the next chapter.

EFFICIENT MARKETS VERSUS PERFECT MARKETS

In thinking about what the EMT does and does not say, it is useful to clarify the difference between a *perfect* market and one which is simply *efficient*. The general conditions necessary for a market to be perfect are as follows:
1 There is full and costless information available to all participants
2 There are no transaction costs and the tax system is neutral with respect to the market
3 There are many buyers and sellers, so that participants are 'price-takers'
4 Participants are 'rational': they behave in accordance with certain axioms of rationality

such as preferring more to less of a good thing, and make their choices in a different way.

The appeal of the perfect market concept is that it can be employed to build models of economic systems from which powerful optimality conclusions can be drawn. If all the markets – for products, labour and capital – are perfect in an economy then we can be sure the economy is 'Pareto-efficient' – that is, there is no reallocation of resources that will make someone better off without making someone else worse off. In other words there is no gratuitous wastefulness. Market-prices in such an economy carry a lot of information – they tell us the cost to the supplier of the marginal unit produced, and the consumer's evaluation of the marginal unit consumed.

But the perfect market economy is an unrealised ideal. In reality the necessary conditions for perfect markets do not hold and in the *capital market* it is particularly conditions 1 and 2 which appear unrealistic. In practice information is neither free nor uniformly distributed. There is a gulf between the information about firms that 'insiders' – managers and their advisers such as stock-brokers, merchant bankers, accountants, consultants – have access to, and the information shareholders are given. Shareholders have to spend money to narrow this gap. Secondly, raising finance and buying and selling existing securities is a costly process. We discussed some of the costs of new finance in the previous chapter. In addition, investors who buy and sell securities pay brokerage costs which reduce the gains from trading. Furthermore there are transactions costs in product markets that can have an impact on financial decisions, notably the costs associated with bankruptcy. Thirdly, companies and investors pay taxes of different sorts and at rates which depend on their individual taxpaying positions. So, for example, the marginal rate of income tax for investors can range from 0% to 60%. Tax drives a wedge between what firms earn and investors receive.

As the reader of this book will find out, we usually assume a perfect capital market when we build models to analyse financial decisions. This provides a useful starting point from which we can develop an analysis of real situations by relaxing the assumptions. But though it is possible to figure out in general terms the effects of these market imperfections on financial decisions it is hard to quantify their effects.

Efficiency is a much less demanding notion, and prices can *always fully reflect all available information* even when there are taxes, transactions costs and information costs. What makes for an efficient market? The real dynamic of efficiency is competition, and the capital market becomes *competitive* when there are *many buyers and sellers* constantly searching for information and reappraising security prices in the light of it, looking for the possibility of an abnormal gain. There is an apparent paradox here, which is why many people, particularly active participants in the stock market, find the EMT hard to accept. They say 'How can you expect us to believe its impossible to make abnormal gains on the stock market? For one thing the market is full of people hoping and striving to make an abnormal gain, and for another there is a large and well-paid profession of market analysts and related experts whose job is to analyse company performance and identify profitable opportunities for investors'. In fact the existence of these people is entirely consistent with market efficiency – the market is efficient *because of* them rather than *in spite of* them. Market efficiency does not imply that abnormal gains cannot be made – good luck or the possession of inside information can both yield them. The point is that armed *only* with publicly available information you could not have an expectation of abnormal gain if you buy and sell shares in an efficient market. As for investors and analysts, it is the strivings of investors, and the close monitoring by analysts that create the competitive conditions under which new information is instantaneously capitalised into security prices.

THE MESSAGE OF THE EMT

The main implication of market efficiency is that, as far as we can tell, share prices can be trusted – given the existing stock of publicly available information shares will neither be over- nor under-valued. This is a very important conclusion. Supply and demand in any market are balanced by the price mechanism. In the capital market the 'price' is the cost of capital. The dividend valuation model shows that the cost of equity capital is the discount rate, r_e which equates the value of the share, S_o, and the future dividend stream, DIV_t

$$\text{where, } S_o = \sum_{t=0}^{\infty} \frac{DIV_t}{(1 + r_e)^t}$$

Thus if the share is under-valued the cost of capital will be too high, and vice versa. In general the firm can only be confident in its cost of capital if its shares are correctly valued. By exactly the same argument investors' return depends on the pricing of shares. But if the market is efficient investors and firms can participate in it with some confidence of getting a fair return and paying a fair price.

EMT research yields a crop of more specific insights too. For instance, we now know that cosmetic accounting changes are unlikely to mislead the market, and that stock splits are not a magical and costless method of enhancing share price, and so forth. Similarly investors should be duly suspicious of claims by experts and advisers to be able to beat the market.

III SUMMARY

This chapter asked whether the capital market is 'efficient'. On one aspect of this question we have abundant evidence, albeit mostly relating to the US capital market. The 'efficient markets theory' asserts that the market will be 'efficient' if it fully and instantaneously embodies all relevant information into security prices. Tests of the EMT suggest that the market is efficient in its handling of publicly available information but that possession of 'insider' information, information ahead of the market, can yield abnormal gains. The implication is that market participants, investors and firms, can 'trust' market prices. They can buy and sell securities, lend money and raise it, with some confidence that they will pay a fair price and get a fair return.

But there are important areas the EMT does not cover – it cannot tell us much about finance that is not transacted on the securities markets. Moreover efficient markets are not necessarily perfect markets.

In the next chapter we look at some other important aspects of market performance.

REFERENCES AND BIBLIOGRAPHY

Alexander, S S	'Price Movements in Speculative Markets: Trends or Random Walks' Industrial Management Review, May 1961, pp 7–26.
Bachelier, L	*Theorie de la Speculation*'. Gauthier-Villars, Paris, 1900, in Cootner (1964).
Baumol, W J Heim, P Malkiel, B G and Quandt, R F	'Earnings Retention, New Capital and the Growth of the Firm' Review of Economics and Statistics, Nov 1970, pp 345–355.

Beaver, W H and Dukes, R E	'Tax Allocation and δ Depreciation Methods', Accounting Review, July 1973, pp 549–559.
Brealey, R A	'The Distribution and Independence of Successive Rates of Return from the British Equity Market' Journal of Business Finance, Summer 1970, pp 29–40.
Briloff, A	Unaccountable Accounting (1972) Harper and Row, New York.
Cohn, R A and Lessard, D R	'The Effect of Inflation on Stock Prices: International Evidence', Journal of Finance, May 1981, pp 277–290.
Coutner, P H (ed)	The Random Character of Stock Market Prices (1964) MIT Press, Cambridge, Mass.
Copeland, T E and Mayers, D	'The Value Line Enigma (1965–1978): A Case Study of Performance Evaluation Issues', Journal of Financial Economics, Nov 1982, pp 289–321.
Dann, L Mayers, D and Raab, R	'Trading Rules, Large Blocks and the Speed of Adjustment', Journal of Financial Economics, Jan 1977, pp 3–22.
Davis, E W and Yeomans, K A	'Company Finance and the Capital Market', Cambridge University Press, Occasional Paper 39, Cambridge, England 1974.
Dryden, M M	'Filter Tests of UK Share Prices', Applied Economics, Jan 1970a.
Dryden, M M	'A Statistical Study of UK Share Prices', Scottish Journal of Political Economy, Nov 1970b.
Dukes, R E	'An Investigation of the Effects of Expensing Research and Development Costs on Security Prices', in M. Schiff, G. Sorter (eds) Proceedings of the Conference of Topical Research in Accounting (1976) New York University, New York.
Fama, E F	'The Behaviour of Stock Market Prices', Journal of Business, Jan 1965, pp 34–105.
Fama, E F	'Efficient Capital Markets: A Review of Theory and Empirical Work', Journal of Finance, May 1970, pp 383–417.
Fama, E F and Blume, M	'Filter rules and stock market trading' Journal of Business, Jan 1966, pp 226–41.
Fama, E, Fisher, L, Jensen, M and Roll R	'The Adjustment of Stock Prices to New Information', International Economic Review, 10 Feb 1969, pp 1–21.
Feldstein, M	'Inflation and the Stock Market', American Economic Review, Dec 1980, pp 839–847.
Firth, M A	'An Empirical Investigation of the Impact of the Announcement of Capitalisation Issues on Share Prices', Journal of Business Finance and Accounting, Spring 1977a, pp 47–60.
Firth, M A	The Valuation of Shares and the Efficient–Markets Theory (1977b) Macmillan, London.
Foster, G	Financial Statement Analysis (1978) Prentice-Hall, Englewood-Cliff, New Jersey.
French C	'Stock Returns and the Weekend Effect' Journal of Financial Economics, 1980.
Jaffe, J	'Special Information and Insider Trading', Journal of Business, July 1974.

Jensen, M	'The Performance of Mutual Funds in the Period 1945–64', Journal of Finance, May 1968, pp 389–416.
Kaplan, R S and Roll, R	'Investor Evaluation of Accounting Information; Some Empirical Evidence', Journal of Business, April 1972, pp 225–257.
Kendall, M G	'The Analysis of Economic Time Series, Part 1: Prices'. Journal of the Royal Statistical Society, Part I 1953, pp 11–25.
Lintner, J	'The use of Volatility Measures in Assessing Market Efficiency – Discussion', Journal of Finance, May 1981, pp 307–312.
Little, I M D and Rayner, A C	*Higgledy Piggledy Growth Again* (1966) Basil Blackwell, Oxford.
Lorie, J H and Niederhoffer, V	'Predictive and Statistical Properties of Insider Trading', Journal of Law and Economics, April 1968.
Modigliani, F and Cohn, R A	'Inflation, Relation Valuation and the Market' Financial Analysts Journal, March/April 1979.
Moore, A B	'Some Characteristics of Changes in Common Stock Prices', from Cootner P. H. (ed) *The Random Character of Stock Market Prices* (1964) MIT Press.
Moore, B	'Equity Values and Inflation: The Importance of Dividends'. Lloyds Bank Review, July 1980.
Reddaway, W B, Potter, S T and Taylor, C T	*Effects of UK Direct Investment Overseas* (1968) Cambridge University Press.
Reinganum, M R	'A Direct Test of Roll's Conjecture on the Firm Size Effect', Journal of Finance, 1982.
Schiller, R J	'The Use of Volatility Measures in Assessing Market Efficiency', Journal of Finance, May 1981(a), pp 291–303.
Schiller, R J	'Do Stock Prices Move Too Much to be Justified by Subsequent Changes in Dividends?', American Economic Review, June 1981(b).

QUESTIONS

1 On the financial page of any daily paper you will see charts of the price history of individual shares and market sectors. What does weak-form EMT say about the value of charts like this?

2 When Bowtie plc had a 1 for 3 stock split, the share price fell from £2.40 to £2. Barry Bowtie, saw the value of his shares rise 11%. So he plans another stock split next year. Advise him.

3 Is the production by most large firms of expensive, glossy annual reports consistent with a semi-strong efficient market?

4 What difficulties exist in ever getting the necessary information for testing strong form efficiency?

5 Why is it sometimes claimed that inflation distorts stock-market prices? How is this problem related to that of stock market efficiency?

6 What is the difference between an efficient market and a perfect market?

7 What is the significance of EMT for investors and financial managers?

CHAPTER 19

Capital market efficiency: small-firms and crowding-out

The EMT concerns aspects of capital market efficiency that can be tested. In this chapter we consider some aspects of market performance that are rather harder to test, but are important all the same. We do this by simply widening the view. The EMT suggests that the finance associated with securities that are traded on a stock-market is fairly priced. In Section I we discuss the notion of a 'fair price' for finance and consider whether even large quoted companies are paying a fair price for the finance they raise in other ways – through bank borrowing and retained earnings. Section II considers the controversial question of the financing of small and medium-sized firms, which fall outside the scope of the EMT. In Section III we widen the scope even further and examine some of the 'crowding-out' arguments which imply that the whole of the business sector is being starved of funds by the other sectors in the economy.

One reason that the Efficient Markets Theory has been so well-researched is that the necessary data – the price histories of quoted securities – are available on computer data-bases. The characteristic of all the issues we discuss in this chapter is lack of hard evidence, but this does not mean they should be ignored. These are important issues for understanding the workings of the capital market so we need to outline the problem and such evidence as exists.

I DO FIRMS PAY A FAIR PRICE FOR FINANCE?

We saw in Chapter 17 that the price of finance is likely to depend on the quantity, the duration and particularly the risk involved. We will say the price is 'fair' if all firms have the same cost of capital, with appropriate allowance for these factors. We are not concerned here with the question of what constitutes an 'appropriate allowance'. The question is whether a project of given risk, duration and scale would face the same cost of capital in different situations, for example, if it were financed by retained earnings instead of by a share issue, if it were undertaken by a division of a large corporation rather than a small firm, or if it were undertaken in the public sector instead of in the private sector.

Suppose market prices were not 'fair' in this sense, and there were two identical firms, A and B, both equally risky and both wanting to raise the same quantity of finance for the same duration, but A could raise funds at 10% while B had to pay 14%. Firm A would find it worthwhile to undertake projects yielding an IRR of only 11% while Firm B would be deterred from investing in 13% projects. From the standpoint of the economy as a whole there is inefficiency here with 11% projects being undertaken in preference to 13% ones.

The EMT is implicitly investigating one aspect of the question of a fair price of finance by investigating whether securities themselves appear to be fairly priced, since the value of a security determines the cost of capital associated with it. But the positive findings of the tests of the EMT directly relate only to that part of a firm's finance associated with the issue of securities.

Bank borrowing

Many quoted firms raise a major part of their finance as bank borrowing. Hence we would like to be sure that comparable firms are paying similar prices for their bank finance. However, the data on this issue are not publicly available. There is simply no way we can check whether banks are charging a fair price for loans. What we can do, though, is start at the other end and examine the structure of the capital market in the area of the supply of bank loans to firms. There are many banks – commercial banks, merchant banks, foreign banks – competing to supply finance to larger firms. And the supply of information in both directions appears good: the terms and rates offered by competing banks are easily available to firms, and banks have access to the same information about firms and to the same expertise in firm analysis as is available in the stock market. In other words the market appears *competitive*, and we would expect interest-rate differentials between comparable firms not to exist for long in this situation.

DO FIRMS INVEST EFFICIENTLY?

Another intriguing question is, given the cost of capital, do firms invest their finance efficiently? We saw in Part II that efficiency in investment meant investing up to the point where the return on the marginal project equals the market price of finance, that is, where the marginal project has an $NPV = 0$. This is the value-maximising position for the firm. But in practice firms may not undertake this amount of investment. They may do less, and leave some positive-valued projects undone – this is effectively 'capital rationing', which is usually self-imposed by the firm as a device for limiting investment.

On the other hand the firm may invest beyond the point of efficiency and undertake projects which yield a return below the cost of capital. This might come about for example, if managers viewed retained earnings as free finance. It is often pointed out that retained earnings are unencumbered by the requirement to provide the supplier of finance with some evidence of investment intentions, as is often required with other types of finance. Little and Raynor (1966) considered this issue in the context of the UK and in the US Baumol, Heim, Malkiel and Quandt (1970) investigated the profitability of retained earnings. Baumol *et al* concluded that 'the rate of return on new equity capital is very much higher than the rate of return on either plough-back or new debt', but they did not conclude that managers were indifferent to the cost of retentions, or treated it as free, but rather that the required return on new equity and retentions reflected the different costs associated with these forms of finance.

The issue here is the one we discussed at some length in Chapter 2 as to whether firms are value-maximisers. There may be firms which invest less or more than is efficient, but evidence on this is hard to obtain. Similarly, the legal and market forces which constrain firms to maximise value may not be strong, but we have no consistent evidence of a failure in those constraints.

II SMALL AND MEDIUM-SIZED FIRMS

The EMT has provided us with a good deal of information about the market in which larger, quoted, firms raise their finance. We now consider the controversial issue of whether the other, small and medium-sized, firms in the economy are paying a fair price for their finance. There has been a long tradition of concern about small firms, reflected in the reports of a succession of government committees from Macmillan in 1931 to Wilson in 1980. The common view has been that small firms are very important for the health of the economy, but that they are disadvantaged in raising funds. This is a common concern in most western economies. As we will see these views tend to be strongly held and so have to be taken seriously, but there is little hard evidence available on them.

THE IMPORTANCE OF SMALL FIRMS

Though we are interested in the financing of small and medium-sized firms, most of the debate tends to centre on small firms. We will briefly discuss the medium sized firms later on. The definition of a 'small firm' is of necessity arbitrary. The Bolton Committee used different definitions of 'small firms' in different industries, for example in manufacturing it was interested in anything under 200 employees whereas the cut-off was 25 employees in construction and mining, and 5 vehicles in road transport. In other industries it set turnover criteria, ranging from £50,000 to £200,000 at 1963 prices. (See Bolton (1971) p 3).

Compared to other competitor nations, the UK seems to have a relatively small small-firms sector. The Bolton Committee collected statistics on this, which are reproduced in Table I.

Table I   Proportion of manufacturing employment in smaller establishments in countries with comparable statistics

Country	Date of figures	%
UK	1963	31
USA	1963	39
West Germany	1963	34
Canada	1968	47
Sweden	1965	53
Norway	1967	64

Source: Bolton (1971)

People have looked for an explanation of Britain's relative economic failure in the figures reproduced in Table I, since a healthy small-firm sector is seen as a necessity for a healthy economy.

The argument tends to depict small firms as young saplings from which the large trees of the future will grow, and without which the forest would eventually die. Small firms are seen to be flexible, not over-centralised, good at innovating new technology, and also nice places to work. The following are excerpts from an article by John Carvel in the Guardian 29.4.1977 entitled 'Case for the Small Firm' which expresses this view:

The revival of interest in the small firm springs from the breakdown of the growth economy. The decline of the small firm is no longer just a matter of sentimental regret. It can be seen as the symptom of the social and economic sickness of the 1970s.

Big business, big finance, and big government now all look to the renewal of the small firms sector as one of the keys to economic recovery . . .

. . . the case for the small firm runs like this. It employs more people because it depends more on human work than machine work. Yet it can often show a superior economic performance because it does not suffer the diseconomies of overlarge organisations with their rigidities, top-heavy bureaucracies, and ponderous inability to change course. The small firm is more flexible, it can respond quickly to market demand, it is more ready to innovate, and to provide specialised services. The consumer gets greater variety from small firms than from large organisations with their standardised products and take-it-or-leave it services.

For the employee small firms offer a wider choice of jobs and a working community which is small enough to be sociable and even convivial. . . .

. . . The social objection to large industrial organisations is that they may have to be a long distance from the places where the workers live, with all that implies for travel costs and travel stress. The social advantage of small firms is that they can be fitted into the urban scene as a natural part of the community, . . .

There is enough recent experience to show what holds back the small firms from making a start: the difficulty of finding a small workplace, the difficulty of getting small-scale starting-up finance, the difficulty of meeting planning regulations and coping with the paperwork required by government. Enough is known about this to clear these obstructions out of the way.

These are attractive ideas, but the reality may be less simple. In fact, it is not proven that a large small-firm sector is necessary for economic growth or success, or that small firms are better at innovating new ideas and technology, and are more flexible and responsive to change. Indeed, in Chapter 24 when we look at *merger*, we see that some people have argued just the opposite – that to exploit new opportunities quickly and powerfully you need large resources. In Chapter 24, we argue caution on the grounds that anything a large firm could do can also be done by a suitable coalition of small firms. But the reverse applies too; and each case needs to be analysed separately and carefully on its merits.

Are small firms nicer places to work? Although the entrepreneur running his own small firm may be happier than he would be half way up a large firm there is some evidence that this may not apply to the other employees. Bolton (1971) while conceding that workers typically get paid 20% less in small firms, argued that 'in many respects the small firm provides a better environment for the employee than is possible in most large firms' and '. . . generally the non-material satisfaction . . . more than outweigh any financial sacrifice involved' (p 21). But Curran and Stanworth (1978) challenged this view. Their study of ten firms in the printing and electronics industries suggested that the notion that communications were better in small firms was a myth promoted by management. Workers in small firms were just as likely to see the work place as a place of conflict. For Curran and Stanworth small firms were largely a refuge for the 'socially marginal', be it as employees or employers.

THE FINANCING OF SMALL FIRMS

Whether or not 'small is beautiful' it remains important that small firms should pay a fair price for their finance. Unfortunately this is hard to test. The data we would need – the market valuations of small firms and the cost of their various types of finance – are not available. So the debate usually involves a review of arguments for inefficiency at a theoretical level that are hard to prove or disprove. Over the years a variety of official committees have examined these problems and taken them seriously enough to recommend new institutional arrangements to alleviate them. Essentially the arguments are as follows: Small firms are precluded from the new issues market by the high fixed costs of new issues and the unwillingness of the institutional investor to take small holdings. However, there has also been a lack of long-term loan finance available externally – banks and similar institutions have been unwilling to lend beyond the short- to medium-term to small firms. Small firms are thus forced to raise money short-term from banks, or to rely on retained earnings. But banks tend to be excessively cautious in lending to small firms, either charging high interest rates or not lending at all. And in times of economic squeeze small firms suffer more severely than other firms – banks tend to give priority to larger firms, and trade credit tends to be squeezed at the expense of smaller firms. Small firms are thus forced to rely heavily on retained earnings, and this puts a limit on their growth potential.

The Macmillan Committee on Finance and Industry, reporting in 1931, identified the well known 'Macmillian Gap', which was the difficulty for small firms of raising external long-term finance in amounts up to, say, £200,000. As a result a variety of new institutions specialising in small-firm financing was established before and immediately after the Second World War. These included the Industrial and Commercial Finance Corporation (ICFC), Finance Corporation for Industry (FCI), Leadenhall Securities, and Charterhouse Industrial Development. The purpose of these institutions was to provide longer term funds to small firms. The Radcliffe Committee on the Working of the Monetary System, reporting in 1959, was satisfied with the response to the Macmillan Gap, but identified the need for more help in financing the exploitation of technical innovation. In turn, by the time the Bolton Committee of Inquiry on Small Firms reported in 1971, it found that institutional developments had met the main criticisms in Radcliffe. But Bolton noted that despite these improvements there was still a widespread view that institutions were failing in the provision of finance to small firms. Between the Bolton Report and the report of the Wilson Committee to Review the Functioning of Financial Institutions in 1980 there were further institutional developments including the creation of the National Enterprise Board, and Equity Capital for Industry, but Wilson still concluded that small firms needed more help.

In its Interim Report on the Financing of Small Firms, Wilson (1979(a)) recommended the following:

1 A state-backed Loan Guarantee Scheme.
2 A Small Firm Investment Company (SFIC), issuing shares bearing personal tax relief to holders.
3 An English Development Agency to match the existing Scottish and Welsh Agencies and the Council for Small Industries in Rural Areas (COSIRA).
4 The encouragement of 'over the counter' (OTC) markets in unlisted shares.
5 A change in the law to permit small firms to issue redeemable shares which would reduce the risk of loss of control to the original owners when raising new equity finance.

Since Wilson, some of these recommendations have been implemented. For example, we noted in Chapter 17 that the Unlisted Securities Market has proven successful since its inception. It is designed to provide an institutional setting for the public issue of securities which will prove attractive to smaller firms. Moreover, under a small business 'start-up' scheme investment in the shares of new small businesses now qualifies for tax-relief within certain limits.

Loan Guarantee Scheme

In June 1981 a Loan Guarantee Scheme was instituted under which the government would guarantee 80% of bank-loans up to £75,000 in exchange for a premium of 3%. This scheme proved popular and the initial endowment of £300m provided by the government was consumed ahead of schedule. However the Financial Times of 6 December 1982 reported that a confidential accountants' report commissioned by the government had expressed concern at the number of small firms with guaranteed loans which had subsequently failed. It suggested that some banks were insufficiently skilled at assessing risk. Also, by making loans easier to get, with no requirement on the entrepreneur to provide security or mortgage his house, the scheme may require insufficient commitment from him.

ANALYSING THE SMALL FIRM FINANCING PROBLEM

A firm's cost of capital is likely to reflect the length of time it wants the money for, the quantity raised, and in particular, the associated risk. So if small firms are riskier than large, or raise funds in inefficiently small quantities then they would be expected to pay more for their finance. We could only conclude that small firms were being unfairly treated in the capital market if they paid a higher price for their finance even after taking these factors into account.

Quantity

It is clear that small firms will seek finance in smaller quantities than large firms. In general we expect 'economies of scale' to occur wherever there are fixed or indivisible costs associated with the supply of a commodity. Finance appears to be such a commodity, since the information and administration costs associated with the provision of finance are relatively invariant to the amount of money involved. It costs as much to process a loan application for £1,000 – to analyse the applicant, check his security and credit-worthiness – as it does for £1 million.

One type of financing which appears to entail high fixed costs is the public issue of securities, debt or equity. We will see in Chapter 19 estimates prepared for the Wilson Committee which show significant economies in transactions costs per pound of finance, as the size of the issue increases. Davis and Yeomans (1974) identified another apparent cost disadvantage suffered by smaller firms in the public issue of securities, associated with the phenomenon known as 'market discount on new issue'. Whenever new shares are issued it is necessary to offer them to the market at a price less than their expected equilibrium price once they have been absorbed into the market. The purpose of this discount is to draw the shares to the attention of the market and bring forward sufficient demand to absorb them. Clearly there is a level of discount which will be sufficient for this, and any discount allowed beyond this will merely add to the cost of the finance at no benefit to the firm. However it has been shown by Davis and Yeomans that discounts on new issues vary according both to the method of issue used and to the size of the issuing firm. On 'method' they say 'Issues by tender displayed the lowest average discount at 6.95% of issue price, with levels of 8.88% for offers for sale and 19.08% for placings'. On size they say '. . . in the case of the unbiased group of offers for sale in stable markets, one could expect revealed discount to be 4% lower for a firm with £2,000,000 net assets than for a firm with £1,000,000 net assets'. But, though Davis and Yeomans make adverse conclusions on the efficiency of the new issues market – 'Our research results confirm earlier findings that levels of market discount on advisory price issues are much higher than appears necessary' – they do not conclude that the new issues market discriminates against smaller firms, but rather that smaller firms are not as well advised by issuing houses. But this issue discount problem is unlikely to affect small firms under the Bolton definition since, as we see below, firms of this size are effectively excluded from public issues anyway.

The trend from individual to institutional investment in the capital market also appears to introduce a bias in favour or large firms. Wilson (1979a) observed 'Most of the major institutions prefer investments in companies with a market capitalisation of £50 million or more, which effectively means the top 20% or so of the companies listed on The Stock

Exchange. Few are prepared to make direct investments to any significant extent in businesses valued at less than £5 million'.

Again this may reflect the institutions' desire to economise on the fixed costs of processing investments, and of appraising and monitoring the investment afterwards. Also institutions are reluctant to take a large proportion of the equity of any single company. They are not interested in acquiring a controlling interest, and like to be able to buy and sell their holdings without disturbing the share price too much, which gives them a preference for easily marketable shares. These factors indicate a policy of investing in large quoted firms.

Risk

The riskiness or variability of the returns of a firm will depend on (1) the extent to which the risk of individual projects cancels-out (is diversified away) in aggregate, and (2) the riskiness of the projects themselves. On both counts one would expect small firms to be riskier. First small firms are unlikely to be as diversified as larger ones and, second, they may find it harder to protect themselves from external fluctuations because of a lack of market power.

One aspect of the market power of small firms was explored by Davis and Yeomans in the study mentioned earlier. Davis and Yeomans examined the balance of trade credit given and received by small and large firms in periods of credit 'ease and squeeze' in the economy. They found that during periods of credit squeeze, when the scarcity of funds pushes up their opportunity cost, large firms are able to move the balance of trade credit in their favour by taking more and giving less. They said

> ... although the liquidity and profitability of all companies fell sharply during squeeze years the deterioration was most marked for the small companies. The differential impact on levels of liquid assets, profits, and bank lending is most marked in 1970, when the small company became more illiquid relative to large companies ... There is also much evidence to suggest that the credit behaviour of firms and their reactions to squeeze conditions was closely associated with financial vulnerability as measured by size and relative liquidity. In general, the smaller firm gave substantially more credit under squeeze conditions, yet had little control over his own trade creditors and was apparently less able to take credit than the large firms.
> (Davis and Yeomans, op cit).

Researchers have confirmed that the returns to small firms are more variable. For example, Gupta (1971) found size to be inversely related to profit variability and sales variability, and small firms appeared more likely to fail in economic recessions.[1]

Suppliers of finance may be afflicted with the uncertainty, as well as the risk, associated with small firms: they feel relatively less confident in believing forecasts of the prospects of small firms. This is partly a small firm problem as small firms are less able to deploy skilled manpower in the analysis and presentation of forecasts. But it is in part a 'new firm' problem, rather than a small firm problem. The relative youth of some small firms means they do not have well-documented histories of successful operations. Hence there are good reasons associated with economics of scale and differences in risk why we would expect a higher cost of capital for small firms. Wilson (1979a) noted in the context of bank lending that 'Rates of interest around 2% higher than those charged to larger businesses appear to be fairly typical and the level of security demanded also tends to be high, with personal guarantees often being required' (p 23). But they were unable to conclude

---

1   See also Singh and Whittington (1968) and Samuels and Smith (1968). However it seems that small firms tend to earn a higher return than large ones, as the survey by Wilson (1979b) also found.

categorically that the rates charged and security arrangements made were *inappropriate* given the risk and cost associated with financing smaller firms.

DOES CAPITAL STRUCTURE MATTER?

One implication of the small-firm financing problem is that small firms tend to have different capital structures from larger firms, probably because their access to finance is critically constrained in certain areas. They are precluded from public issues of securities, debt and equity, by the high fixed costs associated with entry to the securities market. And if they are new as well as small they may not have accumulated proportionately as much retained earnings as other firms. So small firms tend to rely more heavily on external borrowing from banks. Surveys conducted by Wilson (1979a) confirmed this general picture, but noted one or two interesting features. One was the importance of personal loans from directors, which effectively supplemented the equity base of many small firms. The other was that though small firms were generally slightly more profitable than large, they paid a much lower proportion of profit out as dividend. This may reflect the crucial importance for small firms of building reserves of retained earnings. But does this difference in capital structure matter? Does it really matter where the firm gets its money from? In a perfect capital market the capital structure of a firm – the particular mix of finance it employs – should have no effect on its cost of capital. We demonstrated this classic conclusion of finance theory in Chapter 14. But we also see that, in practice, the existence of market imperfections means that firms may be able to find a lowest-cost financing mix, so that being prevented from raising finance in the cheapest way would impose a cost on the firm. One outcome may be an absolute limit on the quantity of finance the firm can raise. This would happen if lenders imposed conventional limits on the ratio of debt to equity they would tolerate in a firm so that the limitation on the availability of equity will become a limit on the growth of the firm as a whole. There is some evidence that lenders do behave this way. Wilson noted that 'In many countries the banks are said to be prepared to envisage gearing (i e debt to equity) ratios as high as 2:1 or 3:1. In this country a ratio of 1:1 is more common.' (Wilson (1979a) p 23). However a well-established loan-guarantee scheme may change this. In Germany the loan guarantee system is well established and permits new investment by small and medium-sized firms of which only 20% may be contributed by the owner.

The problem with debt finance from the point of view of the lender is that he shares in the failure of the firm without being able to participate in its success, and this disparity increases the higher the gearing of the firm.

Small firms often find outside financiers wanting an equity stake as the price of further funds and this poses a dilemma for the owner of the small firm. As the price of growth he is being forced to lose some independence and share the potential fruits with someone else. Of course, this may be a fair price to pay. In demanding a high gearing ratio he is effectively asking someone else to bear the risks of his own wealth creation – this is something that needs to be borne in mind whenever small firms complain about lack of funds. But governments may be prepared to accept this as the price of encouraging small firms. In 1981 the National Enterprise Board, which normally takes an equity stake in firms it supports, created its Oakwood subsidiary for financing smaller businesses. Oakwood would provide unsecured loans, but would normally purchase a warrant from the client firm, permitting Oakwood to subscribe for up to 20% of its equity, six or seven years later. However, importantly, the client would have the right to buy back the option if it wanted to preserve its independence.

SOME FINAL COMMENTS ON SMALL FIRMS

There are good reasons, associated with the extra risk and costs of small firm financing, why a fair price for finance might be higher in the case of a small firm. Although there is no difficulty identifying special difficulties and extra costs facing small firms it is hard to prove that these are inappropriate. Hence the Wilson Report, which represents the most recent survey of small firm financing available, made various recommendations about enhancement of the markets, institutions and information available to small firms, but was not able to *prove* significant inefficiency in the status quo.

In practice, however, it is not necessary to prove unfairness. If governments want to single out small firms for special attention they are quite entitled to do so, even if it means 'positive discrimination', or subsidy of small firms at the expense of fairness with the rest of the economy. There is no doubt that the arguments for encouraging small firms are almost universally accepted in all the western economies. Most of the devices we have mentioned to encourage small firms – specialised agencies, loan guarantees, unlisted securities markets – are already up and running in countries such as the US and Germany.

The efficiency debate tends to be polarised into a discussion of small, and large firms. Wilson commissioned a survey of the investment and financing of 'medium-sized' firms which consisted of a questionnaire survey of 48 assorted companies with turnovers between £5 million and £150 million. Thirty four companies were quoted, fourteen unquoted. The results of the survey were interesting. The companies interviewed displayed very little evident dissatisfaction with the operation of the capital market with respect to them, and in fact they displayed little interest in the financing side of things at all. Their major concern was the lack of attractive investment opportunities which they partly saw as reflecting the climate of uncertainty fostered by successive governments' economic policy. Wilson concluded '. . . we could not find a single individual example of an investment project that had not gone ahead because of the inability to raise external finance . . .' (Wilson (1978) p 20). The Wilson Committee reached a similar conclusion on the performance of the UK capital market as a whole. They found that it was 'not generally the case' that real investment in the UK has been unnecessarily constrained by shortages in the supply of external capital. The problem seemed to be a lack of sufficiently profitable projects. They concluded that 'the perceived real cost of capital is now almost certainly higher than the average real profitability of industrial and commercial companies'.

The same comments might apply to small-firm financing. It is hard to see why an apparently competitive capital market would systematically fail to finance profitable investment opportunities, and not learn by its mistakes. We noted that there is some recent evidence that the marginal projects brought forth by the loan guarantee scheme included a significant number of uneconomic ones. Maybe there is a lack of profitable small firm opportunities in the UK.

What factors inhibit the supply of profitable small firm opportunities? There are those factors which affect the level of activity in the economy as a whole – in the UK commentators have produced many explanations for her low growth rate and low investment levels, but there is no consensus on the causes. Additionally there are those factors which might inhibit small firms particularly. For example small firms often complain about the complexity of government legislation and form-filling as it affects them, and they complain that the tax-system discourages initiative and innovation. We noted that lack of market power makes it harder for them to pass on economic pressures such as rising input prices and interest rates. A more fundamental problem may be the level of skill and knowledge of small firm managers. We saw that a lot of uncertainty surrounds lending to small firms. They often have little history to show lenders, and their management may lack the specialist skills to develop and present a sound economic argument for a loan.

Another problem is lack of knowledge about available financing opportunities. Bolton (1971) found 'many small firms are prevented by lack of information, by inexperience in presenting applications for finance and by a formidable barrier of prejudice against borrowing of all kinds from making use of the full range of facilities available to them.'

III CROWDING-OUT

So far we have been talking about the allocation of finance between firms, but widening the efficiency discussion still further we can ask whether the business sector as a whole is paying a fair price relative to the other sectors in the economy: the personal, public and overseas sectors. These are the sectors with which business must compete for funds and people often argue that in the UK too much is invested in private housing, too much is invested by government, and too much invested overseas, all to the detriment of business. We will briefly sketch these arguments.

Housing

The editorial column of the Financial Times of 23 June 1982 asserted the following:

> Twenty years ago private individuals held broadly the same proportion of their wealth in land and dwellings as they did in company securities.
>
> By the mid-1970s, according to the Diamond Commission, they held twice as much in the form of land and dwellings and half as much in the form of securities.
>
> Much of the explanation for this none too healthy change in the pattern of investment preferences of individuals lies in the quirks of the British tax system, which provides numerous reliefs on a wide and arbitrarily chosen range of assets and liabilities.
>
> There is a growing consensus outside Westminster that home ownership enjoys more than its fair share of tax relief and that haphazard fiscal largesse is an important cause of the inefficiency of the housing finance system in this country.

The FT went on to note that the tax system favours house purchase in the UK in two ways. Roughly speaking interest on borrowing for house purchase is tax deductible for individuals, and capital gains made on the main residence of an individual are exempt capital gains tax. Wilson (1980) lists other subsidies, too, which are implicit in the overall fiscal treatment of housing, for example since 1963 the imputed benefit from enjoying housing has not been taxable, and transfers of houses between a wide range of values are wholly or partly exempt from stamp duty unlike transfers of, say, ordinary shares.

The public sector

There are two 'public sector' arguments which are commonly heard, and which we might call a 'micro' and a 'macro' argument. The micro argument is essentially about the efficiency with which investment decisions are made in the public sector, the macro argument concerns the effects of public sector investment activity on the financing of other sectors.

There is a common view that the public sector, be it central or local government or 'nationalised' industries, can undertake investment projects with a yield below the cost of capital. They are protected from the consequences because of the public sector's ability to raise taxes to cover its deficits – the public sector cannot go 'bankrupt'. The consequence is that the public sector uses funds that could be better invested elsewhere.

The 'spendthrift public sector' argument has not been tested – we do not have full data on returns to public sector investment, and these would in any case be difficult to measure, involving social costs and benefits which are expensive to quantify. But the argument gets a lot of momentum from observing the losses of certain publicly-owned industries such as railways and steel, even though paradoxically these are probably as sophisticated as any in the private sector in their investment decision-making techniques. Of course as we saw in Chapter 2, we cannot be completely confident that private-sector firms failing to yield their cost of capital will be suitably penalised either.

Whether or not the public sector invests inefficiently, your opinion about the impact of this on the investment of other sectors depends on which side you take in what is probably the central economic controversy of the time. In recent years a notable feature of the UK and many other Western economies has been the growth of government borrowing. We saw in Chapter 17 that the public sector is far and away the largest borrower in the capital market. What effect does this have on, for example, the level of activity in the business sector?

Crudely there are two positions on this.[2] One view sees the borrowing of the public sector as directly competing with business for available savings funds. By the scale of its borrowing the public sector drives up the market price – the cost of capital – and thus *crowds-out* the business sector by reducing the number of its projects that remain worthwhile at the higher market price of funds. The other view emphasises the effect of public sector expenditure in increasing the level of demand in the economy. If the economy is operating at a level below full employment the income created by increased public spending may lead to higher saving and by stimulating demand actually engender an increase in the investment of the business sector as more profitable projects become available to firms. Proponents of the first theory tend to advocate reducing public expenditure, and of the second, increasing it. Despite the centrality of this debate and the vehemence with which it is pursued, it remains unresolved. This is largely because of the difficulty of proving causation in a situation where either theory is broadly consistent with the facts.

Overseas

The UK invests heavily overseas, though it also receives a good deal of overseas investment. The outflow of capital from the UK has a long tradition, as has poor industrial performance in the UK, so that inevitably people have tried to link the two and to suggest that overseas investment is made at the cost of domestic investment. The arguments here resemble other crowding-out arguments. The question is whether the indirect benefits from overseas investment – stimulated demand from abroad for UK capital goods and other goods and services – are enough to outweigh the direct loss of investment in the UK. Reddaway, Potter and Taylor (1968) examined the effects of overseas investment by 100 UK multinationals. They concluded that overseas investment did have an initial beneficial effect on the export of UK capital goods and a small continuing effect thereafter. But a full answer would need an ability to identify the opportunity cost of overseas investment, but as we saw above the extent to which one investment crowds out another is an unresolved issue.

The nature of the problem

Some people suggest that the UK tax system encourages the domestic sector to over-invest in housing. Others that the impossibility of bankruptcy in the public sector has been

2　See Wilson (1980) chap 11 for a valiant attempt to summarise these positions.

claimed to induce public sector decision-makers to adopt inadequate decision criteria, and accept returns below the competitive level. These tend to be arguments that there are barriers to the free operation of the market process. But unless you are completely wedded to the free market concept, you might wish to go further and argue for positive discrimination for firms – introducing distortions, taxes, quotas and so forth to induce a bias towards investing in firms. The overseas sector argument tends to be of this sort. It is argued that domestic savings invested overseas deprive the home economy of investment and employment, and that quotas or tariffs should be imposed to limit the export of capital.

Once we start to think about the efficiency with which capital is allocated at the level of the whole economy we confront two closely-related issues that are at the centre of modern ideological debate. The first is whether one investment, be it housing, public, or overseas investment, 'crowds-out' another, such as business investment, or whether on the contrary it generates income which might stimulate other investment in an economy at less than full employment. The second is the extent to which governments should intervene in the market process with taxes, subsidies, public expenditure programmes and so forth; and if they do, what the objects of their intervention should be: higher business investment, a larger stock of dwellings, or whatever. Both these issues are largely political and ideological.

These issues will continue to be contested in future years and the student of finance needs to be aware of them and aware that despite the feeling of serenity that the EMT has induced in him about the effeciency of allocations in the capital market, the price firms pay for their finance is contingent on allocations at the level of the economy as a whole whose efficiency is controversial.

IV SUMMARY

The EMT contains very important information for our understanding of the capital market, but it is also important to understand the limits on what it is telling us. In this chapter we broadened the scope of the 'efficiency' discussion and examined some other aspects of market performance that, though harder to measure, are nonetheless important. In the case of finance such as bank loans and retained earnings we cannot directly observe their price, so we have to base our confidence that they are being properly allocated on the apparent competitiveness of the market for them. On the question of whether small firms are fairly treated in the capital market we find two things. First, there are sound economic reasons why small firms might pay more for their money, and it is rather hard to know whether the actual treatment they receive is inappropriate in the light of these factors. Second, the notion of fairness may not be strictly relevant. So long as governments feel as they apparently do, that small firms need encouragment they can adjust the supply of finance to achieve this objective.

The essentially political nature of these choices is clearer still when we review some of the arguments that are commonly heard that investment in firms is 'crowded-out' by investment in housing by investment overseas, or by public expenditure. We see that the cost of capital of the firm is determined in an economic process whose operation is controversial and which is subject to decisions about resource allocation that are political in nature.

REFERENCES AND BIBLIOGRAPHY

'Bolton Report' Report of the Committee of Inquiry on Small Firms ('Bolton Report') (Cmnd 4811).

Curran, J and Stanworth, J 'Some Reasons Why Small is Not Always Beautiful', New Society, 14 Dec 1978.

Davis, E W and Yeomans, K A 'Company Finance and the Capital Market' Cambridge University Press, Occasional Paper 39, Cambridge, England 1974.

Gupta, M C 'Differential Effects of Tight Money: A Rationale' Journal of Finance, Sept 1972, pp 825–838.

Little, I M D and Rainer, A C *Higgledy Piggledy Growth Again* (1966) Basil Blackwell, Oxford.

'Macmillan Report' Committee on Finance and Industry (Cmd 3897).

'Radcliffe Report' Committee on the Working of the Monetary System (Cmnd 827).

Reddaway, W B, Potter, S T and Taylor, C T *Effects of UK Direct Investment Overseas* (1968) Cambridge University Press.

Samuels, J M and Smith, D J 'Profits, Variability of Profits and Firm Size', Economica, May 1968.

Singh, A and Whittington, G *Growth, Profitability and Valuation* (1968) Cambridge University Press.

'Wilson Report' Committee to Review the Functioning of Financial Institutions. ('Wilson Committee') – 'Report' (Cmnd 7937).

also

— 'Survey of Investment Attitudes and Financing of Medium-Sized Companies' Research Report No 1, HMSO, 1978.

— Interim Report – The Financing of Small Firms (Cmnd 7503).

— 'Studies of Small Firms' Financing', Research Report No 3, HMSO, 1979.

QUESTIONS

1 'Small firms are the backbone of the capitalist economy'. Do you agree?

2 What particular obstacles face small firms in raising finance?

3 Are there legitimate reasons why a bank would lend on different terms to a small and a large firm, against an identical project?

4 'Increased public expenditure financed by bankruptcy – free borrowing is driving out viable private sector projects'. Do you think this can happen?

CHAPTER 20

Equity

Equity is the finance the firm raises from the owners of the business. Equity can be raised in two ways: by issuing new shares, and by retaining profits in the firm. In terms of importance, retained earnings are the major source of finance for most firms. We have examined the firm's decision as to how much of its profit to pay out as dividend and how much to retain earlier in the book. In the present chapter we concentrate on new issue finance.

Section I discusses some of the concepts and terminology of equity finance. Section II discusses the pricing of share issues and the nature and costs of different methods of issue. New issues entail costs of two sorts: there are transactions costs, and in addition shares are usually issued at a discount, which is effectively another cost of issue. Section III tells the story of a share issue by Hesketh Motorcycles in 1980. It shows the problems that can face investors in trying to decide the value of a new and 'unseasoned' share. Section IV shows the steps in determining the issue price and quantity of a new share issue.

A side effect of issuing shares to new shareholders at a discount is a dilution of the wealth of existing shareholders. This happens because the new shareholders are being allowed to buy cheap a part of something that currently belongs to the existing shareholders, namely the present and future earnings power of the firm. This problem can be avoided by giving pre-emptive 'rights' over the new shares to the existing shareholders. In Section V we consider the dilution problem and show how 'rights' issues avoid it.

I EQUITY FINANCE – CONCEPTS AND TERMINOLOGY

Table I details the equity financing of the General Electric Company which is one of the UK's largest companies. It is extracted from the group accounts at 31.3.85:

Table I General Electric Company – shareholders' interest 31.3.85

	%	1985 £m	1984 £m
Share capital[a]	4	133.6	137.3
Share premium account	0	8.8	8.8
Reserves	73	2,247.0	2,263.0
Deferred taxation	10	303.0	267.7
Shareholders' interest	87	2,692.4	2,676.8
CAPITAL EMPLOYED	100	3,096.0	3,113.0

(a) Share capital

	£
Ordinary shares of 25p each issued at 31 March 1978 fully paid	137,174,549
Unissued ordinary shares at 31 March 1978 authorised	37,825,451
	175,000,000

We can see that the equity or *shareholders' interest* was 87% of GEC's overall capital employed in 1985, of which *reserves*, which are the retained profit part of equity, accounted for 73%. Deferred Taxation which is a reserve against future tax liabilities, was financing 10% in 1985.

The note says that the share capital is made up of *issued* and *fully paid* 25p shares. Since the shares are 25p ones the number of GEC shares in issue must be £137,174,549 × 4 = 548,698,196. The *authorised* figure of £175,000,000 tells us what value of ordinary shares the company is allowed to issue by the terms of its memorandum of association. Companies sometimes issue shares *partly-paid* which means if the issue price is say 60p perhaps 35p will be payable on issue with the remaining 25p to be *called* at some specified or unspecified future date. The GEC shares are all 'fully-paid'.

The remaining term which needs explaining is *share premium* account. In terms of economics, this is a slightly meaningless figure which is related to the fact that the shares are '25p' shares. In the UK shares have to have a *nominal* or *par* value, 25p in the case of GEC. But the 25p tells us nothing about the shares since it is unrelated to their market value, or to the price they were initially issued at. Supposing GEC had initially issued its 25p shares for 42p. It must then show the 25p part of the proceeds as 'share capital' and the remaining 17p as 'share premium'. Not only do par-values not seem to do anything useful, they may on occasions get in the way since the law says that shares cannot be issued at a price below par. The Wilson Committee recommended that the UK companies should be allowed to issue no par value shares as they can in some other countries.

Another restriction on UK firms that did not apply in some other countries concerned their ability to repay share capital, or what is the same thing, to buy their own shares back. UK firms can re-purchase their own debentures but it has been a principle of company law that they cannot repurchase shares. The reason for this was a desire to protect creditors. The law saw share capital as a fund available to meet creditors' claims, and repurchase of shares could be used as a device to distribute cash to shareholders in priority to other claims. Firms could undertake a capital *reduction*, but only in special circumstances approved by the court. However the Companies Act 1981 changed this so that now companies *can* buy back and cancel shares if they get approval at an AGM. They are also allowed to issue special classes of redeemable shares.

The characteristic of equity is that is is a financing contract that gives ownership rights to the supplier of funds. We will be talking about *ordinary shares*[1] as though they are a homogeneous commodity possessing identical rights, notably a vote and an equal share in the profits and assets of the firm. In practice this is usually the case, but there are some variants on the standard ordinary share contract. One is the ordinary share with limited voting rights, commonly known as the *A-ordinary*, which were often issued by closely-controlled firms which sought to broaden their equity without losing control. The Stock Exchange now only permits issues of limited voting shares if they are clearly labelled as such, though some that were issued in a previous era still exist, lingering in the balance-sheets of companies. The Investor's Chronicle of 3.6.1980 estimated that there were about 100 companies on the London Stock Market with shares in issue that carry partial voting rights or none at all, and that in half the cases the restricted nature of the share was not evident from the name.

Some firms issue *deferred* shares which have the same rights as other equity, except they receive a dividend only when profits are above a certain level, or after a certain date.

---

1   In the US these are called 'common stock', but in the UK the word 'stock' is used when the firm has taken the power for its share capital to be traded by value rather in units – hence rather than 4,000 25p shares, the investor would buy £1,000 of stock.

Table II Common methods of issue of securities

METHOD	OFFER FOR SALE	PUBLIC ISSUE	PLACING	TENDER	STOCK EXCHANGE INTRODUCTION	RIGHTS ISSUE
	Company/Existing Shareholders ↓ Issuing House ↓ Public	Company/Existing Shareholders ↓ Public	Company ↓ Private clients of issuing house or broker, by arrangement	Company → Issuing House → Public	Existing Shareholders ↓ Public via the Stock Exchange	Company ↓ Existing Shareholders
PRICE	Fixed before issue	Fixed before issue		Set by market	Fixed before issue	Fixed before issue
NOTES	Shares are bought by an issuing house or broker which sells them to the public. These may be new shares or a significant group of existing shares being sold by their owners.	Similar to offer for sale, but direct to the public. The issuing house acts as adviser, as agent rather than principal.	Cheaper than offer for sale, and not underwritten. Since placing limits on the publics' chance to participate, the Stock Exchange limits the size of placings and will require some securities to be made available to jobbers.	Identical to offer for sale, but public are invited to tender for a number of shares, and the shares are sold to the highest bidders at the price which clears the issue.	Company seeks to obtain a market for its existing securities on the stock exchange. No new money is raised.	New shares are offered to existing shareholders in proportion to their existing holdings.

Another variant of the equity contract is the *preference share* which gives an entitlement to a fixed rate of dividend prior to other equity, and priority when the company is liquidated. Though preference shares are legally equity the fixed dividend makes them effectively debt, so we look at them in Chapter 21.

II ISSUING SHARES

When a company issues shares it has to decide what method of issue to use, and what price to charge. These are the subjects we consider in this section. The possibilities facing the firm when it issues shares depend rather on the nature of the firm and particularly on whether it is a *private*, *public*, or *public quoted* company. The private company cannot invite the general public to subscribe for shares. The public company is free to offer shares to the public, and the public company that also has a stock exchange listing can offer shares that have a ready market with a continuously recorded market price.

There are a variety of ways of issuing shares, and Table II provides a checklist of the main ones. The variety may seem confusing, but it simply reflects different possibilities as to

1 Who the shares are going to be bought by – the public, or a known group of individuals or institutions (placing), or existing shareholders (rights).
2 Whether the shares will be sold in the first instance to an issuing house, then sold by them to the public (offer for sale, and sometimes a tender) or whether the issuing house acts simply as an adviser.
3 Whether the price is fixed before issue, or is set by competitive bidding (tender).

One event that looks like a new issue but is not is the *stock split*, or *bonus* or *capitalisation* issue as it is more properly called in the UK. In a stock split the firm simply issues existing shareholders with new shares in proportion to their existing holdings. Stock splits raise some interesting efficiency questions which we discussed in some detail in Chapter 17, but no new money is involved.

Another form of share issue is the *scrip dividend*, which is a dividend paid in the form of new shares instead of cash. Scrips were briefly popular in the UK after 1973 when the Revenue started taxing them as capital gains rather than as distributions of cash. This gave advantages all round. Shareholders were taxed at lower CGT rates, and firms got the cash-flow benefits of not having to pay advance corporation tax as well as avoiding a cash distribution. In 1975 however the system was changed, and the Revenue started taxing scrips as cash distributions. Without tax advantages there is no obvious point in a 'scrip', which becomes effectively a bonus issue. If shareholders want more cash they can make their own 'home-made' dividend by selling some shares, without having to be given more pieces of paper. A scrip issue has no effect on the economic value of the firm. Firms which want to pursue a high-retention policy might think scrips will make shareholders feel better, but in efficient capital markets we do not expect considerations like that to carry much weight.

We call a further issue of shares which are already on the market a *seasoned* issue. The Stock Exchange expects issues of seasoned shares to be made to existing shareholders as a 'rights' issue. Hence we see in Table III that rights has been increasingly the dominant method of issue used by quoted companies since the 1960s, with placings second most popular, followed by public issues and offers for sale.

Showing averages, Table III slightly masks the variation there is from year to year in new issues. Table IV shows annual share issues compared to the FT Actuaries Share Index.

Table III   Amount of different methods of issue used by UK quoted companies in certain years

	Annual averages, £ million				
Method	1961–62	1963–67	1968–72	1973–77	1979
Public issues and offers for sale	49	75	114	77	22
Tenders	6	6	23	24	22
Placings	106	296	211	113	81
Rights	367	180	340	684	979
	528	557	688	898	1104

Source: Wilson (1980)

Table IV   Annual Share Issues by UK listed Industrial and Commercial Companies (£m)

	1982	1981	1980	1979	1978	1977	1976	1975	1974	1973
Ordinary share issues	946	1622	892	879	797	710	770	955	37	98
FT Actuaries (Industrial) Index	373	322	286	267	235	209	163	136	109	185

Source: CSO Financial Statistics

Timing of issues

There is a well established tendency for the volume of share issues to follow the level of market prices. We would expect this if they both reflect an increase in profitable opportunities in the economy. But there seem to be other things happening as well, particularly a tendency to move to equity out of debt when the market rises. The best recent example of this was the aftermath to 1974. In 1974 the stock market plummeted and the new issues market dried up altogether. Firms were forced to turn more than ever to the banks for funds. The surge in new issues the following year was partly a refinancing of this bank borrowing. This may sound like a plausible explanation of the fluctuations in new issues: it is essentially the notion that *timing* of new issues is something firms should attend to. But it does not square too well with the idea of an efficient market. We can understand firms thinking about the timing of new issues in one sense – the high fixed costs of issue mean they will want to issue new shares periodically rather than continuously, and in the meanwhile they will probably rely on borrowing. But these cycles for individual firms should cancel out in aggregate. The trouble is, 'timing' does not fit in too well with 'efficient markets'. In an efficient capital market shares are always correctly priced. They are never 'overpriced' or 'underpriced'. In retrospect we can spot peaks and troughs, but not whilst they are happening. The implication is that in an efficient market the firm could never rationally expect that share prices would be higher, and the cost of capital lower, in the future. Business finance still needs to reconcile theory and practice in this area.

THE COSTS OF ISSUE

The decisive factor in choosing between methods of issue is their relative cost, and the costs of issue vary both according to the type of issue and the amount of money being raised. There are two types of cost associated with a new issue: *administrative costs*, and *issue discounts*.

Administrative costs

Table V gives estimates from Wilson (1980) of the cost of an ordinary share issue of £2 million on the stock-market. We can see that some of the component costs are proportional to the value of the issue, but others are fixed. The existence of these fixed costs means that there are significant economies of scale in issuing shares. But the issue cost also depends on the type of issue. Table V shows that although the administrative costs of a £2 million first issue of unseasoned shares are 7.6% of the proceeds, further issues of seasoned shares by placing of rights would only cost 2.6% or 4% respectively because certain listing costs would be avoided.

Underwriting

Whenever investors are invited to subscribe for shares there is inevitable uncertainty as to how many shares they will demand. Offers for sale and public issues are often oversubscribed, and in this case the company has to resort to some sort of *allotment* procedure to allocate shares pro rata to subscribers. Rights issues cannot be over-subscribed, but in common with offers for sale and public issues they can be under-subscribed, and firms tend to insure against this possibility by writing *underwriting* contracts. An underwriter is someone who agrees, in exchange for a commission to buy any shares which are not subscribed. He, in turn, will spread his risk by writing similar contracts with sub-underwriters. Wilson (1980), talking about rights issues, said 'typically there will be 100 to 200 of these [sub-underwriters] none of whom will generally be asked to underwrite more than 2 or 3% of the issue'. The principal underwriter tends to be the issuing house or broker advising the company, while the sub-underwriters tend to be institutional investors. When it writes an underwriting contract the firm is effectively buying a put option from the underwriter, with an exercise price equal to the issue price of the share.

The risk of undersubscription depends on the relation between the issue price and the equilibrium market price of the share, i e on the size of the 'issue discount'. The cheaper the issue price of the shares the less chance of them not being taken up. So 'issue discount' and 'underwriting commission' are effectively substitutes, and some firms have issued at a 'deep discount' when they have had difficulty in getting underwriting on acceptable terms.[2]

Issue discount

The ideal price for an issue of shares would be the price that just 'clears the market' – induces a demand from investors just equal to the number of shares being issued. A higher price means not all the shares are sold. A lower price means foregone revenue from the sale. Moreover, since the share price and the associated cost of capital are inversely related a lower price means an increased cost of capital. It also means a 'dilution' of the wealth of

2 See Wilson (1980) p 208.

Table V Typical costs of ordinary share issues to raise £2m

Item	New issues prospectus or offer for sale	Further issues Placing	Further issues Rights
	£	£	£
Capital duty at 1%	20,000	20,000	20,000
Advertising	25,000	–	–
Accountancy fees ⎫ (Note 1)	20,000	4,000	4,000
Legal fees ⎭	15,000	4,000	4,000
Listing fee	2,400 (Note 2)	1,000	1,200
Receiving bankers/registrars fees	15,000	2,000	5,000
Printers:			
Extel Card	2,000	–	–
Allotment Letters	2,000	1,500	1,500
Share Certificates	1,500	1,000	1,000
Offer for Sale	10,000	–	–
Circular	–	4,000	4,000
Underwriting commission at 1¼%	25,000	–	25,000
Broker's commission at ¼%	5,000	5,000	5,000
Issuing house ½% (Note 3)	10,000	10,000	10,000
Total cost of issue	152,900	52,700	80,700
Cost as percentage of proceeds of issue	7.6% (Note 4)	2.6%	4.0%

Note 1   These figures may be higher depending on the amount of work to be done.

Note 2   This figure relates to the fee for bringing a new company to the market for the first time. Since the percentage of the company's market capitalisation offered to the market on the first occasion is normally a minimum of 35%, the total market capitalisation of the company in this example would be about £5.7 million. The 35% minimum is imposed by The Stock Exchange so as to ensure an adequate spread of shareholdings.

Note 3   This figure can rise to ¾% and the issuing house, whether broker or merchant bank, may also charge an additional fee for pre-issue corporate finance work.

Note 4   This figure appears to be high because it relates to the expenses of bringing a company to the market for the first time (see Note 2). Because of the need for a full prospectus, the advertising, legal, accountancy and printing fees are inevitably higher than would be the case for a company already listed. The figure is expressed as a percentage of the new money being raised but as a proportion of the total market capitalisation of the company is only 2.7%.

Source: Wilson Committee: Evidence on the Financing of Industry and Trade, Vol 3, 1978, p 257.

existing shareholders in the firm, and a transfer of wealth to the new investors. The issue discount – the difference between the market-clearing price and the actual issue price – is the second major cost associated with new issues.

On the face of it, pricing shares should be like pricing most other products; however there are two special features of shares. First, we would expect the demand curve for any individual share to be horizontal, that is, demand should be perfectly (price-) elastic. This is because if properly priced so that the return on each share exactly reflects the riskiness of that share, all shares should be perfect substitutes for each other. If the demand curve for shares were absolutely horizontal then slight overpricing would result in no-one subscribing while a slight underpricing would lead everyone to subscribe. In practice of course it is not quite like that, and demand curves for shares do have some downward slope. Presumably this is because there is a good deal of uncertainty surrounding share valuation and investors may disagree on their valuations of the firm, and also because unless investors are in equilibrium in a perfect capital market, their marginal evaluation of an additional unit of risk may differ. But the 'horizontality' of demand curves in practice is quite impressive all the same, and explains why a small change in price may lead to a significant over or under subscription.

The second difference is the cost of overpricing a share. Initial overpricing of a product can usually be rectified by subsequent price cuts, discounts or simply by holding the price during inflation. In any case the damage may be cushioned by more successful pricing of other products. But a failure to set a market clearing price for a share issue is usually reckoned a near disaster, to be avoided at all costs. The loss is partly financial, though the firm can insure against this by writing underwriting contracts, but is mainly to do with reputation. At best a failed issue reflects badly on the price-setting skill of the company, but more likely it will be interpreted by the financial community as a market judgment on the quality of the firm itself. New issues are large, well-publicised and rarely-repeated events for the firm.

The problem is that the firm is short of information to guide its price-setting. Pricing an issue of seasoned shares is relatively straightforward since the firm already knows how the market values its existing shares. The main uncertainty concerns movements in the market as a whole that might take place between fixing the issue price and issuing the shares. But with an unseasoned issue the uncertainty is much greater for both the company and for potential investors. Not only are the shares new, but the firm itself may be new and have no substantive history to guide investors and possibly even no comparable firms with market prices that the price setter can refer to. In the next section we describe an example of this problem; the Hesketh Motorcycle issue, and we include the relevant parts of the issue document so that the reader can decide for himself what a reasonable price would have been.

Companies react in two ways to this uncertainty. First, they will usually employ experts to handle the issue and bring whatever experience is available to pricing it. Second, they tend to issue at a discount, preferring the cost of underpricing to the risk of overpricing.

Research has shown that discounts can be large, and vary in size depending on the method of issue. Merett, Howe and Newbold (1967) investigated issues in the period 1959 to 1963, and Davis and Yeomans (1974) found similar results for the period 1965 to 1971. Davis and Yeomans found that, overall, 'issues by tender displayed the lowest average discount at 6.95% of issue price, with levels of 8.88% for offers for sale and 19.08% for placings'. Looking just at discounts when markets were stable the disparity between tenders and offers for sale in particular was enhanced with the following average discounts: tender 4.62%, offer for sale 13.80%, placings 17.48%. On the effects of firm size on offers for sale, they found 'one could expect revealed discount to be 4% lower for a firm with £2,000,000 net assets than for a firm of > £1,000,000, . . .'

Is the market efficient with respect to new issues? Ibbotson (1975) found, as would be expected if most shares are being issued at a discount, that abnormal gains could be made in the first month of issue. Ibbotson took a random sample from 1650 new issues in the US between 1960 and 1969 and found an abnormal return of 11.4% in the first month after issue. In subsequent months however, the market appeared to be efficient in pricing shares. So, though firms and their advisers appear to be underpricing issues and leaving abnormal gains to be made by subscribers, the subsequent pricing of newly issued shares appears to be efficient. The existence of positive market discounts has led to the existence of another market creature, the *stag*. Stags are people who subscribe for shares they do not intend to keep in order to take advantage of under-pricing.

TENDERS

The *tender* appears to be an ideal alternative to fixed price issues with all their attendant uncertainty. With a tender issue subscribers indicate how many shares they want and what they are willing to pay. The firm calculates the 'striking price' which is the price that would just clear the market, and shares are allocated at the striking price to everyone who bid at or above this price. Competitive bidding systems such as this are in widespread use in countries such as France, and it is a puzzle why they are not more popular in the UK.

In the UK this topic became highly publicised after a spate of heavily oversubscribed issues achieved large discounts. One of these was the 'privatisation' by the government of Amersham International, a high technology producer of radio-active materials. Amersham's offer price of 142p attracted subscriptions of £1.5 billion for £71 million of shares, a 20-fold oversubscription. On the first day of trading, the shares closed at 188p, a premium of 46p, or 32%.

Discussing the problem in the Financial Times of 26.3.1983, Barry Riley concluded that tender offers remained 'deeply unpopular'. One reason may have been that vested interests in the City like brokers and jobbers made good commissions from the active buying and selling that follows heavily-stagged fixed price issues. But a better reason was that tendering may be unfair to the small 'amateur' investor. Riley suggested that there were two types of applicant, the well-informed professional institutional investors who are in regular touch and tend to develop a consensus on the value of each new issue, and the amateurs with neither the advantages of expertise or of knowing what the market feels, and who will make a broader spread of bids. In a heavily-subscribed tender the price will tend to be set by the higher, outlying amateur bids, and the striking price will probably be above the subsequent equilibrium price for the share. The shares 'will tend to go to investors who have misjudged the price. They will stand in the market at a discount, possibly for several years, and the company will get a list of grumbling and frustrated shareholders'. However, tenders still represented the best hope according to Riley. He suggested that the tendering system would be improved if sponsors were more flexible in setting striking prices and if small investors were helped by being able, for example, to accept a striking price set by the institutional investor.

III   HESKETH MOTORCYCLES: AN EXAMPLE OF AN UNSEASONED ISSUE

An example of the problems facing the firm and its potential investors in determining the appropriate price for an unseasoned new issue was provided by the Hesketh Motorcycles issue.

This prospectus has been prepared for the purpose of giving information with regard to Hesketh Motorcycles Limited ("HML"). The Directors of HML have taken all reasonable care to ensure that the facts stated herein are true and accurate in all material respects and that there are no other material facts the omission of which would make misleading any statement herein, whether of fact or opinion. All the Directors accept responsibility accordingly.

There is no listing on any stock exchange for the shares of HML and application is not being made to any stock exchange for a listing of any part of HML's capital. However, applications may be made to the Council of The Stock Exchange for permission to transact specific bargains in the shares of HML under Rule 163 (2) of the Rules and Regulations of The Stock Exchange. Persons wishing to deal in the Ordinary shares of HML in accordance with Rule 163 (2) should consult their stockbroker or other professional adviser.

A copy of this prospectus, having attached thereto copies of the documents referred to herein, has been delivered to the Registrar of Companies for registration.

The procedure for application and an Application Form are set out at the end of this document.

Hesketh Motorcycles Limited

(Incorporated under the Companies Acts 1948 to 1976. Registered in England No. 1178402)

OFFER
by
Venture Link Limited
on behalf of HML
for subscriptions for

**1,800,000 Ordinary shares of 50p each, fully paid,
at 80p per share, payable in full on application.**

The Application List will open at 10.00 a.m. on Tuesday, 16th September, 1980 and may be closed at any time thereafter.

THE FUNDS RAISED BY THIS OFFER WILL BE USED TO PUT INTO PRODUCTION A NEW DESIGN OF MOTORCYCLE. BEFORE APPLYING FOR ANY OF THE SHARES HEREBY OFFERED, PROSPECTIVE INVESTORS SHOULD CONSIDER THE RISKS INVOLVED. AN INVESTMENT IN HML MUST BE REGARDED AS SPECULATIVE. ACCORDINGLY THE PARAGRAPH IN THIS DOCUMENT HEADED "RISK FACTORS" SHOULD BE READ CAREFULLY.

Share Capital

Authorised	Issued or to be issued fully paid
£1,750,000 in 3,500,000	£1,430,090 in 2,860,180
Ordinary shares of 50p each.	Ordinary shares of 50p each.

Indebtedness

At the close of business on 29th August, 1980 HML had an unsecured bank overdraft of £14,278 and a loan of £530,762 from Hesketh Tristar Limited ("Tristar") of which £530,000 has since been capitalised as described herein. Save as aforesaid, HML had no loan capital outstanding or created but unissued at that date and no outstanding mortgages, charges, borrowings or indebtedness in the nature of borrowings including bank overdrafts and liabilities under acceptances (other than normal trade bills) or acceptance credits, hire purchase commitments, guarantees or other material contingent liabilities.

Introduction

In 1972 Lord Hesketh, now Deputy Chairman of Hesketh Motorcycles Limited ("HML"), became involved on his own account in the business of Grand Prix motor-car racing under the name of "Hesketh Racing". In July, 1974 he promoted the formation of HML (then called Hesketh Racing Limited), which subsequently acquired the business of Hesketh Racing from him. On 1st May, 1979 HML became a wholly-owned subsidiary of Tristar, a company effectively controlled by Lord Hesketh and the Trustees of the estate of his late father. HML had at its disposal a group of talented designers and engineers who produced the Hesketh Formula I car which, driven by James Hunt, finished fourth in the 1975 Grand Prix World Manufacturers Championship.

The financial burden of maintaining a motor racing team without certainty of sponsorship is very heavy and it became evident that motor racing on its own was unlikely to prove consistently profitable. HML therefore eventually withdrew from direct involvement in Formula I racing. However, through its motor-racing experience, the production team had acquired considerable engineering skills which were used to build up a substantial and profitable specialised automotive engineering business involving the contract overhaul of Formula I and Formula II engines, the manufacture of specialist parts, including suspension components, complete chassis, oil tanks, water pumps and engine sumps, the production of high-precision steel and aluminium machinings and the contract testing, using dynamometers, of diesel and petrol engines for leading manufacturers. During 1977, HML began looking for other ways of exploiting its engineering skills, with the particular aim of developing a proprietary volume product. Among the many possibilities considered were various forms of transportation, of which the motorcycle, due to the rising cost of fuel, the increasing congestion of road traffic and the growth of leisure time, seemed to present the most attractive marketing opportunities.

The current share of the world motorcycle market held by British manufacturers had been reduced to negligible proportions, due mainly to the dominance of the large-volume Japanese manufacturers, with their technologically advanced and competitively priced products. Nevertheless HML's assessment was that an opportunity existed, and should continue to exist in both domestic and export markets for a British-made motorcycle in the high capacity (over 750cc), high-performance, 'superbike' sector. After an intensive and critical analysis of competitive designs and engineering, HML decided towards the end of 1977 to embark on the design of a new high-performance 'superbike' combining individuality and exclusivity with the best traditions of British engineering, with the aim of capturing a profitable share of the rapidly growing high-performance sector of the market.

Reason for the Offer

It was not possible for HML to bring the new motorcycle into volume production without the introduction of external capital. Accordingly it was decided to arrange this by way of an Offer of equity capital which would be underwritten by the group of investment trusts and investment trust management companies brought together by Venture Link Limited and listed in Paragraph 5 (b) of Appendix II of this prospectus.

To facilitate this Offer, the engineering business of HML has been transferred to a subsidiary of Tristar (see Paragraph 4 of Appendix II below), so that HML is now only concerned with the development and production of the new motorcycle.

It has taken some 2½ years from the original conception to produce a motorcycle which, following rigorous testing of several prototypes, is now ready for volume production. The overall specification, design, styling and engineering of this machine, the Hesketh V1000, were the responsibility of the HML team and a sub-contractor was employed to assist HML in the design and engineering of the completely new British engine and gear-box. The entire cost of the motorcycle project up to 30th June, 1980, amounting to approximately £530,000, has been borne by HML and financed by loans from Tristar which have since been repaid or capitalised. Expenditure from 1st July, 1980 to the date of this Offer has been financed by temporary bank borrowings.

The Offer will provide HML with funds of approximately £1,305,000, after allowing for the estimated expenses of the Offer, which will enable it to repay the temporary bank borrowings and to bring the motorcycle into production.

Technical Information on the Hesketh V1000

The 'Hesketh V1000' is a 90° in-line Vee-Twin motorcycle of 1,000cc capacity. This configuration allows a low centre of gravity, making for better handling characteristics and permitting a slim compact motorcycle which presents a smaller frontal area, reducing wind resistance and assisting performance and fuel economy. 90° in-line Vee-Twin engines give optimum smoothness, virtually free from the vibration frequently experienced with other types of 'superbike' engine, whilst four valves per cylinder produce exceptional power without detriment to fuel economy. The V1000 has a top speed of over 130 miles per hour and an average fuel consumption in excess of 50 miles per gallon is attainable under normal riding conditions. The Directors believe that the performance, handling and styling of the V1000 compare favourably with those of competing 'superbikes'.

The design of the V1000 combines a number of features not currently available on other 'superbikes', including a co-axial chain lay-out, which maintains a constant chain tension (greatly improving the life of the chain), and a parallelogram brake linkage system on the rear wheel, which allows the rider to apply the brake with greater safety when cornering.

Prototypes of the V1000 have been extensively road and bench tested and have been test driven by some of Britain's leading experts on high-performance motorcycles, who were consulted on its design and styling during all phases of its development. The V1000 has been shown to a number of leading British motorcycle dealers, all of whom subsequently expressed interest in obtaining dealerships for the machine. It has also received favourable comment in the motorcycle trade press and other media, both in the U.K. and overseas, and HML has as a result received numerous letters from individuals indicating an interest in acquiring a V1000 when a production model is available.

The Market For 'Superbikes'

The Motor Cycle Association of Great Britain Ltd ("MCA") circulates to its members monthly statistics relating to the sale and registration in the United Kingdom of motorcycles from which the following table has been compiled:

Year	Total all types (excluding mopeds)	'Superbikes' only (over 750cc)		
		Units	% increase on previous period	% share of total market
1975	174,751	3,806	—	2.1
1976	188,627	4,804	26.2	2.6
1977	176,031	4,481	(6.7)	2.5
1978	174,095	7,747	72.9	4.4
1979	206,812	11,335	46.3	5.5
1979—6 months to June	94,742	6,041	—	6.4
1980—6 months to June	112,645	6,912	14.4	6.1

The estimated shares of the United Kingdom 'superbike' market during 1979 commanded by the various manufacturing countries were Japan: 64 per cent, Germany: 22 per cent, Italy: 12 per cent and others 2 per cent.

Over the period 1975/9 the share of the total U.K. motorcycle market held by 'superbikes' grew from 2.1 per cent to 5.5 per cent, representing an average compound rate of growth in the number of 'superbikes' sold in the U.K. of some 31 per cent per annum, compared with just under 3.5 per cent per annum for non-'superbikes'. The 'superbike' growth rate in the first six months of 1980, as compared with the corresponding period for 1979, dropped to 14.4 per cent, but this was mainly due to a sharp decline in sales of motorcycles with a capacity of between 751cc and 900cc; in the range of 901cc to 1050cc U.K. sales in the first six months of 1980 were up by over 50 per cent on the same period of 1979, although this rate of growth may have been exceptional and is not believed to have occurred in other European countries.

Statistics similar to those published by the MCA are not readily available in relation to the market for motorcycles on the continent of Europe. However the Directors believe that, whilst, as in the U.K., during the early part of the 1970's continental demand for motorcycles of all types grew very rapidly, there was virtually no growth in the demand for motorcycles below the 'superbike' category during the second half of the decade; in marked contrast, sales of 'superbikes' continued to grow at an impressive rate. 'Superbikes' are believed to have constituted about 2½ per cent of all continental motorcycle sales during 1975 but by 1979 estimated 'superbike' sales had risen to over 50,000 machines per annum, representing about 10 per cent of all continental sales. The Japanese manufacturers' share of the continental 'superbike' market appears still to be growing and is probably slightly higher than their share of the equivalent U.K. market.

The Marketing Plan

HML's marketing plan is based on the cautious assumption that the average rate of increase in sales of 'superbikes' in the United Kingdom and the rest of Europe from the beginning of 1981 onwards will only be about 5 per cent per annum. On this assumption, the number of 'superbikes' sold in the U.K. during 1981 to 1983 would be about 12,000 per annum and the number sold in the rest of Europe would be over 50,000 per annum. HML aims to capture between 5 per cent and 7 per cent of the available U.K. 'superbike' market and between 1 per cent and 2 per cent of the continental 'superbike' market during this period and also to make a limited number of sales into other countries such as Japan, Australia, South Africa and Canada, where a substantial demand for 'superbikes' exists. The United States, although potentially a very large market, is difficult for a foreign manufacturer to penetrate, due to the variety of regulations and legislation in force in the individual states; HML intends to restrict the initial marketing of its products in the U.S.A. to California. If the marketing plan is successfully achieved, HML will be exporting well over half its annual production by 1983.

At the present time only one model, the V1000 Sports Tourer, has been brought to the pre-production stage. However, HML intends to add other models to its range, all built around the same basic engine and gearbox unit. These will include:—

Cafe Racer—A machine with a more finely tuned version of the existing engine, a single seat, dropped handlebars and individual styling. The sales statistics of other manufacturers indicate a substantial worldwide demand for this type of machine, which HML plans to introduce in 1983.

Full Tourer—A machine with the standard engine, full weather-protection fairing and rear-detachable luggage. This configuration is very popular on the Continent and in the U.S.A. HML intends to introduce it in the latter part of 1982.

The above models, together with the existing V1000 Sports Tourer, will form the main Hesketh range which will be supplemented by the introduction, in the second or third year of production, of limited runs of specialised types of motorcycles such as low riders, production racer replicas and special-order personalised motorcycles. In addition, it is intended to enter the market for items such as police motorcycles, engine units for specialist frame-makers and accessories of various types, including clothing and headgear, which can be marketed, although not necessarily manufactured or assembled, by HML. A significant proportion of HML's turnover will also arise in due course from the sale of spare parts.

The Hesketh range of motorcycles will be sold through carefully selected dealers, who will be required to give contractual undertakings in regard to the maintenance of stocks of spares and the promotion of HML's product range in their dealership area. HML expects to appoint approximately 25 dealers to cover the British Isles. Overseas dealers will also be appointed in due course.

It is intended that the recommended retail price of the V1000, when first available, will be in the region of £4,000 including VAT. If it were available now, the price would be about £3,750 including VAT. The current prices of 1000cc production 'superbikes' range from approximately £2,050 to approximately £4,800, the price range reflecting widely differing specifications and performances.

The V1000 will be priced towards the upper end of the 'superbike' range, but the Directors believe that the 'superbike' market is not predominantly price-sensitive and that, having regard to its design and performance, there will be a ready market for the V1000. In addition, they are confident that its running costs will be lower than those of its competitors because of its fuel economy and of their intended policy of offering competitively priced spares. The latter policy should also result in U.K. insurance premiums being lower than those for comparable imported motorcycles.

The Production Plan

The first production models of the V1000 should be available for delivery in the early summer of 1981. No significant sales revenues are therefore expected in HML's current financial year ending 31st March, 1981. The sales effort in the following year, ending 31st March, 1982, will be concentrated mainly on the U.K. market; the first sizeable export deliveries are planned to take place during the year ending 31st March, 1983. The present production plan envisages assembly of sufficient motorcycles to permit the following total deliveries of all models in the Hesketh range:—

Year ending 31st March	Deliveries (Units)
1981	Demonstration models only
1982	1,000
1983	1,700
1984	2,000

HML will consider a further expansion of production, having regard to any additional capital expenditure involved, once a level of 2000 units per annum has been achieved.

Production of the V1000 and of subsequent models will be undertaken by means of an assembly operation and, initially, HML will not be significantly involved in the manufacture of components. A substantial proportion of the funds to be raised by the Offer will be used to purchase jigs and tools which will be made available to selected manufacturers for use in the volume production of the relevant components. A system of selective quality assurance testing will be applied to all deliveries of components before they are accepted. HML will then assemble, test, market and deliver the completed motorcycles. These will, in their turn, be subjected to rigorous final inspection and quality control procedures. The Directors will give consideration in due course to the manufacture of a greater proportion of components.

Premises and Staff

HML is currently negotiating to take an underlease for a period of 21 years on industrial premises at Daventry, Northamptonshire, comprising a factory with an area of 25,200 sq. ft., including 3,500 sq. ft. of office accommodation and a parking area sufficient for 60 cars, at a commencing annual rental of £44,000, subject to review every 5 years.

The Directors intend to sub-let, on an annual basis, a self-contained unit of 4,200 sq. ft., including 850 sq. ft. of office accommodation, at a proposed rental of £7,800 annually, until such time as HML requires the additional space. Subject to completion of the negotiations and legal arrangements, occupation of the factory and part of the office space is expected to begin in November, 1980; the remainder of the office space will be ready for occupation in the spring of 1981. These premises will provide sufficient space for HML's requirements in the immediate future. Daventry is some 10 miles from Easton Neston, Towcester, where the development of the V1000 has been carried on to date.

In the initial pre-production stage, following this Offer, the nucleus of the staff required by HML will consist of some 10 experienced employees who have all been engaged in the development of the V1000. Additional staff will be recruited locally, as required, and trained by HML. It is expected that HML will be employing a total workforce, including part-time workers, of some 30 by 31st March, 1981, rising to about 75 when a production rate of 2,000 machines per annum is achieved. Having regard to current employment conditions in the engineering industry in the Midlands, HML expects no difficulty in recruiting staff of the required calibre.

Management

Chairman

Sir Barrie Heath, aged 64, was appointed non-executive Chairman on 20th August, 1980. Until the beginning of 1980 he was Group Chairman of Guest, Keen & Nettlefolds Limited. He is a director of Barclays Bank Limited, Pilkington Brothers Limited, Smiths Industries Limited and Tunnel Holdings Limited and a member of the European Advisory Council of Tenneco Inc. He has wide experience of production engineering, particularly in the motor industry.

Deputy Chairman

Lord Hesketh, aged 29, has, since the appointment of Sir Barrie Heath as Chairman, become Deputy Chairman of HML. The development of the V1000 has been made possible by the financial support provided by Tristar, of which he is Chairman and which is effectively controlled by him and the Trustees of his late father's estate. Lord Hesketh intends to devote a large part of his time to the affairs of HML, particularly in regard to the marketing and promotion of its products.

Managing Director

Antony Horsley, aged 36, is the Managing Director of HML and has been responsible for the overall supervision of the V1000 programme. He was until recently Managing Director of Tristar and of other companies in the Tristar group of companies ("the Tristar Group"), but has now resigned his executive positions within the Tristar Group in order to devote his full time to the affairs of HML. He remains a non-executive director of Tristar and its subsidiary companies and is also a Trustee of the late 2nd Baron Hesketh's estate.

Technical Director

Geoffrey Johnson, AMIET, aged 45, is Technical Director of the Tristar Group. He will be devoting the major part of his time to the affairs of HML and is, and will continue to be, responsible for the design and engineering of the V1000 and for the technical programme required to bring it to the production stage and to introduce additional models to the range. He was formerly Chief Engineer of engine design in the Austin-Morris Division of British Leyland, and, before that, Chief Designer to British Racing Motors Limited (BRM).

Financial Director

Leslie Hartwell, FCCA, MBIM, aged 44, is Financial Director of the Tristar Group and of other concerns connected with the Hesketh family's interests. He has occupied senior executive positions with Slough Estates Limited and Richard Johnson & Nephew Group Limited. He will be responsible for controlling the financial affairs of HML and for introducing the production control, stock control and accounting systems needed to administer its operations. It is planned that a full-time Financial Director of HML will be recruited in the near future, whereupon Mr. Hartwell will relinquish his directorship of HML.

Non-executive Director

David Simpson, aged 46, was appointed a non-executive Director on 20th August, 1980. He is a Director of Heritable Group Holdings Limited and Managing Director of Heritable Industrial Holdings Limited. He is also Managing Director of Godwin Warren Holdings Limited, Chairman of Godwin Warren Engineering Limited and Chairman of Mokes & Co. Limited. Prior to these appointments, he was labour relations manager at Vauxhall Motors Limited, Plant Director of a manufacturing division of Chrysler (UK) Limited and Director of Manufacturing of Leyland Cars Limited.

It is expected that a further appointment to the Board, to fill the post of Production Director, will be made shortly and additional executives, at or below Board level, including a marketing manager, will be recruited as needed. The Directors have also agreed to give consideration to the appointment to the Board in due course of a further non-executive director to be nominated by Venture Link Limited.

To meet HML's short term requirements for administrative and technical assistance, Tristar and HML have entered into a Management and Services Contract (see Paragraph 7 (d) of Appendix II). The cost to HML of the executive services of Lord Hesketh, Mr. Johnson and Mr. Hartwell, who will remain directors and employees of Tristar, but who will devote a large part of their time to the affairs of HML, will be covered by payments under this Contract. Apart from such payments it is not expected that any substantial trading will take place between HML and Tristar or any of its subsidiaries. Such trading as may occur will be strictly on an arm's-length basis.

Mr. Antony Horsley has entered into an Agreement to serve as Managing Director of HML for a period of three years commencing on 1st September, 1980 (see Paragraph 7 (c) of Appendix II).

Proceeds of the Offer and Working Capital

The estimated net proceeds of the Offer, after expenses of £135,000, will amount to £1,305,000, the whole of which will be applied in the provision of working capital, including the repayment of temporary bank borrowings incurred since 30th June, 1980. It is expected that some £500,000 of this sum will be utilised during the pre-production period on the acquisition of jigs, tools, test equipment and other items of a capital nature.

The Directors of HML are satisfied that, having regard to the net proceeds of the Offer and to bank facilities which are available, HML will have sufficient working capital to enable it to achieve its present production plan.

Substantial Shareholding

Following the Offer, Tristar and a subsidiary of Tristar will respectively own 1,060,000 and 180 Ordinary shares in HML, representing in aggregate 37.1 per cent of the total issued capital. Tristar has given an undertaking to Venture Link Limited and to Grieveson, Grant and Co. (see Paragraph 7 (a) of Appendix II), that it will not, save in certain exceptional circumstances, dispose of any part of its holding of 1,060,000 shares before 30th September, 1983.

Preferential Applications

Of the 1,800,000 Ordinary shares which are the subject of this Offer, a total of 20,000 shares are reserved for allotment, at the issue price of 80p, against applications received from Directors and employees of HML and of the Tristar Group, numbering some 87 persons.

Employees' Profit Sharing Scheme

The Directors intend as soon as appropriate to establish an Inland Revenue-approved Profit Sharing Scheme to provide a continuing incentive to employees who have served an appropriate qualifying period of employment by assisting them to become shareholders in HML. Full details of the Scheme would be submitted to the Shareholders for approval.

Future Prospects and Profitability

Full production drawings of, or specifications for, all the components required for the manufacture of the V1000 have been prepared and submitted to possible suppliers for the purpose of obtaining written estimates. The estimates received, together with HML's own estimates of the size and cost of the direct and indirect labour force required and of the overhead and other expenditure involved, have been used to calculate the overall unit production cost of the motorcycle at different levels of production. All estimates have been adjusted, where appropriate, for the possible effects of inflation between the dates of the original estimates and the anticipated start of production. The unit cost would, of course, be affected by the introduction of different models into the range at a later date.

Volume deliveries of the V1000 are not likely to commence before May, 1981. HML will therefore make a trading loss in its current financial year ending 31st March, 1981, partially offset by interest earned on invested funds. Thereafter, profitability will depend on a number of factors including the selling price of the V1000 and associated spares, the number of motorcycles produced and sold, the volume of sales of spare parts and the cost of materials and labour.

However, on the assumption that production is confined to the V1000 Sports Tourer, the table set out below shows the expected profitability of the operation at different levels of production, assuming a constant recommended retail selling price of £3,950 per machine and making no allowance for profits derived from the sale of spare parts or accessories or for interest earned on the temporary investment of surplus funds. The table, which is based on the historical cost convention, provides for the writing off of the deferred research and development expenditure incurred on the motorcycle up to 30th June, 1980, amounting to £494,681, at the rate of £60 per motorcycle sold. At that rate of amortisation it is expected that the whole of the £494,681 will be written off within a period of five years from the start of deliveries. Amortisation provided in this fashion, being in respect of expenditure already incurred, will not involve any additional cash outgoing.

No. of units sold per annum	1,000	1,500	2,000
Turnover	£2,836,000	£4,254,000	£5,672,000
Operating profit after charging current research and development expenditure	£310,000	£700,000	£1,050,000
Exceptional item: Amortisation of deferred research and development expenditure	£60,000	£90,000	£120,000
Operating profit after exceptional item	£250,000	£610,000	£930,000

The figures in the above table should not be taken to represent profit forecasts. However if they were to represent HML's pre-tax profits for any particular financial year, the following hypothetical earnings and ratios, based on the Offer price of 80p per share, would result:—

Pre-tax earnings per share:			
Before exceptional item	10.8p	24.5p	36.7p
After exceptional item	8.7p	21.3p	32.5p
Price/earnings ratios on nil tax basis:			
On earnings before exceptional item	7.4	3.3	2.2
On earnings after exceptional item	9.2	3.8	2.5
Price/earnings ratios on a notional 52 per cent tax charge:			
On earnings before exceptional item	15.4	6.8	4.5
On earnings after exceptional item	19.1	7.8	5.1

The Directors have been advised that the majority of the deferred research and development expenditure of £494,681 incurred on the motorcycle project up to 30th June, 1980 will be allowable as a deduction against future trading profits liable to Corporation Tax. Having regard to this and to tax allowances which will arise from future expenditure on development and on capital items, the need to provide for Corporation Tax in the accounts covering the first two years of production should be extinguished or significantly reduced.

Accounts and Additional Information

There is set out in Appendix I a copy of the Report by the Auditors and Reporting Accountants showing the financial position of HML as at 30th June, 1980 together with a Pro-Forma Balance Sheet showing the position following the outcome of this Offer. It is intended that HML shall prepare its accounts as at 31st March of each year. Interim reports will also be issued, but not in respect of the six months ended 30th September, 1980.

There is set out in Appendix II certain additional statutory and general information.

Dividends

It is the Directors' intention that HML should commence paying dividends once sufficient distributable profits are available. The timing and amount of the first distribution will depend partly on the results achieved and partly on the extent to which funds may be required to finance further expansion of production.

Risk Factors

Prospective investors in HML should recognise that since the motorcycle project is not an established manufacturing and trading operation, the following special risk factors apply:—

(i) the V1000 design is new and, in spite of extensive pre-production testing, the machine could still reveal design faults requiring rectification;

(ii) volume assembly and production has not yet commenced and "teething troubles" could be experienced, with consequent delays in meeting delivery targets; and

(iii) estimates of the potential market for the V1000 and other models to be introduced in due course, which the Directors believe to be realistic, may not be achieved.

In 1980 the public were invited to subscribe for 1,800,000 ordinary shares in Hesketh Motorcycles Ltd. HML was a new company which had been formed to produce and sell a motorbike, the Hesketh V1000. The project was the brainchild of Lord Hesketh, aged 29, who was well-known as the owner of a successful motor racing team. The bike had been developed initially by Lord Hesketh's company, Tristar, and another 1,060,180 shares, or 37.1% of the issued capital of HML had been issued at the same time to Tristar as settlement for the development costs they had borne. The HML shares had a nominal value of 50p, and were being offered at a price of 80p to the public. HML was not seeking a stock exchange quotation, but the shares could be traded under rule 163(2).

The interesting feature of the Hesketh offer was its highly speculative nature, which the offer document did not seek to conceal, and which gave it the flavour of venture capitalism. The bike did not yet exist in production-line form; its cost, reliability and customer appeal were essentially unknown. It was attempting to enter a market from which previous UK manufacturers had been expelled by the immensely powerful and efficient Japanese manufacturers.

When a company issues new shares it has to produce a PROSPECTUS, which is designed to give the potential buyer a reasonable idea of what he is letting himself in for. So, amongst other things it shows the asset position of the issuing firm and a five year history of its profits and dividends, ten years if the shares are to be quoted. In Hesketh's case, of course, there was no history to show. If the issue is for the purpose of acquiring another company, similar information must be given about that company. If the money is wanted for an internal project it is usual to provide some estimate of the prospects for that project.

In the case of Hesketh the investor had to decide upon the future market prospects of a yet-to-be manufactured super-bike. Extracts from Hesketh's prospectus are included on pp 350–356 and the reader can decide for himself whether he has enough information there to value Hesketh's shares and so make a decision about buying them. Compared to many, the Hesketh prospectus is informative about the project in hand. The problem for the investor was how to cope with the unavoidable uncertainty innate in such a project.

Hindsight

September 1980   The Hesketh issue attracted 925 applicants, and was just 3.1% over-subscribed. At close of business on the first day the shares were trading at 78p, compared to the 80p issue price.

September 1981   Hesketh announced the bike had run into engineering problems, and the sales launch would need to be delayed for six months. The owners were asked to subscribe another £590,000 of working capital.

February 1982   The bike went on sale, six months late. Dealers announced that 250 had been ordered. Hesketh shares rose to 54p from a low of 35p at the end of 1981.

May 1982   Hesketh shares were suspended at 22p. Since the launch 100 bikes had been sold. Hesketh's were 'looking for any options which appear to offer a secure future for the manufacturing operations of the company'.

June 1982   A Receiver was appointed, and all production halted. The entire workforce was made redundant.

IV PRICING A NEW ISSUE – A WORKED EXAMPLE

To help envisage the steps in pricing a new issue consider a simple example:

Ralph Cooper is an unquoted public company which wants to raise £1 million from an offer for sale of £1 ordinary shares. The number of shares Cooper has in issue already, N, is 5,000,000. Cooper recently reported the following figures:

Total earnings	£1.2m	Total dividend	£600,000
eps	24p	Dividend per share	12p
		Target payout	50%

The key questions are:

Question 1 How much does Cooper need to raise, £Q? The issue must cover its own transactions costs, and yield £1 million. The administrative costs of an offer for sale of this size are estimated at 6% of the gross. So Cooper must raise

$$Q = £1m \times \frac{100}{100-6} \simeq £1,065,000$$

Question 2 What will be the post-issue value of Cooper, V? To find the market value of Cooper we need to value the firm along the lines we suggested in Chapter 10.

Cooper expects to continue to get a return of 12% from the new injection of £1m, hence earnings will be increased by £120,000 and since target payout is 50%, dividends will increase by £60,000. We elicit that Cooper believes it can maintain a growth rate of 6% indefinitely. A study of firms in the same industry suggests the market is requiring a return of 10% from firms of this riskiness.

Hence, dividend post-issue $= £600,000 + \cdot5 \times £120,000 = £660,000$

$\qquad$ dividend yield $= r_e - g = 10\% - 6\% = 4\%$

$\qquad$ value of Cooper, $V = \dfrac{DIV}{r_e - g} = \dfrac{£660,000}{4\%} = £16,500,000$

Question 3 What is the issue discount, DIS? It is felt that an appropriate issue discount on the expected equilibrium price for an offer for sale of this sort would be 10%, so DIS = 10%.

We can now find the issue price, P′, and the number of shares to be issued, N′. For convenience we will work with P, the equilibrium share price, rather than P′, where P′ is P less the issue discount, so $P' = P(1-DIS)$.

P and N′ are two unknowns, but we have two expressions which determine them:
— We know that the proceeds of the issue, Q, is the number of shares issued, N′, times the issue price, P′.

$$Q = N' \times P'$$
$$= N' \times P(1-DIS)$$
Hence $\underline{1,065,000 = N' \times P \cdot 9}$ $\qquad\qquad$ (1)

— We know that the value of the whole firm, V, is the number of shares in issue, N + N′, times the equilibrium price, P.

$$V = (N + N') .P$$
$$\text{Hence } \underline{16,500,000} = \underline{(5,000,000 + N') - P} \qquad (2)$$

Dividing (2) into (1) to eliminate P

$$\frac{1,065,000}{16,500,000} = \frac{.9N'}{5,000,000 + N'}$$

Hence N' = 386,282
     P   = £3.06

Cooper should issue 386,282 shares at an issue price of £2.75, which gives a discount of 10% on £3.06.

You may doubt that pricing a new issue can be so exact, with a unique issue price and quantity. We wanted to show the necessary relationships between issue price, the number of shares issued and so forth. But in practice there is much more room for manoeuvre because Q, V and D are not single-valued. The firm will not be committed to raising exactly a net £1 million, the post-issue value of the firm is a matter for estimation with a degree of inherent uncertainty, and the issue discount is a matter of choice. In practice pricing a new issue is an iterative process in which different assumptions about Q, V and D generate different values of N' and P until the firm and its advisers find an acceptable strategy for the issue.

V   RIGHTS ISSUES AND THE DILUTION PROBLEM

If an already quoted company issues new shares, Stock Exchange rules require it to make a *rights* issue. This means that the new shares must be offered to the existing shareholders in proportion to their existing holdings. Suppose a company has 1 million shares issued and wants to issue 200,000 more, it will make a 'one-for-five' rights offer to its existing shareholders. Each shareholder has the right to buy the new share for every five he already owns. He does not have to exercise the right, he can sell it, and if he prefers, the company must sell it for him. Rights issues are made at a discount on market value which can often be around 15%, which is why the 'rights' have a value in themselves.

The issue discount on rights is usually high. However the great virtue of 'rights' is that this does not damage the interests of existing shareholders, which is the reason the Stock Exchange insists on it. If we consider a simple numerical example we can see how giving existing shareholders pre-emptive rights avoids the dilution of their interest when new shares are issued at a discount.

Consider a company which currently has 1 million shares issued and profits of £500,000 pa. The firm is valued at 10 × earnings, which is £5 million or £5 per share. It has a project in mind which will earn another £100,000 pa. The project will cost £1 million, and if the market continues to value the company in the same way it should add £1 million (10 × £100,000) to the value of the company.

To raise the £1 million, 250,000 new shares are to be issued at £4 each (transactions costs will be ignored throughout this example). After the issue the value of the company will be £6 million, and there will be 1,250,000 shares, so we can work out the new equilibrium share price as £6 million ÷ 1,250,000 = £4.80. The issue price of £4 is giving an effective discount of $\frac{4.80 - 4.00}{4.80} = 17\%$.

We will examine the implications of the above if the shares are issued (1) without, and (2) with pre-emptive rights to existing shareholders.

No pre-emptive rights As we see in the box, the old shareholders suffer an immediate loss of wealth because the value of their shares has fallen by 20p. In effect, by allowing new shareholders to buy an equal share in the earnings of the company cheaper than the new equilibrium market price part of the firm that previously belonged to the old shareholders have been given to the new. The existing shareholders' interest in the firm has been *diluted*.

WEALTH POSITION: NO PRE-EMPTIVE RIGHTS	Before issue	After issue
Existing shareholders	£5 million	1,000,000 × £4.80 = £4,800,000
New shareholders	£1 million	250,000 × £4.80 = £1,200,000

With pre-emptive rights Suppose a rights issue is made of 1 for 4 (1,000,000 ÷ 250,000) and, since it makes no difference to the answer, assume that all existing shareholders SELL their rights. We would expect the market price of the right to buy something worth £4.80 for £4 to be 80p. So for selling their rights the existing shareholders should receive 80p × 250,000 rights = £200,000. This has the effect, as the box shows, of just restoring the initial positions.

WEALTH POSITION: WITH RIGHTS	Before issue	After issue
Existing shareholders	£5 million	£4,800,000 + proceeds or rights, £ 200,000 = £5 million
New shareholders	£1 million	£1,200,000 − cost of rights, £ 200,000 = £5 million

One simplifying assumption in the previous example was that the value of the new project was the same as its cost, in other words that the internal rate of return of the project equalled the firm's required return, the project had a zero NPV. But suppose the project yields 15% compared to the required return of 10%, everything else as before so the project is worth £1.5 million and the market values the enhanced firm at £6,500,000. The new share price is 6,500,000 ÷ 1,250,000 shares = £5.20. The danger here is that existing shareholders might feel they have done well since, whatever happens, their wealth increases. In fact if the issue was made straight to the public without pre-emptive rights their loss would be even greater than before, in terms of opportunity cost. We can see this by calculating the value of the rights, were it a rights issue. Recall that the value of the rights measures the compensation the shareholders receive for their dilution if it is a rights issue, and thus their loss if it is not. In this case the rights should sell for £5.20 − £4.00 = £1.20 each, or 250,000 × £1.20 = £300,000 in total.

Some final comments on rights

The important point in the previous example was that unless a rights issue is used, a new issue at a discount must lead to dilution − a transfer of wealth from old shareholders to new. But the corollary is that *the issue price, and the discount, is of no significance in a rights issue.*

An example of a rights issue: BP

On 19 June 1981 British Petroleum Limited made one of the largest rights issues on record when it announced it was raising £600 million by offering 226,859,583 ordinary 25p shares to its existing shareholders. Since BP already had 1,588,017,084 shares in issue, the new issue was a 1 for 7 rights issue. Shareholders could subscribe for one share for every seven they held on the 29 May. The offer price was 275p. The offer had to be accepted, and a first instalment of 125p paid, by 13 July. The balance of 150p had to be paid by the 2 December, but if the whole 275p were paid on 3 July the share would qualify for an interim dividend in November of 'not less than 6.25p per share'. So the shareholder had to decide if a net 6.25p received after 4 months was worth more than foregone interest on 150p for 5 months.

One novel feature of the issue was the role of the UK government. The government was a major shareholder in BP, but in line with its policy at that time of reducing its stake in enterprises, it told BP beforehand that it would not take up its rights. So private shareholders were offered the government's rights, another 1 for 8.69 they already held. But they had to pay 290p for these shares, the extra 15p going to the government for selling their rights.

People sometimes worry about the equilibrium price after rights, the ex-rights price, being lower than the cum-rights price. As we saw, this is predictable and unimportant in a rights issue. Perhaps because this price effect, though unimportant, is unsettling, there has some times been a view that a rights issue does depress a firm's value. Marsh (1979) confronted this view in a study of 254 rights issues in the UK between 1962 and 1972. He found only a very small hiccup associated with the rights issue in the time-trend of the share's prices. On average share prices fell by 0.5% in the months surrounding the rights issue.

VI   SUMMARY

There are two sorts of cost involved in issuing equity − administrative costs and issue discount. Both costs vary with the size and method of issue. Issue discount, which arises when the firm sells shares at an issue price below their equilibrium market value, is perhaps the most perplexing. Firms regularly issue shares at a price which offers big gains to new shareholders at the expense of the existing shareholders. To avoid this problem The Stock Exchange requires 'seasoned' shares to be made issued by a 'rights issue' to existing shareholders. In a public issue the discount can be reduced by asking applicants to 'tender' for the shares, though in the UK this practice remains relatively unpopular.

REFERENCES AND BIBLIOGRAPHY

Davis, E W and Yeomans, K A	'Company Finance and the Capital Market' Cambridge University Press, Occasional Paper 39, Cambridge, England, 1974.
Ibbotson, R G	'Price Performance of Common Stock New Issues' Journal of Financial Economics, 1975, pp 235–272.
Marsh, P R	'Equity Rights Issues and the Efficiency of the UK Stock Market', Journal of Finance, Dec 1982, pp 839–862.
Merrett, A J, Howe, M and Newbould, G D	*Equity Issues and the London Capital Market* (1967) Longmans, London.
'Wilson Report'	Committee to Review the Functioning of Financial Institutions, Report (Cmnd 7937).
'Wilson Report'	'Evidence on the Financing of Industry and Trade' Vol 3, 1978.

QUESTIONS

1 What are the distingushing characteristics of equity and debt from the point of view of an investor?

2 Dombey plc is considering 'rights', 'offer for sale' and 'tender' as methods of share issue. Report to Dombey advising them on their new issue strategy. Indicate the advantages and disadvantages of the main alternative methods, and the relative costs of each.

3 Dombey currently has 20 million shares in issue and a share price of £1. The shares sell at a P/E of 10 and a dividend yield of 5%. Dombey's directors are planning to raise £4 million of cash through the share issue and they hope this new investment in the business will increase earnings by £500,000 per annum.

Making some reasonable assumptions about costs of issue, calculate the effect on shareholders' wealth of the three alternatives which Dombey is considering. State clearly any assumptions you have made.

CHAPTER 21
Debt finance

Debt finance comes in many forms: as loan stock, 'convertibles', and preference shares; as bank loans and overdrafts; but also in disguise in the form of leasing and factoring arrangements and trade credit. By far the main source of debt finance for UK firms is short-term bank borrowing, particularly in the form of 'overdraft' arrangements. Long term debt has become a relatively minor source of company finance, though there is still some interest in loan-stock that is 'convertible' into shares.

Section I gives an overview of debt financing, and discusses the risks of debt and the valuation of a debt contract. Section II considers long-term debt including preference shares, and Secion III considers the special problems in analysing convertible loan-stock and warrants. In Section IV we consider the raising of shorter-term loans. The analysis of 'quasi-debt' finance is left to the next chapter.

I AN OVERVIEW OF DEBT-FINANCE

THE RISKS OF DEBT FINANCE

In a *debt* contract the supplier of funds becomes a *creditor* of the firm for the principal and interest it owes him. The contrast is with equity where the supplier becomes an *owner* of the firm. The debt/equity distinction is only meaningful in an uncertain world. If the future were known with certainty everyone would receive a known stream of returns, and since there would be no risk involved, we would expect everyone to require the same rate of return. In reality though, financing firms is risky. Firms may prosper exceedingly, or they may fail and dissipate all their assets, and ahead of time we cannot be sure which is going to happen. By investing in firms the equity shareholder runs the risk of losing some or all of his money, but this risk is balanced by the possibility of sharing in any surplus the firm makes. The problem for the debt-holder is that he has 'downside risk' too, he stands to lose his money. But he cannot participate in the firm's positive variances since his claims have an upper limit.

We need to understand the various ways in which debt-holders can protect themselves from this asymmetry in their risk. First, they write protective *covenants* into the debt contract to try and reduce the risk of the firm failing to meet their claims. Second they will often look to take a title over some of the firm's assets as *security* for the loan. Debt claims have, in any case, priority over equity, and so thirdly it might seem wise for debt to prevent the *gearing* of the firm, the ratio of debt to equity, from getting too high. This way there will not be too many people making prior claims on the same cake. Any residual risk after all this will be reflected in the cost of debt capital.

One of the fundamental lessons of finance is that risk cannot be *reduced* by writing financial contracts, but it can be *shifted* somewhere else. It is useful to bear this in mind when we look at the efforts of individual debt-holders to protect themselves.

Restrictive covenants

Debt-holders have a problem of downside risk, and this is compounded by the fact that, unlike equity, they have no general right to control the firm. Debt contracts often contain quite complex sets of *restrictive covenants* designed to give debt some control and the right to void the contract if the firm commits certain future acts that damage debt-holders' interests. Table I shows the sort of restrictions commonly found in debt contracts.

Table I Typical restrictions on a debt agreements

- Limitations on the amount the firm may borrow, secured or unsecured; or undertakings that certain specified ratios will be maintained.
- A prohibition on the creation of any further changes on the assets of the business (sometimes known as a 'negative pledge').
- Limitations on the amount of remuneration that the directors may draw, and on dividends; and continuance of existing directors' loans to the business.
- The right of the investor or lender to monitor the performance of the business and to receive regular financial information.
- The right of the investor or lender to appoint a director to the board (this is more usual in the case of an equity investment).
- The right to be consulted about specific developments or unusual transactions.

Source: 'Money for Business' Bank of England.

The problem facing debt-holders is that after writing the contract, with terms specifying the duration and amount of the loan and the rate of interest, the firm can do things which materially alter the debt-holder's position. It may issue more debt of equal or greater *seniority*; it may distribute as dividends or salaries assets the creditors were looking to as security; it may develop a more risky investment strategy, the benefits of which would be reaped by equity but the costs of which might be borne by debt. Restrictive covenants attempt to limit the power of firms to do these things.

The effects of restrictive covenants can be dramatic. We see an example of this in Chapter 25 when we study the bankruptcy of Stone-Platt. Amongst other conditions, Stone-Platt's lenders had included a clause requiring a particular level of gearing to be maintained. When Stone-Platt wrote off some big losses against reserves this pushed gearing over the limit, and a good part of Stone-Platt's debt became repayable on demand. Stone-Platt also had *cross-default* covenants which mean that once it defaulted on one debt, other debts became repayable too.

Security

Debt-holders have priority over equity in the payment of interest, and in repayment of the principal if the firm is wound-up. But if a debt is *secured* it has priority over other creditors too. Loans can be secured by a *fixed* or a *floating* charge. If the charge is fixed the debt contract identifies specific assets and restrictive covenants identify particular events which will permit the debt holders to sell those assets to recover the debt. Once the sale is triggered the debt-holders or a *trustee* representing them will appoint a *receiver* to enter the firm and arrange for the sale of the assets.

Effectively, by securing an asset, a part of the ownership rights is being transferred to the debt-holder, namely the right to dispose of it in certain circumstances, though not the right to use it. And when he does dispose of it any surplus remaining after he has discharged his debt belongs to the shareholders. An alternative to the fixed charge is the 'floating' charge. Under a 'floating' charge there are no restrictions on the firm's right to dispose of its assets prior to default.

Because taking security puts a lender at the front of the queue of creditors it reduces his risk at the expense of other creditors by reducing the fund of assets available to meet their claims. To help creditors assess their risk, company law requires each company to make available at Companies House a list of the prior charges over its assets.

The firm's ability to offer security depends on having the right sort of assets, that is, assets with a relatively secure realisable value and assets whose continued existence is easy to monitor. Offices and houses form good security, while highly specialised plant and machinery, or stocks of raw materials or bank accounts might not. The creditor will usually look for security whose face value is some multiple of the debt to be secured. Given the inherent uncertainty of future realisable values, and the transactions costs associated with selling assets, a creditor might well look for £75,000 to £100,000 of security to secure a loan of £50,000.

When the firm does not have adequate securable assets it is quite common, particularly in smaller firms, for creditors to accept personal security from directors or third parties. Directors might pledge personal property: houses, insurance policies, jewellery; or give a personal *guarantee*, which is effectively a floating charge on the individual's assets.

VALUING DEBT

When we learned how to value shares in Chapter 10 we used the 'dividend valuation' model. The value of a share was the present value of the future stream of cash flows to the investor. We can use the same approach in valuing debt. In the simplest case where the firm raises a loan D and agrees to pay a constant annual *coupon* or interest charge, C, and to repay an amount P after n periods, then

$$D = \sum_{t=0}^{n} \frac{C}{(1 + r_d)^t} + \frac{P}{(1 + r_d)^n} \tag{1}$$

As with equity we can use this expression either way round. The investor who knows his required return from debt, r_d, can value a debt contract using (1), and the firm which observes the value, D, of its debt can calculate its cost of capital using the formula.

The big problem in valuing shares was uncertainty about future dividends; but in valuing debt there should be less uncertainty. The cash flows are known, save for the risk of default which will guide the investor's choice of required return.

Suppose Othello plc has £1 million of loan-stock in issue, redeemable on 31.12.1995 at a premium of 10%. The loan-stock bears an 8% coupon and interest is payable at the end of each calender year. How should the market evaluate the loan-stock on 1.1.1984 if the required return on comparable risk loan-stock is 12%?

Using equation (1) we can find the value of the loan-stock as

$$D = \sum_{t=0}^{11} \frac{80,000}{(1 + .12)^t} + \frac{1,100,000}{(1 + .12)^{11}}$$
$$= 80,000 \times 5.937 + 1,100,000 \times .287$$
$$= £790,660$$

We saw when we looked at equity that 'nominal' or 'par' values are irrelevant and have no economic significance. The same applies to debt. Loan-stocks are issued with a nominal value and the coupon interest rate will be expressed as a percentage of that value. But the nominal value will not necessarily be the sum raised or repaid at the end. Loan-stock is often issued at a *discount* and redeemed at a *premium*. Either way, the *value* of a debt contract once issued reflects current interest rates in the market. If market rates fall after issue, the value of the security and all other securities in the market, will rise, and vice versa.

The Othello example assumed a known and constant annual coupon, but there are other possibilities. Short-term finance such as bank overdrafts typically has a variable interest rate related to the bank's base lending rate. Long-term loans can be at a variable rate too, though these are not yet common – an example is in the 'index-bond' we discuss in the next section. Second, even when the schedule of interest payments is predetermined it may not be constant through the duration of the loan. It is common for institutional lenders to tailor repayment schedules to the tax and financing needs of the client. Sometimes payments may be stepped up or down, 'rolled-up' until the end or 'front-end loaded'. Thirdly, interest is more likely to be half-yearly, quarterly or monthly than annual. Equation (1) can be modified to accommodate this variety.

Coupon yields and redemption yields

In the case of a perpetual debt, $n = \infty$ and the loan is never repaid, so

$$D = \sum_{t=0}^{\infty} \frac{C}{(1 + r_d)^t} \qquad (2)$$

which, summing the infinite series, gives

$$D = \frac{C}{r_d} \qquad (3)$$

$$\text{or } r_d = \frac{C}{D} \qquad (4)$$

So in this case the so-called 'coupon yield', $\frac{C}{D}$, which would be our instinctive estimate of the cost of debt, does indeed tell us the cost. But otherwise the cost of debt has two components, as in expression (1), the cost of the annual interest payment, and the cost of eventually repaying or 'redeeming' the loan. We call the cost of redeemable debt calculated as in (1) and taking into account the final repayment of the loan, the 'redemption yield'. Clearly the redemption yield is the correct estimate of the cost of a debt contract of finite duration, and is different from the coupon yield, C/D. But the longer the duration of the loan and the further away is redemption the closer the redemption yield converges on the coupon yield, and the more faith we can put in the coupon rate as an approximation of r_d.

Taxation

A key difference between debt and equity is in the tax treatment of interest and dividends. The Revenue treats interest payments as an allowable expense against profit. If the corporation tax rate is 40% the effective cost of debt is only .6 of the nominal return received by the supplier of finance. If the firm pays £100 interest, its taxable profit is reduced by £100 and its CT bill by £40. So the effective cost of the interest is £60. But dividends paid to equity are treated as a *distribution* of profit rather than as a business *expense*, so dividends are not tax-deductible.

If the firm is using the debt valuation formula to find its cost of debt capital when it has a marginal rate of corporation tax of T, we need to modify equation (1) thus:

$$D = \sum_{t=0}^{n} \frac{(1 - T)C}{(1 + r_d')^t} + \frac{P}{(1 + r_d')^n} \tag{5}$$

And in the case of a perpetuity we can rearrange to get

$$r_d' = \frac{(1 - T)C}{D} = (1 - T)\frac{C}{D} \tag{6}$$

Now r_d' is the after-tax cost of debt.

In fact (6) is rather inexact, since it ignores the lags in tax payments. Firms pay their corporation tax with a lag, L, so they suffer the same lag in capturing the benefits of any tax deductibility. Developing (6), the general model for the cost of debt with lags in tax payments is

$$D = \sum_{t=0}^{n} \frac{C_t}{(1 + r_d')^t} - \sum_{t=0}^{n} \frac{C_t.T}{(1 + r_d')^{t+L}} + \frac{P}{(1 + r_d')^n} \tag{7}$$

where the second term on the RHS reflects the lagged tax relief on the interest payment.

II LONG-TERM DEBT

In this section we discuss long-term debt, which we will call any debt with a duration of over ten years.

Firms can arrange *term-loans and mortgage loans*. A term-loan may have a fixed or variable rate of interest, will normally be secured, and have a duration of up to twenty years. The prime sources of term-loans are the clearing banks and merchant banks, and the institutions – pension funds and insurance companies. A mortgage-loan tends to be of longer duration and is usually raised from a pension fund or insurance company against the security of land or property. Alternatively the firm can issue securities such as loan-stock, preference shares or convertibles.

Loan-stock

Loan-stock, 'debentures', or 'bonds' as they are commonly known in the US, are similar to share capital in some respects. The firm issues securities embodying a written acknowledgement of the loan. These securities can be traded by their owners and the company can change their marketability by having them listed on The Stock Exchange. Like shares, public issues of loan-stock must be accompanied by a prospectus. The holders of the loan-stock have their rights specified in a 'trust-deed' rather like the articles of association which protect equity, and it is usual to appoint a *trustee* to monitor the firm and act on behalf of the holders if the terms are infringed.

Unlike equity capital loan stock is usually repaid after a finite period though irredeemable loan-stocks is also found. Often the trust deed will give the firm a range of opportunities to *call* or *redeem* the loan-stock. So '10½% loan-stock 1991–93' indicates that the loan-stock is redeemable at the firm's option some time between these dates. However, the firm can repurchase its loan-stock and so effectively redeem it at any time. Unless the firm thinks it can outguess the market about future interest rates repurchasing loan-stock in the market is fairly uninspiring behaviour. It is simply a repayment of capital, a zero-NPV transaction which seems to imply the firm has insufficient positive-NPV projects in the offing. But redemption can be worthwhile. Redeemable loan-stock has a fixed redemption price. Falling interest rates can drive the market price of debt above the redemption price. When this happens the firm should redeem at the first opportunity and refinance at the new lower interest rates.

Preference shares

Preference shares are annoying analytically because they are on the margin between debt and equity; they look like equity, but are effectively debt. There are several variants of the preference share contract but in a 'basic' preference share the holder receives a fixed and predetermined 'dividend', and a repayment of capital if the firm is liquidated in priority to other equity but after the claims of other creditors, including loan-stock, have been met. In common with equity, the firm does not *have to* pay the agreed dividend on a basic preference share, and if it misses the dividend one year the missed dividend does not become a debt of the firm to be made up in future periods. But this characteristic is remedied in a *cumulative* preference share – in this case the firm must make good previous years' preference dividends before paying a dividend to ordinary shares.

Preference shares are usually permanent finance, i e irredeemable. But firms sometimes issue 'redeemable preference shares', which are redeemable in a predetermined period in a similar way to loan-stock. Since company law views preference shares as equity and a basic tenet of company law is that equity should not be repaid, firms are only allowed to redeem preference shares under strict conditions, one of which is that the preference capital of the business should be replaced by an equivalent reserve so that the equity of the firm as a whole is not reduced.

Our criterion for equity was that it yields 'ownership' of the surplus or residue generated by the firm. On this criterion the basic preference contract does not qualify as equity but appears to have the features of loan-stock but with a lower priority in the distribution of income and capital. However another variant of the preference contract appears to qualify. Firms sometimes issue *participating* preference shares which give their owners a share in the surplus of the firm on top of a fixed dividend. If preference shares truly ranked equally with other equity for the surplus of the firm, they would be equity. In practice this is uncommon, and we treat preference shares as debt.

We do not need to spend too much time agonizing whether preference shares are equity or debt. Given the great variety of finance contracts that can be written in practice it should be no surprise that we can find contracts combining elements of debt and equity. Fortunately for our classification system preference shares are unpopular in practice. This is a direct result of their nominal 'equity' status. The Revenue does not allow preference 'dividends' against tax, thus greatly increasing the cost to the firm of servicing this form of finance relative to equivalent loan-stock. Under present tax law, preference shares do not have much appeal.

The market for long-term debt

We can think of good reasons not to issue preference shares, but Table II shows that long-term debt has also varied in popularity with redemptions exceeding new issues in some years.

The collapse of the UK corporate bond market is usually attributed to the combination of high interest rates and great uncertainty. The argument is that firms are reluctant to commit themselves to long-term loans at high, fixed, interest rates because of the danger

Table II Annual Debt Issues by UK listed Companies (£mn)

	1984	1983	1982	1981	1980	1979	1978	1977	1976	1975
Loan capital	115	218	187	(266)	(220)	(104)	(93)	(70)	(12)	8
Convertibles	101	47	8	194	178	23	(21)	(5)	8	84
Preference shares	42	59	8	66	31	54	22	16	31	40

Source: CSO Financial Statistics, HMSO

of being burdened with a crippling interest bill if the rate of inflation fell, and with it nominal returns. The obvious alternative would be floating-rate or *index-bonds*, where the interest rate is linked to a general price index. These are in widespread use in some countries that have experienced chronic high inflation. In the UK the sticking point has been the government, whose borrowing requirement dominates the bond market. Though the UK government has offered some index-linked arrangements to investors, there has been no major move to indexing, which may reflect the confidence that governments, free of the risk of bankruptcy, can have about their ability to meet future claims.[1] What action there has been in the market for long-term corporate debt has involved 'convertible loan-stock' which we analyse in the next section.

III CONVERTIBLES AND WARRANTS

The problem with debt is the 'downside-risk' – the investor runs the risk of loss but cannot share in the success of the firm. In a world of high interest rates and uncertain inflation investors may be particularly reluctant to tie themselves to lending long-term at fixed-interest. In finance theory our usual belief is that risk can be assessed and compensated by a suitable risk-premium, but in practice this may not be so. A way round this problem is to offer loan-stock that is *convertible* into shares or, similarly, loan-stock with *warrants* attached that give the investor the right to buy shares. We will start by looking at warrants.

WARRANTS

A *warrant* is an option which gives the holder the right to buy shares in the firm at a given exercise price at some time in the future. Firms issue warrants for various reasons; they can be attached to loan-stock, they are sometimes issued as part of the consideration for a merger or issued to favoured individuals associated with the firm. The share-options that employees get under the share-participation schemes that many firms run are akin to warrants except that the employee's rights are usually limited – he cannot usually sell the share-option and often has to hold the share for a certain period after he has exercised the option.

Warrants are options on the underlying share. The only difference between warrants and the traded options we analysed in Chapter 11 is that warrants tend to have a longer term, usually several years, and they are issued by the firm rather than being sold by another investor. When the warrant is exercised, new shares come into being. We know from Chapter 11 that the value of the warrant will be as shown in Figure I.

On the day the warrant is exercised its value is the greater of the share price less the

1 See the Bank of England Quarterly Bulletin, March 1981, for a fuller discussion of these issues.

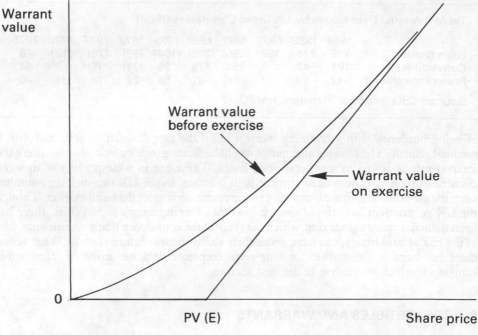

Figure I The value of a warrant

exercise price, and zero. Prior to that the warrant's value will be a convex function lying above this. A warrant with 'time to go' will always sell at some positive value. This value will also be an increasing function of the time to expiry, the riskless interest rate, and the variance on the underlying share, and a decreasing function of the exercise price.

CONVERTIBLES

In a convertible issue the investor buys loan-stock, but has the option to convert it into shares at some time in the future. Issuing convertibles is rather like issuing loan-stock with warrants attached although there are some differences. For example the convertible-holder forfeits his loan-stock when he converts, while the holder of loan-stock with warrants retains his loan-stock when he exercises the warrants. So from the firm's point of view, it gets an extra cash injection when the warrants are exercised. Also, the holder can detach the warrant from the loan stock and sell it separately. Another difference, as we see later, is that convertibles can get rather complicated to analyse.

In 1982 Habitat issued £37,502,847 of 9½% convertible unsecured loan-stock as part of the consideration for its purchase of the Mothercare chain of childswear shops. Interest on the loan-stock was payable on the 15 April and the 15 October each year and the loan-stock would be redeemed at par in four equal instalments from 1998 to 2001. However, before then the holder had the right to convert the stock into 10p ordinary shares at the rate of £145 per 100 shares. This right could be exercised on 30 November in any of the years 1985 to 1998.

To sacrifice £145 of loan-stock for 100 shares puts a price of £1.45 on each Habitat share. This is the *conversion price*. At the date of the issue Habitat shares were actually standing at 103p, 42p less than the conversion price. This difference is normally called the *conversion premium*. It is usual to issue convertibles at a positive conversion premium – the expectation is that by the time conversion is possible the price of the underlying share may have risen enough to make conversion worth while. On the other hand the convertible will sell at a premium over the value of equivalent 'straight' loan-stock, simply because the convertible is more attractive to investors, it is loan-stock plus an option. So the firm will raise more per £1 of interest payments by issuing loan-stock that is convertible, or put the other way round, the *apparent* cost of convertibles is less than for ordinary loan-stock. People sometimes calculate the *rights premium* to describe this difference, where

$$\text{rights premium} = \frac{\text{value of convertible} - \text{value of}}{\text{loan-stock without conversion rights}}{\text{number of underlying shares}}$$

In the UK, since very few loan-stocks are quoted it is hard to find a comparable stock without conversion rights. However, at the time of the Habitat issue, preference shares in ICI, a blue-chip UK stock, were giving a gross yield of 14.1%, compared to the nominal yield of 9½% on Habitat's convertible.

Warrants and convertible that have yet to be exercised are 'overhanging'. Recognising that *overhanging* convertibles threaten to dilute the equity interest, firms are required to publish earnings-per-share data in undiluted and fully-diluted form. In the latter case the firm works out what its EPS would be if all outstanding convertibles and warrants were converted. Habitat's 1982 EPS was 9.9p. but 'fully-diluted', if all outstanding loan-stock were converted, it was 9.3p.

THE VALUE OF A CONVERTIBLE

In the simplest case a convertible is just loan-stock with warrants attached. Figure II shows how its value will behave. Now the lower boundary which is the thick line has two components: the value of a 'straight' bond which is an increasing function of the share value because bond and share both depend on the underlying value of the firm, and the conversion value, which is the 45° line through the origin. We can see how the convertible's 'option' properties determine its value. The convertible with some life left will sell at a premium over the lower boundary and is shown by the dotted line in Figure II. We could find the specific value of such a convertible by valuing the 'straight' loan-stock, and using Black-Scholes to value the warrant component. However the problem in practice is that convertibles are rarely so simple. Convertibles usually have two features that make them rather complicated to value: they are *callable*, and the underlying share pays *dividends*. When we talked about a 'simple' convertible earlier, we meant a convertible without these features. Theorists have made some progress in valuing convertibles with calls and dividends, but the solutions are rather complex.[2] We will simply give some insights into the problem.

Dividends and dilution

In deriving the Black-Scholes model it was convenient to assume the underlying share did not pay dividends. Amongst other things this meant we could use the BS model for European call valuation to value the American options we usually meet in practice.

But if the underlying share pays dividends the option holder might want to exercise early, which he could with an American call. So he values the American call more highly,

2   For a systematic development of convertible valuation see Ingersoll (1977a).

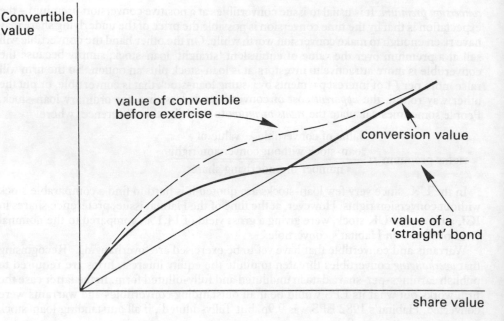

Figure II Value of a Convertible

and the Black-Scholes model is no longer appropriate. Just the same problem arises in valuing warrants and convertibles as dividend-paying shares. If the share pays a dividend it might be in the bond-holders interest to convert just before the share goes ex div. Once the share goes ex div the conversion value of the convertible will drop.

There is a general problem that all debt-holders face – the risk that management will subsequently make decisions, after the debt contract is written, that harm debt. We saw that debt-holders try to protect themselves by writing restrictive covenants into the debt contract. One particular risk for convertible holders is that the firm will make a stock split and so reduce the conversion value of the convertible. Convertible contracts usually *protect* holders from this risk by acquiring that conversion rights be adjusted after a stock split to maintain the value of the conversion rights. So if convertibles have a right to buy 100 shares for £145 stock, and the firm subsequently makes a 1 for 5 stock split, the conversion rights will need to be adjusted to 120 shares for £145 stock.

Sometimes however the convertible contract consciously specifies conversion rights that change over the life of the bond. The conversion value of the bond may be stepped-up or down at discreet intervals. A change in conversion rights has the same effect as a dividend on the underlying share, and can similarly lead bond-holders to convert early. Generally speaking there is a large range of managerial actions that can have the effect of changing the bondholders' conversion rights by changing the value of the underlying share. Convertible contracts cannot provide full protection from these risks.

Calls

Another feature which complicates the analysis of convertibles to the call provision. The firm can usually *call* its convertibles in just the same way as it can redeem ordinary loan-stock. The firm has an option to call the convertible at a specified call price, and the convertible-holder must either accept the cash or convert immediately. So the call option has the effect of forcing conversion. Now, the convertible is a compound of three things: an ordinary bond plus a warrant to buy shares, less a call option sold to the firm.

Ingersoll (1977a) shows that the value-maximising policy for the firm is to call a convertible only when its conversion value equals the call price. To call earlier or later than that means that the firm is making its convertible-holders richer than it needs to. When Ingersoll investigated what firms actually do, in a subsequent paper (Ingersoll (1977b)), he found a strange thing. On average, the 124 US firms which called convertibles between 1968 and 1975 and which Ingersoll investigated did not call until conversion value was 44% higher than the call price. In other words they allowed convertible-holders to convert at a price 44% higher than they needed to. No-one has yet explained why this happens.

THE APPEAL OF CONVERTIBLES

Convertibles, loan-stock-with-warrants, and other variants such as convertible preferance shares are complex financing contracts combining elements of debt and equity. Convertibles look very attractive to all concerned. The investor gets the best of both worlds; the relative security of creditor status plus the chance of participating if things go well. The firm raises finance at a cost apparently below even the cost of debt. There may be firms which analyse convertibles this way, but we expect firms to be more rational! When the investor buys a convertible he is effectively buying two things: an ordinary loan-stock plus an *option* to buy shares at a given price sometime in the future. It is the value of this option that accounts for the increased value of the convertible. But to calculate the cost of funds raised this way by relating it to the cost of servicing the debt-plus-option bundle, would be misleading. There is a hidden cost in issuing convertibles, it is the series of dividend payments, starting some time in the future, that the holder will become entitled to as and when he exercises the conversion option. Put another way, the 'something extra' the purchaser of a convertible pays for does not come from nowhere; it is taken away from existing shareholders. Shareholders are accepting that at some time in the future they may have to sell a share in the firm to outsiders at below its market value. In return for this they get a relative interest 'holiday' in the early years of the new money they are raising. The apparent cheapness of convertibles is an illusion that comes from ignoring the equity aspect. Correctly valued, convertibles do not offer cheap finance. So why do firms issue them?

To suggest a rationale for convertibles we perhaps need to challenge one of the underlying assumptions of finance – the assumption that all risk can be priced. Convertibles tend to be issued in situations where neither debt nor equity is, on its own, attractive enough. Convertibles are commonly issued as consideration in a merger. Here, there can be a great deal of uncertainty surrounding the future prospects of the merged firm, and if the firms involved are relatively small or relatively new there may simply not be enough information to permit investors to happily accept debt or equity on their own.

IV SHORT AND MEDIUM TERM LOANS

It is common to distinguish 'medium-term' finance of between 3 and 10 years, and 'short-term' finance of less than 3 years duration. In either case the main source of this finance is the banks.

Term-loans

In principle term-loans provide a predetermined amount of finance for a fixed period, though often there will be provision for the borrower to draw less than the full amount or to repay early. The interest may be fixed, or periodically varied in line with the banks base-rate. Banks are capable of being fairly flexible about terms, and in the case of project-finance may be prepared to offer an interest schedule that matches the cash flow of the project, with interest 'loaded' towards the end of the project. Conversely the borrowers tax position may indicate loading the interest towards the front of the loan.

Overdrafts

The basic term-loan is for a fixed amount and duration, but the *overdraft* works differently. The bank sets an upper limit to the amount the firm can borrow, in the form of a drawing limit on the firm's current account. The firm only pays interest on the daily balance outstanding. The duration of the arrangement is usually specified at the outset, and is typically 3, 6 or 12 months, with the possibility of renewal for further periods. The interest rate will vary with the bank's base lending rate. The beauty of overdrafts, from the point of view of the firm, or the individual for that matter, is that interest is only paid on the daily borrowing requirement. So it is very attractive to finance at least the fluctuating component of the total financing need this way. The problem with overdrafts is their short-term nature. The firm cannot be certain that the facility will be renewed, and because it operates on the firm's current account the bank is powerfully placed to hinder the normal operations of the firm until the overdraft is cleared.

Export finance

A whole host of special provisions has developed to help firms finance their exports. These have come about for two reasons. For one thing there are special financial problems associated with exporting: there is uncertainty as to exchange-rates, and possible as to the credit-worthiness of the customer and to the political risks involved, and payment can take longer. But also, governments have seen exports as an important part of the national economic effort and worthy of support.

A large part of an exporter's risk can now be insured through the government's Export Credit Guarantee Department (ECGD). The firm is expected to insure a reasonable part of his business, and pays a premium based on his previous claims record. In return he gets coverage against the default of the buyer and political risks such as the blockage of remittances. ECGD is also prepared to guarantee export finance bank loans on behalf of its policy-holders for an additional premium. Certain insurance companies also offer these services.

The traditional instrument for financing foreign trade is the *bill of exchange*. A bill 'may be thought of as a post-dated cheque that can be sold for cash at a discount. It is a legal document covered by the Bills of Exchange Act 1881, in which the consequences of default are clearly defined. It enables the seller of goods to obtain cash for them as soon as possible after their dispatch, while allowing the buyer to defer payments until the goods reach him . . .' ('Money for Business' (1983)). Bills are usually for 30 or 90 days. They can be drawn by the seller ('trade bill') or the bank will attach its own name to the bill ('bank bill'). In the latter case the bank 'accepts' the bill and is said to have given the drawer a 'banker's acceptance' which will make the bill easier to negotiate. Upon receipt a bill can be *discounted* by another bank or more likely by one the discount houses who specialise in this work. They pay cash to the extent of the future value of the bill less an appropriate financing charge.

Bill finance has several attractions; it is project specific, and the buyer's uncertainty about payment is resolved early. Because bill discounting takes place in a well developed market, the cost of bill finance is normally competive with overdraft rates.

In looking for export finance the exporter is usually looking for expertise and advice, as well as funds. There are now many sources of export finance available to firms, including clearing banks, merchant banks, discount houses, export houses and finance houses.[3]

V SUMMARY

Debt finance is commonly divided into short, medium and long-term. By far the most important type of debt in practice is short-term bank finance, and particularly overdraft finance. Next to retained earnings this is the major source of company finance in the UK. By contrast, probably because of high levels of inflation and uncertainty, the use of long-term debt has dwindled to insignificance in the UK in recent years.

The key to understanding debt financing is to think of debt's risk relative to equity. Like equity, debt runs a risk of losing its money, but unlike equity it cannot share in the success of the firm. Debt protects itself in several ways: by priority in distributions, by taking 'security', by writing protective covenants into the debt contract. Investors' evaluation of the risk that remains to debt after taking these measures will be reflected in the relative cost of debt finance. If the firm wishes to enhance the attractiveness of debt further it can issue 'convertibles' or 'loan-stock-with-warrants' to give debt-holders a participation in equity.

In the next chapter we examine some types of financing that are effectively debt in disguise.

REFERENCES AND BIBLIOGRAPHY

Bank of England	'Money for Business', Periodically.
Bank of England	'UK Corporate Bond Market', Bank of England Quarterly Bulletin, 1981.
Ingersoll, J E	'A Contingent-Claims Valuation of Convertible Securities', Journal of Financial Economics, 1977 (a), pp 289–321.
Ingersoll, J E	'An Examination of Corporate Call Policies on Convertible Securities', Journal of Finance, 1977 (b).
Llewellen, W G and Racette, G A	'Convertible Debt Financing', Journal of Finance, 1976.
Myers, S C	'Determinants of Corporate Borrowing' Journal of Financial Economics, Nov 1977, pp 147–175.
Pinches, G E	'Financing with Convertible Preferred Stock, 1960–1967.' Journal of Finance, March, 1970, pp 53–64.
Van Horne, J C	'Implied Fixed Costs of Long-Term Debt Issues' Journal of Financial and Quantitative Analysis, 1973.

---

3 For a comprehensive survey of export finacing see 'Money for Exports' published free by the Bank of England. This is the sister publication to the excellent 'Money for Business', a regularly updated review of types and sources of finance for UK firms.

QUESTIONS

1 'Debt shares in the downside risk of the firm, but not in the upside, moreover the control of these risks belongs to equity'. How do debt-holders protect themselves?

2 What is the difference between the coupon-yield and the redemption-yield of a bond? On 1 January 1987 £1,000 of Arkwright plc 10% loan stock is selling for £750. The loan stock is redeemable at par on 31 December 1990. What is the coupon-yield, and the redemption-yield on the debt? Ignore tax.

3 Suppose Arkwright pays tax at 40%, one year in arrears. What is its after-tax cost of debt in the above example?

4 When companies issue long-term debt, they usually do it in the form of convertibles. How do you account for the apparent popularity of convertibles, and unpopularity of straight-debt?

5 How much does the Black-Scholes option pricing model help in valuing convertible loan stock?

6 Cute plc has 1,000,000 Ordinary shares outstanding at present. Earnings per share are 25p, before tax, and the shares sell at a P/E of 12. The company plans to issue £500,000 of 10%, 20 year convertible loan stock, convertible at the stockholders' option at a conversion price of £4. The new capital is expected to generate increased annual earnings of £100,000. The company tax rate is 40%.

Compute the new earnings per share before and after conversion.

Compute the conversion premium on issue and explain under what circumstances it will pay stockholders to convert.

7 You work in the planning department of the High Street Bank. The bank is worried about the criteria its branch managers are employing in granting overdrafts and making term-loans. Write a note to managers defining the information they should be getting from potential applicants. [You might want to look at Chapters 12, 13, 19 and 25 as well].

CHAPTER 22

Leasing and quasi-debt

You do not have to own an asset in order to use it. An alternative is to *lease* it. In leasing the firm avoids owning certain assets and contracts with someone else who finances their acquisition. The lessee is effectively borrowing from the lessor, so leasing is a form of debt finance. At first glance the lessor will bear the same costs as the lessee would have done, and is likely to charge an appropriate rental, so what are the gains to leasing? It turns out that if the lessee is paying tax at a lower rate than the lessor, they can jointly benefit at the expense of the Inland Revenue. In Section I we show how to analyse the leasing decision when there are tax benefits to leasing.

In finance we tend to see leasing as purely tax motivated, and to assume other benefits are more illusory than real. In Section II we review some of these other arguments, and consider the future of leasing in a world where the tax benefits appear to be waning. In Section III we conclude by looking at some other financial strategies, such as factoring and stretching credit, that like leasing are debt finance in disguise.

I   THE LEASE OR BUY DECISION

THE TAX GAINS TO LEASING

In Chapter 3 we discovered that the Inland Revenue allows companies to deduct 'capital allowances' in calculating taxable profit. Let us assume a simple world in which the capital allowance is 100% in the first year, and the corporation tax rate is 40%, and companies pay tax a year in arrears. Consider the situation where a firm qualifies for capital allowances, but cannot use them because it has not got enough taxable profits. Exhibit I describes two alternative states of Reagon plc, which is buying a £4,000 machine. Cases A and B show Reagon's tax position if its taxable profit before capital allowance is £10,000 and £1,000 per annum respectively. The only difference between the two cases is that in the low profits case, profits are insufficient to absorb all the allowance in the first year, so it has to be used up gradually over four years. So what? Reagon seemingly cannot complain because, either way, it ends up saving £1,600 tax, indeed in Case B Reagon pays no tax for four years. But in columns 8 and 9, we calculate the present value of the cost of the machine in each case, assuming a 10% discount rate. Since the outlay of £4,000 is made in year 0 in each case, the PV is simply the discounted tax savings less £4,000. The effect of postponing the tax relief is that the relief is worth less in PV terms, so that the PV of the machine's cost is £2,731 in Case B but only £2,545 in Case A.

The way is now open for a mutually advantageous trade. Suppose in Case B Smith, a firm with £100,000 of taxable profit per annum, arrives on the scene and offers to buy the machine and lease it to Reagon for five annual payments of £1,000, payable in advance. The PV of this lease-schedule is:

Exhibit I

	CASE A			CASE B			Present values		
	Reagon with high profits			Reagon with low profits					
	(1)	*(2)*	*(3)*	*(4)*	*(5)*	*(6)*	*(7)*	*(8)*	*(9)*
Time	π per annum	Capital Allowance	Tax saved 40% of (2)	π per annum	Capital Allowance	Tax saved 40% of (5)	10% PV Factors	A (3) × (7)	B (6) × (7)
1	10,000	4,000	1,600	1,000	1,000	400	.9091	1,455	364
2	10,000	–	–	1,000	1,000	400	.8264	–	331
3	10,000	–	–	1,000	1,000	400	.7513	–	301
4	10,000	–	–	1,000	1,000	400	.6830	–	273
		£4,000	£1,600		£4,000	£1,600			
							Less initial outlay	(4,000)	(4,000)
							PV of COST	(2,545)	(2,731)

Time	10% PV factors	Lease payments	Tax paid/ saved at 40%	Net PV
0	1	(1,000)		(1,000)
1	.9091	(1,000)	400	(545)
2	.8264	(1,000)	400	(496)
3	.7513	(1,000)	400	(451)
4	.6830	(1,000)	400	(410)
5	.6201		400	248
				(2,654)

So if Reagon leases the machine at £1,000 per annum from Smith, he saves £2,731 and pays £2,654 instead, a net gain of £77. Since Smith has plenty of taxable profit he is in the same position as Reagon in Case A, so the machine costs him £2,545 and he receives £2,654, so his net gain is £109. When firms are in different tax paying positions they may both be able to benefit by writing a lease contract. The loser is the Inland Revenue.

THE ANAYSIS OF THE LEASE OR BUY DECISION

The essence of a lease contract is that the user and owner remain separate and the former pays the latter a regular rental for the use of the asset. Some lease contracts give the user the right to buy after a certain period, and in this case leasing becomes similar to *hire purchase*. In an HP contract both parties set out with the intention that ownership will transfer at the end of the hire period. Another sort of contract which can generate a similar profile of cash flows is the *instalment sale*. In this case the user of the asset acquires ownership at the outset, but pays the purchase price in instalments. In terms of economics there may not seem much difference between these arrangements. But there is a legal difference concerning ownership, and in the case of leasing this legal difference turns out to be all important since it determines the tax allowances that the lessor and lessee are able to claim. The drafters of lease contracts have to take care to differentiate them from instalment sale agreements robustly enough to withstand the scrutiny of the Inland Revenue.

If the lessee is only leasing the asset for part of its useful life, as is normally the case with property, or equipment like a bulldozer required for a particular job, and the asset is then leased to someone else, the lease is known as an *operating* lease. But in many leases the lessee intends to use the asset for its full useful life. There is no particular expectation that the asset will be leased again after the first user has finished with it, and the lessor may well then sell it on the second hand market. In this case the user is making a real choice between leasing and buying the asset. It is these '*financial*' leases that we are interested in.

The lessee makes a series of payments to the lessor, and in leasing jargon this series of payments is called the *lease schedule*. Leasing is worthwhile when, allowing for the tax effects, the lessor values the lease schedule at more than the asset would cost him to buy, while the lessee values it at less than it would cost him. This happy situation can arise when lessor and lessee are in different tax positions. First we will consider how people in different tax positions will value a *given* lease schedule, then we will consider how to find the *optimal* schedule from the point of view of either or both parties. Lease evaluation is simple so long as we remember that leasing is a *financing* decision not an *investment* decision. On occasion the financial benefits to leasing might be enough to tip a negative NPV project into surplus. But in general by the time the lease analysis is undertaken, the investment appraisal should already have been done. The alternative to leasing is to buy the asset, financed by a loan secured on the asset. Since the comparison is with borrowing, two things follow:

— The relevant numbers to compare are the cash flows associated with leasing and with purchasing. The operating flows of the underlying assets are *irrelevant* since they are the same in each case.
— The appropriate discount rate is the firm's marginal borrowing rate on secured loans. The rationale is that lease payments are a low risk stream and, given the prevailing tax system, so are the tax effects. Of course, the ability of the firm to *take advantage* of tax effects depends on its uncertain future profits, so it could be argued we should discount tax effects at a rate which reflects this risk. We will follow usual practice and use a single low risk borrowing-rate throughout.

We will develop our analysis step-by-step, making different assumptions about the lessee's tax position.

Lessee: permanent non-taxpayer

A lessee can be permanently non-taxpaying either because, like local authorities or pension funds, it is tax-exempt, or because it does not expect to earn taxable profits in the foreseeable future. Suppose Dean is such a firm, and is choosing between the purchase of an £8,660 lathe today, and a lease contract for the same asset involving an annual payment of £2,200, payable in advance, for five years. Dean's marginal borrowing rate is 14%.

The analysis of Dean's decision is relatively simple and is shown in Exhibit II. We can find the NPV of the difference between the lease payments and the purchase payment using the firm's marginal cost of borrowing, 14%, as the discount rate. The calculation is presented in terms of what happens if Dean leases: it saves the purchase cost of the machine but has to incur the cost of the lease payments. Since we did it this way round, a positive NPV of £49 indicates a preference for leasing, because its discounted cost is the lesser of the two.

Exhibit II   Lessee in a permanent non-tax paying position

Year	0	1	2	3	4	TOTALS
PURCHASE	8660					8,660
LEASE	(2200)	(2200)	(2200)	(2200)	(2200)	11,000
	6460	(2200)	(2200)	(2200)	(2200)	
Discount factor	1	$\dfrac{1}{(1+.14)}$	$\dfrac{1}{(1+.14)^2}$	$\dfrac{1}{(1+.14)^3}$	$\dfrac{1}{(1+.14)^4}$	
PRESENT VALUES	6460	(1930)	(1693)	(1485)	(1303)	49

NPV = £49 DECISION-LEASE

Our method, here, was to find the *NPV* of the difference between the lease and purchase alternatives. Another way of going about the analysis is to find the 'equivalent loan' to the lease contract directly and compare this with the purchase cost. The equivalent loan is the loan which would generate the same schedule of interest and repayment as the lease schedule. In Exhibit III we see that the lease payments would service a loan of

Exhibit iii   Finding the Equivalent Loan

Year	0	1	2	3	4	5
Balance on loan	8611	6411	5109	3624	1931	0
Interest at 14%	–	898	715	507	270	
Repayment of principal	2200	1302	1485	1693	1931	
Lease payments	2200	2200	2200	2200	2201*	

* difference due to rounding

£8,611. If Dean borrowed £8,611 at the outset, the initial repayment of £2,200 would give a balance at the end of the first year of £6,411. Dean would pay interest on this of £898 (= £6,411 × 14%) so the rest of the year's £2,200 can repay £1,302 of principal giving a new balance of £5,109 (= £6,411−£1,302) and so forth. How did we find the £8,611 to start with? In this case we could cheat – the lease schedule is simply a four year, 14% annuity of £2,200 plus the initial £2,200 and we can find the PV of this from annuity tables as £6,411 + £2,200 = £8,611. Usually though, when tax and other complications yield an uneven stream of cashflows for the lease, we have to find the loan equivalent by trial and error, trying different initial amounts until we find the one that generates a final balance of zero.

The NPV we calculated earlier was simply the purchase cost less the loan equivalent of the lease, £8,660 − £8,611 = £49. Whenever we calculate an NPV, be it for a lease or a project, we are effectively calculating a loan equivalent. Projects are worth undertaking when the future cash flows from the project could service a loan which is larger than the initial outlay on the project. This is what a positive NPV means, and is an important insight. Finding the loan equivalent directly is just another way of doing the same computation, and in the present case it does not offer any benefits. However, it can be a more convenient way of analysing the lease when tax effects are more complicated.

Lessee – fully tax-paying

The case of the fully tax-paying lessee is not very interesting in practice since he does not benefit from leasing; but it helps us develop our analysis of tax effects. Assume the lessee has plenty of taxable profits so that the tax effects of the purchase and lease alternatives result in cash flows with a payment lag of one year. We assume capital allowances are 25%, reducing balance. There is another point to note here:

— When the firm is paying tax the *after-tax* discount rate should be used. In this case the after tax cost of capital is 8.4% which at a CT rate of 40% is 14% × (1 − .4) = 8.4%.

Exhibit IV shows how Dean will evaluate the lease when he is fully tax paying. With the introduction of tax, leasing has become less attractive than purchasing. However a moment's thought shows that when both are fully taxpaying there can never be a lease schedule at which lessor *and* lessee will find it worthwhile to lease. If the lessee if a normal taxpayer, the lessor's and lessee's analysis will be the mirror image of each other. In the present example, the lessor's evaluation will be exhibit IV with the signs reversed. He has an outlay of £8,660 on the machine, and *receives* the lease payments. His NPV will be plus £16 and he will want to lease, but unfortunately the lessee will not accept his proposal, nor any lease schedule that gives the lessor a positive NPV.

Exhibit IV   Lessee fully tax paying

Year	0	1	2	3	4	5	TOTALS
PURCHASE							
Cost	8,660	–	–	–	–	–	8,660
Capital allowances	–	(866)	(650)	(487)	(365)	(1,096)	(3,464)
LEASE							
Payments	(2,200)	(2,200)	(2,200)	(2,200)	(2,200)	–	(11,000)
Tax on payments	–	880	880	880	880	880	4,400
	6,460	(2,186)	(1,970)	(1,807)	(1,685)	(216)	
Discount factor	1	$\dfrac{1}{(1+.084)}$	$\dfrac{1}{(1+.084)^2}$	$\dfrac{1}{(1+.084)^3}$	$\dfrac{1}{(1+.084)^4}$	$\dfrac{1}{(1+.084)^5}$	
PRESENT VALUES	6,460	(2,017)	(1,676)	(1,419)	(1,220)	(144)	(16)

NPV = (£16) DECISION-PURCHASE

NOTE: The capital allowances have been calculated as 25%, reducing balance, with a balancing allowance in the final year. We have assumed a tax rate of 40%, so it is useful to check that the total capital allowances are 40% of the purchase cost (£3,464 = 40% of £8,660). Note that if the assets are 'pooled' (see Chapter 3) there is no balancing allowance or charge, and capital allowances continue to accrue indefinitely.

The tax rate of 40%, so it is useful to check that the total capital allowances are 40% of the purchase cost (£3,464 = 40% × £11,000), and the tax relief on lease payments is 40% of the total payments (£4,400 = 40% × £11,000). Note that if the assets are 'pooled' (see Chapter 3) there is no balancing allowance or charge, and capital allowances continue to accrue indefinitely. Throughout this chapter we are assuming assets are not pooled.

Lessee: temporary non-tax paying

When the situation arises, which is not uncommon, that the firm is in a temporary non-tax paying position, we have a combination of the previous two cases. Suppose in our example that Dean's tax advisers estimate the firm will start to be in a tax paying position after two years. Exhibit V shows the revised analysis.

There are two new points to note:

— The backlog of tax allowances can be claimed as soon as the firm resumes tax paying and it enters the analysis as a cash-flow of that period. So tax of £2,003 (= £866 + £650 + £487) and £2,640 (= 3 × 880) are entered in year 3.
— Cash flows are discounted at the rates prevailing year-by-year until they are received. So taking the fourth-year cash flows as example they are discounted by $\dfrac{1}{(1+.14)^2(1+.084)^2}$ because during two of the years before they are received the firm's marginal borrowing rate is 14% since it is not in a tax paying position and so cannot get tax relief on interest payments. In the third and fourth years, however, the after tax-rate can be used.[1]

Given the lessee's particular tax-position, leasing has a positive NPV of £495.

FINDING THE OPTIMAL LEASE SCHEDULE

When we discuss *merger* we will see that there are often other more efficient ways of achieving the same economic ends. Leasing is a good example. Leasing is an arrangement whereby two firms write a contract which is mutually profitable, in this case at the expense of the Inland Revenue. Mergers have sometimes been argued on the grounds of tax benefits, but merger is a permanent and all embracing solution that can be costly, disruptive and uncertain in its effects. In leasing a specific benefit is perceived, and a specific contract written to exploit it.

When looking at merger we ask two questions: How large are the gains? Who gets them? We can ask the same questions about leasing, and will start with the second.

Sharing the gains

The gains to leasing come from the differences in tax position of lessor and lessee, but the share of the gains to each party depends on the particular schedule of lease payments they agree. Take the example of the previous section where a machine costing £8,660 was to be leased for five annual payments of £2,200 payable in advance. Our lessee, who was a temporary non-taxpayer for three years, found this lease to have a positive NPV of £495, and it gave the lessor a positive NPV of £16.

We can find the range of acceptable lease schedules by seeing what is the minimum the lessor would accept and the maximum the lessee would pay, i e the schedules of payments that just give each party a zero NPV. Exhibit IV, with the signs reversed, gives us the layout of the lessor's analysis, and Exhibit V the lessee's. One way of proceeding is to replace £2,200 by x in each calculation, then get an expression for the present value of the lease in

---

1   Strictly speaking our analysis here is incomplete, because there is a backlog effect on interest payments to be recognised as well. In the third year the firm can claim tax relief on the interest implied in the discount factor for the earlier years. Calculating the appropriate tax effect to include in year three is a little complicated though, since it depends on the size of the cash flows which were discounted back through the first three years, of which it is itself one. Franks and Hodges (1978) suggest a method for calculating this tax effect.

Exhibit V   Lessee temporary non tax paying

Year	0	1	2	3	4	5	TOTALS
PURCHASE Cost	8,660	–	–	–	–	–	8,660
Capital allowances	–	–	–	(2,003)	(365)	(1,096)	(3,464)
LEASE Payments	(2,200)	(2,200)	(2,200)	(2,200)	(2,200)	–	(11,000)
Tax on payments	–	–	–	2,640	880	880	4,400
	6,460	(2,200)	(2,200)	(1,563)	(1,685)	(216)	
Discount factor	1	$\dfrac{1}{(1+.14)}$	$\dfrac{1}{(1+.14)^2}$	$\dfrac{1}{(1+.14)^2(1.084)}$	$\dfrac{1}{(1+.14)^2(1+.084)^2}$	$\dfrac{1}{(1+.14)^2(1+.084)^2(1+.084)^3}$	
PRESENT VALUES	6,460	(1,930)	(1,693)	(1,109)	(1,103)	(130)	495

NPV = £495   DECISION-PURCHASE

terms of the lease payment x. The present value is then set to zero to find the breakeven x. A quicker way is to inspect Exhibits IV and V and to ask in each case what difference an incremental rental of £1 makes to the present value of the lease. This involves adding-up discount factors, and not forgetting the tax effects. We find that decreasing the lease payment by £1 makes the lessee £2.657 better off, increasing it makes the lessor £2.701 better off. Conversely, a reduction in the lease payment of $\frac{16}{2.701} = 6$ will just wipe out the lessor's present value, while an increase of $\frac{495}{2.657} = 186$ will wipe out the lessee's. Hence:

Annual payment	Lessor's NPV	Lessee's NPV	Total NPV
£2,194	0	511	511
£2,200	16	495	511
£2.386	502	0	502

£2,194 and £2,386 are the limits within which a mutually advantageous leasing contract can be written. The *actual* payment will depend on relative bargaining strength. If there is strong competition amongst lessors then we can expect the lease payment to be at the lower end. Edwards and Mayer (1983) examined 100 UK leases written by the banks between 1977 and 1982 and computed their value in terms of an equivalent loan, assuming the lessees were permanently non taxpaying. They found that 80% of the value gains went to lessees and 20% to lessors. The best piece of advice we can give the lessee is to calculate the lessor's NPV as well as his own. That way he knows the total gain available to be shared.

Increasing the gains to both parties

We have seen how the leasing schedule determines the split of the overall gains to leasing between lessor and lessee. The previous arrangement with five annual payments yielded tax advantages to both parties, but they could do better still by pursuing the logic of leasing even further. So far in our example we have assumed a particular *profile* of lease payments, i e equal payments in advance over five years. But suppose lessor and lessee were to agree a lease schedule which involved no payment at all until the end of year three, then two annual payments of, say, £6,000. The reader can confirm, assuming tax positions as before, that this will give the lessor an NPV of £265 and the lessee £1,179, a total of £1,444. The problem with the former lease schedule was that for the first three years the lessor was receiving lease payments and paying tax on them though the lessee was not able to claim the equivalent tax relief until after the three years had elapsed. In the interim, the Inland Revenue holds the cash. By agreeing to postpone lease payments the lessor and lessee capture this cash flow benefit for themselves. They generate a value gain which they can share between them. As a general rule the gains to leasing are maximised if *no lease payments are made until the lessee is paying tax*. In the case of a permanent non taxpayer, it will be profitable to postpone for ever! This strange and rather impractical result follows once we see we are simply postponing the tax payment and so reducing its present value. In reality we do not find many lessors and lessees agreeing to settle-up on the Day of Judgement, but schedules in which payments increase, or 'balloon' at the end of the lease, are found.

In this section we have discussed the determination of the lease schedule. But for smaller leases the lessee usually faces a fixed schedule, the lessor's standard terms. It is usually only for larger leases that the parties find it worth negotiating a specific schedule, tailored to the lessee's needs.

II   ARE THERE OTHER REASONS FOR LEASING?

The idea of taking a lease on a flat or an office block has been familiar for a long time, but a significant change during the 1970s was the dramatic growth in the leasing of other types of business asset, from oil tankers to typists' chairs.[2] Leasing becomes worthwhile when the user of the asset has not got enough taxable profit to take immediate advantage of the tax allowance that comes with the asset. The growth in leasing in the UK was stimulated by the introduction of 100% capital allowances in 1972 and was given a further spurt in 1975 when the new Stock Relief provisions reduced company taxable profits further. By 1982 UK manufacturing industry was leasing 22½% of its plant, machinery and vehicles, and the manufacturing, distributive and service sectors as a whole were leasing 26%. However, in 1984 the tax environment changed dramatically, stock relief was withdrawn, and the corporate tax rate was reduced and first year capital allowances eliminated, by stages, over the next three years. Though the initial effect of these measures was an increase in leasing contracts in anticipation of the changes, there is no doubt that the longer term effect is to significantly reduce the gains to leasing. These gains still exist, so long as there are some firms with lower effective tax rates than others, but the effect of the 1984 budget was to reduce the likely number of such firms.

The market imperfections argument

In this chapter so far we have analysed 'lease-or-buy' as a purely tax-driven decision, but are there any other motives for leasing? Lessors will usually quote a list of advantages, with tax benefits as perhaps the main but not the only one. Usually these other arguments are saying that there may be *imperfections* in either the *product* or *capital* markets and the lessor may be better-placed to capture them than the lessee. Finance books tend to ignore these arguments. The reason is that market imperfections are often more apparent than real, and where they do exist there is usually some way other than leasing of capturing the benefit so they are irrelevant as far as the leasing decision goes.

We need to examine these other arguments. Leasing is often argued on the basis of product market imperfections:

Through leasing the lessee can avoid the risk of owning an asset which may become technologically superseded or otherwise redundant at some time during its life.

Leasing a micro-computer sounds like a better idea than buying while technological change is still so rapid in that area – risk of obsolescence is transferred to the lessor. But the lessor is likely to have noticed this, and if he is rational he will have raised the lease payment to compensate himself for the risk that the resale value of the equipment might slump.

The lessor may be able to buy the asset cheaper, perhaps because he writes a lot of leases for this sort of asset and gets volume discounts.

The lessor may be able to provide servicing and maintenance more economically than the lessee could because of indivisibilities in the provision of a service department. So, for example, it may not be worthwhile for the lessee to employ and equip a full time service engineer.

The lessor may have better access to the second hand markets and thus be able to dispose of the asset at a higher price.

Even if economies of scale confer these benefits, the lessee can share them in other ways

---

2   A good survey of the current UK scene and introduction to leasing is 'Recent developments in equipment leasing'. Bank of England Quarterly Bulletin, September 1982.

than by leasing. The lessor has the alternative of buying through a large wholesaler, arranging a service-contract, finding a second hand dealer to dispose of the asset.

Capital market imperfections are often implied as justification for leasing:

> The lessee may not have been able to raise the cash to buy the asset outright, OR he could only get the cash at a higher cost of capital than the lessor. Also a leasing contract finances 100% of the asset and is secured only on the asset.

The same argument applies in the capital market. The inability of a firm to finance an asset purchase at all, or to finance it on reasonable terms, may be due to capital market imperfections, or it may simply reflect the risk of the venture. In the latter case the rational lessor will 'cost' the capital involved in the lease at a rate appropriate to the riskiness of the lessee, rather than at his own marginal cost of capital. Anyhow the view that leasing is an easy way to get 100% financing of an asset, and that it leaves the gearing and borrowing power of the firm intact, does not take account of the mechanisms of an efficient capital market. Most leasing companies are subsidiaries of the big banks. The leasing company is likely to subject the lessee to just the same credit-review, and subsequent monitoring, as any other provider of finance would.

> Since leasing involves a source of finance and productive assets which do not appear on the balance sheet, it leaves a healthier balance sheet.

This raises the question of the accounting treatment of leases. Leasing is often argued in terms of its beneficial effect on the balance sheet. The equivalent asset-purchase financed by a loan will show a higher book value of assets, and so a lower return, and also higher apparent financial gearing. It is now required under SSAP 23 that UK companies 'capitalise' their leases in the balance sheet, that is, add the capital value of the leased assets to both the asset and the finance sides of the balance sheet. This should have the effect of improving the realism of measures such as the gearing ratio, which will go up, and the return on gross assets, which will decrease. But were readers of accounts fooled by non-disclosure of leases? They were already given a pointer that leases were lurking somewhere, because companies had to disclose hire charges. A full-blooded application of the 'efficient market' doctrine might suggest that all this extra disclosure is unnecessary since analysts can see through the 'veil of accounting practice' and accurately appraise the financial position of the firm whatever its accounting practices.

Leasing as project finance

Subjected to the hard logic of finance these non-tax arguments for leasing seem to lose some of their force. But we still need to explain the fact that leasing activity has also grown rapidly even in countries without the favourable tax conditions the UK has had; and it may well be that product- and capital-market imperfections are an important factor in practice. We can suggest another reason for leasing that also fits ill with our usual approach to financial decision-making. The models of MM and Miller showed that a company's financing and investment decisions are quite independent of each other, under certain assumptions. When we relax these assumptions we see financing and investment as interrelating with the cost of capital as the messenger, but even so we tend to treat them as sequential – the company raises a branch of capital, and the cost of capital then serves as a cut-off rate for investment decisions. However, particularly in small and medium-sized firms, but sometimes in the largest firms too, managers tend to think in terms of *project finance*. In other words they identify a project or asset for investment, then go and raise the funds specifically to finance it. Firms like this may be investment rather than finance oriented, and may not feel they have the skills or time required for a sophisticated search for financing. Leasing offers an exceptionally convenient way of raising project finance. One important reason, that even in larger firms with conventional financing operations we find managers leasing, is that it can provide a convenient way round head office limits on capital expenditure.

III   DEBTOR AND CREDITOR STRATEGIES

There are other financial strategies that are debt financing in disguise. In leasing some of the fixed assets one firm uses are owned by someone else. Many firms do something similar with their debtors by *factoring* or *invoice discounting*.

In its excellent businessman's guide to financing, the Bank of England describes factoring as follows:

> Factoring is a continuing arrangement by which the factoring company purchases all the trade debts due to a business as they arise, providing a sales ledger accounting service and relieving the businessman of debt-collection, and in this way providing cash for his day-to-day needs. Early payment by the factor to the supplier of a substantial percentage of the value of his trade debts reduces his need to extend trade credit to his customers from his own resources. The factor may provide funds either by making cash payments of up to 80% of the value of each new sales invoice raised (the balance, less charges, being paid on the date the invoice is settled), or by paying 100% less charges, of the value of invoices at an agreed average maturity date.[3]

By factoring its debts the firm is doing two things. Firstly, it is buying certain services it would otherwise have to provide for itself.

The factor runs its debtor-ledger for it: keeps accounting records and pursues debtors for cash; and most factors will accept the risk of bad-debts on behalf of clients as well. The cost of the service is expressed as a percentage of the debts factored and depends on the services the factor is providing and, if he is insuring against bad debts, on the riskiness of the debts. Second, the firm is raising finance to the extent on the early payment it receives from the factor. The cost of the financing component is usually a little above bank overdraft rates. As with leasing, the main factoring houses tend to be subsidiaries of the large banks.

The firm can take the ledger management service of factoring without the financing. Conversely, if it has its own sales-ledger department but wants to raise finance on debtors it can use 'invoice discounting'. Institutions which provide this service are often factoring houses. They agree to buy the whole sales ledger, or just invoices relating to approved debtors, and the firm assigns these invoices to the discounting house in exchange for an agreed proportion of their value. The firm itself collects the debts in the normal way, and retains responsibility for bad debts, and when it receives the cash it reimburses the discounting house. Invoice discounting is a parallel system to the bill discounting which is long established in international trade and which we discussed in the previous chapter. Again the discount rate in these arrangements is closely related to the bank overdraft rate.

THE RATIONALE FOR FACTORING

It is rather harder to find a powerful rationale for factoring than it was for leasing. The decisive argument for leasing was a taxation one: by postponing tax payments lessor and lessee could jointly generate economic value at the expense of the Inland Revenue. But

---

3   From *Money for Business* Bank of England and City Communications Centre (4th edn 1983) pp 43–44.

there is no tax argument for factoring, so factoring has to justify itself in terms of exploiting market imperfections. The ledger-management service is likely to appeal to firms that are too small for it to be economic to have their own book-keeper and credit-controller, or are growing fast and want to avoid the disruption of reorganising the sales-ledger function. Otherwise we would not expect there to be much to choose between the firm running its own sales-ledger and paying another firm to run it. Insurance against bad debts might similarly be attractive to the firm which is too small to withstand the default of a major customer, though there are other ways the firm could insure itself against this.

On the financing side, we usually consider that capital market imperfections are more apparent than real. If the firm sees factoring or invoice discounting as an easier or cheaper source of finance, it is probably deluding itself. Factoring is essentially bank borrowing secured against particular assets, debts in this case. As we saw, most of the factoring houses are bank subsidiaries, and the cost of capital is closely related to the bank overdraft rate. The factoring house is likely to apply typical bank lending criteria in assessing the client. Like leasing, factoring is off-balance-sheet finance. But we would not expect the financial community to be misled by that. Aware that existing factoring agreements will reduce the potential security for further loans, borrowers commonly ask for full disclosure of existing agreements when assessing further loans.

When they are advertising their services factors tend to play-up two financing advantages. It is a 'flexible' source of finance, and it helps to avoid cash shortages. They emphasise that, being linked to turnover, the finance from factoring grows with the business. In practice the factoring agreement will often contain credit limits which the firm will need to negotiate periodically as debtors grow, so the difference with an overdraft may not be so great. In general we recommend the firm to ask two questions when it contemplates factoring. What am I getting that I could not get some other way? What is it costing me?

SQUEEZING DEBTORS, STRETCHING CREDITORS

The message of this chapter is that sometimes things that look like investment decisions are actually financing decisions. When we looked at working-capital investment in Chapter 23 we saw that it would pay the firm to make debtors pay as early as possible and to postpone paying creditors as long as possible. This is certainly true so long as these operations are costless and represent merely more efficient working capital management. But beyond a certain point real costs will set in, and with hindsight we can see what they are. Squeezing debtors and stretching creditors are effectively financing operations, and impose financing costs on outsiders. It is likely that eventually, and if they have the market power to do it, debtors and creditors will pass these costs back to the firm. Suppliers will ask a higher price for their goods and services and customers will want a discount for early payment. And as we see in Chapter 23, in terms of the equivalent loan, offering discounts for early payment can be very expensive finance.

IV SUMMARY

In this chapter we looked at some strategies that are debt-financing in disguise. The most important of these is leasing, which now accounts for a significant proportion of the new assets that firms acquire. There are two sorts of argument for leasing, one is that it confers tax advantages, the other is that it permits the firm to exploit market imperfections. Only the first is relevant to the analysis of leasing. In practice market imperfections are often more apparent than real, and when they do exist there are usually other ways in which they can be exploited.

Once we have examined leasing we can view arrangements such as factoring and invoice discounting with a fairly cool eye. They do not offer tax advantages, and the firm which uses them ought to think hard about the benefits they yield.

REFERENCES AND BIBLIOGRAPHY

Bank of England	*Money for Business* (4th Ed.) Bank of England and City Communications Centre, London.
Clark, T	*Leasing* (1978) McGraw-Hill, Maidenhead.
DeMetz, G L R	*Off Balance Sheet Finance* (1985) Graham & Trottman.
Edwards, J and Mayer, C	*Issues in Bank Taxation* (1983) Institute for Fiscal Studies, London.
Fawthrop, R A and Terry, B	'The Evaluation of an Integrated Investment and Lease-Finance Decision', Journal of Business Finance and Accounting, Autumn 1976, pp 79–111.
Franks, J R and Hodges, S D	'Valuation of Financial Lease Contracts: a Note', Journal of Finance, May 1978, pp 657–669.
Gordon, M J	'A General Solution to the Buy or Lease Decision: A Pedagogical Note', Journal of Finance, March 1974, pp 245–250.
Lewellen, W G, Long, M S and McConnell, J J	'Asset Leasing in Competitive Capital Markets', Journal of Finance, June 1976, pp 787–798.
Ma, R	'Comparative Analysis of Lease Evaluation Models: A Review Article', Accounting and Business Research, Spring 1981, pp 153–162.
Miller, M H and Upton, C W	'Leasing, Buying and the Cost of Capital Services', Journal of Finance, June 1976, pp 761–86.
Myers, S, Dill, D A and Bautista, A J	'Valuation of Financial Lease Contracts', Journal of Finance, June 1976, pp 799–819.

QUESTIONS

1 Assuming rational and fully-informed lessors and lessees, where does the mutual advantage in leasing come from? Why do textbooks treat leasing as a 'tax-induced' phenomenon?

2 Guest and Smith are considering whether to buy or lease their own lathe. If bought, it will cost £5,000 and qualify for a first-year allowance of 100%. It is expected to have a useful life of five years, and no terminal value. If leased, there will be five annual payments of £1,150, payable in advance and qualifying for tax relief. The rate of corporation tax is 40% and the firm has a one year lag in tax payments. The firm's marginal cost of borrowing is 8% before tax, and it uses an after tax discount rate of 12% for appraising risky projects.

Advise the firm, whether they should buy or lease, showing your calculations.

Suppose Guest and Smith are not in a tax-paying position in the first two years. Without calculating the outcome, set out the cash flows to show how this will affect the analysis.

3 Loose Ltd is wondering whether to lease or buy a new laser-printer. The printer costs £2,000 to buy. Alternatively it could be leased from Lois Leasing Ltd for four equal annual rentals payable in advance. The machine qualifies for a 50% first-year allowance and 25% writing down allowances subsequently. Lois is a full taxpayer, but Loose is non-taypaying for the first two years. The corporation tax rate is 40%. Loose's cost of borrowing is 10% and its cost of equity is 17%.

What is the minimum lease payments Lois would accept, and the maximum it would be worth Loose's while paying? Can you suggest a strategy that might improve the value of the lease to the two parties?

4 In 1984 the UK Chancellor announced the abolition of stock relief, the phased abolition of first year allowances, and a phased reduction in the corporation tax rate. What effect would you expect these changes to have had on the level of leasing activity in the short- and the long-term?

Part VI
Investment decisions in practice

CHAPTER 23

Investment in working capital

When we talk about working capital we are particularly concerned with three types of asset: cash, stocks and debtors. Why single out these assets from the general approach to investment decision-making we developed in the previous chapters? We do this because of the special features its *short-term* nature gives to working capital. Though firms tend to have a permanent need for balances of cash, stocks and debtors, the internal composition of these balances is constantly changing. On the one hand this reduces the risk associated with working capital investment decisions – they are relatively easy to change. But on the other hand it makes the task of managing working capital a continuous one that consumes a lot of finance-department time.

The chapter starts by considering the special characteristics of the working capital investment decision. It then examines in turn how the optimal balance can be determined for the main classes of working capital: STOCKS (Section II), DEBTORS (Section III), and CASH (Section IV).

Table I Summary balance-sheets of UK companies 1979 and 1982 (£mn)		
	1979	*1982*
Net fixed assets	89,859	140,265
Current assets		
Stocks and work-in-progress	63,334	75,191
Debtors and repayments	59,043	79,162
Investments	14,594	17,030
Cash	13,256	24,620
Sundry	157	182
Gross assets	240,243	336,450
Current liabilities		
Bank loans and overdrafts	25,457	35,391
Short-term loans	5,781	12,981
Creditors and amounts payable	68,207	96,975
Dividends	2,289	3,090
Taxation	6,558	9,355
Sundry	74	43
	(108,366)	(157,835)
NET ASSETS	£131,877	£178,615

Source: Business Monitor MA3

I　THE NATURE OF WORKING CAPITAL

We use the term 'working capital' to describe three types of asset:
1　STOCKS – balances of raw materials, partly completed work ('work-in-progress'), and finished goods.
2　DEBTORS less CREDITORS – amounts owned by customers and to suppliers.
3　CASH and SHORT-TERM INVESTMENTS.

The significance of these assets in the asset structure of firms can be gauged from Table I which shows the aggregate balance sheets of UK companies in 1982 and 1979. UK companies had £196 billion, or 58% of their gross assets, as current assets[1] of which 29% was balanced by creditors.

THE 'CASH CYCLE' AND THE NEED FOR WORKING CAPITAL

To see how working capital fits into the scheme of things we will consider the so-called 'cash-cycle' of the firm. The starting point and finishing point of economic activity is *cash*. We are leaving aside the cash the firm raises from outside financing, or spends on acquiring fixed assets and concentrating on the process of paying for raw materials, converting them into the finished product and finally recovering cash by selling the product. Figure I depicts this process and shows how the firm's need for working capital depends on the balance between its production period and payment lags.

In Figure I a firm acquires £X-worth of raw materials at time t_1. These spend some time

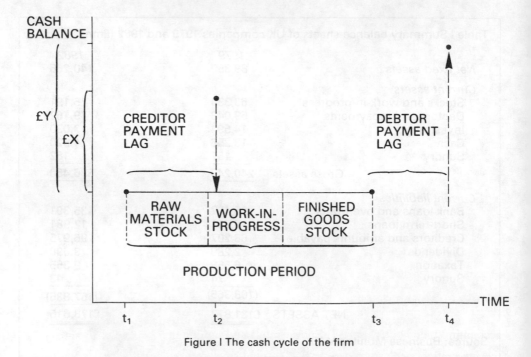

Figure I The cash cycle of the firm

1　Accountants usually define as 'current', any asset or liability which is liable to be liquidated within twelve months.

in raw materials stock, in work-in-progress, and finally in the finished goods stock, before being sold for £Y at t_3. However, there was a lag before the firm had to pay for its inputs, at t_2, but a corresponding lag before its own customers paid, at t_4. So, in this case, the firm had to finance working-capital to the tune of £X for the period $t_2 \rightarrow t_3$, and £Y for the period $t_3 \rightarrow t_4$. Hopefully, if the enterprise is profitable, Y is sufficiently larger than X to cover the cost of financing this investment and the other fixed costs of the firm.

Clearly, the working capital requirement is a function of the payment lags and production period. The task of the firm is to get the working capital requirement down to its optimum level by efficient management. But this optimum level will vary from firm to firm – the production period depending on technology, the payment lags on market conditions in input and output markets. To take two extreme examples, think of a supermarket and a whisky distillery.

In Figure II we depict an imaginary cash cycle for each of these. The supermarket sales are preponderantly for cash. They have no payment lag on outputs, but they are able to extract two months credit from their suppliers. Because shelf-life, which is the production period in the case of a supermarket, is on average three days, the supermarket has a negative working capital requirement – indeed it is able to use its negative net balance on these items to finance other assets. The whisky distillery on the other hand has normal payment lags on inputs and outputs, but keeps its finished product in stock for ten years.

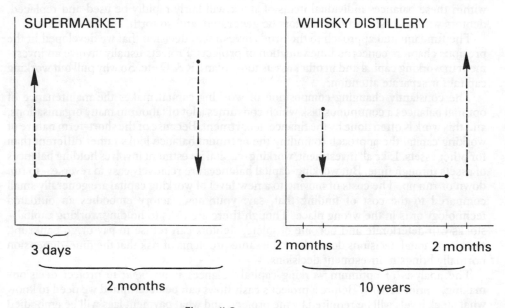

Figure II Some cash cycles

A note on working capital ratios

When they are examining the firm's working capital position, analysts commonly use accounting ratios of two sorts; turnover ratios and liquidity ratios. We encountered the turnover ratios, debtor turnover $= \dfrac{\text{debtors}}{\text{sales}}$, and stock turnover $= \dfrac{\text{stocks}}{\text{sales}}$, in Chapter 13. They relate the firm's investment in working capital to sales, and can signal the efficiency with which the firm is investing in debtors and stocks. The two common liquidity ratios are:

$$\text{current ratio} = \frac{\text{current assets}}{\text{current liabilities}}$$

$$\text{'quick ratio'} = \frac{\text{cash and liquid assets}}{\text{current liabilities}}$$

These ratios tend to be used to signal liquidity problems that could lead to insolvency, though as we see in Chapter 25 the prediction of failure is not so simple.

Making due allowance for the care needed in using accounting data, these ratios can tell us about trends in working capital efficiency, and applied to truly comparable firms, about relative performance. But as we saw the efficient levels of working capital depend very much on the particular firm's lag structure. There are no 'correct' values. The idea sometimes proposed that 2:1 is the right current ratio and 1:1 the right quick ratio has no foundation.

THE ANALYSIS OF WORKING CAPITAL

The characteristic of working capital which distinguishes it from other assets and liabilities of the firm is its short-term nature. The continued need for stocks, debtors and creditors, and cash means that the firm will permanently hold balances of these items, but within these balances individual items of stock will fairly rapidly be used and replaced, debtors will pay cash and new debtors be generated, and so forth.

The fundamental approach to the firm's investment decision that we developed in the previous chapters concerned the valuation of projects. Projects usually involve an investment in working capital and in other assets too – plant, R & D etc. So why pull out working capital for separate attention?

The constantly changing composition of working capital makes the maintenance of optimal balances a continuous task which consumes a lot of labour in many organisations, and this work is often done by the finance department. Because of the short-term nature of working capital the approach to finding the optimum balance looks rather different than for other assets. Like all investment, working-capital investment involves holding balances of assets through time. But working-capital balances are relatively easy to reverse – to run down or run up. The costs of moving to a new level of working capital are generally small compared to the cost of finding that, say, your new factory embodies an outdated technology or is in the wrong place. Though there are risks to holding working capital – stocks can deteriorate and become obsolete, debtors can refuse to pay or go bankrupt, working-capital decisions do not have the same problems of risk that the time-dimension normally brings to investment decisions.

The analysis of optimum working capital balances is an *input* to project decision-making, a prior activity. Before a project's cash flows can be determined we need to know what stock levels will be required by the project, and what payment lags will be embodied in the debtors and creditors generated by the project. In this respect the data on working capital requirements is no different from other technical data the project appraiser will collect from appropriate specialists when he is assembling the cash flows of a project. But though project appraisal is a vital activity, in most firms it consumes much less finance department time than the continuing task of managing the working capital investment generated by the firm's existing activities. It is this investment task we are looking at in this chapter.[2]

2   The reader who wishes to go into working-capital management in more depth can consult various texts, for example Mehta (1974).

The cost-benefit analysis

It is useful to distinguish two aspects of working-capital investment, the *investment decision* – the task of calculating the optimal balance of working capital, and the *control* task – the task of ensuring that actual balances are kept at optimal levels. In subsequent sections we review the decision-making and control of the three main types of working-capital in turn. In each case the optimal investment is found where the marginal cost of holding another unit just equals the marginal benefit.

The *costs* of holding working-capital are fairly straightforward to estimate: they are the financing and storage costs. The financing cost is the opportunity cost of the funds invested in working capital balances. The 'storage' costs include accounting costs, and in the case of stocks, physical storage costs such as warehousing and insurance.

In the main the firm's demand for working capital is a derived demand: stocks, debtors, and cash are all necessary to service the economic activity of the firm. If the firm did not carry balances of these items it would either have to secure the supply of the corresponding service some other way, incurring the cost of the alternative source of supply, or would have to curtail its economic activity, incurring the cost of the loss of contribution from the lost output. The firm would choose the least costly of these alternatives as an alternative to holding working-capital balances. Hence the *benefit* to holding working capital balances, which is the cost saved, is the lower of these two.

In the case of stocks, running lower stock levels means incurring the increased transactions costs of ordering more frequently. But lower stocks may also bring an attendant risk of running out of the input altogether, in which case the benefit of stock-holding is the avoided loss of contribution from curtailed sales. In the case of cash, lower cash balances will mean the firm must buy and sell securities more frequently. The costs of running out of cash altogether are hard to predict. They range from perhaps a slight loss of face with creditors, and the attendant cost of resorting to quick sources of finance, to the costs of complete liquidation of the firm at the other.

The provision of credit is tantamount to the payment of a subsidy to the customer, so the 'alternatives' to this service are, say, price reductions and discounts. If the firm curtails credit without offering any alternative incentive the cost will be, again, the loss of contribution from curtailed sales.

Sometimes the firm will find holding stocks a worthwhile project in itself. This will occur when, independent of the other activity of the firm, the act of holding yields a return which exceeds the carrying cost. In the case of stocks, this will happen if the firm expects input prices to rise sufficiently to justify early purchase.

Since Keynes[3] it is common to call the balances that firms hold to service their economic activity 'transactions balances' for anticipated needs, and 'precautionary balances' for balances held to cover unanticipated needs. Balances held to profit from price changes are known as 'speculative'.

Decision-making and control

Though it is analytically useful to distinguish decision-making and control tasks the two are often combined. The process of monitoring levels tends also to be the occasion for

3   Keynes suggested three motives for liquidity-preference amongst investors:
     'The three divisions of liquidity-preference . . . may be defined as depending on (i) the transactions-motive, i e the need of cash for the current transaction of personal and business exchanges; (ii) the precautionary-motive, i e the desire for security as to a future cash equivalent of a certain proportion of total resources; and (iii) the speculative motive, i e the object of securing profit from knowing better than the market what the future will bring forth.' (Keynes (1936) ch 13).

judgemental decision-making about what they should be. In the case of debtors, the firm may have a standard collection policy, say '30 days net' which might have been calculated in some optimising process or simply be convention. The implementation of this policy may differ from customer to customer depending on a fairly subtle judgement by the credit controller as to the costs and benefits of extending credit in each case, considering relative market power, the contribution generated by the sale, the value of the customer's goodwill now and in the future, and so forth.

The *costs* of holding working capital are still, essentially, and to summarize, they are the *holding* and *ordering* costs. The financing costs, the opportunity cost of the funds invested in working capital, always. The *storage* costs include economic of the cost of excess physical wastage such as we find in the oil business.

II   STOCKS

Stock management is essentially the production manager's concern. The finance manager's interest is simply that the stock balance which results is an investment that needs financing. In other words the finance manager should expect to be handed an optimal stock figure by the production manager. In this section we will only be looking at the simplest of stock-control models in order to get a view of the factors that influence the optimal investment in stocks. Another motive for looking at a simple stock-management model here is that it provides a useful comparison when we come to analyse the optimisation of cash and debtor balances – tasks which do tend to fall on the finance manager's desk.

THE TRANSACTIONS BALANCE

Firms hold balances of raw materials, work-in-progress and finished goods, but we will restrict our analysis to raw materials stocks. The first question to ask is why do firms hold stocks of raw materials at all? After all we can conceive of running a business without stocks of raw materials. You find this behaviour in everyday life – for example in the jobbing builder who sizes up the day's work each morning then spends the next two hours touring round buying the necessary pound of nails or half bag of cement. This behaviour may seem rather eccentric to outsiders but presumably indicates that he puts a lower valuation on the cost of acquiring supplies than he does on the cost of carrying stocks.

We can develop the logic of this trade-off between the costs of *acquiring* and the costs of *holding* in a simple model.

The EOQ model

Assuming the following:
1 A firm has a steady and known demand of S units each period for a particular input.
2 The firm consumes the input at a uniform rate.
3 The costs of carrying stocks are a constant amount, C, per unit per period.
4 The costs of ordering more inputs are a fixed amount, O, per order. Orders are delivered instantly.

If the firm replenishes its stocks periodically by placing an order for Q units when stocks are exhausted, its stock-holding through time will follow the 'saw-tooth' pattern in Figure III.

Clearly the average balance is $Q/2$, so we can find the optimal balance in terms of the recorder quantity Q. Hence this model is sometimes known as the *economic order quantity*, 'EOQ', model.

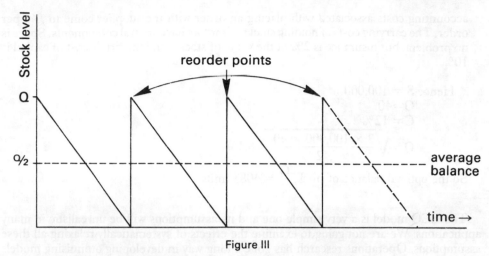

Figure III

The total stock-carrying cost for this firm per period is $C.\dfrac{Q}{2}$, the average stock times the cost per unit. The total ordering costs are $\dfrac{O.S}{Q}$, the cost per order, O, times the number of orders in the period, $\dfrac{S}{Q}$.

So we can define total period stock costs, T, as

(1) $T = \dfrac{CQ}{2} + \dfrac{OS}{Q}$

From this the order quantity, Q, which minimises stock costs, T, emerges[4] as

(2) $Q = \sqrt{\dfrac{2SO}{C}}$

To show how we might use this formula, consider a firm which uses 10,000 electric motors per annum in making washing machines. The motors cost £20 each. The

4   PROOF: Differentiating T with respect to Q in (1) and setting to zero,

$\dfrac{\delta T}{\delta Q} = \dfrac{C}{2} - \dfrac{OS}{Q^2} = 0$

rearranging, and solving for Q

$Q^2 = \dfrac{2SO}{C}$

$Q = \sqrt{\dfrac{2SO}{C}}$

Testing for a minimum:

$\dfrac{\delta^2 T}{\delta\delta Q^2} = + \dfrac{2OS}{Q^3}$, which is +ve, for +ve O, S, Q.

accounting costs associated with placing an order with the supplier come to £40 per order. The carrying costs of holding stocks of motors have several components. Space is no problem, but insurance is 2% of the value of stocks, and the firm's cost of capital is 10%

Hence $S = 100,000$
$$O = 40$$
$$C = 12\%$$
$$Q = \sqrt{\frac{2 \times 100,000 \times 40}{.12}} = 8,165$$

So the optimal balance of stock, $\frac{Q}{2} = 4083$ units.

The ECQ model is a very simple one and its assumptions will be unrealistic in many applications. We are not going to examine the effects of systematically relaxing all these assumptions. Operations research has gone a long way in developing otpimising models for stock which work well in complex real applications. However, it is useful for our purposes to develop one or two of the assumptions further.

The EOQ model assumed that the demand for the input was steady and known and that orders were delivered instantly. In practice orders are not delivered instantly, so we will assume in addition that there is a known lag between order and delivery. Now, the problem is merely one of working out what stock level is observed the period of the delivery lag prior to being out of stock, and ordering at that level, as Figure IV shows.

Storemen, shopkeepers and the like often put a marker on appropriate numbers of items from the bottom of the bin, or from the back of the shelf, to signal reorder. The re-order slip in a cheque book serves the same purpose.

We are still assuming that the moment before the economic order quantity is delivered the firm entirely exhausts its previous stock. But in practice, the firm is likely to hold a 'precautionary balance' as well.

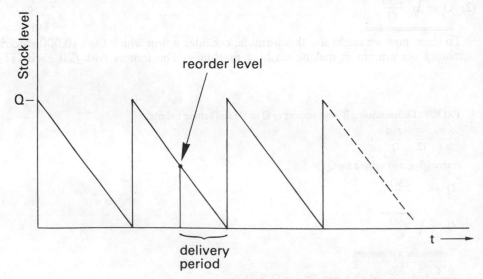

Figure IV

THE PRECAUTIONARY BALANCE

The firm may hold a precautionary balance of stock if it is uncertain about future demand and supply conditions – it may want to keep some raw material in reserve in case of an unexpected order, and it may be uncertain about supply of the raw material itself and seek to cover unexpected holdups in supply. Neither of these problems would arise if there was instantaneous delivery so that inputs could be got as and when they were needed.

Suppose the smooth consumption and replenishment pattern of Figure IV represented the firm's expectation, but that it also holds a safety stock, X, against contingencies. Figure V depicts this, and also shows two unexpected events which would otherwise have led the firm to be out-of-stock. At A the supplier delivered his usual quantity, Q, but a week late. At B an unexpected demand for the input depleted stocks and they had to be replenished in the next order.

In Figure V the safety stock comfortably accommodates these contingencies, but safety stocks are expensive to hold and the optimal safety stock will be one which still permits the firm to go out-of-stock on occasion. How is the optimal safety stock determined? The firm must balance the carrying-cost with the benefits of holding a safety stock, which are avoided costs of going out of stock. So the firm should increase its safety stock until at the margin the carrying costs of another unit of stock equal the expected 'stock-out' costs avoided. Alternatively we can say:

The optimal safety stock minimises the sum of safety stock carrying costs and expected out-of-stock costs.

Consider an example:

In Table II we show some of the relevant data for calculating the optimal precautionary balance of screw shafts the Archimedes Pump Co. should keep. For each level of safety stock under review we calculate the carrying cost and the expected out-of-stock cost. The carrying cost is the firm's cost of capital, 10%, plus 2% which is the estimated storage and insurance cost, times the value of the extra stock. Screw-shafts cost £1,000 each so the carrying cost is £1,000 × 12% = £120 per unit per annum. The costs of being out-of-stock are by definition uncertain. They consist of the combined probabili-

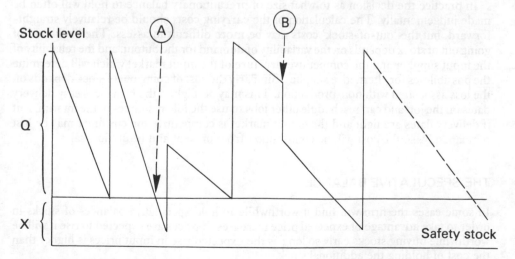

Figure V

ties of being out-of-stock by various amounts times the costs associated with those
levels of 'stock out'. Archimedes estimates that without any safety stock at all it will run
out of stock with the following frequencies:

Extent of	*Probability*
stockout (units)	*of occurrence*
10	.30
20	.05
30	.02

These are the occasions when demand for a screw shaft will exceed the transactions
balance the firm holds. Each time Archimedes finds itself short of a shaft it estimates it
incurrs extra costs of £400. Combining this information is Table II we can see that
Archimedes should hold a safety stock of 10 shafts: this is the lowest cost position.

Table II

Safety stock ⒶA	Carrying cost (£) @ £150 ⒷB	Out of stock = excess demand – Ⓐ	Probability	Expected cost (£) ⒸC	TOTAL COST
0	0	10	.30	1200 ⎫	
		20	.05	400 ⎬ 1840	1840
		30	.02	240 ⎭	
10	1200	10	.05	200 ⎫	
		20	.02	160 ⎭ 360	1560
20	2400	10	.02	80	2480
30	3600	0	0	0	3600

In practice the decision as to what size of precautionary balance to hold will often be
made judgementally. The calculation of the carrying costs should be relatively straightforward, but the 'out-of-stock' costs may be more difficult to assess. The likelihood of
going out of stock depends on the variability of demand for the output, and the reliability of
the input supplier and the competitive structure of the input market which will determine
the possibilities for alternative supplies. Similarly the cost of going out of stock depends on
the loss associated with non-production. This may be slight if the firm faces easy delivery
dates on the job and can reschedule other jobs to use the idle resources in the interim. But
if delivery dates are tight and the output market is competitive the customer may be lost
permanently, so the cost will be contribution from present and future lost sales.

THE SPECULATIVE BALANCE

In some cases the firm will find it worthwhile to hold speculative balances of stocks in
order to take advantage of expected price increases. If prices are expected to rise it will be
worthwhile buying stocks early so long as the expected rise in input prices is higher than
the cost of holding the additional stock.

At first glance we might expect this to occur approximately half of the time. After all, the major component in holding costs is the cost of capital, and the major component of nominal interest rates is the expected general inflation rate – yet this rate is a composite of specific rates which will lie equally above and below the average. In reality though the odds are more heavily loaded against speculative balances. In general we expect interest rates to contain a positive real component over and above the expected general rise in prices, and on top of that the firm will have to pay a positive risk premium to finance a project such as speculative investment in stocks. Further, the cost of carrying stocks contains items such as storage and insurance. Figure VI is a pictorial representation of all this. In it we assume (arbitrarily) that the specific inflation rates for commodities in the economy are normally-distributed. We can see that only if the expected inflation rate on a commodity is in the shaded area, A, will it be worthwhile holding speculative balances of stock.

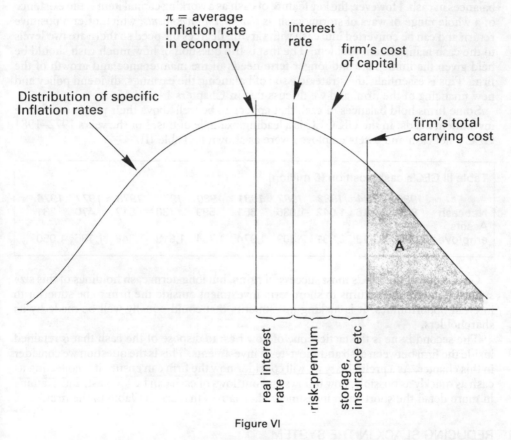

Figure VI

Moreover, in an efficient market the market process will work to eliminate the potential for speculative gains. If the market shares the firm's expectations about inflation the current price of the input will be bid up until no potential exists for speculative gains – that is, until no firm has a total carrying cost less than the expected rate of future inflation. In such a world there will only be speculative behaviour when a firm feels it can 'outguess' the market.

We have talked about advance purchase as speculative behaviour. But there is no reason why the firm should restrict its speculative purchases to its production needs or indeed to the commodities it happens to use. This brings us into the area of 'futures' trading. In practice firms do engage in futures trading though usually restricted to commodities they know well.

III   CASH AND SHORT-TERM INVESTMENTS

Firms need to have cash available to meet their liabilities – payments to suppliers, wages, taxation etc – when they fall due and to pay for the replacement and expansion of the assets of the firm. Some of these payments will be anticipated and some unanticipated. Receipts of cash – from trading, from selling assets, from raising new finance – will be in part unpredictable too. The firm will want to hold transactions balances and precautionary balances of cash. However, the key feature of cash as a working capital item is the existence of a whole range of ways of storing cash as *short-term investments*, which offer a positiive return and can be converted into cash with varying degrees of speed so there are two levels to the cash management problem. The first is the question of how much cash should be held given the immediate and longer term needs of the maintenance and growth of the firm. This is essentially the strategic issue of balancing the earnings, dividend policy and new financing of the firm, and we discuss this in Chapters 14 and 15.

Some firms hold balances of cash that appear to be well above their present or future investment needs. In the UK GEC is a leading example of this. For the years 1972–1981 GEC's net cash and assets employed were as shown in Table III.

Table III GEC's cash position (£ million)									
	1985	1984	1983	1982	1981	1980	1979	1978	1977	1976
Net cash	879	1,116	1,042	1,036	661	599	730	617	470	231
Assets employed	3,096	3,113	2,881	2,309	1,974	1,754	1,613	1,346	1,185	1,050

GEC is one of the UK's most successful firms, but long-term cash holdings of this size suggest it judges the returns to short-term investment outside the firm to be superior to internal opportunities. It is making investments that could equally well be made by its shareholders.

The second issue is the tactical one of how best to dispose of the cash that *is* retained inside the firm between cash and short-term investments. This is the question we consider in this chapter. As a preliminary we will consider how the firm can ensure it is collecting its cash as quickly as possible, how inflows and outflows of cash can be forecast, and examine in more detail the short-term investment alternatives that are available to the firm.

REDUCING SLACK IN THE SYSTEM

Before the firm considers how best to deploy its cash it should ensure it is collecting cash as effectively as possible. Of course, all the firm's activities are directed towards the generation of cash, but we are thinking particularly of the final stage in the process, between the issue of a cheque by the debtor and its crediting to the firm's bank account. By this stage all the problems of producing and supplying a satisfactory product and getting the customer to pay for it are over, and it is in the firm's interests to get hold of the cash as quickly as possible. There are three stages in the process:

  1 the cheque is in the post

2 the cheque is received but waiting to be paid into the bank

3 the bank is 'clearing' the cheque.

2 and 3 are commonly known as the 'float' stage. There is not much the firm can do about the time it takes banks to clear cheques – this is an institutional fact about banks. But it may be able to speed the other two stages. In the US many firms attack 1 and 2 by operating a *lock-box* system. In a lock-box system customers mail cheques to a regional collection box in a bank branch. The box is opened each day by the bank and the account credited. This way postal delays are reduced by regional mailing, and 'paying in' delays are eliminated because the cheques are already in the bank. In the UK though, perhaps because of the smaller distances involved lock-boxes do not seem to have become popular.

The most useful thing a firm can do is to tighten up stage 2 of the process, and make sure that cash is paid into the bank as soon as possible. The firm should consider daily banking, and if the receipt of cash is decentralised – if cash is collected by local offices or salesmen for example – arrangements should be made for cash to be paid in to local banks each day. There are costs associated with increasing the frequency of banking, largely the costs of clerical time, and the firm should calculate if the interest saving merits these costs. The best solution is to encourage customers to pay direct into your bank by making a bank giro transfer, thus avoiding stages 1 and 2 entirely. This might appeal to customers since it is a much more economical method of payment in terms of clerical effort if there is some volume of transactions, though the increased speed of clearance brings an interest cost to the customer.

In terms of strict logical symmetry we should be recommending the firm to do all it can to *increase* the slack on the payments side just as it seeks to reduce it for receipts. By increasing its creditors' float it will save interest charges. Of course, firms can stoop to all sorts of chicanery, particularly when they are in financial difficulties, to slow down payments to creditors. But as a general rule, though firms will take as much credit as they can from creditors, once they have decided to pay they do so promptly.

Cash forecasting

A necessary preliminary to cash management is a careful forecast of receipts and payments of cash. The more confident the firm can be about future cash balances the less it will need to invest in costly precautionary balances. Interest rates tend to be positively associated with the 'term' of the investment so the further ahead the firm can anticipate its cash balance the more cash it can store in higher yielding investments.

The cash forecast is a task for the accountant. In Chapter 10 we saw that some accounting numbers, notably profits, are remarkably difficult to forecast. Research has shown that the time series properties of profit approximates a 'random walk'. This problem may be less severe in cash forecasting. Cash forecasts are usually relatively short-term and hence are more likely to embody cash flows about which the firm can be fairly confident and which may reflect contractual commitments that already exist or are expected to be made fairly soon. How far ahead should cash be forecast? Management will need to judge the tradeoff between the usefulness and the increasing unreliability of longer forecasts.

WAYS OF STORING CASH

Instead of holding cash in a current account offering zero return, there is a variety of alternative investments available to the firm offering different returns and different *degrees of liquidity*. By 'degree of liquidity' we refer to the speed with which an asset can be converted into cash, and our general expectation is that the more illiquid an investment the higher its return. It is important to note that the 'liquidity' of a security is not the same as its 'term'. So long as a market exists for a security, it represents a highly liquid investment whatever its term. Hence 'Treasury 12%, 1987' bonds can be sold tomorrow on The Stock Exchange and cash received at the end of the account a few days later. However, marketability also introduces uncertainty into the outcome. If you hold a bond until redemption the cash you will receive is known with certainty from the outset but the intermediate market price of the bond will fluctuate as interest rates change. If the short-term investment is a company share, which is effectively an irredeemable investment, the firm can have no certainty as to the cash that will be realised when it is sold. In the latter case we would recomend the firm to reduce the risk associated with its position in company shares by diversification. These are some of the common short-term investments for firms:

Bank deposits

The most popular destination for spare cash is a deposit account at a bank. This can be the firm's own clearing bank which offers the advantage of quick and economical transfer of funds from and to current account, or some other banking institution such as a merchant bank, overseas bank, acceptance or finance house. All of these will take short term deposits from firms, though we can expect the rate they pay to be slightly less than on less liquid investments.

Certificates of deposit

Certificates of deposit are written acknowledgements of deposits issued by banks. They are associated with longer-term deposits which tend to be between three months and five years, but they offer an accordingly higher return, and are negotiable.

Public sector securities

Public sector securities are government or local authority bonds. Local authority bonds tend to have a term of up to five years, government bonds are available in any term up to irredeemable. More relevant than their term, though, is their marketability. Government

Table IV Selected current assets of large industrial and commercial companies, at the end of 1st quarter 1985

	£mn
Bank deposits*	10,960
Other commercial paper and company loans	882
Negotiable certificates of deposit	623
British government securities	1,649
Local authority securities	395
Overseas assets	970
Tax instruments	2,218
Notes, coins and treasury bills	609
TOTAL	£18,306 million

*including loans to licensed deposit takers
Source: CSO, Financial Statistics, HMSO

bonds are saleable on the stock market, but the market for local authority bonds may be much smaller.

Company securities

Company securities are shares and debentures in other companies. If these securities are quoted there will be a ready market for them.

We can see how the larger UK industrial and commercial companies dispose their current assets in Table IV.

MODEL-BUILDING APPROACHES TO CASH MANAGEMENT

The 'EOQ' model

Suppose (1) a firm's consumption of cash follows the 'sawtooth' pattern, ie cash is consumed at a constant rate and is replenished occasionally by the injection of a fixed amount of cash from deposit or the sale of securities, (2) we can calculate a percentage 'carrying cost' per period for cash, and (3) there is a fixed cost of replenishing cash. In this case we can use the EOQ stock control model to find the optimum balance.[5]

If, S = total requirement for cash in the period
  O = fixed transactions cost associated with liquidating deposits or selling securities to raise cash
  C = holding cost of cash, ie the interest foregone on deposits or marketable securities
  Q = optimal quantity of cash to raise at a time
then we know that

$$Q = \sqrt{\frac{2S0}{C}}$$

If a firm expects to disburse £800,000 of cash in the year, sales of securites cost £50 to effect, and the return on securities is 15%, then

D = 800,000
K = 50
r = .15

$$Q = \sqrt{\frac{2 \times 50 \times 800,000}{.15}} \approx £23,100$$

Hence the firm should sell securities in lots of £23,100. This implies an average cash balance of $\frac{£23,000}{2} = £11,550$, and suggests that cash will be replenished $\frac{800,000}{23,100} = 35$ times per year.

In reality the cost of replenishing cash has a fixed component – the managerial effort involved and any fixed charge by the bank or broker – but if securities are sold there will also be a variable cost of brokerage which will be a decreasing proportion of the quantity transferred. But the real limitation of the EOQ model is its assumption of certainty and constancy in future cash flows. The EOQ model best describes a situation like the one facing the student who pays his grant into the building society at the beginning of the term,

5   This application of the EOQ model was first suggested by Baumol (1952).

then has to decide how often to go and draw it to pay his weekly rent, food and spending money. His carrying cost is the interest he loses, and he can minimise this by increasing the frequency of his trips to the building society. But the transactions cost for him is the effort of going there.

The 'Miller-Orr' model

Miller and Orr[6] developed a cash management model for use in the situation where the firm's inflows and outflows of cash are unpredictable. They derive a formula to calculate upper and lower 'control limits' for cash. These limits indicate the optimal cash levels at which to buy and sell securities, to reduce and replenish cash respetively. Figure VII shows the operation of control limits.

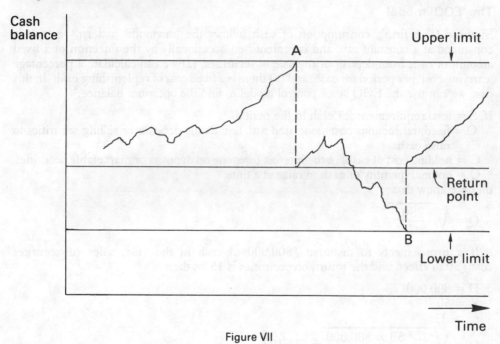

Figure VII

A sustained inflow of cash brings the firm to A (see Figure VII), which is the level of cash at which it is appropriate to buy securities and reduce the cash balance. At B, on the other hand, the firm sells securities to replenish cash.

To implement the Miller-Orr model in practice we take the following steps:
1 Choose the lower limit, which is the precautionary balance – the minimum cash balance the firm can accept.
2 Find the upper limit. Miller and Orr provide a formula for the interval between the limits:

$$\text{interval} = 3 \left(\frac{3}{4} \frac{\text{transaction cost} \times \text{variance of daily cash flows}}{\text{interest rate per day}} \right)^{1/3}$$

6   The initial model is presented in Miller and Orr (1966). Miller and Orr (1968) extend the model to handle long-term and short-term securities.

The interval is an increasing function of the transactions cost, and a decreasing function of the interest rate. The wider the interval the less frequent are security transactions and the higher the average balance of cash. Hence, the Miller-Orr model is consistent with the EOQ model in this respect. However, Miller-Orr also show that the interval is an increasing function of the variance of the cash flows of the firm, which implicitly measures the likelihood of cash flows restoring themselves without the need for costly security transactions.

3 Find the 'return point' which is one third the way up from the lower limit:

$$\text{Return point} = \text{lower limit} + \frac{\text{interval}}{3}$$

Consider an example:

A firm can buy or sell securities at a fixed cost of £30, and gets a daily return of .05% on those securities. It sets out to estimate its control limits as follows:

1 The firm chooses a lower limit of £2,000.
2 The interval between upper or lower limits can be calculated once the variance of daily cash flows is ascertained. A sample of daily cash flows is analysed and found to have a variance of £1,000,000 (standard deviation of £1,000).

$$\text{So interval} = 3 \left(\sqrt[3]{\frac{3}{4}\frac{30 \times 1,000,000}{.05}} \right)$$

$$= £2,298$$

Hence the upper limit is £2,000 + £2,298 = £4,298

3 The return point is:

£2,000 + £2,298 = £2,766.

CASH MANAGEMENT IN PRACTICE

Researchers have tested to see whether cash management models such as 'Miller-Orr' are valuable in practice. On the whole the answer seems to be that in many cases they do not offer significant advantages over the experienced manager guided by rules of thumb and judgement[7]. However, a study of cash management models can guide managers in developing their judgement.

In practice we can recommend certain steps to the manager:

1 Eliminate any slack or inefficiency in the collections system. In other words reduce the 'float' to a minimum.
2 Ensure the accounting section is producing regular cash forecasts and assess their reliability by comparing past forecasts to outcome.
3 Generate a 'list' of the alternative short-term investments that are available to the firm, in terms of return and liquidity.
4 Minimise the 'precautionary' balance. Other things being equal the more confidence you have in your cash forecast, the lower the precautionary balance you need, and similarly a store of cash in short-term investments that are highly liquid will reduce the importance of holding idle cash.
5 Make full use of the deposit account at the bank. In both the 'EOQ' and the 'Miller-

---

7 See, for example, Daellenbach (1974). Mullins and Homonoff (1976) provide a review of these tests. See also Budin and Van Handel (1975).

Orr' models the average balance is an increasing function of transactions costs. The transactions costs associated with transferring from and to deposit accounts are usually negligible and both models correctly predict that in this case the rational firm will run very small transactions balances. In practice many firms respond in just this way – investing their surplus each evening on 'overnight' deposit. By doing this the firm can retain a high level of liquidity at a positive return, and the task of cash management is then to seek securities that offer a higher return and trade this off against the sacrifice of liquidity.

We have talked so far as though firms all have positive cash balances. In reality a great many firms run on overdraft either through choice or necessity, and others, often multidivisional firms, run overdrafts in some divisions and surpluses in others. If the bank is prepared to provide overdraft finance it becomes a matter of relative costs whether the firm decides to hold a cash balance which is always positive, always negative or somewhere in between. We consider the question of the inclusion of bank borrowing in the capital structure of the firm in a subsequent chapter. The point to note is that even with negative cash balances much of what we have said about cash management carries through. Now, the firm's transactions and precautionary balances measure the leeway it will seek to keep above its overdraft limit. It is feasible that the firm would want to invest in securities with cash raised on overdraft, though the relative returns and costs involved make this unlikely.

IV DEBTORS[8]

Debtor balances are amounts owed by customers who have received delivery but have yet to pay. Whether or not sales are made on credit depends on the nature of the business – for example retail stores may sell predominantly for cash, whereas a manufacturer of inter-mediate goods such as vehicle components might have no cash sales. In some businesses the product is largely paid for before it is delivered: in industries such as construction the product is specially ordered and takes some time to manufacture. In this case the customer defrays some of the manufacturer's stock-carrying cost by making payments on-account.

Similarly the period of credit varies from one trade to another – the period of credit allowed tends to be conventional and an individual firm's ability to offer terms other than the ones that are customary in the trade is dependent on the structure of the market in which it is selling.

The debtor balance is determined by the number of customers the firm allows credit to, and the length of credit it allows. In principle the credit decision is the same as any other working-capital decision: the firm should extend credit just so far as the marginal benefit exceeds the marginal cost.

The cost of extending credit has two components. There is a carrying cost – the cost of capital plus the administrative costs associated with credit decision-making and with controlling outstanding debtors. There is also a cost associated with the risk of default – a certain proportion of debtors will never pay, and will become 'bad debts'. The benefit of extending credit – the cost of not extending it – is the additional contribution that results from increased sales.

8　Cole (1972) provides a good introduction to this topic. See also Bierman and Hausman (1970) and Atkins (1978).

THE BENEFITS OF CREDIT

Firms offer longer credit to customers in the hope of attracting more business. The benefit is the contribution from that increased turnover. But forecasting the outcome of a given change in credit policy is no easy matter since it is rather hard to know how existing and potential customers will react. This very much depends on the structure of the market in which the firm is selling.

Though it often falls the lot of the finance section to make the credit decision, credit is as much a marketing decision and should be taken in full consultation with the marketing department. If the product is highly differentiated and competition is weak the firm can offer less credit than when the market is highly competitive. On the other hand if the market is competitive any credit concession will fairly quickly be matched by competitors, and the benefit annulled. The ability of the firm to enforce the credit policy it has chosen on its customers depends very much on the same factors – it will depend on relative market power.

Much the same calculus applies to the decision on when to pay suppliers. Hence we tend to find that the larger manufacturer extracts lengthy credit from its suppliers, particularly those which depend on it for a significant proportion of their sales, yet will be 'firm' with its own customers particularly smaller ones.

The individual consumer is in the same position. If we are unfortunate enough to get the bill for the rates and the telephone on the same day, there is a good chance we will pay the telephone first. Both suppliers are monopolists in their market, but the telephone company can and will curtail supplies very quickly if the bill is not paid, while the local authority is not in the same position and must resort to enforcing its claim through the courts, which is a lengthy and expensive remedy.

Davis and Yeomans (1974) studied the effects of firm size on credit terms. They found that when money was 'tight' in the economy and interest rates rose, there was a shift in the balance of credit terms with larger firms exacting more credit from smaller firms. This is consistent with our analysis. As the cost of borrowing rises, all firms will seek to reduce their debtor balances and increase their credit balances, other things being equal. But the costs of doing this are likely to be higher for the small firm, their relatively weaker market power means that they are more likely to lose customers and suppliers than the larger firm. In short, the effects of a credit policy change depend on market conditions and the responses of competitors. A major drawback of credit policy as an instrument for increasing sales is that the more generous credit terms may have to be extended to existing customers, incurring extra costs for no gain.

ALTERNATIVE MARKETING STRATEGIES

Credit-period is an aspect of price since, if the customer has a positive cost of capital, extending his credit is tantamount to giving him a price discount. We call the overall package of attributes a product possesses, which determine its market appeal, its 'marketing mix'. The marketing mix includes aspects of the product such as its price, quality, packaging, advertising, distribution system and so forth. Therefore, a change in credit policy should only be made if it is more profitable than any of the alternative marketing policies the firm could adopt – increased advertising, a change in the product or the package, a price reduction etc. All of these should be appraised and quantified.

Discounts

One alternative which is sometimes offered to customers instead of extended credit is a discount for early payment. Hence the terms of sale might be '3/10 net 30' – if the customer pays in ten days he can deduct 3%, otherwise the normal credit interval of thirty days applies.

It is important to know the implicit cost of making an offer like this. If the offer has induced customers to pay in 10 instead of 30 days the supplier gets 20 days usage of cash for an extra 3%. This is equivalent to an annual cost of capital of $3\% \times \frac{365}{20} = 55\%$.

However, what matters is when customers *would have* paid. If customers were in the habit of taking 60 days credit rather than the theoretical 30 then the cost is $3\% \times \frac{365}{50} = 21\%$. If the discount is viewed merely as a payment-hastening device then rates like this, assuming they are higher than the firm's cost of capital, will be prohibitive. But if the offer of a discount is seen as an alternative marketing policy which might yield extra sales the cost may be worthwhile.

There are problems associated with using discounts for early payment. One is that many customers with computerised payments systems on a monthly cycle are not geared to taking advantage of them without using a more costly alternative payments procedure. Another is the problem of what to do with the customer who takes the discount then pays at his usual time. It may be unjustifiably expensive to pursue the balance of the cash.

THE COST OF CREDIT

The carrying cost   The carrying cost of extending credit is relatively straightforward – it is the financing cost and the administrative cost associated with the increase in debtor balance. The financing cost is the firm's cost of capital, the accounting and clerical costs are the *incremental* accounting and clerical costs associated with running increased debtors.[9]

Suppose the Aristotle Manufacturing Co is trying to calculate the cost of a policy which would increase debtors by £1 million. Aristotle's cost of capital is 12% and its extra annual administrative cost tends to be 3% of any additional debtor balance. Hence the CARRYING COST of the new policy is £1 million × 15% = £150,000 per annum.

THE RISKS OF CREDIT

Wherever sales are made on credit there is a risk that the goods or services will be delivered but the customer will not pay. Customers fail to pay for various reasons, some good, some bad. Sometimes there is a valid dispute about the quality of the product which would have perhaps led to a refund even if the goods had been bought for cash. In other cases, though, the customer either cynically refuses to pay, or goes into liquidation. There are remedies in law for a cynical refusal to pay, but these are expensive and time consuming.

The risk of non-payment is relevant in two ways to the credit decision. First, the firm

9   Not the departmental costs allocated on what accountants call a 'full-cost basis – i e total departmental costs times the proportion of new debtors to total debtors – since this may be significantly misleading if departmental costs are part-fixed, part-variable.

should expect that a percentage of its new debtors will fail to pay. The prevalence of non-payment will depend very much on the nature of the business, and the firm should estimate the non-payment rate from its previous experience. Second, though, if the change in credit policy is to generate increased sales it is likely to involve new credit customers with the attendant danger that these will be more risky than the existent customers. Indeed the firm may consciously decide to extend credit to higher risk customers in order to generate sales.

This raises the question of how the credit risk of a customer can be assessed. Firms may use a variety of sources of information to help form expectations about the default risk of a customer. They ask for bank and credit references to see if the customer has managed to achieve a successful trading relationship with its bank and with other suppliers. They try to gauge the reputation of the customer by enquiries in the trade. They make enquiries of one of the credit rating agencies who specialise in the collection and analysis of data on the credit-worthiness of firms. They may insist that earlier sales are paid cash-before-delivery or on-delivery, before a credit relationship is established.

The problem is that enquiries about a customer's past performance as a debtor will assist in judging the 'moral hazard' and will help eliminate the unscrupulous or fly-by-night customer, but they will not tell you much about the risk of the customer going into liquidation in the future. Our inability to know what will happen in the future is the central problem in finance and it poses a problem in making the credit decision. Traditionally people have tried to assess the risk of liquidation by combining the sort of enquiries we mentioned above with a ratio analysis of the customer's accounts. However there is no clear link between this sort of analysis of the past and the probability of future liquidation – especially if liquidation is to be anticipated sufficiently far in advance usefully to warn the potential supplier. Increasingly, the credit analyst has access to statistical techniques such as multiple discriminant analysis to assemble and analyse the predictive evidence. We examine the prediction of liquidation and the interpretation of the so-called 'Z-scores' generated by multiple discriminant analysis in some detail in Chapter 25.[10]

Separation of decision-making and control

In theory the decision-making and control aspects of debtors can be separated – the company's credit policy can be determined centrally and applied to the individual debtor accounts by clerks in the credit control department. In practice though the separation is not usually so easy. Though the firm will have a standard credit policy, it may well apply it with different degrees of flexibility to different customers. This is almost inevitable since we saw that the benefits of credit vary according to the market conditions. So, for example, the firm may decide to allow more credit to larger customers, or customers for products with easily available alternative sources of supply. These decisions tend to be made customer by customer on the basis of the credit controller's experience and judgement, preferably in discussion with the marketing department.

Creditors

The firm's position vis-a-vis its creditors is a mirror image of its debtor position. In the case of creditors the firm's interest is to postpone payment until the marginal benefit in terms of interest saved is just matched by the marginal cost in terms of loss of goodwill of its suppliers. Again, the extent to which the firm can do this will depend on market structure and relative market power.

10   For some other approaches see Cyert, Davidson and Thompson (1962) and Beranek (1963).

V SUMMARY

Both in terms of the sums involved, and the amount of finance function time consumed in managing these assets, the working capital investment decision is important in most firms. Though operations researchers have had some success in developing mathematical techniques for optimising stock balances, in the main firms tend to make judgemental investment decisions for cash and debtors. In either case the fundamental principle is the same – the firm should hold working capital balances up to the point where the marginal benefit of an extra unit is equalled by the marginal cost. Put another way, the firm should minimise the sum of the costs associated with holding and not holding working capital balances. The holding costs are essentially the cost of capital and 'storage' costs – administrative and accounting costs and, in the case of stocks, physical storage costs too. The benefits to holding working-capital balances, which are the costs of not holding them, are associated with the derived nature of the demand for these assets. Working capital is needed to support the economic activity of the firm. If the firm reduces its balances of cash, stocks and debtors too far it will have to acquire the service they provide in some other way, or sacrifice contribution from reduced economic activity. Additionally, in the case of stocks there is an increased cost associated with more frequent replacement.

REFERENCES AND BIBLIOGRAPHY

Atkins, J C	'Evaluating Investments in Accounts Receivable: A Wealth Maximising Framework', Journal of Finance, May 1978, pp 403–412.
Baumol, W J	'The Transactions Demand For Cash: an Inventory Theoretic Approach' Quarterly Journal of Economics, Nov 1952.
Beranek, W	Analysis for Financial Decisions (1963) Irwin, Homewood, Illinois.
Bierman, H Jr and Hausman, W H	'The Credit Granting Decision', Management Science, 16 April 1970.
Budin, M and Van Handel, R J	'A Rule of Thumb Theory of Cash Holdings by Firms', Journal of Financial and Quantitative Analysis, March 1975, pp 86–108.
Cole, R H	Consumer and Commercial Credit Management (4th edn, 1972), Irwin, Homewood, Illinois.
Cyert, R M Davidson, H J and Thompson, G L	'Estimation of the Allowance for Doubtful Accounts by Markov Chains', Management Science, April 1962, pp 287–303.
Daellenbach, H G	'Are Cash Management Optimisation Models Worthwhile' Journal of Financial and Quantitative Analysis, Sept 1974, pp 607–626.
Davis, E W and Yeomans, K A	'Company Finance and the Capital Market', Cambridge University Press, Occasional Paper No 39, 1974.
Hadley, G and Whitin T M	Analysis of Inventory Systems (1973) Prentice-Hall.
Kaleberg, J G and Parkinson, K	Current Asset Management: Cash, Credit and Inventory (1984), New York, John Wiley and Sons.

Keynes, J M	*The General Theory of Employment Interest and Money* (1936) Macmillan, London.
Kraus, A, Janssen, C and McAdams, A	'The Lock-Box Location Problem', Journal of Bank Research, Autumn 1970, pp 50–58.
Lee, G A	'Working Capital: Theory of Control', Accountancy, July and Sept 1970.
Levy, F K	'An Application of Heuristic Problem Solving to Accounts Receivable Management', Management Science, Feb 1966, pp 236–44.
Lewis, C D	*Scientific Inventory Control* (2nd edn, 1981), Butterworths.
Mehta, D R	*Working Capital Management* (1974) Prentice-Hall, Englewood-Cliffs, New Jersey.
Miller, M H and Orr, D	'A model of the Demand for Money by Firms' Quarterly Journal of Economics, Aug 1966, pp 413–455. 'The Demand for Money by Firms: Extension of Analytic Results' Journal of Finance, Dec 1968, pp 735–759.
Mullins, D and Homonoff, R	'Applications of Inventory Cash Management Models', in Myers, S C (ed) *Modern Developments in Financial Management* (1976) Frederick A. Praeger.
Smith, K J	*Guide to Working Capital Management* (1979) New York, McGraw-Hill.

QUESTIONS

1 What is the difference between working-capital investment decisions, and project investment decisions?

2 The Pidgeon Corporation manufactures pooms, using one raw material, the drimp. For each poom manufactured, twelve drimps are needed. Assume that the company manufactures 450,000 pooms per year, that it costs £600 to order drimps, and that carrying costs are £24 per drimp per year. Determine the economic order quantity of drimps and how many times per year inventory would be ordered.

What are total inventory costs for Pidgeon?

Describe the effect on the economic order quantity of (i) an increase in demand (ii) a decrease in carrying costs (iii) an increase in ordering costs.

3 Why do people need to hold cash?

4 State the assumptions of Baumol's model for the transactions demand for cash, and derive the model. How does the model change if the cost of transferring funds has a variable as well as a fixed component?

The Tropicana Company expects to have £120,000 each week in cash outlays next year. It plans to obtain such cash by equal transfers from its portfolio of marketable securities which it expects to earn 10% per year interest. The company predicts that it will incur a fixed charge of £3,000 each time it makes a transfer. How often should cash be transferred?

5 Explain how Miller and Orr developed Baumol's model, and assess the usefulness of cash management models in practice.

6 Squeezem Limited sells on credit, allowing customers one month to pay. The sales manager is having great difficulty in expanding sales, as competitors are offering more generous credit terms. He has prepared estimates of the effect of increasing the credit period to two or three months. These show a rise in sales revenue from the present level of £600,000 a year to £750,000 with two months credit, or to £810,000 with three months credit. However, bad debts, which at present average 1% of credit sales, may be expected to rise to 2.5% with two months credit, or to 5% with three months credit. Variable costs are two-thirds of selling price. Squeezem's required rate of return is 25%.

Advise Squeezem on the optimal credit policy, and suggest if any other factors should be taken into account.

7 The Aggro Collection Company employs agents who collect hire purchase instalments and other outstanding accounts on a door to door basis from Monday to Friday. The agents bank the cash collected to be remitted to head office once per week at the end of the week. The budget for next year shows that the total collections will be of the order of £5,200,000 and that the estimated bank overdraft rate is 9%. The collection manager has suggested that a daily remitting system should be introduced for collectors.

Advise him, pointing out any other factors he should be taking into account.

CHAPTER 24

Merger and growth

Previous chapters have talked about investment in terms of building *new* projects. This is 'internal' or 'organic' growth. But very often firms choose to grow by *merger* – by buying *existing* projects through the acquisition of the whole or part of another firm. As with organic investment, merger is worthwhile if it leads to an increase in the *value* of the firm.

In Section I we introduce the necessary terminology and concepts for talking about merger. We look at some of the 'stylised facts' of merger: the prevalence of merger activity and the nature of the firms that merge, and we consider the legal and institutional constraints on merging. In Section II we describe a recent example of a contested merger, the takeover of Thomas Tilling by BTR.

To have any chance of making good merger decisions managers need a clear understanding of the effect of merger on the value of the firm. We examine the potential costs and benefits of merger in Section III and in Section IV review the evidence on the success of mergers in practice. In considering this question we shall be throwing some light on the economics of organic growth, too, and on an issue that is widely debated – the rationale for the larger firm. In the final section we discuss the arithmetic of the merger decision, and contrast how a merger should and should not be evaluated.

I THE BACKGROUND TO MERGER

THE CONCEPTS AND TERMINOLOGY

There are various terms for merger. In this chapter we use the word 'merger' to cover a range of situations from a simple change in ownership of a firm to the situation where the operations of a firm, its physical and human assets, are fully integrated into those of another firm. People sometimes talk about *takeover* or *acquisition* when the main feature of the investment is a change in control, where one firm is fairly clearly buying another and perhaps the merger is contested by one party, and save the word *merger* for the situation where the two firms are of similar size or perhaps the merger is not contested. However, this distinction is not easy to apply in practice. We will use the words interchangeably, and also will talk as though there is an *acquiror* which initiates the merger and an *acquiree* or victim.

But it *is* useful to distinguish mergers according to the association between the *activities* of the firms involved:

—A HORIZONTAL merger occurs when the merging firms produce in the same industry, and a VERTICAL merger where one firm produces inputs to the production of the other.

> For example a brewery which buys up another brewery is growing horizontally; if it buys a hop farm it is pursuing 'backward' vertical integration, and if it buys a chain of pubs, 'forward' vertical integration.

—A CONCENTRIC merger involves the extension of a range of products or services, using the same core of expertise in, say, production, engineering, R & D, and marketing.

For example a computer manufacturer which buys an office equipment firm or a software house, is growing concentrically.

—A CONGLOMERATE or DIVERSIFICATION merger is one between firms in unrelated product areas. In this case there is no core of technical or product expertise common to the firms involved. Within conglomerate mergers we can make a further distinction between *managerial* conglomerates, where the new group shares management skills, probably at the strategic and control level, and *financial* conglomerates which are the loosest groupings of all – here the conglomerate is effectively just a holding company, a portfolio of autonomous firms.

For example a building group which buys a newspaper chain is indulging in conglomerate merger. Whether it is 'financial' or 'managerial' depends on the degree of control exercised over the operations of the new subsidiary.

This distinction is useful because, as we will see in the next section, the degree of association dramatically affects the potential benefits from merger. Because the economic logic of vertical/horizontal and concentric mergers is rather plainer to see, firms sometimes go to some pains to label their mergers this way.

The Financial Times (25.3.1981), describing the recent expansion of certain oil companies into mining said

Oil companies, which . . . now like to be known as 'energy' or 'resource-based' undertakings, thus argue that diversification into mining and minerals operations is logical.

In practice it is not always very easy to classify a merger. The merging firms may have a variety of activities, some of which are associated and some of which are not.

THE STYLISED FACTS OF MERGER

The scale of merger activity

Table I shows the scale of merger activity in the UK in recent years, and how it was financed.

Table I UK mergers 1977–1984					
Number of companies acquired	Expenditure Total	Cash	Cash as %	Ord shares	Prefs & com stock
1977 481	824	512	62%	304	8
1978 567	1,140	654	57%	463	23
1979 534	1,656	933	56%	515	208
1980 469	1,475	760	52%	669	46
1981 452	1,144	775	68%	338	31
1982 463	2,206	1,282	58%	701	223
1983 447	2,343	1,026	44%	1,261	57
1984 568	5,475	2,946	54%	1,837	690
Source: CSO, Financial Statistics, HMSO					

Fifty to seventy percent of the consideration for these mergers was cash and the rest was mainly ordinary shares. To relate these figures to the overall investment of firms is less straightforward but Meeks (1977) calculated the growth achieved by firms in a sample of UK industrial and commercial companies during the periods 1948–64 and 1964–71. Meeks divided achieved growth into 'internal', and 'external', which we are calling growth by merger. His results, reproduced in Table II, show that in the period 1948–64 about one third of growth achieved by firms was 'external' and in the period 1964–71 over half.

Table II Meeks' estimates of the sources of growth in total net assets		
Rate of growth %	1948–64	1964–71
by internal means	6.1	5.8
by external means	2.9	6.0
total	9.0	11.8

Source: Meeks (1977)

Merger waves

Table III extends the merger statistics from Table I back to 1963 and shows that merger activity appears to go in waves. In the UK recent peaks of merger activity have occurred around 1964–5 and 1972–3.

Table III Mergers of industrial and commercial companies: 1963–1981			
Year	Number of Mergers	Year	Number of Mergers
1963	888	1972	1,210
1964	940	1973	1,205
1965	1,000	1974	504
1966	807	1975	315
1967	763	1976	353
1968	946	1977	482
1969+	907	1978	567
1969+	846	1979	534
1970	793	1980	469
1971	884	1981	452
		1983	447
		1984	568

Sources: CSO Financial Statistics; Green Paper, cmnd 7198

Researchers have tried to explain these merger waves. There seems to be no association between merger activity and the business cycle[1], however it is firmly established that mergers are most likely to occur at stock-market peaks[2], though we have no clear explanation why this is so from orthodox theory.

1 Nelson (1959) claimed to find a link between merger activity and the business cycle, but Maule (1968) questioned these findings and supported the earlier conclusion of Markham (1955) that merger activity was unconnected with the business cycle.
2 See Nelson (1959).

Types of merger

In the US there is a historic tendency for mergers to be 'conglomerate' and this is usually explained in terms of the obstacles US anti-trust legislation puts in the way of vertical and horizontal mergers. In the UK, though, mergers have been predominantly horizontal. Studies of UK mergers in the 1950s and 1960s found that 70–80% of mergers were horizontal.[3] However the 1978 Green Paper suggested there may be a trend towards diversification mergers in the UK. Between 1965–1969 only 7% of the mergers referred to the Mergers Panel were diversification mergers, but the figure had risen to 39% in 1970–76.

THE CHARACTERISTICS OF ACQUIRORS AND ACQUIREES

Singh (1971) made a study of UK mergers between 1955 and 1960 in the food, drink, clothing and footwear, and non-electrical engineering industries to determine the characteristics of acquiror and acquiree firms and thus discover which firms were most likely to be taken over, or to take over others.[4] He repeated the study in Singh (1975) for the period 1967–70, adding the electrical engineering industry. In the later study Singh concluded that acquiror companies were on average bigger, more profitable, faster growing, more liquid and more highly geared than those they acquired, also that they showed greater recent improvement in profits and retained more profits. Singh found *size* to be the *main* distinguishing factor between acquirors and acquirees. As to *profitability* the difference between the average levels of the two groups was not very big but there was a 'very marked' difference between the rates of change in profitability – 'acquiring firms, on average, showed a small improvement [over the last two years] in their profit records while acquired ones showed a marked decline'. In his 1955–60 study, Singh had found a stronger set of differences between acquirors and acquirees, and that growth was a more important distinguisher, but liquidity less so. Singh's results suggested a survival strategy – above a certain minimum size-class, varying from industry to industry, the best way a firm could avoid being taken over would be by growing.[5] Increasing the firm's profitability, on the other hand, would not be a very useful survival strategy.

THE MECHANICS OF A MERGER

Usually in merger one firm is buying the other – there is an acquiror and an acquiree. This will happen simply for legal convenience even in a marriage of equals, though sometimes in this case a new company might be formed to buy the two existing firms. So usually the acquiree becomes a *subsidiary* of the acquiror. One firm is a subsidiary of another if that firm owns > 50% of its voting equity, hence a parent does not need to buy *all* the shares in a subsidiary. We would only call the acquiree a 'subsidiary' if it retained its separate legal status after the merger, and this usually happens. Indeed it must happen if the parent has not bought all the equity. Whether the acquiree remains a separate legal entity or not is of no great consequence economically except for one fact: by maintaining a subsidiary's company status the parent is protected by limited liability for the subsidiary's debts. At

3   See Singh (1971), Kuehn (1975), Utton (1969), Newbould (1970).
4   For other recent studies of the characteristics of firms that get involved in merger see Kuehn (1975) and Newbould (1970).
5   Below this minimum size Singh suggested, the best thing would be to get smaller, though he recognised this to be impracticable in a dynamic economy.

worst the subsidiary can be allowed to go bankrupt – though few parents, conscious of their business reputation, would allow this.

The consideration

The consideration for mergers is either *shares* or *cash*. In the former case the acquiror issues its own shares in exchange for the acquiree's shares. In the latter case the offer is made in cash, either from the acquiror's reserves or raised specially by a public issue of shares. Often the acquiree's shareholders will be offered a choice or a mixture of the two.

The acquiror's decision whether to offer cash or shares will depend on several things. The obvious one is the size of his cash reserves. If these are insufficient he would have to incur issue costs in raising cash, as well as the transactions costs associated with the merger. A second is the degree of confidence the acquiree-shareholders have in the value of the acquiror's shares – cash has a certainty about it which may appeal to shareholders. A third factor is the tax position of the acquiree shareholders – to the extent that the offer is for cash it becomes liable to capital gains tax whereas a share exchange does not.

The law

There is nothing to stop an acquiror buying up shares in the normal way in the market place, and this sort of activity usually precedes a takeover bid. But once a general offer is made it falls under certain codes and law. The 'CITY CODE on takeovers and mergers' lays down in some detail the procedure that must be followed in a merger. Amongst other things it specifies who should be informed of the bid and when, how acquiror and acquiree shareholders will be protected, what happens in the case of a partial offer, and so forth. Certain aspects of merger are covered by company law. For example, company law protects the acquiror from the risk that a few shareholders will block his attaining full control. If the acquiror has had acceptances on 90% of the shares for which he is bidding, he can enforce the sale of the remainder at the offer price.

Tactics

Sometimes mergers are agreed by both parties from the outset – the acquiree directors agree the terms and recommend them to their shareholders. Often, though, the merger is *contested* and the acquiree directors recommend rejection. There are two good reasons why they would do this. For one thing, the acquiree directors may be the first people to go after a merger and are thus likely to resist it at any price. But anyhow early resistance makes sense in a price bargaining situation. A key question in merger is how the potential gains are divided between acquiror and acquiree shareholders. To a large extent this depends on the tactical skill of the respective managements in the bargaining process. As we will see later on, the evidence is that on the whole, it is the acquiree shareholders who capture most of the gains in mergers.

The tactics of the acquiror will often be to appeal directly to the acquiree shareholders by painting as attractive a picture as possible of the new firm, while perhaps reducing the resolve of the acquiree directors through offering them some sort of role after the merger. If there are single shareholders with significant holdings, such as institutions, pressure may be brought to bear on them directly. The acquiree directors, on the other hand, may set out to attack the claims and credibility of the acquiror, and will often publish revised profit forecasts for the firm under existing management. They often encourage a third firm to make a rival bid in order to introduce some auction-like competitiveness into the bidding. This preferred bidder who gallops to the rescue is commonly known as a 'white knight'.

Public policy

Occasionally mergers fall foul of public policy as reflected in the operation of monopolies and mergers policy. In the US there is a strong anti-trust stance in public policy – i e public policy sees the need to actively maintain competition by countering monopoly. In the UK responsibility for these matters resides with the Monopolies (defined as 'dominant firm' situations in which one firm has over 25% of a market) and mergers which are *referred* to them. References are made by the Secretary of State on the recommendation of the Mergers Panel, serviced by the Office of Fair Trading. Between 1965 and 1980 only 55 mergers were referred to the MMC. Of these 16 were subsequently judged against the public interest, 18 of the mergers were abandoned during the proceedings and the rest were judged not against the public interest. The total of 55 reflects only a very small percentage of mergers that occurred during the period. The MMC has been criticised by firms engaged in merger on the grounds that it holds mergers up while it investigates and this often kills them. Of course in a contested merger this is exactly what the acquiree may want. More generally, UK merger policy has often been criticised for lack of bite or direction. The 'ad hoc' approach to merger policy is enshrined in the OFT guide to the Fair Trading Act 1973 – 'Each case falling within the scope of the Act is looked at on its own particular merits and not in accordance with any fixed rules and assumptions . . .' (Office of Fair Trading 1973). This approach is reasonable, given the difficulty of legislating for the variety of cases in the real world. The real problem is at the level of philosophy, rather than implementation. There has never been the same settled view in the UK as in the US about whether mergers are a 'good thing' or a 'bad thing'. On the one hand mergers have been seen as yielding firms of the size and efficiency needed to compete in the world economy, on the other hand there is a 'small is beautiful' lobby which sees evils in the all-powerful conglomerate corporation. For a long while the former view predominated and there was a presumption in merger policy that mergers were beneficial. However the 1978 Green Paper, influenced by evidence such as that by Meeks (1977) that mergers are unprofitable, recommended that the official presumption be downgraded to one of neutrality. Mr Nott, the Conservative trade minister, subsequently rejected this proposal, though he did suggest that conglomerate mergers should get a more critical look in future, since firms which were 'shopping around when flush with funds might lead to a diminution of competition and no evident efficiency gain' (quoted in FT 23.11.1981). Overall, the relative lack of interventionism in the UK probably reflects a feeling that the health of the UK industrial economy is too weak to stand it, and all signs of life need encouragement.

II BTR/THOMAS TILLING: THE TIMETABLE OF A CONTESTED BID

In this section we describe the chronology of a typical contested takeover.

In March 1983 Thomas Tilling announced its 1982–3 results. Tilling was an industrial conglomerate with interests in energy, health care, construction materials, Cornhill Insurance, Heinemann Publishers, Pretty Polly tights, and Pilkington's Tiles. Sales had risen £187.5 million to £2.24 billion, but taxable profits fell from £73.6 million to £43.7 million. The main contributors to this slump were the energy equipment division where a profit the previous year of £24.8 million turned into a loss of £16.4 million and higher interest charges, up £15.8 million.

On Tuesday, 5 April the BTR group instructed its brokers, Cazenove, to launch a '*dawn raid*' by buying up Tilling's shares in the market at an offer price of 175p. Under the

Council for the Security Industry's rules BTR could acquire not more than 15% of Tilling's shares this way, but in the event BTR had only acquired 6% before buying drove Tilling's share price above 175. City commentators concluded that the BTR raid was badly timed, a lot of fund managers were just returning from a long weekend and were anyhow not inclined to act with a new tax year just around the corner. BTR's shares fell from 454 to 428. But BTR were not daunted, and during Tuesday their chairman and chief executive Sir David Nicholson and Mr Owen Green paid a 'brief courtesy call' on the office of Tilling chief executive, Sir Patrick Meaney, in recognition of their status as largest single shareholder in Tilling.

Following the dawn raid a full bid was expected by the City and this arrived a week later. BTR offered Tilling shareholders either paper or cash. The current Tilling shareprice was 186p as against a price before the dawn raid of 128p. The paper offer was 10 BTR shares for every 21 Tilling. At the ruling BRT price of 418p this valued Tilling shares at 199p. The cash offer was 185p.

If the cash offer was chosen by all Tilling's shareholders, BTR would need to issue 97 million shares to raise the cash and Morgan Grenfell had agreed to underwrite such an issue.

BTR's main activity was as a manufacturer of components such as heat exchangers valves and rubber products for oil, mining, transport and paper manufacturing. It argued it had 'contiguity' with some of Tilling's interests. In 1982 BTR made a pre-tax profit of £107m on sales of £725m. Since 1978 BTR's profits had shown steady growth from £40.1 million, while Tilling's profits had fallen from £64.9 million to £43.7 million. In terms of margin, BTR's margin had climbed from 11% to 14.7%, while Tillings had fallen from 6.3% to 2.0%. BTR explained the difference in performance by saying that BTR was 'an industrial manager rather than an industrial banker'. The implication was that Tilling was merely a financial conglomerate in which all operating decisions were decentralised, while in BTR there was a strong central management team distributing management skills and a coherent management philosophy.

Tilling's directors quickly countered the bid. In a novel move they took out a restraining order on BTR in Cook County, Illinois, via a branch of their Cornhill Insurance subsidy, in order to exploit a US Law requiring authorisation by the relevant insurance bodies before there is a change in control of an insurance company. This order was withdrawn a week later. More conventionally, they set out to discredit BTR's bid. Sir Patrick Meaney expressed the view that Tilling would be a perfectly 'logical and proper' vehicle for growth in the 1980s and so as to indicate that BTR were not the only people interested in Tilling he said he had received offers 'as long as your arm' for Tilling subsidiaries. And he wrote to BTR shareholders saying 'how can such a massive and illogical expansion by acquisition be sensible?' He questioned the 'contiguity' argument and raised doubts about the effect of the bid on BTR's share price:

> You are being asked to pass a resolution approving adjusted, revised, additional or other offers and you should presume that BTR will need to make further increases in its offer price if your board does not want to back down. If in the end some increased offer did succeed there would be a huge number of BTR shares to be issued and liable to come on the market. What effects will this have on the BTR share price and for how long?

Green of BTR retorted:

> Tilling's attempts to make their conglomeration of businesses seem so different that it cannot yield to the application of the principles of sound business management evidently arises from their having become captives of their own experience.

Tilling also predicted that 1983 earnings would be 113% higher at £95 million a forecast which the Financial Times commented 'appears to be right at the top end of most independent analysts' estimates for 1983'. On the 5 May, the day after this forecast and the announcement by the Department of Trade that it had cleared the BTR bid, BTR held 9% of Tilling and Tilling's shares stood at 211p compared to the 204p value of BTR's paper offer. On the 6 May BTR sent Tilling's shareholders a four page rebuttal of Tilling's defence document. They asserted that the profit forecast 'is in reality no more than an ambitious profit plan – a plan based on a string of highly questionable assumptions and dependent on a substantial upturn in the world economy in 1983'. They said 'Tilling has become obsessed by size – but of sales rather than profits. It has invested heavily and indiscriminately in a range of unconnected businesses at the expense of continuous issues of shares and substantial additions to debt'.

BTR's initial offer expired on the 10 May, but was extended to 24 May. On 17 May BTR increased their bid and gave Tilling shareholders until June 8 to choose between a shares or cash offer each worth 225p. The new bid valued Tilling's at £659.4 million, compared to £375 million before the dawn raid, a premium of £28 million or 76%. This was the largest bid in UK history. Tilling rejected the new bid as 'derisory'. Tilling issued a new defence document in which it claimed that the break-up value of the Tilling group was between £802 million and £960 million. If the BTR bid failed, Tilling now proposed to *demerge* itself in order to realise some of the breakup value for shareholders. In particular 45% of the Intermed health care division would be released, and the whole of Cornhill Insurance. The document also reaffirmed the earlier profit forecast of £95 million for the year.

BTR was increasing its holding in Tilling daily by purchases in the market so that by 6 June with two days before the offer closed, BTR held 27.5%. However some major institutional shareholders were still not declared. The Prudential stated 'A decision will be made at the last moment, which is our normal policy'. In response to suggestions that the Pru would declare for Tilling, it said it had 'a predisposition to support incumbent management who are of good standing'.

By the closing date, counting indicated that BTR held 61.3% of Tilling shares, and in accepting defeat Tilling directors recommended acceptance to their shareholders. Amongst the remaining shareholders were the larger insurance companies, and they were later strongly attacked by Mr Owen Green for failing to support the bid.

By late June Tilling's five non executive directors had resigned including the chairman Sir Arthur Norman, and had been replaced by six BTR directors.

III THE ECONOMIC RATIONALE FOR MERGER

THE VALUE-MAXIMISING MERGER

In business finance the test of any decision is its impact on *value*. The firm should accept positive-NPV projects because these will increase the firm's value. The same principle applies to merger: the question of whether a merger is worthwhile comes down to two questions (1) Does the merger yield value gains? (2) Who gets them?

Suppose firm A with a current market value of £1 million buys firm B, value £.5m. The new firm A* has a market value of £1.75 million – together the two firms are worth £.25m more than they were separately. Clearly economic benefits have flowed from bringing A and B together, so was the merger a 'good thing' from the point of view of A's shareholders? Not necessarily. It depends what they paid for B. We define the *cost* of a merger as the premium the acquirer must pay over the existing market value of the acquiree. If they paid £.5 million they have done well, they paid no premium.

VALUE GAIN ON A*   .25m
COST OF MERGER   –
NET GAIN   .25m

In practice though it never happens that you can buy a firm at its existing market value. There are two reasons for this. The first is that when we talk about the 'market value' of a firm we are talking about the current price at which its shares are traded, multiplied by the shares in issue. However, we can never expect to buy *all* the shares in a company at the price at which the *marginal* share is trading, and would expect to pay a premium to dislodge 'inframarginal' shareholders.

But the main reason for a premium is that shareholders in B will spot the potential value gain to the merger and hold out for a share of it. So A might easily finish up paying £.7 million for B. In this case the position of A's shareholders is as follows:

VALUE GAIN ON A*   .25m
COST OF MERGER   .20m
NET GAIN   .05m

When we look at the empirical evidence on mergers in a subsequent section we will see that this second scenario is fairly realistic. Even when there are overall value gains to merger they often finish up being captured in the bargaining process by the acquiree, 'B' in our example.

To sum up, value gains are not enough to justify merger from the point of view of an acquiror's shareholders. The value gains must exceed the cost of merger, in other words the merger negotiation must leave some of the value gains in the hands of acquirors.

The sources of value gains

Why might the value of a merged ·firm be greater than the value of the two firms independently? Why might a merger yield

$$V_{A^*} > V_A + V_B?$$

In general we know that the rational shareholder will value firm j thus:

$$V = \sum_{t=0}^{\infty} \frac{DIV_t}{(1 + r_e)^t}$$

This is the '*dividend valuation model*'. The rationale of the dividend valuation model is that the value of a firm to its owner 'V' is the present value of the dividend stream he receives from it, DIV, discounted at a cost of capital r_e, which reflects its riskiness. In the long run the dividend a firm can pay must be determined by its earnings, so the model tells us that the value of a firm is a function of the earnings of the firm and the cost of capital. If merger is to yield value gains it must do it by increasing *earnings* or reducing the *cost of capital* compared to what they would have been. It must yield what is commonly called *synergy*, the situation where 2 + 2 = 5.

THERE ARE ALTERNATIVES TO MERGER

When reviewing the often plausible arguments for merger it is useful to bear in mind that there are other ways of achieving the same thing. The alternative method of *growing* is *organic* growth – the construction of projects within the firm rather than the purchase of ready-made projects. But both merger and organic growth represent what we call 'hierarchical' or 'organisational' methods of achieving a particular economic goal. In both cases the activity in question takes place inside one firm using inputs belonging to the firm. The alternative method of capturing the benefits of size is to make *contracts* in the market-place with other independent firms to capture some scale economy or other. The arrangements of this sort we see in practice are joint-ventures, franchises, sub-contracts, service contracts and the like. A merger must prove clear superiority over these if it is to be justified.

The key advantage of merger over organic growth as methods of growing is speed, and the reduced uncertainty associated with acquiring projects that are already up and running. The relative merits of hierarchical and market approaches to economic activity reflect the *costs of writing contracts*.[6]

In the rest of this section we will examine some of the common arguments for merger. Most of them are actually arguments for growth, arguments why it might be better to be big. As such they have a wider relevance than the simple study of mergers. They shed some light on the rationale for organic growth, and on the current debates in most western economies about the virtues of 'large' and 'small' as forms of economic organisation. We encountered some of them in Chapter 19 when we discussed the small firm financing problem.

THE EFFECT OF MERGER ON EARNINGS

Merger can improve earnings by increasing revenues, reducing costs, or both. It can do this by improving the prices which the firm pays for inputs and receives for its outputs, and by improving the efficiency with which it converts inputs to outputs.

Market power

By buying up competitors a firm may increase its market power in output markets. Economic theory suggests that this may enable it to charge a higher price for its product. What it also does is give the firm more 'control' over the market so that it can soften the impact of economic fluctuations by passing their effects on to others. The *market power* argument applies to input markets too. By increasing its purchases of a certain input the firm may be able to enforce a keener price on suppliers. A good example of this is food retailing, where a large supermarket chain can account for a significant proportion of the sales of certain branded items and can enforce significant quantity discounts from suppliers. These arguments only seem to favour *horizontal* mergers, since only these are likely to increase market power in a given input or output market.

Vertical merger is an *alternative* way of securing control over inputs and outputs. In this case the relationship with the supplier or customer is *internalised* rather than being left to a market transaction. So if the firm already has a powerful market position there may be little advantage in vertical integration.

Operating efficiency

In the market power argument firms improve profit by improving the prices of their outputs and inputs. The operating efficiency arguments suggest ways in which merger can improve the efficiency with which inputs are converted into outputs. This is usually a

6   See Chapter 2 for a more detailed discussion of this.

question of exploiting *individualism* in inputs by building a larger firm – in other words of achieving *economies of scale*. Though the economies of scale argument springs readily to mind when we think about large firms, it is an argument which often does not bear close inspection. The scope for scale economies depends on the extent to which the merging firms share common inputs, and on the minimum efficient scale for deploying those inputs.

(a) Manufacturing economies of scale   It is well established that the technology of certain processes indicates a large plant and the cost savings associated with such plants give their owners a competitive advantage. But significant technical economies of scale only exist in certain industries. In Table IV we reproduce some of the data from a fascinating list of research findings on optimum plant size in various industries collected in the Merger Green Paper (1978). While the minimum efficient scale in, say, automobiles, aluminium and calculators is high; in bricks and paint it is small. Anyhow, on the face of it, merger does not look like the best way to achieve technical economies of scale. By merging the acquiror is getting two plants when what he really wants is one big one – he is buying some capacity he will probably have to close down. More likely the merger will be a permissive factor designed to create the market needed to sustain the larger plant. Either way, the manufacturing economies of scale argument can relate only to *horizontal* mergers.

Table IV Some engineering-type estimates of minimum efficient plant size (MEPS)

Product	MEPS	MEPS as % of UK produced sales	
Potato crisps	30–35,000 tons per annum	10%	
Cigarettes	36 billion per annum	21%	
Paint	10 million US galls pa	7%	
Steel	2–3 million tons pa	8–12%	different studies
	4–9 million tons pa	17–37%	
	4 million tons pa	17%	
Aluminium semi-manufacturers	200,000 tons pa		
Electronic calculators	3–4 million	>100%	
Automobiles	½–1 million pa	29–57%	
Bricks	25 million pa	.4%	different studies
	50–62.5 pa	.7–.9%	

Source: Merger Green Paper (1978)

(b) Administrative economies of scale   There can be economies to be made in the deployment of other inputs too – doubling the size of the firm may not mean a doubling in the size of the marketing, advertising, finance and administration needed to service the bigger firm.

The cost savings got by exploiting indivisibilities may occur outside the firm instead of inside, and sometimes it is this that accounts for the lower price larger firms pay for their inputs, rather than the exercise of market power. For example, in the case of a raw material such as steel rods there may be some indivisibilities in transport if it costs as much to send a half full lorry of rods as it does a full lorry, and there may be fixed costs in the accounting department of the stockist that make it relatively cheaper to process a larger order. Thus when a big firm pays a lower price for its steel this may reflect its market power *or* cost savings of the supplier.

In a competitive market such as the capital market we do not expect any participant to be able to influence the price ie market power cannot be relevant. If big firms are paying a lower price for their finance we must attribute it to indivisibilities in supply – for example financing costs which are partly invariant to the amount of finance raised. In the case of an input such as advertising bought in from an agency we might expect the price to reflect cost savings and market power. There are fixed costs associated with preparing a campaign which make large campaigns relatively cheaper, but whether the agency passes these costs savings on to the customer depends on the customer's market power.

We have been talking about what we can call *administrative economies of scale*. Since inputs such as marketing, advertising, finance and administration tend to be less specific to particular products than is plant, it is feasible that cost savings of this sort could arise in *concentric* and even *conglomerate* mergers too. However size does not always yield administrative cost savings. Large firms may become slow, inflexible and maintain large bureaucracies. These effects can follow a merger either because of a reluctance to dispose of surplus personnel post-merger, or because of a perceived need to add additional levels of authority in the bigger firm.

Management skills

Merger usually involves a change in management, and mergers are often promoted for just this reason. The argument is that managers differ in skill, and that the new team will be able to generate more earnings from the existing human and physical capital. When mergers are argued in terms of the acquiree being undervalued, or having assets that could be better used or could be profitably sold off, this is essentially a 'management skills' argument. As we saw in Chapter 2 the threat of a change in the management team is usually reckoned to be the main sanction shareholders have against inefficient management.

There is no doubt that some managements are more dynamic than others, and we see examples of this everywhere. The problem with the management skills argument is that it is rather hard to quantify beforehand and to prove afterwards. In the build up to a merger it is very easy for the acquiror to assert that he will run things better. Ex post, an attempt to judge the performance of the new management team is beset by the problems of measuring the performance and efficiency of firms that we discussed in Chapter 9. Management can argue that the merger has paid off, but for the outsider it becomes difficult to disentangle the relevant performance data from the aggregate results of the new group, and to eliminate the influence of other factors from those results.

Since 'management skills' are often appealed to as a justification for merger we need to ask just how significant these are, and what sort of mergers they appear to favour. The question is how *specific* are management skills? We can easily conceive that the transfer of management skills can be beneficial in a *horizontal* and perhaps a *concentric* merger, but can it justify *vertical* and especially *conglomerate* merger. In other words can a good manager manage anything? The answer seems to be – it depends on the manager. Examples are legion of powerful chief executives who impose a tight economic discipline on diverse groups. There is also a legion of successful enterprises who have got into difficulties through diversifying into areas, whose culture they did not properly understand.[7]

Views about the omnipotent manager seem to differ internationally. It is noteworthy that in Germany the expectation is that managers are best at those things they know about,

---

7   Studies in the UK and the US suggest, however, that firms often do not tend to diversify too far from their prime activity – diversification tends to be *concentric* rather than *conglomerate*. Utton (1977) studied the diversification of the 200 largest UK manufacturers in 1974 and found that the majority of diversification was into closely connected areas. Gorecki (1975) found similar results, as did Berry (1971) in the US.

and this may explain the relatively low diversification of German firms compared to those in the UK and US.

The management skills argument is rather akin to other economy-of-scale arguments. The acquiror's management team is seen as a specially valuable asset which can be exploited more fully by using it in other firms but human assets have features physical assets do not have. Since the abolition of slavery it is rather harder to enforce property rights over humans – they are inclined to get up and walk away. The ability to do this, allied to their ability to perceive their own worth, means that managers will constantly seek to capture a larger share of the value gains they generate, by defecting to other firms, setting up their own firms, or using the threat of these as a lever on their present firms. So acquirors cannot be certain about the continued ownership of superior management skills. Nor can they rely on the acquiree management remaining in place post-merger. Often the inevitable disruption surrounding a merger is increased by the loss of key staff.

Taxation

A final and rather specific earnings-type argument which is sometimes used to justify merger is *tax-benefits*. We reviewed the potential for this in Chapter 3. Essentially, there will be tax benefits whenever a firm which is paying corporation tax can pool its earnings with a firm which has more tax-deductions – losses or capital allowances than it has earnings to set them off against. The benefits are in the form of interest savings through the postponement of tax payments. Arrangements which permit this yield value-gains at the expense of the Revenue. In fact merger is only one of several devices for capturing tax benefits by joining forces with another firm. As we saw in Chapter 19, leasing provides a less permanent method of doing this.

If it is past trading losses or past excess capital allowances that are hoped to be used to generate tax benefits, the scope is rather restricted. Tax law permits some carry over of tax losses or capital allowances *against the same trade*, but the transfer is not automatic and special rules limit the period in which losses can be transferred.

THE EFFECT OF MERGER ON THE COST OF CAPITAL

If merger brings down the cost of capital it will yield value-gains. We usually consider that cost of capital of a firm will reflect the amount it raises, the period for which it raises the finance and the risk involved. It is hard to see how merger will systematically affect the term or duration of firms' financing. But it may affect the amounts in which the firm raises funds, and the risk involved.

Risk

If the firm diversifies by indulging in conglomerate merger the variance or 'riskiness' of its earnings stream should fall. Will this reduce the cost of capital? In other words, is corporate diversification a thing of value to shareholders?

In a perfect capital market diversification by the firm is of no value to shareholders – the reason is that they can achieve this for themselves by building a portfolio of shares in individual firms. In reality shareholders may not be indifferent between diversification by the firm and doing it themselves, though it is not entirely clear which they will prefer. The loss of *limited liability* will lead them to prefer homemade diversification; the existence of bankruptcy costs will make them prefer the firm to do it. It is rather hard to know which will predominate in practice[8].

Capital market imperfections

Merger is sometimes promoted on the grounds that larger firms can exploit capital market imperfections and get funds cheaper than smaller firms, or even get funds smaller firms could not get at all. The 'group' operates as a mini-capital market for its subsidiaries.

There are fixed costs in raising new finance on the capital market which make it relatively expensive for small firms so the group may be able to raise funds more cheaply on behalf of its subsidiaries. But if the group contains some firms which are net investors and some which are net savers – i e have spare retained earnings, it can avoid the capital market and its costs altogether. This is the *'spare cash'* argument for merger. The retained earnings of one part of the group can be deployed in another part costlessly whereas if the two firms were independent the finance would need to be passed through the capital market – paid out as divided and raised as new capital. Apart from the transactions costs involved there is a lack of speed and flexibility in this process.

Another financial argument for merging is to exploit the *unused debt capacity* of a firm which could be borrowing more than it is. The firm with the ability to raise further low cost debt seems to be in a similar position to the firm with spare cash or excess retained earnings. It possesses an asset that can be better exploited by joining up with a firm with an excess of investment projects. What is really implied here, again, is imperfections in the capital market. In a perfect capital market, as we shall see in Chapter 22, the amount of 'cheap' debt a firm employs has no effect on its overall cost of capital. But in practice the existence of tax-benefits to debt might make unused debt capacity a positive argument for merger.

The enhanced supply of capital can be used as a justification for any merger and indeed it provides the only argument for the sort of loose confederacy we described as the *financial conglomerate* since finance is the only input those firms share.

A REVIEW OF THE ARGUMENTS FOR MERGER

The arguments for merger essentially provide reasons why bigger firms might be better.

Certain things are clear. The first is that it is impossible to generalise about the virtues of size. The arguments for technical economies of scale, managerial skills, financial benefits etc are highly specific to the context of the merger: they depend on the nature of the particular market and industry, the personalities of the management involved and so forth. These are questions the acquiror must study very carefully before going ahead with the merger. The benefits to merger must be robust enough – large enough and certain enough – to cover the costs – the premium paid to the acquiror and the transactions costs, professional fees etc, of the merger.

The second thing is that there are often other ways of achieving the benefits of size. There is a good example of this in the modern automobile industry. The costs of research and development in this highly competitive industry are now very high and can only be borne if the subsequent market is seen in global terms. However car manufacturers have responded to this indivisibility not by creating monolithic worldwide corporations but by a series of joint ventures in which R & D costs are shared, and in some cases one partner

---

8   See Chapter 2 for the effect of diversification on limited liability. Bankruptcy costs are discussed in the next chapter.

manufactures a component for both parties so as to capture manufacturing economics of scale as well. Examples are Honda/BL, Ford/Mazda.

Some firms have clearly become sceptical about the economic benefits to merger even to the extent of considering 'demerger'.

Managerial objectives

So far we have assumed the acquiror's managers are value-maximisers, but they may not be. Once we admit that managers might be pursuing goals such as *growth* with scant regard for value, our examination of the economic rationale for merger becomes rather redundant – merger is likely to be justified simply because it offers speedy growth. Another managerial objective is *risk reduction*. The costs to the manager of bankruptcy can be a loss of income, status, and security, and the damage to his reputation of being associated with failure. The growth objective can be served by any type of merger, but it is clear that *diversification* mergers may be particularly attractive to this sort of manager since they will yield quick growth and risk reduction.

Various writers have developed the notion of merger as a managerial response to uncertainty. In these theories mergers and merger waves tend to be triggered by events in the external environment that increase the uncertainty felt by managers – mergers by other firms, macroeconomic changes and so forth.[9]

The importance of clout

It is often said that in the modern economy firms need to be big in order to have *clout*.

Hence in the 1960s European governments actively encouraged the formation of firms that could match US competitors in scale. A key requirement for competing effectively in an era of rapid technological change is the ability to *innovate* successfully. Are big firms good at innovation? Innovation involves the generation of new product ideas, their development and subsequent implementation. Small firms are sometimes said to be good at idea generation, although there is no real evidence that the culture of the small firm is more conducive to creative thought. However it is the case that the development stage – bringing the idea to the market – can be very expensive and very risky. The advantages the large firm has in innovation are several. For one thing its size will help it to survive the failure of a particular innovative thrust or a heavy research programme which proves fruitless.

This is the diversification argument again. A second virtue of size is that the large firm can deploy the necessary financial and human resources very quickly and flexibly, transferring them from other operations as needed, without resort to the market place. We have already seen how this argument works in the case of finance. The same argument applies to labour. A small firm could hire the necessary labour, but the large firm has certain advantages – it avoids all the costs of recruitment and selection, and it avoids the risks of joining a new and untried firm from the point of view of the employees. Finally, the uncertainty surrounding some innovatory projects might make them hard to finance in the normal way – the large firm with adequate internal resources is not constrained in this way. Hence there are various ways in which being a well endowed firm can aid in innovation.

9   See for example Newbould (1970), Aaronovitch and Sawyer (1975), George and Silberson (1975).

IV   HOW MERGERS PERFORM – THE EVIDENCE

There have been a great many studies of the success or otherwise of mergers.[10] In this section we look at some of the results. On the whole research seems to show that mergers generate value gains which are most captured by the acquiree. Paradoxically though it seems that mergers do not lead to increased profitability. Less surprisingly, perhaps, we find that conglomerate mergers are less likely to succeed than vertical and horizontal mergers.

Value gains

The key test is whether mergers lead to value gains. If firm A and firm B merger to form A*, we want to check that the value of A* is greater than the values of A and B *would have been*. The problem for the investigator is figuring out what the values of A and B would have been. Mandelker (1974) used the CAPM to estimate this. If shares are priced in a way consistent with the Capital Asset Pricing Model there will be a proportional relationship between the return on the market and the return on an individual share which is stable through time and is measured by the share's 'beta'. So by estimating the share's beta pre-merger, and applying it to the return on the market in subsequent periods – the investigator can calculate what 'would have been' in terms of the return on the share.[11]

Mandelker calculated the cumulative 'abnormal' returns, that is the excess of 'actual' over 'would have been', of the acquirors and acquirees involved in his sample of 252 US mergers. On average the returns of the *acquired* firms moved with the market up to 8 months prior to the merger.[12] But, 8 months prior, the market started to anticipate the merger, yielding abnormal gains of about 15% by the announcement date. On the other hand Mandelker found abnormal gains of only about 3½% for *acquirors*, and this result was not statistically significant. So he concluded that there were value gains to merger, but they mostly accrued to the acquiree.

Franks, Broyles and Hecht (1977) used a similar approach in studying mergers in the UK Breweries and Distilleries sector from 1955 to 1972. They found a similar pattern in that acquirees made gains of up to 26% during a shorter period of three months prior to the merger announcement, with acquirors gaining 2½%. Moreover, Franks et al note that in the UK these small gains to acquirors were temporary and subsequently disappeared.

Profitability

The key test of success in a merger is its effect on *value*, but it is hard to avoid regarding profitability as the major determinant of value. Several researchers have studied whether mergers lead to increases in profitability. The most recent and thorough of UK studies was by Meeks (1977). Meeks found that on average mergers lead to a decline in profitability. This perplexing result has yet to be reconciled with the value based studies.

Meeks examined the profitability of a sample of 233 UK mergers representing over a third of all mergers between quoted companies from 1964 to 1972. He studied the profitability of the merged firm for seven years after the merger and compared it with the average profitability the two firms were achieving in the three years before the merger. Meeks used historic-cost return on capital employed as the measure of profitability and

---

10   A good recent survey of the evidence in this area is Mueller (1977).
11   We examine this methodology in more detail in Chapter 15 in the context of the effect of 'stock splits'.
12   Having previously fallen in the period 30 to 40 months prior to merger.

made some fairly sophisticated adjustments to allow for accounting bias and economic and industry distortions. Meeks found that on average the firms in his sample experienced a decline in profitability relative to pre-merger levels in all seven years after merger – numerically, half to two-thirds of the firms in the sample showed this decline. Since it is hard to conceive that the benefits to a merger would not have shown up by the end of seven years, the conclusion of the Meeks study is that mergers are unprofitable.

Meeks methodology required a 'clear run' of data for firms in his sample and this meant the exclusion of frequently merging firms from the sample. This has been a common criticism of his approach. But other profitability studies in the UK and the US have also found mergers to be, on balance, unprofitable.[13]

The results of these profitability-based research studies have been taken seriously by a lot of commentators, and the question-mark they put over the worth of mergers partly led to the conclusion of the 1978 Green Paper that the official attitude towards merger should be downgraded from one of encouragement to one of neutrality. However some doubt must remain over the appropriateness of this methodology. For one thing the results of theoretically more appropriate 'value' studies tend to be more encouraging. Appleyard (1980) has produced some convincing arguments why post-merger profitability will tend to fall merely for accounting reasons. He finds that there tends to be a downward bias in accounting rates of return whenever company results are grouped together under present accounting conventions, and that this bias is likely to be enhanced if accounting policy is harmonised after the merger. It is possible that these effects account for the observed results in profitability studies.

Other studies

Some researchers have preferred a case-study approach to surveying mergers, to get a richer insight into their effects. Cowling *et al* (1977) looked at some horizontal mergers in the UK and found that in these cases efficiency gains were not a significant outcome, but that substantial increases in market power were. Hart, Utton and Walshe (1973) found a high incidence of managerial dis-economies arising in mergers within product groups. These studies show that even in the case of mergers between firms in closely related fields there is no promise of success. However the evidence suggests that vertical and horizontal mergers are more likely to be successful than conglomerate. Weston (1970) studied, like Meeks in the UK, the performance of mergers in terms of measures of return on investment. He examined mergers in the US from 1937–58, and found conglomerate performance 'average', but with very high variability in the performance of particular conglomerates. However concentric mergers had a very high probability of success. Kitchen (1974) used a questionnaire to elicit managerial opinions. Thirty per cent of UK mergers emerged as failures, with a further 12 per cent classed as not worth repeating. He found that vertical and horizontal mergers were highly successful, conglomerates had a high failure rate, and that concentric mergers fell somewhere in between.

Kitching (1967) supplemented financial analyses with a questionnaire to survey the opinion of managers involved in 69 US mergers. He asked them how the merger had turned out, relative to their original plans and aspirations. He found that vertical and horizontal tended to be successful, whereas conglomerate mergers had a high incidence of failure. Concentric mergers fell somewhere in between.

---

13   See for example Newbould (1970), Utton (1974), Singh (1971) and the surveys by Meeks (1977) and Utton of merger studies in the UK and the US.

V   THE MERGER DECISION

A merger will be worthwhile if it leaves the shareholders of the acquiror firm better off. As we have seen this will depend on two things: (1) the BENEFIT – the *value gains* arising from the merger (2) the COST – how much of the value gain is transferred to the acquiree shareholders in the merger negotiation. This is the *premium* paid over the market value of the acquiree's shares.

The best way to evaluate a merger is in these two stages, first estimating the value gains, then the premium the acquiror will have to pay for the acquiree.

VALUE GAINS

If firms A and B merger to form firm A*, we can define the benefit to merger as the difference between the value of the new firm and the two original firms, i e

$$\text{BENEFIT} = V_{A*} - (V_A + V_B)$$

This is what the managers of A must try to predict. The first problem they will face is in knowing if the values V_A and V_B are 'correct'.

A characteristic of an efficient stock market is that it anticipates events such as mergers and starts to embody expected value gains into share prices well before the event. So when managers sit down to evaluate a proposed merger they may be working with share prices which already reflect to some extent the market's expectations about the proposed merger and they will need to try and estimate what the true share price of the independent A and B would be.

The real problem facing management, however, is to estimate V_A, to quantify the value of the new firm. To do this they must estimate the extra cash flows that will be generated by the merger. This may be difficult, probably much more so than in normal project appraisal. The benefits may reflect things such as market power and improved management skills that are hard to quantify. But if management cannot put a value on the benefits, they should not be contemplating the merger.

The wrong way to value a merger

Analysts commonly use an earnings price ratio or P/E in valuing the firm. They multiply the firm's earnings by an 'appropriate' P/E to find its value.

Consider an example:
Firm X is contemplating a merger with either firm Y or firm Z. The details of these firms are as follows:

	X	Y	Z
Market value of firm	£20m	£5m	£2.5m
Earnings	£2m	£1m	£1m
P/E	10	5	2½

Assume for convenience that X can buy both Y and Z at their current market value, i e no premium will be involved. Which should it buy? If the market capitalises the earnings of the new firms at a P/E of 10 then we can assess the two alternatives as follows:

Buy Y

earnings of new firm = 2m + 1m =	3m
P/E	×10
Value of new firm	£30m
Values of old firms £20m + £5m =	£25m
VALUE GAIN	£5m

Buy Z

earnings of new firm =	2m + 1m =	3m
P/E		×10
Value of new firm		£30m
Values of old firms £20m + £2.5m	=	£22.5m
VALUE GAIN		£7.5m

Since the premium is the same in each case, i e NIL by assumption, buying Z emerges as the better strategy.

'P/E' is usually taken as a measure of the quality of a firm – *given* the firm's earnings we expect a firm to have a higher P/E the better its growth prospects and the lower its riskiness. The message of the previous example seems to be that the firm should find the *worst* acquirees it can. This is because each £1 of earnings bought adds £10 to the value of X irrespective of where it came from. So X ought to buy up earnings as cheaply as it can. In fact it should be clear that the purchase of *any* firm with a P/E less than that of X will increase the value of X, and yield what has come to be known as an *instant merger profit*. This all hangs on the use of the acquiror's P/E for valuing the new earnings. What economic rationale could we provide for doing this? Clearly there is none. The null hypothesis must be that the earnings will continue to have the value they had before – as measured by the *acquiree's* P/E. If there are value gains to merger they need to be explicitly identified and measured. The best we could say for a procedure of valuing new earnings at the acquiror's P/E is that it is a convenient way of expressing confidence in the ability of the acquiror management to achieve a certain level of growth and risk in any context. It is hard to conceive that such confidence could ever be justified.

That analysts should value firms this way conflicts with our view of market efficiency, but there is some evidence that at least in the 1960s this was happening. Newbould (1970) produced evidence that this was taking place.

THE COST

The cost of a merger depends on whether the offer is in shares or cash, but either way it is the *premium* the acquiror pays over the existing market price, V_B, of the acquiree. As before, to estimate the premium we need a figure for V_B which excludes any anticipated merger gains. Hence the price of B immediately prior to the merger, say on the day before, will not do.

Suppose we have the following two firms

Firm	A	B
Share price	£7.50	£1.50
No of shares in issue	1,000,000	600,000
Market value of firm	£7.5m	£900,000

A is planning to buy B. It anticipates merger gains of £600,000 and is contemplating either a cash offer of £2 per share, or an exchange of one A share for every three in B.

Cash

In the case of the cash offer the total cost of B is 600,000 × £2 = £1,200,000 giving a premium of £300,000. Hence the net gain to A shareholders from the merger is £600,000 − £300,000 = £300,000.

Shares

The calculation of the cost is less direct in a share-for-share merger since the 'cost' is a portion of the value of the new firm. In this case A estimates the value of the new firm will be £7.5 million + £900,000 + £600,000 = £9 million. The B shareholders are being given the proportion of this value represented by their shares as a proportion of the total shares in issue in A post merger. Since they are being given 200,000 (= ⅓ × 600,000) shares this proportion is

$$1m + \frac{200,000}{200,000} = 1/6$$

Hence their new shares are worth 1/6 × £9m = £1.5m. The premium on issue is £1.5 million − £900,000 = £600,000, and the net gain to A's shareholders is £600,000 − £600,000 = NIL.

VI   SUMMARY

Merger is a popular method of growing. Like other investment decisions the key question in appraising a merger is its effect on the value of the firm. In this chapter we reviewed the economic rationale for merger, the reasons why mergers might lead to value gains. We saw that the potential for gains depends very much on the type of merger, and that merger has to demonstrate its superiority over other ways of achieving the same outcome. From the point of view of the acquiring firm, though, an overall value gain is not enough. There is a cost to merger in the form of the premium it must pay the acquiree shareholders, and the merger will only be worthwhile if the value gain exceeds this premium. Research has shown that on average mergers do seem to lead to value gains but that most of these gains go to the aquiree shareholders. In other words, acquiree shareholders are able to enforce a premium that captures most or all of the gains to merger.

REFERENCES AND BIBLIOGRAPHY

Appleyard, A R	'Takeovers: Accounting Policy, Financial Policy and the case against Accounting Measures of Performance' Journal of Business Finance and Accounting' Winter 1980, pp 541–554.
Appleyard, A R and Yarrow, G K	'The Relationship between Take-over Activity and Share Valuation' Journal of Finance, Dec 1975, pp 1239–1250.
Cowling, K et al	'Mergers and Economic Performance' Research Study for the Office of Fair Trading, 1977.

Ellert, J C	'Mergers, Antitrust Law Enforcement and Stockholder Returns' Journal of Finance, 1976.
Firth, M	'Takeovers, Shareholder Returns and the Theory of the Firms' Quarterly Journal of Economics, March 1980, pp 235–260.
Franks, J R, Broyles, J E and Hecht, M J	'An Industry Study of the Profitability of Mergers in the United Kingdom' Journal of Finance, Dec 1977, pp 1513–25.
Gorecki, P	'An Inter-industry Analysis of Diversification in the UK Manufacturing Sector' Journal of Industrial Economics, 1975.
Gort, M	'An Economic Disturbance Theory of Mergers' Quarterly Journal of Economics, 1969.
Grossman, S J and Hart, O O	'Takeover Bids, the Free-Rider Problem and the Theory of the Corporation' Bell Journal of Economics, Spring 1980, pp 42–64.
Haugen, R A and Langetieg, T C	'An Empirical Test for Synergism in Merger' Journal of Finance, Sept 1975, pp 1003–1026.
Hogarty, T F	'The Profitability of Corporate Mergers' Journal of Business, 1970.
Kitchen, M	'Why Acquisitions are Abortive' Management Today, 1974.
Kitching, J	'Acquisitions in Europe: Causes of Corporate Successes and Failures,' Geneva, Business International, 1973.
Kuehn, D	*Takeovers and the Theory of the Firm* (1975) Macmillan, London.
Lee, K W	'Co-insurance and Conglomerate Mergers' Journal of Finance, Dec 1977, pp 1527–37.
Levy, H Sarnat, M	'Diversification, Portfolio Analysis, and the Uneasy Case for Conglomerate Mergers' Journal of Finance, June 1970, pp 295–802.
Lewellen, W G	'A Pure Financial Rationale for the Conglomerate Merger' Journal of Finance, 1971.
Mandelker, G	'Risk and Return: The Case of Merging Firms' Journal of Financial Economics, Dec 1974, pp 303–335.
Maule, C J	'A Note on Mergers and the Business Cycle' Journal of Industrial Economics, April 1968.
Meeks, G	*Disappointing Marriage: A Study of the Gains from Merger* (1977) Cambridge University Press.
Merger Green Paper	A Review of Monopolies and Mergers Policy (Cmnd 7198).
Mueller, D C	'A Theory of Conglomerate Mergers' Quarterly Journal of Economics, 1969.
Mueller, D C	'The Effects of Conglomerate Mergers: A Survey of the Empirical Evidence' Journal of Banking and Finance, 1977.
Nelson, R	*Merger Movements in American Industry, 1895–1956* (1959) National Bureau of Economic Research, Princeton University Press.
Newbould, G	*Management and Merger Activity* Githstead, Liverpool, 1970.
Office of Fair Trading	'Mergers' HMSO, London, 1978.
Scott, J H Jr	'On the Theory of Conglomerate Mergers' Journal of Finance, Sept 1977, pp 1235–1250.

Singh, A   *Takeovers* (1971) Cambridge University Press, London.
Singh, A   'Takeovers, Economic Natural Selection, and the Theory
                  of the Firm: Evidence from the Postwar United Kingdom
                  Experience' Economic Journal, Sept 1975, pp 497–515.
Utton, M A   'On Measuring the Effects of Industrial Mergers' Scottish
                  Journal of Political Economy, 1974.

QUESTIONS

1 Distinguish the different classes of merger and the costs and benefits likely to accrue to
each.

2 Is there an economic rationale for conglomerate mergers?

3 In terms of profitability, mergers seem to have been on average unsuccessful, but in
terms of value gains, successful. Can we explain this paradox?

4 Why would mergers come in waves?

5 Large is thinking of taking-over Helpless. Large presently has 10 million shares in
issue, with a market price of £4. Helpless has 4 million shares selling at £2.50. Large
believes that, together, the two firms could be worth £55 million and Large is considering financing the merger either through a cash offer of £3.50 per Helpless share or by a
one for one share exchange. Find the gains to the merger, and the cost under each of the
financing alternatives. What factors would affect the choice of cash versus shares for
financing a merger in practice?

6 The Heavy Speaker Company has made an offer to acquire all the ordinary shares of
Red Rectangle Turntables. The offer document states that the merger should create
gains for the combined group due to the complementary nature of the products. The
offer document provides the following information:

	Heavy	Red Rectangle
Shares in issue	5 million	7 million
Earnings per share	160p	110p
Price earnings ratio (P/E)	9	6

The profits forecast indicates an earnings per share of £2.20 for the combined group.
Stockbrokers to the group expect the P/E of the combined group to be one point above
the weighted average on the basis of pre-merger market values of the firm.

Heavy has offered one new share in exchange for two Red Rectangle shares. The
cash alternative is £6.50 for one Red Rectangle share.

Assuming the prevailing P/E for the new group is:

(a) Heavy's
(b) Red Rectangle's
(c) a weighted average of the two

calculate the gain from the merger and the cost to Heavy under the cash and share
alternatives. Also calculate the bid-premiums.

CHAPTER 25

Failure and disinvestment

When we study investment decision-making we tend to emphasise the positive and talk about techniques for choosing the best projects and making the best merger decisions. But it is important that disinvestment decisions are well made too. On occasion economic activities 'fail' – projects and even whole firms or parts of firms cease to have a positive economic value. In a world of uncertainty we need not be surprised by this. Our approach to decision-making under uncertainty has been to envisage a range of possible outcomes and failure represents one tail of this distribution. However the people involved in failure tend not to be so philosophical about it. In the case of a single project, failure can seriously damage the reputation of those managers who sponsored and implemented the project. Larger scale failure can mean a significant financial loss to owners and creditors but also, if it means redundancy, a loss to employees – workers and managers – or income, status, and the social relationships of the workplace. Not surprisingly people are reluctant to recognise failure and this means that disinvestment decisions are often forced from outside.

There has been much less research into failure than, say, merger. We do not have a rich, empirically developed economic theory of why firms fail, or any evidence on whether the right firms are failing.[1] Hence our approach in this chapter is rather different from the last. We examine the legal and institutional circumstances surrounding failure and see if they are likely to be conducive to efficient disinvestment.

In Section I we examine the prevalence of failure and the legal and institutional background. In Section II we consider whether the failure process is likely to be efficient in practice, and present a case-study of an actual failure – the failure of Stone-Platt Ltd – in which we can see the process at work. In Section III we look at the related question of 'bankruptcy costs'. If there are costs associated with liquidation this will provide an incentive to arrange companies' affairs so as to avoid liquidation. Section IV examines how disinvestment decisions should be made from the point of view of society as a whole. We see that accounting losses may be an unreliable signal for closure. The main research effort in the field of company failure has gone into the development of statistical models of failure prediction, and in Section V we examine the use of such models.

I THE BACKGROUND TO FAILURE

CONCEPTS AND TERMINOLOGY

We cannot talk about company failure without sorting out the slightly confusing terminology. In the UK when a company ceases to exist in law we say it is *wound up* or goes into *liquidation*. *Bankruptcy* is something that, strictly speaking, happens only to individuals or partnerships who cannot meet their debts. However in the US they apply the word

---

1 This is partly because of lack of information – we can trace the records of firms before they fail, but then they disappear – and also perhaps because of lack of interest in the past when company failure was less prevalent.

'bankruptcy' to companies as well and the same tends to happen in the UK in everyday parlance.

A firm or an individual is *insolvent* if it does not have the cash to pay its debts as and when they fall due. Insolvency is the economic event that often gives rise to the legal event of liquidation, but other outcomes are possible. Creditors may be persuaded to hold off while the company's fortunes are revived. Sometimes it is possible to undertake a legal *reconstruction* of the firm. The old firm is liquidated and all parties agree to accept reduced claims on a new legal entity constructed round a viable part of the former business. Failed companies of some importance have been prone to being rescued by government on public policy grounds – examples in the UK have been Rolls Royce, British Leyland, Ferranti, Alfred Herbert, Chrysler. Often these companies are able to be relaunched successfully in due course.

Just as not all failed firms are wound up, not all liquidated firms have failed. An interesting albeit uncommon example of this occurred in 1982 when the Manville Corporation filed for bankruptcy – the biggest US bankruptcy since the 1930s. On the face of it Manville was a very healthy company, with assets of $2.2 billion against liabilities of $1 billion. But Manville was an asbestos manufacturer, and was facing 52,000 asbestos-health lawsuits whose combined damages could run to $2 billion. Mr John McKinney, Manville's chairman, did not intend to wind-up the company – quite the reverse. The filing for bankruptcy was a device 'to preserve the company's continuing operations, protect its assets, and achieve even-handed treatment of asbestos-health lawsuits and the claims of lending institutions and trade creditors'.

THE LEGAL PROCESS

Many companies are wound up each year for reasons which have nothing to do with failure, they may simply have outlived their usefulness and their owners see no further point in continuing the registration. However, our main concern is with companies which are liquidated through insolvency.

Insolvency is an inability to pay a debt. It is this event that usually triggers the legal process of liquidation. The law defines certain exact tests of 'failure to pay' which we outline in Table I.

If the company fails on one of these counts the court can be *petitioned* for an order for *compulsory winding-up*. The company or a shareholder can present such a petition, but it is more likely to be an unsecured creditor. There will be a hearing at which the petition will either be dismissed, adjourned or a winding-up order passed. At the same time the petitioner can ask for a provisional liquidator, probably the *official receiver*, to be put in to

---

Table I   Tests of insolvency

1 A creditor has served on the company a signed demand for payment of the sum due and the company has not either paid, secured or compounded for the sum to the creditor's satisfaction within three weeks.

2 Execution issued on a judgement in favour of a creditor is returned unsatisfied.

3 It is proved to the satisfaction of the court that the company is unable to pay its debts, taking into account its contingent and prospective liabilities.

safeguard the assets of the company, and if the court eventually decides to wind up the firm, he becomes the *liquidator*. Alternatively a company can be wound-up without going to the court. The company can initiate a member's or creditor's *voluntary winding-up* by passing an extraordinary resolution to that effect, and calling a meeting of creditors. The winding-up then proceeds in a similar fashion to a compulsory winding-up. Sometimes creditors will ask for the supervision of the court to give added protection in a voluntary winding-up.

The job of a liquidator is to wind up the affairs of the firm and realise its assets as quickly as possible. A receiver's task is to manage the business as a continuing entity and on occasion, if he is more successful than the previous management, he can nurse the business back to life. If a debt contract gives the lender a charge over the company's assets then the trust deed will empower him to appoint a receiver to safeguard his assets if the company breaks one of the specified covenants in the deed. Hence receivers are often appointed by banks or debenture-holders ahead of the legal winding-up process.

Table II shows the *order* in which the assets of a company are distributed to people with claims on them, in a winding-up. Apart from its interest to the people involved, the existence of a pecking-order amongst creditors is of some interest from the point of view of the efficiency of the liquidation process. It is sometimes suggested that the existence of preferential creditors who can install a receiver to protect their interests may lead to firms being liquidated which would otherwise not need to be, and assets being sold below their economic value. We return to this question when we discuss bankruptcy costs.

Table II   Statutory order of distribution in a winding-up

- Creditors having a fixed charge over a particular asset, to the extent of the proceeds of sale of that asset after payment of the realisation expenses of the receiver or liquidator. This includes the fixed charge over book debts, which has become more common in recent years.

- Costs of receivership in relation to a floating charge, and costs of liquidation where a receiver has not been appointed.

- Preferential creditors including, subject to various limitations, claims for local rates, income and corporation taxes, VAT, wages and salaries, social security contributions and superannuation contributions. The wages preference is for a maximum of four months wages with an overall limit of £800 per employee.

- Liabilities for tax arising from the activities of the receiver.

- Debenture holders, to the extent that their claims are covered by a floating charge over the company.

- Costs of the liquidator, where the company has first been placed in receivership.

- Unsecured creditors.

- Shareholders.

Source: Bank of England Quarterly Bulletin. Dec 1980.

THE PREVALENCE OF LIQUIDATION

Table III shows the number of companies entering compulsory or creditors' voluntary liquidation in England and Wales in the years up to 1984. The scale of these figures can be gauged by recalling that the population of active companies is presently around 300,000. So in 1984 approximately 4½% of these companies were liquidated.

Table III   Companies liquidated in England and Wales

	TOTAL	COMPULSORY	CREDITORS' VOLUNTARY
1975	5,398	2,287	3,111
1976	5,939	2,511	3,428
1977	5,831	2,425	3,406
1978	5,086	2,265	2,821
1979	4,537	2,064	2,473
1980	6,891	2,935	3,956
1981	8,596	2,771	5,825
1982	12,067	3,745	8,322
1983	13,406	4,807	8,599
1984	13,721	5,260	8,461

Source: CSO, FINANCIAL STATISTICS, HMSO

II   THE ECONOMICS OF DISINVESTMENT

THE THEORY

In theory it is easy enough to specify when a project should be abandoned, or a firm liquidated. It depends on their *value*. We advocate *investment* whenever NPV is positive – ie the present value of the net cash flows generated by a project exceeds the investment required to establish it. This investment will be measured by the opportunity cost of the assets employed, and if the assets are specially acquired this will generally be their 'replacement cost'. By the same token there should be *disinvestment* when NPV is negative – when the value of the assets in their present use is below their opportunity cost. The only difference is that now this will be measured by the 'realisable value' of the assets. So a project should be abandoned when

$$V_o > \sum_{t=1}^{n} \frac{C_t}{(1+r)^t} - I_o \tag{1}$$

where C_t = cash-flow in period t
　　　　 r　 = required return from the project
　　　　 I_o　 = the realisable value of the project's assets at t_o

In the case of a firm, its market value, V_o, measures the present value of future cash flows – so the firm should be abandoned when

$$V_o < I_o \tag{2}$$

We examined the relationship between replacement cost and realisable value in Chapter 12. Assets which are highly specific may have a very 'thin' market with realisable values well below replacement cost. This divergence can create a 'trap' in which projects or whole firms that with the benefit of hindsight would not have been worth creating, are worth preserving simply because of the low value of their assets in other uses.

Project abandonment

Projects should be abandoned as soon as the value of maintaining them becomes negative. To check this the firm should regularly revalue existing projects in order to compare the present value of the remaining cash flows with the value of the projects' assets in their next best use. In the unrealistic world of 'certainty' this problem never arises because the point at which the project will cease to be worthwhile is fully anticipated and defines the project life. In reality, though, project lives are uncertain. The decision-maker makes his best guess and some allowance for the riskiness of the forecast, but if the actual outcome is at the lower end of his expectations the project may need to be terminated early.

The risk is that the firm will not spot failing projects promptly. We saw that many firms do not even use DCF for initial project appraisal, preferring potentially misleading 'rules-of-thumb'. But still less firms have a formal DCF system for subsequent monitoring of projects. More commonly firms rely on signals from the accounting system or the perceptions of the marketing department to trigger doubts about a project; projects will only be abandoned at the right time if these signals are reliable indicators of value.

Abandonment is not always caused by failure. An increase in I_o can have the same effect when new and more lucrative uses come along for the project's assets.

The occasional failure and abandonment of individual projects is an inevitable side-effect of the uncertainty of economic life. In most firms it is a sustainable event – some reputations may suffer but the loss is borne by other projects and the human and physical capital is transferred elsewhere. Sometimes, though, the failure engulfs the whole firm and the loss can be severe, financially to investors and creditors, and for employees in terms of unemployment with its attendant costs. Hence the failure and liquidation of the firm is an event that tends to be resisted by all concerned.

The link between cash and value

The firm should be liquidated when $V_o < I_o$. In practice, though, liquidation does not seem to be about *value* so much as about *cash* – companies are insolvent and face liquidation if they cannot meet their debts as and when they fall due. The key to understanding the economics of liquidation is that *in a perfect capital market a firm should never be insolvent if it has a positive NPV*. This is because such a firm can always borrow against future cash inflows to meet temporary cash deficits and be confident of being able to pay the necessary interest on borrowing – this ability is precisely what present values measure.

How does liquidation work in practice? The best way to see this is by looking at the case of Stone-Platt.

STONE-PLATT – AN EXAMPLE OF COMPANY FAILURE

Stone-Platt was a UK manufacturer with long traditions, producing textile and other engineering machinery. In the early and mid-1970s it was exporting two-thirds of its UK output and earning an ROI of over 20%. However its fortunes started to change dramatically because of changes in the economic environment and because of Stone-Platt's failure to respond. Stone-Platt's heavy export emphasis had partly reflected the decline in the domestic textile industry, but the world market for textile machinery was undergoing significant changes too. Stone-Platt found that the world textile industry was losing its buoyancy, competitors were eroding its technical lead, sterling was rising, and perhaps most significantly the market for the 'big deal' – the supply and implementation of complete textile plants – which Stone-Platt had dominated, dwindled. Now they were forced increasingly to compete in more conventional product markets for individual items of capital equipment.

In 1976 Stone-Platt achieved a profit of £15.8 million. By 1979 this had turned into a pre-tax loss of £2.9 million. Fairly rapidly the following sequence of events took place.

— In 1979 the big Oldham plant was closed and £17.5 million was written-off against reserves. However a covenant in one of Stone-Platt's loan contracts required the maintenance of a certain level of equity. This clause was triggered by the write-off and in turn breached 'cross-default clauses' in other loan agreements. Hence a significant part of Stone-Platt's debt finance became repayable on demand and Stone-Platt's bankers were now in a position to decide its future.

— The Bank of England intervened and appointed a former Governor, Sir Jasper Hallam, to chair a process of renegotiation and settlement with creditors. The creditors led by the Midland Bank agreed to hold off whilst Stone-Platt, which was perceived to contain some viable sections, reorganised. Under the new arrangements the firm was given loans and overdraft facilities until January 1982.

— Certain divisions of Stone-Platt remained viable and it was possible to sell these off. In November 1980 the pumps division was sold for £11 million and in February 1981 the marine propeller division. These sales reduced borrowings by £16 million. Unfortunately these sales of profitable divisions which had been subsidising other activities, depressed the returns on the 'rump' even further. The 1981 loss was £5.7 million pre-tax. There were further write-offs of £15 million in 1981.

— It had been clear all along that a long term settlement with creditors would only be possible if the equity base could be increased. This required investors who would be prepared to subscribe equity to Stone-Platt. On the 12 March 1981 this was achieved and a settlement was made. Forty million new shares were issued raising £10 million. Two city institutions, Equity Capital for Industry and Finance Corporation for Industry, were to take up 12 million with the rest being offered to existing shareholders and underwritten by Hill Samuel, Stone-Platt's financial advisers, and ECI and FCI. In return four clearing banks provided £40 million of borrowing facilities, of which £25 million was a five-year loan and standby credit. This settlement gave Stone-Platt a healthy balance-sheet – £50 million of equity to £30 million of debt – and time for further reorganisation.

The Stone-Platt case shows up some interesting features of the failure process. In principle the capital market should extend cash to firms with positive value. In practice, lack of information about the future prospects of the firm and about available alternative uses for its assets make a spot decision impossible. Instead time is needed. If the firm's position can be held the future may unfold and a *search* can be undertaken to find the most valuable method of deploying the firm's assets. The search involves a thorough study by the firm and its consultants of possible internal reorganisations, and an assessment of external possibilities through attempts to sell-off parts of the firm. In a world of imperfect information this may be a good way of appraising 'value'. In the case of Stone-Platt the process seemed to work well – the activities of the firm came under close scrutiny from inside and outside. Valuable activities were identified and in some cases floated off, and management changes and policy changes were made in order to salvage perceived problem areas. New finance was provided when investors convinced themselves they had enough information from which to forecast an adequate return to debt and equity finance.

Coda   The settlement of 12 March 1981 did not stem the Stone-Platt losses; the ailing textile division was still at the heart of Stone-Platt's problem. Losses mounted during the ensuing year so that by March 1982 the directors were proposing another capital reconstruction. Reckoning that at the present rate shareholders funds would soon fall to £15 million the Midland Bank led the clearing banks in putting a receiver in. The company was dismantled in a series of sales and management buy-outs which raised £40 million. This was not even sufficient to pay the outstanding debt and preferential creditors. At the beginning of June 1982 shareholders, including FCI and ECI, received letters telling them they could not hope to receive anything from the dismantling of Stone-Platt.

The decision of Midland Bank to 'blow the whistle' on Stone-Platt was criticised in several quarters. Mr Geoffrey Robinson, Labour MP for Coventry NW, felt it marked 'the nadir of the failure of the banks to understand and cater for manufacturing industry'.

IS THE LIQUIDATION PROCESS EFFICIENT?

In theory the firm should be liquidated when $V_o < I_o$. In practice there is imperfect information about the value of the firm's assets in different uses: it takes time to search out possibilities for selling-off profitable divisions or salvaging and reconstructing part of the firm. In the case of Stone-Platt the search was largely made possible by the status of the company and by the willingness of the Bank of England and Sir Jasper Hallam to be involved. Holding-off while a search takes place is an act of faith by investors, and they run the risk that new money is being thrown after bad. This turned out to be the case at Stone-Platt. In general it seems likely that the decision to hold-off will be influenced by factors such as size, status and reputation, and by public policy considerations acting through the influence of agencies such as the Bank of England. Unless factors such as these are reliable signals of value, we cannot rely on the process being efficient. There are clear examples of large companies being rescued by government on public policy grounds. Furthermore we know that small firms are more likely to fail than large. There may be good reasons for this – small firms are more vulnerable to economic fluctuations and less likely to be diversified. We have no evidence on whether the right firms fail, and we never get to know what would have happened if they had not.

The effect of 'me-first'

There is a pecking order amongst creditors when a company is liquidated. Secured lenders come first and very often, as in the Stone-Platt case, liquidation is triggered by their decision to appoint a receiver to protect their interests. Does the existence of so-called 'me-first' rules affect the efficiency of the process?

One possibility is that liquidation will be triggered sooner, and 'equity' often accuse debt-holders of withdrawing too early. This argument looks attractive – since the secured assets are usually vital to the survival of the company, the ability to withdraw them means that the company's survival is effectively dependent on the welfare of one group of investors. On the other hand equity usually have very little to lose by shouting 'foul' when debt-holders send in a receiver. In the case of Stone-Platt, equity shareholders were reported to be disgruntled by the Midland Bank's action. But since the equity interest turned out to be worth nothing at that time, it was in their interests to use any ploy to lengthen Stone-Platt's life – even if the chances of a turnaround were infinitesimal.

Furthermore, since the receiver's prime task is to recover debt-holders funds he may not bother to realise the firm's assets for their full value. Searching out the best price will involve him in additional costs at no gain to debt-holders. Similarly the receiver may well find it 'easier' to sell off a firm's assets than to seek to return the firm to sound health even though this might yield a higher value. In extreme cases the aggrieved residue of creditors are able to sue the receiver for negligence. The argument may have some force – it is another issue in company failure on which we have no hard evidence.

Diversification and efficient disinvestment

Large firms are less likely to fail than small, and research shows that the returns of large firms are less 'risky', less variable, than those of small firms. This is partly explained by the greater diversification of large firms. But it is wrong to jump to the conclusion that diversification is an attractive cure to company failure. Economic failure is not avoided by diversification – the difference is that rather than leading to company failure the loss is borne inside the firm. We know that managers, employees and even investors may be reluctant to recognise company failure so that firms may continue to trade after their net present value becomes negative. But is failure more quickly recognised and loss-making activities more speedily terminated inside a diversified firm? This is a moot point. It should be – the firm is both the investor and the manager and has the best information on net present value; the firm may be able to transfer resources smoothly to other uses; the 'cost of bankruptcy' – which we discuss in the next section – will be avoided. In practice though, without the sanction of the market-place firms may continue loss-making activities, *cross-subsidised* by profitable ones, for lengthy periods of time. This may be because of optimism, a relectance of the project's sponsors to besmirch their reputations, or a failure in the accounting system to properly allocate costs. In this case the shareholder bears costs he might avoid under limited liability and this may well exceed any benefit from avoiding bankruptcy costs.

III   BANKRUPTCY COSTS

When we are building theories in finance we like, at least as a starting point, to assume a perfect capital market in which there are no obstacles to the free operation of market forces. One potential set of obstacles in practice is costs to liquidation or 'bankruptcy costs' and these have assumed great importance in finance. For example, in a 'pure' Capital Asset Pricing Model world it is shareholders who build diversified portfolios, and diversification by the firm is not a thing of value to them. But if there are *bankruptcy costs* diversification by the firm may be in the interests of shareholders. Similarly if there are bankruptcy costs the value of the firm may be maximised by restricting the amount of debt the firm uses, whereas in a pure Modigliani and Miller world capital structure is irrelevant to the value of the firm.

How significant are bankruptcy costs? The answer is that we have little hard evidence, but people often behave as though bankruptcy is something to be avoided if at all possible – in other words they behave as though there are severe costs to bankruptcy. In a perfect capital market bankruptcy is painless – it is the event of a smooth and costless transfer of assets to their next best use, outside the firm. Bankruptcy costs are leakages – losses of value – that occur when the firm is liquidated. Suppose a proportion L of the value of the firm, V, is lost when the firm is liquidated. Then if there is a probability, p, of the firm failing, the expected value of bankruptcy costs is p.L.V.

The most tangible costs to bankruptcy are the 'transactions costs' associated with winding up the firm – the expenses of liquidation and particularly the costs of the receiver and liquidator, Warner (1977) examined these costs associated with railroad bankruptcies in the US. On average he found that the costs were 5.3% of the market values of the firms involved, in terms of their values just before liquidation. In terms of the value of these firms a few years prior to liquidation these costs emerged as quite small.

If the assets of a bankrupt firm were sold off at less than their true value this would be another cost to bankruptcy. People often claim that this happens – liquidators may go for a quick sale, or being the creditors' representatives may have little incentive to achieve a price beyond what is needed to pay off the creditors. The implication is that asset markets are inefficient around bankruptcy. This idea is attractive, but we have no hard evidence on it. There is no doubt that asset values often *seem* very low in liquidation, but this may be an illusion. People are often reluctant to recognise the decline in value of a failing firm, and its liquidation value comes as a shock. The temptation to cry 'we've been done!' is irresistible.

The third component of bankruptcy cost is also hard to measure. It is the effects of restrictions and limitations put on failing firms by their creditors. Creditors routinely impose certain constraints on the freedom of management – these are embodied in the restrictive covenants written into debt agreements and in the normal course of events these restrictions are not too onerous. But if these covenants are breached as the firm fails, creditors are likely to impose much tighter limits and closer monitoring. The creditors' aim now is to give managers just enough leeway to exploit any possibilities for salvaging the firm whilst avoiding the risk of further losses. We saw this happening in the Stone-Platt example. In practice this does limit management's ability to pursue new projects, and involves them in a good deal of time negotiating and being monitored by bankers and creditors.

A final cost of bankruptcy is the damage to managers' reputations from association with failure and the loss of income while they are looking for new jobs. This appears to be a cost to managers rather than shareholders, but it could be argued that managers will seek to transfer it to shareholders by asking higher rewards for managing risky firms.

IV SOCIAL DISINVESTMENT DECISIONS

The intervention of government can be decisive in averting the failure of companies. Many well-known firms have been saved by UK government support in recent years, and some have been nursed back to health and relaunched as viable entities. But how should governments decide which firms to save? We know from our study of decision-making that there is a recurrent problem with 'rules-of-thumb'. People are inclined to make decisions on the basis of accounting measures of performance that may not be good signals of value. This problem can be particularly acute with social disinvestment decisions. It stems from the very reasonable and generally-held view, shared by many politicians, that profitable operations in the economy should be expanded and loss-making ones closed. So profit or loss becomes a criterion for investing or disinvesting.

Consider the following problem:

Burton and Williams Ltd owns a steelworks in South Wales. The steelworks has made a heavy loss this year and Burton and Williams has asked the government for financial support.

BURTON & WILLIAMS: INCOME STATEMENT y/e 31.12.1985

	(£ million)	
Sales		180
Materials	90	
Purchased fuels	20	
Employment costs	65	
Other charges	20	
Depreciation	10	(205)
		(25)
Interest charges by government		(14)
	Loss	£(39)

Should the government support a loss-making firm? If it does not, the steelworks will close, so the financial decision is effectively a disinvestment decision. It is worth recalling some principles of sound decision-making from earlier chapters. First, only the 'effects' of the decision should be taken into account, and the appropriate measure of costs and benefits is opportunity cost. Second, investment and disinvestment decisions will have effects in several future time periods. The surplus of benefits over costs is termed 'contribution' in the case of short-term decisions, 'net present value' in the case of long-term. In the light of this, we have to ask: Is the current loss of Burton and Williams a correct measure of its contribution? And what happens in other years?

The accounting loss of Burton and Williams will only measure its contribution relative to this decision if the accounting costs are correct measures of the opportunity cost to the government of the resources used by the firm and if the accounting revenue correctly measures the benefits.

A whole branch of economics has evolved around this issue. 'Social cost-benefit analysis' examines under what conditions we can expect a divergence between public ('social' or 'government') costs and benefits, and private ones, and it has developed techniques for estimating these public costs and benefits.[2] In this section we sketch some of the arguments. Clearly if there is a divergence, the use of private costs and benefits will not necessarily yield correct social investment decisions. It is common to refer to the set of prices that would yield an optimal decision as 'shadow prices'.[3] The problem is thus to find the appropriate set of shadow prices underlying the actual prices we observe.

To get the flavour of the adjustments that would be necessary to convert a historic cost profit or loss figure into a measure of social contribution, we will look at just three of Burton and Williams' inputs, and assume for simplicity that the rest can stand as they are.

Labour

The opportunity cost of an idle resource is zero. We estimate that if they are made redundant 80% of the workers will not find other employment. The private cost of employing these workers, the cost to the firm, is measured by their wages. But viewed from a government point of view the problem is one of an internal transfer of resources from one use to another within the decision-unit, the economy. If some workers will be otherwise

2 Good introductions to this topic are Prest and Turvey (1965) in Layard (1972), and Layard's own introduction. A recent text on cost-benefit analysis is Pearce and Nash (1981).
3 See Chapter 12 for a description of shadow pricing in the context of project choice.

unemployed the cost of using these workers at Burton and Williams is zero.[4] So, if we can assume that the remaining 20% will find work elsewhere which enables them to earn a contribution equivalent to their current salary, the opportunity cost measure of the labour expense is £65m × 20% = £13m.

Depreciation

Depreciation attempts to measure the cost of using fixed assets. It is an allocation of part of the initial cost to a particular time period. But for decision making what is needed is a measure of the opportunity cost of using the fixed assets. It appears that no offers have been received for the plant and equipment of the steelworks, and that if the steelworks closes they will be idle resources. In this case the opportunity cost of using them is zero. Zero is presumably the private opportunity cost as well, since depreciation does not represent a cash flow of the firm, the associated cash has been spent and is now a 'sunk cost'.

Raw materials

To demonstrate another problem in the transition from private to public costs, consider the opportunity cost of resources acquired from other firms. The private cost of using such resources is in 'normal' conditions of regular purchase, what is paid for them. But what is the public opportunity cost? What is the relationship between the price of the resources and their opportunity cost? Basic micro-economics shows this to be a function of the degree of monopoly of the supplier. Consider Figure I which shows the conventional prediction of theory about the pricing behaviour of rational monopolists.

The rational monopolist produces up to the point where marginal cost equals marginal revenue, up to q^* with a corresponding marginal cost of c^*. But because of the divergence

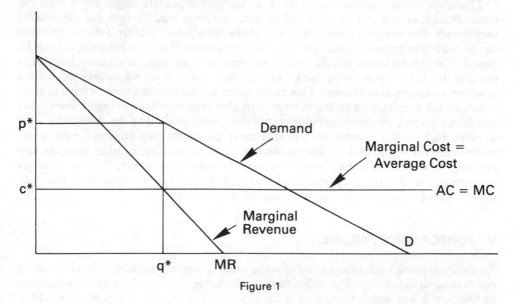

Figure 1

4   What about unemployment pay, 'dole', which appears to put an extra cost on government when workers are unemployed? Does this make the opportunity cost actually negative? No, dole is irrelevant since it is merely a *transfer* of income from one group in society to another. It does not involve the generation of contribution.

of the demand and marginal cost curves he is able to charge a price of p* at this output level. We assume here that AC = MC. The key perception is that part of the price of the monopolist's output, p* − c*, will be 'monopoly profit', and this will constitute a divergence between the price of inputs provided by a monopolist, and the real cost of the resources being supplied. It has been estimated that 20% of the price of the raw materials bought by the steelworks is 'monopoly profit' of the supplier. So to find the public opportunity cost it is necessary to reduce the private cost proportionately,

£90m × 80% = £72m.

Making these three adjustments will convert the measure of private profit or loss into a measure of public contribution as follows:

	(£m)
Sales	180
Materials 90 × 80%	72
Purchased fuels	20
Employment costs 65 × 20%	13
Other charges	20
Depreciation 10 × 0%	0
	(125)
	55
Interest charges by government	(14)
	41

On this basis it appears that the steelworks is currently making a positive contribution.

Though it is hard to fault the logic of all this, some readers might argue with the conclusion. It seems that by a sleight of hand we have made a case for subsidising inefficiency. But so far we have only looked at one time period. Before a proper decision can be made about closure, future periods must be examined too. The plant should only be closed if the present value of all the future contributions it will make is negative. It is clearly possible that in the future, even using social measures of cost, the steelworks will indeed generate a negative contribution. This might happen if for instance there were a general return to full employment in the economy. In this case increased demand from other activities will drive up the opportunity cost of the resources used by the steelworks – the workers might find jobs elsewhere, an alternative use might even emerge for the steel-works.[5] So a full appraisal of this problem is going to require a rather complex and conjectural analysis of future events in the economy as a whole. Not surprisingly governments tend to shy away from doing this explicitly, though we would hope they take these factors into account in their judgemental decision-making.

V   FORECASTING FAILURE

An ability to predict failure is a thing of some value to anyone planning to lend or supply goods or services to a firm. The technique for calculating a 'Z-score' for a firm to measure its failure risk was largely developed in the US by Ed Altman. Z-scores are now widely available for UK firms, and in this section we review their use.

5   Though in this economy there will probably be increased demand for steel too which might raise the opportunity cost of closing the steelworks!

Traditionally financial analysts studied the accounts of firms whose credit worthiness they were trying to assess. They concentrated particularly on measures of solvency, such as 'current ratio' and 'quick ratio', and on measures of financial strength such as 'gearing', and compared these with industry norms or rules of thumb. The problem with this sort of approach is that in a world of complex industrial types it may be hard to define a 'norm'. Moreover ratios share the limitations of the accounting data from which they are prepared. In particular, the data is historic, it describes what has already happened, whereas the analyst actually wants to know what is going to happen, and as far in advance as possible. Obviously this is no surprise, this is always our problem in finance and it cannot be avoided.

The approach of researchers into failure prediction has been to use statistical analysis to make the best use possible of historical data. Various approaches have been used but most recent work uses a technique called *multiple discriminant analysis* (MDA). The MDA approach works by finding the 'model', in this case a function containing ratios with various weights attached, that best discriminates between certain prespecified groups of objects, in this case the set of failed and the set of non-failed firms.

Note that in this section we are using the word 'failure' rather than 'liquidation'. As we saw, liquidation is a legal event that *usually* follows the economic event of insolvency. But since it is at least possible that the capital market is inefficient with respect to liquidation we could get a situation where, out of two identical insolvent firms, one was liquidated and one survived – the difference being institutional or 'human' factors reflecting such things as the optimism of the creditors and the status of the firm. Because of the potential difficulty of modelling these non-economic factors researchers have restricted themselves to predicting 'failure', rather than liquidation.

We will look at two studies by Altman.

ALTMAN'S 1968 PAPER

Altman took 33 US manufacturers that filed for bankruptcy between 1946 and 1965. He paired each of these with a firm of similar *size* and *industry* that did not go bankrupt. Twenty-two ratios falling into 5 categories – liquidity, profitability, leverage, solvency, and activity ratios – were calculated, chosen on the basis of their apparent relevance and popularity with users. MDA was used to find the five ratios, one from each category, X_1 – X_5, and the linear weighting of those ratios, that yielded the best discriminant statistic, Z. The process is essentially an 'iterative search' by computer; repeated combinations of variables are tried until one that 'works best' emerges. Unlike economic model-building, there is no theoretical basis to the choice of variables and weights and for this reason the MDA approach to failure prediction has been called 'brute empiricism'.[6]

Altman found the following model worked best:

	weight	ratio		contribution to discrimination
Z =	.012 .	working capital to total assets	X_1	3.29
+	.014 .	retained earnings to total assets	X_2	6.04
+	.033 .	earnings before interest and taxes to total assets	X_3	9.89
+	.006 .	market value of equity to book value of total debt	X_4	7.42
+	.010 .	sales to total assets	X_5	8.41

---

6   See Foster (1978) ch 14 for this, and for an excellent summary and critique of approaches to failure prediction. Dev (1974) provides a survey of earlier uses of ratio analysis in predicting failure. For recent critiques
of the MDA methodology see Eisenbeis (1977), Mayer (1977).

Though the performance of the variables in a discriminant function is interdependent, the relative contribution of the variables in MDA can be measured by 'scaled-vectors'[7] and we can see that on this basis X_3, £BIT/total assets, is the main contributor.

There are two types of possible error in failure prediction. We call forecasting as non-failed a firm that subsequently fails a 'type-I error' and forecasting as a failure a firm that does not fail a 'type-II error'. Will the user of Z-scores be indifferent between these two types of error? This is unlikely. Suppose he is a bank or finance house receiving loan applicants. The cost to him of a type-II error, if it leads him to reject a loan applicant who subsequently does not go bankrupt, is the loss of profit on the loan, and if he is lending under capital rationing this cost may approximate zero. Type-I errors are likely to have a much higher cost. Accepting a client who subsequently fails can mean interest and all or part of the principal may be jeopardised. Moreover, considerable administrative costs will be incurred in the process. In his 1977 paper Altman estimated the cost of a type-I error at 35 times the cost of a type-II.

Altman found that using data for one year prior to bankruptcy on the sample of firms on which the model was estimated, the model accurately classified 95% overall, but within this there were 6% of type-I errors, and 3% of type-II. Using data two years prior to bankruptcy, overall 83% were classified accurately within which there were 28% type-I errors and 6% type-II errors. The success rate of the model fell off dramatically beyond two years prediction, overall accuracy for three years prior data was 48%, four years – 29%, 5 years – 36%.

ALTMAN'S 1977 STUDY

In 1977 Altman *et al* produced an improved model for failure predictions. Their 1977 sample of failures had a larger average size and included some non-bankrupt failures – firms whom the government had had to support, had been forced to merge, or had been taken over by the banks. They used an augmented list of variables and a refined discriminant technique. This time the best predictor was a seven-variable model comprising the following variables: return on assets, stability of earnings, interest cover, cumulative profitability, liquidity (= current ratio), equity/total capital, size (= total assets). The relative performance of the 1977 and 1968 models is shown in Table IV.

Table IV   Classification accuracy of the 1968 and 1977 models compared

Year prior to bankruptcy	1977 model		1968 model	
	bankrupt	non-bankrupt	bankrupt	non-bankrupt
1	96.2	89.7	93.9	97.0
2	84.9	93.1	71.9	93.9
3	74.5	91.4	48.3	n.a.
4	68.1	89.5	28.6	n.a.
5	69.8	82.1	36.0	n.a.

Source: Altman et al (1977)

---

7   Calculated by multiplying corresponding elements by the square roots of the diagonal elements of the variance-co-variance matrix.

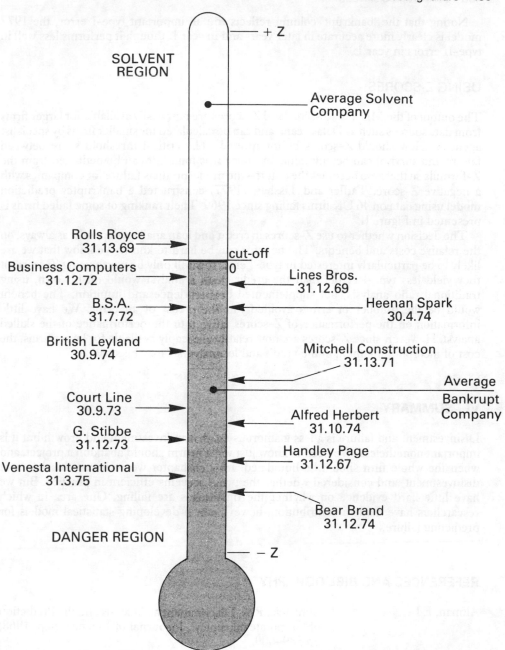

SOLVENT
REGION

+ Z

Average Solvent
Company

Rolls Royce
31.13.69

cut-off
0

Business Computers
31.12.72

Lines Bros.
31.12.69

B.S.A.
31.7.72

Heenan Spark
30.4.74

British Leyland
30.9.74

Mitchell Construction
31.13.71

Average
Bankrupt
Company

Court Line
30.9.73

Alfred Herbert
31.10.74

G. Stibbe
31.12.73

Handley Page
31.12.67

Venesta International
31.3.75

Bear Brand
31.12.74

DANGER REGION

– Z

Source: Taffler & Tisshaw (1977)

Figure II The Solvency Thermometer

Noting that the 'bankrupt' column reflects the all important type-I error, the 1977 model is clearly more accurate in later years and in year 1, though it performs less well in type-II errors in year 1.

USING Z-SCORES

The output of the MDA is a Z-score and Z-scores are now easily available for larger firms from data sources such as Datastream, and can be calculated for smaller firms by specialist agencies. How should Z-scores be interpreted? The critical threshold score between failure and survival can be any value, but once it is found, it can be deducted from the Z-formula so that zero becomes the cutoff – the model predicts failure for companies with a negative Z-score. Taffler and Tisshaw (1977) constructed a bankruptcy prediction model using data on 46 UK firms failing since 1969. Their ranking of some failed firms is presented in Figure II.

The decision whether to use Z-scores in credit and loan analysis depends, as always, on the relative costs and benefits. The benefits can be hard to know. We know that we are likely to be particularly interested in type-I errors. It will only be worth using Z-scores if they yield less type-I errors than the credit or loan analyst would on his own, using traditional ratio analysis, but supplemented by experience and intuition. The benefit would be the number of errors avoided times the cost of an error. We have little information on the performance of Z-scores relative to the performance of the skilled analyst. However, since Z-scores are now relatively cheaply available for larger firms, the cost of incorporating them in the credit and loan analysis may be small.

VI SUMMARY

Disinvestment and failure is a less glamorous topic than investment and growth but it is important nonetheless. We need to know just when a firm should abandon a project, and when the whole firm should be liquidated. In this chapter we reviewed the theory of disinvestment, and considered whether the process seems efficient in practice. But we have little hard evidence on whether the right firms are failing. One area in which researchers have made a contribution, however, is in developing statistical models for predicting failure.

REFERENCES AND BIBLIOGRAPHY

Altman, E I	'Financial Ratios, Discriminant Analysis and the Prediction of Corporate Bankruptcy', Journal of Finance, Sept 1968, pp 589–609.
Altman, E I	*Corporate Bankruptcy in America* (1971) Heath Lexington Books, Lexington, Mass.
Altman, E I, Haldeman, R G and Naraianan, P	'Zeta Analysis: A New Model to Identify Bankruptcy Risk of Corporations', Journal of Banking and Finance, 1977, pp 29–54.
Danbolena, I G and Khoury, S J	'Ratio Stability and Corporate Failure', Journal of Finance, Sept 1980, pp 1012–1026.

Dev, S	'Ratio Analysis and the Prediction of Company Failure', in Edey H S & B S Yamey, *Debits, Credits, Finance and Profits* (1974) London.
Eisenbeis, R A	'Pitfalls in the Application of Discriminant Analysis in Business, Finance and Economics', Journal of Finance, June 1977, pp 875–900.
Foster, G	*Financial Statement Analysis* (1978) Prentice-Hall, Englewood-Cliffs, New Jersey.
Gordon, M J	'Towards a Theory of Financial Distress', Journal of Finance, May 1971, pp 347–356.
Layard, R (ed)	*Cost-Benefit Analysis* (1972) Penguin, Harmondsworth.
Mayer, R C	'Forecasting Financial Failure: A Re-examination', Financial Management, Spring 1977.
Norton, C L and Smith, R E	'A Comparison of General Price Level and Historical Cost Financial Statements in the Prediction of Bankruptcy', Accounting Review, Jan 1979, pp 72–87.
Ohlson, J A	'Financial Ratios and the Probabilistic Prediction of Bankruptcy', Journal of Accounting Research, Spring 1980.
Pearce, D W and Nash, C A	*The Social Appraisal of Projects* (1981) Macmillan, London.
Prest, A R and Turvey, R	'Cost-Benefit Analysis – A Survey', Economic Journal 1965, in Layard (1972).
Stapleton, R C	'Some Aspects of the Pure Theory of Corporate Finance: Bankruptcies and Take-overs: Comment', Bell Journal of Economics, Autumn 1975, pp 708–710.
Stiglitz, J E	'Some Aspects of the Pure Theory of Corporate Finance; Bankruptcies and Take-overs: Reply', Bell Journal of Economics, Autumn 1975, pp 711–714.
Taffler, R J and Tisshaw, H	'Going, Going, Gone – for Factors which Predict', Accountancy, March 1977.
Van Horne, J C	'Optimal Initiation of Bankruptcy Proceedings', Journal of Finance, June 1976, pp 897–910.
Warner, J B	'Bankruptcy Costs: Some Evidence', Journal of Finance, 1977, pp 337–348.

QUESTIONS

1 Define a decision-rule for liquidating projects and whole firms. Are there barriers to the efficient liquidation of projects and firms in practice?

2 In a perfect capital market there are no costs to bankruptcy. In reality, bankruptcy is an outcome everyone seeks to avoid. What are the costs?

3 You have been asked by a bank how they can most efficiently predict which of their customers are bad credit risks. Explain in detail the alternatives available.

4 You are the chairman of Lameduck Ltd, a Midlands manufacturing company. Lameduck's most recent P & L a/c was as follows:

	£ million
Sales – Home	10
– Overseas	5
	15
Expenses –	
Materials	6
Labour	6
Depreciation	3
Interest	1
Other	3
	19
Profit/(Loss)	(4)

Lameduck's creditors are threatening liquidation. You decide to write to the government to ask for a subsidy to cover your losses.

(a) List the arguments you might use in your appeal and explain why they should influence a government which was maximising the welfare of society as a whole.

(b) Say how you would reply if you were the government, and what extra information you might require.

Part VII
International finance and investment

Part VII
International finance and
investment

CHAPTER 26

International finance and investment

So far we have been discussing finance and investment in a domestic setting. We now remove this restriction to see how the analysis is affected if the firm can invest in projects and raise finance abroad. We find the logic of finance is unaffected, but there is a new dimension we need to take account of. The prices of the goods and services and of the finance embodied in finance and investment decisions may depend on the exchange rates between the countries concerned. This introduces a new source of risk, albeit one which can be hedged. We discuss these issues in Section I, and show that if currency markets are working freely financial decisions should be unaffected by exchange rates. In Section II we show that given certain institutional features of the real world, the company will need to give some thought to its international finance and investment decisions.

This chapter is necessarily an overview of the main issues, moreover we restrict the discussion to the 'financial' rather than the more general 'business' issues. There are many good texts on international financial management, and on international business and multinational enterprises. We reference some at the end of the chapter.

I PRICES ACROSS EXCHANGES

FIXED AND FLOATING EXCHANGES RATES

We know that different countries have different currencies. In itself, that has no significance for financial decisions. Suppose Anglo-Moldavian is considering building a new factory in Moldavia and most of the costs and revenues of the project will be incurred in the local currency, dinars. Suppose also the dinar/sterling 'rate of exchange', the rate at which AM can convert one pound into dinars is fixed at 8. Then it is of no importance whether AM figures out the NPV of its new project in pounds or dinars, the answer will be the same. In a world of fixed exchange rates investing and financing in another country will be no different from investing and financing in another region of the same country.

The history of fixed and floating exchanges

In the years leading up to the First World War exchange rates were regulated through the 'gold standard'. Under the gold standard the pound sterling was deemed to contain 113 grains of gold, and the US dollar 23.22. This fixed the dollar/sterling exchange rate as \$4.87 to £1. Demand and supply was balanced by movements of gold. If more Americans were demanding British goods than vice versa gold would flow into the UK to pay for them, and in principle, the increase in UK money supply would push up the prices and reduction in US supply would deflate US prices until the demand imbalance was eliminated. In retrospect the gold standard probably survived because the period before the First World War was particularly stable. During the upheaval of the First War it was suspended and never successfully re-established again.

The appeal of stable currencies is strong and in 1944 the international monetary authorities meeting at Bretton Woods agreed a new system of fixed exchange rates between the member nations. Under 'Bretton Woods' only the US dollar was convertible into gold, and movements in domestic prices were not to be entirely relied on to maintain parity. Member countries were expected to try and maintain the value of their currencies within 1% of the official level, but if this proved impossible up to a 10% devaluation could be made without reference to the ruling authority, the International Monetary Fund,and devaluations of over 10% if approved by the IMF. At the outset this 'adjustable peg' system had some features of the gold standard with the US dollar proxying for gold. This system worked so long as the US had far and away the most powerful economy. However as the pre-eminence of the US currency waned, the 1960s became an era of perpetual balance of payments surpluses in West Germany and Japan and deficits in the US, which the IMF seemed powerless to do anything about. In 1973 the fixed rate system was abandoned and a period of freely floating rates ensued. Towards the end of the 1970s this crystallised into a mixed system known as the 'managed float'. Under this system some countries try to maintain a fixed parity between their currencies, while others float. Some smaller nations will maintain a fixed rate with their major trading partner; often this means the US dollar. Another fixed group are the members of the European Monetary System which was founded in 1979. The EMS was formed by all the members of the European Community except Britain, and acts like a local Bretton Woods. Even amongst those floating currencies, the float is not free, but is controlled by the intervention of the respective central bankers.

The politicians who create fixed exchange rate systems are sometimes pursuing broader sorts of unity; but the desire for stable currencies is a powerful one. However fixed rate systems tend not to survive under the constant pressure of market forces towards 'purchasing power parity'.

PURCHASING POWER PARITY

'Purchasing power parity theory' says that exchange rates must be such that they permit someone with a given amount of wealth to exchange it for the same bundle of goods and services in any country. If PPP does not hold arbitrage will be possible.

An example should make this clear.

Doris has got £100 which she desperately wants to spend on brass door knobs. In England knobs cost £5 each, in Moldavia 40 dinars. suppose the dinar/sterling exchange rate is 10. While Doris could get 20 knobs in England, by changing her money into dinars and buying in Moldavia she could get 25. Indeed it will pay Doris not only to spend her £100 but to borrow more and to buy large quantities of knobs in Moldavia and sell them in England. By the same token if the exchange rate were 6 the flow would be the other way, and Moldavians would be importing door knobs from England. As we have noted before in other contexts, 'arbitrage' will take place wherever the same commodity is selling for different prices. Arbitrage only ceases when prices are driven into line. Across exchanges this can happen in two ways, by domestic prices changing, and by exchange rates changing. So in the first case, when Doris can buy 20 knobs in England and 25 in Moldavia, her demand for Moldavian knobs will tend to drive their price up, while her lack of demand for English knobs wil push their price down. At the same time, however, Doris's demand for dinars to buy the knobs, and her desire to supply sterling, will tend to drive the dinar/sterling exchange rate down. The equilibrium will come when there is 'purchasing power parity'. In the present case, this will occur when the exchange rate is 8.

The question of whether it is domestic prices, or the exchange rate, which does the adjusting is rather important. The assumption behind the gold standard was that it would be domestic prices which did all the adjustment, so the exchange rate could be fixed. But the heyday of the gold standard corresponded with a period of economic stability. In more recent times the volatility of the world economy would have required much greater adjustments in domestic economies; and social and political changes meant that the necessary adjustments were less acceptable, hence the burden fell on exchange rate adjustment.

Of course our Doris example was excessively simple. In reality there is a variety of barriers to arbitrage:

—There are costs to finding out about international prices, to converting currency, and to importing and exporting.

—Some goods and services are hard to trade internationally, and so are partly sheltered from international competition: transport, education, labour are examples.

—National governments sometimes control competition by limiting the freedom to import and export, or by limiting the freedom to exchange currency. And if imbalance between demand and supply of a currency does put exchange rates under pressure governments will sometimes hold out against a change by borrowing or lending the deficit.

However, the underlying pressure towards purchasing power parity remains. So once an equilibrium system of exchange rates is established why cannot rates remain fixed? Where does the disequilibrium come from?

The main factor which destabilises exchange rates is differences in domestic inflation rates. Suppose the English and Moldavian brass door knob prices were £5 and 40 dinars in January 1986, with an exchange rate of 8 giving purchasing power parity, but during the next year English and Moldavian prices inflate by 5% and 15% respectively, to £5.25 and 46 dinars. By the end of 1986 an exchange rate of $\frac{46}{5.25} = 8.76$ will be needed to maintain purchasing power parity. The exchange rate must inflate to keep pace with domestic prices, ie,

$$8 \times \frac{1.15}{1.05} = 8.76$$

To summarise, for equilibrium we require purchasing power parity, but with differential domestic inflation this is inconsistent with exchange rate parity.

INTEREST RATE PARITY

We can now say something about the relationship between interest rates and exchange rates. We call the rate at which one currency can be exchanged for another *today*, the *spot* exchange rate. The rates you see hanging on the wall in the bank or bureau de change are spot rates. However you can also make a contract to buy or sell currency forward, and the rate at which you agree to exchange in the future is the *future rate*. You can get a forward rate for any term, but rates are commonly quoted for 1-, 3-, 6- and 12-months ahead. For example for 10 October 1985 the Financial Times showed the following dollar/sterling rates:

Day's spread	Close	One month	% pa	Three months	% pa
1.4095 − 1.4150	1.4105 − 1.4115	0.44 − 0.41	3.61	1.16 − 1.11	3.22
		cents per month		cents per month	

Hence for immediate delivery on the 10 October you could buy (taking the mid-point) 1.4124 dollars per pound, the spot rate was 1.4124. However, the three month future rate showed a premium of 1.11–1.16, let us say 1.135 cents. In other words the forward rate was 1.4238 which as the FT tells us, was an annualised increase of 3.22%.

This immediately leads us to some conclusions about relative interest rates. *Interest rate parity* requires that the difference between the interest rates on loans in the two currencies should be the same as the % difference between the spot rate and the forward rate of the same duration. We can check this, because the FT of 10 October 1985 also shows that three months sterling loans on the Euromarket paid 11½–11⅝%, while three month dollar loans were quoted at 8⅛–8¼, a differential of 3.375%, close to the 3.22% we noted earlier.

Purchasing power parity said that a given amount of wealth should be able to purchase the same bundle of goods in any country. Interest rate parity is just an inter-temporal extension of purchasing power parity, and in the same way there will be arbitrage possibilities unless it holds. Suppose we have £1,000 and need dollars in three months: we have two routes to getting them, both of which involve no uncertainty about future exchange rates. We can:

1 buy dollars spot, and invest them at the dollar rate for three months, or
2 make a forward contract and invest at the sterling rate for three months. These should yield as follows:

(1) £1,000 converted at 1.4124   = $1,412
    $1,412 invested at 8⅛% for three months   = $1,441

(2) £1,000 invested at 11½% for three months   = £1,029
    £1,029 converted at 1.4238   = $1,465

Though there is some difference between the outcomes, it is too small to exploit, relative to the transactions costs involved. The market for Eurocurrency loans and the foreign exchange markets are highly competitive, and given that both the rates we observed are riskless means that we always observe interest rate parity to hold in practice. Indeed it almost holds by definition since dealers in the Eurocurrency markets fix relative currency loan rates by observing differences in spot and forward rates.

THE ROLE OF EXPECTED INFLATION

The theme linking the last two sections is 'expected inflation'. We started by noting that if two countries are expected to have different domestic inflation rates exchange rate parity will not be possible. Their exchange rate will have to inflate at the difference between their domestic inflation rates to maintain purchasing power parity. But the forward rate is simply the market's expectation, its current best guess, of the future spot rate, so the differences between spot and forward rates, and thus interest rates, which we discussed in the last section reflect these differences in domestic inflation rates:

expected difference in inflation ⟶ difference between 'spot and 'forward' exchange *which is the same as* difference in interest rates

Notice we say *expected* inflation. In the figures we looked at the sterling interest rate was

11½%, and the dollar, 8⅛%, which seems to imply that on the day those rates were fixed the market expected UK prices to inflate 3.375% per annum faster than US prices over the next three months. The reader may recall that we encountered the relationship between inflation and interest rates in a domestic setting earlier in the book. We found that according to Fisher, the nominal interest rate, r, has two components, the real rate r', and the inflation rate, i.

$$r = r' + i$$

Now, since we are saying that differences in international interest rates are accounted for by differences in inflation, we are implicitly saying that all countries have the same real interest rate, r'. This, however, would be going too far. Though it probably applies to rates in the Eurocurrency market, which is a particularly free market, it does not always hold between domestic interest rates. Between these rates we can find the same sorts of obstacles to interest rate parity as we did to purchasing power parity: constraints and costs to the individual's ability to borrow and lend freely internationally; and governments intervening to maintain disequilibrium rates. Between domestic interest rates we now and then observe differences that do not seem explicable in terms of expected inflation.

Another important question for our understanding of prices across exchanges, is whether the market gets its expectations right. Are forward rates a good predictor of future spot rates? The evidence is that forward rates do tend to predict future spot rates[1] correctly on average, but they are not strong predictors and tend to overstate future changes in spot rates. So although forward rates seem to be set efficiently, they simply reflect the very great uncertainty associated with predicting exchange rates.

II FINANCIAL DECISIONS ACROSS EXCHANGES

In the previous section we pointed up some of the effects on the prices of finance, and of goods and services, when exchange rates are not fixed. In this section we conclude with some comments on financial management across exchanges.

Hedging currency risks

One lesson to emerge clearly from our discussion of currency markets is that currency risk – the problem that future cash flows in foreign currencies are dependent on unknown exchange rates – can be eliminated by hedging using forward markets. Moreover the cost of this insurance is low, so firms are free to make overseas contracts and appraise foreign ventures without having to worry about exchange rates. Of course it is only possible to hedge *expected* cash flows this way. If future cash flows have some uncertainty, as they often have with real investment projects, then there will be an associated risk of over- or under-covering the cash flows, so to this extent a currency risk will remain.

Financing

Our analysis of interest rate parity and purchasing power parity resembles our 'perfect market' discussions in other parts of the book and taken literally it yields the familiar conclusion that financing policy is 'irrelevant' across exchanges. In a world of interest rate parity and purchasing power parity, real interest rates are the same everywhere, so it does not really matter where you borrow, and exchange rates always ensure the same real

1 See for example B Cornell (1977)

consumption opportunities, so it does not really matter when you remit funds. In reality we need to temper these conclusions somewhat.

International capital markets

We can view the world's capital markets as consisting of a set of more or less regulated domestic markets and a free international market. The 'Eurocurrency' market is an international market which arose partly to escape from the constraints of domestic governments. It is a market without a formal location, though a lot of its transactions take place in London. The characteristic of a Eurocurrency transaction is that a deposit is created in a bank outside the country whose currency it is denominated in. So a Eurodollar deposit is a dollar deposit outside the US. The Eurocurrency market deals in shorter-term loans. The longer end of the market is referred to as the Eurobond market.

The Eurocurrency market is unrestricted and very competitive, and real interest rates appear to be uniform across currencies in the market. But this may not apply between domestic markets: governments pursue policies which mean domestic rates can diverge from world rates; and they create barriers to prevent arbitrage restoring equilibrium. Sometimes governments will make cheap money available to favoured investment projects. In this case by defining the investment and providing the funds they can prevent mobility of the funds. More generally, governments may hold domestic rates above or below world levels as part of their economic policy, and prevent mobility by running exchange controls. Many countries run foreign exchange controls, as did Britain until recently, and particularly in developing countries for whom investment funds are particularly important, the illegal import or export of finance, often attracts Draconian penalties. Hence it may well be beneficial to look carefully at where to source the financing of a project.

Financing risk

Purchasing power parity should ensure that a project's cash flows retain their home currency value even if the country in which the project is located devalues relative to the home currency. However many countries prefer not to rely on this, and consider carefully the effect of winding up the project and repatriating it after a devaluation. This often argues for only financing from home those assets with a buoyant world market value, and financing other assets locally.

Taxation and repatriation

Another complicating factor the company needs to be aware of is differing international tax systems. Though the rules differ, in general we can expect overseas projects to be taxed in the country in which they are located. The parent will be subject to further home tax on payments remitted from overseas, though there may be some relief of domestic tax if there is a double taxation agreement between the two countries. Needless to say there are considerable opportunities for exploiting the diversity of tax rules by choice of structure, and of location for the parent and the subsidiary.

The main cash flows between subsidiary and parent tend to be for management fees, royalties, payment for goods and other services supplied, dividends and interest and repayment of principal. Though all of these appear to offer a vehicle for moving cash, to combat tax avoidance and to help enforce exchange controls domestic authorities keep a close check on the repatriation of funds, and expect to see these amounts as reasonable.

International diversification

Unless market returns in different markets around the world are perfectly correlated, which they are not, there will be portfolio gains to international diversification. This seems to provide a motive for investing overseas. Solnick (1974) showed that an international portfolio would be only half as risky as a well diversified portfolio of US securities though as Cooper and Kaplanis (1985) show, international security investment seems to fall well short of exploiting the full benefits from this source. This raises the question of how to price risk. We know that in a domestic economy, if investors are fully diversified we can use CAPM to derive a price for risk in terms of 'beta', measured against the domestic stock market. Maybe for international investment appraisal we can use an international beta measured against a world market index? Various researchers have developed an International Asset Pricing Model (IAPM) along these lines, and found some, usually weak, evidence for its superiority to the domestic CAPM in pricing risk. For practical purposes though, we cannot yet rely on the international capital market being sufficiently integrated, or investors sufficiently diversified internationally to use an international beta to measure the risk.

III SUMMARY

In this chapter we examined the implication for financing and investment decisions if the company is operating internationally. We found that if markets are operating freely arbitrage will establish some important relationships. There will be purchasing power parity, so that a given amount of wealth will buy the same bundle of goods and services in any country, and interest rate parity, so that international differences in interest rates correspond to differences between spot and forward rates. In a world like this, the firm does not need to worry too much about currency risk, or where to borrow. We have our familiar 'irrelevance' conclusion.

In reality institutional constraints mean that domestic real interest rates may diverge, and not all the risk associated with exchanges can be hedged away. The firm will need to recognise these issues in its financial decisions.

REFERENCES AND BIBLIOGRAPHY

Aliber, R Z   *The International Money Game* (3rd edn 1979) Basic Books, New York.

Cooper, I A and Kaplanis, E   'Costs to Crossborder Investment and International Security Market Equilibrium'. Paper presented to ESRC/CEPR conference, Oxford, 1985.

Cornell, B   'Spot Rates, Forward Rates and Exchange Market Efficiency', Journal of Financial Economics, 1977, p 55–65.

Cornell, B and Reinganun, M R   'Forward and Future Prices: Evidence from the Foreign Exchange Markets', Journal of Finance, 1981.

Eiteman, D K and Stonehill, A I   *Multinational Business Finance* (3rd edn 1982) Addison-Wesley Publishing Corporation Inc, Reading, Mass.

Frenkel, J A and Levich, R M   'Covered Interest Arbitrage: Unexploited Profits?' Journal of Political Economy.

Robock, S H and Simmonds, K   *International Business and Multinational Enterprises* (3rd edn 1983), Irwin Homewood, Illinois.

Rodriguez, R and Carter, E   *International Financial Management* (1976) Prentice-Hall, Inc Englewood-Cliffs, New Jersey.

Solnik, B   'The International Pricing of Risk: An Empirical Investigation of World Capital Market Structure', Journal of Finance, 1974.

QUESTIONS

1 What is the relationship between domestic inflation and exchange rates?

2 Explain the terms 'purchasing power parity' and 'interest rate parity'. Are there any barriers to their prevailing in practice?

3 What difference does it make to international finance and investment decisions if purchasing power parity and interest rate parity do, and do not, hold?

Appendix
Present values and annuities

Present value of one Pound at the end of n years

n	1%	2%	3%	4%	5%	6%	7%	8%	9%	10%
1	.99010	.98039	.97007	.96154	.95238	.94340	.93458	.92593	.91743	.90909
2	.98030	.96117	.94260	.92456	.90703	.89000	.87344	.85734	.84168	.82645
3	.97059	.94232	.91514	.88900	.86384	.83962	.81630	.79383	.77218	.75131
4	.96098	.92385	.88849	.85480	.83370	.79209	.76390	.74503	.70843	.68301
5	.95147	.90573	.86261	.82193	.78353	.74726	.71299	.68058	.64993	.62092
6	.94204	.88797	.83748	.79031	.74622	.70496	.66634	.63017	.59627	.56447
7	.93272	.87056	.81309	.75992	.71068	.66506	.62275	.58349	.54703	.51316
8	.92348	.85349	.78941	.73069	.67684	.62741	.58201	.54027	.50187	.46651
9	.91434	.83675	.76642	.70259	.64461	.59190	.54393	.50025	.46043	.42410
10	.90529	.82035	.74409	.67556	.61391	.55839	.50835	.46319	.42241	.38554
11	.89632	.80426	.72242	.64958	.58468	.52679	.47509	.42888	.38753	.35049
12	.88745	.78849	.70138	.62460	.55684	.49697	.44401	.39711	.35553	.31863
13	.87866	.77303	.68095	.60057	.53032	.46884	.41496	.36770	.32618	.28966
14	.86996	.75787	.66112	.57747	.50507	.44230	.38782	.34046	.29925	.26333
15	.86135	.74301	.64186	.55526	.48102	.41726	.36245	.31524	.27454	.23939
16	.85282	.72845	.62317	.53391	.45811	.39365	.33873	.29189	.25187	.21763
17	.84438	.71416	.60502	.51337	.43630	.37136	.31657	.27027	.23107	.19784
18	.83602	.70016	.58739	.49363	.41552	.35034	.29586	.25025	.21199	.17986
19	.82774	.68643	.57029	.47464	.39573	.33051	.27651	.23171	.19449	.16351
20	.81954	.67297	.55367	.45639	.37689	.31180	.25842	.21455	.17843	.14864
21	.81143	.65978	.53755	.43883	.35894	.29415	.24151	.19866	.16370	.13513
22	.80340	.64684	.52189	.42195	.34185	.27750	.22571	.18394	.15018	.12285
23	.79544	.63416	.50669	.40573	.32557	.26180	.21095	.17031	.13778	.11168
24	.78757	.62172	.49193	.39012	.31007	.24698	.19715	.15770	.12640	.10153
25	.77977	.60953	.47760	.37512	.29530	.23300	.18425	.14602	.11597	.09230

Present value of one Pound at the end of n years (cont.)

n	11%	12%	13%	14%	15%	16%	17%	18%	19%	20%
1	.90090	.89286	.88486	.87719	.86957	.86207	.85470	.84746	.84034	.83333
2	.81162	.79719	.78315	.76947	.75614	.74316	.73051	.71818	.70616	.69444
3	.73119	.71178	.69305	.67497	.65752	.64066	.62437	.60863	.59342	.57870
4	.65873	.63552	.61332	.59208	.57175	.55229	.53365	.51579	.49867	.48225
5	.59345	.56743	.54276	.51937	.49718	.47611	.45611	.43711	.41905	.40188
6	.53464	.50663	.48032	.45559	.43233	.41044	.38984	.37043	.35214	.33490
7	.48166	.45235	.42506	.39964	.37594	.35383	.33320	.31392	.29592	.27908
8	.43393	.40388	.37616	.35056	.32690	.30503	.28478	.26604	.24867	.23257
9	.39092	.36061	.33288	.30751	.28426	.26295	.24340	.22546	.20897	.19381
10	.35218	.32197	.29459	.26974	.24718	.22668	.20804	.19106	.17560	.16151
11	.31728	.28748	.26070	.23662	.21494	.19542	.17781	.16192	.14756	.13459
12	.28584	.25667	.23071	.20756	.18691	.16846	.15197	.13722	.12400	.11216
13	.25751	.22917	.20416	.18207	.16253	.14523	.12989	.11629	.10420	.09346
14	.23199	.20462	.18068	.15971	.14133	.12520	.11102	.09855	.08757	.07789
15	.20900	.18270	.15989	.14010	.12289	.10793	.09489	.08352	.07359	.06491
16	.18829	.16312	.14150	.12289	.10686	.09304	.08110	.07078	.06184	.05409
17	.16963	.14564	.12522	.10780	.09293	.08021	.06932	.05998	.05196	.04507
18	.15282	.13004	.11081	.09456	.08080	.06914	.05925	.05083	.04367	.03756
19	.13768	.11611	.09806	.08295	.07026	.05961	.05064	.04308	.03669	.03130
20	.12403	.10367	.08678	.07276	.06110	.05139	.04328	.03651	.03084	.02608
21	.11174	.09256	.07680	.06383	.05313	.04430	.03699	.03094	.02591	.02174
22	.10067	.08264	.06796	.05599	.04620	.03819	.03162	.02622	.02178	.01811
23	.09069	.07379	.06014	.04911	.04017	.03292	.02702	.02222	.01830	.01509
24	.08170	.06588	.05322	.04308	.03493	.02838	.02310	.01883	.01538	.01258
25	.07361	.05882	.04710	.03779	.03038	.02447	.01974	.01596	.01292	.01048

Present value of one Pound at the end of n years (cont.)

n	21%	22%	23%	24%	25%	26%	27%	28%	29%	30%
1	.82645	.81967	.81301	.80645	.80000	.79365	.78740	.78125	.77519	.76923
2	.68301	.67186	.66098	.65036	.64000	.62988	.62000	.61035	.60093	.59172
3	.56447	.55071	.53738	.52449	.51200	.49991	.48819	.47684	.46583	.45517
4	.46651	.45140	.43690	.42297	.40960	.39675	.38440	.37253	.36111	.35013
5	.38554	.37000	.35520	.34111	.32768	.31488	.30268	.29104	.27993	.26933
6	.31863	.30328	.28878	.27509	.26214	.24991	.23833	.22737	.21700	.20718
7	.26333	.24859	.23478	.22184	.20972	.19834	.18766	.17764	.16822	.15937
8	.21763	.20376	.19088	.17891	.16777	.15741	.14776	.13878	.13040	.12259
9	.17986	.16702	.15519	.14428	.13422	.12493	.11635	.10842	.10109	.09430
10	.14864	.13690	.12617	.11635	.10737	.09915	.09161	.08470	.07836	.07254
11	.12285	.11221	.10258	.09383	.08590	.07869	.07214	.06617	.06075	.05580
12	.10153	.09198	.08339	.07567	.06872	.06245	.05680	.05170	.04709	.04292
13	.08391	.07539	.06780	.06103	.05498	.04957	.04472	.04039	.06350	.03302
14	.06934	.06180	.05512	.04921	.04398	.03934	.03522	.03155	.02830	.02540
15	.05731	.05065	.04481	.03969	.03518	.03122	.02773	.02465	.02194	.01954
16	.04736	.04152	.03643	.03201	.02815	.02478	.02183	.01926	.01700	.01503
17	.03914	.03403	.02962	.02581	.02252	.01967	.01719	.01505	.01318	.01156
18	.03235	.02789	.02408	.02082	.01801	.01561	.01354	.01175	.01022	.00889
19	.02673	.02286	.01958	.01679	.01441	.01239	.01066	.00918	.00792	.00684
20	.02209	.01874	.01592	.01354	.01153	.00983	.00839	.00717	.00614	.00526
21	.01826	.01536	.01294	.01092	.00922	.00780	.00661	.00561	.00476	.00405
22	.01509	.01259	.01052	.00880	.00738	.00619	.00520	.00438	.00369	.00311
23	.01247	.01032	.00855	.00710	.00590	.00491	.00410	.00342	.00286	.00239
24	.01031	.00846	.00695	.00573	.00472	.00390	.00323	.00267	.00222	.00184
25	.00852	.00693	.00565	.00462	.00378	.00310	.00254	.00209	.00172	.00142

ANNUITY

Present value of one Pound per year for n years

n	1%	2%	3%	4%	5%	6%	7%	8%	9%	10%
1	0.9901	0.9804	0.9709	0.9615	0.9524	0.9434	0.9346	0.9259	0.9174	0.9091
2	1.9704	1.9416	1.9135	1.8861	1.8594	1.8334	1.8080	1.7833	1.7591	1.7355
3	2.9410	2.8839	2.8286	2.7751	2.7232	2.6730	2.6243	2.5771	2.5313	2.4868
4	3.9020	3.8077	3.7171	3.6299	3.5459	3.4651	3.3872	3.3121	3.2397	3.1699
5	4.8535	4.7134	4.5797	4.4518	4.3295	4.2123	4.1002	3.9927	3.8896	3.7908
6	5.7955	5.6014	5.4172	5.2421	5.0757	4.9173	4.7665	4.6229	4.4859	4.3553
7	6.7282	6.4720	6.2302	6.0020	5.7863	5.5824	5.3893	5.2064	5.0329	4.8684
8	7.6517	7.3254	7.0196	6.7327	6.4632	6.2098	5.9713	5.7466	5.5348	5.3349
9	8.5661	8.1622	7.7861	7.4353	7.1078	6.8017	6.5152	6.2469	5.9852	5.7590
10	9.4714	8.9825	8.5302	8.1109	7.7217	7.3601	7.0236	6.7101	6.4176	6.1446
11	10.3677	9.7868	9.2526	8.7604	8.3064	7.8868	7.4987	7.1389	6.8052	6.4951
12	11.2552	10.5753	9.9539	9.3850	8.8632	8.3838	7.9427	7.5361	7.1607	6.8137
13	12.1338	11.3483	10.6349	9.9856	9.3935	8.8527	8.3576	7.9038	7.4869	7.1034
14	13.0038	12.1062	11.2960	10.5631	9.8986	9.2950	8.7454	8.2442	7.7861	7.3667
15	13.8651	12.8492	11.9379	11.1183	10.3796	9.7122	9.1079	8.5595	8.0607	7.6060
16	14.7180	13.5777	12.5610	11.6522	10.8377	10.1059	9.4466	8.8514	8.3125	7.8237
17	15.5624	14.2918	13.1660	12.1656	11.2740	10.4772	9.7632	9.1216	8.5436	8.0215
18	16.3984	14.9920	13.7534	12.6592	11.6895	10.8276	10.0591	9.3719	8.7556	8.2014
19	17.2261	15.6784	14.3237	13.1339	12.0853	11.1581	10.3356	9.6036	8.9501	8.3649
20	18.0457	16.3514	14.8774	13.5903	12.4622	11.4699	10.5940	9.8181	9.1285	8.5136
21	18.8571	17.0111	15.4149	14.0291	12.8211	11.7640	10.8355	10.0168	9.2922	8.4687
22	19.6605	17.6580	15.9368	14.4511	13.1630	12.0416	11.0612	12.2007	9.4424	8.7715
23	20.4559	18.2921	16.4435	14.8568	13.4885	12.3033	11.2722	10.3710	9.5802	8.8832
24	21.2435	18.9139	16.9355	15.2469	13.7986	12.5503	11.4693	10.5287	9.7066	8.9847
25	22.0233	19.5234	17.4131	15.6220	14.0939	12.7833	11.6536	10.6748	9.8226	9.0770

Present value of one pound per year for n years (cont.)

n	11%	12%	13%	14%	15%	16%	17%	18%	19%	20%
1	0.9009	0.8929	0.8850	0.8772	0.8696	0.8621	0.8547	0.8475	0.8403	0.8333
2	1.7125	1.6901	1.6681	1.6467	1.6257	1.6052	1.5852	1.5656	1.5465	1.5278
3	2.4437	2.4018	2.3612	2.3216	2.2832	2.2459	2.2096	2.1743	2.1399	2.1065
4	3.1024	3.0373	2.9745	2.9137	2.8550	2.7982	2.7432	2.6901	2.6386	2.5887
5	3.6959	3.6048	3.5172	3.4331	3.3522	3.2743	3.1993	3.1272	3.0576	2.9906
6	4.2305	4.1114	3.9976	3.8887	3.7845	3.6847	3.5892	3.4976	3.4098	3.3255
7	4.7122	4.5638	4.4226	4.2883	4.1604	4.0386	3.9224	3.8115	3.7057	3.6046
8	5.1461	4.9676	4.7988	4.6389	4.4873	4.3436	4.2072	4.0776	3.9544	3.8372
9	5.5370	5.3282	5.1317	4.9464	4.7716	4.6065	4.4506	4.3030	4.1633	4.0310
10	5.8892	5.6502	5.4262	5.2161	5.0188	4.8332	4.6586	4.4941	4.3389	4.1925
11	6.2065	5.9377	5.6869	5.4527	5.2337	5.0268	4.8364	4.6560	4.4865	4.3271
12	6.4924	6.1944	5.9176	5.6603	5.4206	5.1971	4.9884	4.7932	4.6105	4.4392
13	6.7499	6.4235	6.1218	5.8424	5.5831	5.3423	5.1183	4.9095	4.7147	4.5327
14	6.9819	6.6282	6.3025	6.0021	5.7245	5.4675	5.2293	5.0081	4.8023	4.6106
15	7.1909	6.8109	6.4624	6.1422	5.8474	5.5755	5.3242	5.0916	4.8759	4.6755
16	7.3792	6.9740	6.6039	6.2651	5.9542	5.6685	5.4053	5.1624	4.9377	4.7296
17	7.5488	7.1196	6.7291	6.3729	6.0472	5.7487	5.4746	5.2223	4.9897	4.7746
18	7.7016	7.2497	6.8399	6.4674	6.1280	5.8178	5.5339	5.2732	5.0333	4.8122
19	7.8393	7.3658	6.9380	6.5504	6.1982	5.8775	5.5845	5.3162	5.0700	4.8435
20	7.9633	7.4694	7.0248	6.6231	6.2593	5.9288	5.6278	5.3527	5.1009	4.8696
21	8.0751	7.5620	7.1016	6.6870	6.3125	5.9731	5.6648	5.3837	5.1268	4.8913
22	8.1757	7.6446	7.1695	6.7429	6.3587	6.0113	5.6964	5.4099	5.1486	4.9094
23	8.2664	7.7184	7.2297	6.7921	6.3988	6.0442	5.7234	5.4321	5.1668	4.9245
24	8.3481	7.7843	7.2829	6.8351	6.4338	6.0726	5.7465	5.4509	5.1822	4.9371
25	8.4217	7.8431	7.3300	6.8729	6.4641	6.0971	5.7662	5.4669	5.1951	4.9476

Present value of one pound per year for n years (cont.)

n	21%	22%	23%	24%	25%	26%	27%	28%	29%	30%
1	0.8264	0.8197	0.8130	0.8065	0.8000	0.7937	0.7874	0.7813	0.7752	0.7692
2	1.5095	1.4915	1.4740	1.4568	1.4400	1.4235	1.4074	1.3916	1.3761	1.3609
3	2.0739	2.0422	2.0114	1.9813	1.9520	1.9234	1.8956	1.8684	1.8420	1.8161
4	2.5404	2.4936	2.4483	2.4043	2.3616	2.3202	2.2800	2.2410	2.2031	2.1662
5	2.9260	2.8636	2.8035	2.7454	2.6893	2.6351	2.5827	2.5320	2.4830	2.4356
6	3.2446	3.1669	3.0923	3.0205	2.9514	2.8850	2.8210	2.7594	2.7000	2.6427
7	3.5079	3.4155	3.3270	3.2423	3.1611	3.0833	3.0087	2.9370	2.8682	2.8021
8	3.7256	3.6193	3.5179	3.4212	3.3289	3.2407	3.1564	3.0758	2.9986	2.9247
9	3.9054	3.7863	3.6731	3.5655	3.4631	3.3657	3.2728	3.1842	3.0997	3.0190
10	4.0541	3.9232	3.7993	3.6819	3.5705	3.4648	3.3644	3.2689	3.1781	3.0915
11	4.1769	4.0354	3.9018	3.7757	3.6564	3.5435	3.4365	3.3351	3.2388	3.1473
12	4.2785	4.1274	3.9852	3.8514	3.7251	3.6060	3.4933	3.3868	3.2859	3.1903
13	4.3624	4.2028	4.0530	3.9124	3.7801	3.6555	3.6381	3.4272	3.3224	3.2233
14	4.4317	4.2646	4.1082	3.9616	3.8241	3.6949	3.5733	3.4587	3.3507	3.2487
15	4.4890	4.3152	4.1530	4.0013	3.8593	3.7261	3.6010	3.4834	3.3726	3.2682
16	4.5364	4.3567	4.1894	4.0333	3.8874	3.7509	3.6228	3.5026	3.3896	3.2832
17	4.5755	4.3908	4.2190	4.0591	3.9099	3.7705	3.6400	3.5177	3.4028	3.2948
18	4.6079	4.4187	4.2431	4.0799	3.9279	3.7861	3.6536	3.5294	3.4130	3.3037
19	4.6346	4.4415	4.2627	4.0967	3.9424	3.7985	3.6642	3.5386	3.4210	3.3105
20	4.6567	4.4603	4.2786	4.1103	3.9539	3.8083	3.6726	3.5458	3.4271	3.3158
21	4.6750	4.4756	4.2916	4.1212	3.9631	3.8161	3.6792	3.5514	3.4319	3.3198
22	4.6900	4.4882	4.3021	4.1300	3.9705	3.8223	3.6844	3.5558	3.4356	3.3230
23	4.7025	4.4985	4.3016	4.1371	3.9764	3.8273	3.6885	3.5592	3.4384	3.3254
24	4.7128	4.5070	4.3176	4.1428	3.9811	3.8312	3.6918	3.5619	3.4406	3.3272
25	4.7213	4.5139	4.3232	4.1474	3.9849	3.8342	3.6943	3.5640	3.4423	3.3286

Index